SQL

Hans Ladányi, Ph.D.

SAMS
PUBLISHING

201 West 103rd Street
Indianapolis, IN 46290

UNLEASHED

Copyright © 1997 by Sams Publishing

FIRST EDITION

International Standard Book Number: 0-672-31133-X

Library of Congress Catalog Card Number: 97-66950

2000   99   98   4   3

Interpretation of the printing code: the rightmost double-digit number is the year of the book's printing; the rightmost single-digit, the number of the book's printing. For example, a printing code of 97-1 shows that the first printing of the book occurred in 1997.

Composed in AGaramond and MCPdigital by Macmillan Computer Publishing

Printed in the United States of America

Trademarks

President	Richard K. Swadley
Publisher and Director of Acquisitions	Jordan Gold
Director of Product Development	Dean Miller
Executive Editor	Rosemarie Graham
Managing Editor	Kitty Wilson Jarrett
Indexing Manager	Johnna L. VanHoose
Director of Marketing	Kelli S. Spencer
Associate Product Marketing Manager	Jennifer Pock
Marketing Coordinator	Linda Beckwith

Acquisitions Editor
Steve Straiger

Development Editor
Kristi Asher

Software Development Specialist
John Warriner

Production Editor
Colleen Williams

Copy Editors
Mary Ann Abramson,
Sarah Burkhart,
Kimberly K. Hannel,
Kris Simmons,
Kate Shoup Welsh

Indexers
Christine L. Nelsen, Ben Slen

Technical Reviewer
Jeff Bankston

Editorial Coordinators
Mandie Rowell, Katie Wise

Technical Edit Coordinator
Lorraine E. Schaffer

Resource Coordinators
Charlotte Clapp,
Deborah Frisby

Editorial Assistants
Carol Ackerman, Andi Richter,
Rhonda Tinch-Mize,
Karen Williams

Cover Designer
Jason Grisham

Book Designer
Gary Adair

Copy Writer
David Reichwein

Production Team Supervisor
Brad Chinn

Production
Rick Bond, Michael Henry,
Ayanna Lacey,
Chris Livengood,
Mary Ellen Stephenson

Contents

Foreword

In the course of working extensively with SQL as a systems developer, database and system administrator, consultant, technical manager/trainer/coach, and teacher, I have gained first-hand experience about the difficulties understanding and using the language. While I don't think that understanding SQL takes the brains of a rocket scientist, I did get frustrated with the books and training that are available for learning this language.

While there are quite a few resources on SQL, I have never seen any SQL manual, text, or training that was pragmatic. Most texts go through all the features, demonstrate a few standard tables, and then it is up to the user to figure out how to make SQL work in a practical context. I would argue that most good SQL programmers learned their skill despite the materials available to them and not because of them.

Being comfortable with the technical issues involved, as well as the organizational and people context in which systems are built, and having enjoyed to share my knowledge with others, I felt that I could create a useful resource—a practical and pragmatic guide to SQL. This book seeks to be useful in day-to-day SQL programming, in understanding the underlying concepts both of SQL and relational databases, and in ways to get the job done.

Acknowledgments

Many individuals have contributed significantly to the success of this project. They all deserve credit and thanks. Foremost, the Publishing team at Sams, true masters of their trades who know how to work with an author—leaving a lot of room for an involved writing process yet making sure that the project stays on target in the end. Most involved were Steve Straiger and Kristi Asher, always returning those phone calls; willing to provide advice, encouragement, and support; providing creative solutions when necessary; and mastering carrot (advance checks) and stick ("when can I get that chapter").

Without such a support system, writing a large book and testing everything that it contains would be almost impossible within a reasonable time frame. With that support system, writing was really a great experience leaving all the fun—writing, exploring, and testing—for me and sparing me all the tasks that I would not have liked that much. Therefore, while I did work day and night on the manuscript, it was a good time and I enjoyed myself.

Many others at Sams contributed, among them John Warriner, who put the CD together, the copy editors, proofreaders, and last but not least, the graphic artists. My handwriting has always been atrocious (I never got better than a C in penmanship and only that because the teacher took mercy on me). To take my line drafts and convert them to real graphs, without even complaining, is a feat for which I am very grateful.

I have received technical advice, feedback, and encouragement from David Austin, Oracle Corporation, on database topics; from Klaus Witz, University of Illinois, on mathematics and set theory; from Scott Hollows, Uniscape, on some tricks with indexing; from Jurek Safar, Infosolv, on a whole series of issues; and from Laurie Martin on creative solutions and good programming habits. I started considering to write this book in connection with the AIR Technology Institute organized by Victor Borden, for which I provided the SQL workshops. The anonymous staff at Oracle Support clarified a few issues and helped me put together my system a couple of times—as usual only an 800 call away.

Arial Zach, Rich Dobinsky, and Dan Maier from Platinum Technology were most helpful and encouraging with all matters related to SQL station and provided the enclosed trial version of the software. Arial also spent the better part of a day guiding me through the workings of the program.

Very special thanks go to my family, especially my wife Kay, a busy professional herself, who has been most supportive through all these years, professionally and personally. It is a blessing to have a spouse who can live with a lot of ambiguity yet who can provide a lot of perspective, intellectual and intuitive alike. I owe spirited discussions and solid insights to her. Thank you, it would have been difficult to accomplish this without you.

My son Jakob had to be very patient at times, too, trying to understand what it means to write a book and having a hard time accepting that although I am at home with him much more, I can't build him all the paper airplanes and cardboard ships he wants. Jakob also makes me look at things from a completely different perspective—his. My father and my brother Christoph provided some sanity checks, as usual with an old-world perspective. My father has also shared a wealth of experience in control methodology, management, and the reality of bringing complex projects to completion.

Over the years I had the privilege of being influenced by many friends, teachers, and colleagues who encouraged me to pursue educational and professional alternatives and provided valuable perspectives. I would not be who I am without them, and I doubt that I would have ever written this book. My immediate family is part of this group too. Klaus Witz keeps sharing insights on a range of topics encompassing spiritual writings, arts, creativity, and research methods, just to list a few. He, Keith Thompson, and Ronald Hedlund offered invaluable discussion, support, and constructive criticism during and subsequent to the time I wrote my thesis. Ronald also was my voice teacher for many years. James Marchand, Mike Goldstein, and William Bowen shared many of their insights, conclusions, and methods concerning systems, large projects, networks, and spacial analysis, as well as lifestyles and many other things of interest.

To this day I approach projects with the methodology learned back in Austria, from Rudi Hofstötter in a musical context and from Charlotte Teuber-Weckersdorff, who introduced me to research methods in independent study sessions, which usually lasted from a late breakfast to a midnight supper. She also encouraged me to seek my future in America, a step I have never regretted. Friedrich Meixner helped me to clarify the relationship of professional endeavors to other aspects of life.

Last but not least, thanks are due to those who financed most of my professional work—the taxpayers of Austria and the United States, in particular those in California, Maine, and Illinois. A cursory estimate makes me believe that they got a good return on their investment, yet their trusting support is nevertheless appreciated.

This book is dedicated to the people in the last three paragraphs—the friends, teachers, and colleagues who helped me become who I am, my family who has to put up with the results, and the taxpayers who footed the bill.

About the Author

Hans Ladányi is president of Derived Systems Corporation in Los Angeles, Calif., which provides consulting and development services in the areas of client/server system development, system and application integration, troubleshooting and debugging, technology and project support, as well as software training and coaching. He serves as an independent IT expert for GIGA Information Group/Expert Net in Cambridge, Massachusetts.

Hans has built or cooperated with the building of large- and medium-sized decision support and research systems that integrate a wide variety of governmental, financial, commercial, and internal data into consistent client/server systems. He developed the database and data analysis component for several research systems. He has built or contributed to the building of transactional database systems in educational and financial industries. Most systems were implemented using Oracle Server under AIX, Windows NT and 95, and Oracle Developer/2000 and Designer/2000 client tools.

Hans has taught and presented many training seminars, workshops, presentations, and demonstrations in the United States, Europe, and Australia on SQL, decision support systems, and C.

He holds a doctorate and a master's degree from the University of Illinois, a master's degree from the University of Vienna, and a teaching certificate for Recorder from the State Academy for Music and Performing Arts in Wien.

Hans lives in Los Angeles with his wife Kay and son Jakob. He can be reached through e-mail at `ladanyi@bigfoot.com`.

Tell Us What You Think!

As the reader of this book, *you* are our most important critic and commentator. We value your opinion and want to know what we're doing right, what we could do better, what areas you'd like to see us publish in, and any other words of wisdom you're willing to pass our way.

As the Executive Editor for the Database team at Macmillan Computer Publishing, I welcome your comments. You can fax, email, or write me directly to let me know what you did or didn't like about this book—as well as what we can do to make our books stronger.

Please note that I cannot help you with technical problems related to the topic of this book, and that, due to the high volume of mail I receive, I might not be able to reply to every message.

When you write, please be sure to include this book's title and author, as well as your name and phone or fax number. I will carefully review your comments and share them with the author and editors who worked on the book.

```
Fax:    317-817-7070
Email:  databases@mcp.com
Mail:   Rosemarie Graham
        Database
        Macmillan Computer Publishing
        201 West 103rd Street
        Indianapolis, IN  46290 USA
```

Introduction

The hottest developments in the information technology market are coming from relational database products and services. There are thousands of vendors who sell applications that are implemented on Relational Database Management Systems (RDBMSs) and tens of thousands of people who build, consult, train, or use these products. Income from software sales (server, client, and specialty plug-ins), consulting, integration, and training adds up to many billion dollars a year annually and grows steadily. With the maturing of client/server and three- or multi-tier approaches, databases are integrated in or accessed by many other systems such as analysis or GIS applications. The growth of the World Wide Web has had a huge impact there as well because once a site abandons the serve-one-page-at-a-time approach, it needs a well-tuned database as a back end. The same is true for the large-scale decision support and research systems that may maintain several terabytes of data; the industry is now talking about pedabytes. A huge number of application software packages such as spreadsheets, statistical analysis tools, or geographic information systems can be interfaced with relational databases as well.

Structured Query Language (SQL) is the standard command set used to communicate with the most important RDBMS on the market today. All tasks such as creating database objects or retrieving, inserting, updating, and deleting information are ultimately done through SQL statements. The basic features of the language are implemented almost identically across-the-board by competitors. Implementation of the most advanced features differs, as do vendor extensions, but even conceptual similarities exist. It is, therefore, easy to transfer skills learned on one platform to another one.

 Many software packages generate SQL statements or eliminate the need for creating SQL statements manually. For example, browser software generates SQL code for queries and updates. CASE tools can construct the SQL code for building an entire system. One tool, SQL Station, a trial version of which is included on the CD accompanying this book, creates whole statements or least templates. As a result, detailed manual coding of SQL has become not quite as necessary.

Code thus generated is not always correct or may not suffice for more complex tasks. While the database management systems parse the syntax of statements and resolve references to database objects, they provide little or no warning in the case of logical errors. Even then, error messages can be rather cryptic and sometimes misleading.

Therefore, it is easy to generate code that corrupts data, returns the wrong information, or severely deteriorates database performance. SQL code, whether generated or written from scratch, must, therefore, be carefully examined, verified, and optimized. A fundamental understanding of SQL is still essential to create and maintain efficiently performing systems and to avoid rather dangerous pitfalls that can lead to undesirable and sometimes unpredictable results.

Considering the fact that there are many client tools available, some of which are truly impressive, less and less SQL work is actually performed in a command-line SQL interface. Most SQL code is now embedded somewhere in a client session, either generated by the client tool or the starting point of a module. It is, therefore, assumed that those working with SQL will mostly work through such interfaces. SQL code remains and needs to be understood, altered, and tweaked as such.

For Whom This Book Is Written

Given the explosive growth of the RDBMS industry, it is fair to say that every IT professional ought to have at least a rudimentary understanding of SQL.

This book provides in-depth coverage of all important SQL topics and is structured so that most chapters build on the content of previous ones. Therefore, the experienced user can use it as a reference and developer's guide while beginners can work through the chapters in order. Those in need of a quick yet solid review can use it as a refresher. Experienced IT professionals who need to use SQL for projects and so on can use it for a crash course.

More specifically, *SQL Unleashed* is intended to be a resource for everybody who needs to master SQL, including

- Database administrators who need to go beyond the menu-driven options of management tools and who need to write SQL scripts that perform complex tasks
- Application developers who must understand, enhance, correct, and refine the SQL code that is created through integrated development tools
- Managers of programming or administration teams who need some understanding of RDBMS and SQL concepts, even if they do not program themselves
- Anybody who uses SQL-based software, such as Oracle, Microsoft Access (which is part of Office Professional) and SQL Server, Sybase, Informix, and DB2.

For individuals who use SQL primarily for data retrieval, this book should suffice, especially if combined with reference manuals provided by vendors. Those responsible for database administration should also have one or more good books on that topic.

Who Should Buy This Book?

If you do or intend to use SQL all the time or occasionally, this book is a fine reference. For all others, SQL is likely somewhere in your future and having this book available should make tasks a lot easier.

Power users, independent and corporate IT professionals, and technical professionals who are seeking a definitive reference book for their migration to Access 97 programming and development will benefit from using *SQL Unleashed*.

Helpful Prerequisites

This book is structured so that a beginner can follow it chapter by chapter, while an experienced user can quickly find relevant information. As such, there are really no prerequisite skills to speak of. The uninitiated reader is advised, however, to use books on databases and the operating system in use concurrently. Knowledge on the use of Windows 95 or NT would help, as would the ability to operate a personal computer including the use of Notepad or another common text editor, and be experienced with data management (such as through statistical analysis, spreadsheets, or similar tools).

The examples can be run on any SQL-compliant database, although slight changes for some scripts will be necessary if non-Oracle servers are involved.

Contents and Structure of *SQL Unleashed*

The most important focus of the book has been put on effective SQL statements for a number of reasons:

- Everybody using SQL needs to use `select` statements, yet many developers are never allowed to create database objects. Large shops may have a few dozen developers that may not create objects and only a few administrators/analysts that may.
- Even if you create objects, you will still use a lot of `select` statements to load or test.
- Many `create`, or, `insert`, or `update` statements use subqueries and therefore `select` statements.
- Databases isolate the user from the guts of storage, datafiles, and so on. Therefore, it is quite feasible to start out with retrieval only using predefined and loaded tables.
- If information cannot be retrieved from a database, there is no point to have it in the first place. Databases also need to be designed to optimize query performance. Without understanding data retrieval, such an optimization is difficult to achieve.

The next section of this book deals with manipulating data, defining database objects such as tables, views, and features such as indexes and keys. It also covers security issues.

The third section deals with performance tuning and with the steps involved when data downloaded from another system is cleaned up.

How to Best Use the Guide

Learning is an individual issue, and therefore no general way of using *SQL Unleashed* is proscribed. You can work cover to cover, pick out some chapters of interest, or simply use it as a reference. Do whatever else works best for you.

Few people, however, master software without extensive work with it. Therefore, every script included in the book is provided on the accompanying CD as well. You are encouraged to try and adapt the statements on your own.

Conventions Used in This Book

This book uses certain conventions that make it easier for you to use.

A monospaced font is used to identify program code.

 Materials that appear on the CD are noted by an icon appearing next to the paragraph.

The Oracle vs. SQL icon brings your attention to aspects of Oracle SQL and ANSI/ISO SQL-92 that are different.

NOTE

Notes like this are used to call your attention to information that is important to understanding and using SQL.

TIP

Tips are used to identify ways that you can use SQL or related topics more efficiently.

DEBUG ALERT

Debug alerts provide practical information about debugging code. They also note things to look out for while reading through this book.

REAL-WORLD EXPERIENCES

Real-world experiences apply things you have learned to familiar surroundings or situations. These notes should help you better grasp the subject matter by connecting more difficult material to something easily understood.

Sources Used for This Book and Suggestions for Further Reading

The contents of this book are based on my experience and experimentation with SQL over approximately seven years. A big help came from several colleagues who shared their insights.

I also had an opportunity to attend a great number of courses offered by Oracle Education—a good part of which touched on SQL. I learned many of the techniques described in this book from a number of books about databases and the SQL language. The ones that I found most useful and that I have consulted repeatedly during the writing of this book are presented here.

Chris J. Date with Hugh Darwen's *A Guide to The SQL Standard* (4th Edition, Addison Wesley, 1997, ISBN 0-201-96426-0) is an indispensable compendium. The senior author is one of the most respected writers on SQL, and this book is an improvement on the previous editions. Basically, the book meticulously summarizes, criticizes, and comments on the standard, sometimes with a welcome dry wit.

Joe Celko's *SQL for Smarties: Advanced SQL Programming* (Morgan Kaufmann, San Francisco, 1995, ISBN 1-55860-323-9) presents a lot of useful material, written by someone who knows SQL really well. For an advanced SQL user and developer, it is also quite enjoyable reading. It has a practical focus in the sense that it comments on the best way to do a certain statement. Many of the advanced SQL programming tricks and techniques are culled from the author's columns in *DBMS* magazine.

Whenever you find the *SQL standard*, *SQL-89*, or *SQL-92* referenced in this book, it means as interpreted by Date/Darwen and Celko. The standard proper consists of many pages that are essentially unreadable, as shown in Date/Darwen (p. viii).

Most software vendors sell SQL user's guides and reference guides. These are indispensable for reference purposes, especially when extended features are concerned. All of the following can be found on a reference CD:

- *Oracle 7, Server SQL Reference, Release 7.3*, 1996, Part No. A32538-1—Very useful if you have a good understanding of what's going on.
- *Oracle 7, Server Reference, Release 7.3*, 1996, Part No. A32589-1.
- *Oracle 7, Server Application Developer's Guide, Release 7.3*, 1996, Part No. A32536-1.
- *Oracle 7, Server Administrator's Guide, Release 7.3*, 1996, Part No. A32535-1.
- *Oracle 7, Server Concepts, Release 7.3*, 1996, Part No. A32534-1.
- *Oracle 7, Server Messages, Release 7.3*, 1996, Part No. A32539-1.
- *Oracle 7, Server Utilities User's Guide, Release 1995*, Part No. A19485-2—Describes the use of utilities (such as SQL Loader), exporting, and importing.

Those attending training courses usually receive course materials. These are written from a how-to perspective and how a company thinks its products should be used. Therefore, they can be extremely useful references.

A topic that this book only briefly touches on is performance tuning. One book solely devoted to this topic, specific to Oracle databases, is Guy Harrison's *Oracle SQL High-Performance Tuning* (Prentice Hall, 1997, ISBN 0-13-61-614231-1). Harrison includes a freeware tuning toolkit.

A number of introductory SQL books are also on the market, some of which might serve as a complement to and a different perspective from this book. I have Larry Newcomer's *Select...SQL: The Relational Database Language* (Macmillan, 1992, ISBN 0-02-386693-4).

Retrieving Information

The purpose of a database is to allow for efficient and reliant storage of data. The purpose of any storage facility is to allow the keeper to retrieve the stored objects in reasonable shape. Anyone who has lost food stored in a freezer because of a power outage is painfully aware of that. Most of the people who have gone through this experience probably would rather not have saved and frozen the food in the first place. The opposite of storage is disposal, which has the intent to never confront the disposer with the item again. Examples are toilets, graveyards, and waste baskets.

The same thing is true for a database: If one cannot get anything out of a database, there is no point in putting it in there in the first place. Otherwise, if data is to be disposed of, it would be much easier to overwrite the storage media with some random characters and not bother about systematic storage. Databases, therefore, must be designed to optimize query performance. Without understanding data retrieval, such an optimization is difficult to achieve. The full meaning of SQL—Structured Query Language—indicates this emphasis as well. Everybody using SQL needs to use select statements, yet many developers do not create database objects other than views.

Even if your professional emphasis is to create objects or manipulate information, you will likely use many select statements to test your work and in subqueries

continues

of many `create`, `insert`, and `update` statements. Many of these statements use subqueries and, therefore, `select` statements. If you are a database administrator, you will find almost all the information about your database through `select` statements, even if these are generated by some management interface.

Therefore, the first and largest section of the book covers data retrieval. It starts with the simple `select` statement against one table. Building on that, the next thirteen chapters introduce ways for ever more powerful queries—through conversions, aggregations, conditions, and by taking advantage of the various datatypes available in SQL and their associated functions.

The second half of this section deals with `select` statements from multiple tables by means of joins, set and pseudoset operators, and subqueries.

Introduction to SQL

CHAPTER 1

IN THIS CHAPTER

The Database Server Approach and Its Predecessors

You can best understand SQL and its underlying database server concept by comparing them with the procedural data processing approach that had to be used before their emergence. Some concepts have not changed much, but others are completely different.

Predecessors of Database Server Systems

What really seemed to open up data processing was the use of sequential electronic storage devices such as tape drives, which are still in use for backup purposes. Figure 1.1 shows a conceptual overview of a computing system based on such sequential storage devices. The central processing unit (CPU) has access to memory and a sequential storage device such as a tape drive. It can provide output through a device such as a printer. The operating system provides basic functionality such as tape reading and writing or printing.

Figure 1.1.

The architecture of a typical sequential computing system.

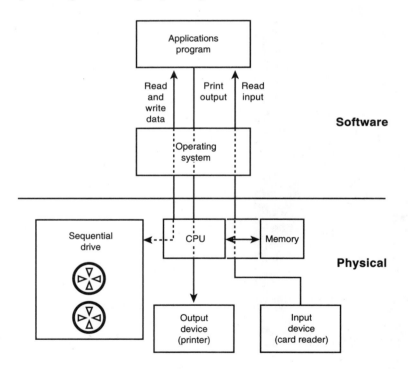

To work in the sequential configuration, the programmer must create and compile applications programs in a procedural language such as COBOL. Such programs in turn access computing resources through the operating system and manipulate tape information or create output as directed in the program code.

Flat File Systems

Typically, data systems of this sequential age (a lot of which are still in use) maintain information in flat file systems:

- Data is laid out in predefined records with fields of a predetermined length and type.
- Every record has the same length.
- A new record starts every x bytes.
- Records do not have to be ordered.

To find one specific record, you must search the entire file. One record is read at a time, and some processing is performed on each record. Figure 1.2 outlines the necessary steps.

FIGURE 1.2.

The steps of sequential file reading.

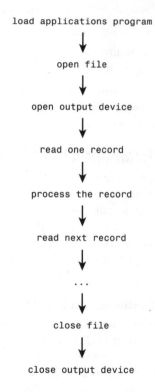

```
load applications program
            ↓
        open file
            ↓
    open output device
            ↓
      read one record
            ↓
     process the record
            ↓
      read next record
            ↓
           ...
            ↓
        close file
            ↓
    close output device
```

The program must contain every procedural step, including low-level memory initialization and file manipulation tasks. Incidentally, some procedural languages such as C let you use variable-length character strings. This benefit results in even more programming complexity.

Sequential (Ordered) Flat File Systems

The sequential ordering of records based on a key field results in a major improvement in access speed. To find one record, it is not necessary to search those sections of the file that you know do not contain it. For example, if you want to retrieve a record whose key starts with the letter E, and the first 40 and last 200 meters of tape contain no E records, then you can immediately skip those parts of the tape.

Indexed Sequential Flat File System

The emergence of affordable random access storage devices such as hard disks was a major improvement. With these devices, you do not need to spool forward or backward through a sequential file. You can direct the read/right head to any block on the disk. Hard disks make improved multiple-file access schemes feasible. In its simplest form, two files are used:

■ A flat file that contains full records and includes the key field

■ An index file that contains only the key field in sequential order and the matching record's location on the flat file

You must search the much shorter key file fully or partially until the key value is found. You need to access only the block of the long flat file that contains the desired record. It is also possible to apply much faster search algorithms such as B-trieve to the key search.

Non-Procedural Computing Paradigms

The procedural paradigm outlined previously works well when a computing task has a logical beginning and a logical end—a procedure. Examples are printing address labels from a data file, converting one data set to a different one, creating complex scheduled reports, or performing the complex computations necessary to design certain physical objects such as a space telescope. On the other hand, in transactional environments, such as those of many management information systems, this paradigm is cumbersome, especially where a good end-user interface is important.

Creating a Non-Procedural Interface in a Procedural Environment

In essence, the programmer must fake a non-procedural environment through infinite loops. C programmers are well aware of the constructs `for(,,)` or `while(true)`, which keeps executing until some operator action causes a break. In the following example, an infinite `for` loop keeps calling a function that prints a menu on screen and assigns the choice to a variable called `response`. The next function executes something based on the value of `response`. If either of the functions returns -1, the loop terminates:

```
for(,,) {
  if response = printmenu()  == -1 break;
  if execmenu(response)      == -1 break;
  }
```

Figure 1.3 illustrates this approach graphically.

FIGURE 1.3.

Creating a non-procedural menu structure in a procedural environment.

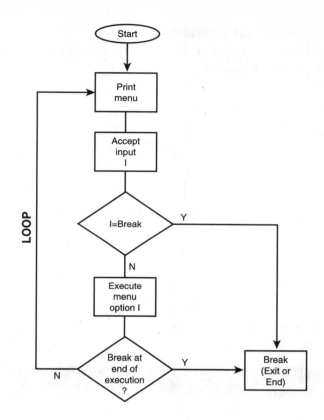

Essentially, the CPU polls all devices periodically to see whether anything is happening that needs its attention.

Event-Driven Environments

The rise of microcomputers and graphical user interfaces brought the other extreme to the forefront—the event-driven computing paradigm. In this approach, the computer is booted up and waits until something happens that interrupts the wait. This something might be a keystroke, a mouse click, or some activity through a modem. In each of these cases, the device through which this activity occurs sends a signal, or an interrupt, to the CPU. In that moment, the CPU directs its attention to that particular device and processes the information. Contrary to a procedural environment, no CPU resources are wasted on polling devices. Today, almost all GUI-based programs are event driven.

NOTE

Have you realized that nobody uses block diagrams any more? Twenty years ago, every self-respecting programmer had a special template for drawing block diagram symbols.

Record Versus Set Operations

Procedural languages work on one record at a time. A loop is necessary if a set of records is to be processed (see Figure 1.4).

(see Figure 1.4).

FIGURE 1.4.

Working with one record at a time.

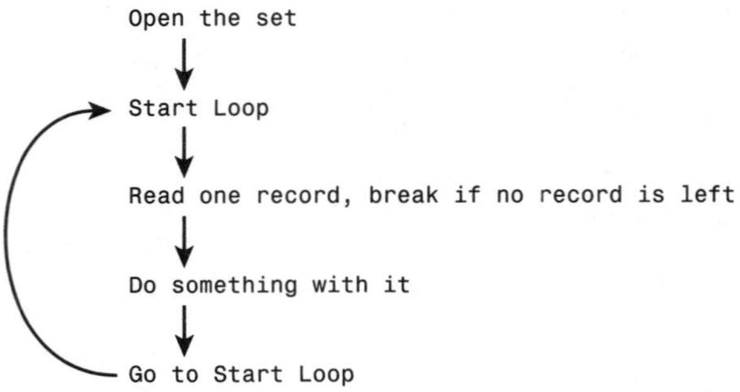

```
Open the set
      |
      v
 Start Loop
      |
      v
 Read one record, break if no record is left
      |
      v
 Do something with it
      |
      v
 Go to Start Loop
```

The other extreme, implemented through SQL, is operating on sets (or, more accurately, pseudosets). When you work with SQL, you always work with a set of records such as all the records in a table. You can limit the number of records to one through WHERE conditions, but even then, you work with a set of size 1. You do not have to work with loops, however; that functionality is provided for you.

> **NOTE**
>
> There is one difference between the use of the word "set" in mathematics and in SQL. In mathematics theory, every member of the set must be unique, meaning that no two members can have identical characteristics. In SQL, duplicate members, or rows, are permitted. This issue is discussed more in Chapter 18, "Combining Output from Similar Tables Through Set and Pseudoset Operators."

Fourth-Generation Languages (4GL)

A typical third-generation language (3GL) such as COBOL or C requires the programmer to determine how certain tasks are performed and to operate on small units of data such as a variable or a record. Furthermore, application designers and programmers must take care of low-level functionality such as setting aside storage, opening or closing files, searching, and so on.

A fourth-generation language handles most of these tasks for the programmer who, at least in theory, no longer needs to worry about how a task is performed but can concentrate on what tasks should be performed in the first place.

> **CAUTION**
>
> Note that I mentioned "at least in theory" in my description of 4GLs. Optimizing and debugging 4GL modules often require intricate understanding of the inner workings of software. A dichotomy between highly specialized caretakers such as database managers or software gurus who have this intricate knowledge, and low-skilled users or applications programmers who don't, is a frequent reality.

Database Servers

Although dissertations could be written to define and explain Relational Database Management Systems (RDBMS) in detail, all you need is a quick definition to understand SQL. A database server combines highly efficient database management with a non-procedural approach. An RDBMS

- Performs the low-level tasks necessary to maintain data in an organized form
- Takes care of all data reading or writing with files or raw memory devices of the host computer
- Provides fast data access mechanisms
- Reduces or eliminates the need to hold redundant data
- Optimizes storage
- Ensures integrity and consistency of data

Figure 1.5 shows that a number of components must work together in an RDBMS.

At the physical level is a computer unit with CPUs, BIOS, bus, and memory. This machine can range in size from a small laptop to a supercomputer. Random access storage in the form of one or more disks is attached to this unit. The unit is connected to a network through interface cards.

As with sequential systems, an operating system such as UNIX, Windows, or MVS provides basic functionality, including disk input and output, memory management, process management, communications, and so on. Database server software interacts with the system in the following three ways:

- It uses operating system data files or raw system devices for data storage.
- It uses CPU time and memory for itself and for the data it processes.
- It uses system-provided communications facilities to make the database resource available to interface systems, which are run on the computer (host-based) or on other computers connected through a network (client/server or distributed).

FIGURE 1.5.
*A typical database
server implementation.*

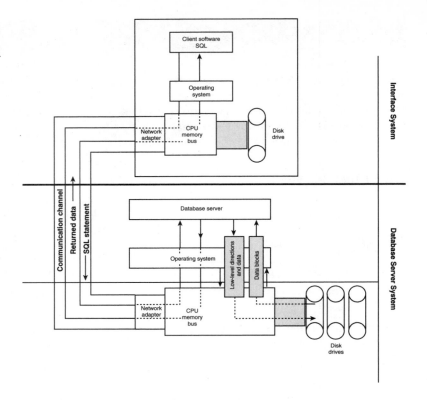

In a typical transaction, as shown in Figure 1.5, a SQL statement is routed from a user interface to the database server via a communications channel supported by the operating system.
The statement is processed by the database server, which in turn reads and writes blocks to the
disk drive, which is also supported by the operating system. Finally, data and a status feedback
are sent back to the user interface via the communications channel.

The primary distinction is between the data, which is stored in some physical form and can be
backed up and moved if necessary, and the software, which maintains the data in an organized
fashion. Once the database manager is started, it is possible to connect client programs to it.
These programs in turn have SQL embedded.

Although this book works mostly with a SQL command-line interface, thousands of other
programs can interact with the database manager. Examples are user interface screen modules
such as Oracle Forms, reporting applications, geographic information systems, system development tools, management interfaces, or WWW interfaces.

With extremely rare exceptions, there is only one way to interface client software to the database
server: the Structured Query Language (SQL). The database server waits for SQL commands
from the clients and executes them as fast as it can manage. To the end user, the database server
presents data in a non-procedural interface through SQL.

Structured Query Language (SQL)

Dr. Edgar F. Codd published the paper "A Relational Model of Data for Large Shared Data Banks," in the journal *Communications of the ACM* in June 1970. In this paper, he outlined the relational database model that he developed. It took almost a decade for the idea to take hold. IBM, where Codd worked for a considerable time, developed the Structured English Query Language (SEQUEL) as an interface to relational databases based on his concept. The "English" was eventually dropped, and the abbreviation changed to SQL.

Relational Software, Inc. released the first commercial database server software based on SQL in 1979; IBM had DB2 ready in 1981. Other important SQL-based database server software released over the years includes Sybase, Microsoft SQL Server, Informix, Rbase by Microrim, and Microsoft Access.

Within a few years, SQL became standardized. The American National Standards Institute (ANSI) and the International Standard Organization (ISO) published the first standard in 1986, a second one in 1989 (SQL-89), and the most recent one in 1992 (SQL-92 is also sometimes called SQL2). The SQL-92 standard has three levels: entry, intermediate, and full. Full implementations comply with SQL-89 and the entry level of SQL-92.

By a wide margin, SQL is the most important relational language. The most important non-SQL relational database products, dBASE and FoxPro, both owned by Microsoft, are slowly fading.

It is a reasonable assumption that SQL will maintain and even enhance its position for quite a while. The two big pushes in the market right now are the universal server, a database that can maintain information such as videos, music, or images as well as character data, and object-oriented databases.

It is quite obvious that the database vendors have too much of an investment in the relational model to initiate a dramatic change of direction. Instead, the two new features are implemented as extensions to the relational model and thus to SQL.

At this point, it is totally irrelevant whether SQL is good, bad, ugly, or even appropriate for its purpose. It is widely implemented, and if you are not using it now, you probably will use it sometime in the near future.

SQL in Database Applications

Basically, the only thing that database management software understands is SQL. Whether the client tool is a command-line interface or a complicated user interface, all statements that go from the client to the database must be SQL.

The two basic approaches of communicating using SQL are including statements in client modules or using software that creates SQL statements based on other information that you specify.

For example, a command-line interface such as SQL*Plus (which has some added functionality) requires the user to create all the statements, which are then passed to the server. It is also possible to run scripts that are stored in the file system.

Screen modules also interact with the server using SQL. In the cruder ones, the programmer must paint or set up the screen and then link the fields to variables in SQL statements. As a user retrieves information, the returned values are inserted into the fields. Values that a user provides are copied into the variables and shipped to the RDBMS as a SQL statement. Some powerful screen software generates necessary SQL statements from the context; all the programmer must specify is the basic relationship between a table and a module.

 Finally, some client software generates SQL either in the process of doing something else or as its very purpose. Browser software allows the user to select tables and columns, and the program creates the necessary SQL statement. A program such as SQL-Station by Platinum (a trial version is provided on the CD-ROM) can extract a SQL statement from a database that could in turn be used to create an identical table.

Procedural Extensions to SQL

At times it is necessary to perform operations that SQL proper cannot handle. These operations might include procedural steps where some processing is done line by line or a necessary conversion beyond the functionality of operators and built-in functions. To deal with such a situation, most vendors provide extensions.

In one option, you can embed SQL calls in a program written in a procedural language such as C, COBOL, or FORTRAN. The program flow is handled in the procedural program, but database access is handled through SQL statements within the program. To allow the program to access information, you set up a join memory area, also called a cursor, which can be accessed by both the program and SQL. The same approach is used by database procedures, which offer similar flow of control options, but procedures can be stored in the database itself and run from any session that can connect to the database, provided that the user has the appropriate privileges.

Another option is to create a function that then can be accessed within SQL. A function is a short module that can accept some values and that returns exactly one value. By calling the function from a select statement, for instance, you can perform a complex computation on a few numbers and then directly include the result in the result set.

A third option is to use a database trigger, which causes some processing to be performed in the event of a predefined database action such as insert, update, or delete on a table. This action can be a function call, some data manipulation, or a check for allowable values.

Installing Oracle and Customizing the Workstation

 The Oracle Web site (www.oracle.com) includes a 90-day trial license for Personal Oracle, which you can use to run all the examples in this book.

This section has three purposes:

- It guides you through the software installation process.
- You can copy all sample files from the CD-ROM to hard disk.
- It shows how you can customize the environment so that SQL development work is more efficient.

Installing Personal Oracle

The first step is to install Oracle Server. Personal Oracle is a single machine version of Oracle Server that has (almost) all the features of Oracle Server on other platforms.

> **NOTE**
>
> All the examples assume that your CD-ROM drive is assigned to drive letter D: and that you are installing into the c:\0rawin95 directory. If your settings are different, please substitute the appropriate drive letters or folders.

Download Personal Oracle to a directory and run the executable file. Then type a string similar to the following:

`d:\oraserv\setup`

Click OK. (See Figure 1.6.)

FIGURE 1.6.
Starting the install.

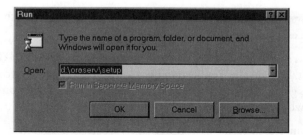

This loads the Oracle Installer program, which takes a few seconds. The first dialog box asks for the language you want to use. You will probably select English, the default. Selecting a different language affects error messages, the order of sorts, and in some cases, the number of bytes per character. If you want English, click OK. Otherwise, click the button next to English to get a selection of available languages, select your preferred language, and click OK. (See Figure 1.7.)

FIGURE 1.7.

The Language dialog.

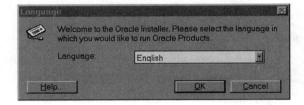

Next appears a welcome screen. Read what's there and click OK. The next dialog asks for a company name and the Oracle home directory. (See Figure 1.8.) Complete these fields and click OK.

FIGURE 1.8.

The Oracle Installation Settings dialog.

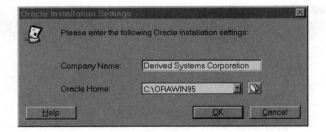

Now comes a warning stating that this directory is included in the Registry path. If you are installing on Windows NT, you should now reboot the system. In this case, you click Yes and then start the install again. Otherwise, you can just click No. However, unless you reboot, you cannot start the services.

Windows 95 adds the Oracle home directory to your AUTOEXEC.BAT path statement, which is only necessary if you run DOS utilities.

The next screen asks for installation options. (See Figure 1.9.) Usually, you should click Custom Installation. The Application Developer option installs all components on the CD-ROM, which is generally not necessary. The Runtime option installs only the database and documentation, which are not enough. Click Custom Installation and then OK.

Now comes the Software Asset Manager, where you can select all the options you want. The very minimum that you need to install to run the examples on a local database (meaning that the SQL*Plus session and the database server are installed and run on the same computer) is Personal Oracle and SQL*Plus. It is also convenient to install the documentation on hard disk if you have enough space.

FIGURE 1.9.
The Installation Options dialog.

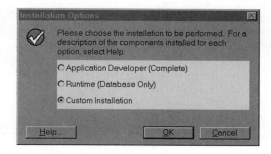

Control-click your choices. Then click the Install button. Figure 1.10 shows the selection of these two options.

FIGURE 1.10.
The Software Asset Manager dialog.

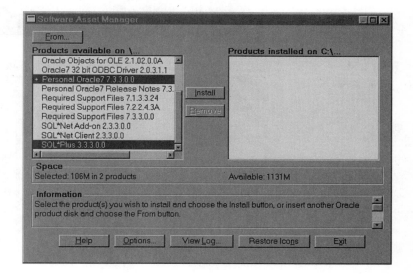

Now the install begins; a few screens will whiz by. The next dialog asks for the database installation options. (See Figure 1.11.) Click Standard, which is 20MB for Windows 95 and 30MB for Windows NT. Then click OK.

The next dialog asks you to confirm the choice of a character set fitting the chosen language. (See Figure 1.12.) Click OK if the selection is fine. If not, click No and a list of other options appears.

Next is a screen that reports the progress of the file copy. This process takes awhile. No message informs you, "This will take a while; now is a good time to fill in the registration card."

In the course of the copying, a few program groups are created. (See Figure 1.13.) Don't worry about these right now; you will customize these later.

Figure 1.11.

The Starter Database Installation Options dialog.

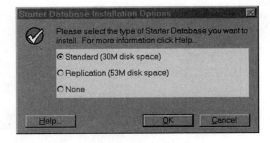

Figure 1.12.

Character set confirmation.

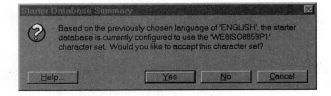

Figure 1.13.

Program groups.

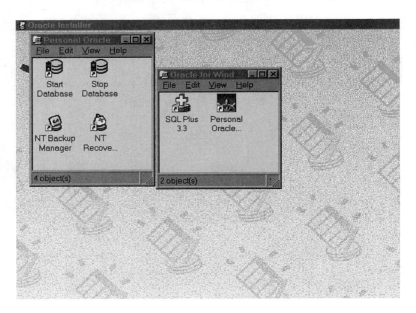

When the copying is finished, an installation complete dialog appears. Click OK to continue. The Software Asset Manager reappears, but this time, the right pane shows all the software that was installed. (See Figure 1.14.)

The setup program installed a few more things than what you selected. The required support files are, as the name says, required, and the release notes come along for good measure.

FIGURE 1.14.

*The Software Asset
Manager after install.*

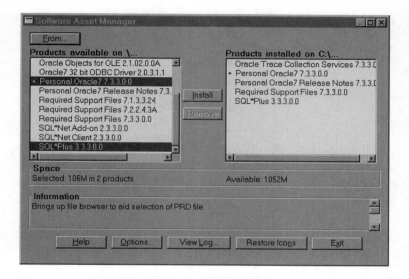

Notice the Restore Icons option on the Asset Manager. In the next steps, you will customize icon locations. If that fails or icons get lost, you can restore them from this pane.

Click OK to continue. Click Yes on the Confirmation dialog. On Windows NT, if you have not rebooted the system, you will get another dialog reminding you. Click OK. Now everything is installed.

Customizing the Work Environment

The install created two program groups where one would suffice. It might also be desirable to move some shortcuts in the Start menu; it is just not efficient to go through three or four levels to get anywhere. This section describes the customization process.

As a first step, consolidate the two program groups into one and rename that group. Simply drag the icons of one group into the other one. Point the cursor to the icon, hold the left mouse button down, and drag it over.

Now open Windows Explorer. Click Start | Programs | Windows Explorer. Keep expanding the tree by clicking the plus button next to a node. On Windows NT, expand C, WINNT, Profiles, All Users, and Start Menu. On Windows 95, expand C, Windows, and Start Menu.

If you click the folder name into which you dragged everything, the Explorer window looks similar to Figure 1.15.

Highlight the folder you do not want any more and press the Delete key. Then highlight the other folder and click the right button of the mouse. A menu appears. (See Figure 1.16.) Select Rename.

FIGURE 1.15.

The Start Menu in Windows Explorer.

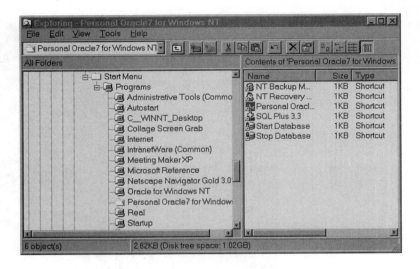

FIGURE 1.16.

Changing the name of the program group.

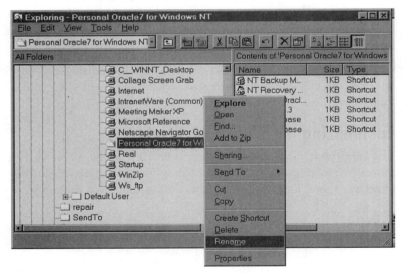

Type Oracle, or anything else you want, and you are set.

Finally, if you use Oracle a lot, you might want to move the Oracle group to the top of the Start Menu tree. Just drag the Oracle group to the Start Menu node.

If you now click the Start Menu, Oracle is an option in the top section. (See Figure 1.17.) If you highlight it, the six icons appear in a submenu.

If you want some of these icons directly on the desktop, simply copy them from the Oracle group. Highlight the icons to copy, press Ctrl+C, click the desktop, and press Ctrl+V.

FIGURE 1.17.
The customized Start Menu.

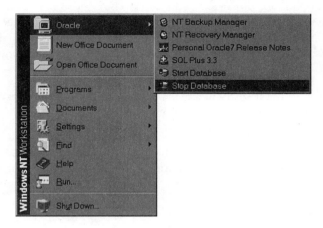

Copying the Provided Scripts

 The CD-ROM contains a source directory by chapter. The CD install program will copy the folders to your file's hard drive.

The CD-ROM also contains third-party software essential to using many examples in this book.

Simply copy the whole squ directory including subdirectories to one of your hard drives. You can simply do that in Explorer. For the rest of this chapter, the C drive is assumed.

Now it is necessary to change the SQL_PATH key in the Registry, so that SQL*Plus searches these directories for scripts. Click Start | Run. A dialog box appears. (See Figure 1.18.) Type regedit and click OK. The Registry Editor appears.

FIGURE 1.18.
Starting regedit.

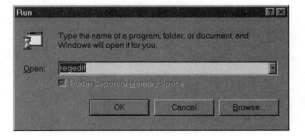

> **CAUTION**
>
> To be safe, you should export the Registry before you work on it. If you accidentally delete a major part of the Registry keys, the affected software no longer works correctly. Should you have to reset the Registry without a backup, consult the Registry help under *resetting the Registry*. Read that entry before you start working on the Registry.

First, export the Registry to a file. Click Registry | Export Registry File to get the Export Registry File dialog. Fill in a filename and click Save.

You are ready to customize entries. Click the + button next to HK_LOCAL_MACHINE and then the + button next to SOFTWARE. Click the folder icon next to ORACLE. Then click anywhere on the right pane and press the letter S until the key SQLPATH is highlighted. Double-click it. (See Figure 1.19.)

FIGURE 1.19.
The Registry Editor.

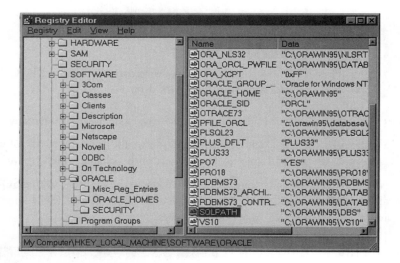

You get a dialog to edit that key. In the Value data field, click once on the right of the highlighted portion. (See Figure 1.20.) Add the following string (assuming that you copied to the C drive) or a similar string that include the source directory of the book's examples:

```
;c:\squ\objects;c:\squ\scripts;c:\squ\user
```

Click OK and close the Registry Editor. (Click the X button on the top-right corner of its window.)

FIGURE 1.20.
Value data string.

Customizing Notepad

For the purposes of working through the examples, Notepad is perfectly fine. You should make a shortcut to it that points directly to the `c:\squ\user` directory. It is also desirable to have a special icon that shows up with all SQL files.

Following these steps creates a shortcut to Notepad in the new Oracle directory:

1. Start Explorer and return to the Start Menu directory.
2. Expand the tree by clicking the + button.
3. Click the folder next to Oracle.
4. Click File | New | Shortcut.

Following these steps also accomplishes the task:

1. Right-click in the right pane and then click New | Shortcut.
2. A Create Shortcut Wizard pane appears. (See Figure 1.21.)

FIGURE 1.21.
The Create Shortcut Wizard pane.

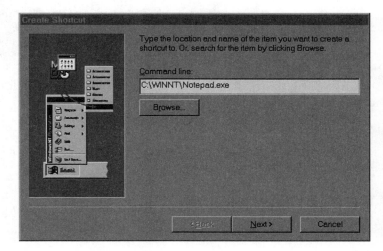

Click Browse and work through the directories until you find `c:\windows\notepad.exe` in Windows 95 or `c:\winnt\notepad.exe` in Windows NT. Click it only once. It now appears in the filename window. Click Open. Now the full filename appears in the Shortcut Wizard pane. Click Next.

The wizard prompts for a shortcut name. Use something like Notepad SQL. Click Finish.

The shortcut appears in the right pane of Explorer. Right-click the new icon and select Properties. A new window appears; click the Shortcut tab. (See Figure 1.22.)

FIGURE 1.22.

The Notepad SQL Properties window.

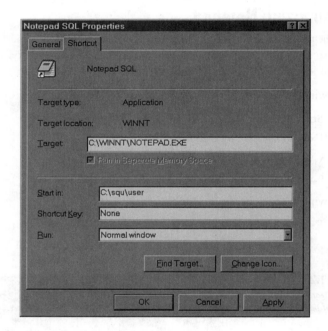

Change the field labeled Start in to `c:\squ\users`. This is the default directory for Notepad launched through that shortcut.

If you want, you can use a different icon. Click Change Icon and either choose one or browse to find another one.

Click OK to leave the properties window.

Creating SQL Icons for SQL Scripts

It is definitely convenient to have all scripts with SQL endings displayed with a SQL icon. You can do this through Windows Explorer.

Click the View Menu option and select Options. The Options window appears. Make sure that the checkbox left of "Hide file extensions for known file types" is unchecked. Because Notepad occasionally adds a .TXT to a file, it is important to see that and be able to fix it.

Click the File Types tab. Click the New Type button. Yet another window appears with the title Add New File Type. In the Description of Type field, enter SQL Scripts. In the Associated extension field, enter sql. Now click the New button.

A New Action dialog appears. Type open into the Action field and c:\winnt\notepad.exe or c:\windows\notepad.exe into the Application field. The completed forms for Windows NT look like Figure 1.23.

FIGURE 1.23.

The New Action dialog.

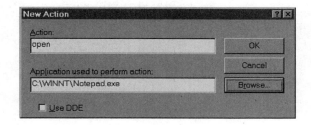

Click OK on the New Action dialog. Back on the Add New File Type dialog, check all three boxes at the bottom. Then click the Change Icon button.

The Change Icon dialog appears. (See Figure 1.24.) Click Browse and go to c:\orawin95\bin or c:\orant\bin directory and find the SQL*Plus icon. Click it. That icon now appears in the dialog.

FIGURE 1.24.

The Change Icon dialog.

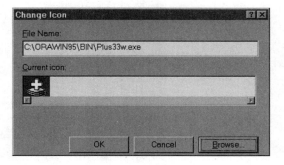

The complete Add New File Type dialog should look like Figure 1.25.

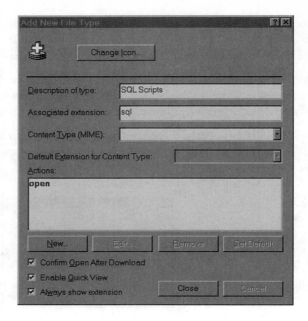

Figure 1.25.

The completed Add New File Type dialog.

Click the Close button. The Options window reappears and looks like Figure 1.26.

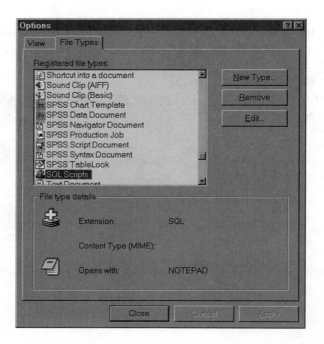

Figure 1.26.

The Options dialog with a new file type.

Click Close. You now are back in Explorer.

Copying Custom Items on the Desktop

Some users prefer to put the most important icons also on the desktop. This is easy to accomplish; simply copy them from the Oracle program group. Control-click the four icons of interest and type Ctrl+C or click Edit|Copy. (See Figure 1.27.)

FIGURE 1.27.

Highlight the options to copy to the desktop.

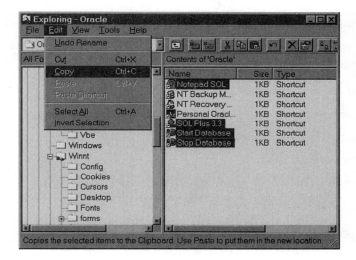

Click anywhere on the desktop and click Edit|Paste or type Ctrl+V. If you minimize all the other windows (click the – button), you see the four new icons.

Database Customization

Whenever Oracle sets up a default database, it creates a few standard users:

- System with the password `manager`
- Sys with the password `change_on_install` (hint, hint)
- Internal with the password `manager`
- Scott with the password `tiger`

A few sample tables such as `dept` and `emp` are provided as well.

One script is provided: `squ.sql`. This script performs the following steps:

1. It changes the first three passwords to squ. (When the sys password changes, internal changes with it.)
2. It creates a user squ with the password squ, under which you can run all the examples.
3. It sets custom storage parameters for the user_data tablespace. This is more efficient here because all the tables used for the book are very short.

> **CAUTION**
>
> If you want to run these scripts on a multi-user database, run `postinmu.sql` instead. This script does not change the preset passwords.

The following code shows the `postinstall.sql` script:

```
--      Filename: postinstall.sql
--       Purpose: setting up squ user
--                resetting default passwords
--
connect system/manager

alter user sys identified by squ;

alter user system identified by squ;

drop user squ cascade;

alter tablespace user_data default storage
    (initial 2K
     next    2K
     minextents 1
     maxextents 121
     pctincrease 0);

create user squ identified by squ
   default tablespace user_data
   temporary tablespace temporary_data
   quota unlimited on  user_data
   quota unlimited on temporary_data
;

grant create session, standard to squ;
```

Starting the Database and SQL*Plus

You are now ready to start the database and SQL*Plus.

To start the database, either double-click the Startup ORCL icon on the desktop or click Start | Programs | Oracle (or whatever you called that group on install) and then click once on Start Database.

To start SQL*Plus, either double-click the SQL*Plus icon on the desktop or click Start | Programs | Oracle (or whatever you called that group on install) and then click once on SQL*Plus.

Summary

Relational Database Management Systems (RDBMS) performs the low-level tasks necessary to maintain data in an organized form, provide fast data-access mechanisms, optimize storage, and ensure integrity and consistency of data.

With extremely rare exceptions, there is only one way to interface client software to the database server: the Structured Query Language (SQL). The database server waits for SQL commands from the clients and executes them as fast as it can manage. To the end user, the database server presents data in a nonprocedural interface through SQL.

Started as SEQUEL in the 1970s, SQL eventually became standardized through both the American National Standards Institute (ANSI) and the International Standard Organization (ISO). SQL-89 and SQL-92 are still active, meaning that most implementations comply with SQL-89 and the entry level of SQL-92.

It is a reasonable assumption that SQL will maintain and even enhance its position with new features being implemented as extensions to the relational model and thus to SQL.

For purposes of efficiency and effectiveness, it is desirable to customize the Start Menu, the desktop, and the Windows 95/NT Registry.

PART

I

Single Tables/Single Rows

The Simple select Statement

CHAPTER 2

IN THIS CHAPTER

The single most important statement in SQL is the simple select statement, which retrieves information from just one table. Many queries access only one table or view in the first place. While the major beauty of relational databases is the ease and flexibility with which they integrate related yet different information stored in different tables, all work is ultimately done on single tables. In the case of multiple table queries, whether through join, set/pseudoset operators, or subqueries, you are ultimately presented with a virtual single table to work with.

Database Tables

The way the Relational Database Managing System (RDBMS) physically maintains data is beyond the scope of this book and should be amply explained in books about database server (system) administration. On a logical level, the RDBMS presents only one kind of object-to-client software: *database tables*. The server maintains all other database objects—such as views, schemes, stored procedures, or user information—in system database tables.

What is a database table? It is a two-dimensional column/row representation of data. The column dimension is created when a database table is defined. The row dimension grows whenever a row is loaded into the table. Tables are set up as follows:

- Data that logically belongs to the same larger unit (referred to as an *entity*) is organized in database tables.
- Each data element (attribute) is assigned a *field* (also called a *column*) in the table.
- Each record is assigned a row in the table.
- Redundant information does not need to be maintained or, if normalization rules are strictly implemented, must not be maintained (see Chapter 32, "Relational Database Design and Normalization").
- Each record is identified by a unique primary key.

 The pers1 table, provided on the CD-ROM, is designed to hold information about people. Its columns are labeled as follows: ID, Last name, First and middle name/ initial, SSN, and Age.

If you run the provided script crper1,

```
SQL> @crper1,
```

SQL will respond like this:

```
Table created.
```

Now run the script ldper1. SQL> @ldper1 returns

```
insert into persl values (
1, 'Jones',          'Davis N.',   '895663453',34, 'M');

1 row created.

insert into persl values (
2, 'Martinelli',     'A. Emery',   '312331818',92, 'M');

1 row created.
```

```
insert into persl values (
3, 'Talavera',        'F. Espinosa','533932999',19, 'F');

1 row created.

insert into persl values (
4, 'Kratochvil',      'Mary T.',    '969825711',48, 'F');

1 row created.

insert into persl values (
5, 'Melsheli',        'Joseph K.",  '000342222',14, 'M');

1 row created.

commit;

Commit complete.
```

Chapter 28, "Creating Tables," covers the creation of database tables.

Once a table is created, meaning that it is defined in the database, rows that correspond to its columns can be inserted, updated, deleted (see Chapter 24, "Manipulating Single-Table Data"), or retrieved, the latter of which is covered in this chapter.

The definition of a table can be queried from the database through the SQL*Plus command desc, which returns a description of the table. The syntax of the command is

```
SQL> desc pers1
```

It returns this:

```
Name                            Null?     Type
------------------------------- --------- ----
ID                              NOT NULL  NUMBER(2)
LNAME                                     VARCHAR2(15)
FMNAME                                    VARCHAR2(15)
SSN                                       CHAR(9)
AGE                                       NUMBER(3)
SEX                                       CHAR(1)
```

> **CAUTION**
>
> Normally, an ID field is at least five digits long, and a name field is at least 30 characters. This example uses shorter fields to make the display more readable without reformatting. Chapter 3, "Readability and Formatting Issues," covers this in more detail.

Numerical and Character/Character String Datatypes

Like most other computer programs, SQL provides a number of different datatypes for the efficient storage of integers, floating-point numbers, fixed- and variable-length character strings, dates, and binary data. The first part of this book deals with only three datatypes, all of which are used in the pers1 table:

■ Integer: `number(n)`
■ Fixed character or character string: `char(n)`
■ Variable-length character string: `varchar2(n)`

The *n* specifies the length of the field.

Other datatypes and extensions to these datatypes are covered in Chapter 11, "Numerical Data: The `number` Datatype," Chapter 12, "Dates and Times: The `date` Datatype," and Chapter 13, "Extended Datatypes."

The Integer Datatype: `number()`

The integer datatype is a place where Oracle differs from ANSI SQL. For Oracle, any type of number is expressed with the keyword `number`, whether it is an integer, a small integer, a floating-point number, or a decimal number with specified precision. Chapter 11 discusses numeric datatypes in detail. Until then, we'll use only integers:

Datatype	Description
number(1)	Can hold exactly one digit
number(8)	Can hold exactly eight digits
number	This is not an integer, but a floating-point number

The Fixed-Length Character String: `char()`

The `char()` datatype allows for the storage of a character string with a defined length from 1 to 255 characters. The default length is one character. If a string value is shorter than the defined length of a column, the missing characters are padded with blanks. In other words, the database always enforces exactly that particular length. The following are the `char()` datatypes:

Datatype	Description
char(1)	Can hold exactly one character
char	Can hold exactly one character (default length)
char(8)	Can hold exactly eight characters

TIP

Do not rely on default lengths or values—I would never use the `char` notation. The reason is that in a multi-vendor, multi-platform world, most of us are working with way too many programs to reliably remember their (often conflicting) defaults. If, on the other hand, the length or value is explicitly specified, you may reap one or more of the following benefits:

■ There is no ambiguity.
■ What is meant is immediately clear when describing the table or looking at the script.
■ The vendor can change defaults to his heart's desire without unexpected impact on the system.

This, of course, goes against the pride of us who came from a C background and love to write obfuscated code. Sometimes less macho is safer.

Fixed-length character strings work well in situations where the length of a value is guaranteed. Examples are

- State codes in the United States or province codes in Canada, which are always two characters long
- Codes such as M and F for male and female
- Zip codes (five characters) in most countries and extensions (four characters)
- Social Security numbers (SSN), which are always nine characters

> **CAUTION**
>
> The previous examples are a major reason why a number such as zip code or SSN should be represented as fixed-length characters: First, they can start with zeros, such as the zip codes for Maine, which start with 04. This can create problems in number representations that treat 04769 the same as 4769. In character representations, however, 0 is a letter just like all others.

Variable-Length Characters: `varchar2()` and `varchar()`

The `varchar()` datatype allows for the storage of a variable-length character string whose length must be defined from 1 to 2,000 characters. If a string value is shorter than or exactly as long as the defined length of a column, the value will be stored exactly as specified. If the value is longer than defined, an error will result. No blank-padding of missing characters is necessary.

> **CAUTION**
>
> Never use fixed-length strings in variable-length situations. You will have nothing but problems if you do. Remember that the unused space is padded with blanks, so technically, you end up with your value *and* blanks, which bloat data storage unnecessarily. Whether a fixed- or variable-length string is used can also affect string comparisons. Oracle's CASE tool, Designer/2000, "feels" so strongly about this issue that it will insert the warning `char is not a suitable datatype for an Oracle 7 database` if you use the `char` datatype and generate table-creation scripts.

Sample Database Tables

The `pers1` table, described previously, will serve as the basis for the examples in this chapter. It is shown in Figure 2.1. Other tables are used for examples throughout the course of the book; some of them are entirely different, some are complementary, and some are similar to `pers1`. Similar tables will be named similarly, such as `pers1`, `pers2`, and so on.

FIGURE 2.1.

Contents of the pers1 *table.*

ID	LNAME	FMNAME	SSN	AGE	S
1	Jones	David N.	895663453	34	M
2	Martinelli	A. Emery	312331818	92	M
3	Talavera	F. Espinosa	533932999	19	F
4	Kratochvil	Mary T.	969825711	48	F
5	Melsheli	Joseph K.	000342222	14	M

The Basic `select` Statement

The most important word in SQL is `select`. Whenever you want to retrieve information from the database, you do so with a statement that begins with the word `select`.

Retrieving All the Rows and Columns of a Table

To use `select`, you have to identify what data to select and how to select it. The following case uses `*`, which means all columns. Next is the keyword `from`, which must be in every `select` statement, followed by the name of the table from which to select. Finally, there must be a semicolon (;) to finish the statement.

DEBUG ALERT

If a statement does not do anything, check whether you have it properly ended, meaning that it ends with a ;. This problem is probably as frequent as technicians making service calls only to find a device not plugged into an outlet.

The simplest statement, shown here, retrieves all rows from the pers1 table:

```
SQL> select * from pers1;
```

Here is what it returns:

ID	LNAME	FMNAME	SSN	AGE	S
1	Jones	David N.	895663453	34	M
2	Martinelli	A. Emery	312331818	92	M
3	Talavera	F. Espinosa	533932999	19	F
4	Kratochvil	Mary T.	969825711	48	F
5	Melsheli	Joseph K.	000342222	14	M

Retrieving All Rows and Exactly One Specific Column of a Table

The statement for retrieving all rows but only one column is identical to the simple statement, except that the `*` is replaced with the name of the column that you want to retrieve. Then comes the keyword `from`, the table names, and then a semicolon (;).

In the following example, you want to see only the last names:

```
SQL> select lname from pers1;
```

This returns the following:

```
LNAME
- - - - - - - - - - - - - -
Jones
Martinelli
Talavera
Kratochvil
Melsheli
```

Retrieving All Rows but Only Specific Columns of a Table

When you want to retrieve all rows but more than one column, the statement you use is again identical to the simple one, except that the * is replaced with an explicit subexpression in which you identify the columns that you want selected, separated by commas. Then comes the keyword from, the table name, and a semicolon (;).

The following example asks to see only the last and the first/middle names:

```
SQL> select lname, fmname from pers1;
```

It returns this:

```
LNAME            FMNAME
- - - - - - - - - - - - - -   - - - - - - - - - - - - - -
Jones            David N
Martinelli       A. Emery
Talavera         F. Espinosa
Kratochvil       Mary T.
Melsheli         Joseph K.
```

Comma Lists

The construct lname, fmname is called a *comma list*. If a comma list contains more than one term, they are separated by commas—thus the name. The following constructs are all valid comma lists:

```
*

lname, fname

lname, fname, sex, age

age

pers1, inc2

1, 3, 6, 9

'uiu','eee','2dd'
```

SQL uses comma lists on various occasions:

- ■ The select comma list determines the columns retrieved in a query.
- ■ The from comma list lists the tables to be selected from.

■ The order by comma list sets the order criteria.

■ The group by comma list is used for aggregations.

■ A comma list is used for the in construct.

An important variation of comma lists results from *aliasing*, which is a way to give an alias—a nickname—to the term immediately preceding the alias. When an alias is listed after a term, the term can be referred to by its name or by the alias except in some special cases where the alias must be used. The following are valid comma lists with aliases:

```
lname last_name, fname first_name

lname, fname, sex gender, age years

pers1 p, inc2 i
```

DEBUG ALERT

By far the most frequent reason for errors in my own SQL code, as well as that of others I have fixed and debugged, is either too few or too many commas. There must be exactly one comma after each variable except the last variable before the from.

In the following example, one column is missing in the select set:

```
SQL> select id lname, fmname, ssn from pers1;

   LNAME FMNAME            SSN
--------- ---------------- ---------
       1 David N.          895663453
       2 A. Emery          312331818
       3 F. Espinosa       533932999
       4 Mary T.           969825711
       5 Joseph K.         000342222

SQL> select lname fmname, ssn from pers1;

FMNAME           SSN
---------------- ---------
Jones            895663453
Martinelli       312331818
Talavera         533932999
Kratochvil       969825711
Melsheli         000342222
```

In both cases, the first column has been omitted, as shown here:

```
SQL> select lname, fmname, ssn age, sex from pers1;

LNAME            FMNAME           AGE        S
---------------- ---------------- --------- -
Jones            David N.         895663453 M
Martinelli       A. Emery         312331818 M
Talavera         F. Espinosa      533932999 F
Kratochvil       Mary T.          969825711 F
Melsheli         Joseph K.        000342222 M
```

In the preceding example, note that SSN, which was not followed by a comma, has been omitted.

In the following example, the database server doesn't interpret the statement any longer. Note that the * is under the s from sex, not after the ssn, where the logical error occurred:

```
SQL> select lname, fmname, ssn age sex from pers1;
select lname, fmname, ssn age sex from pers1
                          *
ERROR at line 1:
ORA-00923: FROM keyword not found where expected
```

The error message is much more consistent when there are too many commas, as is the case in the following examples. In both cases, the comma is close to the source of the error; it is placed at the next comma or the keyword from. In essence, the RDBMS expects another variable instead. This is illustrated here:

```
SQL> select lname, fmname, ssn, ,age, sex from pers1;
select lname, fmname, ssn, ,age, sex from pers1
                          *
ERROR at line 1:
ORA-00936: missing expression

SQL>  select lname, fmname, ssn,age, sex, from pers1;
 select lname, fmname, ssn,age, sex, from pers1
                              *
ERROR at line 1:
ORA-00936: missing expression
```

Reordering the Columns

You can retrieve columns in any order and as often as you want. The columns will be retrieved as specified between the select and from keywords.

In the following example, the age, first/middle name, last name, and the age are retrieved again:

```
SQL> select age, fmname, lname, age from pers1;
```

This code returns

AGE	FMNAME	LNAME	AGE
34	David N.	Jones	34
92	A. Emery	Martinelli	92
19	F. Espinosa	Talavera	19
48	Mary T.	Kratochvil	48
14	Joseph K.	Melsheli	14

Retrieving All Rows Versus Retrieving Distinct Combinations of Fields

A query can select either all rows or only those rows that are distinctly different from one another.

The all Keyword

By default, the `select` statement retrieves all rows in a table. This default can be explicitly specified through the `all` keyword, but this is rarely done. The following example retrieves all rows of `pers1` using the `all` keyword:

```
SQL> select all * from pers1;
```

Here is what it returns:

```
    ID LNAME           FMNAME          SSN            AGE S
--------- --------------- --------------- --------- --------- -
     1 Jones           David N.        895663453       34 M
     2 Martinelli      A. Emery        312331818       92 M
     3 Talavera        F. Espinosa     533932999       19 F
     4 Kratochvil      Mary T.         969825711       48 F
     5 Melsheli        Joseph K.       000342222       14 M
```

The distinct Clause

distinct, on the other hand, returns only those rows that are distinctly different. Note that these are rows as defined in the select statement, not rows in the table. In other words, distinct strictly considers only those variables that are listed in the select statement. select distinct statements on *, id, ssn, lname, or fmname will all retrieve five rows, because each of these columns happens to be unique. A select distinct on sex, on the other hand, will retrieve only two values because only two values exist in that column:

```
SQL> select distinct lname from pers1;

LNAME
--------------
Jones
Kratochvil
Martinelli
Melsheli
Talavera

SQL> select distinct * from pers1;

    ID LNAME           FMNAME           SSN             AGE S
--------- --------------- ---------------- --------- ---------- -
     1 Jones           David N.         895663453        34 M
     2 Martinelli      A. Emery         312331818        92 M
     3 Talavera        F. Espinosa      533932999        19 F
     4 Kratochvil      Mary T.          969825711        48 F
     5 Melsheli        Joseph K.        000342222        14 M

SQL> select distinct sex from pers1;

S
-
F
M
```

A select distinct is the simplest case of an aggregation, where one set of rows is reduced to a representative subset. Chapter 8, "Aggregations and Group Functions," expands on this feature through group functions, in which for each row a count, a sum, or some other aggregation can be attached.

NOTE

Whether the table has two rows or three million, if there are only two distinct values in a column, and you include only this column in a select distinct, you will get only two rows.

CAUTION

A `select distinct` requires the database server to scan through the entire table (or through an index, if the column in question is indexed). If this is a large table, processing could take a while.

TIP

If you inherit the data of some other system, `select distinct` is extremely useful for code control purposes. You can use it to immediately see whether invalid codes have made it into the data set.

Sorting Output Using the order by Clause

A relational database does not guarantee the order in which rows are maintained in a table. For example, if a record is deleted and another record is added, the new record may take the space of the old one without concern about the order. The only exception are tables that are loaded once in the desired order and never updated.

Ordering of output, however, is provided through the `order by` clause of the `select` statement, which provides a number of convenient options.

Specifying a Sort Column by Name

It is possible to order the output of a `select` statement by any column selected by the statement. The following example selects all columns ordered by last name:

```
SQL> select * from pers1
  2  order by lname;

    ID LNAME           FMNAME           SSN        AGE S
---------- --------------- --------------- --------- --------- -
     1 Jones           David N.         895663453    34 M
     4 Kratochvil      Mary T.          969825711    48 F
     2 Martinelli      A. Emery         312331818    92 M
     5 Melsheli        Joseph K.        000342222    14 M
     3 Talavera        F. Espinosa      533932999    19 F
```

Specifying a Sort Column by Position

The same result can be accomplished through *positional notation*, which specifies the order column by its position in the selected column set. In this case, `order by 2` replaces `order by lname`:

```
SQL> select * from pers1
  2  order by 2;
```

```
    ID LNAME           FMNAME           SSN          AGE S
--------- --------------- --------------- ---------- ---------- -
     1 Jones           David N.        895663453        34 M
     4 Kratochvil      Mary T.         969825711        48 F
     2 Martinelli      A. Emery        312331818        92 M
     5 Melsheli        Joseph K.       000342222        14 M
     3 Talavera        F. Espinosa     533932999        19 F
```

CAUTION

Positional notation is useful when a script is developed. However, for production code, it is preferable to name the sort columns. Invariably, scripts need to be adapted to new uses. If these changes affect the order in which columns are retrieved, the sort order will be affected as well. This is a source of errors that can be easily avoided. Positional notation must be used in some cases, however, such as ordering output from set operations.

Specifying the Sort Order: asc and desc

If no sort order is specified, the output is sorted in ascending order of the sort column. The same result can be achieved explicitly by adding asc after the sort column name, as in order by 2 asc:

```
SQL> select age from pers1 order by 1 asc;

    AGE
---------
     14
     19
     34
     48
     92
```

desc does the opposite; it sorts the output in descending order. The next example lists all columns sorted by age, beginning with the oldest person in the set:

```
SQL> select * from pers1 order by age desc;

    ID LNAME           FMNAME           SSN          AGE S
--------- --------------- --------------- ---------- ---------- -
     2 Martinelli      A. Emery        312331818        92 M
     4 Kratochvil      Mary T.         969825711        48 F
     1 Jones           David N.        895663453        34 M
     3 Talavera        F. Espinosa     533932999        19 F
     5 Melsheli        Joseph K.       000342222        14 M
```

Sorting Based on Several Sort Columns

More than one column can be specified in the order by comma list as a basis for sorting. In this example, the pers1 output can be sorted by sex as the primary sort column, and then by age as the secondary sort column:

2

THE SIMPLE SELECT
STATEMENT

```
SQL> select * from pers1 order by sex, age;

        ID LNAME             FMNAME            SSN              AGE S
---------- ----------------- ----------------- ---------- ---------- -
         3 Talavera          F. Espinosa       533932999         19 F
         4 Kratochvil        Mary T.           969825711         48 F
         5 Melsheli          Joseph K.         000342222         14 M
         1 Jones             David N.          895663453         34 M
         2 Martinelli        A. Emery          312331818         92 M
```

You can add asc or desc to any of the sort columns as desired. The following example illustrates this:

```
SQL> select * from pers1 order by sex desc, age desc;

        ID LNAME             FMNAME            SSN              AGE S
---------- ----------------- ----------------- ---------- ---------- -
         2 Martinelli        A. Emery          312331818         92 M
         1 Jones             David N.          895663453         34 M
         5 Melsheli          Joseph K.         000342222         14 M
         4 Kratochvil        Mary T.           969825711         48 F
         3 Talavera          F. Espinosa       533932999         19 F
```

```
SQL> select * from pers1 order by sex, age desc;

        ID LNAME             FMNAME            SSN              AGE S
---------- ----------------- ----------------- ---------- ---------- -
         4 Kratochvil        Mary T.           969825711         48 F
         3 Talavera          F. Espinosa       533932999         19 F
         2 Martinelli        A. Emery          312331818         92 M
         1 Jones             David N.          895663453         34 M
         5 Melsheli          Joseph K.         000342222         14 M
```

REAL-WORLD EXPERIENCES

Most, if not all, address books are ordered by last name. That can pose a problem. In my first job after completing my Ph.D., I worked for a small college in Northern Maine where the staff was quite friendly. The result was that for quite a while I remembered only the first names of my colleagues, yet the telephone list was done by last name. Finally, I asked the receptionist for the file with the address list, which happened to be a WordPerfect file. I wrote a little macro that rearranged and re-sorted everything by first name, which took care of the problem. In SQL, a simple select fmname, lname from pers1 order by 1, 2; would have done the trick quite nicely. The statement returns the following output:

```
FMNAME            LNAME
----------------- ----------------
A. Emery          Martinelli
David N.          Jones
F. Espinosa       Talavera
Joseph K.         Melsheli
Mary T.           Kratochvil
```

Sorting by Columns That Are Not Contained in the Selected Column Set

One of the fundamental facts of SQL is that *all* variables of a table selected from are available as sorting columns, not just those in the selected set. Even if only one column is selected, this one column *and* all other columns can serve as sort columns. In the following example, the names of people listed are sorted by age, starting with the oldest person:

```
SQL> select fmname, lname from pers1 order by age desc;

FMNAME          LNAME
--------------- ---------------
A. Emery        Martinelli
Mary T.         Kratochvil
David N.        Jones
F. Espinosa     Talavera
Joseph K.       Melsheli
```

Whether or not age is included, the sort order is exactly the same, as the next example shows:

```
SQL> select fmname, lname, age from pers1 order by age desc;

FMNAME          LNAME                 AGE
--------------- --------------- ---------
A. Emery        Martinelli             92
Mary T.         Kratochvil             48
David N.        Jones                  34
F. Espinosa     Talavera               19
Joseph K.       Melsheli               14
```

This feature is extremely useful in cases where the required sort order is neither ascending nor descending, but some other ordering of the values. For example, many businesses use fiscal years that are different from calendar years. The fiscal year may start on July 1 and end June 30 of the following year. The quarters, however, may be numbered according to calendar year, so that 1 would be winter, 2 would be spring, 3 would be summer, and 4 would be fall. If a sort by fiscal year is desired, the sort order is 3, 4, 1, 2, which does not fit into an ascending or descending scheme. The problem can be solved by adding a *sort order* column. Run the scripts `crquar1.sql` and `ldquar1.sql` to create the quar1, which will be used in the following examples. (See Figure 2.2.)

FIGURE 2.2.

A quarter lookup table with a sort order column.

YEAR	QUARNO	SORTORDER	SHNAME	LNNAME	FISCYEAR
1996	3	1	SU96	Summer	1996/97
1996	4	2	FA96	Fall	1996/97
1997	1	3	WI97	Winter	1996/97
1997	2	4	SP97	Spring	1996/97
1997	3	1	SU97	Summer	1997/98
1997	4	2	FA97	Fall	1997/98
1998	1	3	WI98	Winter	1997/98
1998	2	4	SP98	Spring	1997/98

Because this is a lookup table, which is loaded once, the rows are sorted in a desirable order:

```
SQL> select * from quar1;

    YEAR   QUARNO SORTORDER SHNA LNNAME      FISCYEA
--------- --------- --------- ---- ----------- -------
     1996        3         1 SU96 Summer 1996 1996/97
     1996        4         2 FA96 Fall 1996   1996/97
     1997        1         3 WI97 Winter 1997 1996/97
     1997        2         4 SP97 Spring 1997 1996/97
     1997        3         1 SU97 Summer 1997 1997/98
     1997        4         2 FA97 Fall 1997   1997/98
     1998        1         3 WI98 Winter 1998 1997/98
     1998        2         4 SP98 Spring 1998 1997/98
```

But sorting by fiscal year and quarter, which would be desirable in a report, would not be appropriate, as shown here:

```
SQL> select fiscyear, lnname from quar1 order by 1,2;

FISCYEA LNNAME
------- -----------
1996/97 Fall
1996/97 Spring
1996/97 Summer
1996/97 Winter
1997/98 Fall
1997/98 Spring
1997/98 Summer
1997/98 Winter

8 rows selected.
```

Sorting by fiscal year and sort order, however, takes care of the problem:

```
SQL> select fiscyear, lnname from quar1 order by 1, sortorder;

FISCYEA LNNAME
------- -----------
1996/97 Summer
1996/97 Fall
1996/97 Winter
1996/97 Spring
1997/98 Summer
1997/98 Fall
1997/98 Winter
1997/98 Spring

8 rows selected.
```

Summary

The key to SQL is mastering the select statement—the only way to retrieve information from a database. The simplest of these—select * from tablename;—retrieves all rows and all columns from the named table. Specific columns may be selected in any desired order by listing them after the select keyword, separated by commas. You can retrieve the entire set of rows in a table or just distinctly different sets of selected columns. You can order the output using the order by clause based on any selected or nonselected column in the table, or on combinations thereof.

Readability and Formatting Issues

IN THIS CHAPTER

CHAPTER 3

SQL is fairly unconcerned how statements are formatted. When the statement is processed, the first step involves removing extraneous spaces, returns, and tabs. The only thing that seems to have an impact are too many returns in a row. SQL interprets the second return as an indication that the statement is complete. Because this is usually not the case, errors are returned.

This lack of concern can be an advantage in that the programmer has greater leeway on how to format code. The disadvantage is that it is easy to format code in a way that it is hard to understand what the code was intended to do. This chapter presents a set of pragmatic standards that greatly improve the readability of code. It also covers an efficient way to work with scripts that are stored in the file system.

REAL-WORLD EXPERIENCES

My son attends a Waldorf kindergarten. This approach to education seeks to work with and foster the creativity, interest, and motivation of children. It works quite well; not only do they learn to think, create, and express themselves well, but they also enjoy going to school. One of the keys to this approach is to instill good habits at the outset.

It is difficult to be successful without creativity, interest, and motivation. If one instills these good habits on the outset, then the code will work better and work will be much more fun. If habits are poor, extensive rework of code will result, which is only frustrating. Whether you are working by yourself or you are responsible for a group of good programmers, insist on good habits.

Formatting SQL Code

Despite the rather clever marketing choice of its name, Structured Query Language (SQL) is not that English-like or as readable as the name might imply. Error messages that SQL returns tend to be fairly unspecific as well. It takes quite a bit of experience to trace somewhat cryptic error messages back to the cause of a problem. It is, therefore, an important time-saver to write clean code in the first place. That will be next to impossible to do so without using equally clean formatting standards, unless you have a mind that can handle complex formulas easily.

TIP

Follow a ground rule of quality control: Do it right the first time. A script should perform flawlessly the first time you submit it. Good formatting habits will help you with that goal. A trial and error method is costly because

- The cycling through saving, submitting, interpreting of error messages, fixing, and resubmitting steps costs time, which adds up in the course of a day.

> ■ Flawed queries, especially of the runaway kind (see Chapter 16, "Retrieving Data from Multiple Tables") may take a long time to execute without returning anything useful. You will waste your time waiting for output. It can also waste other users' time in a multiuser environment because their jobs will run that much slower as well.

Formatting SQL Scripts

The formatting system that I have been using follows a few basic rules:

■ Left-align key words such as SELECT, FROM, ORDER BY

■ Indent listed items such as column or table names

■ List only one listed item per line

■ Keep the semicolon at the end of a statement on a separate line

The only exception is the case where only one listed item follows a keyword. In that situation, the item can be listed on the same line as the keyword.

The following example reformats code from Chapter 2, "The Simple select Statement," according to these standards.

The following is the original code:

```
select fmname, lname from pers1 order by age desc;
```

The following is the reformatted code:

```
select
    fmname,
    lname
from
    pers1
order by
    age desc;
```

The following is an acceptable format:

```
select
    fmname,
    lname
from pers1
order by age desc;
```

CAUTION

Do not include extraneous lines without comment indicators (- -) in your code. SQL interprets these as end commands in a script, as the following example shows:

```
select
    *
from
    pers1
order by
    1
;
```

This code returns the following errors:

```
SQL> @lines
unknown command "from" - rest of line ignored.
unknown command "pers1" - rest of line ignored.
unknown command "order by" - rest of line ignored.
  1* select
  1  select
  2*     *
```

CAUTION

 You will get the same errors if there is only one extra line each. If you want extra lines, use the comment (- -). This, however, makes the code less readable, thus you are best off not using extra lines at all. The following example (`linesqu.sql` on the CD) works fine:

```
select
    *
--
from
    pers1
--
order by
    1
;
```

Exceptional Situations Where Formatting Is Not Useful

There are a few situations where it is not preferable to engage in a full formatting effort:

- Command line mode—Short SQL queries in command line mode may as well be typed on one or two lines.

- SQL code that is input into code windows or dialogs that are provided for that purpose in GUI client tools—These windows are usually small. Formatting SQL code, as described in this chapter, makes it impossible to see the entire statement at once, which is a nuisance. In this case, use a modified approach.

- SQL code that is created by other software tools should be left unchanged if it works satisfactorily. If it is copied into another program, however, it should be cleaned up.

- For the sake of saving paper, SQL code examples that are included as examples in books, for example, do not need to contain the full documentation.

Figure 3.1 shows the standard size SQL window in Oracle Reports 2.5. While this window can be enlarged, it will resize itself every time it is closed and reopened. If the SQL statement is fully formatted, part of it will be obscured.

FIGURE 3.1.

SQL code obscured by the standard GUI input window.

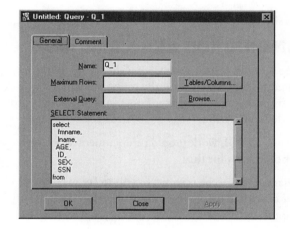

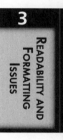

A slightly modified formatting, as shown in Figure 3.2, will solve this issue. It starts all keywords on a new line. If there are more column names than can fit on a line, the following line or lines that contain column names should be indented.

FIGURE 3.2.

Unobscured, slightly modified formatting.

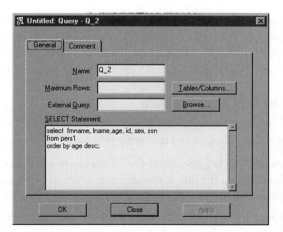

> **CAUTION**
>
> Typing SQL statements directly into the command line interface is a bad habit. Most tasks with a database are done repeatedly, perhaps with small modifications. Having well-documented scripts available saves time the next time a similar task has to be performed. Furthermore, editing or correcting code can be performed much easier on scripts where a familiar text editor can be used. Although most SQL interfaces offer limited editing functionality, there is no point in learning another set of editing commands.

Documentation and Comments

One of the beauties of 4GL languages is the brevity of most scripts. This makes it fairly easy for the initiated to understand what the script was supposed to do in the first place. This is quite different from the code of a large program written in a procedural language that may need extensive documentation.

Nevertheless, all SQL work should be documented through appropriate comments. There are a number of reasons for this:

- What appears to be obvious to you today may not be obvious at all six months or a year down the road. A few hints, therefore, will greatly help you to revise or rerun the script then.

- In a team or corporate environment, the viability of a development project must be maintained if a key member moves on to greener pastures or is hit by a truck. Good documentation is a necessary insurance policy.

A comment in SQL proper starts with a - - and ends at the end of the line.

Similarly, relational databases force a structure on a system which makes design choices, or the lack thereof, fairly obvious. In addition, comments on tables, views, snapshots, or columns can be maintained in the Data Dictionary. These will be covered in Chapters 26, "Insertable Single-Table Views," 27, "Multi-Table, Distinct, and Aggregate Views," and 28, "Creating Tables."

Extent of Documentation

Good documentation should be brief, simple, to the point, yet complete. The documentation of a script should contain the following points:

- Filename—It is a good hint that there might be problems if a script has a filename different from the one it should have. It could be an undocumented revision, or it could be simply misfiled.

- Purpose—This is a key field to search when a new request is received and a suitable script needs to be identified.

- Creation history—This documents who created the script and when. Obviously, if questions arise later, at least the creator could be asked.

- Stage of design—Indicates whether a script is fully tested, production quality, first cut, or a stage to a better version.

- Continued with—Often it is desirable to save intermediate scripts that lead to a final version that is good for production use. In this case, it is helpful to list the next script in a series. With that information, it would be at least possible to follow the steps of creation. Otherwise, you will find yourself puzzling over which of a series of similar scripts is the one you should use.

- Revision history—Lists every update and improvement, together with the name of the reviser and the date.

- General notes—Should be included if any notes beyond the purpose statement appear to be necessary.

Standard Script Files and Templates

The easiest way to ensure standard layout and documentation is to use a script template that includes all these points. This may simply be a file that gets copied as needed, or it could be a word processor macro/template. The following example shows such a template; this is also included on the CD (`format01.sql`). Please note that the keywords `select`, `from`, `order by`, and `;` are already included as appropriate.

The following example is a code template with all the documentation categories that were described above:

```
--        Filename:
--         Purpose:
--
--
-- Continued with:
--
-- Revised Revised    Revision
--   on      by       Notes
--
--
select
from
order by
;
```

Formatting SQL Output

The times when entire reports are created through SQL are slowly drawing to a close. If clean, presentable output is desired, it is preferable to postprocess the output of SQL through a GUI spreadsheet program or to use an integrated report writer that uses SQL for database calls, but processes the output in a standard GUI fashion. Nevertheless, some straight SQL reporting is still useful:

- The straight SQL interface is the lowest level access to a database; it is usually available when everything else fails. As a matter of fact, if everything else fails, there are even lower-level interfaces, such as server manager, around. Examples include piecing a database together from a far distance either through a modem or the Internet. In that case, character mode may be the only feasible choice.

- Often it is much faster to develop a standard SQL script in character mode instead of through some integrated tool. Only when a script works as desired will it be included in a GUI tool. If the output is properly formatted, this task is much easier.

- Some scripts are simply convenient to have, especially those necessary for database administration. Clean output aids these tasks as well.

Most command-line interfaces include a set of formatting options. Because of better SQL-based reporting tools being around, the full set of these formatting codes is hardly necessary anymore. A few of these formatting options are quite convenient, however. The commands used here work with SQL*Plus, Oracle's command line SQL interface, which contains a few useful extensions.

Adding Titles: `ttitle` and `btitle` Clauses

These clauses set title lines that will print once per page:

- `ttitle` at the top
- `btitle` at the bottom of each page

Both can be formatted as left-, center-, and right-aligned, and both can contain multiple lines.

It would be most appropriate to use `ttitle`s to summarize what a report is about and to include important cautions and notes in `btitle`s. Listing 3.1 shows their use.

Listing 3.1. Adding titles to output.

```
--  Filename: 03squ01.sql
--  Purpose: Show top and bottom titles ttitle left 'Person Data'

btitle left 'run by ' SQL.USER ' on 15-APR-1997'
select
    fmname,
    lname
from
    pers1
order by
    age desc
;
```

This returns

```
SQL>  @03squ01
Person Data
```

```
FMNAME           LNAME
--------------   ------------
A. Emery         Martinelli
Mary T.          Kratochvil
David N.         Jones
F. Espinosa      Talavera
Joseph K.        Melsheli
... about 15 empty lines
```

> **CAUTION**
>
> Never print a report that will leave your hands without proper titles and notes. If there is any ambiguity about the date or the meaning of the report, especially if there are discrepancies with other published reports, then such omissions are likely to haunt you.

Titles need to be properly cleared at the end of a report script. Otherwise, SQL*Plus will use the same titles for the next report that happens to be run, as the next example shows:

```
SQL> select * from pers1;
Person Data
        ID LNAME            FMNAME           SSN           AGE S
--------- ---------------  ---------------  ---------  --------- -
         1 Jones            David N.         895663453      34 M
         2 Martinelli       A. Emery         312331818      92 M
         3 Talavera         F. Espinosa      533932999      19 F
         4 Kratochvil       Mary T.          969825711      48 F
         5 Melsheli         Joseph K.        000342222      14 M
... about 15 empty lines ...
```

To properly clear `btitle` and `ttitle`, Listing 3.2 shows the statements necessary to suppress the display of titles.

Listing 3.2. Suppressing `btitle` and `ttitle`.

```
--        Filename: 03squ02.sql
--         Purpose: Show top and bottom titles;
--                  Suppress display after running query
--
ttitle left 'Person Data'
btitle left 'run by ' SQL.USER ' on 15-APR-1997'
select
   fmname,
   lname
from
   pers1
order by
   age desc
;
ttitle off
btitle off
```

Length of Output Pages

The length of output pages is usually set in one of three ways:

- ■ To fit the screen—Usually 20 to 25 lines long.
- ■ To fit a page—Usually between 54 and 60 lines long. Fifty-four lines at 6 lines per inch leaves 1-inch margins on a letter-size page.
- ■ To suppress the printing of headings, title lines, page breaks, and initial blank lines— Set to 0. This option is especially important if the output is spooled to a file and subsequently processed through another program.

These options are set through the `set pagesize` SQL*Plus subcommand. The following example sets a short page size of 8, runs a query, and resets the page size to 25, which is reasonable for a screen. To show the use of this command, Listing 3.3 sets the page length to eight lines.

Listing 3.3. Setting page length.

```
--        Filename: 03squ03.sql
--        Purpose: Set page length to 8 lines
--
set pagesize 8
ttitle left 'Person Data'
btitle left 'run by ' SQL.USER ' on 15-APR-1997'

select
   fmname,
   lname
from
   pers1
order by
   age desc
;

ttitle off
btitle off
set pagesize 25
```

The statement returns

```
Person Data
FMNAME          LNAME
--------------- ---------------
A. Emery        Martinelli
Mary T.         Kratochvil
David N.        Jones
run by HANS on 15-APR-1997
Person Data
FMNAME          LNAME
--------------- ---------------
F. Espinosa     Talavera
Joseph K.       Melsheli
```

Listing 3.4 suppresses the initial blank line, all titles, headings, and page breaks.

Listing 3.4. Suppressing the printing of the initial blank line, all titles, headings, and page breaks.

```
--      Filename: 03squ04.sql
--       Purpose: suppress printing of
--                the initial blank line, all titles,
--                headings, and pagebreaks.
--
set pagesize 0
ttitle left 'Person Data'
btitle left 'run by ' SQL.USER ' on 15-APR-1997'
select
   fmname,
   lname
from
   pers1
order by
   age desc
;
ttitle off
btitle off
set pagesize 25

This code returns
A. Emery       Martinelli
Mary T.        Kratochvil
David N.       Jones
F. Espinosa    Talavera
Joseph K.      Melsheli
```

Length of Output Lines

The set linesize command sets the number of characters that are displayed on one line. The overflow beyond that number is wrapped to the next line(s). The default value is 80. Usually this command is only used to set the lines longer, which is useful in small print, on large screens, or when the output is spooled to a file where a new line indicates a new record.

Listing 3.5 sets the line size shorter to show how overflow lines are displayed. In this case, title lines are truncated, and column headers and values are wrapped to the next line. This makes inconvenient reading, and appropriate formatting should be used to avoid that kind of a situation.

Listing 3.5. Setting line length.

```
--      Filename: 03squ05.sql
--       Purpose: set linesize (length) to 20
--
set linesize 20
ttitle left 'Person Data'
btitle left 'run by ' SQL.USER ' on 15-APR-1997'
select
```

continues

Listing 3.5. continued

```
    fmname,
    lname
from
    pers1
order by
    age desc
;
ttitle off
btitle off
set linesize 80
```

This code returns

```
Person Data
FMNAME
--------------
LNAME
--------------
A. Emery
Martinelli
Mary T.
Kratochvil
David N.
Jones
F. Espinosa
Talavera
Joseph K.
Melsheli
```

Column Formats and Headings

Two features help a reader to make sense of a report column: a meaningful title and proper formatting that makes reading easier. Titles can and sometimes must be created through column aliases and headings. Aliases are a feature of SQL; headings are a feature of SQL*Plus. The formatting is controlled through the formatting command.

Column Aliases

Just as a person can assume an alias such as a writer's or actor's name, columns can be assigned an alias and subsequently be referred to by this name. This requires listing the alias immediately after the column to which it applies. There must be no comma between a column and its alias.

TIP

If you find aliases to be confusing, just imagine them as nicknames. For example, if Jacob is known to his friends as Jake, Jake is an alias to Jacob. Both Jake and Jacob refer to the same person. If a column is followed by an alias, both the column name and the alias refer to the same column.

In the output, the column titles print the alias rather than the original column name. Listing 3.6 assigns the aliases FIRST_MIDDLE and LAST to the fmname and lname columns.

Listing 3.6. Assigning column aliases.

```
select
   fmname First_Middle,
   lname Last
from
   pers1
order by
   fmname
;
```

This code returns

```
FIRST_MIDDLE    LAST
--------------- ---------------
A. Emery        Martinelli
David N.        Jones
F. Espinosa     Talavera
Joseph K.       Melsheli
Mary T.         Kratochvil
```

It is also possible to refer to the alias rather than the column in the order by clause, as Listing 3.7 shows. This feature will be useful once report columns are derived through a more complex expression.

Listing 3.7. Referring to an alias.

```
select
   fmname First_Middle,
   lname Last
from
   pers1
order by
   First_Middle
;
```

This code returns

```
FIRST_MIDDLE    LAST
--------------- ---------------
A. Emery        Martinelli
David N.        Jones
F. Espinosa     Talavera
Joseph K.       Melsheli
Mary T.         Kratochvil
```

Column Headings

The col *colname* heading *heading* SQL*Plus command provides for more elaborate options such as multiline column titles. This feature is demonstrated in Listing 3.8, which also uses the ¦ character to split a column heading over several lines.

Listing 3.8. Showing a column heading based on a column name.

```
--      Filename: 03squ08.sql
--      Purpose: Show column heading based on column name
--
col fmname heading 'First and¦Middle Name'
col lname heading 'Last¦Name'
--
select
   fmname,
   lname
from
   pers1
order by
   fmname
;
clear columns
```

This returns

```
First and       Last
Middle Name     Name
--------------- ---------------
A. Emery        Martinelli
David N.        Jones
F. Espinosa     Talavera
Joseph K.       Melsheli
Mary T.         Kratochvil
```

CAUTION

Just as was the case with titles, always clear column-formatting directives at the end of a script with the `clear columns` option. If you don't, you risk unpredictable output that could lead to time wasted in unnecessary debugging.

For the sake of convenience, column-formatting commands are often combined with column aliases. You can also retrieve a column several times with a different alias each time and then assign different titles to each alias, as Listing 3.9 shows.

Listing 3.9. Showing column headings based on column aliases.

```
--      Filename: 03squ09.sql
--      Purpose: Show column heading based on column alias
--               Refer to the same column more than once
--
col fmn heading 'First and¦Middle Name'
col fmo heading 'First/Middle'
col ln  heading 'Last¦Name'
col ln2 heading 'Family¦Name'
--
select
   fmname fmn,
   fmname fmo,
```

```
   lname ln,
   lname ln2
from
   pers1
order by
   fmname
;

clear columns
```

This returns

```
First and                         Last            Family
Middle Name      First/Middle     Name            Name
-------------    -------------    -------------    -------------
A. Emery         A. Emery         Martinelli       Martinelli
David N.         David N.         Jones            Jones
F. Espinosa      F. Espinosa      Talavera         Talavera
Joseph K.        Joseph K.        Melsheli         Melsheli
Mary T.          Mary T.          Kratochvil       Kratochvil
```

Formatting Character Columns

If no formatting commands are used for character columns (defined as char or varchar2), the width of the report column is the same as the width of the column, as defined in the database. With formatting codes, it is possible to set the width of the report column to a different, usually shorter, value and to specify whether values that are longer than the formatted column width should wrap into the next line or be truncated. Wrapping is the default.

The column width is set with the format subcommand of the col command; the wrapping style is set through set wrap on and set wrap off. Listing 3.10 demonstrates this.

Listing 3.10. Setting report column widths.

```
--       Filename: 03squ10.sql
--        Purpose: Set report column widths
--                 Show column heading based on column alias
--                 Refer to the same column more than once
--
col fmn heading 'First and¦Middle Name' format a10
col fmo heading 'First/Middle'          format a6
col ln  heading 'Last¦Name'             format a6
col ln2 heading 'Family¦Name'           format a8
--
select
   fmname fmn,
   fmname fmo,
   lname ln,
   lname ln2
from
   pers1
order by
   fmname
;
--
clear columns
```

This returns

```
First and          Last    Family
Middle Nam First/   Name    Name
---------- ------  ------  --------
A. Emery   A. Eme Martin Martinel
           ry      elli    li
David N.   David  Jones  Jones
           N.
F. Espinos F. Esp Talave Talavera
a          inosa   ra
Joseph K.  Joseph Melshe Melsheli
           K.      li
Mary T.    Mary T Kratoc Kratochv
           .       hvil    il
Input truncated to 13 characters
```

> **TIP**
>
> For readability's sake, always line up the heading and format subcommands.

Rather than wrapping overflow values to the next line, Listing 3.11 simply truncates them using the set wrap off option. Notice that at the end of the script the wrapping style is reset to on.

Listing 3.11. Using set wrap off to truncate overflow values.

```
--       Filename: 03squ11.sql
--        Purpose: Set report column widths
--                 truncate overflow portions of values
--                 Show column heading based on column alias
--                 Refer to the same column more than once
col fmn heading 'First and¦Middle Name' format a10
col fmo heading 'First/Middle'        format a6
col ln  heading 'Last¦Name'           format a6
col ln2 heading 'Family¦Name'         format a8
set wrap off
--
select
   fmname fmn,
   fmname fmo,
   lname ln,
   lname ln2
from
   pers1
order by
   fmname
;
--
clear columns
set wrap on
```

This returns

```
First and              Last    Family
Middle Nam First/ Name  Name
---------- ------ ------ --------
A. Emery   A. Eme Martin Martinel
David N.   David  Jones  Jones
F. Espinos F. Esp Talave Talavera
Joseph K.  Joseph Melshe Melsheli
Mary T.    Mary T Kratoc Kratochv
Input truncated to 11 characters
```

Formatting Numerical Columns

Just as was the case with character columns, the length and title of the number columns can be set through the col SQL*Plus command. Instead of just specifying the length, however, the length and the way a number should be displayed are set through a format mask.

A number is stored in the database in a format that is internal to the database. It can be displayed only by translating it to a character string—letters on a screen or on paper are always characters. Format masks, shown in Table 3.1, determine how this translation is performed.

Table 3.1. Number formats.

Mask element	Description
9	Sets the display width; one digit is displayed for each 9 entered.
0 at the beginning of the mask	Pads the value with leading zeroes.
0 trailing	Prints a zero and not a blank if the value is zero.
$	Inserts a dollar sign.
B	Prints blanks in case of a zero value.
,	Prints a comma character.

Listing 3.12 shows the use of format masks. To demonstrate the impact of zero values, the example runs against the table pers2, which is identical to pers1 except that Messrs. Jones and Melsheli are listed as being 0 years old. You need to run crper2.sql first to create this table.

Listing 3.12. Using format masks.

```
--       Filename: 03squ12.sql
--       Purpose: Demonstrate the use of number format masks
--
col fma heading 'age¦fmt¦99'     format 99
col fmb heading 'age¦fmt¦00'     format 00
col fmc heading 'age¦fmt¦099'    format 099
col fmd heading 'age¦fmt¦0,999'  format 0,999
col fme heading 'age¦fmt¦09'     format 09
```

continues

Listing 3.12. continued

```
col fmf heading 'age¦fmt¦90'    format 90
col fmg heading 'age¦fmt¦$90'   format $90
col fmh heading 'age¦fmt¦B99'   format B99
--
select
   age fma,
   age fmb,
   age fmc,
   age fmd,
   age fme,
   age fmf,
   age fmg,
   age fmh
from
   pers2
order by
   age
;
clear columns
```

This code returns

```
age age  age      age age age  age age
fmt fmt  fmt      fmt fmt fmt  fmt fmt
99  00   099    0,999  09  90  $90 B99
--- ---  ----  ------- --- --- ---- ---
  0  00  000   0,000   00   0   $0
  0  00  000   0,000   00   0   $0
 19  19  019   0,019   19  19  $19   19
 48  48  048   0,048   48  48  $48   48
 92  92  092   0,092   92  92  $92   92
Input truncated to 13 characters
```

Summary

SQL code needs to be properly formatted and documented to ensure that its purpose and the way that purpose is achieved can be easily understood by yourself and others at a later point in time. Incomplete documentation and poor formatting lead to costly errors, bugs, and misunderstandings. It is much better to develop good working habits on the outset. This chapter recommends formatting and documentation standards that serve that purpose.

For those situations where output is directly produced from a SQL command-line interface, the second part of the chapter has presented the most important output-formatting options that allow you to

- Set top and bottom titles
- Set the column length and titles, and control column formatting (such as width) and format masks
- Set page length and size

In the days of GUIs and fancy reporting tools, there should be no need for more sophisticated reporting from a SQL command-line interface.

IN THIS PART

PART

II

Converting Output

Operator Conversions and Value Decoding

IN THIS CHAPTER

CHAPTER 4

This chapter deals with those conversions that are built into the basic nomenclature of the SQL language. Constant numbers, characters, and strings constants can be inserted into the output. Numerical field values can be converted through arithmetic operators. Characters and strings can be concatenated. Some nontable data, such as the system date or the current user, are always available for retrieval either through pseudocolumns or specific functions. Finally, the `decode` expression allows you to replace values in a search list with those in a replace list.

Working with Constants

SQL works with data strictly in a row and column context. At times it is necessary to include constant values in the output. To do so, constants have to be specified as virtual columns, which is done by including and specifying them in the `select` statement. These specifications are slightly different for numerical and character values, as you'll see in the next few sections.

Numerical Constants

Numerical constants are simply listed like a column and may be followed by an alias. If SQL encounters a number where it expects a column, it treats that number as a numerical constant. Listing 4.1 inserts the constant number 100 after displaying the last name and the constant 50 at the end of each line.

Listing 4.1. Inserting numerical constants into output.

```
--      Filename: 04squ01.sql
--       Purpose: Insert numerical constants into output

select
   fmname,
   lname,
   100 cons,
   age,
   sex,
   50 cons2
from
   pers1
;
```

This code returns

FMNAME	LNAME	CONS	AGE	S	CONS2
David N.	Jones	100	34	M	50
A. Emery	Martinelli	100	92	M	50
F. Espinosa	Talavera	100	19	F	50
Mary T.	Kratochvil	100	48	F	50
Joseph K.	Melsheli	100	14	M	50

Character and String Constants

SQL treats character and string constants the same: They must be enclosed between single quotes to distinguish them from code. Just as with numerical constants, they may be followed by an alias. Listing 4.2 inserts the string constant is after displaying the last name and inserts years old. after age.

Listing 4.2. Inserting string constants into output.

```
--        Filename: 04squ02.sql
--        Purpose: Insert string constants into output

select
   fmname,
   lname,
   'is ',
   age,
   ' years old.'
from
   pers1
;
```

This code returns

```
FMNAME           LNAME            'IS      AGE 'YEARSOLD.'
---------------  ---------------  ---  ---------- ----------
David N.         Jones            is        34  years old.
A. Emery         Martinelli       is        92  years old.
F. Espinosa      Talavera         is        19  years old.
Mary T.          Kratochvil       is        48  years old.
Joseph K.        Melsheli         is        14  years old.
```

In the "Concatenation" and "The decode Expression" sections, you will alter this example to return properly formatted sentences.

If a single quote needs to be returned as part of the string constant, it must be preceded by another single quote that serves as an escape character. Listing 4.3 shows this use of the single quote character. Chapter 23, "Generating SQL Statements Through SQL," demonstrates the use of single-quote escape codes in depth.

Listing 4.3. Using the single-quote character.

```
--        Filename: 04squ03.sql
--        Purpose: Use ' as escape character
--
select
   age,
   ' years'' work'
from
   pers1
;
```

This code returns

```
    AGE  'YEARS''WORK
---------  ------------
       34   years' work
       92   years' work
       19   years' work
       48   years' work
       14   years' work
```

Converting Numerical Data Through Arithmetic Procedures

SQL provides six built-in arithmetic operators, two of unary nature and the other four of binary nature. These can be used to calculate values using numerical constants and any numerical columns on a row-by-row basis.

Unary Operators

There are two unary operators:

- The minus sign (-) reverses the sign of a value.
- The plus sign (+) appears to do absolutely nothing useful.

The unary operator must immediately precede the value to which it pertains. It makes no difference whether there is a space between the unary operator and the value to which it pertains. In output, the minus operator is printed before the value without space. The plus operator is only printed in the column heading for constants but not for table columns. Listing 4.4 shows how unary operators affect the output.

Listing 4.4. Using unary operators.

```
--        Filename: 04squ04.sql
--        Purpose: Change or don't change output
--                 with unary operators - and +

select
    +age,
    + age,
    -age,
    - age,
    +5,
    -5,
    + 5,
    - 5
from
    pers1
;
```

This code returns

```
    AGE        AGE       -AGE       -AGE        +5         -5         +5         -5
---------- ---------- ---------- ---------- ---------- ---------- ---------- ----------
    34         34        -34        -34         5         -5          5         -5
    92         92        -92        -92         5         -5          5         -5
    19         19        -19        -19         5         -5          5         -5
    48         48        -48        -48         5         -5          5         -5
    14         14        -14        -14         5         -5          5         -5
```

Binary Arithmetic Operators

SQL provides four basic arithmetic operators (+, -, *, and /) that allow you to add, subtract, multiply, and divide. SQL uses customary arithmetical standards for operands and operators. It also makes no difference whether there are spaces between an operator and the value to which it pertains. Any column or constant may be used as an operand.

Listing 4.5 shows how arithmetic operators affect the output.

Listing 4.5. Performing calculations with arithmetic binary operators.

```
--       Filename: 04squ05.sql
--        Purpose: Perform calculations with
--                 arithmetic binary operators +,-,*,/
select
   age / 2,
   age/age,
   65 - age,
   65 - age active,
   5 * 100,
   8+19
from
   pers1
;
```

This code returns

```
  AGE/2    AGE/AGE     65-AGE     ACTIVE      5*100      8+19
---------- ---------- ---------- ---------- ---------- ----------
    17         1         31         31         500        27
    46         1        -27        -27         500        27
   9.5         1         46         46         500        27
    24         1         17         17         500        27
     7         1         51         51         500        27
```

Calculations with More than Two Operands

Operators can be combined to create complex numerical expressions. The customary mathematical operator precedence rules apply. What that means is that a unary minus gets applied first, multiplications and divisions are performed next, and finally additions and subtractions are applied. (See Table 4.1.)

Table 4.1. Precedence of unary and arithmetic operators.

Operator	Precedence
Unary + and -	Highest
Multiplication * and division /	Lower
Addition + and subtraction -	Lowest

As in most programming languages and mathematics proper, parentheses can be used to change this order.

 The `pers3` table, which can be created and loaded by running the `crper3.sql` script, contains columns on interest, salary, profit, royalty, and wealth in addition to the information of `pers1`.

Listing 4.6 uses these data to compute total income, income over wealth, and tax, if a flat 30% income tax and a flat 2% wealth tax are assumed.

Listing 4.6. Performing complex calculations with arithmetic binary operators.

```
--         Filename: 04squ06.sql
--          Purpose: Perform (somewhat) complex calculations with
--                   arithmetic binary operators +,-,*,/
--
--                   Computes total income,
--                   income / wealth, and
--                   tax, (assuming a flat 30% income tax and
--                       a flat 2% wealth tax)
--
select
   lname,
   age,
   interest,
   salary,
   profit,
   royalty,
   wealth,
   interest + salary + profit + royalty,
   (interest + salary + profit + royalty) / wealth,
   (interest + salary + profit + royalty) * 30/100
        + wealth * 2/100
from
   pers3
;
```

This code returns

```
LNAME                AGE  INTEREST   SALARY    PROFIT   ROYALTY    WEALTH
---------------- --------- --------- --------- --------- --------- ---------
INTEREST+SALARY+PROFIT+ROYALTY (INTEREST+SALARY+PROFIT+ROYALTY)/WEALTH
------------------------------ ----------------------------------------
(INTEREST+SALARY+PROFIT+ROYALTY)*30/100+WEALTH*2/100
----------------------------------------------------
Jones                 34       200     80000     12000         0     43000
                   92200                                 2.144186
                                                 28520
Martinelli            92     24000         0      5000     63900    645000
                   92900                                .14403101
                                                 40770
Talavera              19       110      4870         0         0     24000
                    4980                                    .2075
                                                  1974
Kratochvil            48      4800         0    184000         0   2400600
                  188800                                 .078647
                                                104652
Melsheli              14        50         0         0         0       800
LNAME                AGE  INTEREST   SALARY    PROFIT   ROYALTY    WEALTH
---------------- --------- --------- --------- --------- --------- ---------
INTEREST+SALARY+PROFIT+ROYALTY (INTEREST+SALARY+PROFIT+ROYALTY)/WEALTH
------------------------------ ----------------------------------------
(INTEREST+SALARY+PROFIT+ROYALTY)*30/100+WEALTH*2/100
----------------------------------------------------
                      50                                    .0625
                                                    31
```

As this example shows, the formatting becomes so unwieldy that the output is essentially un-
usable. SQL also tends to set the columns much wider than is usually necessary. If SQL code
of that sort is included in some other client program, this issue does not matter. When working with the command-line interface, however, the formatting needs to be fixed. In most cases,
therefore, an alias should be used with arithmetic expressions. If readability and formatting are
issues, the alias can be combined with a proper column heading and format. (See Listing 4.7.)

Listing 4.7. Using column aliases to format output.

```
--        Filename: 04squ07.sql
--         Purpose: Performs (somewhat) complex calculations with
--                  arithmetic binary operators +,-,*,/
--                  Uses column aliases
--
--                  Computes total income,
--                  income / wealth, and
--                  tax, (assuming a flat 30% income tax and
--                      a flat 2% wealth tax)

col lname format a10
col age format 99

select
   lname,
   age,
```

continues

4

Listing 4.7. continued

```
    interest,
    salary,
    profit,
    royalty,
    wealth,
    interest + salary + profit + royalty tot_income,
    (interest + salary + profit + royalty) / wealth inc_ov_wealth,
    (interest + salary + profit + royalty) * 30/100
        + wealth * 2/100 tax
from
    pers3
;
```

This code returns

LNAME	AGE	INTEREST	SALARY	PROFIT	ROYALTY	WEALTH	TOT_INCOME
Jones	34	200	80000	12000	0	43000	92200
Martinelli	92	24000	0	5000	63900	645000	92900
Talavera	19	110	4870	0	0	24000	4980
Kratochvil	48	4800	0	184000	0	2400600	188800
Melsheli	14	50	0	0	0	800	50

INC_OV_WEALTH	TAX
2.144186	28520
.14403101	40770
.2075	1974
.078647	104652
.0625	31

Concatenation

The only string and character operator that SQL understands is the *concatenation operator* (¦¦). This operator allows you to join the values of two or more columns or constants to one another, or themselves for that matter. Concatenation is extremely useful; it allows you to convert a set of fields to plain English text (or text in any other applicable language). Concatenation also allows tasks such as inserting column values into form letters or address labels. Listing 4.8 is a variation of the second example in this chapter. Instead of tabular output, each record will be returned as one straight sentence.

Listing 4.8. Inserting string constants into the output.

```
--          Filename: 04squ08.sql
--          Purpose: Insert string constants into output
--                   to create one plain English sentence
--             Note: adaptation of 04squ02.sql

select
    fmname ¦¦
    ' ' ¦¦
    lname ¦¦
```

```
   ' is ' ||
   age ||
   ' years old.'
from
   pers1
;
```

This code returns

```
FMNAME||''||LNAME||'IS'||AGE||'YEARSOLD.'
-----------------------------------------------------------------------------
David N. Jones is 34 years old.
A. Emery Martinelli is 92 years old.
F. Espinosa Talavera is 19 years old.
Mary T. Kratochvil is 48 years old.
Joseph K. Melsheli is 14 years old.
```

Just as is the case with complex conversions, concatenation blurs the tight relationship of table columns to report columns. The previous example combined three database columns and three string constants to create one report column.

In a command-line environment, further formatting is necessary because SQL sets aside a width of 85 characters. This is considerably more than the combined length of all columns and constants used. Even using an alias does not help, as Listing 4.9 shows.

Listing 4.9. Using aliases to insert string constants into the output.

```
--       Filename: 04squ09.sql
--        Purpose: Insert string constants into output
--                 to create one plain English sentence
--                 use alias
--           Note: adaptation of 04squ02.sql
--
select
   fmname ||
   ' ' ||
   lname ||
   ' is ' ||
   age ||
   ' years old.' statement,
   age
from
   pers1
;
```

This code returns

```
STATEMENT                                                          AGE
-----------------------------------------------------------------  ---------
David N. Jones is 34 years old.                                     34
A. Emery Martinelli is 92 years old.                                92
F. Espinosa Talavera is 19 years old.                               19
Mary T. Kratochvil is 48 years old.                                 48
Joseph K. Melsheli is 14 years old.                                 14
```

4

CONVERSIONS
AND VALUE
DECODING

The length of the output can be affected using a `format` statement. Listing 4.10 illustrates this.

Listing 4.10. Using aliases and column formatting to insert string constants into the output.

```
--         Filename: 04squ10.sql
--          Purpose: Insert string constants into output
--                   to create one plain English sentence
--                   use alias and column formatting
--             Note: adaptation of 04squ02.sql
--
column statement format A45

select
   fmname ||
   ' ' ||
   lname ||
   ' is ' ||
   age ||
   ' years old.' statement,
   age
from
   pers1
;
```

This code returns

```
STATEMENT                                       AGE
----------------------------------------------- ---------
David N. Jones is 34 years old.                  34
A. Emery Martinelli is 92 years old.             92
F. Espinosa Talavera is 19 years old.            19
Mary T. Kratochvil is 48 years old.              48
Joseph K. Melsheli is 14 years old.              14
```

Working with Pseudocolumns

For purposes of data retrieval, pseudocolumns act like any other table column, but the data is not stored in the table. Three types of pseudocolumns are available:

- Row address (`rowid`) and number of row retrieved (`rownum`)
- Current and next sequence values (`currval` and `nextval`)
- Level in a hierarchical query, which will be discussed in Chapter 22, "Trees and Hierarchical Subqueries"

CAUTION

Pseudocolumns can only be used for data retrieval. *It is not possible to delete, insert, or update them.*

Number of Row Retrieved: rownum

The rownum pseudocolumn returns the number of rows in the order retrieved from the database thus far. If a query returns three rows, rownum returns 1 for the first, 2 for the second, and 3 for the third. Listing 4.11 illustrates this.

Listing 4.11. Retrieving data using rownum.

```
--        Filename: 04squ11.sql
--         Purpose: Display ROWNUM
--
-select
   rownum,
   fmname,
   lname,
   age,
   sex
from
   pers1
;
```

This code returns

```
ROWNUM FMNAME          LNAME            AGE S
------- --------------- ---------------- ---- -
      1 David N.        Jones              34 M
      2 A. Emery        Martinelli         92 M
      3 F. Espinosa     Talavera           19 F
      4 Mary T.         Kratochvil         48 F
      5 Joseph K.       Melsheli           14 M
```

CAUTION

The number assigned is determined by the order of retrieval, not the order of display. In other words, rownum is unaffected by the order by clause, unless the ordering is accomplished by means of an index. The latter case is discussed in Chapter 29, "Keys, Indexes, Constraints, and Table/Column Comments." Listing 4.12 shows the effect of ordering on the rownum values.

4

CONVERSIONS AND VALUE DECODING

Listing 4.12. Retrieving data using rownum and order by.

```
--        Filename: 04squ12.sql
--         Purpose: Display ROWNUM
--                  order output rows
--
select
   rownum,
   fmname,
   lname,
   age,
   sex
```

continues

Listing 4.12. continued

```
from
    pers1
order by age
;
```

This code returns

```
 ROWNUM FMNAME          LNAME            AGE S
 ------- --------------- ---------------- ---- -
      5 Joseph K.       Melsheli          14 M
      3 F. Espinosa     Talavera          19 F
      1 David N.        Jones             34 M
      4 Mary T.         Kratochvil        48 F
      2 A. Emery        Martinelli        92 M
```

Row Address: `rowid`

The row address pseudocolumn `rowid` returns the physical address of a row in the database, as shown in Listing 4.13.

Listing 4.13. Using `rowid`.

```
--        Filename: 04squ13.sql
--        Purpose: Display ROWID
--
select
    rowid,
    fmname,
    lname,
    age,
    sex
from
    pers1
;
```

This code returns

```
ROWID             FMNAME           LNAME             AGE S
----------------- ---------------- ---------------- ---- -
00000158.0000.0002 David N.        Jones             34 M
00000158.0001.0002 A. Emery        Martinelli        92 M
00000158.0002.0002 F. Espinosa     Talavera          19 F
00000158.0003.0002 Mary T.         Kratochvil        48 F
00000158.0004.0002 Joseph K.       Melsheli          14 M
```

As the previous example shows, `rowid` returns three numbers that identify the following, in hexadecimal notation:

- The block address within the datafile
- The row address within the datablock
- The number of the datafile

In the example, the rows are stored in datafile 2, datablock 158, and rows 0, 1, 2, 3, and 4.

> **NOTE**
>
> rowid has its own datatype. This fact has little practical impact. When rowid values are retrieved, they are translated to character strings for display purposes. If they are used in a condition, they are written as a character string, which is then automatically translated to rowid. See Chapter 9, "Conditional Operands," for an example. There are also rowidtochar and chartorowid functions available that provide explicit-type conversions.

The values returned by rowid uniquely identify the rows of a table and usually those in the database.

> **CAUTION**
>
> Rows of *different* clustered tables may share the same rowid. This can only happen if these rows are stored together in the same cluster. Refer to your SQL reference if you use rowid on clustered tables.

Database Sequence Values: currval and nextval

Oracle provides a sequence-generation feature. A database sequence creates unique sequential values. These are most frequently used to generate primary and unique key values (see Chapter 29 for the creation of sequences and their use for that purpose).

ORACLE vs. SQL

If a sequence is defined in the database, its values can be retrieved in a query.

Two pseudocolumns provide access for sequence values:

- *sequencename*.currval returns the current value of the sequence.
- *sequencename*.nextval increments the sequence by a number specified in its definition.

 The script crseq01.sql, available on the CD-ROM attached to this book, creates two sequences that are used for the following examples:

- step1 starts with the value 1 and increments by 1.
- step3 starts with the value 3 and increments by 3.

The script drops the sequences before creating them. When you run it the first time, there are no sequences to drop. This will result in the following error messages, which may be disregarded:

```
drop sequence step1
          *
ERROR at line 1:
ORA-02289: sequence does not exist
Sequence created.
```

```
drop sequence step3
             *
ERROR at line 1:
ORA-02289: sequence does not exist
Sequence created.
```

> **NOTE**
>
> Because the sequence values are retrieved from the sequence and not from the table, and because these are augmented every time nextval is called, you will likely retrieve values that are different from the examples.

Listing 4.14 shows the retrieval and incrementing of sequence values with nextval.

Listing 4.14. Retrieving next sequence values.

```
--        Filename: 04squ14.sql
--         Purpose: Retrieve next sequence values
--
column onxv1 heading 'NEXT¦STEP1'
column tnxv1 heading 'NEXT¦STEP3'
--
select
   fmname,
   step1.nextval onxv1,
   step3.nextval tnxv1
from
   pers1
;

Clear columns
```

This code returns

```
FMNAME              STEP1      STEP3
---------------  ---------  ---------
David N.               31         33
A. Emery               32         36
F. Espinosa            33         39
Mary T.                34         42
Joseph K.              35         45
Input truncated to 13 characters
```

If you run it another time, it returns the following:

```
FMNAME              ONXV1      TNXV1
---------------  ---------  ---------
David N.               36         48
A. Emery               37         51
```

```
F. Espinosa            38         54
Mary T.                39         57
Joseph K.              40         60
```

currval only retrieves the current sequence value; it does not augment it, as Listing 4.15 shows.

Listing 4.15. Retrieving current sequence values.

```
--        Filename: 04squ15.sql
--         Purpose: Retrieve current sequence values
--
column ocrv1 heading 'CURR.¦STEP1'
column tcrv1 heading 'CURR.¦STEP3'

select
   fmname,
   step1.currval ocrv1,
   step3.currval tcrv1
from
   pers1
;
```

This code returns

```
                   CURR.     CURR.
FMNAME             STEP1     STEP3
--------------- --------- ---------
David N.              40        60
A. Emery              40        60
F. Espinosa           40        60
Mary T.               40        60
Joseph K.             40        60
```

Do not combine or repeat currval and nextval of one sequence in the same row. The results of doing so do not make a whole lot of sense. (See Listing 4.16.)

Listing 4.16. Retrieving current and next sequence values together in a statement.

```
--        Filename: 04squ16.sql
--         Purpose: Retrieve several current and next sequence values
--                  together in a statement
--                  DOES NOT WORK
--
column ocrv1 heading 'CURR.¦STEP1'
column onxv1 heading 'NEXT¦STEP1'
column ocrv2 heading 'CURR.¦STEP1'
column tcrv1 heading 'CURR.¦STEP3'
column tnxv1 heading 'NEXT¦STEP3'
column tcrv2 heading 'CURR.¦STEP3'

select
   fmname,
   step1.currval ocrv1,
   step1.nextval onxv1,
   step1.currval ocrv2,
   step3.currval tcrv1,
```

4

CONVERSIONS AND VALUE DECODING

continues

Listing 4.16. continued

```
   step3.nextval tnxv1,
   step3.currval tcrv2
from
   pers1
;
```

This code returns

FMNAME	CURR. STEP1	NEXT STEP1	CURR. STEP1	CURR. STEP3	NEXT STEP3	CURR. STEP3
David N.	41	41	41	63	63	63
A. Emery	42	42	42	66	66	66
F. Espinosa	43	43	43	69	69	69
Mary T.	44	44	44	72	72	72
Joseph K.	45	45	45	75	75	75

System Functions

System functions return values that pertain to

■ The current system date and time

■ The database user

■ The user environment

These system functions can be used in a `select` statement similar to pseudocolumns. The first two will be covered in this section; the third is briefly demonstrated in Part X, "Security."

Current System Date and Time: sysdate

`sysdate` returns the current date and time in the default date format, which is shown in Listing 4.17. The time portion is not displayed because the default date format is set to date only. How to retrieve the time portion will be covered in Chapter 12, "Dates and Times: The `date` Datatype."

Listing 4.17. Retrieving system date.

```
--        Filename: 04squ17.sql
--         Purpose: Retrieve sysdate as report column
--
select
   fmname,
   sysdate
from
   pers1
;
```

This code returns

```
FMNAME           SYSDATE
---------------  -----------
David N.         18-APR-1997
A. Emery         18-APR-1997
F. Espinosa      18-APR-1997
Mary T.          18-APR-1997
Joseph K.        18-APR-1997
```

User Information: uid and user

The current user can be uniquely identified through two functions:

- user returns the username as known to the database.
- userid is a unique integer that is assigned to each user.

Both are extremely useful for security and audit trail tables. Listing 4.18 demonstrates their use.

Listing 4.18. Retrieving user ID and username.

```
--       Filename: 04squ18.sql
--        Purpose: Retrieve uid and username as report columns
--
select
   fmname,
   uid,
   user
from
   pers1
;
```

This code returns

```
FMNAME              UID USER
---------------  ------- ----------------------------------
David N.             11 HANS
A. Emery             11 HANS
F. Espinosa          11 HANS
Mary T.              11 HANS
Joseph K.            11 HANS
```

The decode Expression

The decode expression allows you to specify a matched pair list of search and replace values. decode substitutes the replace value for the search value of an expression. This can be a column, a constant, or the result of a conversion. If the value cannot be found among the search values, decode uses a default value.

The syntax of decode is like that of a function call with arguments (see Figure 4.1). A comma list with at least three and up to 255 expressions can be passed into decode by including it between the parentheses as follows:

- The column, constant, or expression that is being decoded

- Between one and 126 matched pairs of search value and replacement value; 127 pairs if no default value is used

- A default value to be returned if the value of the expression, column, or constant cannot be found among the search values

FIGURE 4.1.

The structure of the decode expression.

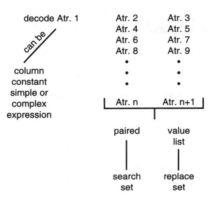

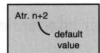

DEBUG ALERT

Always include a default value in a decode expression unless you are absolutely sure that all the possible values in the expression are represented in the search list. If no default value is specified and decode cannot find the value among the search values, it will return a null value that may lead to undesired or unexpected results. See Chapter 15, "Missing Data, Null, and Zero Values," for more information.

Use a formatting standard, similar to that of Figure 4.1 and the following examples. This allows you to scan through the matched sets of values quickly.

For brevity's sake, values are often stored using a code scheme that has to be translated to appropriate value labels in order to make sense to an uninitiated user. The decode expression provides a standard method for such a translation. Listing 4.19 translates the codes of the sex column to Mr. and Ms. and then again to male, female, and missing, respectively.

Listing 4.19. Using the decode expression.

```
--       Filename: 04squ19.sql
--        Purpose: decode string values
--
select
   decode(sex,'M','Mr.',
              'F','Ms.','??') salut,
   fmname,
```

```
   lname,
   'is ',
   decode(sex,'M','male',
              'F','female','??') what
from
   pers1
;
```

This code returns

```
SAL FMNAME            LNAME            'IS WHAT
--- ---------------   ---------------  --- ------
Mr. David N.          Jones            is  male
Mr. A. Emery          Martinelli       is  male
Ms. F. Espinosa       Talavera         is  female
Ms. Mary T.           Kratochvil       is  female
Mr. Joseph K.         Melsheli         is  male
```

The datatypes of the search and replace values do not need to be the same. Thus numerical codes can be translated to strings, and vice versa. The datatype of the search values should correspond to the expression, and all replace and default values should be of the same datatype. SQL, however, will not even return an error if they are not the same. Listing 4.20 translates the ID column—which is a number—to a string with its corresponding ordinal number.

Listing 4.20. Using decode to translate a number to a string.

```
--        Filename: 04squ20.sql
--         Purpose: Decode a number to a string
--
select
   'The',
   decode(id,1,'first',
             2,'second',
             3,'third',
             4,'fourth',
             5,'fifth','??') ordering,
   'is',
    decode(id,1,'first','not first') what
from
   pers1
;
```

This code returns

```
'TH ORDERI 'I WHAT
--- ------ -- ---------
The first  is first
The second is not first
The third  is not first
The fourth is not first
The fifth  is not first
```

Summary

SQL allows you to retrieve more data than is stored in a table. System functions return the system date and time as well as information on the user or the current session. Numerical and string constants can be retrieved as part of a query. Pseudocolumns return information such as the physical database address of a row, the order in which a row is retrieved, or current and next values of sequences. Finally, SQL provides a small set of operators that allows you to convert values from columns, constants, pseudocolumns, and functions through simple expressions.

Single-Row Numerical Functions

IN THIS CHAPTER

Similar to numerical operators, single-row numerical functions provide a means to convert numerical values. While the operators are limited to simple calculations, these functions provide comparably higher mathematical conversions. Their syntax is similar to that of the decode function—the function name is followed by one or more numerical arguments within parentheses. A number function returns always exactly one number.

ORACLE VS SQL

All functions in this chapter are vendor extensions, meaning that they are not part of the SQL-89 and SQL-92 standards. Most vendors provide similar functions, but the syntax might be slightly different.

This chapter presents these functions in four distinct groups:

- Simple numerical functions, such as absolute value (abs), the rounded value (round), or the sign (sign)
- Higher-level mathematical functions, such as power and exponent (exp)
- Trigonometric functions, such as sine (sin) and cosine (cos)
- Hyperbolic functions, such as the hyperbolic sine (sinh) and cosine (cosh)

> **TIP**
>
> You are not limited to the SQL functions provided to you; you can also create your own so-called user functions through procedural extensions to SQL, such as PL/SQL. Functions created this way can be used in a number of SQL statements.

Simple Numerical Functions

Simple numerical functions provide for the simple conversion of numbers. The absolute value (abs), the rounded value (round), and the sign (sign) are described in the following sections.

The Absolute Value (abs) and the Sign (sign)

The function abs(*number*) returns the absolute value of a number. The absolute value of

- A positive number is the number
- A negative number is the number times -1
- Zero is zero

In plain English, if you omit the sign of a number, you get its absolute value.

The function sign(*number*) is the complement of the function abs; it returns the sign of a number. The sign of

- A positive number is +1
- A negative number is -1
- Zero is zero

If you multiply the absolute value of a number with its sign, you get the number (abs(*number*) * sign(*number*) = *number*).

 Run the script cper4.sql, which and be found on the CD accompanying this book, to create a variation of the pers3 table that includes negative and zero values.

Listing 5.1 demonstrates the use of the abs and sign functions. This example contains three select statements that are interpreted as three independent queries. Each of these returns one set of five rows.

Listing 5.1. Using abs and sign functions.

```
--        Filename: 05squ01.sql
--         Purpose: Performs (somewhat) complex calculations with
--                  arithmetic binary operators +,-,*,/
--                  Uses column aliases
--                  Returns absolute values and signs.
--
--                  Computes total income,
--                  income / wealth, and
--                  tax, (assuming a flat 30% income tax and
--                        a flat 2% wealth tax)
--
--                  Adapted from 04squ07.sql

col lname format a10
col age format 99
select
   interest + salary + profit + royalty tot_income,
   abs(interest + salary + profit + royalty) absinc,
   sign(interest + salary + profit + royalty) signinc
from
   pers4
;

select
   (interest + salary + profit + royalty) / wealth inc_ov_wealth,
   abs((interest + salary + profit + royalty) / wealth) abs_inc_ov_wealth,
   sign((interest + salary + profit + royalty) / wealth) sign_inc_ov_wealth
from
   pers4
;

select
   (interest + salary + profit + royalty) * 30/100
       + wealth * 2/100 tax,
   abs((interest + salary + profit + royalty) * 30/100
       + wealth * 2/100) abs_tax,
   sign((interest + salary + profit + royalty) * 30/100
       + wealth * 2/100) sign_tax
from
   pers4
;
```

5

SINGLE-ROW
NUMERICAL
FUNCTIONS

This code returns

```
TOT_INCOME    ABSINC   SIGNINC
----------  ---------- ---------
     92200       92200         1
     92900       92900         1
      4980        4980         1
    188800      188800         1
         0           0         0


INC_OV_WEALTH ABS_INC_OV_WEALTH SIGN_INC_OV_WEALTH
------------- ----------------- ------------------
    -.6447552        .64475524                  -1
   .14403101        .14403101                   1
       .2075            .2075                   1
     .078647          .078647                   1
           0                0                   0


       TAX   ABS_TAX  SIGN_TAX
---------- --------- ---------
     24800     24800         1
     40770     40770         1
      1974      1974         1
    104652    104652         1
        16        16         1
```

Rounding Up or Down to the Next Integer: `floor` and `ceil`

The `floor` function truncates a floating point value to an integer. In other words, it strips all digits right of the decimal point from the number. Complementary to it is the ceiling function `ceil(number)`, which returns the smallest integer that is greater than or equal to a number.

Listing 5.2 demonstrates both functions. Please note that if *number* is an integer, both the ceiling and floor functions return *number*.

Listing 5.2. Using `ceil` and `floor` functions.

```
--       Filename: 05squ02.sql
--        Purpose: demonstrates the ceil and floor functions
--                 Adapted from 04squ07.sql
--
select
   interest + salary + profit + royalty tot_income,
   ceil(interest + salary + profit + royalty) ceilinc,
   floor(interest + salary + profit + royalty) floorinc,
   (interest + salary + profit + royalty) / wealth incowea,
   ceil((interest + salary + profit + royalty) / wealth) ceiliow,
   floor((interest + salary + profit + royalty) / wealth) flooriow
from
   pers4
;
```

This code returns

TOT_INCOME	CEILINC	FLOORINC	INCOWEA	CEILIOW	FLOORIOW
92200	92200	92200	-.6447552	0	-1
92900	92900	92900	.14403101	1	0
4980	4980	4980	.2075	1	0
188800	188800	188800	.078647	1	0
0	0	0	0	0	0

Truncating and Rounding Functions: round and trunc

The round and trunc functions can be called with either one or two arguments. If called with one argument only, they return an integer value:

- trunc(*number*) truncates (drops or omits) the digits right of the decimal point.

- round(*number*) rounds the number up or down to the next integer. Positive numbers are rounded up if their decimal portions are greater than 0.5 and are rounded down otherwise. Negative numbers are rounded *down* if their decimal portions are greater than 0.5 and rounded up otherwise.

> **NOTE**
>
> Although it may appear so on first sight, trunc and round are not quite equivalent to floor and ceil because they deal differently with negative and positive numbers:
>
> - If the number is positive, trunc(*number*) returns the same value as floor(*number*). If the number is negative, trunc(*number*) returns the same value as ceil(*number*).
>
> - If the number is positive, round(*number*) returns the same value as floor(*number* + 0.5). If the number is negative, round(*number*) returns the same value as ceil(*number* - 0.5).
>
> Thus trunc(16.1) returns 16 just as floor(16.1) and round(16.1) do. Whereas, round(16.5), round(16.7), round(17), and round(17.49) all return the same value, 17.
>
> You are most likely to need the round and trunc functions because a truncation or rounding in an arithmetic sense is usually desired.

If these functions are called with two arguments, the second argument, an integer, specifies to *how many digits right of the decimal point the number should be rounded and truncated.* Thus, if the second argument is 4, four digits right of the decimal point will be maintained. If it is zero, the function will return an integer, just as it would have done if *no* second argument had been passed in. The second argument may also be set to a negative integer, in which case it determines how many digits to the *left* of the decimal point will be set to zero by the truncating or rounding process.

5

Listing 5.3. Using `trunc` and `round` functions.

```
--        Filename: 05squ03.sql
--         Purpose: demonstrates the trunc and round functions

select
   interest + salary + profit + royalty tot_income,
   round(interest + salary + profit + royalty) roundinc,
   trunc(interest + salary + profit + royalty) truncinc,
   (interest + salary + profit + royalty) / wealth incowea,
   round((interest + salary + profit + royalty) / wealth, 0) roundiow,
   trunc((interest + salary + profit + royalty) / wealth, 0) trunciow
from
   pers4
;

select
   interest + salary + profit + royalty tot_income,
   round(interest + salary + profit + royalty, -2) roundinc,
   trunc(interest + salary + profit + royalty, -4) truncinc,
   (interest + salary + profit + royalty) / wealth incowea,
   round((interest + salary + profit + royalty) / wealth, 4) roundiow,
   trunc((interest + salary + profit + royalty) / wealth, 6) trunciow
from
   pers4
;
```

This code returns

TOT_INCOME	ROUNDINC	TRUNCINC	INCOWEA	ROUNDIOW	TRUNCIOW
92200	92200	92200	-.6447552	-1	0
92900	92900	92900	.14403101	0	0
4980	4980	4980	.2075	0	0
188800	188800	188800	.078647	0	0
0	0	0	0	0	0

TOT_INCOME	ROUNDINC	TRUNCINC	INCOWEA	ROUNDIOW	TRUNCIOW
92200	92200	90000	-.6447552	-.6448	-.644755
92900	92900	90000	.14403101	.144	.144031
4980	5000	0	.2075	.2075	.2075
188800	188800	180000	.078647	.0786	.078647
0	0	0	0	0	0

Mathematical Functions

SQL provides four kinds of mathematical functions:

- The remainder function, which is treated as an operator in some programming languages
- The functions that raise a number to its power or calculate the square root
- Exponential and logarithmic functions
- Trigonometric functions

It would be desirable to have other mathematical functions available, such as a random number generator. On the other hand, most calculations on database data are fairly simple, so these functions suffice. It is also possible to combine these functions to perform much more complex calculations. Therefore, the following sections provide detailed examples to show what these functions can and cannot do. For example, compound interest and related financial calculations can be performed by use of the power function.

The Remainder Function: mod

The remainder function—mod(*numerator, denominator*)—returns the remainder of the division of the numerator by denominator.

Listing 5.4. Using the mod function.

```
--        Filename: 05squ04.sql
--        Purpose: demonstrates the mod function
--
column tot_income heading 'Total¦Income'
column remain1k   heading 'Remainder¦after¦division¦by 1000'
column incowea    heading 'Income¦------¦wealth'
column remainp5   heading 'Remainder¦after¦division¦by 0.5'

select
   interest + salary + profit + royalty tot_income,
   mod(interest + salary + profit + royalty, 1000) remain1k,
   (interest + salary + profit + royalty) / wealth incowea,
   mod((interest + salary + profit + royalty) / wealth, .5) remainp5
from
   pers4
;

clear columns
```

This code returns

```
           Remainder           Remainder
              after   Income      after
    Total  division   ------   division
   Income  by 1000    wealth    by 0.5
--------- --------- --------- ---------
    92200       200 -.6447552 -.1447552
    92900       900 .14403101 .14403101
     4980       980    .2075     .2075
   188800       800  .078647   .078647
        0         0        0         0

Input truncated to 13 characters
```

Exponential Functions: power, exp, and sqrt

The power function power(*number, exponent*) raises the number to the power of an exponent. This function accepts all positive integers and floating point numbers. With some limitations, which are discussed in the following section, it also accepts negative values. Because the exponent may be a fraction, it can also be used to extract the nth root of a number.

The following examples run against the dual table, which contains only one dummy row and one column. It is mostly used to extract exactly one value from system functions.

ORACLE
vs SQL

All examples in this section are contained in the file 05squ05.sql, which is available on the CD-ROM at the back of this book. If you are using them in an installation of SQL that does not have a dual table installed, you can run the script crfkdual.sql. This creates the similar fkdual table against which you can run the examples. Just replace from dual with from fkdual. You should also check the syntax of the arithmetic and mathematical functions proper in your vendor-provided SQL reference guide.

Listing 5.5 uses only positive integers for both the number and exponent.

Listing 5.5. Using the power function.

```
select  power(10,3),
        power(2,1),
        power(1,1000),
        power(1000,0)
from dual;
```

This code returns

```
POWER(10,3) POWER(2,1) POWER(1,1000) POWER(1000,0)
----------- ---------- ------------- -------------
       1000          2             1             1
```

These are straightforward cases, where the number is raised to a power. The same can be done if the first argument is a floating point number, as shown in the following:

```
select  power(10.55,3),
        power(29.886,1),
        power(1.001,1000),
        power(1000.9812,0)
from dual;
```

This code returns

```
POWER(10.55,3) POWER(29.886,1) POWER(1.001,1000) POWER(1000.9812,0)
-------------- --------------- ----------------- ------------------
     1174.2414          29.886         2.7169239                  1
```

You also can raise a negative number, whether integer or floating point, to a power. If the exponent is even, the result will be even. If the exponent is odd, the result will be odd:

```
select  power(-10,3),
        power(-2,4),
        power(-29.886,1),
        power(-1.001,1000),
        power(-1000.9812,0)
from dual;
```

This code returns

```
POWER(-10,3) POWER(-2,4) POWER(-29.886,1) POWER(-1.001,1000) POWER(-1000.9812,0)
------------ ----------- ---------------- ------------------- --------------------
       -1000          16          -29.886           2.7169239                    1
```

A special case is the number *e* (~2.71828182845904) on which natural logarithms are based (see the following section). The exponent function exp is equivalent to the power function where the first argument is *e*. The following example returns slightly different numbers because *e* has many more digits than the ones supplied:

```
select exp(10),
       power(2.7182818,10)
from dual;
```

This code returns

```
EXP(10) POWER(2.7182818,10)
--------- --------------------
22026.466           22026.463
```

A more powerful use of this function is the extraction of roots. This is done by supplying a simple fraction as the second argument, such as 1/2 for the square root, 1/3 for the third root, 1/4 for the fourth root, and so on. The sqrt(*number*) function is a special case equivalent to power(*number*, 1/2). The following example shows root procedures with whole positive integers:

```
select  power(1000,1/3),
        power(3,1/3),
        power(1,1/1000),
        power(4,1/2),
        sqrt(4)
from dual;
```

This code returns

```
POWER(1000,1/3) POWER(3,1/3) POWER(1,1/1000) POWER(4,1/2)   SQRT(4)
--------------- ------------ --------------- ------------ ---------
             10    1.4422496               1            2         2
```

Despite the fact that expressions such as the third root of a negative number are defined in real number space, the power function does not permit root operations if the first argument is negative. This is what the manual means by the cryptic comment that the exponent has to be an integer if the number is negative. The following example demonstrates that treatment:

```
select  power(-1000,1/3) from dual;
```

This code returns

```
ERROR:
ORA-01428: argument '-1000' is out of range
no rows selected
```

You can try to get around this by applying a combination of the abs and sign functions, but only if you can guarantee that the denominator of the exponent is odd, meaning that you extract an odd, not an even, root. In the latter case, you will get a result, but the result will be wrong because an even root of a negative number is not defined in real number space. The following example shows that:

```
select sign(-27)*power(abs(-27),1/3),
       sign(-16)*power(abs(-16),1/4)
from dual;
```

This code returns

```
SIGN(-27)*POWER(ABS(-27),1/3) SIGN(-16)*POWER(ABS(-16),1/4)
----------------------------- -----------------------------
                           -3                            -2
```

You might try to find a solution to this problem and submit it to the obfuscated SQL code contest. If you use PL/SQL or the procedural language extension provided by your vendor, you could create a function that would return the correct number where it is defined in real number space, and an error, where it is not defined. Listing 5.6 shows the necessary code.

Listing 5.6. Using npower user function to extend the power function.

```
--         Filename: 05squ06.sql
--          Purpose: npower user function
--          extends the power function to handle odd roots of negative numbers
--
create or replace FUNCTION npower
        (base in number,
         exp in number)
        RETURN number IS
basen   number := base;
expn    number := exp;
result number;
BEGIN
  if (base < 0) and (expn > 0) and (mod(1/expn,2) = 1) then
        basen := abs(basen);
        result := -power(basen, exp);
  else result := power(basen,exp);
  end if;
  return result;
END npower;
/
```

This function returns the correct result for the odd root of a negative number and returns a different error upon encountering an even root of a negative number, as shown in the following:

```
select  npower(-1000,1/3) from dual;
```

This code returns

```
NPOWER(-1000,1/3)
-----------------
              -10
```

This code

```
select  npower(-10000,1/4) from dual;
```

returns the following:

```
ERROR:
ORA-06502: PL/SQL: numeric or value error
ORA-06512: at "SYS.STANDARD", line 448
ORA-06512: at "HANS.NPOWER", line 12
ORA-06512: at line 1
no rows selected
```

 This function works with all the examples that are included in the section about the power function, which you can try out by running the script 05squ07.sql, found on the CD-ROM at the back of this book.

REAL-WORLD EXPERIENCES

Have you ever asked an American how many feet fit into a mile, or how many acres fit into a square mile? Some, who have experienced rural areas may know the latter, because if you take ½ of a mile square, you get the standard land grant and farm size of 160 acres. To the American mind, the first question is totally unintuitive because feet are used in one context such as building houses or measuring out twine, and miles are used in a different one such as driving cars. The fact that the two are related—both are measures of length—is simply besides the point. This is not a matter of intelligence but a matter of habit. Kids in many European countries, on the other hand, can convert meters to kilometers and millimeters and are quite good in decimal expressions. But even Canada, which went decimal 25 years ago, still has a $25 bill because it is a convenient quarter of $100.

The same applies to cooking. An American cookbook reads like this: "Take 3½ cups of flour, add ½ tablespoon of cinnamon...." In most American kitchens, you can find a set of measuring cups that are marked 1 cup, ½ cup, ⅓ cup, and so on. Few cooks care how many tablespoons fit into a cup. In the German-speaking parts of Europe, most kitchens have a scale. Cookbook instructions read similar to the following: "Take 430 grams of flour, add 25 grams of cinnamon...."

You may have wondered why the preceding examples always use a fraction, such as ¼, rather than a decimal number, such as 0.25. The reason is that, at least on this continent, it is much more intuitive to use the fraction. The fraction ¼ in the exponent, for example, makes it immediately clear that we are dealing with the fourth root. This will help others who have to understand the code.

5

SINGLE-ROW
NUMERICAL
FUNCTIONS

The last noteworthy situation arises in situations where the exponent is negative. A number raised to a negative power of n is the same as 1 divided by the same number raised to the positive power of n. Thus, 2 to the power of -2 equals 1 over 2 to the power of 2, or 1/4. SQL handles this situation without any problems, as the following example shows:

```
select power(8,1/3),
       1/power(8,1/3) ,
       power(8,-1/3)
from dual;
```

This code returns

```
POWER(8,1/3) 1/POWER(8,1/3) POWER(8,-1/3)
------------ -------------- -------------
           2             .5            .5
```

Logarithmic Functions: `log` and `ln`

The function `log(base, number)` returns the logarithm of the base of a number. It is the complement of the power function. In plain English, it returns the power to which you have to raise *base* in order to get *number*. Thus, in order to raise 2 to obtain 8, an exponent of 3 has to be used; log(2, 8) returns 3. The function log accepts only positive numbers as arguments, but the base must not be 0 or 1:

```
select log(10,1000),
       power(10,3),
       power(10,log(10,1000)),
       log(10,power(10,3))
from dual;
```

This code returns

```
LOG(10,1000) POWER(10,3) POWER(10,LOG(10,1000)) LOG(10,POWER(10,3))
------------ ----------- ---------------------- -------------------
           3        1000                   1000                   3
```

Just as was the case with `exp`, a special `ln(number)` function is provided for natural logarithms based on the number *e*. Again, the number must be positive:

```
select ln(10),
       log(2.7182818,10)
from dual;
```

This code returns

```
LN(10) LOG(2.7182818,10)
--------- -----------------
2.3025851         2.3025851
```

Trigonometric Functions: `sin`, `cos`, and `tan`

The `sin`, `cos`, and `tan` functions return the sine, cosine, and tangent of an angle expressed in radians. The radians of an angle are calculated by multiplying the angle with π and dividing the resulting number by 180.

FIGURE 5.1.
Degrees and radians.

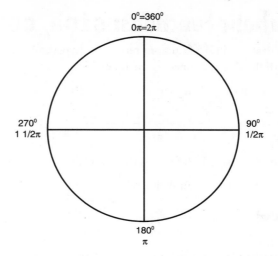

$$\text{Radius} = \frac{\text{Degrees}}{180} * \pi$$

The first example calculates the sine of 60 degrees:

```
select  sin(60/180*3.14159265358979) from dual;
```

This code returns

```
SIN(60/180*3.14159265358979)
----------------------------
                   .8660254
```

The second example calculates the cosine of 60 degrees:

```
select  cos(60/180*3.14159265358979) from dual;
```

This code returns

```
COS(60/180*3.14159265358979)
----------------------------
                         .5
```

The last example calculates the tangent of 60 degrees:

```
select  tan(60/180*3.14159265358979) from dual;
```

This code returns

```
TAN(60/180*3.14159265358979)
----------------------------
                  1.7320508
```

Hyperbolic Functions: `sinh`, `cosh`, and `tanh`

The `sinh`, `cosh`, and `tanh` functions return the hyperbolic sine, cosine, or tangent of a number. The hyperbolic sine is defined as the following:

$$\text{sinh}(\textit{number}) = \frac{e^{\textit{number}} - e^{\textit{number}}}{2}$$

The hyperbolic cosine is defined as the following:

$$\text{cosh}(\textit{number}) = \frac{e^{\textit{number}} + e^{-\textit{number}}}{2}$$

The hyperbolic tangent is defined as the following:

$$\text{tanh}(\textit{number}) = \frac{\text{sinh}(\textit{number})}{\text{cosh}(\textit{number})}$$

The following example calculates the hyperbolic sine, cosine and tangent of the numbers -2, .5, and -1, respectively.

```
select  sinh(-2),
        cosh(.5),
        tanh(-1) from dual;
```

This code returns

```
 SINH(-2)  COSH(.5)  TANH(-1)
--------- --------- ---------
 -3.62686  1.127626 -.7615942
```

Summary

Single-row numerical functions perform value conversions that are more sophisticated than the rather limited functionality of the numerical operators. While these functions are not part of the SQL standard, most vendors provide at least some of them (although the syntax may be different). The simple numerical and the exponential functions will most likely be of use for programming. If other functionality is required, a user function can be written.

Single-Row Character String Functions

IN THIS CHAPTER

CHAPTER 6

If you recall from Chapter 4, "Operator Conversions and Value Decoding," the functionality of the only single string operator in the SQL language—concatenation—is even more limited than that of its numerical counterparts. The much more powerful decode operator can be used for string conversions as well. Compensating for these limitations, the SQL standard includes string functions that will look familiar if you have experience with C. These should be sufficiently powerful to handle most jobs encountered by the typical database system. For tasks beyond that, custom functions can be written through vendor-supplied language extensions such as PL/SQL.

This chapter covers the two distinct subsets of single-row character functions: substring extraction, trimming, and padding functions on the one hand and conversion functions on the other. Chapter 7, "Character/Number Conversions," covers the remaining sets: functions that calculate the string length or the position of one string within another, character set functions, and datatype conversion functions.

Substring Extraction, Trimming, and Padding Functions

Strings frequently are stored in a form different from what is desired for a report. The column definition for a string may be much longer than the average value it is intended to hold, just for the case that a very long string value needs to be taken care of. Several fields that belong together may be stored in a single string because this is how the data is downloaded from a feeder system. Some extraneous padding characters may have been included because this is how a constant width system deals with strings. In all these cases, strings need to be converted to a suitable format. This can be done either in storage, which is usually preferable, or upon reporting. SQL provides a few useful functions for these purposes.

All functions in this chapter are vendor extensions, meaning that they are not part of the SQL-89 and SQL-92 standards. Most vendors provide similar functions, but the syntax may be slightly different.

Substrings: `substr`

The substring function `substr` is by far the most important and most frequently used character function. It allows you to extract a substring from a string beginning at a specified character and for a specified number of characters. The substring function has three arguments:

- A column name, a constant, or any other legal expression
- The position of the string calculated in bytes, at which the substring should start
- The length of the substring in bytes

Substring Counting Forward

The standard use is to begin calculating the position at which the substring should begin from the beginning of the string. In this case, the second argument must be positive.

Listing 6.1 converts the lname and fmname entries of pers1 to initials.

Listing 6.1. Using the substr function.

```
--          Filename: 06squ01.sql
--          Purpose: show use of substr function
--
select
    decode(sex,'M','Mr. ',
               'F','Ms. ','??? ') ||
    substr(fmname,1,1) || '. ' ||
    substr(lname,1,1) || '.!' who
from
    pers1
order by
    substr(lname,2,4)
;
```

This code returns

```
WHO
----------
Ms. F. T.!
Mr. A. M.!
Mr. J. M.!
Mr. D. J.!
Ms. M. K.!
```

Substring Counting Backwards

The substring function can also be used to begin extraction by counting a defined number of bytes from the end of the string backwards. Listing 6.2 first extracts a substring from lname, starting five bytes from the right and three characters long. It then extracts the last character of the fmname column.

Listing 6.2. Using the substr function to count backwards in a string.

```
--          Filename: 06squ02.sql
--          Purpose: show use of substr function
--                   counting from end of string backwards
--
select
    lname,
    substr(lname,-5,3),
    fmname,
    substr(fmname,-1,1)
from
    pers1
;
```

This code returns

```
LNAME           SUB FMNAME          S
--------------- --- --------------- -
Jones           Jon David N.        .
Martinelli      nel A. Emery        y
Talavera        ave F. Espinosa     a
Kratochvil      chv Mary T.         .
Melsheli        she Joseph K.       .
```

Note that the last character of the fmname column is a period if the person uses a full first name.

Trimming Off Parts of Strings: rtrim and ltrim

Substring requires that you specify both the exact position and the exact length of the substring. The trim functions determine both the position and length on the basis of the contents of the string value. Trim functions have two arguments:

- The string to be trimmed—A column, a constant, or a string expression
- The trimset—A string that contains the characters to be trimmed

Beginning from the left or right, respectively, ltrim or rtrim keeps stripping trimset characters from the string until it encounters the first character not included in the trimset. The remaining string is returned.

> **NOTE**
>
> The trim functions do *not* strip out those trimset characters that are encountered after the first nontrimset character. Thus, for example, you can trim leading and trailing spaces from a string without stripping space characters between two words.

The most customary use of these functions is to strip extraneous padding from a value.

 Run the script crper5.sql, which can be found on the CD accompanying this book. This creates and loads the table pers5, which includes many strings with extraneous characters. The content of the table is as follows:

```
ID LNAME                   FMNAME                   SSN
-- ----------------------- ------------------------ --------------
 1 padx. ...Jones  ... pad . *^*^*^*David N.*^*^*^*^*^ ###895663453###
 2 ..padx.Martinelli .pad .. *^*^ ^* *^ A. Emery ^*^ ^ ##312331818####
 3 ...padx..... Talavera pad *^* *^ *F. Espinosa*^* ** #533932999#####
 4 .. .. .. ..Kratochvil pad ***^^^   ^^^ Mary T.***^^ #####969825711#
 5 paMelshelidx..padx .. pad ^^^ Joseph K.**** *** ^^^ ##000342222####
```

Listing 6.3 strips extraneous characters from the left of lname and then from the right of both fmname and ssn.

Single-Row Character String Functions

CHAPTER 6

109

6
SINGLE-ROW
CHARACTER
STRING FUNCTIONS

Listing 6.3. Using `ltrim` and `rtrim` functions to remove characters.

```
--        Filename: 06squ03.sql
--         Purpose: use of ltrim/rtrim functions
--                  to strip the extraneous characters from pers5
--
col id format 99

select
   id,
   ltrim(lname,'padx. ') L_Name,
   rtrim(fmname,'^* ')    FM_Name,
   rtrim(ssn,'#')
from
   pers5
;

clear columns ;
```

The preceding code returns the following:

```
ID L_NAME                        FM_NAME                    RTRIM(SSN,'#')
-- ---------------------------   ------------------------   --------------
 1 Jones  ... pad .              *^*^*^*David N.            ###895663453
 2 Martinelli .pad ..            *^*^ ^* *^ A. Emery        ##312331818
 3 Talavera pad                  *^* *^ *F. Espinosa        #533932999
 4 Kratochvil pad                ***^^^   ^^^ Mary T.       #####969825711
 5 Melshelidx..padx .. pad       ^^^ Joseph K.             ##000342222
```

Note that the letters *a* in Martinelli, Talavera, and Kratochvil are not stripped because there were letters *not* represented in the trimset between the beginning of the string and these letters.

Listing 6.4 does the opposite and strips from the right of `lname` and from the left of the other values.

Listing 6.4. Using `ltrim` and `rtrim` functions to remove characters.

```
--        Filename: 06squ04.sql
--         Purpose: use of ltrim/rtrim functions
--                  to strip the extraneous characters from pers5
--
col id format 99

select
   id,
   rtrim(lname,'padx. ') L_Name,
   ltrim(fmname,'^* ')    FM_Name,
   ltrim(ssn,'#')
from
   pers5
;

clear columns
```

This code returns

```
ID L_NAME                  FM_NAME                   LTRIM(SSN,'#')
--- ---------------------  ------------------------  --------------
  1 padx. ...Jones         David N.*^*^*^*^*^         895663453###
  2 ..padx.Martinelli      A. Emery ^*^ ^             312331818####
  3 ...padx..... Talaver   F. Espinosa*^* **          533932999#####
  4 .. .. .. ..Kratochvil   Mary T.***^^              969825711#
  5 paMelsheli             Joseph K.**** *** ^^^      000342222####
```

CAUTION

Beware of the trim trap: If the trimset characters are part of the string to be retained and there are no nontrimset characters in between, that part of the string will be trimmed as well. For example, see the last a in the name Talavera in the previous example. SQL will follow the rule provided by the trimset, but it cannot read minds.

Finally, Listing 6.5 combines the first two examples and strips on both sides.

Listing 6.5. Using `ltrim` and `rtrim` functions to remove characters from both sides of a string.

```
--        Filename: 06squ05.sql
--        Purpose: use of ltrim/rtrim functions
--                 to strip the extraneous characters from pers5
--                 strips from both sides
--
col id format 99

select
   id,
   ltrim(rtrim(lname,'padx. '),'padx. ')  L_Name,
   ltrim(rtrim(fmname,'^* '),'^* ')    FM_Name,
   ltrim(rtrim(ssn,'#'),'#') SSNo
from
   pers5
;

clear columns
```

This code returns

```
ID L_NAME                  FM_NAME                   SSNO
--- ---------------------  ------------------------  --------------
  1 Jones                  David N.                  895663453
  2 Martinelli             A. Emery                  312331818
  3 Talaver                F. Espinosa               533932999
  4 Kratochvil             Mary T.                   969825711
  5 Melsheli               Joseph K.                 000342222
```

While the error on Talavera stays the same, these functions are clearly capable of stripping out the typical characters that are used for padding (., *, #, $, and blanks).

Single-Row Character String Functions

CHAPTER 6

111

6

SINGLE-ROW
CHARACTER
STRING FUNCTIONS

The functions can also be used to obtain the call name from a field that is organized like `fmname` in `pers1`.

Padding Strings: `rpad` and `lpad`

The padding functions do just the opposite of string functions: They take a string and pad it to a specified length, either to the right (`rpad`) or to the left (`lpad`). Padding functions have three arguments:

- The string to be trimmed—Either a column, a constant, or a string expression.

- The display length of the output in characters—Display length and the number of bytes are the same in 8-bit character sets (most are 8-bit character sets).

- The padset—This is a string that will be repeated by the function until the specified display length is reached. This argument is optional. If it is omitted, a single blank is used as the default.

Padding functions always return a fixed-length string, regardless of whether the string to be trimmed is fixed length or variable.

Listing 6.6 pads both the `first` and `mlnames` from the `pers1` table to the right and `ssn` to the left.

Listing 6.6. Using `lpad` and `rpad` functions.

```
--      Filename: 06squ06.sql
--      Purpose: use of lpad/rpad functions
--               to pad to a specified length.
--               strips from both sides
--
col id format 99

select
   id,
   rpad(lname,20,'* # '),
   rpad(fmname,20,'^* '),
   lpad(ssn,12,'#')
from
   pers1
;

clear columns
```

This code returns

```
ID RPAD(LNAME,20,'*#')    RPAD(FMNAME,20,'^*') LPAD(SSN,12,
--- --------------------    -------------------- ------------
  1 Jones* # * # * # * #    David N.^* ^* ^* ^*   ###895663453
  2 Martinelli* # * # *     A. Emery^* ^* ^* ^*   ###312331818
  3 Talavera* # * # * #     F. Espinosa^* ^* ^*   ###533932999
  4 Kratochvil* # * # *     Mary T.^* ^* ^* ^* ^  ###969825711
  5 Melsheli* # * # * #     Joseph K.^* ^* ^* ^*  ###000342222
```

It is unnecessary to combine rpad and lpad for padding a value on both sides. A padding function returns a string of a fixed length already. All that needs to be done is to concatenate the padding to the other side, as Listing 6.7 shows.

Listing 6.7. Using lpad and rpad functions.

```
--        Filename: 06squ07.sql
--         Purpose: use of lpad/rpad functions
--                  to pad to a specified length.
--                  concatenates padding to other side
--
col id format 99

select
   id,
   '****' || rpad(lname,20,'*'),
   '####' || rpad(fmname,20,'#'),
   lpad(ssn,12,'$') || '$$$'
from
   pers1
;

clear columns
```

This code returns

```
 ID '****'||RPAD(LNAME,20,'* '####'||RPAD(FMNAME,20,' LPAD(SSN,12,'$'
--- ------------------------ ------------------------ --------------
  1 ****Jones*************** ####David N.########### $$$895663453$$$
  2 ****Martinelli********** ####A. Emery########### $$$312331818$$$
  3 ****Talavera************ ####F. Espinosa######### $$$533932999$$$
  4 ****Kratochvil********** ####Mary T.############ $$$969825711$$$
  5 ****Melsheli************ ####Joseph K.########## $$$000342222$$$
```

> **TIP**
>
> Using padding functions on a fixed-length character string is unnecessary because the length of the string is already known. Concatenating the padding will do the trick.

Another way of padding values, format masks, is shown in Chapter 11, "Numerical Data: The number Datatype."

Character Conversion Functions

The functions discussed thus far have either taken something out of a string or added something to it. The functions in the following sections convert strings in different ways—they search and replace characters or substrings, and alter the capitalization.

Character Translations: `translate`

The decode operator deals with an entire argument, which may be a whole string at a time. The `translate` function can convert characters within a string. It has three arguments:

- The string to be translated—A column, a constant, or a string expression.
- The search set—A string that contains the characters to be changed.
- The replace set—A string that contains the characters to be substituted. The first letter replaces the first letter of the search set, the second letter replaces the second letter of the search set, and so on.

The `translate` function processes all the characters of the string. If it encounters a character that is not in the search set, it leaves it as is. If the character is contained in the search set, and a character is listed on the matching spot in the replace set, a substitution is made. If the replace set is shorter than the search set, some search set characters will not have corresponding replace set characters. In this case, `translate` substitutes NULL.

Listing 6.8 uses the `translate` function to convert the case of the characters of both `lname` and `fmname`, and to express the `ssn` entry as lowercase letters—1 equals a, 2 equals b, and so on.

Listing 6.8. Using `translate` function.

```
--        Filename: 06squ08.sql
--        Purpose: use of the translate function
--                 switches cases of name columns
--                 expresses ssn as corresponding letters.
--
col id format 99

select
   id,
   translate(lname,
     'ABCDEFGHIJKLMNOPQRSTUVWXYZabcdefghijklmnopqrstuvwxyz1234567890',
     'abcdefghijklmnopqrstuvwxyzABCDEFGHIJKLMNOPQRSTUVWXYZabcdefghij')
     l_name,
   translate(fmname,
     'ABCDEFGHIJKLMNOPQRSTUVWXYZabcdefghijklmnopqrstuvwxyz1234567890',
     'abcdefghijklmnopqrstuvwxyzABCDEFGHIJKLMNOPQRSTUVWXYZabcdefghij')
     fm_name,
   translate(ssn,
     'ABCDEFGHIJKLMNOPQRSTUVWXYZabcdefghijklmnopqrstuvwxyz1234567890',
     'abcdefghijklmnopqrstuvwxyzABCDEFGHIJKLMNOPQRSTUVWXYZabcdefghij')
     s_s_n
from
   pers1
;

clear columns
```

This code returns

```
 ID L_NAME           FM_NAME          S_S_N
--- ---------------- ---------------- ---------
  1 jONES            dAVID n.         hieffcdec
  2 mARTINELLI       a. eMERY         cabccahah
  3 tALAVERA         f. eSPINOSA      eccicbiii
  4 kRATOCHVIL       mARY t.          ifihbegaa
  5 mELSHELI         jOSEPH k.        jjjcdbbbb
```

Listing 6.9 changes the case and blanks out the letters of the second half of the alphabet and the digits 6-0 as well.

Listing 6.9. Using the `translate` function to blank out letters.

```
--        Filename: 06squ09.sql
--         Purpose: use of the translate function
--                  switches cases of name columns
--                  expresses ssn as corresponding letters
--                  blanks out letters m-z, M-Z, and digits 6-0
--
select
   id,
   translate(lname,
     'ABCDEFGHIJKLMNOPQRSTUVWXYZabcdefghijklmnopqrstuvwxyz1234567890',
     'abcdefghijkl            ABCDEFGHIJKL            abcde      ')
     l_name,
   translate(fmname,
     'ABCDEFGHIJKLMNOPQRSTUVWXYZabcdefghijklmnopqrstuvwxyz1234567890',
     'abcdefghijkl            ABCDEFGHIJKL            abcde      ')
     fm_name,
   translate(ssn,
     'ABCDEFGHIJKLMNOPQRSTUVWXYZabcdefghijklmnopqrstuvwxyz1234567890',
     'abcdefghijkl            ABCDEFGHIJKL            abcdef     ')
     s_s_n
from
   pers1
;

clear columns
```

This code returns

```
 ID L_NAME           FM_NAME          S_S_N
--- ---------------- ---------------- ---------
  1 j    E           dA ID   .          effcdec
  2  A  I ELLI       a. e E           cabcca a
  3  ALA E A         f. e I   A       ecc cb
  4 k A  CH IL        A      .          f  be aa
  5  EL HELI         j  E H k.          cdbbbb
```

Listing 6.10 does the same thing, except that these characters are not blanked but stripped out. For that purpose, the search and replace strings had to be rearranged a little. All matched search/replace character pairs are listed first. The characters to be stripped out are listed at the end of the search string, but have no matching value in the replace string.

Single-Row Character String Functions

CHAPTER 6

115

6

SINGLE-ROW
CHARACTER
STRING FUNCTIONS

Listing 6.10. Using the `translate` function to strip out characters.

```
--         Filename: 06squ10.sql
--         Purpose: use of the translate function
--                  switches cases of name columns
--                  expresses ssn as corresponding letters
--                  strips out letters m-z, M-Z, and digits 6-0
--
col id format 99

select
   id,
   translate(lname,
     'ABCDEFGHIJKLabcdefghijkl12345MNOPQRSTUVWXYZmnopqrstuvwxyz67890',
     'abcdefghijklABCDEFGHIJKLabcde')      l_name,
   translate(fmname,
     'ABCDEFGHIJKLabcdefghijkl12345MNOPQRSTUVWXYZmnopqrstuvwxyz67890',
     'abcdefghijklABCDEFGHIJKLabcde')      fm_name,
   translate(ssn,
     'ABCDEFGHIJKLabcdefghijkl12345MNOPQRSTUVWXYZmnopqrstuvwxyz67890',
     'abcdefghijklABCDEFGHIJKLabcde')      s_s_n
from
   pers1
;

clear columns
```

This code returns

```
ID L_NAME           FM_NAME          S_S_N
--- ---------------- ---------------- ---------
  1 jE               dAID .           ecdec
  2 AIELLI           a. eE            cabccaa
  3 ALAEA            f. eIA           ecccb
  4 kACHIL           A .              beaa
  5 ELHELI           jEH k.           cdbbbb
```

Substring Replacements: `replace`

The `replace` function is equivalent to a global search function in a word processor or text editor utility. It has three arguments:

- The string to be processed—A column, a constant, or a string expression.
- The search string with the exact character pattern to be changed.
- The replace string with the exact character pattern to be substituted—This argument is optional. If it is missing, all occurrences of the search string are stripped.

Listing 6.11 replaces the string `li` in `lname` with `lly` and `ry` in `fmname` with `rri`, and strips out the pattern `000` in `ssn`:

Listing 6.11. Using the `replace` function.

```
--        Filename: 06squ11.sql
--        Purpose: use of the replace function
--                 replaces the sting li in lname with lly,
--                          ry in fmname with rri, and
--                          strips out 000 in ssn.
--
col id format 99
col L_name format A20
col FM_name format A20

select
   id,
   replace(lname,'li','lly') l_name,
   replace(fmname,'ry','rri') fm_name,
   replace(ssn,'000')
from pers1
;


clear columns
```

This code returns

```
ID L_NAME              FM_NAME            REPLACE(S
--- ----------------   ----------------   ---------
  1 Jones              David N.           895663453
  2 Martinellly        A. Emerri          312331818
  3 Talavera           F. Espinosa        533932999
  4 Kratochvil         Marri T.           969825711
  5 Melshelly          Joseph K.          342222
```

Case Conversions

The example `06squ08.sql` uses the `translate` function to globally switch the case of letters in a string. SQL provides three explicit case conversion functions, `upper`, `lower`, and `initcap`, which capitalize all letters, put all letters to lowercase, and capitalize initial letters of words within a string only, respectively. These functions take just one argument—the string to be converted.

Conversions to Uppercase or Lowercase: `upper` and `lower`

The `upper` and `lower` functions return all capitalized or lowercase versions, respectively, of the string passed in. Listing 6.12 uses `decode`, concatenation, and `upper` to create a string that contains a salutation, a first/middle name, and an all-capitalized last name. It also creates a code consisting of the first three letters of the last name and the first initial, all in lowercase.

Listing 6.12. Using `decode`, `concatenation`, and `upper`.

```
--        Filename: 06squ12.sql
--        Purpose: use of the upper and lower functions
--                 Creates salutation string and
--                 last/f code
```

Single-Row Character String Functions

CHAPTER 6

117

6

SINGLE-ROW
CHARACTER
STRING FUNCTIONS

```
--
col id format 99
col L_name format A20
col FM_name format A20

select
   id,
   decode(sex, 'M','Mr. ',
               'F','Ms.','??? ') ||
   fmname || ' ' ||
   upper(lname) Salut,
   lower(substr(lname,1,3) || substr(fmname,1,1)) Code
from pers1
;

clear columns
```

This code returns

```
ID SALUT                               CODE
--- ------------------------------------ ----
  1 Mr. David N. JONES                  jond
  2 Mr. A. Emery MARTINELLI             mara
  3 Ms. F. Espinosa TALAVERA            talf
  4 Ms. Mary T. KRATOCHVIL              kram
  5 Mr. Joseph K. MELSHELI              melj
```

Capitalization of Initial Letters: `initcap`

The `initcap` function capitalizes the initial letters of each word within the string to be converted. The function considers any combination of letters *immediately* preceded by white space or other nonalphanumeric characters as words. Listing 6.13 consists of four `select` statements. The first one is a single string where the words are separated by spaces.

Listing 6.13. Using the `initcap` function.

```
--      Filename: 06squ13.sql
--      Purpose: use of the initcap function
--
select
   initcap('this is a test of the initicap function') spaces
from dual;
```

This code returns

```
SPACES
-----------------------------------------
This Is A Test Of The Initicap Function
```

The initial character of every word is capitalized.

The words of the string in the next two queries are separated by digits. In the second one, all digits are translated to spaces by enclosing the output into a `translate` function. In either case, all words are lowercase:

```
select
    initcap('this1is2a3test4of5the6initicap7function') digits
from dual;

select
    translate(initcap('this1is2a3test4of5the6initicap7function'),
              '1234567','       ') stripped_digits
from dual;
```

This code returns

```
DIGITS
----------------------------------------
This1is2a3test4of5the6initicap7function

STRIPPED_DIGITS
----------------------------------------
This is a test of the initicap function
```

The next example separates the words by nonalphanumeric characters:

```
select
    initcap('this$is''a+test_of?the initicap^function')
        non_alpha_numeric
from dual;
```

This code returns

```
NON_ALPHA_NUM
----------------------------------------
This$Is'A+Test_Of?The    Initicap^Function
```

All words have capitalized initial letters.

The final example includes digits after the nonalphanumeric characters:

```
select
    initcap('this$is''a+test_of?2the    4initicap^5function') mixed
from dual;
```

This code returns

```
MIXED
----------------------------------------
This$Is'A+Test_Of?2the  4initicap^5function
```

The digits cancel the capitalization that the nonalphanumeric would bring about.

Special Functions for National Language Support

Different languages have different rules for sorting and capitalization. Special versions of the `upper`, `lower`, and `initcap` functions can handle these special linguistic requirements. These

Single-Row Character String Functions

CHAPTER 6

119

6

SINGLE-ROW
CHARACTER
STRING FUNCTIONS

functions—`nls_upper`, `nls_lower`, and `nls_initcap`—have a second argument, which specifies the linguistic sort sequence to be used. Consult SQL and server documentation if you are interested in these features.

Identifying Similarly Sounding Strings: soundex

soundex returns a phonetic representation of a word, which is the same word or a similarly sounding word (even if the spelling is different). This function is useful if you want to retrieve all names that sound similar to a particular word. This is done by retrieving those names where soundex returns the same or similar value of the word being compared. Chapter 9 demonstrates this method.

Exactly how soundex works is of little consequence for using the function. If you are interested in the algorithm used for soundex or you would like to learn about other, improved algorithms, see Celko 1995, pp. 83–90, which provides a good discussion. It's sufficient to say that the function returns a four-byte code consisting of the first character of the word and three digits. Listing 6.14 shows these codes for several similarly sounding words.

Listing 6.14. Using the soundex function.

```
--         Filename: 06squ14.sql
--         Purpose: soundex function
--
select soundex('macdugal'),
       soundex('mcdugal'),
       soundex('mcdugle'),
       soundex('macdougal'),
       soundex('macdugee'),
       soundex('mcdog'),
       soundex('mcduck'),
       soundex('mcdonald')
from dual;
```

This code returns

```
SOUN SOUN SOUN SOUN SOUN SOUN SOUN SOUN
---- ---- ---- ---- ---- ---- ---- ----
M232 M232 M232 M232 M232 M232 M232 M235
```

soundex returns the same code for all but the last word, mcdonald. If the mac or mc is omitted, it differentiates a little more, as the next example shows:

```
select soundex('dugal'),
       soundex('dougal'),
       soundex('dugle'),
       soundex('duglee'),
       soundex('douglee'),
       soundex('dog'),
       soundex('duck'),
       soundex('donald')
from dual;
```

This code returns

```
SOUN SOUN SOUN SOUN SOUN SOUN SOUN SOUN
---- ---- ---- ---- ---- ---- ---- ----
D240 D240 D240 D240 D240 D200 D200 D543
```

REAL-WORLD EXPERIENCES

The original soundex, patented in 1918, has six basic rules. An improved soundex, presented in Celko, has approximately 15 rules. Metaphone, another improvement, is four pages of Pascal code. Either of these can only classify words according to how similar they sound. They do not really indicate how a word should be pronounced.

Some educators, on the other hand, try to teach just that. The phonics movement has children sound out words. That works if one understands the Germanic and Romanic roots of the language. Most children to whom this method is targeted, however, have not had this exposure. Therefore, phonics is about as useful for them as road signs are to travellers. If a person has an inkling of the right way, the road signs might actually do some good. Otherwise, they only confuse the traveller.

Concatenation Function: `concat`

The concat function is equivalent to the concatenation operator, as the following examples show:

```
select concat('a ','bx') from dual;
```

The following code produces the same output as the preceding `select` statement:

```
select 'a ' ¦¦ 'bx' conc from dual;
```

The following is the result for both:

```
CONC
----
a bx
```

Summary

SQL, or better, the Oracle implementation of SQL, provides a number of string functions to extract substrings, as well as to trim, pad, and convert strings.

The substring function—by far the most important of these—allows you to extract a substring from the string, beginning at a specified character, and for a specified number of characters. The trim functions determine both position and length on the basis of the contents of the string value. The padding functions take a string and pad it to a specified length.

Single-Row Character String Functions

CHAPTER 6

121

6

SINGLE-ROW
CHARACTER
STRING FUNCTIONS

The conversion functions act on characters or substrings within a string. The `translate` function can globally convert characters to other characters or nulls. The `replace` function converts a search substring to a replace substring. The `upper`, `lower`, and `initcap` functions capitalize all letters, put all letters into lowercase, and capitalize initial letters of words within a string only, respectively.

Character/Number Conversions

IN THIS CHAPTER

CHAPTER

7

The string functions described in Chapter 6, "Single-Row Character String Functions," all return another string. String-analysis functions, which are covered in the first part of this chapter, return an integer that indicates either the length or the position of another string within a string. The second part of the chapter discusses functions that convert datatypes or character representations. These are functions such as to_char or to_number, which convert a number to string or vice versa. Character set functions convert characters to their ASCII representation, or vice versa.

ORACLE vs SQL All functions in this chapter are vendor extensions, meaning that they are not part of the SQL-89 and SQL-92 standards. Most vendors provide similar functions, but the syntax may be slightly different.

String-Analysis Functions

String-analysis functions provide answers to two questions:

■ How long a string is
■ The position at which a particular substring begins within the string

Especially when combined with substring and trimming functions or with decode operations, these functions can provide quite sophisticated string manipulations right from within SQL.

String Length: length

The length function returns the actual number of characters stored in a string. This is useful only for variable-length strings, such as the ones retrieved from variable-length (varchar2) columns. In a fixed-character column defined with char, length always returns the same number as the defined length of the column because the values in fixed-length columns are always blank-padded to the defined length. Listing 7.1 selects lname, fmname, and ssn from pers1 and lists the length of these strings next to their values.

Listing 7.1. Using the length function.

```
--        Filename: 07squ01.sql
--         Purpose: use of length function
--
col id format 99
col l1 format 99
col l2 format 99
col l3 format 99

select
   id,
   lname,
   length(lname) l1,
   fmname,
   length(fmname) l2,
   ssn,
   length(ssn) l3
```

```
from pers1
;

clear columns
```

This code returns

ID	LNAME	L1	FMNAME	L2	SSN	L3
1	Jones	5	David N.	8	895663453	9
2	Martinelli	10	A. Emery	8	312331818	9
3	Talavera	8	F. Espinosa	11	533932999	9
4	Kratochvil	10	Mary T.	7	969825711	9
5	Melsheli	8	Joseph K.	9	000342222	9

The length function is affected by blank padding in variable-length strings; it simply counts the blanks as characters. The following examples demonstrate this.

 Run the Crper6.sql script provided on the CD-ROM; this will create the table pers6. Two select statements are included in the script:

```
col id format 99

select
    id,
    lname || '**',
    '**' || fmname || '**',
    ssn || '**'
from pers6;

select
    id,
    name
from pers6;

clear columns
```

They return the following:

ID	LNAME||'**'		'**'||FMNAME||'**'		SSN||'**'	
1	Jones	**	**	David N.	**	895663453	**
2	Martinelli	**	**	A. Emery	**	312331818	**
3	Talavera	**	**	F. Espinosa	**	533932999	**
4	Kratochvil	**	**	Mary T.	**	969825711	**
5	Melsheli	**	**	Joseph K.	**	000342222	**

ID	NAME
1	Jones, David N.
2	Martinelli, A. Emery
3	Talavera, F. Espinosa
4	Kratochvil, Mary T.
5	Melsheli, Joseph K.

As this output shows, the table is similar to the other pers tables that are used in previous chapters. The lname column has spaces included on the end, and the fmname column has spaces padded to it on both sides. The ssn column, which is of a fixed character length, is blank-padded to the right as well. To clearly show the padding, the select statement concatenates the fields between the ** constants.

In addition to the columns you are already familiar with from other chapters, a column name has been added. It contains the full name in the typical *last name, first name middle name* format.

If the previous example is rewritten for this table (pers6), the effect of blank padding will become obvious. (See Listing 7.2.)

Listing 7.2. Using the length function to pad columns to the same length.

```
--      Filename: 07squ02.sql
--      Purpose: use of length function
--               show effect of padding
--
col id format 99
col l1 format 99
col l2 format 99
col l3 format 99

select
   id,
   lname,
   length(lname) l1,
   fmname,
   length(fmname) l2,
   ssn,
   length(ssn) l3
from pers6
;
```

This script returns the following:

```
ID LNAME              L1  FMNAME                L2 SSN          L3
--- ------------------ --- --------------------- --- ----------- ---
  1 Jones              13  David N.              15 895663453    12
  2 Martinelli         13  A. Emery              15 312331818    12
  3 Talavera           13  F. Espinosa           15 533932999    12
  4 Kratochvil         13  Mary T.               15 969825711    12
  5 Melsheli           13  Joseph K.             15 000342222    12
```

Because of the padding, all three columns are evaluated to exactly the same length. The new column, however, which is not padded, returns values as it should. The following code

```
select
   id,
   name,
   length(name) l1
```

```
from pers6
;

clear columns
```

returns this:

```
ID NAME                    L1
--- ------------------------- ---
  1 Jones, David N.          15
  2 Martinelli, A. Emery     20
  3 Talavera, F. Espinosa    21
  4 Kratochvil, Mary T.      19
  5 Melsheli, Joseph K.      19
```

lengthb

lengthb is equivalent to length, but it returns the length of a string in bytes instead of in characters. The value returned by length and lengthb is identical for all one-byte character sets. Other character sets, however, use two bytes to code a letter, in which case lengthb returns two bytes per character. For example, Listing 7.3 returns exactly the same as 07squ01.sql, the code in Listing 7.1.

Listing 7.3. Using the lengthb function.

```
--      Filename: 07squ03.sql
--       Purpose: use of the lengthb function
--
col id format 99
col l1 format 99
col l2 format 99
col l3 format 99

select
   id,
   lname,
   lengthb(lname) l1,
   fmname,
   lengthb(fmname) l2,
   ssn,
   lengthb(ssn) l3
from pers1
;

clear columns
```

Here is what this listing returns:

```
ID LNAME          L1 FMNAME         L2 SSN        L3
--- -------------- --- -------------- --- ---------- ---
  1 Jones           5 David N.        8 895663453   9
  2 Martinelli     10 A. Emery        8 312331818   9
  3 Talavera        8 F. Espinosa    11 533932999   9
  4 Kratochvil     10 Mary T.         7 969825711   9
  5 Melsheli        8 Joseph K.       9 000342222   9
```

7

CHARACTER/
NUMBER
CONVERSIONS

Substring Comparisons and Position: `instr`

The instring function, `instr`, locates a substring within a string and returns the character position at which the substring begins. It has four arguments:

- The string to be processed—a column, constant, or string expression
- The substring to be located within the string
- An integer that indicates the character position within the string at which the search shall begin
- An integer indicating which of a number of occurrences of the search string should be located

If the last two arguments are omitted, default values of 1 and 1 are substituted. In other words, the search starts at the first character of the string and attempts to locate the first occurrence of the substring.

 `crper7` creates the `pers7` table, which combines the columns of `pers1` with the last column of `pers6`. `crper7` can be found on the CD at the back of this book.

Listing 7.4 uses the instring function to calculate the length of the last, first, and middle names or initials from the name column in `pers7`.

Listing 7.4. Using the `instr` function.

```
--      Filename: 07squ04.sql
--      Purpose: use of instring function
--               to calculate lengths of names
--
col id format 99
col l1 format 99
col l2 format 99
col l3 format 99
col l4 format 99

select
   id,
   lname,
   length(lname) l1,
   instr(name, ',') - 1 l2,
   fmname,
   length(fmname) l3,
   length(name) -  instr(name, ',') -1  l4
from pers7
;

clear columns
```

l1 and l3 calculate the length of `lname` and `fmname`, respectively, using the `length` function. l2 calculates the length of `lname` by determining the position of the period and subtracting 1.

14 first finds the position of the comma in name and then calculates the length of fmname by subtracting this value plus 1 from the total length of name:

```
ID LNAME                L1  L2 FMNAME              L3  L4
--- -------------------- --- --- ------------------- --- ---
  1 Jones                 5   5 David N.             8   8
  2 Martinelli           10  10 A. Emery             8   8
  3 Talavera              8   8 F. Espinosa         11  11
  4 Kratochvil           10  10 Mary T.              7   7
  5 Melsheli              8   8 Joseph K.            9   9
```

The following example extracts the call name from the fmname column. (The *call name* is the name that is spelled out in that column.) A decode of the second character determines whether the first or the middle name is to be extracted. If that character is a period, a substring extracts the portion of the string from character 4 to the end of the string.

This use of the decode operator works for Oracle, but not necessarily for other ANSI SQL RDBMSs.

The instring function is used in the second option for extracting the call name. In this case, the objective is to locate the first blank in the string, which identifies the end of the first name. The substring function uses this value minus one for the length argument. Listing 7.5 shows that approach.

Listing 7.5. Using the instr function to extract the calling name.

```
--        Filename: 07squ05.sql
--         Purpose: use of instring function
--                  to extract the calling name
--
col id     format 99
col called format a10

select
   id,
   fmname,
   decode(substr(fmname,2,1),'.', substr(fmname,4,15),
                              substr(fmname,1,instr(fmname,' ')-1))
         called
from pers7
;clear columns
```

This code returns the following:

```
ID FMNAME               CALLED
--- -------------------- ----------
  1 David N.             David
  2 A. Emery             Emery
  3 F. Espinosa          Espinosa
  4 Mary T.              Mary
  5 Joseph K.            Joseph
```

In fixed-length string systems, names are frequently stored as in the name column of pers6 and pers7. String analysis and single-row string-conversion functions provide help when such a string needs to broken up into its component fields. Besides id, the script extracts three columns:

- The last name is extracted by a substring function that starts at character 1 and proceeds for a length that is one less than what the instring function searching for a comma returns.

- The first name is extracted by a substring function as well. The beginning character is determined through the location of the comma that is found through an instring function. The value 2 is added because the comma is located two characters before the first character of first name. `instr(name,' ') + 1` would work as well. The length is determined by the location of the second space, which is found by `instr(name,' ', 1,2)` minus the location of the comma, minus two.

- The substring that extracts the middle name starts one character after the second space and has a static length of 20, which should be plenty for all circumstances.

Listing 7.6 is an example of this.

Listing 7.6. Culling data from a column using `substr`.

```
--        Filename: 07squ06.sql
--        Purpose: culling first, middle, and last names from the
--                 name column
--
col id     format 99
col name   format a21
col last   format a12
col first  format a12
col middle format a12

select
   id,
   name,
   substr(name, 1                      , instr(name,',')-1     ) last,
   substr(name, instr(name,',') + 2    , instr(name,' ',1,2) -
                                         instr(name,',') -2 ) first,
   substr(name, instr(name,' ',1,2)+ 1 , 20                    ) middle
from pers7
;
```

This code returns the following:

```
ID NAME                     LAST         FIRST        MIDDLE
--- --------------------    ------------ ------------ ------------
  1 Jones, David N.         Jones        David        N.
  2 Martinelli, A. Emery    Martinelli   A.           Emery
  3 Talavera, F. Espinosa   Talavera     F.           Espinosa
  4 Kratochvil, Mary T.     Kratochvil   Mary         T.
  5 Melsheli, Joseph K.     Melsheli     Joseph       K.
```

Just as was the case with substr, the argument that denotes the position may be negative. In this case, the string is processed right to left. The following example returns exactly the same output:

```
select
   id,
   name,
   substr(name, 1                    , instr(name,',')-1     ) last,
   substr(name, instr(name,',') + 2  , instr(name,' ',-1) -
                                        instr(name,',') -2 ) first,
   substr(name, instr(name,' ',-1)+ 1 , 20                   ) middle
from pers7
;

clear columns
```

The Byte Equivalent Instring Function: instrb

instrb is the byte equivalent of instr, which is character based. This function may be, just as lengthb may be, of use in a double-byte character set.

Datatype Conversion Functions

Datatype conversion functions convert numbers to strings, or vice versa. Combined with format masks, these functions provide elaborate formatting or interpretation options.

Converting a Value to a String: to_char

The to_char function converts a value to its character representation. It comes in three versions. In its simplest form, the to_char function has only one parameter, the value to be converted. If more elaborate formatting is required, a format mask can be added as a second parameter. National Language Support (NLS) customization is possible through a third parameter.

The Single-Parameter to_char Function

This single-parameter to_char function returns a variable-length string that is just long enough to hold all significant strings of the value. Listing 7.7 converts the interest column of pers3 as well as the income/wealth ratio to character strings (in order to show what exactly the function returns, these values are enclosed between leading and trailing asterisks).

Listing 7.7. Using the to_char function.

```
--      Filename: 07squ07.sql
--       Purpose: to_char function, simple form
--
col cinterest format a10 heading 'Interest¦Character¦String'
col ratio format a45 heading 'Ratio¦Character¦String'

select
   interest,
```

continues

Listing 7.7. continued

```
    '**' || to_char(interest) || '**' cinterest,
    '**' || to_char((interest +
           salary   +
           profit   +
           royalty)/wealth) || '**' ratio
from pers3
;

clear columns
```

This code returns the following:

```
         Interest    Ratio
         Character   Character
INTEREST String      String
-------- ---------   ----------------------------------------------
     200 **200**     **2.1441860465116279069767441860465116279l**
   24000 **24000**   **.14403100775193798449612403100775193798s**
     110 **110**     **.2075**
    4800 **4800**    **.078647004915437807214862950928934433058**
      50 **50**      **.0625**
```

The to_char Function with a Format Mask

The more powerful version of the to_char function is the one with two parameters, the second being a format mask. This mask is a character string that specifies the appearance of the final string.

While the simple form of to_char returns a variable-length string, the two-parameter form always returns a fixed-length string (except when the FM modifier is used, as you will see later in this section). The length of the string is usually one character more than the mask to provide space for a minus sign, if applicable.

The simplest format mask is a string that contains as many nines as the number should be long. Thus, for example, 999 will return a string that can hold up to three digits and a minus sign. Numbers with fewer digits will be blank-padded, and a zero value will print exactly one zero. This is shown in the first column of Listing 7.8.

Listing 7.8. Using the to_char function with the format mask.

```
--          Filename: 07squ08.sql
--           Purpose: to_char function with format mask: 9, 0, B
--
select
    '**' || to_char(profit,'999999')  || '**' prof9,
    '**' || to_char(profit,'999990')  || '**' prof90,
    '**' || to_char(profit,'999000')  || '**' prof9000,
    '**' || to_char(profit,'099999')  || '**' prof09,
    '**' || to_char(profit,'B999990') || '**' profB90,
    '**' || to_char(profit,'B000000') || '**' profB00
from pers3
;
```

This script returns the following:

```
   PROFIT PROF9        PROF90       PROF9000     PROF09        PROFB90
--------- ----------- ------------ ------------ ------------- -----------
    12000 **  12000** **  12000** **   12000** ** 012000** **  12000**
     5000 **   5000** **   5000** **    5000** ** 005000** **   5000**
        0 **      0** **      0** **     000** ** 000000** **         **
   184000 ** 184000** ** 184000** **  184000** ** 184000** ** 184000**
        0 **      0** **      0** **     000** ** 000000** **         **
```

The padding between asterisks has been maintained to show what exactly the function returns.

A few variations are shown in this code as well:

- A mask consisting of all nines and an otherwise identical mask with one trailing zero return the same output, which is shown in the first and second column.

- A mask with more than one trailing zero pads shorter values up to the number of zeros in the mask, and blank-pads the remaining digits to the left (third column).

- A mask with a leading zero will zero-pad the entire number to the number of digits in the mask (fourth column).

- A B in front of the mask will blank-pad the entire number, and will print only blanks in the case of zero. If this modifier is used, it does not matter whether zeros or nines are used for the rest of the mask (fifth and sixth column).

Three options are provided to deal with minus values:

- MI returns a trailing minus sign if the value is negative, and a trailing blank if it is positive.

- S returns a minus or plus sign, respectively. A leading sign is indicated through preceding the mask with S, and a trailing sign through a trailing S.

- PR returns negative values between angle brackets. When it is used, the string length increases by one.

CAUTION

Note that both MI and PR need to be at the end of the mask.

Listing 7.9 is an adaptation of 07squ08.sql (refer to Listing 7.8) that includes these options to specify the treatment of negative values. Two select statements are included: one for positive numbers and one for negative numbers.

Listing 7.9. Using the to_char function and sign modifiers.

```
--       Filename: 07squ09.sql
--        Purpose: to_char function with format mask: 9, 0, B
--                 and sign modifiers
```

continues

```
select
    '**' || to_char(profit,'999999')    || '**' prof9,
    '**' || to_char(profit,'999990MI')  || '**' prof90,
    '**' || to_char(profit,'S999000')   || '**' prof9000,
    '**' || to_char(profit,'099999S')   || '**' prof09,
    '**' || to_char(profit,'SB999990')  || '**' profB90,
    '**' || to_char(profit,'B000000PR') || '**' profB00
from pers3
;

select
    '**' || to_char(-profit,'999999')    || '**' prof9,
    '**' || to_char(-profit,'999990MI')  || '**' prof90,
    '**' || to_char(-profit,'S999000')   || '**' prof9000,
    '**' || to_char(-profit,'099999S')   || '**' prof09,
    '**' || to_char(-profit,'SB999990')  || '**' profB90,
    '**' || to_char(-profit,'B000000PR') || '**' profB00
from pers3
;
```

This code returns the following:

```
PROF9        PROF90       PROF9000     PROF09       PROFB90      PROFB00
-----------  -----------  -----------  -----------  -----------  -----------
**   12000** **  12000 ** ** +12000** **012000+** ** +12000** ** 012000 **
**    5000** **   5000 ** **  +5000** **005000+** **  +5000** ** 005000 **
**       0** **      0 ** **   +000** **000000+** **       ** **        **
** 184000** **184000 ** **+184000** **184000+** **+184000** ** 184000 **
**       0** **      0 ** **   +000** **000000+** **       ** **        **


PROF9        PROF90       PROF9000     PROF09       PROFB90      PROFB00
-----------  -----------  -----------  -----------  -----------  -----------
** -12000** **  12000-** ** -12000** **012000-** ** -12000** **<012000>**
**  -5000** **   5000-** **  -5000** **005000-** **  -5000** **<005000>**
**      0** **      0 ** **   +000** **000000+** **       ** **        **
**-184000** **184000-** **-184000** **184000-** **-184000** **<184000>**
**      0** **      0 ** **   +000** **000000+** **       ** **        **
```

To return these values as variable-length strings without padding, the FM modifier can be used, as shown in the following example (FM, however, cannot be used together with B):

```
select
    '**' || to_char(profit,'FM999999')   || '**' prof9,
    '**' || to_char(profit,'FM999990MI') || '**' prof90,
    '**' || to_char(profit,'FMS999000')  || '**' prof9000,
    '**' || to_char(profit,'FM099999S')  || '**' prof09
from pers3
;
```

It returns this:

```
PROF9        PROF90       PROF9000      PROF09
-----------  -----------  ------------  ----------
**12000**    **12000**    **+12000**    **012000+**
**5000**     **5000**     **+5000**     **005000+**
**0**        **0**        **+000**      **000000+**
**184000**   **184000**   **+184000**   **184000+**
**0**        **0**        **+000**      **000000+**
```

As you can see, all leading blanks are stripped from the values.

The next set of modifiers allows for the inclusion of currency symbols, decimal points, and group symbols into format mask:

- A leading dollar symbol ($) in the mask prints a leading dollar symbol in the output. L returns the local currency, and C returns the currency according to ISO standards. These are set through NLS_CURRENCY and NLS_LOCAL_CURRENCY.

- A period returns a decimal point. A D returns a decimal point or its equivalent as specified by the initialization parameter NLS_NUMERIC_CHARACTER, or as one of the set of parameters specified by NLS_TERRITORY.

- A comma returns a group separator. A group separator is most commonly used for formatting groups of three digits to indicate thousands, millions, and so on. G returns a group separator or its equivalent as specified by the initialization parameter NLS_NUMERIC_CHARACTER or implicitly by NLS_TERRITORY.

The current NLS settings can be displayed by selecting the values of V$NLS_PARAMETERS:

```
--         Filename: NLS1.sql
--          Purpose: display current NLS Parameters
--
col parameter format a35 heading 'NLS Parameter'
col value      format a30 heading 'NLS Value'

select
   parameter,
   value
from v$nls_parameters
;

clear columns
```

This returns the following:

```
NLS Parameter                       NLS Value
-----------------------------------  ------------------------------
NLS_LANGUAGE                         AMERICAN
NLS_TERRITORY                        AMERICA
NLS_CURRENCY                         $
NLS_ISO_CURRENCY                     AMERICA
NLS_NUMERIC_CHARACTERS               .,
```

```
NLS_DATE_FORMAT              DD-MON-YYYY
NLS_DATE_LANGUAGE            AMERICAN
NLS_CHARACTERSET             WE8ISO8859P1
NLS_SORT                     BINARY
NLS_CALENDAR                 GREGORIAN

10 rows selected.
```

Listing 7.10 demonstrates the use of these modifiers: It displays profit formatted as a dollar value, in local currency and in ISO currency. The first set is based on an NLS_TERRITORY code of AMERICA, the second on SPAIN, and the third on AUSTRIA.

Listing 7.10. Using to_char function with currency modifiers.

```
--        Filename: 07squ10.sql
--         Purpose: to_char function with format mask: 9, 0, B
--                  and currency modifiers
--
select
   '**' || to_char(profit,'$999999')  || '**' Dollars,
   '**' || to_char(profit,'L999990')  || '**' Local_Currency,
   '**' || to_char(profit,'C999000')  || '**' ISO_Currency
from pers3
;

alter session set NLS_TERRITORY = SPAIN;

select
   '**' || to_char(profit,'$999999')  || '**' Dollars,
   '**' || to_char(profit,'L999990')  || '**' Local_Currency,
   '**' || to_char(profit,'C999000')  || '**' ISO_Currency
from pers3
;

alter session set NLS_TERRITORY = Austria;

select
   '**' || to_char(profit,'$999999')  || '**' Dollars,
   '**' || to_char(profit,'L999990')  || '**' Local_Currency,
   '**' || to_char(profit,'C999000')  || '**' ISO_Currency
from pers3
;

alter session set NLS_TERRITORY = America;
```

This script returns the following:

```
DOLLARS        LOCAL_CURRENCY         ISO_CURRENCY
-----------    --------------------   -------------
**    $12000** **         $12000** **  USD12000**
**     $5000** **          $5000** **   USD5000**
**        $0** **             $0** **    USD000**
** $184000** **         $184000** ** USD184000**
**        $0** **             $0** **    USD000**


Session altered.
```

```
DOLLARS        LOCAL_CURRENCY        ISO_CURRENCY
-----------    --------------------  --------------
**   $12000**  **         Pts12000** **   ESP12000**
**    $5000**  **          Pts5000** **    ESP5000**
**       $0**  **             Pts0** **     ESP000**
**  $184000**  **        Pts184000** ** ESP184000**
**       $0**  **             Pts0** **     ESP000**


Session altered.


DOLLARS        LOCAL_CURRENCY        ISO_CURRENCY
-----------    --------------------  --------------
**   $12000**  **          ÖS12000** **   ATS12000**
**    $5000**  **           ÖS5000** **    ATS5000**
**       $0**  **              ÖS0** **     ATS000**
**  $184000**  **         ÖS184000** ** ATS184000**
**       $0**  **              ÖS0** **     ATS000**


Session altered.
```

The decimal and group separators can be affected similarly. Listing 7.11 demonstrates this by choosing a wealth value that is 1,000 times the values contained in pers3.

Listing 7.11. Using the to_char function with decimal and group modifiers.

```sql
--         Filename: 07squ11.sql
--         Purpose: to_char function with format mask: 9, 0, $
--                  and decimal and group modifiers
--
select
   '**' || to_char(profit*1000,'$999,999,999')    || '**' Commas,
   '**' || to_char(profit*1000,'$999G999G990')     || '**' Group_Code,
   '**' || to_char((interest+salary+profit+royalty)
                          /wealth, '9.999')    || '**' Period,
   '**' || to_char((interest+salary+profit+royalty)
                          /wealth, '9D999')    || '**' Dec_Pt
from pers3
;

alter session set NLS_TERRITORY = SPAIN;

select
   '**' || to_char(profit*1000,'$999,999,999')    || '**' Commas,
   '**' || to_char(profit*1000,'$999G999G990')     || '**' Group_Code,
   '**' || to_char((interest+salary+profit+royalty)
                          /wealth, '9.999')    || '**' Period,
   '**' || to_char((interest+salary+profit+royalty)
                          /wealth, '9D999')    || '**' Dec_Pt
from pers3
;

alter session set NLS_TERRITORY = Austria;
```

continues

Listing 7.11. continued

```
select
    '**' || to_char(profit*1000,'$999,999,999')     || '**' Commas,
    '**' || to_char(profit*1000,'$999G999G990')     || '**' Group_Code,
    '**' || to_char((interest+salary+profit+royalty)
                            /wealth, '9.999')        || '**' Period,
    '**' || to_char((interest+salary+profit+royalty)
                            /wealth, '9D999')        || '**' Dec_Pt
from pers3
;

alter session set NLS_TERRITORY = America;
```

This script returns

```
COMMAS               GROUP_CODE          PERIOD      DEC_PT
----------------     ----------------    ----------  ----------
**   $12,000,000** **   $12,000,000** ** 2.144** **  2.144**
**    $5,000,000** **    $5,000,000** **  .144** **   .144**
**            $0** **            $0** **  .208** **   .208**
** $184,000,000** ** $184,000,000** **  .079** **   .079**
**            $0** **            $0** **  .063** **   .063**

Session altered.


COMMAS               GROUP_CODE          PERIOD      DEC_PT
----------------     ----------------    ----------  ----------
**   $12,000,000** **   $12.000.000** ** 2.144** **  2,144**
**    $5,000,000** **    $5.000.000** **  .144** **   ,144**
**            $0** **            $0** **  .208** **   ,208**
** $184,000,000** ** $184.000.000** **  .079** **   ,079**
**            $0** **            $0** **  .063** **   ,063**

Session altered.


COMMAS               GROUP_CODE          PERIOD      DEC_PT
----------------     ----------------    ----------  ----------
**   $12,000,000** **   $12.000.000** ** 2.144** **  2,144**
**    $5,000,000** **    $5.000.000** **  .144** **   ,144**
**            $0** **            $0** **  .208** **   ,208**
** $184,000,000** ** $184.000.000** **  .079** **   ,079**
**            $0** **            $0** **  .063** **   ,063**

Session altered.
```

In the United States, the standard decimal character is a point, and the standard group character is a comma. In Spain and Austria, these characters are used the other way around.

CAUTION

Do not mix periods, dots, and dollar signs on the one hand and L, C, D, and G on the other. If you do, you will get this error:

```
ERROR:
ORA-01481: invalid number format model
```

How these NLS parameters can be changed is shown in the next section of this chapter.

The last set of modifiers provides for a conversion of values to other number types:

- RN and rn convert integers between 1 and 3,999 to uppercase or lowercase Roman numerals.
- V multiplies the value by 10 once for every numeral 9 that follows it.
- EEEE displays the value in scientific notation.

Listing 7.12 converts the ages and 10 times the ages of the pers1 table to upper- and lowercase Roman numerals.

Listing 7.12. Using the to_char function with conversion modifiers.

```
--         Filename: 07squ12.sql
--         Purpose: display age and age*10
--                  as upper case and lower case roman numerals
--
col age     format 99
col age10 format 999    heading 'Age¦*10'
col Age10_Roman_Upper   heading 'Age * 10 ¦Roman Upper'
col Age10_Roman_Lower   heading 'Age * 10 ¦Roman Lower'

select
   age,
   to_char(age,'RN')    Age_Roman_Upper,
   to_char(age,'rn')    Age_Roman_Lower,
   age * 10             age10,
   to_char(age*10,'RN') Age10_Roman_Upper,
   to_char(age*10,'rn') Age10_Roman_Lower
from pers1;

clear columns
```

This script returns

AGE	AGE_ROMAN_UPPER	AGE_ROMAN_LOWER	Age *10	Age * 10 Roman Upper	Age * 10 Roman Lower
34	XXXIV	xxxiv	340	CCCXL	cccxl
92	XCII	xcii	920	CMXX	cmxx
19	XIX	xix	190	CXC	cxc
48	XLVIII	xlviii	480	CDLXXX	cdlxxx
14	XIV	xiv	140	CXL	cxl

7

CHARACTER/
NUMBER
CONVERSIONS

The scientific and 10-multiplied notations are demonstrated in Listing 7.13. All columns renotate the income/wealth ratios of the pers3 table. The first column displays the ratio accurate to four decimals. The second column redisplays the same value in scientific notation. The third column does the same, but multiplies the value by 10E44 first. The last two columns display percentages; the first uses the V modifier, which can only return integers, and the second is accurate to three decimals using a calculation.

Listing 7.13. Using the to_char function with scientific notation.

```
--         Filename: 07squ13.sql
--          Purpose: to_char function with format mask: 9, 0
--                   and scientific/ten-multiplied notation
--
select
    '**' || to_char((interest+salary+profit+royalty)
                            /wealth, '9.9999')      || '**'
        ratio,
    '**' || to_char((interest+salary+profit+royalty)
                            /wealth, '9.999EEEE')   || '**'
        Scientific,
    '**' || to_char(10E44*
                    (interest+salary+profit+royalty)
                            /wealth, '9.999EEEE')   || '**'
        Scientific_large,
    '**' || to_char((interest+salary+profit+royalty)
                            /wealth, '999V99')      || '%**'
        WholePct,
    '**' || to_char(100 *
                    (interest+salary+profit+royalty)
                            /wealth, '999.99')      || '%**'
        Percentage
from pers3
;
```

This script returns

```
RATIO        SCIENTIFIC       SCIENTIFIC_LARG WHOLEPCT      PERCENTAGE
-----------  ---------------  --------------- -----------   ------------
** 2.1442**  **  2.144E+00**  **  2.144E+45** **   214%**  ** 214.42%**
**  .1440**  **  1.440E-01**  **  1.440E+44** **    14%**  **  14.40%**
**  .2075**  **  2.075E-01**  **  2.075E+44** **    21%**  **  20.75%**
**  .0786**  **  7.865E-02**  **  7.865E+43** **    08%**  **   7.86%**
**  .0625**  **  6.250E-02**  **  6.250E+43** **    06%**  **   6.25%**
```

The Three-Argument to_char Function and Other Ways to Affect the NLS Format Parameters

The most powerful version is the to_char function which uses a third parameter to allow an on-the-fly customization of the NLS parameters. The end of this section shows how to alter NLS parameters globally, either for the session or for the instance.

This feature is not as contrived as it might appear at first glance. A currency table would want to display appropriate symbols, which would be different among columns. Listing 7.14 does that and displays the total income from `pers3` in dollars and Austrian schillings. The schilling values are displayed twice, first with the ISO currency symbol and then with the word `Schillinge` using the `NLS_CURRENCY` text string. The exchange rates are made up. Look at the code.

Listing 7.14. Using the `to_char` function to convert NLS parameters.

```
--       Filename: 07squ14.sql
--       Purpose: Display in Dollars and Austrian Schillinge
--
select
   '**' || to_char((interest+salary+profit+royalty),
           'C999G999G999','NLS_ISO_CURRENCY = AMERICA')      || '**'
          ISO_AMERICA,
   '**' || to_char((interest+salary+profit+royalty) * 13,
           'C999G999G999','NLS_ISO_CURRENCY = AUSTRIA')      || '**'
          ISO_AUSTRIA,
   '**' || to_char((interest+salary+profit+royalty) * 13,
           'L999G999G999','NLS_CURRENCY = ''Schillinge''')   || '**'
          NLS_SCHILLING
from pers3
;
```

This script returns

```
ISO_AMERICA          ISO_AUSTRIA          NLS_SCHILLING
-------------------  -------------------  ---------------------------
**       USD92,200** **     ATS1,198,600** **    Schillinge1,198,600**
**       USD92,900** **     ATS1,207,700** **    Schillinge1,207,700**
**        USD4,980** **        ATS64,740** **      Schillinge64,740**
**      USD188,800** **     ATS2,454,400** **    Schillinge2,454,400**
**           USD50** **          ATS650** **         Schillinge650**
```

Listing 7.15 changes the group and the decimal separators, too, in addition to the currency symbols or names. These are affected by the `NLS_NUMERIC_CHARACTERS = '',.''` component of the third argument. Enclosed between the double single quotes is a string with two characters. The first sets the decimal separators, and the second one sets the group separator.

Listing 7.15. Using the `to_char` function to convert NLS parameters.

```
--       Filename: 07squ15.sql
--       Purpose: Display in Dollars, Pesetas, and Pounds
--                using proper group and decimal characters
--
select
   '**' || to_char((interest+salary+profit+royalty),
           'C999G999G999D00','NLS_ISO_CURRENCY = AMERICA')      || '**'
          ISO_AMERICA,
   '**' || to_char((interest+salary+profit+royalty) * 13,
           'C999G999G999D00',
           'NLS_ISO_CURRENCY = ''UNITED KINGDOM''
           NLS_NUMERIC_CHARACTERS = ''.,''')      || '**'
          ISO_UK,
   '**' || to_char((interest+salary+profit+royalty) * 13,
           'C999G999G999D00',
```

continues

7

CHARACTER/
NUMBER
CONVERSIONS

Listing 7.15. continued

```
            'NLS_ISO_CURRENCY = SPAIN
            NLS_NUMERIC_CHARACTERS = '',.''')      ¦¦ '**'
         ISO_SPAIN
from pers3
;
```

This script returns

```
ISO_AMERICA              ISO_UK                  ISO_SPAIN
----------------------   ---------------------   ---------------------
**       USD92,200.00** **    GBP1.198.600,00** **   ESP1,198,600.00**
**       USD92,900.00** **    GBP1.207.700,00** **   ESP1,207,700.00**
**        USD4,980.00** **      GBP64.740,00** **      ESP64,740.00**
**      USD188,800.00** **    GBP2.454.400,00** **   ESP2,454,400.00**
**           USD50.00** **         GBP650,00** **        ESP650.00**
```

Valid territory codes can be selected by running the script nls2, which is provided on the CD-ROM.

```
--       Filename: NLS2.sql
--        Purpose: display valid NLS Parameters

col value      format a30 heading 'Territory'

select
     value
from v$nls_valid_values
where parameter = 'TERRITORY'
order by value
;

clear columns
```

Table 7.1 lists these values.

Table 7.1. Valid NLS territory codes.

Territory	*Territory*	*Territory*	*Territory*
ALGERIA	CHINA	FINLAND	ITALY
AMERICA	CIS	FRANCE	JAPAN
AUSTRIA	CROATIA	GERMANY	JORDAN
BAHRAIN	CZECH REPUBLIC	GREECE	KOREA
BANGLADESH	CZECHOSLOVAKIA	HONG KONG	KUWAIT
BRAZIL	DENMARK	HUNGARY	LATVIA
BULGARIA	DJIBOUTI	ICELAND	LEBANON
CANADA	EGYPT	IRAQ	LIBYA
CATALONIA	ESTONIA	ISRAEL	LITHUANIA

Territory	Territory	Territory	Territory
MALAYSIA	QATAR	SWEDEN	UKRAINE
MAURITANIA	ROMANIA	SWITZERLAND	UNITED ARAB
MEXICO	SAUDI ARABIA	SYRIA	EMIRATES
MOROCCO	SLOVAKIA	TAIWAN	UNITED KINGDOM
NORWAY	SLOVENIA	THAILAND	VIETNAM
OMAN	SOMALIA	THE NETHERLANDS	YEMEN
POLAND	SPAIN	TUNISIA	
PORTUGAL	SUDAN	TURKEY	

to_number

The to_number function does the opposite of to_char—it converts a string to a numeric value. While the single-argument form is used most frequently, in cases where a numerical value is stored as a character value but is needed as a number for comparisons the function also accepts two or three arguments. These arguments are identical to those used by the to_char function. Listing 7.16 shows all three forms of to_number.

Listing 7.16. Using the to_number function.

```
--      Filename: 07squ16.sql
--       Purpose: demonstrate use of to_number function
--
select
to_number('888888.88') arg_1,
   to_number('.88888888E6') arg_1_exp,
   to_number('888,888.88','99,999,999.99') arg_2,
   to_number('$888,888.88','$99,999,999.99') arg_2_curr,
   to_number('888.888,88','99G999G999D99',
             'NLS_NUMERIC_CHARACTERS = '',.''') arg_3
from dual;
```

As the output shows, integers, floating-point, and scientifically notated numbers can be converted by the single-argument function:

```
    ARG_1 ARG_1_EXP     ARG_2 ARG_2_CURR      ARG_3
--------- --------- --------- --------- ---------
888888.88 888888.88 888888.88  888888.88 888888.88
```

If the function has group separators or currency symbols, a second argument, the format mask, is necessary. The three-argument version can be used if the mask follows an NLS_TERRITORY format, with or without custom group and decimal characters.

7
CHARACTER/ NUMBER CONVERSIONS

Character Set Representation Conversions

The functions chr and ascii convert characters to their binary equivalent, and vice versa. In the world of fourth-generation languages, it should not be necessary to worry about such details of data processing. One good use for these functions is to print newlines for SQL generating SQL statements using chr(10). (See Chapter 23, "Generating SQL Statements Through SQL.")

ascii

The ascii function accepts a character and returns its binary equivalent. Listing 7.17 shows the binary equivalent of a blank, of the digits 1 to 3, and of the letters a to c as well as A to Z.

Listing 7.17. Using the ascii function.

```
--        Filename: 07squ17.sql
--        Purpose: demonstrate use of ascii function
--
select
   ascii(' ') bl,
   ascii('1') a1,
   ascii('2') a2,
   ascii('3') a3,
   ascii('a') la
from dual;

select
   ascii('b') lb,
   ascii('c') lc,
   ascii('A') ua,
   ascii('B') ub,
   ascii('C') uc
from dual;
```

This script returns

BL	A1	A2	A3	LA
32	49	50	51	97

LB	LC	UA	UB	UC
98	99	65	66	67

Converting a Binary Representation to its Corresponding Character: chr

chr returns the character representation of a binary value expressed as an integer. Listing 7.18 provides an ASCII character table for the integers 33 to 127. It takes advantage of the rownum pseudocolumn against v$nls_valid_values, which has over 300 records and can thus be used to generate an ordinal scale. The where in the example is explained in Chapter 9, "Conditional Operands."

Listing 7.18. Using chr.

```
--        Filename: 07squ18.sql
--         Purpose: display ASCII code table
--
col   code        format 999
col   letter      format A3

select
    rownum + 32 code,
    chr(rownum +32) lt,
    rownum + 32 + 19 code,
    chr(rownum +32 + 19) lt,
    rownum + 32 + 38 code,
    chr(rownum +32 + 38) lt,
    rownum + 32 + 57 code,
    chr(rownum +32 + 57) lt,
    rownum + 32 + 76 code,
    chr(rownum + 76) lt
from v$nls_valid_values
where rownum < 20
;

clear columns
```

This script returns

CODE	LT	CODE	LT	CODE	LT	CODE	LT	CODE	LT
33	!	52	4	71	G	90	Z	109	M
34	"	53	5	72	H	91	[	110	N
35	#	54	6	73	I	92	\	111	O
36	$	55	7	74	J	93	]	112	P
37	%	56	8	75	K	94	^	113	Q
38	&	57	9	76	L	95	_	114	R
39	'	58	:	77	M	96	`	115	S
40	(	59	;	78	N	97	a	116	T
41	)	60	<	79	O	98	b	117	U
42	*	61	=	80	P	99	c	118	V
43	+	62	>	81	Q	100	d	119	W
44	,	63	?	82	R	101	e	120	X
45	-	64	@	83	S	102	f	121	Y
46	.	65	A	84	T	103	g	122	Z
47	/	66	B	85	U	104	h	123	[
48	0	67	C	86	V	105	i	124	]
49	1	68	D	87	W	106	j	125	]
50	2	69	E	88	X	107	k	126	^
51	3	70	F	89	Y	108	l	127	_

Summary

This chapter covers functions that allow for powerful processing of strings. String analysis returns either the length of a string (`length`) or the position of a substring within a string (`instr`).

Datatype conversion functions (`to_char` or `to_number`) convert a number to a string, or vice versa. There are three versions of these functions, each with one, two, or three arguments, respectively. The first argument always takes the expression or value to be converted. The second argument is a format mask, according to which the conversion is performed. The third argument provides for NLS customizations of the format mask.

Character-set conversion functions (`chr` and `ascii`) convert characters to their binary equivalent, and vice versa, which can be useful for such purposes as printing newlines using `chr(10)`.

PART

Aggregations and Conditions

CHAPTER 8

Aggregations and Group Functions

IN THIS CHAPTER

Until now, every row that was retrieved in a query corresponded to a row in the table from which it was read. If the table had five rows, the output of the query had five rows. The only exceptions were `select distinct` statements, which retrieve one row for each distinct combination of values of the columns selected.

The functions in this chapter expand the `select distinct` functionality. They return summary (aggregate) information on these *aggregate sets of rows* rather than just listing the sets as `distinct` does. The distinction between single-row and aggregate queries is extremely important. From now on, whenever you perform a query, you need to give some thought as to how many rows the query is likely to return.

All Versus Single Rows

The default case of an aggregate set is all the rows in a table. If no further break-outs are specified, group functions will calculate aggregates over all rows. Listing 8.1 calculates the average, the minimum, and the maximum age from `pers1`.

Listing 8.1. Calculating `avg`, `min`, and `max`.

```
--        Filename: 08squ01.sql
--        Purpose: demonstrate group functions
--                 uses entire set of rows
--
select
   avg(age),
   min(age),
   max(age)
from pers1
;
```

This query returns exactly one row reporting aggregates for the entire table, listing the average age as 41.4 years, the minimum age as 14, and the maximum age as 92 years:

```
AVG(AGE)  MIN(AGE)  MAX(AGE)
--------  --------  --------
    41.4        14        92
```

Aggregating Over Subsets of Rows: group by

While aggregating over all rows of a table is quite useful, aggregating over subsets of the table generally is even more so. In SQL, a *subset* of a row is a group that is created by the `group by` subclause. The groups are determined on the basis of a common criterion, such as having the same value in a column.

For example, in the `pers1` table, there are five rows. If `sex` is taken as the criterion, two sets of rows result:

- ■ The female set, consisting of two records
- ■ The male set, consisting of three records

Listing 8.2 breaks down these sets.

Listing 8.2. Grouping data using `order by`.

```
--       Filename: 08squ02.sql
--        Purpose: demonstrate group functions
--
break on sex skip 2
col id format 99

select
   sex,
   id,
   lname,
   fmname,
   ssn,
   age
from pers1
order by sex
;

clear columns
clear breaks
```

This script returns

```
S  ID LNAME            FMNAME           SSN         AGE
-- -- ---------------- ---------------- ---------- ---------

F   3 Talavera         F. Espinosa      533932999       19
    4 Kratochvil       Mary T.          969825711       48


M   1 Jones            David N.         895663453       34
    5 Melsheli         Joseph K.        000342222       14
    2 Martinelli       A. Emery         312331818       92
```

NOTE

Listing 8.2 includes the SQL*Plus statement

`break on sex skip 2`

which inserts two spare lines (`skip 2`) every time the value of sex changes. Because the example is ordered by the same column, sex, this line skip happens only once, effectively separating the groups. Note that this is a SQL*Plus command that is not part of SQL proper. If you use these commands, make sure you clear their definitions at the end of the script with the statement

`clear breaks`

Otherwise, they will stay in effect for future queries.

ORACLE VS. SQL

8

AGGREGATIONS AND GROUP FUNCTIONS

Listing 8.3 combines the `08squ01.sql` and `08squ02.sql` scripts and calculates the average, minimum, and maximum age for each distinct subset of `pers1` that has a common value on the `sex` column.

Listing 8.3. Grouping data using `group by`.

```
--        Filename: 08squ03.sql
--         Purpose: demonstrate group functions
--                  group by sex
--
select
   sex,
   avg(age),
   min(age),
   max(age)
from pers1
group by sex
;
```

This returns two rows, one for males and one for females:

```
S   AVG(AGE)  MIN(AGE)  MAX(AGE)
-   --------- --------- ---------
F       33.5        19        48
M  46.666667        14        92
```

CAUTION

If there is only one column to group by in a query, `group by` returns exactly as many rows as there are distinct values in the single-row column by which the query is grouped. If that column has two values, such as in the previous example, two rows will result.

DEBUG ALERT

If you are not clear how many rows a query returns, run a `select distinct` over the columns included in the `group by`. This is shown in Listing 8.4.

This may sound trite, which it is, indeed. But when you get weird results for a query, `select distinct` statements are the first step when trying to find out what went wrong.

Listing 8.4. Using `select distinct` to determine number of groups.

```
--        Filename: 08squ04.sql
--         Purpose: determine number of groups for sex
--
```

```
select distinct
    sex
from pers1
;
```

This script returns

```
S
-
F
M
```

Single Versus Group Columns

In the previous example, there are two types of columns:

- Single columns that provide group categories
- Group columns that calculate aggregates

In all cases, the single columns have to be included in the group by subclause as well. If that rule is violated, the rather frequent error

```
ERROR at line 1:
ORA-00937: not a single-group group function
```

is returned. In some rare cases when working with substrings, additional variables are included in the group by column comma list. Normally, however, it makes no sense to break out on a column and then not know which aggregate values belong to which value within the break column. For all practical purposes, the only use for even having a group by is to affect the order in which the grouping is performed independently from the order in which the same single columns are selected.

8

AGGREGATIONS AND GROUP FUNCTIONS

> **TIP**
>
> Usually it is best to copy the single column or the whole set of single columns and paste them in the group by subclause. Make sure, however, that you strip out aliases from the latter.

The query is not limited to one single-row column. If too many single columns are included, however, the subsets become smaller and smaller, until eventually no aggregation happens, thus defying the purpose of aggregating.

 The crlaw1.sql script included on the CD-ROM that accompanies this book creates the lawyer1 table, which is laid out as follows:

```
SQL> select * from lawyer1;
```

```
   ID NAME              OFFICE           BHRS    BGROSS
--------- ---------------  -------------  ----------  ---------
    1 Dewey             Boston           2856    426800
    2 Cheetham          New York         1398    280435
    3 Howe              Los Angeles      3480    569338
    4 Clayton           Houston          1789    190045
    5 Roach             Houston          2349    269844
    6 Roll              Los Angeles      3203    498084
    7 Easton            Los Angeles      3800    654832
    8 Bonin             New York         1678    346892
    9 Frankie           New York         2134    469843
   10 Greene            Boston           2854    289435
   11 Cardinal          Boston           2694    277952
   12 Chandler          Los Angeles      2987    423878
   13 Martinez          Los Angeles      2659    403488
   14 Earl              New York         2320    434801
   15 Wright            Boston           2789    204133
   16 Chabot            New York         1680    310897
   17 Miller            Los Angeles      3153    503582
   18 Ming              Los Angeles      2492    359021
   19 Chatham           New York         1759    367944
   20 Paul              Boston           2198    239855

20 rows selected.
```

One obvious way to group is by the value of the office column. (See Listing 8.5.)

Listing 8.5. Grouping data by column.

```
--       Filename: 08squ05.sql
--        Purpose: determine avg, max, and minimum hours of
                   lawyers by office

col avghrs format 9,999.00 heading 'Avg. Hrs'

select
   office,
   avg(bhrs) avghrs,
   min(bhrs),
   max(bhrs)
from lawyer1
group by office
;

clear columns
```

This script returns

```
OFFICE          Avg. Hrs MIN(BHRS) MAX(BHRS)
------------- ---------- --------- ---------
Boston          2,678.20      2198      2856
Houston         2,069.00      1789      2349
Los Angeles     3,110.57      2492      3800
New York        1,828.17      1398      2320
```

But it is also possible to group by any valid SQL column expression. An example is to break down earnings by the number of hours rounded to 1,000. First, a `select distinct` is used to determine the number of group rows. (See Listing 8.6.)

Listing 8.6. Grouping data by SQL column expression, `hrange`.

```
--        Filename: 08squ06.sql
--        Purpose: determine avg, max, and minimum gross income of
--                 lawyers by hour ranges (rounded to 1000)
--
col avgdol format $999,999.00 heading 'Avg. $$$'
col mindol format $999,999.00 heading 'Min. $$$'
col maxdol format $999,999.00 heading 'Max. $$$'

select
   distinct round ( bhrs, -3) hrange
from lawyer1
;
```

This script returns

```
HRANGE
---------
     1000
     2000
     3000
     4000
```

At this point, it turns out that the granularity of steps of 1,000 hours is fine for this purpose. Therefore, a slightly adapted formula is used that groups by 2,000-hour intervals:

```
select
   distinct round ( bhrs / 2, -3)*2 hrange
from lawyer1
;
```

This returns

```
HRANGE
---------
     2000
     4000
```

Now the average, minimum, and maximum billable gross receipts can be calculated, as in the following:

```
select
   round ( bhrs, -3) hrange,
   avg(bgross) avgdol,
   min(bgross) mindol,
   max(bgross) maxdol
from lawyer1
group by round ( bhrs, -3)
;
```

This returns

```
HRANGE     Avg. $$$     Min. $$$      Max. $$$
---------  -----------  ------------  ------------
     2000  $330,953.94  $190,045.00   $469,843.00
     4000  $556,459.00  $498,084.00   $654,832.00
```

Grouping by More Than One Column

group by can be extended to include more than one column. The aggregations could happen on both office and hrange (see Listing 8.7).

Listing 8.7. Grouping data by more than one column.

```
--          Filename: 08squ07.sql
--           Purpose: determine avg, max, and minimum gross income of
--                    lawyers by hour ranges (rounded to 1000)
--
col avgdol format $999,999.00 heading 'Avg. $$$'
col mindol format $999,999.00 heading 'Min. $$$'
col maxdol format $999,999.00 heading 'Max. $$$'

select
   office,
   round ( bhrs / 2, -3)*2 hrange,
   avg(bgross) avgdol,
   min(bgross) mindol,
   max(bgross) maxdol
from lawyer1
group by
   office,
   round ( bhrs / 2, -3)*2
;

clear columns
```

This script returns

```
OFFICE           HRANGE     Avg. $$$     Min. $$$      Max. $$$
---------------  ---------  -----------  ------------  ------------
Boston                2000  $287,635.00  $204,133.00   $426,800.00
Houston               2000  $229,944.50  $190,045.00   $269,844.00
Los Angeles           2000  $395,462.33  $359,021.00   $423,878.00
Los Angeles           4000  $556,459.00  $498,084.00   $654,832.00
New York              2000  $368,468.67  $280,435.00   $469,843.00
```

The aggregate rows in this example are first sorted by office, and then by billable hour range. If these columns are reversed in the group by statement, the output will be sorted accordingly. (See Listing 8.8.)

Listing 8.8. Grouping data by more than one column.

```
--        Filename: 08squ08.sql
--         Purpose: determine avg, max, and minimum gross income of
--                  lawyers by hour ranges (rounded to 2000) and
--                  office name
--
col avgdol format $999,999.00 heading 'Avg. $$$'
col mindol format $999,999.00 heading 'Min. $$$'
col maxdol format $999,999.00 heading 'Max. $$$'

select
   office,
   round ( bhrs / 2, -3)*2 hrange,
   avg(bgross) avgdol,
   min(bgross) mindol,
   max(bgross) maxdol
from lawyer1
group by
   round ( bhrs / 2, -3)*2,
   office
;

clear columns
```

This returns

```
OFFICE            HRANGE    Avg. $$$      Min. $$$      Max. $$$
-------------     -------   -----------   -----------   -----------
Boston               2000   $287,635.00   $204,133.00   $426,800.00
Houston              2000   $229,944.50   $190,045.00   $269,844.00
Los Angeles          2000   $395,462.33   $359,021.00   $423,878.00
New York             2000   $368,468.67   $280,435.00   $469,843.00
Los Angeles          4000   $556,459.00   $498,084.00   $654,832.00
```

Thus, the group by does not only set the columns that determine the aggregation, but also the order in which these columns are broken out.

CAUTION

If several single-row columns are in a query, group by returns exactly as many rows as there are distinct sets of values in all the single-row columns involved in the query. If these columns have five sets of values, as in the previous example, five rows will result. You will never have more than the product of the number of values per column. If there are four offices and two time ranges, you will never have more than eight aggregate rows returned (unless something is seriously wrong with the logic of your statement). A select distinct statement will identify all value sets occurring in your data, as shown in Listing 8.9.

Listing 8.9. Determining value sets using select distinct.

```
--        Filename: 08squ09.sql
--         Purpose: determine distinct value combinations of
--                  hour ranges rounded to 2000 and office name
--
select distinct
   office,
   round ( bhrs / 2, -3)*2 hrange
from lawyer1
;
```

This returns

```
OFFICE              HRANGE
---------------  ---------
Boston                2000
Houston               2000
Los Angeles           2000
Los Angeles           4000
New York              2000
```

which are exactly the same combinations of values as the breakout on these groups in
`08squ08.sql`.

Group Functions

A group column is designated as such through the use of a group function in its definition.
This function also specifies what kind of an aggregate is to be calculated. All these functions
have exactly one parameter: the expression being aggregated.

Counting Rows: count

The count function returns the number of rows retrieved in a query. The default option is to
count all rows retrieved. It does not matter what column, constant, or expression is passed in
as argument, even if it is null. Please see Chapter 15, "Missing Data, Null, and Zero Values,"
for an example. Listing 8.10 counts the rows of the lawyer1 table using several different arguments.

Listing 8.10. Using the count function.

```
--        Filename: 08squ10.sql
--         Purpose: show use of count function
--
select
   count(*),
   count(1),
   count(id),
   count(office),
   count(bhrs)
from lawyer1
;
```

This returns

```
COUNT(*)   COUNT(1)  COUNT(ID) COUNT(OFFICE) COUNT(BHRS)
---------- --------- --------- ------------- -----------
    20         20        20         20            20
```

Regardless of the argument, count returns the same. The use of count(1) has the advantage that no data within a row has to be processed for the calculation.

The same script with a grouping on office will return counts of rows (and thus lawyers) in each office:

```
select
   office,
   count(*),
   count(1),
   count(id),
   count(office),
   count(bhrs)
from lawyer1
group by office
;

select
```

This returns

```
OFFICE          COUNT(*)  COUNT(1) COUNT(ID) COUNT(OFFICE) COUNT(BHRS)
--------------- --------- -------- --------- ------------- -----------
Boston              5         5         5         5             5
Houston             2         2         2         2             2
Los Angeles         7         7         7         7             7
New York            6         6         6         6             6
```

The second option of the count function is the counting of distinct values or of distinct combinations of columns. This option is very valuable when testing tables. The following example counts first the distinct ID and then distinct values when office and the character representation of round (bhrs / 2, -3)*2 are concatenated:

```
select
   count (distinct id)
from lawyer1;

select
   count (distinct office ¦¦
          to_char(round ( bhrs / 2, -3)*2) )
from lawyer1;
```

This returns

```
COUNT(DISTINCTID)
-----------------
             20


COUNT(DISTINCTOFFICE¦¦TO_CHAR(ROUND(BHRS/2,-3)*2))
--------------------------------------------------
                        5
```

> **TIP**
>
> If a distinct count on a column returns the same value as a count, the column is unique. Please see Chapter 29, "Keys, Indexes, Constraints, and Table/Column Comments."

Calculating the Total of a Set of Values: sum

The sum function returns the sum of the values of the expression passed in as argument. sum(1) returns the same as count(1) or count on any other valid value. Listing 8.11 calculates the sum of all numerical fields of lawyer1—first for the entire table, and then broken out by office.

Listing 8.11. Using the sum function.

```
--      Filename: 08squ11.sql
--      Purpose: show use of sum function
--
select
   sum(1),
   sum(id),
   sum(bhrs),
   sum(bgross)
from lawyer1
;

select
   office,
   sum(1),
   sum(id),
   sum(bhrs),
   sum(bgross)
from lawyer1
group by office
;
```

This returns the following:

```
  SUM(1)    SUM(ID) SUM(BHRS) SUM(BGROSS)
--------- --------- --------- -----------
       20       210     50272     7521099
```

```
OFFICE                  SUM(1)   SUM(ID) SUM(BHRS) SUM(BGROSS)
--------------        --------- --------- --------- -----------
Boston                        5        57     13391     1438175
Houston                       2         9      4138      459889
Los Angeles                   7        76     21774     3412223
New York                      6        68     10969     2210812
```

Just as was the case with count, sum can work with a distinct argument, which might be useful for certain statistical analyses. (See Listing 8.12.)

Listing 8.12. Using `sum` with the `distinct` argument.

```
--        Filename: 08squ12.sql
--        Purpose: sum of distinct values
--
select
   sum (distinct round ( bhrs / 2, -3)*2 )
from lawyer1
;
```

This returns

```
SUM(DISTINCTROUND(BHRS/2,-3)*2)
-------------------------------
                           6000
```

Calculating the Highest and Lowest of a Set of Values: `max` and `min`

The `max` and `min` functions return the highest or lowest value, respectively, within a column. Because these pick out just one value, it does not matter whether they do so on all rows or on a distinct set of rows. The lowest value of a large set of values is identical to the lowest value of the distinctly different values of the set. Listing 8.13 shows the use of these functions.

Listing 8.13. Using `min` and `max` functions.

```
--        Filename: 08squ13.sql
--        Purpose: min and max functions
--
select
   min (round ( bhrs / 2, -3)*2)  minrange,
   max (round ( bhrs / 2, -3)*2)  maxrange,
   min (bhrs)                     minbhrs,
   max (bhrs)                     maxbhrs,
   min (bgross)                   minbgross,
   max (bgross)                   maxbgross
from lawyer1
;
```

This script returns

MINRANGE	MAXRANGE	MINBHRS	MAXBHRS	MINBGROSS	MAXBGROSS
2000	4000	1398	3800	190045	654832

It is also possible to apply a group function on top of a group function, such as counting the lawyers per office and then reporting the minimum and maximum number thereof. This operation requires the use of at least a subquery view. Please see Chapter 26, "Insertable Single-Table Views," for an example.

Calculating the Average of a Set of Values: avg

avg is the first of a very limited set of statistical functions that calculates the average value of a set of values. Averaging distinct values is possible, too, and it leads to solutions that are likely to be statistically inappropriate. Listing 8.14 may illuminate the difference:

Listing 8.14. Using avg function.

```
--        Filename: 08squ14.sql
--         Purpose: min and max functions
--
select
   avg (round ( bhrs / 2, -3)*2)          avgrange,
   avg (distinct round ( bhrs / 2, -3)*2) avgdrange,
   avg (bhrs)                             avgbhrs,
   avg (distinct bhrs)                    avgdbhrs,
   avg (bgross)                           avggross,
   avg (distinct bgross)                  avgdgross
from lawyer1
;
```

This returns

```
AVGRANGE AVGDRANGE   AVGBHRS  AVGDBHRS  AVGGROSS AVGDGROSS
-------- --------- --------- --------- --------- ---------
    2400      3000    2513.6    2513.6 376054.95 376054.95
```

The average of the rounded hour ranges is 2,400, and the average of distinct values is 3,000. The averages and distinct averages of hours and gross receipts are the same.

The second part of the example breaks out the count of rows by the hour ranges:

```
select
   round ( bhrs / 2, -3)*2,
   count(1)
from lawyer1
group by
   round ( bhrs / 2, -3)*2
;
```

It shows that 2,000 occurs 16 times, and 4,000 only four times:

```
ROUND(BHRS/2,-3)*2  COUNT(1)
------------------  --------
              2000        16
              4000         4
```

If the objective were to calculate the average from such a frequency table, the weighted average formula should be used—(2000*16+4000*4)/20 equals (32000+16000)/20 equals 48000/20 or 2400—which, not incidentally, is the same as the average of all values returned.

> **CAUTION**
>
> The average of distinct values illuminates another fact: Only because SQL returns it does not necessarily mean that it makes sense. The appropriateness of statement logic is the sole responsibility of the programmer.

The averages of hour-range values and the distinct hour-range values are the same as those of the gross receipts and distinct gross-receipt values. The reason is that the values of these columns happen to be unique.

Calculating the Variance and Standard Deviations of All Values in a Column: `variance` and `stddev`

This and the following functions in this chapter are vendor extensions, meaning that they are not part of the SQL-89 and SQL-92 standards. Most vendors provide similar functions, but the syntax might be slightly different.

ORACLE
vs SQL

Variance and standard deviation are measures of the average distance of a set of values to the mean of the same set of numbers. The variance is a key to statistical significance testing. Without a full complement of statistical functions, however, it is unlikely that it will be used much at all. Statistically, the standard deviation is the square root of the variance.

Listing 8.15 calculates the measures of the distance to the mean and the individual values of the bhours column. Some of these use functions; others do not. The measures that do not use functions statically insert the values for the mean and the number of observations.

8

AGGREGATIONS AND GROUP FUNCTIONS

Listing 8.15. Using `variance` and `stddev` functions.

```
--      Filename: 08squ15.sql
--        Purpose: variance and stddev functions
--
select
   avg (bhrs)                                    avgbhrs,
   count(1)                                      cnt,
   sum (abs(bhrs - 2513.6))/20                   avdst,
   sum ((bhrs - 2513.6)*(bhrs - 2513.6))         sumsquare,
   sum ((bhrs - 2513.6)*(bhrs - 2513.6)) /19     variance1,
   variance (bhrs)                               variance2,
   sqrt(variance (bhrs) )                        stdev1,
   stddev (bhrs)                                 stdev2
from lawyer1
;
```

First the average and the count of rows are displayed. The third column is the average distance of a value to the column's mean. The abs function has to be used; otherwise, the values cancel out. Next is the sum of the squares of the distances to the mean. The next column calculates the variance by dividing the sum of squares by the number of rows minus 1. The `variance` function arrives at the same value. The last two columns display the standard deviation, first by taking the square root of the variance and then by using the `stddev` function. As they should be, both numbers are the same. The output looks like this:

```
AVGBHRS   CNT   AVDST  SUMSQUARE  VARIANCE1  VARIANCE2   STDEV1    STDEV2
---------  ----  ------ ---------  ---------  ---------  ---------  ---------
  2513.6    20   533.9 8100492.8  426341.73  426341.73  652.94849  652.94849
```

Summary

The functions in this chapter expand the `select distinct` functionality and retrieve one row for each distinct combination of values of the columns selected. Group functions return aggregate-information sets of rows, which may be all rows of the table or subsets specified by the `group by` subclause. `group by` allows you to specify one or more columns or expressions by which the results should be broken out. A query with one `group by` column returns exactly as many rows as there are distinct values in the `group by` column. If there are more `group by` columns, the query returns one row for every distinct set of values of all `group by` columns combined.

The following aggregate functions are provided:

- The `count` function returns the number of rows retrieved in a query. It can list the count of all values of a column, or the number of distinct values only.

- `sum` returns the sum of the values of the expression passed in as argument. It can sum up all values or distinct values only.

- The `max` and `min` functions return the highest or lowest value, respectively, within a column.

- The `average` function returns the statistical mean of a column.

- The `variance` and `stddev` functions return the statistical variance or standard deviation, respectively, of a column.

These aggregate functions are extremely useful, especially when combined with views (see Chapter 29) and subqueries (see Chapters 19, "Single-Value Subqueries," 20, "Multiple-Value Subqueries," and 21, "Correlated Subqueries").

Conditional Operands

IN THIS CHAPTER

In the course of the first eight chapters, we have been content to retrieve all rows within a table or at least summarize information from all rows, as was the case in Chapter 8, "Aggregations and Group Functions." This chapter covers the straightforward possibilities that SQL provides for selecting a subset of rows—the `where` clause that qualifies an input row for inclusion or exclusion *before* further processing and the `having` clause that does the same with an aggregate value *after* all accessed rows have been processed. SQL offers another post-processing conditional option, which will be covered in Chapter 21, "Correlated Subqueries." The second part of the chapter covers all comparison operators and predicates available. The last part touches on ways to include conditional processing in the `select` comma list, including some workaround options.

Evaluating Conditional Statements

Conditional statements are formulated so that they can return one of two values: `true` or `false`. Thus, if the condition is stated as `if 2 = 2`, it would evaluate as true, while `2 = 4` would evaluate as `false`. The statement `if age = 43` would evaluate to `true` if the age were indeed 43, and to `false` otherwise. SQL adds a twist in the way it treats null values, which effectively amounts to a third value to which a condition can evaluate—unknown. This special case is covered in Chapter 15, "Missing Data, Null, and Zero Values." In all other cases, SQL behaves like most other computer languages.

Limiting the Selection of Rows: `where`

By far the most important conditional feature is the `where` subclause, which allows you to list the conditions under which a row will be included in the selection. `where` conditions are evaluated upon retrieval of a row from a table. Only those rows in the table that fulfill the condition specified with `where` will be chosen.

Thus, if we want to retrieve information on all the people in `pers1` who are male, Listing 9.1 would do just that.

Listing 9.1. Retrieving data using `where` conditions.

```
--        Filename: 09squ01.sql
--         Purpose: retrieve rows
--                  where sex equals male or female
--
select *
from pers1
where sex = 'M'
;
```

This code returns all male rows, as shown in the following:

```
   ID LNAME           FMNAME          SSN          AGE S
--------- --------------- --------------- -------- ----------- -
    1 Jones           David N.        895663453         34 M
    2 Martinelli      A. Emery        312331818         92 M
    5 Melsheli        Joseph K.       000342222         14 M
```

The following code

```
select *
from pers1
where sex = 'F'
;
```

returns all the female ones, as shown in the following:

```
    ID LNAME          FMNAME           SSN          AGE S
--------- -------------- ---------------- -------- ---------- -
     3 Talavera       F. Espinosa      533932999     19 F
     4 Kratochvil     Mary T.          969825711     48 F
```

The where subclause is always listed after the from comma list.

From the lawyer1 table, Listing 9.2 extracts all lawyers who work in the Los Angeles office.

Listing 9.2. Retrieving data using where conditions.

```
--        Filename: 09squ02.sql
--         Purpose: retrieve rows
--                  where age > avg age which is 41.4
--
select *
from lawyer1
where office = 'Los Angeles'
;
```

This code returns

```
    ID NAME           OFFICE           BHRS    BGROSS
--------- -------------- ---------------- ---------- ---------
     3 Howe           Los Angeles      3480    569338
     6 Roll           Los Angeles      3203    498084
     7 Easton         Los Angeles      3800    654832
    12 Chandler       Los Angeles      2987    423878
    13 Martinez       Los Angeles      2659    403488
    17 Miller         Los Angeles      3153    503582
    18 Ming           Los Angeles      2492    359021

7 rows selected.
```

Note that all characters and character strings must be enclosed between single quotes. This applies to the where clause just as anywhere else where string constants are used. The following example selects those lawyers from the lawyer1 table who work approximately 3,000 hours, meaning that if the values contained in the bhrs column are rounded to thousands, 3,000 would result:

```
select *
from lawyer1
where round(bhrs,-3) = 3000
;
```

This code returns

```
    ID NAME             OFFICE              BHRS      BGROSS
--------- ---------------- -----------------  ---------  ---------
     1 Dewey            Boston              2856      426800
     3 Howe             Los Angeles         3480      569338
     6 Roll             Los Angeles         3203      498084
    10 Greene           Boston              2854      289435
    11 Cardinal         Boston              2694      277952
    12 Chandler         Los Angeles         2987      423878
    13 Martinez         Los Angeles         2659      403488
    15 Wright           Boston              2789      204133
    17 Miller           Los Angeles         3153      503582
```

```
9 rows selected.
```

Values that are included in the condition do not need to be included in the `select` comma list. Every row that is contained in the table from which the query selects can be used in the conditions, as can pseudocolumns and pseudofunctions. Listing 9.3 selects `id`, `name`, `bhrs`, and `bgross` of all lawyers from the Boston office.

Listing 9.3. Retrieving data using where and select.

```
--      Filename: 19squ03.sql
--      Purpose: retrieve id, name, bhrs, and bgross
--               where office is 'Boston'
--
select
   id,
   name,
   bhrs,
   bgross
from lawyer1
where office = 'Boston'
;
```

This code returns

```
    ID NAME              BHRS      BGROSS
--------- ----------------  ---------  ---------
     1 Dewey             2856      426800
    10 Greene            2854      289435
    11 Cardinal          2694      277952
    15 Wright            2789      204133
    20 Paul              2198      239855
```

In many cases, it makes more sense not to include the column that is referenced by the condition because that information is known up front anyway.

Rejecting Group Rows After Calculation: `having`

The result of an aggregate function is not known until all rows to which it pertains have been processed. Because `where` conditions are evaluated at the time when a row is retrieved from a table, they are not suitable for evaluating aggregate results. The value to be evaluated is simply not yet known at that point. Listing 9.4, which is a variation of `08squ07.sql`, groups the `lawyer1` records by office; this results in four rows. For each of these, it reports average, minimum, and maximum gross receipts. To calculate these, all rows of the table have to be read.

Listing 9.4. Grouping and determing average, maximum, and minimum of data.

```
--        Filename: 09squ04.sql
--        Purpose: determine avg, max, and minimum gross income of
--                 lawyers by hour ranges (rounded to 1000)
--                 where count of lawyer = 6
--
col avgdol format $999,999.00 heading 'Avg. $$$'
col mindol format $999,999.00 heading 'Min. $$$'
col maxdol format $999,999.00 heading 'Max. $$$'

select
   office,
   avg(bgross) avgdol,
   min(bgross) mindol,
   max(bgross) maxdol
from lawyer1
group by
   office
having count(1) = 6
;

clear columns
```

The `having count(1) = 6` condition, however, prevents three of these rows from being returned. Only the New York row is returned because the count of lawyers in New York is exactly six, as the `having` condition specifies. As is the case with the `where` condition, the `having` condition can evaluate expressions that do not occur in the `select` comma list. Only one row is returned:

```
OFFICE            Avg. $$$     Min. $$$     Max. $$$
---------------   -----------  -----------  -----------
New York          $368,468.67  $280,435.00  $469,843.00
```

The use of `having` is not limited to aggregate columns. The following example retrieves the same information:

```
select
   office,
   avg(bgross) avgdol,
   min(bgross) mindol,
   max(bgross) maxdol
from lawyer1
group by
   office
having office = 'New York'
;
```

TIP

Using having where where would work is not advisable because it is likely to slow execution down, especially if the column on which the condition acts is indexed. (See Chapter 29, "Keys, Indexes, Constraints, and Table/Column Comments" for more information.) While where works on all columns, having can be used only for aggregate expressions or columns or expressions in the group by comma list.

where and having are frequently combined in a statement: where is used to limit the set of rows that is considered for further analysis, and having is used to select from a smaller set of aggregate rows that is based on the initially selected set of rows. This is demonstrated in Listing 9.5.

Listing 9.5. Using where and having to retrieve data.

```
--        Filename: 09squ05.sql
--        Purpose: determine avg, max, and minimum gross income of
--                 lawyers who work about 3000 hours in an office with
--                 exactly four such lawyers

col avgdol format $999,999.00 heading 'Avg. $$$'
col mindol format $999,999.00 heading 'Min. $$$'
col maxdol format $999,999.00 heading 'Max. $$$'

select
   office,
   avg(bgross) avgdol,
   min(bgross) mindol,
   max(bgross) maxdol
from lawyer1
where round ( bhrs, -3) = 3000
group by
   office
having count(1) = 4
;

clear columns
```

This code returns

```
OFFICE             Avg. $$$      Min. $$$      Max. $$$
---------------    ------------  ------------  ------------
Boston             $299,580.00   $204,133.00   $426,800.00
```

REAL-WORLD EXPERIENCES

When I was in high school, I had to take a few years of business calculations. This was at a time when pocket calculators started to become available, but because the curriculum and equipment in Austrian business high schools were always many years behind (remember the core memory), we spent many hours learning tricks on how to quickly multiply or divide numbers with special characteristics. Although I did not like the subject then, one rule has come in handy: When you perform a calculation of a few numbers, you should always have a reasonably good idea as to approximately what result to expect. This estimate is then used to double-check the results.

The same is true in SQL queries and in any computer-based analysis for that matter. You should always have a good idea what to expect from a query—how many rows it will return, which values these rows should have approximately, and so on. Even if an implausible number turns out to be right, your customer or boss may ask you whether that number is possible and then you can say, "Yes, we tested such and such."

As this is written, Gary Kasparov and IBM were going through another historical man versus machine chess game. This one ended in a tie. The outcome does not really matter; at some point a supercomputer should be able to beat the best chess player at the game. The fact, however, that IBM feels they need a 32-node SP2—1.4 tons of machinery that can consider 200 million moves per second—just to have a crack at winning should say something; it takes incredible computing power to beat a brain. Take advantage of this brain power, and consider the plausibility of the outcomes of your programs.

Comparison Operators

The examples so far have used only one comparison operator, equal (=). The test for equality has an extremely important use when joining tables; this is discussed in Chapter 17, "Joins." In addition, SQL provides the typical set of comparison operators and a few that are used in the context of databases only. Two of these, `exists` and `not exists`, are covered in Chapter 21. Finally, there are two tests for null values, `is null` and `is not null`, which are covered in Chapter 15.

Inequality (<>)

The SQL standard lists only <> as the inequality operator. A number of others (such as !=, ^=, and ~=) work in some implementations as well, but there is really no point to use them. In most cases, an inequality test returns exactly those rows that an equality test does not return. The big exception in SQL are cases where the value of a column referenced in the comparison expression is null. In this case the entire comparison evaluates to null as well. The rows to which this applies cannot be retrieved either with the equality or with the inequality test. Special tests for null values exist, which are covered in Chapter 15. Listing 9.6 is the complement to `09squ04.sql`.

Listing 9.6. Using the inequality operator.

```
--          Filename: 09squ06.sql
--           Purpose: determine avg, max, and minimum gross income of
--                    lawyers by hour ranges (rounded to 1000) where
--                    count of lawyers in the office <> 6
--
col avgdol format $999,999.00 heading 'Avg. $$$'
col mindol format $999,999.00 heading 'Min. $$$'
col maxdol format $999,999.00 heading 'Max. $$$'

select
   office,
   avg(bgross) avgdol,
   min(bgross) mindol,
   max(bgross) maxdol,
   count(1)
from lawyer1
group by
   office
having count(1) <> 6
;

clear columns
```

The code returns those three offices where the count of lawyers is unequal to six:

OFFICE	Avg. $$$	Min. $$$	Max. $$$	COUNT(1)
Boston	$287,635.00	$204,133.00	$426,800.00	5
Houston	$229,944.50	$190,045.00	$269,844.00	2
Los Angeles	$487,460.43	$359,021.00	$654,832.00	7

Less Than and Greater Than: < and >

Greater than and less than tests evaluate to true if the expression at the thin end of the operator is less than the expression at the wide end. Thus 3 < 5 and 6 > 2 evaluate as true and 3 > 5 and 6 < 2 evaluate as false. These operators are used frequently to force a dichotomy on continuous data, such as all lawyers who work more than 2,500 hours, all offices that have more than three lawyers, and so on. Listing 9.7 adapts 09squ05.sql for that purpose.

Listing 9.7. Using the greater than operator.

```
--          Filename: 09squ07.sql
--           Purpose: determine avg, max, and minimum gross income of
--                    lawyers who work more than 2500 billable hours
--                    in offices with more than three such lawyers
--                    where count of lawyer = 6
--
col avgdol format $999,999.00 heading 'Avg. $$$'
col mindol format $999,999.00 heading 'Min. $$$'
col maxdol format $999,999.00 heading 'Max. $$$'

select
   office,
   avg(bgross) avgdol,
```

```
    min(bgross) mindol,
    max(bgross) maxdol,
    count(1)
from lawyer1
where bhrs > 2500
group by
    office
having count(1) > 3
;

clear columns
```

This code returns

```
OFFICE              Avg. $$$     Min. $$$     Max. $$$  COUNT(1)
--------------      -----------  -----------  -----------  --------
Boston              $299,580.00  $204,133.00  $426,800.00         4
Los Angeles         $508,867.00  $403,488.00  $654,832.00         6
```

The where condition limits the analysis to only those lawyers who work more than 2,500 hours. The having condition limits the output to those offices with more than three such lawyers. A different query could be asked, which would allow you to consider the averages of *all* lawyers in the offices that have at least three lawyers working more than 2,500 hours. To answer this question, a subquery will be necessary. (See Chapter 20, "Multiple-Value Subqueries," for more information.)

Greater Than/Equal, Less Than/Equal, and Between: >=, <=, and between ... and

The greater than/equal (>=), less than/equal (<=), and between ... and operators are similar to greater than and less than tests. In the case of integer comparisons, they are equivalent—bhrs > 2500 equates to bhrs >= 2501.

In the case of fixed-point and floating-point numbers (which will be covered in Chapter 11, "Numerical Data: The number Datatype"), the difference can be substantial. There are no values defined between two adjoining integers. In real number space, however, there is an infinite number of values between these. Even in their computer representation, which is definitely not infinite, there can be considerably more values between 1 and 2 than the national debt expressed in nano cents. The difference beween >= 2 and > 1 is all these values.

Because dealing with large distinctions is cumbersome, descriptive statistics summarizes many individual data points into a few numbers that tell essentially the same thing. Every country's statistical abstract is full with tables of income or revenue ranges. The intention might be to list the percentage of the population with an income less than $10,000, between $10,000 and $20,000, between $20,000 and $30,000, and so on. These ranges work fine until somebody makes exactly $20,000. Because the ranges here were defined sloppily, there is an overlap and SQL would count that person twice, once in each range. The issue can be easily resolved, however, if the ranges are defined as in Table 9.1.

Table 9.1. Nonoverlapping value ranges.

Range	Definition
1	0 <= income < 10,000
2	10,000 <= income < 20,000
3	20,000 <= income < 30,000
4	30,000 <= income < 40,000
5	40,000 <= income < 50,000
6	50,000 <= income < 60,000

DEBUG ALERT

If you do not see the same number at the end of one range and at the beginning of the next, there is likely to be something wrong.

Listing 9.8 breaks the lawyer table into two ranges: those making up to $150 per hour and those making more. Because SQL lacks a column-based conditional construct, one query per range will be performed.

Listing 9.8. Retrieving data using operator ranges.

```
--        Filename: 09squ08.sql
--           Purpose: select hourly revenue ranges using
--                    <= and > operators.
--
col hrldol format $999,999.00 heading 'Hourly $$$'
ttitle left 'Lawyers making up to $150 per hour'

select
   id,
   name,
   office,
   bhrs,
   bgross,
   bgross/bhrs hrldol
from lawyer1
where bgross/bhrs <= 150
order by 6
;

ttitle left 'Lawyers making over $150 per hour'

select
   id,
   name,
   office,
```

```
   bhrs,
   bgross,
   bgross/bhrs hrldol
from lawyer1
where bgross/bhrs > 150
order by 6
;

clear columns
ttitle off
```

One set of rows per output range is returned:

```
Lawyers making up to $150 per hour

      ID NAME              OFFICE              BHRS     BGROSS   Hourly $$$
--------- ------------------ ---------------- ---------- ---------- -----------
      15 Wright            Boston              2789     204133       $73.19
      10 Greene            Boston              2854     289435      $101.41
      11 Cardinal          Boston              2694     277952      $103.17
       4 Clayton           Houston             1789     190045      $106.23
      20 Paul              Boston              2198     239855      $109.12
       5 Roach             Houston             2349     269844      $114.88
      12 Chandler          Los Angeles         2987     423878      $141.91
      18 Ming              Los Angeles         2492     359021      $144.07
       1 Dewey             Boston              2856     426800      $149.44

9 rows selected.


Lawyers making over $150 per hour
      ID NAME              OFFICE              BHRS     BGROSS   Hourly $$$
--------- ------------------ ---------------- ---------- ---------- -----------
      13 Martinez          Los Angeles         2659     403488      $151.74
       6 Roll              Los Angeles         3203     498084      $155.51
      17 Miller            Los Angeles         3153     503582      $159.72
       3 Howe              Los Angeles         3480     569338      $163.60
       7 Easton            Los Angeles         3800     654832      $172.32
      16 Chabot            New York            1680     310897      $185.06
      14 Earl              New York            2320     434801      $187.41
       2 Cheetham          New York            1398     280435      $200.60
       8 Bonin             New York            1678     346892      $206.73
      19 Chatham           New York            1759     367944      $209.18
       9 Frankie           New York            2134     469843      $220.17

11 rows selected.
```

> **TIP**
>
> While there are several ways to express a condition, you are much better off to develop one consistent standard and stick to it. Personally, I rarely use <= and >= for integer data, but I use them a lot on fixed- or floating-point ones.

9

CONDITIONAL
OPERANDS

The between ... and operator is intended to identify ranges. Thus, the statement where bgross/ bhrs between 120 and 170 would include all hourly rates that are greater than or equal to $120 on one extreme and less than or equal to $170 on the other, as Listing 9.9 shows.

Listing 9.9. Retrieving data using the between...and operator.

```
--         Filename: 09squ09.sql
--          Purpose: select hourly revenue range
--                   between 120 and 170
--
col hrldol format $999,999.00 heading 'Hourly $$$'
ttitle left 'Lawyers making between $120 and $170 per hour'

select
    id,
    name,
    office,
    bhrs,
    bgross,
    bgross/bhrs hrldol
from lawyer1
where bgross/bhrs between 120 and 170
order by 6
;

clear columns
ttitle off
```

This code returns

```
Lawyers making between $120 and $170 per hour

    ID NAME            OFFICE            BHRS      BGROSS   Hourly $$$
--------- --------------- --------------- --------- --------- ------------
    12 Chandler        Los Angeles       2987      423878     $141.91
    18 Ming            Los Angeles       2492      359021     $144.07
     1 Dewey           Boston            2856      426800     $149.44
    13 Martinez        Los Angeles       2659      403488     $151.74
     6 Roll            Los Angeles       3203      498084     $155.51
    17 Miller          Los Angeles       3153      503582     $159.72
     3 Howe            Los Angeles       3480      569338     $163.60

7 rows selected.
```

CAUTION

Between ... and works fine if only one range is selected or the other ranges are not defined to overlap with the between ... and statement values. Generally, however, between ... and is not suitable to define sets of ranges against fixed- or floating-point columns.

Equal to Any (in) and Not Equal to Any (not in) Operators

The in operator is used to compare a value to a list of values. Thus, 2 in (2,4) is true because the value 2 can be found in the list of values (2,4). On the other hand, 2 in (3,4) is false because it cannot be found in the list of values. not in does the opposite. 2 not in (2,4) is false because the value 2 can be found in the list of values (2,4). 2 not in (3,4), on the other hand, is true.

If all the lawyers who work on the East Coast need to be selected, a condition where office in ('Boston','New York') would do the trick. Listing 9.10 first selects the lawyers in these offices.

Listing 9.10. Using the in operator.

```
--       Filename: 09squ10.sql
--        Purpose: select lawyers in east coast offices.
--                 select lawyer in all other offices
--
col hrldol format $999,999.00 heading 'Hourly $$$'

select
   id,
   name,
   office,
   bhrs,
   bgross,
   bgross/bhrs hrldol
from lawyer1
where office in ('Boston','New York')
order by 3, 6
;

clear columns
```

This code returns

ID	NAME	OFFICE	BHRS	BGROSS	Hourly $$$
15	Wright	Boston	2789	204133	$73.19
10	Greene	Boston	2854	289435	$101.41
11	Cardinal	Boston	2694	277952	$103.17
20	Paul	Boston	2198	239855	$109.12
1	Dewey	Boston	2856	426800	$149.44
16	Chabot	New York	1680	310897	$185.06
14	Earl	New York	2320	434801	$187.41
2	Cheetham	New York	1398	280435	$200.60
8	Bonin	New York	1678	346892	$206.73
19	Chatham	New York	1759	367944	$209.18
9	Frankie	New York	2134	469843	$220.17

11 rows selected.

The second part of the example selects all offices that are not in New York or Boston:

```
select distinct
    office
from lawyer1
where office not in ('Boston','New York')
;
```

This code returns

```
OFFICE
--------------
Houston
Los Angeles
```

Similarity Operators: like and like ... escape

All comparison operators discussed so far have compared one value to one or more exact, other values. Such precision may not be necessary or desirable. The value of interest might be only imprecisely known, such as a name that is half forgotten. A varchar2 column may be set up to hold a few hundred characters, but only those records that are to be retrieved contain one particular word in that field.

In some cases, other functions such as substr or soundex may be of help. But often, a like comparison with a few wildcard characters will work much better.

like allows for a comparison of a string with a shorter string that includes wildcard characters. Two of these wildcards are available:

- The percent sign (%) stands in for any substring of zero or more characters.
- The underscore (_) is a placeholder for exactly one character.

Thus like '__e' evaluates to true for every three letter word where the last letter is a lowercase e. like '%e' will be true for any string that ends with a lowercase e.

For example, the names of lawyers whose names start with 'Cha' could be extracted using like, as shown in Listing 9.11.

Listing 9.11. Retrieving data using the like comparison.

```
--       Filename: 09squ11.sql
--        Purpose: select name like 'Cha%'
--
--
col hrldol format $999,999.00 heading 'Hourly $$$'

select
    name,
    office,
    bhrs,
    bgross,
    bgross/bhrs hrldol
```

```
from lawyer1
where name like 'Cha%'
order by name
;

clear columns
```

This code returns

NAME	OFFICE	BHRS	BGROSS	Hourly $$$
Chabot	New York	1680	310897	$185.06
Chandler	Los Angeles	2987	423878	$141.91
Chatham	New York	1759	367944	$209.18

The same rows would be retrieved by the following query, which uses the substring function:

```
select
    name,
    office,
    bhrs,
    bgross,
    bgross/bhrs hrldol
from lawyer1
where substr(name,1,3) = 'Cha'
order by name
;
```

The next listing queries retrieve every name that contains the combination of the letters *ar*—first using `like` and then `instr`.

Listing 9.12. Retrieving data using `like` and `instr`.

```
--      Filename: 09squ12.sql
--       Purpose: select name like '%ar%'
--
col hrldol format $999,999.00 heading 'Hourly $$$'

select
    name,
    office,
    bhrs,
    bgross,
    bgross/bhrs hrldol
from lawyer1
where name like '%ar%'
order by name
;

select
    name,
    office,
    bhrs,
    bgross,
    bgross/bhrs hrldol
```

9

CONDITIONAL
OPERANDS

continues

Listing 9.12. continued

```
from lawyer1
where instr(name,'ar') > 0
order by name
;

clear columns
```

The preceding code returns the following output twice:

```
NAME              OFFICE               BHRS     BGROSS      Hourly $$$
---------------   ---------------    ---------  ---------  ------------
Cardinal          Boston               2694     277952        $103.17
Earl              New York             2320     434801        $187.41
Martinez          Los Angeles          2659     403488        $151.74
```

If you are familiar with powerful word processors, the `like` functionality will appear a bit primitive. This functionality can be somewhat enhanced through other string functions such as `upper` or `lower`.

For example, if any name were to be retrieved that contained at least one lowercase or uppercase *m*, then `where upper(name) like '%E%'` would work as would `where lower(name) like '%e%'`. Both are shown in Listing 9.13.

Listing 9.13. Retrieving data using where ... like.

```
--        Filename: 09squ13.sql
--          Purpose: select names that contain upper case or lower case e
--
col hrldol format $999,999.00 heading 'Hourly $$$'

select
   name,
   office,
   bhrs,
   bgross,
   bgross/bhrs hrldol
from lawyer1
where upper(name) like '%E%'
order by name
;

select
   name,
   office,
   bhrs,
   bgross,
   bgross/bhrs hrldol
from lawyer1
where instr(upper(name),'E') > 0
order by name
;

clear columns
```

This code returns the same output twice:

```
NAME             OFFICE           BHRS    BGROSS    Hourly $$$
---------------  ---------------  ------  --------  -----------
Chandler         Los Angeles      2987    423878    $141.91
Cheetham         New York         1398    280435    $200.60
Dewey            Boston           2856    426800    $149.44
Earl             New York         2320    434801    $187.41
Easton           Los Angeles      3800    654832    $172.32
Frankie          New York         2134    469843    $220.17
Greene           Boston           2854    289435    $101.41
Howe             Los Angeles      3480    569338    $163.60
Martinez         Los Angeles      2659    403488    $151.74
Miller           Los Angeles      3153    503582    $159.72

10 rows selected.
```

Once in a while, it will be necessary to identify those values that contain underscores or percent signs. For this case, an escape option is provided. If an escape character precedes the underscore or the percent sign, these will be interpreted literally. Thus `like '_^_YFG' escape '^'` will match every string that starts with any character (underscore wildcard), followed by an underscore (underscore escaped), followed by the characters YFG. The `'^'` character after the keyword escape specifies that that character is to be interpreted as an escape character.

Seldom Used Comparison Operators: `any`, `some`, and `all`

If they make any sense, the `any`, `some`, and `all` operators do so in the context of subqueries, where they will be covered (see Chapter 20).

Using Row Number to Limit the Number of Rows Retrieved

ORACLE vs SQL

`rowid` and `rownum` are vendor extensions, meaning that they are not part of the SQL-89 and SQL-92 standards.

Two pseudocolumns, `rownum` and `rowid`, can be conveniently used in comparisons. `rownum`, if you recall from Chapter 4, "Operator Conversions and Value Decoding," identifies the order in which a row is retrieved from the database. It can be used to limit the number of rows retrieved. The problem is that the `order by` construct does not have any effect on `rownum` unless it happens to retrieve via an index. As a result, you may be retrieving different rows than the ones you had in mind. Listing 9.14 shows an accurate `rownum` listing and then the effect of ordering on these values, which is none.

Listing 9.14. Using rownum.

```
--      Filename: 09squ14.sql
--        Purpose: select first 7 rows by rownum
--
col hrldol format $999,999.00 heading 'Hourly $$$'
```

continues

9

CONDITIONAL
OPERANDS

Listing 9.14. continued

```
select
   id,
   rownum,
   name,
   office
from lawyer1
where rownum < 8
;
```

This code returns

```
       ID    ROWNUM NAME             OFFICE
--------- --------- ---------------- --------------
        1         1 Dewey            Boston
        2         2 Cheetham         New York
        3         3 Howe             Los Angeles
        4         4 Clayton          Houston
        5         5 Roach            Houston
        6         6 Roll             Los Angeles
        7         7 Easton           Los Angeles
```

The next statement orders by name:

```
select
   id,
   rownum,
   name,
   office
from lawyer1
where rownum < 8
order by name
;

clear columns
```

It returns the same seven rows, but they are reordered by name:

```
       ID    ROWNUM NAME             OFFICE
--------- --------- ---------------- --------------
        2         2 Cheetham         New York
        4         4 Clayton          Houston
        1         1 Dewey            Boston
        7         7 Easton           Los Angeles
        3         3 Howe             Los Angeles
        5         5 Roach            Houston
        6         6 Roll             Los Angeles
```

```
7 rows selected.
```

There is really no trivial way to limit the rows retrieved by order. One solution will be presented in Chapter 26, "Insertable Single-Table Views."

CAUTION

rownum can be used with a less than operator (<) but not with a greater than operator (except >= 1 or any statement for which >= 1 is true as well as >0, > -10000, and so on). This is shown in the following example:

```
select
    id,
    rownum,
    name,
    office
from lawyer1
where rownum > 8
;
```

This code returns the following:

```
no rows selected
```

The reason that no columns are returned is because the rownum is assigned as the row is retrieved. The first row is assigned 1. If now the condition states that only rows with rownum > 1 should be retrieved, this row is simply skipped and the next row is assigned the rownum 1. This way, execution will run through the entire table and never assign anything higher. If, however, the condition allows a rownum of 1, rows will be returned, as the following part of the example shows:

```
select
    id,
    rownum,
    name,
    office
from lawyer1
where rownum >= 1
;
```

The preceding code returns all 20 rows of the table.

9

CONDITIONAL
OPERANDS

String Comparison Issues

String comparisons pose a few challenges of their own because things that appear equal are not necessarily so. This section discusses three issues germane to strings:

- Case sensitivity
- Trailing blanks
- Comparing sound representations

Case-Insensitive Comparisons

Comparisons of string values, whether fixed or variable length, are case sensitive. Thus, for SQL `Miller` is not equal to `MILLER`, which is not equal to `miller` either. This is of little concern for a simple name, but on the more complex ones, such as `de Vilbiss` or `Schmackers von der Heide`, capitalization is not quite as obvious.

The cheap solution to this problem is to keep all names uppercase. It's cheap because it makes any clean formatting of strings in letters or addresses futile. Of course, if you don't mind presenting your customer in a bleak bureaucratic style, all caps may be fine. In the age of fancy laser printers, however, a letter that starts with "Dear SCHMACKERS VON DER HEIDE" is a turnoff.

The better solution is to have the names as accurate as possible in the database and to use case conversion functions for comparisons. This approach is used in Listing 9.15.

Listing 9.15. Using case conversion functions.

```
--        Filename: 09squ15.sql
--         Purpose: case insensitive name selection
--
select
   id,
   name,
   office
from lawyer1
where upper(name) = 'MARTINEZ'
;

select
   id,
   name,
   office
from lawyer1
where lower(name) = 'martinez'
;
```

Both queries return the same row:

```
     ID NAME              OFFICE
--------- ---------------- --------------
     13 Martinez          Los Angeles
```

They should because functionally there is no difference. Therefore, whether to use `upper` or `lower` is a matter of taste. Personally, I prefer lowercase; I am fond of UNIX and its derivatives, and I dislike it when people "yell" at me in e-mails by using uppercase.

Testing Variable Length String Values for Extraneous Blanks

A nice property of `varchar2` columns is that they can store variable length variables efficiently. The disadvantage is that values with trailing blanks are not equal to the same values without a blank. To `varchar2` columns, a trailing blank is a character. To fixed-length character columns, a trailing blank is padding.

Two approaches can be used to handle this issue:

- Make sure that `varchar2` columns do not have trailing blanks.
- Use the `rtrim` function to strip out blanks in comparisons.

The first approach is always preferable. Obviously, your data should be clean. This section shows a test for trailing blanks and a method to strip them in comparisons. Chapter 24, "Manipulating Single-Table Data," illustrates the use of both to eliminate trailing blanks from the tables.

Testing for Trailing Blanks

The easiest test for trailing blanks is to concatenate a constant to the value to be tested. If there are trailing blanks, they will show up between the value and constant. If not, the constant will follow immediately after the last character of the value. Listing 9.16 shows that with the name column in the `pers6` table, which was created in Chapter 7, "Character/Number Conversions."

Listing 9.16. Testing for trailing blanks.

```
--         Filename: 09squ16.sql
--         Purpose: testing for trailing blanks
--
col id format 99

select
   id,
   lname,
   lname || '**'
from pers6
;
```

This code returns

```
    ID LNAME               LNAME||'**'
--------- ------------------- ---------------------
     1 Jones               Jones            **
     2 Martinelli          Martinelli       **
     3 Talavera            Talavera         **
     4 Kratochvil          Kratochvil       **
     5 Melsheli            Melsheli         **
```

From the `lname` field alone, it is impossible to tell whether there are trailing blanks because SQL*Plus blank-pads the output for display purposes. With the appended asterisks, the padding is immediately clear.

This approach is of little help if the task is to find a handful of blank-padded entries in a table with a few million rows. In that case, eyeballing through such output is simply not an option. A better approach is a test that compares a value with the same value passed into `rtrim` as the first argument and a blank as the second. If these are not equal, trailing blanks are present, as the next example shows:

```
select
    id,
    lname,
    lname || '**'
from pers6
    where lname <> rtrim(lname,' ')
;
```

This statement returns the same five rows as the previous one, which it should because all last names are blank-padded in pers6. The same query against the pers1 table, however, returns the following because the names in this table are clean:

```
no rows selected
```

Coping with Trailing Blanks in Comparisons

It may not be possible to clean up the data; they may be in someone else's control or something else may be more important at the time. In that case, the rtrim function can be used to fix them on-the-fly, just as upper was. The value of the comparison column is processed by rtrim before the comparison. The following example extracts all rows from pers6, where the last name is either Martinelli or Kratochvil:

```
select
    id,
    lname,
    lname || '**'
from pers6
    where rtrim(lname,' ') in ('Martinelli','Kratochvil')
;
```

This code returns

```
ID LNAME                 LNAME||'**'
--- -------------------   --------------------
  2 Martinelli            Martinelli    **
  4 Kratochvil            Kratochvil    **
```

Similar Sounding Comparisons: soundex

In Chapter 6, "Single-Row Character String Functions," the soundex function and its return values were explained. The major purpose of this function is to identify values in a column that sound similar to a comparison value. Telephone information operators often must hear, "I don't really know how to spell the name, but it sounds like…." Using soundex, the operator could enter that word and all similar sounding names would be selected.

The following listing uses the clause where soundex(name) in (soundex('chitum'), soundex('duee'), soundex('erle')) to extract all names from the lawyer1 table that sound similar. The first query shows the soundex representations of these names; the second one extracts similar names.

Listing 9.17. Using soundex to retrieve data.

```
--          Filename: 09squ17.sql
--          Purpose: select names by soundex
--
col chitum format a10
col duee   format a10
col erle   format a10

select
   soundex('chitum') chitum,
   soundex('duee')   duee,
   soundex('erle')   erle
from dual
;

select
   id,
   name,
   soundex(name)
from lawyer1
where soundex(name) in
    (soundex('chitum'),
     soundex('duee'),
     soundex('erle'))
order by soundex(name)
;

clear columns
```

This code returns

```
CHITUM     DUEE       ERLE
---------- ---------- --------
C350       D000       E640


        ID NAME            SOUN
---------- --------------- ----
         2 Cheetham        C350
        19 Chatham         C350
         1 Dewey           D000
        14 Earl            E640
```

The limits of this algorithm become obvious as soon as words are compared that sound similar, but have different first letters such as in the case of write, right, and wright:

```
col write  format a10
col right  format a10
col wright format a10

select
   soundex('write')  write,
   soundex('right')  right,
   soundex('wright') wright
from dual
;

clear columns
```

These are the return values:

```
WRITE        RIGHT       WRIGHT
----------   ----------  ----------
W630         R230        W623
```

It is not even clear how these could be made comparable. Thus, soundex sounds nice but is quite limited.

> **NOTE**
>
> If you need real soundex functionality, other algorithms exist. Celko describes some that could be implemented through a user-defined function. Another option that he recommends is to calculate the soundex values in a program other than SQL and store them in the database in a separate column. That would be the preferred method.

Conditions in the `select` Comma List

ORACLE vs. SQL

One of the biggest shortcomings of SQL, which the SQL-92 standard has overcome, is the lack of good conditional functionality that can be used at the select comma list level. If, depending which value is contained in one column, either the value of a second column or that of a third column should be inserted, then this could be implemented in Oracle through the decode operator. If the test expressions use ranges, however, and not discrete values, there is no straightforward way left.

One SQL implementation, dbQuery, which is part of the RAIMA data manager, has a ternary if function akin to that used in spreadsheets—if(col_a == 'A',col_b, col c). The case operation in the SQL-92 standard provides for case operations that are even more convenient:

```
case bgross/bhrs
    when > 170 then 'high'
    when > 120 then 'medium'
    else       then 'low'
end
```

This statement sorts the rows into nonoverlapping ranges. The when clauses are tested from the top to the first time the condition evaluates to true. Therefore, while a value of 180 would fulfill all three conditions, it would be evaluated only once at the first condition, when > 170, resulting in an output value of 'high'.

> **NOTE**
>
> For a full explanation of the case statement in SQL-92, see Date and Darwen, pp. 89–90.

The use of the decode operator for similar purposes has been shown in Chapters 4 and 7. Another option is to try numerical conversions that rework one range into another one. This is possible, especially in the case where the original scale is proportional to the newly defined one. Such conversions should be thoroughly tested and documented because they are prone to errors. The use of a range lookup table to join with the base table is an option that works in all implementations.

Summary

This chapter presents the standard options for selecting a subset of rows only—the where clause that qualifies an input row for inclusion or exclusion *before* further processing, and the having clause that does the same with an aggregate value *after* all accessed rows have been processed.

The typical set of comparison operators is provided. The = operator tests for equality; the <>, <, >, <=, and >= operators test for inequality. The in and not in operators allow you to compare an expression to a list of values. Limited wildcard comparison functionality is provided by like and like ... escape.

String comparisons pose challenges in terms of the handling of case sensitivity, trailing blanks, and sound representations.

SQL provides only limited functionality for conditional expressions in the select comma list. This is likely to improve as the SQL-92 standard is implemented by vendors.

CHAPTER 10

Compound Conditions and Logical Operators

IN THIS CHAPTER

Chapter 9, "Conditional Operands," introduced conditions that limit the retrieval of rows—the where condition eliminates rows for further processing and the having condition rejects group rows after completion of the aggregation process. This chapter expands on the condition statements of Chapter 9 in two ways:

- It introduces the logical operators and, or, and not.

- Using these operators, it combines conditional statements to execute in parallel or nested mode.

Logical Operators

Logical operators, also called boolean operators to honor the mathematician who invented them, have been implemented in just about every computer language. Their use in SQL follows standard rules.

REAL-WORLD EXPERIENCES

As is the case with many other features, especially where algorithms are concerned, computer science is deeply indebted to mathematics and logic, which developed its foundation long before the advent of electronic computing machinery. George Boole (1815-1864) established modern symbolic logic and the algebra of logic with his "A mathematical analysis of logic" in 1847 and "An investigation into the laws of thought on which are founded the mathematical theories of logic and probabilities." Augustus De Morgan (1806-1871) formulated and investigated the laws that are named after him, drawing on writings of William Ockham (1285-1347/49), a Franciscan monk and *theologicus logicus*. Only De Morgan had a mainstream education. Boole never attended college; Ockham dropped out from his master's program over some theological dispute and eventually found himself excommunicated. Yet these three men, of vastly different backgrounds, created the foundation for conditional expressions.

The Logical Not Operator: not

The logical not operator (not) is an unary operator, the logical equivalent to the minus operator. It reverses a true evaluation to false, and vice versa. In Chapter 9 not in was used to select rows where a field was not contained in a list. not in, however, is its own conditional operator that has to be written exactly that way. A similar case is not exists (see Chapter 21, "Correlated Subqueries"), which is also a logical operator in its own right.

The not operator, on the other hand, has to be written before a conditional statement and negates its outcome. Thus, if the conditional statement is where x = 2, the opposite condition will be where not x = 2, which evaluates to the same as where x <> 2.

There should be only limited use for the not operator because most not conditions can be rewritten using different operators. Table 10.1 shows not conditions with their unnegated equivalents.

Table 10.1. Equivalents of not conditions.

not *condition*	*Equivalent operator*
not x = y	x <> y
not x <> y	x = y
not x > y	x <= y
not x >= y	x < y
not x < y	x >= y
not x <= y	x > y

The only exceptions to this are situations where negating a simple condition avoids the need to rephrase it as an overly complex one. not can also be combined with the and and or operators, which are demonstrated in this and the following sections.

Listing 10.1 shows the effect of not on the equality and inequality condition, using the sex column in the pers1 table. It consists of two sets of pairs of queries; the second of each is equivalent with the first one but does not use the not operator.

Listing 10.1. Retrieving rows using the not operator.

```
--       Filename: 10squ01.sql
--        Purpose: retrieve rows
--                 where not sex = male
--                 where not sex  <> male
--
ttitle left 'not sex = ''M'' // sex <> ''M'''

select *
from pers1
where not sex = 'M'
;

select *
from pers1
where sex <> 'M'
;
```

This code returns the following twice:

```
not sex = 'M' // sex <> 'M'
```

```
        ID LNAME           FMNAME          SSN            AGE S
--------- --------------- --------------- --------- --------- -
        3 Talavera        F. Espinosa     533932999        19 F
        4 Kratochvil      Mary T.         969825711        48 F
```

and

```
ttitle left 'not sex <> ''M'' // sex = ''M'''

select *
from pers1
where not sex <> 'M'
;

select *
from pers1
where sex = 'M'
;

ttitle off
```

This code also returns the following twice:

```
not sex <> 'M' // sex = 'M'

        ID LNAME           FMNAME          SSN            AGE S
--------- --------------- --------------- --------- --------- -
        1 Jones           David N.        895663453        34 M
        2 Martinelli      A. Emery        312331818        92 M
        5 Melsheli        Joseph K.       000342222        14 M
```

Listing 10.2 consists of four sets of pairs of queries; the second of each is equivalent with the first one but uses the not operator.

Listing 10.2. Retrieving rows using the not operator.

```
--        Filename: 10squ02.sql
--        Purpose: retrieve rows
--                where age > 48
--                    not age <= 48
--                where age < 48
--                    not age >= 48
--                where age >= 48
--                    not age < 48
--                where age <= 48
--                    not age > 48
--
ttitle left 'where age > 48 // not age <= 48'

select *
from pers1
where age > 48
;

select *
from pers1
where not age <= 48
;
```

```
ttitle left 'where age < 48 // not age >= 48'

select *
from pers1
where age < 48
;

select *
from pers1
where not age >= 48
;

ttitle left 'where age >= 48 // not age < 48'

select *
from pers1
where age >= 48
;

select *
from pers1
where not age < 48
;
ttitle left 'where age <= 48 // not age > 48'

select *
from pers1
where age <= 48
;

select *
from pers1
where not age > 48
;

ttitle off
```

This code returns each of the following sets twice:

```
where age > 48 // not age <= 48

      ID LNAME            FMNAME           SSN              AGE S
--------- ---------------- ---------------- ---------- ---------- -
       2 Martinelli       A. Emery         312331818          92 M

where age < 48 // not age >= 48

      ID LNAME            FMNAME           SSN              AGE S
--------- ---------------- ---------------- ---------- ---------- -
       1 Jones            David N.         895663453          34 M
       3 Talavera         F. Espinosa      533932999          19 F
       5 Melsheli         Joseph K.        000342222          14 M

where age >= 48 // not age < 48
```

```
      ID LNAME            FMNAME           SSN            AGE S
--------- ---------------- ---------------- ---------- ---------- -
       2 Martinelli       A. Emery         312331818          92 M
       4 Kratochvil       Mary T.          969825711          48 F
```

where age <= 48 // not age > 48

```
      ID LNAME            FMNAME           SSN            AGE S
--------- ---------------- ---------------- ---------- ---------- -
       1 Jones            David N.         895663453          34 M
       3 Talavera         F. Espinosa      533932999          19 F
       4 Kratochvil       Mary T.          969825711          48 F
       5 Melsheli         Joseph K.        000342222          14 M
```

The Logical And Operator: and

The binary logical and operator (and) is used to compound two conditional statements into one. Only if both statements are true will the compound statement be true. In all other cases, where either one or both statements are false, the compound and statement will be false as well. Figure 10.1 summarizes the outcome of compound and conditions.

Figure 10.1.
The return value of compound and conditions.

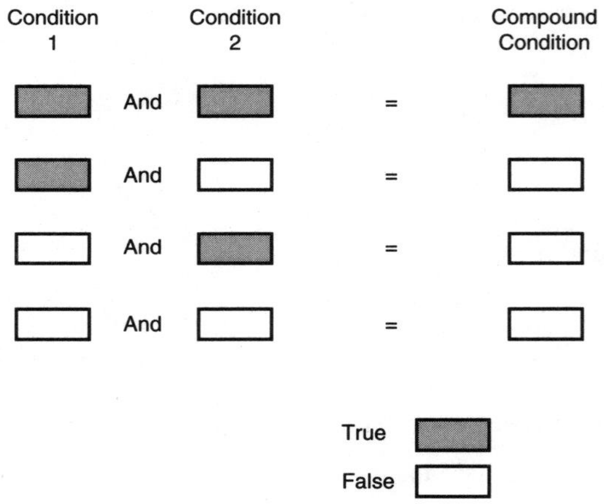

Listing 10.3 selects all lawyers from the lawyer1 table, who work in the Boston office and who generate at least 2,800 billable hours.

Listing 10.3. Retrieving rows using and.

```
--        Filename: 10squ03.sql
--        Purpose: select Boston lawyers who generate more than
--                 2800 billable hours
--                 (and more than $350,000 revenue)
--
select
   id,
   name,
   office,
   bhrs,
```

```
    bgross
from lawyer1
where bhrs > 2800 and
      office = 'Boston'
;
```

This code returns

ID	NAME	OFFICE	BHRS	BGROSS
1	Dewey	Boston	2856	426800
10	Greene	Boston	2854	289435

It is also possible to combine more than two conditions with and. In this case, *all* conditions must be true in order for the compound statement to return true as well. In all other cases, the compound statement returns false. The return values of compound three element and statements are summarized in Figure 10.2.

FIGURE 10.2.
Return value of compound and condition with three elements.

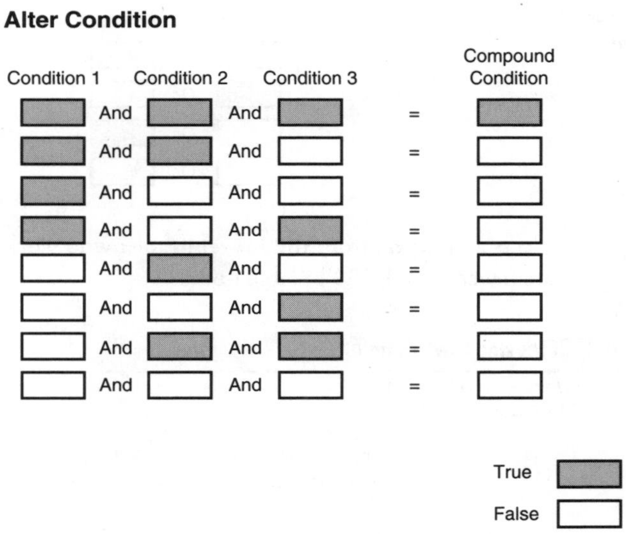

Alter Condition

The following example combines three conditions:

```
select
   id,
   name,
   office,
   bhrs,
   bgross
from lawyer1
where bhrs > 2800       and
      office = 'Boston' and
      bgross > 350000
;
```

It selects all Boston lawyers with more than 2,800 billable hours and more than $350,000 gross receipts. One record is returned:

```
ID NAME              OFFICE              BHRS     BGROSS
--------- --------------- -------------------- --------- ---------
 1 Dewey             Boston              2856     426800
```

Only Dewey fulfills all conditions because he works in the Boston office, bills more than 2,800 hours, and has more than $350,000 in gross receipts.

The Logical Or Operator: or

Just like and, the binary or operator is also used to compound two conditional statements into one. The compound statement will only be true if at least one statement is true. Only if both statements are false will the compound or statement return false as well (see Figure 10.3).

FIGURE 10.3.

The return value of compound or conditions.

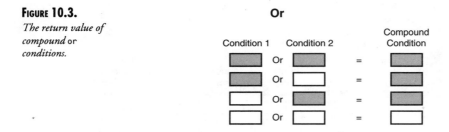

Listing 10.4 selects all lawyers from the lawyer1 table, who work either in the Houston office or who generate fewer than 1,400 billable hours.

Listing 10.4. Retrieving rows using or.

```
--          Filename: 10squ04.sql
--           Purpose: select lawyers
--                    who work either in the Houston office or
--                    who generate fewer than 1400 billable hours (or
--                        who generate less than $220,000 revenue)
--
select
   id,
   name,
   office,
   bhrs,
   bgross
from lawyer1
where bhrs < 1400 or
      office = 'Houston'
;
```

This code returns

```
ID NAME              OFFICE            BHRS    BGROSS
--------- ----------------  ----------------  --------  --------
 2 Cheetham          New York           1398    280435
 4 Clayton           Houston            1789    190045
 5 Roach             Houston            2349    269844
```

As was the case with and, more than two conditions may be combined with or. This results in a compound three (four ...) element or statement. In this case *at least one* condition must be true in order for the compound statement to return true as well. Only if all conditions are false will the compound condition be false as well. Figure 10.4 shows the return values of compound three element or statements.

FIGURE 10.4.

The return value of compound or *condition with three elements.*

Alternative

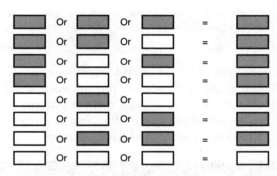

The following example adds one more condition, gross receipts of less than $220,000, to the statement:

```
select
   id,
   name,
   office,
   bhrs,
   bgross
from lawyer1
where bhrs < 1400       or
      office = 'Houston' or
      bgross < 220000
;
```

This code returns one more lawyer, Wright, who works neither in Houston, nor less than 1,400 hours, but grosses $204,133, less than the criterion of $220,000. The following are the results from the preceding code:

10

LOGICAL OPERATORS

```
  ID NAME            OFFICE            BHRS    BGROSS
-------- --------------- --------------- --------- ---------
   2 Cheetham        New York          1398    280435
   4 Clayton         Houston           1789    190045
   5 Roach           Houston           2349    269844
  15 Wright          Boston            2789    204133
```

Nesting Logical Statements

The first part of this chapter has dealt with the case where only two conditions were compounded, or where only one compound operator was used when compounding more than two conditions. Frequently, however, it is necessary to formulate more complex compound conditions. The following are a few examples:

- When a question that a query should answer may be fairly complex
- When a complex join is used (see Chapter 17, "Joins"), which requires equally complex where clauses
- When there is a combination of both, which occurs quite frequently.

SQL provides great leeway for the nesting of conditions through use of a combination of and, or, and not. Similar to calculations where multiplication and division have precedence over addition and multiplication, meaning that they are performed first, not has precedence over and, which in turn has precedence over or. If necessary, parentheses can be used to override or simply clarify the precedence order in which the conditions are evaluated.

DEBUG ALERT

Clarify the order of precedence with parentheses, even if these may be redundant. If you format the statement cleanly, it will be immediately clear what was intended. This saves a lot of time during debugging.

One typical nested construct is a compound or condition nested in an and condition. Figure 10.5 shows the outcome of such a statement. If Condition 1 is false, the total condition is false, too. If Condition 1 is true, the outcome of the total condition is equal to that of the compound one.

Listing 10.5 uses such a construct. It selects those lawyers from lawyer1 who have an even id value (such as 2, 4, 6, and so on) and who either work fewer than 1,700 hours or gross less than $300,000.

FIGURE 10.5.

The return value of a compound or condition nested in an and condition.

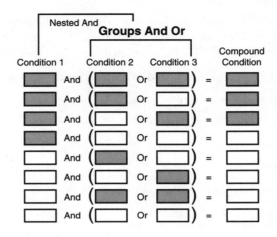

Listing 10.5. Retrieving rows using nested conditions.

```
--        Filename: 10squ05.sql
--         Purpose: Nested conditions
--                  select lawyers with even ID numbers
--                  who work fewer than 1700 hours or bill less revenue
--                  than $300,000
--
select
   id,
   name,
   office,
   bhrs,
   bgross
from lawyer1
where mod(id,2) = 0       and
      (bhrs < 1700 or bgross < 300000)
order by
   bhrs,
   bgross
;
```

The preceding code returns six rows:

```
    ID NAME               OFFICE           BHRS    BGROSS
--------- ------------------ ---------------- --------- ---------
     2 Cheetham           New York          1398    280435
     8 Bonin              New York          1678    346892
    16 Chabot             New York          1680    310897
     4 Clayton            Houston           1789    190045
    20 Paul               Boston            2198    239855
    10 Greene             Boston            2854    289435

6 rows selected.
```

10

LOGICAL OPERATORS

Cheetham qualifies under both criteria. Bonin and Chabot make more than $300,000 but qualify because they work less than 1,700 hours. On the other hand, Clayton, Paul, and Greene, who all work more than 1,700 hours, qualify because they make less than $300,000.

Omitting the parentheses will lead to a wrong result, as shown in the following:

```
break on even_odd skip 1

select
   id,
   name,
   office,
   bhrs,
   bgross,
   mod(id,2) even_odd
from lawyer1
where mod(id,2) = 0        and
      bhrs < 1700 or bgross < 300000
order by
   mod(id,2),
   bhrs,
   bgross
;

clear breaks
```

This returns nine rows:

ID	NAME	OFFICE	BHRS	BGROSS	EVEN_ODD
2	Cheetham	New York	1398	280435	0
8	Bonin	New York	1678	346892	
16	Chabot	New York	1680	310897	
4	Clayton	Houston	1789	190045	
20	Paul	Boston	2198	239855	
10	Greene	Boston	2854	289435	
5	Roach	Houston	2349	269844	1
11	Cardinal	Boston	2694	277952	
15	Wright	Boston	2789	204133	

Figure 10.6 shows the effect of omitting the parentheses: It has changed the logic of the compound statement. Two more cases will return a true now, where the Condition 1 is false (odd id value) but Condition 3 is true (less than $300,000 gross receipts). The last three rows fall into that category. To qualify now, a lawyer has to either have an even id value and work less than 1,700 hours, or have to gross less than $300,000 regardless of the value of the ID.

The last example in this section uses a nested compound condition to select those lawyers who work significantly more hours than the average in their offices. First a query is written that determines the reference values for the offices by adding average and standard deviation of hours. Then the values returned by this query (see Listing 10.6) are inserted into a compound condition.

FIGURE 10.6.

The return value of a compound and condition nested in an or condition.

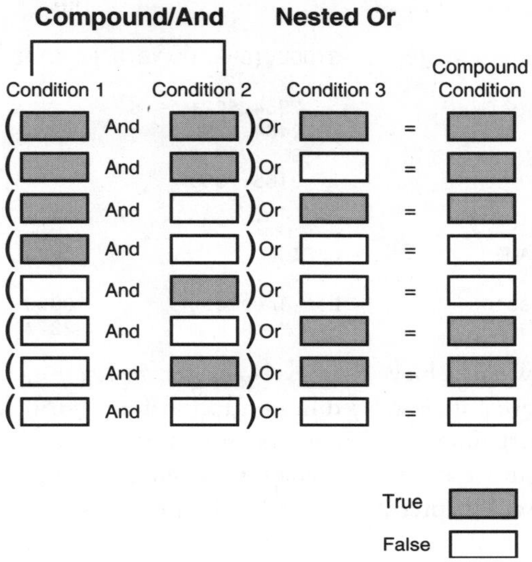

Listing 10.6. Retrieving rows using nested conditions.

```
--          Filename: 10squ06.sql
--           Purpose: Nested conditions
--                    select lawyers
--                    who work significantly more hours than
--                    office averages
--
select
   office,
   avg(bhrs) + stddev(bhrs),
   avg(bgross) + stddev(bgross)
from lawyer1
group by office
;

select
   id,
   name,
   office,
   bhrs,
   bgross
from lawyer1
where (office = 'Boston'      and bhrs > 2954.6221 ) or
      (office = 'Houston'     and bhrs > 2464.9798) or
      (office = 'Los Angeles' and bhrs > 3562.2257) or
      (office = 'New York'    and bhrs > 2165.7359)
order by
   office,
   bhrs
;
```

10

LOGICAL
OPERATORS

This code returns

```
OFFICE          AVG(BHRS)+STDDEV(BHRS)  AVG(BGROSS)+STDDEV(BGROSS)
--------------  ----------------------  --------------------------
Boston                      2954.6221                    372369.01
Houston                     2464.9798                    286370.91
Los Angeles                 3562.2257                    589669.96
New York                    2165.7359                    440866.16


       ID NAME            OFFICE              BHRS       BGROSS
--------- --------------- --------------- --------- ----------
        7 Easton          Los Angeles          3800     654832
       14 Earl            New York             2320     434801
```

Only two lawyers achieve that level—Easton in Los Angeles, because he or she works really hard to achieve a stress-related heart attack before age 50, and Earl in New York. That office has a lot of part-timers, which lowers the comparison criterion. Views (see Chapter 18, "Combining Output from Similar Tables Through Set and Pseudoset Operators") and correlated subqueries (see Chapter 21, "Correlated Subqueries") offer better, one-shot solutions to this question.

The Exclusive or Compound Statement

SQL does not provide an exclusive or operator, such as the bitwise exclusive or operator ^ in C. Exclusive or returns true if only one of the conditions is true, and false if both are true or both are false. Figure 10.7 illustrates the effect of such an operator.

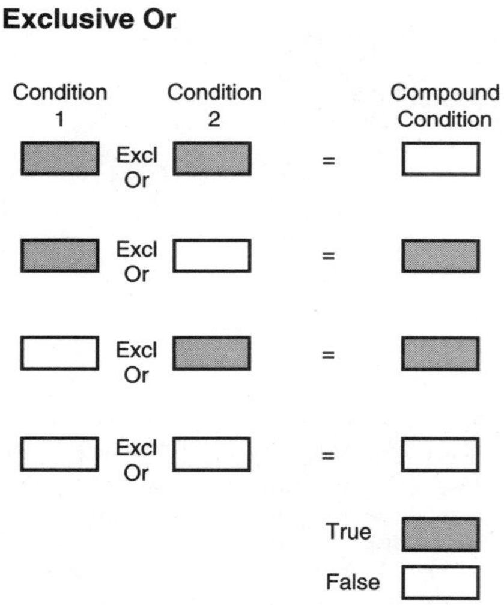

FIGURE 10.7.

The return value of compound exclusive or conditions.

Exclusive Or

Listing 10.7 includes only those lawyers who either work in Houston or work less than 1,400 hours, but not both.

Listing 10.7. Using the exclusive or compound statement.

```
--        Filename: 10squ07.sql
--        Purpose: exclusive or: select lawyers
--                 who work either in the Houston office or
--                 who generate fewer than 1400 billable hours
--                 but not both
--
select
   id,
   name,
   office,
   bhrs,
   bgross
from lawyer1
where (bhrs < 1400   and office <> 'Houston') or
      (bhrs <= 1400  and office = 'Houston')
;
```

This code returns

```
    ID NAME              OFFICE             BHRS   BGROSS
--------- ---------------- ---------------- --------- ---------
     2 Cheetham          New York           1398   280435
```

Because of the precedence of and over or, the where statement returns the same if the parentheses are omitted, which is shown in the last part of this example:

```
where bhrs < 1400   and office <> 'Houston' or
      bhrs <= 1400  and office = 'Houston'
```

Negated Compound Conditional Statements (De Morgan's Laws): not or and not and

Compound conditional statements can be negated by preceding them with a not operator. According to the mathematical laws of De Morgan, the outcomes of such operations are as follows:

- Not (A and B) is the same as Not A or Not B.
- Not (A or B) is the same as Not A and Not B.

CAUTION

Negated compound statements are a good way to get confused and to confuse others who have to work with your code. Resolve them to straightforward compound statements, unless absolutely necessary.

The following example negates the query in `10squ03.sql`, which selected all Boston lawyers with more than 2,800 billable hours and returned two rows:

```
  ID NAME                OFFICE             BHRS    BGROSS
--------- ------------------- ------------------ --------- --------
   1 Dewey               Boston             2856    426800
  10 Greene              Boston             2854    289435
```

The negation of the compound condition, as coded in the following example, must then return the other 18 rows. This is demonstrated in Listing 10.8.

Listing 10.8. Using negated conditional statements.

```
--        Filename: 10squ08.sql
--         Purpose: select lawyers who are not
--                  Boston lawyers generating
--                  more than 2800 billable hours
--
select
   id,
   name,
   office,
   bhrs,
   bgross
from lawyer1
where not (bhrs > 2800 and
           office = 'Boston')
;
```

It returns these 18 rows:

```
  ID NAME                OFFICE             BHRS    BGROSS
--------- ------------------- ------------------ --------- --------
   2 Cheetham            New York           1398    280435
   3 Howe                Los Angeles        3480    569338
   4 Clayton             Houston            1789    190045
   5 Roach               Houston            2349    269844
   6 Roll                Los Angeles        3203    498084
   7 Easton              Los Angeles        3800    654832
   8 Bonin               New York           1678    346892
   9 Frankie             New York           2134    469843
  11 Cardinal            Boston             2694    277952
  12 Chandler            Los Angeles        2987    423878
  13 Martinez            Los Angeles        2659    403488
  14 Earl                New York           2320    434801
  15 Wright              Boston             2789    204133
  16 Chabot              New York           1680    310897
  17 Miller              Los Angeles        3153    503582
  18 Ming                Los Angeles        2492    359021
  19 Chatham             New York           1759    367944
  20 Paul                Boston             2198    239855

18 rows selected.
```

The equivalent statement, according to De Morgan, returns the same 18 rows. This is shown in the following part of the example:

```
select
    id,
    name,
    office,
    bhrs,
    bgross
from lawyer1
where not bhrs > 2800 or
      not office = 'Boston'
;
```

The final part of the example returns the same 18 rows as well. It selects all lawyers who work less than or equal to 2,800 hours or who do not work in Boston:

```
select
    id,
    name,
    office,
    bhrs,
    bgross
from lawyer1
where bhrs <= 2800 or
      office <> 'Boston'
;
```

That final version is, obviously, the preferable one.

Summary

Compound where and having conditions can be created by combining simple conditions using the logical operators and, or, and not. The not operator is the logical equivalent of the unary minus operator. It reverses a true evaluation to false, and vice versa. In most cases, it is preferable and it is just as easy to rewrite the condition to avoid not.

The binary and operator is used to compound two conditional statements into one. Only if both statements are true will the compound statement be true. If more than two conditions are combined with multiple and operators, *all* conditions must be true in order for the compound statement to return true as well.

The binary or operator compounds two conditional statements into one as well, but the compound statement will be true if at least one statement is true. If more than two conditions are combined with or, *at least one* condition must be true in order for the compound statement to return true as well.

Through the use of a combination of and, or, and not operators, logical statements can be nested or executed in parallel. not has precedence over and, which in turn has precedence over or. Parentheses can override or clarify the precedence order.

10

LOGICAL
OPERATORS

A few cases of nested queries are of special interest:

■ SQL does not provide an exclusive or operator; this operation has to be expressed as a nested and condition that contains two compound or conditions.

■ Negated compound conditional statements, such as not or and not and, can be resolved using De Morgan's laws.

Datatypes and Null Values

Numerical Data: The number Datatype

11

CHAPTER

Earlier chapters in this book deal with numerical data without considering how SQL defines and treats them. All the examples in those chapters include integer data, and in some examples, decimal numbers have resulted from some conversions. Chapter 7, "Character Number/ Conversions," gave you the biggest clue of things to come when you learned how the to_char function converts numerical data to cleanly formatted character strings.

This chapter initiates the postponed discussion on numerical datatypes.

The SQL standard supports five numerical datatypes, which are summarized in Table 11.1.

Table 11.1. SQL standard numerical datatypes.

Datatype	*Description*
Integer	Signed integer that might be decimal or binary; no size specified
Smallint	An integer that must be the same size or smaller than Integer
Numeric(*precision, scale*)	Fixed-point decimal number of *exactly* the specified precision and scale
Decimal(*precision, scale*)	Fixed-point decimal number of *at least* the specified precision and scale
Float(*precision*)	Floating-point number with a specified precision

ORACLE vs SQL

Oracle uses the number datatype to specify all numerical data, integers, fixed points, and floating points alike. It also allows you to specify floating-point numbers using the float datatype.

Please consult the reference manual if you use a different dialect of SQL. The difference matters if you port an application from one dialect to another, but scripts that access tables and columns should not be affected by such differences once the tables are defined, and table names and column names stay the same.

This chapter covers the datatypes as Oracle defines them and lists which ANSI SQL datatype would be applicable to a specific case.

Integers: number(*precision*)

Oracle treats integers as a special case of a fixed-point number where the scale argument is 0. In good object-oriented overloading tradition, the second argument can be omitted, and the integer datatype number(*precision*) is born.

Numerical Data: The number *Datatype*

CHAPTER 11

213

11

NUMBERICAL
DATA: THE
NUMBER DATATYPE

 Run the script `crint.sql`, included on the CD accompanying this book, to create the `int1` table, which contains a set of integer columns.

A column defined with number(*precision*) can hold a signed (positive or negative) integer with as many digits as are specified by *precision*. Although table creation is covered in Chapter 28, "Creating Tables," let's digress here a bit to examine the following `crint.sql` script for creating table `int11`. It can show how Oracle deals with ANSI datatypes:

```
create table int1 (
    int1        number(1),
    int2        number(2),
    int3        number(3),
    int4        number(4),
    int38       number(38),
    ansiint     int,
    ansiinteger integer,
    ansismint   smallint)
;
```

The first four columns define signed integers of lengths from 1–4; the last four columns define signed integers of length 38. The script specifies these in four different ways: first in Oracle format, and then using the ANSI SQL keywords `int`, `integer`, and `smallint`. The first part of Listing 11.1 shows the resulting data definition.

Listing 11.1. Describing a table.

```
--      Filename: 11squ01.sql
--       Purpose: describe int1 table
--                select int1 - int4
--                select int38 ... smallint
--
desc int1
```

This returns

Name	Null?	Type
INT1		NUMBER(1)
INT2		NUMBER(2)
INT3		NUMBER(3)
INT4		NUMBER(4)
INT38		NUMBER(38)
ANSIINT		NUMBER(38)
ANSIINTEGER		NUMBER(38)
ANSISMINT		NUMBER(38)

It doesn't matter to Oracle how you call them; `int`, `integer`, and `smallint` will always be defined as number(38).

> **CAUTION**
>
> Although the Oracle Server might be forgiving, Oracle's client tools, such as Forms, are not. Forms allows an int datatype. Designer/2000, Oracle's CASE product, allows the specification of many different datatypes, but when it comes to the generation of forms, an error will result from some of these. Therefore, to avoid unpleasant surprises later on, it is best to stick with the native datatypes of the SQL implementation used—even in client tools that interact with the implementation.

Retrieval of integers is straightforward as long as the integers aren't too long. The following example, which retrieves the data in the first four columns,

```
select
    int1,
    int2,
    int3,
    int4
from int1;
```

returns this:

```
    INT1        INT2        INT3        INT4
--------- --------- --------- ---------
       1          12         123        1234
       9          99         999        9999
      -1         -12        -123       -1234
      -9         -99        -999       -9999
```

No surprise here: The columns can hold and display what they are supposed to. A long integer, however, like the following

```
select
    int38
from int1;
```

is displayed in scientific notation:

```
INT38
---------
1.235E+37
1.000E+38
-1.23E+37
-1.00E+38
```

A specification of a format mask, identical to that used in the second argument of the to_char function, allows you to display all 38 digits. Note how the second and fourth numbers have been rounded up in the previous output section:

```
col generic format 999,999,999,999,999,999,999,999,999,999,999,999

select
    int38 generic
from int1;
```

```
GENERIC
-----------------------------------------------------
  12,345,678,901,234,567,890,123,456,789,012,345,678
  99,999,999,999,999,999,999,999,999,999,999,999,999
 -12,345,678,901,234,567,890,123,456,789,012,345,678
 -99,999,999,999,999,999,999,999,999,999,999,999,999
```

select statements of the last three columns return the same:

```
select
   ansiint generic
from int1;

select
   ansiinteger generic
from int1;

select
   ansismint generic
from int1;

clear columns
```

If an update or insert statement (see Chapter 24, "Manipulating Single-Table Data") attempts to load an integer with more digits than defined, an error will result (which is illustrated in Listing 11.2).

Listing 11.2. Inserting integers that are larger than defined.

```
--       Filename: 11squ02.sql
--          Purpose: inserting integers that are larger than defined
--
insert into int1 (int4)
values (12345);
```

This returns the following output:

```
values (12345)
      *
ERROR at line 2:
ORA-01438: value larger than specified precision allows for this column
```

Representing Boolean Data

SQL has no dedicated boolean datatype. Such a datatype would have only two values, representing true and false. However, it is possible to use a single-digit integer for boolean values. The integer proper would allow you to store the values -9 to +9. Using a check constraint (see Chapter 29, "Keys, Indexes, Constraints, and Table/Column Comments"), that range can then be limited to 1, representing true, and 2, representing false. The added advantage of using 1 for true and 0 for false is that you can use mathematical formulas that provide the equivalent of column-level conditional statements. Listing 11.3 shows the steps necessary to implement this approach.

Listing 11.3. Using integer notation to represent boolean data.

```
--          Filename: 11squ03.sql
--          Purpose: Boolean data representation using integer notation
--
create table boole1 (
    boolecol        number(1)
        constraint chk_boole1
            check (boolecol in (1, 0)))
;

alter table boole1
  enable constraint chk_boole1
;

insert into boole1 values (1);

insert into boole1 values (0);

commit;
```

These statements return the following output:

```
Table created.

Table altered.

1 row created.

1 row created.

Commit complete.
```

Using a `decode`, the values can be translated into `true` and `false`:

```
select
    decode (boolecol,1,'TRUE',
                    0,'FALSE')
from boole1;
```

This statement returns the following:

```
DECOD
----
TRUE
FALSE
```

If, however, values other than 0 or 1 are inserted, an error will result. For example, the following code

```
insert into boole1 values (7);

insert into boole1 values (-9);
```

returns this:

```
insert into boole1 values (7)
            *
```

Numerical Data: The number *Datatype*

CHAPTER 11

217

11

NUMERICAL
DATA: THE
NUMBER DATATYPE

```
ERROR at line 1:
ORA-02290: check constraint (HANS.CHK_BOOLE1) violated

insert into boole1 values (-9)
                *
ERROR at line 1:
ORA-02290: check constraint (HANS.CHK_BOOLE1) violated
```

NOTE

The efforts of vendors to include object-oriented notions into relational databases should be of interest here. Because it will be possible to create user-defined datatypes, it should be possible to create a generic datatype, boolean, which can then be used for subsequent definitions.

Decimal Numbers

Decimal numbers use the mantissa-exponent representation well known from the time when Hewlett-Packard put out its first engineering pocket calculator. The mantissa is the precision of the number in question. The exponent is used in two different ways:

■ The definition of the data, as used in the create table statement and the desc SQL*Plus command, denotes the maximum number of digits to the right of the decimal point. In this representation the exponent is the second argument of the number definition.

■ In the display and entry of data, the exponent indicates to which power the number 10 has to be raised so that multiplication of the mantissa with that number will result in the correct number. In this case the exponent follows the letter e or E.

Decimal numbers can be expressed in fixed-point notation, meaning that the scale always remains the same, or in floating-point notation, where the precision can be up to 38 characters and the scale can change as needed to hold a particular number.

Fixed-Point Numbers: number(*precision, scale*)

A fixed-point number is specified in such a way that the scale always remains the same within the column that is thus defined. As in the case of integers, the precision specifies the number of integers that will be recorded. The scale specifies the number of digits to the right of the decimal point. Normally, the scale is positive and smaller than the precision. Two special cases exist, however, when the scale is negative or larger than the precision. Both cases will be discussed later in this section.

The following example shows the normal case when the scale is positive and smaller than the precision. A fixed-point table, fix1, which is similar to the int1 table, will hold several fixed-point columns up to the maximum size.

Run the script `crfix1.sql`, included on the CD accompanying this book, to create the `fix1` table, which contains a set of fixed-point columns and loads a few records.

Oracle allows the ANSI definitions `decimal` and `numeric` and treats them just as another `number` column for comparison with the table creation script and the table description show. The `crfix1.sql` script can serve as an example:

```
create table fix1 (
    fix1        number(2,1),
    fix2        number(4,2),
    fix3        number(6,3),
    fix4        number(8,4),
    fix38       number(38,19),
    ansidecimal decimal(8,3),
    ansinumeric numeric(8,3))
;
```

The first four columns define signed fixed-point decimals of lengths from 2–8, with half of the length reserved for the decimal portions. The next column defines a signed fixed-point integer of length 38 with 19 decimals. The last two columns define signed fixed-point numbers of length 8 with 3 decimal positions using the ANSI keywords `decimal` and `numeric`. The first part of Listing 11.4 shows the resulting data definition.

Listing 11.4. Describing a table.

```
--          Filename: 11squ04.sql
--           Purpose: describe fix1 table
--                    select from fix1
--
desc fix1
```

This listing returns

```
Name                            Null?    Type
------------------------------- -------- ------------
FIX1                                     NUMBER(2,1)
FIX2                                     NUMBER(4,2)
FIX3                                     NUMBER(6,3)
FIX4                                     NUMBER(8,4)
FIX38                                    NUMBER(38,19)
ANSIDECIMAL                              NUMBER(8,3)
ANSINUMERIC                              NUMBER(8,3)
```

Oracle treats `numeric` and `decimal` in a similar fashion as `int`, `integer`, and `smallint`: They are converted to the corresponding `number` definitions and never heard of again. The caution to not rely on the server to do such conversions applies here as well.

Retrieval of short fixed-point numbers is straightforward. The following example retrieves the data in the first four columns:

```
select
    fix1,
    fix2,
```

```
    fix3,
    fix4
from fix1;
```

It returns this output:

```
    FIX1       FIX2        FIX3       FIX4
--------- --------- --------- ---------
      1.2      12.34    123.456 1234.5678
      9.9      99.99    999.999 9999.9999
     -1.2     -12.34   -123.456 -1234.568
     -9.9     -99.99   -999.999    -10000
```

Although the columns can hold and display what they are supposed to, the last value, -9999.9999, cannot be fully displayed in the standard column output but is rounded to -10000. A format mask would take care of this issue. As was the case with large integers, longer values like this

```
select
    fix38
from fix1
;
```

are displayed in scientific notation with a very limited precision, as shown here:

```
FIX38
----------
1.235E+18
1.000E+19
-1.23E+18
-1.00E+19
```

A specification of a format mask allows the display of all 38 digits properly:

```
col generic format 99,999,999,999,999,999,999.9999999999999999999
```

```
select
    fix38 generic
from fix1;
```

```
GENERIC
-----------------------------------------------
  1,234,567,890,123,456,789.0123456789012345678
  9,999,999,999,999,999,999.9999999999999999999
 -1,234,567,890,123,456,789.0123456789012345678
 -9,999,999,999,999,999,999.9999999999999999999
```

select statements of the last two columns return the same values. The formatting of -99999.999 is afflicted by the same problem as the formatting of fix4; a rounded number is displayed for space reasons, as in the following example:

```
select
    ansinumeric,
    ansidecimal
from fix1;
```

```
clear columns
```

It returns

```
ANSINUMERIC ANSIDECIMAL
----------- -----------
  12345.678   12345.678
  99999.999   99999.999
  -12345.68   -12345.68
    -100000     -100000
```

There are two cases in which a number being inserted does not quite fit the definition of the column:

■ The precision of the number is larger than that of the column. In this case, the number will be rounded to fit the column's precision, and the number will load.

■ The number is too large to fit the column. If a number has a higher value than what will fit into the definition, an error will result and the number will not load.

Listing 11.5 demonstrates how larger numbers are handled, either in terms of precision or in terms of scale. The first number inserted has a larger precision—meaning that there are extra decimals. After the display of the number using `is null` on a different column to display only the row of interest (see Chapter 15, "Missing Data, Null, and Zero Values"), the new value table is returned to its original state through a rollback (see Chapter 25, "Control Transactions").

Listing 11.5. Inserting numbers with higher precision or scale.

```
--        Filename: 11squ05.sql
--         Purpose: insert numbers with higher precision or scale
--                  into fixed length integer
--
insert into fix1(fix4)
values (6648.9696421)
;

select
   fix4
from fix1
where fix1 is null
;

rollback;
```

This listing returns

```
1 row created.
```

```
FIX4
---------
6648.9696
```

```
Rollback complete.
```

In this case, the digits 421 that do not fit into the definition are simply trimmed, and the remaining digits are loaded into their respective spots.

The second number inserted has the same precision as the column (eight digits), but a smaller scale:

```
insert into fix1(fix4)
values (6.6489697)
;

select
   fix4
from fix1
where fix1 is null
;

rollback;
```

This code returns

```
1 row created.


FIX4
----------
     6.649

Rollback complete.
```

The precision does not matter in this case. Because of the scale, which is less by two, the number only starts at the third digit of the definition. The digits 697, which do not fit into the definition, which are simply trimmed. Because 697 is greater than 499, the next digit is rounded up. Because this digit happens to be 9, the next digit is rounded as well, and 6.6490 ends up being loaded. Because the last digit is 0, the number is displayed as if it had only a precision of four digits.

The third number inserted has the same precision but a larger scale—five digits to the left of the decimal, rather than the four in the definition:

```
insert into fix1(fix4)
values (66489.696)
;

select
   fix4
from fix1
where fix1 is null
;

rollback;
```

This code returns

```
values (66489.696)
        *
ERROR at line 2:
ORA-01438: value larger than specified precision allows for this column
```

```
no rows selected

Rollback complete.
```

Because the five digits to the left of the period do not fit into the space of four, an error results. The error message is a bit peculiar: It is not the precision that is off but the scale. Because the error number is the same as the one that occurred in 11squ02.sql, where too great of an integer was attempted to be loaded, one error seems to catch a number of problems.

Fixed-Point Numbers with Very Large or Negative Scales

The typical case of a fixed-point number specifies a scale that is smaller than the precision and positive, such as 8 and 3. It is also possible to specify a negative scale or a very large scale.

 Run the script crfix2.sql, included on the CD accompanying this book, to create the fix2 table, which contains a set of fixed-point columns and loads a few records.

Listing 11.6 describes the table and displays data once you use the default and a format mask.

Listing 11.6. Working with very small or very large fixed point numbers.

```
--      Filename: 11squ06.sql
--      Purpose: work with very small or very large scale
--               fixed point numbers
--
desc fix2
```

This returns

```
Name                            Null?    Type
------------------------------- -------- ----
FIXTELLER                                NUMBER(3,-1)
FIXSMALL                                 NUMBER(4,50)
FIXBIG                                   NUMBER(6,-50)
FIX38SMALL                               NUMBER(38,19)
FIX38BIG                                 NUMBER(38,-84)
```

The first column is defined with a scale of -1. Upon insertion into that column, values are rounded to the nearest 10 if necessary. FIXSMALL takes very small numbers—consisting of a period, 46 zeroes, and up to four digits. FIXBIG takes a very large number—six digits followed by 50 zeroes. The last two numbers use the full precision possible, the latter of which is very big—38 digits followed by 84 zeroes.

REAL-WORLD EXPERIENCES

The teller machines I use dispense $20 bills only. Nevertheless, they require me to enter the desired amount down to the cent (consisting of zeroes, of course). This, of course, makes no sense whatsoever. In commemoration of this folly, the first column, which accepts multiples of 10 only, is named fixteller. This column would improve on the teller machine by also being able to dispense $10 bills.

Unformatted retrieval uses mostly scientific notation to express values, as follows:

```
desc fix2

select
  *
from fix2
;
```

This code returns the following:

```
FIXTELLER  FIXSMALL    FIXBIG FIX38SMALL   FIX38BIG
---------  --------- --------- ---------- ---------
     1230 1.234E-47 1.235E+55  1.235E+18 1.23E+121
    -1230 -1.23E-47 -1.23E+55  -1.23E+18 -1.2E+121
```

Formatting improves the display of data, as in the following example:

```
col FIXSMALL    format .00000000000000000000000000000000000000099999999
col FIXBIG      format 99999999999999999999999999999999999999999999999999
col FIX38SMALL  format 9999999999999999999.9999999999999999999
col FIX38BIG    format 9.9999999999999999999999999999999999999EEEE

select
  fixsmall
from fix2
;
select
  fixbig
from fix2
;
select
  fix38small
from fix2
;
select
  fix38big
from fix2
;

clear columns
```

This returns

```
FIXSMALL
---------------------------------------------------
 .000000000000000000000000000000000000000000001234
-.000000000000000000000000000000000000000000001234
```

```
                                            FIXBIG
---------------------------------------------------
 123456000000000000000000000000000000000000000000000
-123456000000000000000000000000000000000000000000000
```

```
                              FIX38SMALL
-----------------------------------------------
  1234567890123456789.0123456789012345678
 -1234567890123456789.0123456789012345678


                                   FIX38BIG
-----------------------------------------------
  1.2345678901234567890123456789012345678E+121
 -1.2345678901234567890123456789012345678E+121
```

As with floating-point numbers, it is not possible to display more than 99 digits of a number. Hence FIX38BIG can only be displayed in scientific format, but at least it shows the full precision.

The rest of the example shows how underflow and overflow values are handled. Similar to the situation with floating-point numbers, which are demonstrated at the end of this chapter, underflow values keep getting trimmed and rounded until they are zero. Inserting overflow values returns an error, as in the following example:

```
insert into fix2 (fixteller) values (4.5);

select
    fixteller
from fix2
where fixsmall is null
;

rollback;

insert into fix2 (fixteller) values (44000)
;
```

These statements return the following output:

```
FIXTELLER
---------
        0

rollback;

Rollback complete.

insert into fix2 (fixteller) values (44000)
                                     *
ERROR at line 1:
ORA-01438: value larger than specified precision allows for this column
```

Floating-Point Numbers: number

Floating-point numbers provide the most flexible storage, by storing numbers with a precision of 38 digits, ranging from ±.99999999999999999999999999999999999999 E-126 to ±.99999999999999999999999999999999999999 E126. In plain English, this means that these numbers translate to a period, 88 zeroes, and 38 nines on the low end, and 38 nines followed by 88 zeroes on the high end. This should be sufficient for most numbers occurring in databases anywhere.

There are three ways to define floating-point numbers. The standard way is to use the keyword number without any parameters. Oracle translates the keyword float without parameters to number. It is also possible to specify float with a parameter for binary precision. This parameter can range from 1 to 126. A decimal equivalent can be calculated by dividing this value by the value .30103.

A definition with float*(binary precision)* affects only the precision with which a number will be stored. The scale range remains the same.

 Run the script crfloat1.sql, which can be found on the CD at the back of this book, to create the float1 table. The float table contains three columns: one specified as number, one as float, and one as float(14). One row of sample data is loaded as well. The table float1 is defined as follows:

```
create table float1 (
    f1        number,
    ansifloat float,
    ansiflb   float(14))
;
```

Listing 11.7 describes the table and displays data, once using default and once using a format mask.

Listing 11.7. Describing a table using the default and a format mask.

```
--        Filename: 11squ07.sql
--         Purpose: describe float1 table
--                  select without and with format mask

desc float1
```

This code returns

```
Name                              Null?     Type
-------------------------------   --------  ----
F1                                          NUMBER
ANSIFLOAT                                   FLOAT(126)
ANSIFLB                                     FLOAT(14)
```

This time the ANSI datatype keywords are actually maintained: float got translated to float(126), which is equivalent to number, and the binary float definition is maintained as defined.

The next part of the example retrieves the four rows of the table, which show almost the maximum ranges that the number datatype can store—all digits of the mantissa could be nines:

```
select
    *
from float1
;
```

It returns

```
       F1 ANSIFLOAT    ANSIFLB
--------- ---------   ---------
1.23E+125 1.23E+125 1.23E+125
-1.2E+125 -1.2E+125 -1.2E+125
1.23E-127 1.23E-127 1.23E-127
-1.2E-127 -1.2E-127 -1.2E-127
```

Note that the ANSIFLB column displays exactly as the other ones because the precision that amounts to five decimal characters is larger than that displayed as default.

Applying the following format mask will show the full values as stored. This script

```
col generic format 9.9999999999999999999999999999999999999EEEE

select
    f1 generic
from float1
;

select
    ansifloat generic
from float1
;

select
    ansiflb generic
from float1
;

clear columns
```

returns this twice:

```
GENERIC
-----------------------------------------------
 1.2345678901234567890123456780E+125
-1.2345678901234567890123456780E+125
 1.2345678901234567890123456780E-127
-1.2345678901234567890123456780E-127
```

and this once:

```
GENERIC
-----------------------------------------------
 1.2346000000000000000000000000000000000E+125
-1.2346000000000000000000000000000000000E+125
 1.2346000000000000000000000000000000000E-127
-1.2346000000000000000000000000000000000E-127
```

Thus, ANSIFLB lost the precision of the last 33 digits. The number is rounded to a precision of five, and the scale is the same.

> **NOTE**
>
> It is not possible to display the full range that can be stored in floating-point numbers other than using scientific notation. The format mask must have only up to 99 characters. A format mask as the second parameter of the to_char function is limited in length as well.

Exceeding the Allowable Range of Floating-Point Numbers

There are three cases in which a floating-point number definition might not be sufficient to hold a number to be inserted:

- The precision of the number is larger than that of the column. Although it might be needed in some physics applications and the like, it is hard to imagine why anyone would need a higher precision than 38 digits. In real life a difference of less than a few percentages does not seem to make much of a difference. To use a previous note, it takes only 13 digits to fully state the national debt in U.S. dollars. At any rate, in this case, the number will be rounded to fit the column's precision, and the number will load. This is exactly what happened with the ANSIFLB column, where 33 digits precision disappeared and will not be demonstrated again.

- The number is too large to fit the scale. If a number has a higher value than what will fit into the definition, an overflow error will result and the number will not load.

- The number is too small to fit the scale. This case is handled consistently with the integer case. Rather than resulting in an underflow error, the number will simply load as zero. This can cause unexpected results.

> **DEBUG ALERT**
>
> In the huge range of allowable values for a floating-point column, it is highly unlikely that you will get an overflow error. Such an error, therefore, should trigger some serious debugging.

Listing 11.8 demonstrates how numbers beyond the range of floating-point numbers are handled. The first number inserted has an excessively large scale that results in an error. The second number inserted has an excessively small scale that results in the insertion of a zero value. As before, the new value table is returned to its original state through a rollback (see Chapter 25).

Listing 11.8. Exceeding allowable scale for a floating-point column.

```
--          Filename: 11squ08.sql
--           Purpose: exceeding allowable scale for floating-point column
--
col generic format 9.9999999999999999999999999999999999999EEEE

insert into float1 (f1)
values (.99999999999999999999999999999999999999E127)
;
```

This listing returns an error:

```
values (.99999999999999999999999999999999999999E127)
        *
ERROR at line 2:
ORA-01426: numeric overflow
```

The rest of the example inserts smaller and smaller values, until the underflow leads to the storage of the following zero value:

```
insert into float1 (f1)
values (-.99999999999999999999999999999999999999E-126)
;

select
    f1 generic
from float1
where ansifloat is null
;

rollback;

insert into float1 (f1)
values (-.99999999999999999999999999999999999999E-129)
;

select
    f1 generic
from float1
where ansifloat is null
;

rollback;

insert into float1 (f1)
values (-.99999999999999999999999999999999999999E-130)
;

select
    f1 generic
from float1
where ansifloat is null
;

rollback;

clear columns
```

The return of these statements is as follows:

```
1 row created.

                                        GENERIC
-----------------------------------------------
-9.99999999999999999999999999999999999990E-127

Rollback complete.

1 row created.

                                        GENERIC
-----------------------------------------------
-9.99999999999999999999999999999999999990E-130

Rollback complete.

1 row created.

                                        GENERIC
-----------------------------------------------
   .000000000000000000000000000000000000000E+00

Rollback complete.
```

The first two numbers (.99 ... E -126, .99 ... E -129) loaded fine. Once the exponent becomes smaller than -130, a value of zero is stored.

Summary

Numerical data can be defined as one of three types:

- ■ Integer
- ■ Fixed point
- ■ Floating point

The number datatype is overloaded so that it can be used to define all three:

- ■ number(*precision*) allows you to specify a signed integer with a precision of up to 38 digits. If the ANSI SQL keywords int, integer, and smallint are used, a definition of a 38-digit integer will result.

- ■ number(*precision, scale*) specifies a fixed-point decimal number with up to 38 digits precision and a scale between -84 and 127. The number results from multiplying the precision part of the number with 10 to the power of scale. The ANSI SQL keywords decimal and numeric result in the same definitions.

- ■ number specifies a floating-point column with up to 38 digits precision and a scale between 125 and -127. The keyword float can be used to specify floating-point numbers as well; float is equivalent to number, and float(*binary precision*) allows you to specify a precision between 1 and 126 binary digits that corresponds to between 1 and 38 decimal digits.

The attempt to load numbers that are too small (in the sense of approaching zero) or too large (in the sense of approaching ± infinity) is dealt with consistently throughout datatypes. If numbers are too small, precision is lost until the number is loaded as a zero. If numbers are too large, an overflow error will result.

Dates and Times: The date Datatype

IN THIS CHAPTER

Dates are a fascinating phenomenon. They have been around almost as long as "civilized" mankind. They also pose interesting issues for computer systems, which use dates in a number of ways. Information content, time stamping, and key generation are a few of their uses. The use of dates is interesting even without touching on the obscene sums of money being spent to fix poorly designed applications to keep them churning beyond the year 2000. This chapter covers the following date-related issues:

- Expressing the length of the year in days
- Breaking the year into months of unequal length and weeks
- Synchronizing time zones and daylight time-zone shifts in international systems (every Web page is international in some way)
- Representing dates and times in storage
- Representing date and time intervals in storage

Dates and times were not included in the SQL-89 standard. SQL-92, on the other hand, elaborates on them in great detail. Software vendors have been incorporating their own date-and-time schemes and are likely to standardize in the course of upcoming upgrades. These schemes differ from one another, but because they deal with the same phenomenon and issues, they do not differ that much.

ORACLE vs. SQL

This chapter presents date and time issues as Oracle handles them.

Representing Points in Time: The date Datatype

Oracle uses only one datatype to represent points in time: date, which can range from January 1, 4712 B.C., to December 31, 4712 A.D. A date column can store time points down to the second.

REAL-WORLD EXPERIENCES

The length of the year is determined by the earth's course around the sun; the length of the day is determined by the amount of time it takes the earth to rotate once. In brief, the scheme that makes these jibe is as follows:

- There is a leap year every four years.
- The leap year is skipped every 100 years, except
- The leap year is not skipped every 400 years.

Not until the sixteenth century did anyone figure out the length of the year and its correction every hundred years with reasonable accuracy. Because by then the calendar had been out of joint by 10 days, Pope Gregory XIII fixed the problem by having the calendar drop 10 days from October 5 to October 14, 1582. It is funny to think that most people did not even realize it, when today just the change to and from daylight saving time is such a big deal. The Russians did not go along with the change, so the October revolution happened when it was November in most other places.

A number of years ago, when I taught C at a university, I assigned the programming of an eternal calendar as a short project. In essence, the program was to ask for a date and return the 15 days before and after, including the applicable days of the week. Although some students went so far as to add moon phases and tidal tables, most students could not complete the assignment. I still wonder whether the year 2000 problem has less to do with applications and programs that outlasted their expected usable life and more with the fundamental difficulty of grasping the concepts of timekeeping.

The date datatype is quite versatile: It supports adding and subtracting time intervals from dates. It allows you to extract the day of the week and the month of a year for a date. It knows which infamous days did or did not exist. It also provides some support for time-zone issues.

The examples in this chapter use a default data format string of DD-MMM-YYYY, which is the format string for a date such as 31-JUL-1974. If you use Personal Oracle, this string has to be set as the NLS_DATE_FORMAT parameter in the Registry. This is done in the following steps:

ORACLE vs SQL

1. Click on the Start Menu icon.

2. Click on Run.

3. Type regedit in the Open field (see Chapter 1, "Introduction to SQL," for a screenshot of this).

4. Watch the screen, shown in Figure 12.1, appear.

FIGURE 12.1.
Windows 95 Registry—top level.

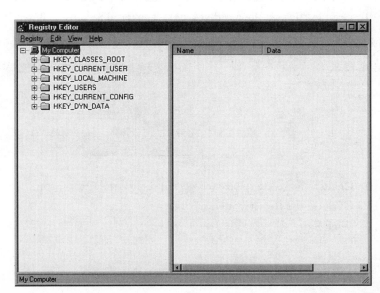

5. Click on the + next to HKEY_LOCAL_MACHINE.

6. Click on the + next to SOFTWARE.

7. Click on the folder icon next to ORACLE, which will display all the entries pertaining to Oracle proper on the right pane of the screen. You will see a screen like the one in Figure 12.2.

FIGURE 12.2.

Windows 95 Registry—Oracle entries.

8. Scroll down the entries until you find NLS_DATE_FORMAT.

9. Double-click on the word NLS_DATE_FORMAT. The screen shown in Figure 12.3 will appear.

FIGURE 12.3.

Windows 95 Registry—edit string for NLS_DATE_FORMAT.

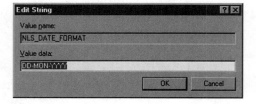

10. Change the string to DD-MON-YYYY and click the OK button.

11. Click on the Registry menu.

12. Click Exit.

If you use these scripts on a different platform, you must include the line

```
NLS_DATE_FORMAT='DD-MON-YYYY'
```

in the `init____.ora` file, where the ____ stands for the so-called `sid` of the database you are using. If you have no control over this, which is likely to be the case in a multi-user environment with a database administrator, you can change the default for your SQL session by issuing the following command:

```
alter session set NLS_DATE_FORMAT = 'DD-MON-YYYY';
```

This code allows only your session to be affected by the change. Note that the new format will only be in effect for the duration of the session during which you issued it.

Features of the date Datatype

Conceptually, `date` columns are based on days. Adding 1 to a date will return the date of the next day. Adding 7 will return the date of a week later. Times within a day are represented as their fraction of the day. Thus 12 hours is half, 1 hour is 1/24, 1 minute is 1/1440, and 1 second is 1/86400. If you have worked with dates and times in spreadsheets, this approach should be familiar to you.

 Run the provided script `crdate1.sql`. It will create table `dates1`, which contains only one date column `dte`.

The table `dates1` contains six records with various dates. Listing 12.1 describes the table and selects all rows.

Listing 12.1. Creating and loading the sample table.

```
--       Filename: 12squ01.sql
--       Purpose: Creates and loads table dates1
--
....
....

desc dates1;

select
   dte,
   to_char(dte,'HH24:MI:SS')
from dates1
;
```

The statements return

```
Name                            Null?    Type
------------------------------- -------- ----
DTE                                      DATE


DTE          TO_CHAR(DTE,'HH24:MI:SS')
-----------  --------------------------------------------------------------
08-MAY-1997  00:00:00
08-MAY-1997  12:00:00
08-MAY-2010  00:00:00
03-FEB-1997  04:53:59
14-JUL-1910  00:00:00
08-MAY-2010  00:00:00

6 rows selected.
```

The first column of the output shows the date in default format. The second column shows the time portion extracted through the date version of the to_char function, which we will discuss in detail toward the end of the chapter. Note the excessive width of the second column. The following examples, therefore, will format converted columns.

Adding and Subtracting from Dates and Times

The inconsistency of day- and year-based values requires a separate kind of treatment when calculating with these. For days and times, it is necessary to add or subtract only numbers reflecting days or fractions thereof. For adding months and years, special functions are necessary.

Adding Days

The next example demonstrates the day/fraction-of-day basis of the date datatype. In the first set 1, 3, 7, 14, and 28 days will be added to the date. This is done simply by adding the number of days to the date, as shown in Listing 12.2.

Listing 12.2. Adding days to the date datatype.

```
--      Filename: 12squ02.sql
--      Purpose: Add days
--
select
   dte,
   dte + 1,
   dte + 3,
   dte + 7,
   dte + 14,
   dte + 28
from dates1;
```

The preceding code returns this:

```
DTE         DTE+1       DTE+3       DTE+7       DTE+14      DTE+28
----------- ----------- ----------- ----------- ----------- -----------
08-MAY-1997 09-MAY-1997 11-MAY-1997 15-MAY-1997 22-MAY-1997 05-JUN-1997
08-MAY-1997 09-MAY-1997 11-MAY-1997 15-MAY-1997 22-MAY-1997 05-JUN-1997
08-MAY-2010 09-MAY-2010 11-MAY-2010 15-MAY-2010 22-MAY-2010 05-JUN-2010
03-FEB-1997 04-FEB-1997 06-FEB-1997 10-FEB-1997 17-FEB-1997 03-MAR-1997
14-JUL-1910 15-JUL-1910 17-JUL-1910 21-JUL-1910 28-JUL-1910 11-AUG-1910
08-MAY-2010 09-MAY-2010 11-MAY-2010 15-MAY-2010 22-MAY-2010 05-JUN-2010

6 rows selected.
```

Indeed, the dates of 1 day to 28 days later are returned. Note, however, that if the date is B.C., that calculation returns still a later month, which it should. The last row is a B.C. date, which leads to peculiarities; a later day is reflected as a later date within the same year but as a lower year value if applicable. The following example repeats the first and fourth column, formatted to show the A.D. indicator:

```
col dtf1 heading 'to_char(dte,''DD-MON-YYYY AD'')' format A30
col dtf2 heading 'to_char(dte+7,''DD-MON-YYYY AD'')' format A32

select
    to_char(dte,'DD-MON-YYYY AD')      dtf1,
    to_char(dte + 7,'DD-MON-YYYY AD') dtf2
from dates1;

clear columns
```

It returns

```
to_char(dte,'DD-MON-YYYY AD')  to_char(dte+7,'DD-MON-YYYY AD')
------------------------------ -------------------------------
08-MAY-1997 AD                 15-MAY-1997 AD
08-MAY-1997 AD                 15-MAY-1997 AD
08-MAY-2010 AD                 15-MAY-2010 AD
03-FEB-1997 AD                 10-FEB-1997 AD
14-JUL-1910 AD                 21-JUL-1910 AD
08-MAY-2010 BC                 15-MAY-2010 BC
6 rows selected.
```

Adding a day to a B.C. date reveals the treatment of days in time, which is not exactly equivalent with that of integers. The day after May 8th is always May 9th. The year 2010 B.C. is followed by the year 2009 B.C. Good thing the people living then did not know that they were living in B.C.; the system would have been quite confusing.

Adding and Subtracting Time

Time is represented as a fraction of day in the date datatype. Therefore,

- One hour is 1/24 of a day.
- One minute is 1/(60*24) or 1/1440 of a day.
- A second is 1/(60*60*24) or 1/86400 of a day.

Adding these values will add an hour, a minute, or a second, respectively, to the time. Subtracting them will do the opposite.

Listing 12.3 adds times. After repeating the time as stored in the table, 3 hours, 3 minutes, and 3 seconds will be added. The third column will have 21 hours added.

Listing 12.3. Adding time.

```
--        Filename: 12squ03.sql
--         Purpose: Add time
--
col dtf1 heading 'dte'          format A22
col dtf2 heading 'dte + 3/3/3' format A22
col dtf3 heading 'dte + 21hrs' format A22

select
   to_char(dte,'DD-MON-YYYY HH24:MI:SS') dtf1,
   to_char(dte + 3/24 + 3/1440 + 3/86400,'DD-MON-YYYY HH24:MI:SS') dtf2,
   to_char(dte + 21/24,'DD-MON-YYYY HH24:MI:SS') dtf3
from dates1
;

clear columns
```

The preceding code returns

```
dte                    dte + 3/3/3            dte + 21hrs
--------------------   -------------------   -------------------
08-MAY-1997 00:00:00   08-MAY-1997 03:03:03   08-MAY-1997 21:00:00
08-MAY-1997 12:00:00   08-MAY-1997 15:03:03   09-MAY-1997 09:00:00
08-MAY-2010 00:00:00   08-MAY-2010 03:03:03   08-MAY-2010 21:00:00
03-FEB-1997 04:53:59   03-FEB-1997 07:57:02   04-FEB-1997 01:53:59
14-JUL-1910 00:00:00   14-JUL-1910 03:03:03   14-JUL-1910 21:00:00
08-MAY-2010 00:00:00   08-MAY-2010 03:03:03   08-MAY-2010 21:00:00

6 rows selected.
```

The date portion in the third column reflects the change in the dates accurately.

Subtracting time works the same way, as Listing 12.4 shows.

Listing 12.4. Subtracting time.

```
--        Filename: 12squ04.sql
--         Purpose: Subtract time
--
col dtf1 heading 'dte'          format A22
col dtf2 heading 'dte - 3/3/3' format A22
col dtf3 heading 'dte - 21hrs' format A22

select
   to_char(dte,'DD-MON-YYYY HH24:MI:SS') dtf1,
   to_char(dte - 3/24 - 3/1440 - 3/86400,'DD-MON-YYYY HH24:MI:SS') dtf2,
   to_char(dte - 21/24,'DD-MON-YYYY HH24:MI:SS') dtf3
```

```
from dates1
;

clear columns
```

The preceding code returns

```
dte                      dte - 3/3/3              dte - 21hrs
-------------------      -------------------      -------------------
08-MAY-1997 00:00:00     07-MAY-1997 20:56:57     07-MAY-1997 03:00:00
08-MAY-1997 12:00:00     08-MAY-1997 08:56:57     07-MAY-1997 15:00:00
08-MAY-2010 00:00:00     07-MAY-2010 20:56:57     07-MAY-2010 03:00:00
03-FEB-1997 04:53:59     03-FEB-1997 01:50:56     02-FEB-1997 07:53:59
14-JUL-1910 00:00:00     13-JUL-1910 20:56:57     13-JUL-1910 03:00:00
08-MAY-2010 00:00:00     07-MAY-2010 20:56:57     07-MAY-2010 03:00:00

6 rows selected.
```

Adding or Subtracting Months: add_months

Because months are from 28 to 31 days long, adding and subtracting days does not allow you to accurately reflect months and years. However, the add_months function allows you to add months to a date.

Listing 12.5 adds 1, 3, and 9 months, and subtracts 6 months to the values stored in dates1.

Listing 12.5. Adding and subtracting months.

```
--        Filename: 12squ05.sql
--        Purpose: Adding and subtracting months
--
select
   dte,
   add_months(dte,1)   mo1pls,
   add_months(dte,3)   mo3pls,
   add_months(dte,9)   mo9pls,
   add_months(dte,-6)  mo6min
from dates1;
```

This code returns

```
DTE          MO1PLS       MO3PLS       MO9PLS       MO6MIN
-----------  -----------  -----------  -----------  -----------
08-MAY-1997  08-JUN-1997  08-AUG-1997  08-FEB-1998  08-NOV-1996
08-MAY-1997  08-JUN-1997  08-AUG-1997  08-FEB-1998  08-NOV-1996
08-MAY-2010  08-JUN-2010  08-AUG-2010  08-FEB-2011  08-NOV-2009
03-FEB-1997  03-MAR-1997  03-MAY-1997  03-NOV-1997  03-AUG-1996
14-JUL-1910  14-AUG-1910  14-OCT-1910  14-APR-1911  14-JAN-1910
08-MAY-2010  08-JUN-2010  08-AUG-2010  08-FEB-2009  08-NOV-2011

6 rows selected.
```

Note that the B.C. row now reflects the change of the year accurately: the year after 2010 B.C. is 2009, the year before it is 2011.

Adding or Subtracting Years

Years are either 365 or 366 days long (except for the infamous year 1582, which had only 355 days). As with months, adding and subtracting days does not accurately reflect years. No special function is provided though, so the add_months function has to serve this purpose as well. Listing 12.6 adds 1, 3, and 1,000 years, and subtracts 60.

Listing 12.6. Adding and subtracting years.

```
--      Filename: 12squ06.sql
--       Purpose: Adding and subtracting years
--
select
   dte,
   add_months(dte,1*12)    yr1pls,
   add_months(dte,3*12)    yr3pls,
   add_months(dte,1000*12) yr1000pls,
   add_months(dte,-60*12)  yr60min
from dates1;
```

This code returns

```
DTE          YR1PLS       YR3PLS       YR1000PLS    YR60MIN
-----------  -----------  -----------  -----------  -----------
08-MAY-1997  08-MAY-1998  08-MAY-2000  08-MAY-2997  08-MAY-1937
08-MAY-1997  08-MAY-1998  08-MAY-2000  08-MAY-2997  08-MAY-1937
08-MAY-2010  08-MAY-2011  08-MAY-2013  08-MAY-3010  08-MAY-1950
03-FEB-1997  03-FEB-1998  03-FEB-2000  03-FEB-2997  03-FEB-1937
14-JUL-1910  14-JUL-1911  14-JUL-1913  14-JUL-2910  14-JUL-1850
08-MAY-2010  08-MAY-2009  08-MAY-2007  08-MAY-1010  08-MAY-2070

6 rows selected.
```

As the output shows, only the year values are affected.

DEBUG ALERT

Although it would certainly have been easy to express the months parameter as a single number, it is in many cases preferable to state it as a calculated number. In the latter case it is immediately clear that it was intended to add or subtract years and not months.

Calculating the Difference Between Dates

Just as it was possible to arrive at a new date when adding a number or using the add_month function, it is possible to subtract dates from each other to yield the period between them, or you can use a function called months_between to calculate months or years passed.

Days

The period in days between dates can simply be calculated by subtracting one from the other and truncating or rounding the result. Listing 12.7 does just that: It calculates the days between the values in the `dte` column and

- `01-JAN-1997`

- `31-DEC-1997`

- `01-JAN-0001`, the first day A.D. (remember, there is no year 0)

- The first day of the year 2000, `01-JAN-2000`

Listing 12.7 demonstrates this procedure.

Listing 12.7. Calculating the number of days between dates.

```
--        Filename: 12squ07.sql
--        Purpose: Calculating the number of days between dates
--
select
   trunc(dte - to_date('01-JAN-1997')) since1_1,
   trunc(to_date('31-DEC-1997') - dte) till31_12,
   trunc(dte - to_date('01-JAN-0001')) sinceyr1,
   trunc(to_date('01-JAN-2000')-dte)   tillyr2000
from dates1
;
```

This code returns

```
SINCE1_1 TILL31_12  SINCEYR1 TILLYR2000
--------- --------- --------- ----------
      127       237    729153        968
      127       236    729153        967
     4875     -4511    733901      -3780
       33       330    729059       1061
   -31583     31947    697443      32678
 -1463417   1463781   -734391    1464512
```

The negative sign results from subtracting a later date from an earlier one. The example uses the `trunc` function to eliminate the effect of times.

Time

Because subtracting one date from another yields the days and fraction of days between them, you can calculate the difference in time either including the days or truncating them. Listing 12.8 demonstrates this by calculating the time passed between a day and 22:40 hours of the same day. To extract the date portion of the values, it will use the `trunc` function, which we will examine in detail at the end of this chapter. Using mathematical functions, it then converts the number into hours, minutes, and seconds.

Listing 12.8. Calculating the time between date values.

```
--        Filename: 12squ08.sql
--          Purpose: Calculating the time between date values
--
col dtf1 heading 'dte'  format A12
col hrs                 format 9999
col mins                format 9999
col secs                format 9999

select distinct
   to_char(dte,'HH24:MI:SS') dtf1,
   22/24+40/1440 + trunc(dte) - dte fract_val,
   trunc(   (22/24+40/1440 + trunc(dte) - dte)*24) hrs,
   trunc(mod((22/24+40/1440 + trunc(dte) - dte)*1440,60)) mins,
         mod((22/24+40/1440 + trunc(dte) - dte)*86400,60) secs
from dates1
;

clear columns
```

This code returns

```
dte          FRACT_VAL   HRS  MINS  SECS
-----------  ---------   ---  ----  ----
00:00:00     .94444444    22    40     0
04:53:59     .74028935    17    46     1
12:00:00     .44444444    10    40     0
```

The first column simply displays the time portion of dte. The second column adds the fractional day for 22:40 hours to the value of dte truncated to days and subtracts all of dte. The date portion of dte cancels out, and the difference between the times remains. Multiplying this fractional value with 24 and truncating the result yields the whole hours (column 3). Multiplying the fractional value with 1440 and then calculating the modulus on the basis of 60 yields the whole minutes after truncation, that is column 4. The seconds are calculated by multiplying the fractional value with 86,400 and then calculating the modulus on the basis of 60. A select distinct is chosen because four of the rows contain the same time fraction: 0 hours.

It is obvious from this example that an interval datatype with its own formatting options and functions is preferable to this roundabout way of extracting time periods.

Calculating the Number of Months Between Dates: months_between

The complement to the add_months function is the months_between function, which calculates the number of months between two dates. The integer portion represents the full number of months passed. The fractional portion represents the remaining number of days divided by 31.

Listing 12.9 is a variation of `12squ07.sql`; it will calculate the months passed between the `dte` values and four dates: `01-JAN-1997`, `1-DEC-1997`, `01-JAN-0001`, and `01-JAN-2000`. The last number will be displayed a second time in month and day format.

Listing 12.9. Calculating the number of months between dates.

```
--        Filename: 12squ09.sql
--        Purpose: Calculating the number of months between dates
--
col since1_1   format 999,999.99
col till31_12  format 999,999.99
col sinceyr1   format 999,999.99
col tillyr2000 format 999,999.99
col days       format 99.9

select
   months_between(dte,to_date('01-JAN-1997'))        since1_1,
   months_between(to_date('31-DEC-1997'),dte)        till31_12,
   months_between(dte,to_date('01-JAN-0001'))        sinceyr1,
   months_between(to_date('01-JAN-2000'),dte)        tillyr2000,
   trunc(months_between(to_date('01-JAN-2000'),dte)) months,
   mod( months_between(to_date('01-JAN-2000'),dte) -
        trunc(months_between(to_date('01-JAN-2000'),dte)),31) * 31 days
from dates1
;
clear columns
```

This code returns

SINCE1_1	TILL31_12	SINCEYR1	TILLYR2000	MONTHS	DAYS
4.23	7.74	23,956.23	31.77	31	24.0
4.24	7.73	23,956.24	31.76	31	23.5
160.23	-148.26	24,112.23	-124.23	-124	-7.0
1.07	10.90	23,953.07	34.93	34	28.8
-1,037.58	1,049.55	22,914.42	1,073.58	1073	18.0
-48,079.77	48,091.74	-24,127.77	48,115.77	48115	24.0

6 rows selected.

Years

As was the case with the `add_months` function, `months_between` has to double up to calculate the number of years between dates as well. The number of months returned by this function divided by 12 and then truncated or rounded gives the years.

Listing 12.10 adapts `12squ09.sql` to return values in years. The last set of columns is now changed to display the years, months, and days.

Listing 12.10. Calculating the number of years between dates.

```
--         Filename: 12squ10.sql
--         Purpose: Calculating the number of years between dates
--
col since1_1   format 999,999.99
col till31_12  format 999,999.99
col sinceyr1   format 999,999.99
col tillyr2000 format 999,999.99
col days       format 99.9

select
   months_between(dte,to_date('01-JAN-1997'))/12        since1_1,
   months_between(to_date('31-DEC-1997'),dte)/12        till31_12,
   months_between(dte,to_date('01-JAN-0001'))/12        sinceyr1,
   months_between(to_date('01-JAN-2000'),dte)/12        tillyr2000,
   trunc(months_between(to_date('01-JAN-2000'),dte)/12) years,
   trunc(mod(months_between(to_date('01-JAN-2000'),dte),12)) months,
   mod( months_between(to_date('01-JAN-2000'),dte) -
        trunc(months_between(to_date('01-JAN-2000'),dte)),31) * 31 days
from dates1
;

clear columns
```

This code returns

SINCE1_1	TILL31_12	SINCEYR1	TILLYR2000	YEARS	MONTHS	DAYS
.35	.65	1,996.35	2.65	2	7	24.0
.35	.64	1,996.35	2.65	2	7	23.5
13.35	-12.35	2,009.35	-10.35	-10	-4	-7.0
.09	.91	1,996.09	2.91	2	10	28.8
-86.47	87.46	1,909.53	89.47	89	5	18.0
-4,006.65	4,007.65	-2,010.65	4,009.65	4009	7	24.0

6 rows selected.

Special-Day Functions: last_day and next_day

Together with the other month functions, the last_day function takes into account the fact that months can last from 28 to 31 days, except for October 1582, which had only 21 days. The last_day function returns the last day of the month, which contains the date passed into it. The following example shows the dte values and the last days in the month of each of these values.

The next_day function returns the date after a date is passed into it on which a day of the week, specified as its second argument, falls. If, for example, a company pays on every first Monday of the month, then next_day('30-APR-1997','Monday') would identify the payday for May 1997. The following example shows the dte values, the dte day of the week, and the dates of the following Monday, Wednesday, Friday, and Sunday.

Julian Dates

A Julian date is the number of days that have passed between January 1, 4712 B.C., and the date passed in. It is obtained by specifying the J format parameter into the to_char function. The term *Julian* is misleading because days are counted using a Gregorian calendar.

Rounding and Truncating Dates: round and trunc

Like their number equivalents, the round and trunc functions can be called with either one or two arguments.

Rounding and Truncating Dates to the Date Portion (Years, Months, and Days)

If called with one argument only—the date to be processed—round and trunc return the date portion (year, month, day) of the date only in the following ways:

- ■ trunc(date) truncates (drops or omits) the time portion.
- ■ round(date) rounds the number up to the next date if the time portion equals or is greater than 12:00 noon. B.C. dates work the same way.

Listing 12.11 rounds and truncates the dte values.

Listing 12.11. Rounding and truncating dates.

```
--        Filename: 12squ11.sql
--        Purpose: rounding and truncating dates
--
col dateportion format a12
col timeportion format a8
col rounded     format a12
col truncated   format a12
col roundtime   format a8
col trunctime   format a8

select
   dte                               dateportion,
   to_char(dte,'HH24:MI:SS')         timeportion,
   round (dte)                       rounded,
   to_char(round(dte),'HH24:MI:SS')  roundtime,
   trunc (dte)                       truncated,
   to_char(trunc(dte),'HH24:MI:SS')  trunctime
from dates1;

clear columns
```

This code returns

```
DATEPORTION   TIMEPORT ROUNDED        ROUNDTIM TRUNCATED     TRUNCTIM
------------  -------- ------------   -------- ------------  --------
08-MAY-1997   00:00:00 08-MAY-1997    00:00:00 08-MAY-1997   00:00:00
08-MAY-1997   12:00:00 09-MAY-1997    00:00:00 08-MAY-1997   00:00:00
08-MAY-2010   00:00:00 08-MAY-2010    00:00:00 08-MAY-2010   00:00:00
03-FEB-1997   04:53:59 03-FEB-1997    00:00:00 03-FEB-1997   00:00:00
14-JUL-1910   00:00:00 14-JUL-1910    00:00:00 14-JUL-1910   00:00:00
08-MAY-2010   00:00:00 08-MAY-2010    00:00:00 08-MAY-2010   00:00:00

6 rows selected.
```

All dates are rounded down, except the second one in which the time is 12:00 noon.

> **NOTE**
>
> Columns four and six show what truncating a date really means: Truncating a date returns the very same date with the time portion set to zeroes. In other words, the time portion has not been removed from the date; it has only been set to 0 hours, 0 minutes, and 0 seconds.

The following sections show the use of the trunc and round functions with a second argument— a format mask. Using DD, DDD, and J as format masks returns the same output as using no format mask at all. The examples will not demonstrate these.

> **CAUTION**
>
> If you compare dates that were generated through the sysdate command, these dates will be identical only if they were generated in the same second. In all likelihood you will have to use trunc to get the date portion only. Listing 12.12 attempts to retrieve all rows where the date equals May 8, 1997.

Listing 12.12. Comparing dates using trunc.

```
--        Filename: 12squ12.sql
--        Purpose: comparing dates using trunc
--
col dateportion format a12
col timeportion format a8

select
   dte                             dateportion,
   to_char(dte,'HH24:MI:SS')       timeportion
from dates1
where dte = to_date('08-MAY-1997')
;
```

It returns only one row, as shown here:

```
DATEPORTION   TIMEPORT
------------  --------
08-MAY-1997   00:00:00
```

This is the row where the time portion is zero. To retrieve the second row with that date, you must change the statement as follows:

```
1   select
2     dte                           dateportion,
3     to_char(dte,'HH24:MI:SS')     timeportion
4   from dates1
5*  where trunc(dte) = to_date('08-MAY-1997')
6   ;
```

This returns both rows:

```
DATEPORTION   TIMEPORT
------------  --------
08-MAY-1997   00:00:00
08-MAY-1997   12:00:00
```

Through the `trunc` command, only the date portion is compared; the time portions in both dates are zero.

Rounding and Truncating Dates to Other Units of Time

If these functions are called with two arguments, the second argument is a format string that indicates the time unit to which a date should be truncated or rounded. The function again returns a full date with the smaller time units set to zeroes.

Rounding and Truncating Dates to Centuries and Years

A number of format masks allow you to truncate or round dates to centuries (CC and SCC) or years (SYYYY, YYYY, YYY, YY, Y, YEAR, and SYEAR). The century truncation returns the first day of the first year of the century; the year truncation returns the first day of the year. This is demonstrated by Listing 12.13.

Listing 12.13. Truncating dates using format strings.

```
--      Filename: 12squ13.sql
--       Purpose: truncating dates using format strings
--
select
  dte             ,
  trunc (dte,'CC')   CC,
  trunc (dte,'SCC')  SCC,
```

continues

Listing 12.13. continued

```
   trunc (dte,'YEAR')   YEAR,
   trunc (dte,'SYEAR')  SYEAR
from dates1
;

select
   dte                     ,
   trunc (dte,'SYYYY')   SYYYY,
   trunc (dte,'YYYY')    YYYY,
   trunc (dte,'YYY')     YYY,
   trunc (dte,'YY')      YY,
   trunc (dte,'Y')       Y
from dates1
;
```

This code returns

```
DTE          CC           SCC          YEAR         SYEAR
-----------  -----------  -----------  -----------  -----------
08-MAY-1997  01-JAN-1900  01-JAN-1900  01-JAN-1997  01-JAN-1997
08-MAY-1997  01-JAN-1900  01-JAN-1900  01-JAN-1997  01-JAN-1997
08-MAY-2010  01-JAN-2000  01-JAN-2000  01-JAN-2010  01-JAN-2010
03-FEB-1997  01-JAN-1900  01-JAN-1900  01-JAN-1997  01-JAN-1997
14-JUL-1910  01-JAN-1900  01-JAN-1900  01-JAN-1910  01-JAN-1910
08-MAY-2010  01-JAN-2000  01-JAN-2000  01-JAN-2010  01-JAN-2010

6 rows selected.

DTE          SYYYY        YYYY         YYY          YY           Y
-----------  -----------  -----------  -----------  -----------  -----------
08-MAY-1997  01-JAN-1997  01-JAN-1997  01-JAN-1997  01-JAN-1997  01-JAN-1997
08-MAY-1997  01-JAN-1997  01-JAN-1997  01-JAN-1997  01-JAN-1997  01-JAN-1997
08-MAY-2010  01-JAN-2010  01-JAN-2010  01-JAN-2010  01-JAN-2010  01-JAN-2010
03-FEB-1997  01-JAN-1997  01-JAN-1997  01-JAN-1997  01-JAN-1997  01-JAN-1997
14-JUL-1910  01-JAN-1910  01-JAN-1910  01-JAN-1910  01-JAN-1910  01-JAN-1910
08-MAY-2010  01-JAN-2010  01-JAN-2010  01-JAN-2010  01-JAN-2010  01-JAN-2010

6 rows selected.
```

Rounding does essentially the same thing as truncating, but dates on or after July 1 are rounded up to the next January 1; dates on or after the first day of year 50 in a century are rounded up to the next century's first day. This is shown in Listing 12.14.

Listing 12.14. Rounding dates using format strings.

```
--          Filename: 12squ14.sql
--           Purpose: ROUNDING dates using format strings
--
select
   dte                  ,
   round (dte,'CC')     CC,
   round (dte,'SCC')    SCC,
   round (dte,'YEAR')   YEAR,
   round (dte,'SYEAR')  SYEAR
```

```
from dates1
;

select
   dte                       ,
   round (dte,'SYYYY')    SYYYY,
   round (dte,'YYYY')     YYYY,
   round (dte,'YYY')      YYY,
   round (dte,'YY')       YY,
   round (dte,'Y')        Y
from dates1
;
```

This code returns

```
DTE         CC          SCC         YEAR        SYEAR
----------- ----------- ----------- ----------- -----------
08-MAY-1997 01-JAN-2000 01-JAN-2000 01-JAN-1997 01-JAN-1997
08-MAY-1997 01-JAN-2000 01-JAN-2000 01-JAN-1997 01-JAN-1997
08-MAY-2010 01-JAN-2000 01-JAN-2000 01-JAN-2010 01-JAN-2010
03-FEB-1997 01-JAN-2000 01-JAN-2000 01-JAN-1997 01-JAN-1997
14-JUL-1910 01-JAN-1900 01-JAN-1900 01-JAN-1911 01-JAN-1911
08-MAY-2010 01-JAN-2000 01-JAN-2000 01-JAN-2010 01-JAN-2010

6 rows selected.

DTE         SYYYY       YYYY        YYY         YY          Y
----------- ----------- ----------- ----------- ----------- -----------
08-MAY-1997 01-JAN-1997 01-JAN-1997 01-JAN-1997 01-JAN-1997 01-JAN-1997
08-MAY-1997 01-JAN-1997 01-JAN-1997 01-JAN-1997 01-JAN-1997 01-JAN-1997
08-MAY-2010 01-JAN-2010 01-JAN-2010 01-JAN-2010 01-JAN-2010 01-JAN-2010
03-FEB-1997 01-JAN-1997 01-JAN-1997 01-JAN-1997 01-JAN-1997 01-JAN-1997
14-JUL-1910 01-JAN-1911 01-JAN-1911 01-JAN-1911 01-JAN-1911 01-JAN-1911
08-MAY-2010 01-JAN-2010 01-JAN-2010 01-JAN-2010 01-JAN-2010 01-JAN-2010

6 rows selected.
```

Rounding and Truncating Dates to Months and Quarters

The format masks to truncate or round dates to quarters or months are Q, MONTH, MON, MM, and RM, respectively. The quarter truncation returns the first day of the quarter. The quarter rounding returns the same up to the 15th day of the second month, and the first day of the next quarter thereafter. The month truncation returns the first day of the month. The month rounding returns the same up to the 15th day of the second month, and the first day of the next month thereafter. Listing 12.15 demonstrates this.

Listing 12.15. Truncating/rounding dates to months and quarters.

```
--       Filename: 12squ15.sql
--       Purpose: truncating/rounding dates to months and quarters
--
select
   dte                   ,
   trunc (dte,'Q')       truncQ,
```

continues

Listing 12.15. continued

```
    round (dte,'Q')       roundQ,
    round (dte+33,'Q')    roundQ_33,
    trunc (dte,'MM')      truncM,
    round (dte,'MM')      roundM
from dates1
;
```

This code returns

```
DTE          TRUNCQ       ROUNDQ       ROUNDQ_33    TRUNCM       ROUNDM
-----------  -----------  -----------  -----------  -----------  ----------
08-MAY-1997  01-APR-1997  01-APR-1997  01-JUL-1997  01-MAY-1997  01-MAY-1997
08-MAY-1997  01-APR-1997  01-APR-1997  01-JUL-1997  01-MAY-1997  01-MAY-1997
08-MAY-2010  01-APR-2010  01-APR-2010  01-JUL-2010  01-MAY-2010  01-MAY-2010
03-FEB-1997  01-JAN-1997  01-JAN-1997  01-APR-1997  01-FEB-1997  01-FEB-1997
14-JUL-1910  01-JUL-1910  01-JUL-1910  01-OCT-1910  01-JUL-1910  01-JUL-1910
08-MAY-2010  01-APR-2010  01-APR-2010  01-JUL-2010  01-MAY-2010  01-MAY-2010

6 rows selected.
```

Rounding and Truncating Dates to the Same Weekday as the First of the Year or Month

The format masks to truncate or round dates to the same weekday as the first day of the year or month are WW, IW, and W. These format masks are a bit confusing but quite useful. They answer questions such as, "What is the date of the weekday before a given date that is the same weekday as the first of the year?" The question might sound contrived, but rules like that are used in accounting systems all the time. Rounding answers the same question but replaces "before" with "closest to." Listing 12.16 shows the use of rounding and truncating.

Listing 12.16. Truncating/rounding dates to the same weekday as the first day of the year or month.

```
--        Filename: 12squ16.sql
--          Purpose: truncating/rounding dates to same weekday as
--        first of year or first of month
--
col dtew          format a16
col first_of_year format a16
col first_of_month format a16

select
    to_char(dte,'DY, DD-MON-YYYY') dtew,
    to_char(trunc(dte,'YEAR'),'DY, DD-MON-YYYY') first_of_year,
    trunc (dte,'WW')       truncWW,
    round (dte,'WW')       roundWW
from dates1
;
```

This code returns

```
DTEW              FIRST_OF_YEAR   TRUNCWW      ROUNDWW
----------------  --------------- -----------  -----------
THU, 08-MAY-1997  WED, 01-JAN-1997 07-MAY-1997 07-MAY-1997
THU, 08-MAY-1997  WED, 01-JAN-1997 07-MAY-1997 07-MAY-1997
SAT, 08-MAY-2010  FRI, 01-JAN-2010 07-MAY-2010 07-MAY-2010
MON, 03-FEB-1997  WED, 01-JAN-1997 29-JAN-1997 05-FEB-1997
THU, 14-JUL-1910  SAT, 01-JAN-1910 09-JUL-1910 16-JUL-1910
SAT, 08-MAY-2010  FRI, 01-JAN-2010 07-MAY-2010 07-MAY-2010

6 rows selected.
```

The weekday of the first of the year of rows 1, 2, and 5 was a Wednesday. Truncation with the WW format mask returns the date of the Wednesday on or previous to the date passed in as the argument. In the fourth row, the first of the year was a Wednesday as well, but the weekday of the date was a Monday. Therefore trunc returns the date of the Wednesday before (29-Jan), but round returns the Wednesday after (5-Feb).

The same question for the first weekday of the month can be answered using the W format mask. The following example adds four days to the date column because the eighth of a month is always the same weekday as the first of the month, in which case the function would not show much:

```
select
    to_char(dte+4,'DY, DD-MON-YYYY') dtew,
    to_char(trunc(dte+4,'MONTH'),'DY, DD-MON-YYYY') first_of_month,
    trunc (dte+4,'W')       truncW,
    round (dte+4,'W')       roundW
from dates1
;

clear columns
```

This code returns

```
DTEW              FIRST_OF_MONTH   TRUNCW       ROUNDW
----------------  --------------- -----------  -----------
MON, 12-MAY-1997  THU, 01-MAY-1997 08-MAY-1997 15-MAY-1997
MON, 12-MAY-1997  THU, 01-MAY-1997 08-MAY-1997 15-MAY-1997
WED, 12-MAY-2010  SAT, 01-MAY-2010 08-MAY-2010 15-MAY-2010
FRI, 07-FEB-1997  SAT, 01-FEB-1997 01-FEB-1997 08-FEB-1997
MON, 18-JUL-1910  FRI, 01-JUL-1910 15-JUL-1910 15-JUL-1910
WED, 12-MAY-2010  SAT, 01-MAY-2010 08-MAY-2010 15-MAY-2010

6 rows selected.
```

Rounding and Truncating Dates to the Starting Day of the Week

The format masks to truncate or round dates to the starting day of the week are DAY, DY, and D. round will return the first of the next week, if applicable. The NLS_TERRITORY mask determines which day of the week is the first. In the UNITED_STATES setting, the week starts on Sunday and ends on Saturday.

These masks can be adapted to return the date of any day of the week by adding or subtracting the number of days to that value. Listing 12.17 shows rounding and truncating to the first day of the week and truncating to the last day of the week.

Listing 12.17. Truncating/rounding dates to the first day of the week and truncating to the last day of the week.

```
--        Filename: 12squ17.sql
--         Purpose: truncating/rounding dates to first day of the week
--                  truncating dates to the last day of the week
--
col dtew            format a16
col trunc_f_o_w     format a16
col trunc_l_o_w     format a16
col round_f_o_w     format a16

select
   to_char(dte,'DY, DD-MON-YYYY') dtew,
   to_char(trunc(dte,'DAY'),'DY, DD-MON-YYYY')   trunc_f_o_w,
   to_char(trunc(dte,'DAY')+6,'DY, DD-MON-YYYY') trunc_l_o_w,
   to_char(round(dte,'DAY'),'DY, DD-MON-YYYY')   round_f_o_w
from dates1
;

clear columns
```

This code returns

```
DTEW             TRUNC_F_O_W      TRUNC_L_O_W      ROUND_F_O_W
---------------- ---------------- ---------------- ----------------
THU, 08-MAY-1997 SUN, 04-MAY-1997 SAT, 10-MAY-1997 SUN, 11-MAY-1997
THU, 08-MAY-1997 SUN, 04-MAY-1997 SAT, 10-MAY-1997 SUN, 11-MAY-1997
SAT, 08-MAY-2010 SUN, 02-MAY-2010 SAT, 08-MAY-2010 SUN, 09-MAY-2010
MON, 03-FEB-1997 SUN, 02-FEB-1997 SAT, 08-FEB-1997 SUN, 02-FEB-1997
THU, 14-JUL-1910 SUN, 10-JUL-1910 SAT, 16-JUL-1910 SUN, 17-JUL-1910
SAT, 08-MAY-2010 SUN, 02-MAY-2010 SAT, 08-MAY-2010 SUN, 09-MAY-2010
```

Rounding and Truncating Dates to Hours and Minutes

The format masks to truncate or round dates to hours are HH, HH12, and HH24. The MI mask truncates or rounds dates to minutes. Listing 12.18 shows their use. In this example, 3/48 plus 30/86400 of a day have been added to each date—the time fraction for 1 1/2 hours and 30 seconds.

Listing 12.18. Truncating/rounding dates to hours and minutes.

```
--        Filename: 12squ18.sql
--         Purpose: truncating/rounding dates to hours and minutes
--
col dtf1 heading 'dte'        format A22
col trunc_hh     format a9
col round_hh     format a9
col trunc_mi     format a9
```

```
col round_mi      format a9
select
to_char(dte+3/48+30/86400,'DD-MON-YYYY HH24:MI:SS') dtf1,
    to_char(trunc(dte+3/48+30/86400,'HH'),'HH24:MI:SS') trunc_hh,
    to_char(round(dte+3/48+30/86400,'HH'),'HH24:MI:SS') round_hh,
    to_char(trunc(dte+3/48+30/86400,'MI'),'HH24:MI:SS') trunc_mi,
    to_char(round(dte+3/48+30/86400,'MI'),'HH24:MI:SS') round_mi
from dates1
;

clear columns
```

This code returns

```
dte                      TRUNC_HH  ROUND_HH  TRUNC_MI  ROUND_MI
--------------------     --------- --------- --------- ---------
08-MAY-1997 01:30:30     01:00:00  02:00:00  01:30:00  01:31:00
08-MAY-1997 13:30:30     13:00:00  14:00:00  13:30:00  13:31:00
08-MAY-2010 01:30:30     01:00:00  02:00:00  01:30:00  01:31:00
03-FEB-1997 06:24:29     06:00:00  06:00:00  06:24:00  06:24:00
14-JUL-1910 01:30:30     01:00:00  02:00:00  01:30:00  01:31:00
08-MAY-2010 01:30:30     01:00:00  02:00:00  01:30:00  01:31:00

6 rows selected.
```

If the minute portion is 30 or more, round returns the next hour. If the second portion is 30 or more, round returns the next minute.

Conversions from One Time Zone to Another: new_time

The new_time function converts a date from one time zone to another. It has three arguments:

- The date to be converted
- A text string indicating to which time zone the date pertains
- A text string indicating to which time zone the date is to be converted

The text strings for the North American time zones and Greenwich mean time are listed in Table 12.1.

Table 12.1. Time zone text string codes for North America and Greenwich mean time.

Standard code	Daylight code	Time zone
GMT		Greenwich mean time
NST		Newfoundland
AST	ADT	Atlantic
EST	EDT	Eastern

continues

Table 12.1. continued

Standard code	Daylight code	Time zone
CST	CDT	Central
MST	MDT	Mountain
PST	PDT	Pacific
YST	YDT	Yukon
HST	HDT	Hawaii-Alaska
BST	BDT	Bering

This function is useful in a number of situations:

- Systems that span several time zones, perhaps distributed, where local users want to see times as applicable for their own time zones
- Systems that span several time zones, perhaps distributed, where all dates are translated and maintained as of one time zone only
- Systems that support environments, such as aviation, that express most times in terms of Greenwich mean time

You could do the same conversions adding or subtracting numbers, but why think if you don't have to? Furthermore, the time zone code can often be obtained through a system call.

Listing 12.19 converts pacific daylight time to all the other standard and daylight time zones as applicable. In the first example, 6 hours are added to dte; in the second, 18 are added.

Listing 12.19. Converting dates using the `new_time` function.

```
--        Filename: 12squ19.sql
--         Purpose: using new_time function
--
col dtf1 heading 'dte'  format A6
col GMT     format a5
col NST     format a5
col AST     format a5
col EST     format a5
col CST     format a5
col MST     format a5
col PST     format a5
col YST     format a5
col HST     format a5
col BST     format a5

select
   to_char(dte+8/24,'HH24:MI') dtf1,
   to_char(new_time(dte+8/24,'PDT','GMT'),'HH24:MI') GMT,
   to_char(new_time(dte+8/24,'PDT','NST'),'HH24:MI') NST,
   to_char(new_time(dte+8/24,'PDT','AST'),'HH24:MI') AST,
   to_char(new_time(dte+8/24,'PDT','EST'),'HH24:MI') EST,
```

```
    to_char(new_time(dte+8/24,'PDT','CST'),'HH24:MI') CST,
    to_char(new_time(dte+8/24,'PDT','MST'),'HH24:MI') MST,
    to_char(new_time(dte+8/24,'PDT','PST'),'HH24:MI') PST,
    to_char(new_time(dte+8/24,'PDT','YST'),'HH24:MI') YST,
    to_char(new_time(dte+8/24,'PDT','HST'),'HH24:MI') HST,
    to_char(new_time(dte+8/24,'PDT','BST'),'HH24:MI') BST
from dates1
;

col ADT     format a5
col EDT     format a5
col CDT     format a5
col MDT     format a5
col PDT     format a5
col YDT     format a5
col HDT     format a5
col BDT     format a5

select
    to_char(dte+8/24,'HH24:MI') dtf1,
    to_char(new_time(dte+8/24,'PDT','GMT'),'HH24:MI') GMT,
    to_char(new_time(dte+8/24,'PDT','NST'),'HH24:MI') NST,
    to_char(new_time(dte+8/24,'PDT','ADT'),'HH24:MI') ADT,
    to_char(new_time(dte+8/24,'PDT','EDT'),'HH24:MI') EDT,
    to_char(new_time(dte+8/24,'PDT','CDT'),'HH24:MI') CDT,
    to_char(new_time(dte+8/24,'PDT','MDT'),'HH24:MI') MDT,
    to_char(new_time(dte+8/24,'PDT','PDT'),'HH24:MI') PDT,
    to_char(new_time(dte+8/24,'PDT','YDT'),'HH24:MI') YDT,
    to_char(new_time(dte+8/24,'PDT','HDT'),'HH24:MI') HDT,
    to_char(new_time(dte+8/24,'PDT','BDT'),'HH24:MI') BDT
from dates1
;

clear columns
```

This code returns

```
dte    GMT   NST   AST   EST   CST   MST   PST   YST   HST   BST
------ ----- ----- ----- ----- ----- ----- ----- ----- ----- -----
08:00  15:00 11:30 11:00 10:00 09:00 08:00 07:00 06:00 05:00 04:00
20:00  03:00 23:30 23:00 22:00 21:00 20:00 19:00 18:00 17:00 16:00
08:00  15:00 11:30 11:00 10:00 09:00 08:00 07:00 06:00 05:00 04:00
12:53  19:53 16:23 15:53 14:53 13:53 12:53 11:53 10:53 09:53 08:53
08:00  15:00 11:30 11:00 10:00 09:00 08:00 07:00 06:00 05:00 04:00
08:00  15:00 11:30 11:00 10:00 09:00 08:00 07:00 06:00 05:00 04:00

6 rows selected.

dte    GMT   NST   ADT   EDT   CDT   MDT   PDT   YDT   HDT   BDT
------ ----- ----- ----- ----- ----- ----- ----- ----- ----- -----
08:00  15:00 11:30 12:00 11:00 10:00 09:00 08:00 07:00 06:00 05:00
20:00  03:00 23:30 00:00 23:00 22:00 21:00 20:00 19:00 18:00 17:00
08:00  15:00 11:30 12:00 11:00 10:00 09:00 08:00 07:00 06:00 05:00
12:53  19:53 16:23 16:53 15:53 14:53 13:53 12:53 11:53 10:53 09:53
08:00  15:00 11:30 12:00 11:00 10:00 09:00 08:00 07:00 06:00 05:00
08:00  15:00 11:30 12:00 11:00 10:00 09:00 08:00 07:00 06:00 05:00

6 rows selected.
```

Date-Formatting Options: `to_char`

The `to_char` date function has been used in some of the examples already. It converts a date to a formatted character string. Through format masks, passed to it as a second argument, dates and times can be formatted in many different ways, which, needless to say, spares the need for extensive programming. Most formatting codes are the same as those used for the `trunc` and `round` functions.

Formatting the Date Portion (Years, Months, and Days)

If called with one argument only—the date to be processed—`to_char` returns the date in the format specified under `NLS_DATE_FORMAT`. The function is also affected by the setting of the `NLS_DATE_LANGUAGE` parameter, which sets the language in which month and day names are printed.

> **CAUTION**
>
> The length of the entire format string must not exceed 22 characters.

Inserting Text Strings

The characters -, /, ,, ., ;, and : , as well as blanks, can be inserted into the mask and will be inserted into the formatted string accordingly. Any text string can be inserted between double quotes.

Spelling Out Month and Week Days

`DAY` inserts the day name padded to nine characters; `DY` inserts a three-character day abbreviation. `MONTH` and `MON` do the same, respectively, for months. `RM` returns the month as a Roman numeral (I–XII). Listing 12.20 prints all these formats in English and German using the following code.

Listing 12.20. Printing month and day names in English and German.

```
--       Filename: 12squ20.sql
--        Purpose: printing months and days in English and German
--
col dtew    format a16
col days    format a12
col months  format a9
col digits  format a6
col roman   format a6

select
   to_char(dte,'DY, DD-MON-YYYY') dtew,
   to_char(dte,'DAY')             days,
```

```
    to_char(dte,'MONTH')               months,
    to_char(dte,'MM')                  digits,
    to_char(dte,'RM')                  roman
from dates1
;

alter session set NLS_DATE_LANGUAGE = German;

select
    to_char(dte,'DY, DD-MON-YYYY') dtew,
    to_char(dte,'DAY')                 days,
    to_char(dte,'MONTH')               months,
    to_char(dte,'MM')                  digits,
    to_char(dte,'RM')                  roman
from dates1
;

alter session set NLS_DATE_LANGUAGE = English;

clear columns
```

This code returns

```
DTEW                 DAYS           MONTHS     DIGITS  ROMAN
----------------     ------------   --------   ------- ------
THU, 08-MAY-1997 THURSDAY           MAY        05      V
THU, 08-MAY-1997 THURSDAY           MAY        05      V
SAT, 08-MAY-2010 SATURDAY           MAY        05      V
MON, 03-FEB-1997 MONDAY             FEBRUARY   02      II
THU, 14-JUL-1910 THURSDAY           JULY       07      VII
SAT, 08-MAY-2010 SATURDAY           MAY        05      V

6 rows selected.

Session altered.

DTEW                 DAYS           MONTHS     DIGITS  ROMAN
----------------     ------------   --------   ------- ------
DO, 08-MAI-1997  DONNERSTAG         MAI        05      V
DO, 08-MAI-1997  DONNERSTAG         MAI        05      V
SA, 08-MAI-2010  SAMSTAG            MAI        05      V
MO, 03-FEB-1997  MONTAG             FEBRUAR    02      II
DO, 14-JUL-1910  DONNERSTAG         JULI       07      VII
SA, 08-MAI-2010  SAMSTAG            MAI        05      V

6 rows selected.

Session altered.
```

Displaying Dates in Other Units of Time

It is possible to convert a date to a character string that displays it in other units of time, such as a century, week of the year, day of the year, and so on.

Options for Displaying Centuries and Years

There are many options for displaying years:

- ■ YYYY returns the four-digit year.

- ■ SYYYY does the same as YYYY but inserts a minus for B.C. dates as well.

- ■ YYY returns the last three digits.

- ■ YY returns the last two.

- ■ Y returns the last digit of the year.

- ■ YEAR writes out the year in English.

- ■ SYEAR does the same as YEAR but inserts a minus for B.C. dates.

Listing 12.21 demonstrates this.

Listing 12.21. Using century and year formatting options.

```
--         Filename: 12squ21.sql
--         Purpose: Century and year formatting options
--
col dtew    format a14
col SYYYY   format a5
col YYY  format a3
col YY  format a2
col Y  format a1
col YEAR  format a21
col SYEAR format a22

select
   to_char(dte,'DD-MON-YYYY B.C.')  dtew,
   to_char(dte,'SYYYY')             SYYYY,
   to_char(dte,'YYY')               YYY,
   to_char(dte,'YY')                YY,
   to_char(dte,'Y')                 Y,
   to_char(dte,'YEAR')              YEAR,
   to_char(dte,'SYEAR')             SYEAR
from dates1
;

clear columns
```

This code returns

```
DTEW           SYYYY YYY YY Y YEAR                 SYEAR
-------------- ----- --- -- - -------------------- --------------------
08-MAY-1997 AD  1997 997 97 7 NINETEEN NINETY-SEVEN NINETEEN NINETY-SEVEN
08-MAY-1997 AD  1997 997 97 7 NINETEEN NINETY-SEVEN NINETEEN NINETY-SEVEN
08-MAY-2010 AD  2010 010 10 0 TWENTY TEN           TWENTY TEN
03-FEB-1997 AD  1997 997 97 7 NINETEEN NINETY-SEVEN NINETEEN NINETY-SEVEN
14-JUL-1910 AD  1910 910 10 0 NINETEEN TEN         NINETEEN TEN
08-MAY-2010 BC -2010 010 10 0 TWENTY TEN           -TWENTY TEN

6 rows selected.
```

The YEAR format is definitely the one to use for all those fancy wedding and graduation announcements.

> **TIP**
>
> Because a whole industry has sprung up to make billions of dollars fixing the so-called year 2000 problem, it is not advisable to represent years with two digits, even if it works (as it does in SQL—at least the Oracle variety) and would be convenient. You can trust that even a manager who is so computer illiterate that he cannot distinguish a keyboard from a monitor will take issue with a two-digit year, especially after shelling out big bucks to fix this "bug" elsewhere.

Centuries are displayed using CC and SCC—the S before the year being minus for dates B.C. AD, BC, A.D., and B.C. display the respective indicators instead. Listing 12.22 demonstrates century and year formatting options.

Listing 12.22. Using century and year formatting.

```
--        Filename: 12squ22.sql
--         Purpose: Century and year formatting options
--
col dtew format a14
col CC    format a5
col SCC   format a5
col AD   format a3
col BC   format a3
col A_D_  format a5
col B_C_  format a5

select
   to_char(dte,'DD-MON-YYYY B.C.') dtew,
   to_char(dte,'CC')          CC,
   to_char(dte,'SCC')         SCC,
   to_char(dte,'AD')          AD,
   to_char(dte,'BC')          BC,
   to_char(dte,'A.D.')        A_D_,
   to_char(dte,'B.C.')        B_C_
from dates1
;

clear columns
```

This code returns

```
DTEW            CC    SCC   AD  BC  A_D_  B_C_
--------------  ----- ----- --- --- ----- ----
08-MAY-1997 AD  20       20 AD  AD  AD    AD
08-MAY-1997 AD  20       20 AD  AD  AD    AD
08-MAY-2010 AD  21       21 AD  AD  AD    AD
```

```
03-FEB-1997 AD 20      20   AD  AD  AD    AD
14-JUL-1910 AD 20      20   AD  AD  AD    AD
08-MAY-2010 BC 21     -21   BC  BC  BC    BC
```

6 rows selected.

Displaying Quarter, Day of Year, Week of Year, and Week of Month

The next set of format masks provides convenient conversions that calculate the quarter within a year, day of the year, week of the year, and week of the month of a date.

The conversions function as follows:

- ■ Q returns the quarter of the year.

- ■ DDD returns the day of the date within the year.

- ■ D returns the day of the week.

- ■ WW returns the week of the date within the year.

- ■ IW does the same as WW using the ISO standard.

- ■ W returns the week of the date within the month.

Listing 12.23 demonstrates these options.

Listing 12.23. Using date conversion functions.

```
--      Filename: 12squ23.sql
--       Purpose: quarters, day of year, week of year, and week of month
--
col dtew format a14
col Q     format a5
col DDD   format a5
col D     format a3
col WW    format a3
col IW    format a5
col W     format a5

select
    to_char(dte,'DD-MON-YYYY B.C.') dtew,
    to_char(dte,'Q')               Q,
    to_char(dte,'DDD')             DDD,
    to_char(dte,'D')               D,
    to_char(dte,'WW')              WW,
    to_char(dte,'IW')              IW,
    to_char(dte,'W')               W
from dates1
;

clear columns
```

This code returns

```
DTEW             Q      DDD   D   WW  IW    W
-------------- ----- ----- --- --- ----- ----
08-MAY-1997 AD 2      128   4   19  19    2
08-MAY-1997 AD 2      128   4   19  19    2
08-MAY-2010 AD 2      128   6   19  18    2
03-FEB-1997 AD 1      034   1   05  06    1
14-JUL-1910 AD 3      195   4   28  28    2
08-MAY-2010 BC 2      128   6   19  18    2

6 rows selected.
```

Time Display Options

Time can be displayed in various formats with or without a.m./p.m. indicators. HH is the format mask that truncates or rounds dates to hours, HH12 displays the hours in a 12-hour format, and HH24 displays hours in a 24-hour format. MI displays the minutes and SS displays the seconds. SSSSS provides a convenient conversion of seconds since midnight. AM, A.M., PM, and P.M. insert a.m. or p.m. indicators. Listing 12.24 shows the use of these masks—3/48 plus 30/86400 of a day have been added to each date (the time fraction for 1 1/2 hours and 30 seconds).

Listing 12.24. Using time display options.

```
--        Filename: 12squ24.sql
--         Purpose: time display options
--
col dtf1 heading 'dte'          format A22
col HH12      format a4
col HH24      format a4
col HH        format a3
col AM        format a3
col PM        format a3
col A_M_      format a4
col P_M_      format a4
col SSSSS     format a6

select
   to_char(dte+3/48+30/86400,'DD-MON-YYYY HH24:MI:SS') dtf1,
   to_char(dte+3/48+30/86400,'HH12')  HH12,
   to_char(dte+3/48+30/86400,'HH24')  HH24,
    to_char(dte+3/48+30/86400,'HH')   HH,
   to_char(dte+3/48+30/86400,'SSSSS') SSSSS,
   to_char(dte+3/48+30/86400,'AM')    AM,
   to_char(dte+3/48+30/86400,'PM')    PM,
   to_char(dte+3/48+30/86400,'A.M.')  A_M_,
   to_char(dte+3/48+30/86400,'P.M.')  P_M_
from dates1
;

clear columns
```

This code returns

```
dte                   HH12 HH24 HH   SSSSS   AM   PM   A_M_  P_M_
--------------------  ---- ---- ---  ------  ---  ---  ----  ----
08-MAY-1997 01:30:30  01   01   01   05430   AM   AM   AM    AM
08-MAY-1997 13:30:30  01   13   01   48630   PM   PM   PM    PM
08-MAY-2010 01:30:30  01   01   01   05430   AM   AM   AM    AM
03-FEB-1997 06:24:29  06   06   06   23069   AM   AM   AM    AM
14-JUL-1910 01:30:30  01   01   01   05430   AM   AM   AM    AM
08-MAY-2010 01:30:30  01   01   01   05430   AM   AM   AM    AM

6 rows selected.
```

Inserting Dates with Special Formatting Codes: to_date

Although sometimes it is possible to rely on an automatic conversion of a character string to a date, the to_date function does so explicitly. Similar to the to_char date function, it takes one or two arguments—one argument converts from a format that conforms with that of the NLS_DATE_FORMAT. A format string identical to those for the to_char date function can be passed in as a second argument. In that case, the format of the first argument must conform to the format string. The function will then extract the correct date from this string.

Summary

Although it falls short of the SQL-92 standard, the date datatype and the date and time functions provide a rich set of functionality for storing points in time in a native format, for calculating with these values, and for extracting and displaying specific information.

One datatype—date—is used to represent points in time that can range from January 1, 4712 B.C., to December 31, 4712 A.D. You can store values that are accurate down to the second.

Conceptually, date columns are based on days. Adding one to a date will return the date of the next day. Adding seven will return the date of a week later. Times within a day are represented as their fraction of the day. Thus 12 hours is half, 1 hour is 1/24, 1 minute is 1/1440, and 1 second is 1/86400. If you have worked with dates and times in spreadsheets, this approach will be familiar to you.

Because months are from 28 to 31 days long, adding and subtracting days does not allow you to accurately reflect months and years. However, the add_months function allows you to add months, as well as years, to a date. Although the number of days between dates can be calculated by subtracting one from another, the months_between function allows you to do the equivalent for months and years.

Other convenient functions are provided to deal with dates:

- The last_day function returns the last day of the month that contains the date passed into it.

- The next_day function returns the date after a date passed into it on which a day of the week, specified as its second argument, falls.

- Julian dates are the number of days that have passed between January 1, 4712 B.C., and the date passed in. They are obtained by specifying the J format parameter into the to_char function.

- Dates can be rounded and truncated to the date portion (years, months, days) with the round and trunc functions with one argument. In most cases trunc should also be used to compare dates, unless accuracy of the second is of concern.

- Dates can be rounded and truncated to other units of time with the round and trunc function with two arguments—a format string that indicates the time unit to which a date should be truncated or rounded.

- The new_time function provides conversions between time zones.

- Extensive formatting options of dates and times are provided through the to_char date formatting function.

- The complementary function to_date converts formatted date strings to a date, either using the NLS_DATE_FORMAT as a default or a format string passed to it as a second argument.

Extended Datatypes

IN THIS CHAPTER

ORACLE
vs SQL

Oracle provides four datatypes that are not part of the SQL standard:

- `rowid`—A unique identifier of the storage address where a record is stored
- `long`—An extension to `varchar2`, which can hold a string up to 2GB
- `raw`—A binary data string that holds up to 255 bytes
- `long raw`—A binary data string that holds up to 2GB

The `rowid` is typically used for data control work. The other three datatypes are used for special purposes, such as storing long documents or for maintaining binary data, such as sound files or graphics in the database.

Database Storage Addresses: `rowid`

To recap from Chapter 4, "Operator Conversions and Value Decoding," the row address pseudocolumn `rowid` returns the physical address of a row in the database.

> **NOTE**
>
> One of the key purposes of a database is to isolate the user from low-level tasks such as I/O or data storage. The user issues a few commands, and the database takes care of such things. It is then contrary to the purpose of a database to worry about the physical location of a record. Thus, under most circumstances, there should be no reason to use `rowid`.

However, the key features of `rowid` make this pseudocolumn valuable for data control and database administration work. These features include the following:

- `rowid` stays the same for the life of a record.
- `rowid` uniquely identifies the rows of a table and usually those in the database, except in the case of rows of *different* clustered tables, which may share the same `rowid` value. (Please see the SQL reference manual if you use the latter.)

The fact that `rowid` has its own datatype has little practical impact, except that it illustrates the need to translate between `rowid` and character strings. Conversions are usually not necessary in SQL*Plus:

- `rowid` values that are retrieved from the database are translated to character strings for display purposes.
- `rowid` values that are entered, as would be the case if they were used in a `where` clause, are written as a character string that is automatically translated.

Two functions, however, perform this conversion explicitly: `chartorowid` and `rowidtochar`.

The three numbers of rowid are, in hexadecimal notation, the following:

- The block address within the data file
- The row address within the data block
- The number of the data file

Using rowid

As the preceding note indicates, rowid is unlikely to be used for ongoing database work. There are two purposes for which using rowid values can be very convenient:

- To identify a record for deletion by its rowid
- To determine the data files in which the records of a table are stored

The fact remains that rowid is the fastest way to access a single row of data. Therefore, rowid could be used for some optimized row access scheme or as the primary key.

Using rowid to Identify Records for Deletion

The use of rowid for duplicate record deletion is explained in Listing 13.1. First, it inserts a few duplicate rows into lawyer1 to create the situation to be rectified. (For more on the insert statement, see Chapter 24, "Manipulating Single-Table Data.")

Listing 13.1. Using rowid for duplicate record deletion.

```
--        Filename: 13squ01.sql
--         Purpose: Working with ROWID
--
insert into lawyer1
   select * from lawyer1
   where id in (2,5)
;

insert into lawyer1
   select * from lawyer1
   where id in (2,5)
;
```

The next statement identifies duplicate ID numbers, which, not surprisingly, turn out to be 2 and 5—the very same numbers that the previous statements entered:

```
select
   id,
   name,
   office,
   count(*)
from
   lawyer1
having count(*) > 1
group by
```

```
   id,
   name,
   office
;
```

This code returns the following output:

```
      ID NAME              OFFICE            COUNT(*)
--------- ----------------  ----------------  ---------
       2 Cheetham          New York                 4
       5 Roach             Houston                  4
```

These values are then inserted into the next statement to list all the rows where the ID equals 2 or 5. Note that the two statements can be combined as a subquery (see Chapter 20, "Multiple-Value Subqueries," for more information about subqueries):

```
select
   id,
   name,
   office,
   rowid
from
   lawyer1
where id in (2,5)
;
```

This returns the following output:

```
      ID NAME              OFFICE            ROWID
--------- ----------------  ----------------  -------------------
       2 Cheetham          New York          00000392.0001.0002
       5 Roach             Houston           00000392.0004.0002
       2 Cheetham          New York          00000392.0014.0002
       5 Roach             Houston           00000392.0015.0002
       2 Cheetham          New York          00000392.0016.0002
       5 Roach             Houston           00000392.0017.0002
       2 Cheetham          New York          00000392.0018.0002
       5 Roach             Houston           00000392.0019.0002

8 rows selected.
```

In the example, the rows are stored in data file 2, data block 392, and rows 1, 4, and 14–19. In this case, rows 14–19 will be deleted, and the original two rows, 1 and 4, will remain.

However, if you run these examples, different `rowid` values are likely to appear; therefore, you need to edit your copy of `13squ01.sql` to reflect these different numbers. Even if you simply rerun the script, the redundant rows may have different `rowid` values.

Why is a `rowid` value used at all for this purpose? Because it is the only (pseudo) column with which these rows can be uniquely distinguished from one another.

Listing 13.2 finishes the example. The `rowid` values are copied into the next statement, which will delete the rows (see Chapter 24 for more on `delete`).

Listing 13.2. Deleting rows using rowid.

```
--        Filename: 13squ02.sql
--          Purpose: delete rows using ROWID
--
delete from lawyer1
where rowid between
   chartorowid('00000392.0014.0002') and
   chartorowid('00000392.0019.0002') ;

select
   id,
   name,
   office,
   count(*)
from
   lawyer1
having count(*) > 1
group by
   id,
   name,
   office
;

commit;
```

This code returns the following output:

```
6 rows deleted.

no rows selected

Commit complete.
```

Rerunning `13squ01.sql` results in partially different rowids for the extra rows:

```
ID NAME            OFFICE           COUNT(*)
--------- --------------- --------------- ---------
        2 Cheetham        New York               4
        5 Roach           Houston                4


     ID NAME            OFFICE          ROWID
--------- --------------- --------------- ------------------
        2 Cheetham        New York        00000392.0001.0002
        5 Roach           Houston         00000392.0004.0002
        2 Cheetham        New York        00000392.0014.0002
        5 Roach           Houston         00000392.0015.0002
        2 Cheetham        New York        00000392.0016.0002
        5 Roach           Houston         00000392.0017.0002
        2 Cheetham        New York        00000392.001A.0002
        5 Roach           Houston         00000392.001B.0002

8 rows selected.
```

13

EXTENDED
DATATYPES

Therefore, a different delete statement will be necessary. See Listing 13.3.

Listing 13.3. Deleting rows using `rowid`.

```
--        Filename: 13squ03.sql
--         Purpose: delete rows using ROWID
--
delete from lawyer1
where rowid between
   chartorowid('00000392.0014.0002') and
   chartorowid('00000392.0017.0002')
or rowid in
   (chartorowid('00000392.001A.0002'),
    chartorowid('00000392.001B.0002'));

commit;

select
   id,
   name,
   office,
   count(*)
from
   lawyer1
having count(*) > 1
group by
   id,
   name,
   office
;
```

This code returns the following:

```
6 rows deleted.


Commit complete.


no rows selected
```

Using `rowid` to Identify Data Files in Which Table Information Is Stored

The third portion of the `rowid` uniquely identifies the data file in which the row is located. Using a Data Dictionary view, the corresponding filename(s) can be found. In a small table under Personal Oracle, there is usually only one data file per tablespace (a unit of storage with which the database works). In large systems and tables, however, many files can be part of a tablespace, and knowing the file(s) in which records of a table are stored may be of value for system optimization purposes.

Listing 13.4 consists of two statements: a `distinct select` on the data file portion of `rowid` of `lawyer1`, and a query against the Data Dictionary view `dba_data_files`, from whose results the corresponding data file can be looked up.

Listing 13.4. Identifying data files using `rowid`.

```
--        Filename: 13squ04.sql
--        Purpose: Identifying datafiles through ROWID
--
select distinct
   substr(rowidtochar(rowid),instr(rowidtochar(rowid),'.',1,2) + 1,20)
from
   lawyer1
;
```

This code returns the following:

```
SUBSTR(ROWIDTOCHAR
------------------
0002
```

The second statement lists the file ID, filename, tablespace name, bytes, and status of all data files:

```
col tablespace_name  format a14   heading 'TABLESPACE¦NAME'
col file_name         format a35   heading 'FILE¦NAME'
col file_id           format 9999 heading 'FILE¦ID'
col bytes             format 999,999,999
col status            format a10

select
FILE_ID ,
TABLESPACE_NAME,
FILE_NAME,
BYTES,
STATUS
from dba_data_files
order by file_id
;
```

This code returns the following:

FILE ID	TABLESPACE NAME	FILE NAME	BYTES	STATUS
1	SYSTEM	C:\ORAWIN95\DATABASE\sys1orcl.ora	20,971,520	AVAILABLE
2	USER_DATA	C:\ORAWIN95\DATABASE\usr1orcl.ora	3,145,728	AVAILABLE
3	ROLLBACK_DATA	C:\ORAWIN95\DATABASE\rbs1orcl.ora	37,748,736	AVAILABLE
4	TEMPORARY_DATA	C:\ORAWIN95\DATABASE\tmp1orcl.ora	2,097,152	AVAILABLE

```
4 rows selected.
```

Note that these queries could be rewritten into one using joins (see Chapter 17, "Joins," for more information) and a conversion of a hexadecimal number to a decimal one.

13

EXTENDED
DATATYPES

rowid **and Character String Conversion Functions:** rowidtochar **and** chartorowid

Two functions are provided to explicitly convert rowid values to character strings, and vice versa. The rowidtochar function converts a rowid to its equivalent character string. The chartorowid function does the opposite. Both functions have been used in previous examples of the chapter: chartorowid in 13squ03.sql and rowidtochar in 13squ04.sql.

Very Long Strings: long

Columns of type long can store variable length character strings, up to 2GB long, subject to memory constraints of the host computer. In many ways, the long datatype is similar to the varchar2 datatype. There are, however, serious limitations of this datatype; the most important ones are listed here. Please consult the Oracle Server SQL Reference for all the limitations:

- They can be used only in the select comma list, set clauses of the update statement, and the values clause of the insert statement (see Chapter 24).

- Only one long column may be contained in a table.

Along with other restrictions, they cannot be used

- In the where, group by, order by, and connect by clauses of select statements

- In select distinct queries

- In SQL functions, such as the character functions available for varchar2 columns

- In aggregate queries

- In subqueries

- In queries combined through set operators (see Chapter 18, "Combining Output from Similar Tables Through Set and Pseudoset Operators")

So, basically, if you want to store long strings that otherwise would have to be stored in the filesystem in the database, the long datatype allows you to do so. Other than storing, retrieving, updating, and deleting these fields, you cannot do most other things that can be done with other columns.

Binary Datatypes: raw **and** long raw

raw and long raw datatypes are used to maintain binary data in the database. Data loaded into columns of these datatypes are stored without any further conversion. On the other hand, char, varchar2, and long datatypes may be converted to different character sets by import and export utilities, as well as SQL*Net, which is in place whenever an Oracle-based client/server or distributed setup is involved.

In essence, using binary datatypes guarantees that a string will come out of the database exactly the same way as it went in, without any conversions, and so on.

`raw(bytes)` can be up to 255 bytes long, where the argument determines the length in bytes. `long raw`, which is not defined with arguments at all, can contain up to 2GB. `long raw` columns presumably have the same limitations as `long` columns.

There are two major purposes for these datatypes. Both go beyond the scope of this book and will therefore only be touched on:

- Including bitmap or sound files in the database—It used to be that it was preferable to store lengthy sets of data as operating system files and then store only the name in the database. Because RDBMS now can handle very large databases, this is not always the case anymore. Thus, smaller files can be efficiently maintained right in the database.

- Storing whole programs or program units in the database—In an international multiuser client/server system, a user needs two things: access to the database and access to the up-to-date version of the client module necessary to run the application. Because the first must be in place at all times or else a user simply does not have access to the system, it may be worthwhile to store the modules there as well. Only one networking mechanism is then necessary for both. Oracle Forms and Reports include dedicated database tables just for that purpose. A similar approach can be used for storing modules based on third-party software.

Raw to Hexadecimal Digit String Conversion Functions: rawtohex and hextoraw

Two functions are provided to explicitly convert `raw` and `long raw` character strings to their hexadecimal digit representation, and vice versa. The `rawtohex` function converts a raw value to its equivalent hexadecimal digit string; `hextoraw` does the opposite.

Summary

Oracle provides four extended datatypes that are not part of the SQL standard.

`rowid` is a unique identifier of the storage address where a record is stored. It can be used to uniquely identify a duplicate row that needs to be deleted. `rowid` values can also be used for identifying the data files in which records of a table are stored and for fast access of single rows. Two functions—`rowidtochar` and `chartorowid`—explicitly convert `rowid` values to character strings, and vice versa.

The `long` datatype is an extension to `varchar2`. It may hold a string up to 2GB long, which is useful for storing long strings that otherwise would have to be stored in the filesystem. Other than for storing, retrieving, updating, and deleting, its use is limited.

The binary datatypes—raw and long raw—can be used to maintain binary data in the database. While char, varchar2, and long datatypes may be converted to different formats upon loading and retrieval, raw and long raw data remain unconverted.

Two functions—rawtohex and hextoraw—explicitly convert raw and long raw character strings to their hexadecimal digit representations, and vice versa.

CHAPTER 14

Datatype Conversions and Comparison Issues

The same piece of information can be represented in several different formats. A number can be represented as a fixed- or variable-length character string or as a fixed-point, a floating-point, or an integer value. A date can be represented as a date, as a floating-point number, as an integer (Julian date), or as a fixed- or variable-length character string.

Only values of the same datatype can be used in a calculation or comparison. If that condition is not met, some or all values must be converted to create consistent datatypes. In many cases, the conversion is performed automatically, but often it is necessary or at least safer to explicitly specify the use of a conversion function for this purpose.

In previous chapters, the to_char, to_number, and to_date functions have been used mainly to deal with special formatting issues. This chapter covers their use for the purpose of datatype conversions only.

Datatype conversions are most frequent when retrieving or entering data through user interfaces and when moving data from a datasource or table to another table. Comparisons across datatypes occur frequently when data from different sources are compared or when a column is compared to a constant.

Implicit Datatype Conversion

SQL, at least the Oracle version, is fairly forgiving (as far as mismatched datatypes are concerned) and will convert a value to a different datatype, except in a few ambiguous cases.

A constant in a statement—be it a comparison value, a part of a numerical conversion, an argument for a function, or a value to be inserted or updated—is acceptable to SQL only in two ways: as a number in a valid format or a string.

A number in a valid format includes the following:

- An integer, such as 50
- A fixed-point number, such as 3.1456 (a constant, by definition, is not a floating point)
- As expressed in scientific format, such as 3.7899999999E66
- A valid numerical expression, such as a fraction

If the number format is not valid, the following error will be returned:

```
ERROR:
ORA-01722: invalid number
```

A string can contain

- Characters
- A number in any of the preceding formats
- A date in the appropriate format
- A row ID in the appropriate format

If the string is properly enclosed in single quotes, the string is accepted as such. If, however, the string contains a number, date, or `rowid`, and the format is not correct, a corresponding error, such as the following, will be returned:

```
ERROR:
ORA-01722: invalid number

ERROR:
ORA-01843: not a valid month

ERROR:
ORA-01410: invalid ROWID
```

If a string is not enclosed in single quotes, one of the following errors will be returned:

```
ERROR at line 4:
ORA-00932: inconsistent datatypes
ERROR at line 4:
ORA-00904: invalid column name

ERROR at line 4:
ORA-00933: SQL command not properly ended
```

Converting Character Strings to Numeric Expressions

In a numeric expression, character-string arguments are converted to the `number` datatype. Therefore, dividing age by `'2'` (the character-string representation of 2) rather than by 2 (its numerical representation), as shown in Listing 14.1, makes no difference.

Listing 14.1. Using character and numerical representations of numbers in a numeric expression.

```
--       Filename: 14squ01.sql
--       Purpose: Implicit conversion to number

select
   age / '2',
   age / 2
from pers1
;
```

The listing code returns the following:

```
AGE/'2'    AGE/2
--------- ---------
       17        17
       46        46
      9.5       9.5
       24        24
        7         7
```

Comparing a Number and a Character String

In a comparison between a number and a character string, the character string is converted to the number datatype if its contents can be converted validly. Listing 14.2 retrieves all pers1 rows where the age is greater than 40. This happens to retrieve the same rows where the age is greater than 40.5. The last two statements return errors because the number contained in the string is not valid.

Listing 14.2. Using numeric and character representations of numbers in a comparison.

```
--      Filename: 14squ02.sql
--      Purpose: Implicit conversion to number in comparison
--
select
    *
from pers1
where age > '40'
;

select
    *
from pers1
where age > '40.5'
;

select
    *
from pers1
where age > '40.5.2'
;

select
    *
from pers1
where age > '40 1/2'
;
```

The code in the listing returns the following output:

```
    ID LNAME           FMNAME          SSN            AGE S
---------- --------------- --------------- ---------- ---------- -
     2 Martinelli      A. Emery        312331818        92 M
     4 Kratochvil      Mary T.         969825711        48 F

    ID LNAME           FMNAME          SSN            AGE S
---------- --------------- --------------- ---------- ---------- -
     2 Martinelli      A. Emery        312331818        92 M
     4 Kratochvil      Mary T.         969825711        48 F

ERROR:
ORA-01722: invalid number
```

```
no rows selected

ERROR:
ORA-01722: invalid number


no rows selected
```

Comparing a Date with a Number or a Character String

In a comparison between a date and a character string, the character string will be converted to its equivalent in the `date` datatype, if it contains the date in the same format as the `NLS_DATE_PARAMETER` active for the session. A comparison between a date and a number results in an error.

Listing 14.3 retrieves all rows from `dates1` where `dte` is greater than January 1, 1997. First, the date is entered without a single quote, which results in an error. Then the date is entered as a character string within single quotes. The string is converted to a date, after which the values are compared. The next statement is the same, except that it uses a two-digit year. This value is converted properly as well. The next statement uses the number `01` for the month. Because this is not consistent with the `NLS_DATE_FORMAT`, an error is returned. The last statement, which compares itself with the Julian date value for that date, returns an error as well.

Listing 14.3. Using numeric and character representations for dates.

```
--      Filename: 14squ03.sql
--      Purpose: Implicit conversion to date
--
select
    *
from dates1
where dte > 01-JAN-1997
;

select
    *
from dates1
where dte > '01-JAN-1997'
;

select
    *
from dates1
where dte > '01-JAN-97'
;

select
    *
from dates1
where dte > '01-01-97'
;
```

continues

Listing 14.3. continued

```
select
    *
from dates1
where dte > 2450450
;
```

This code returns the following output:

```
where dte > 01-JAN-1997
            *
ERROR at line 4:
ORA-00904: invalid column name


DTE
----------
08-MAY-1997
08-MAY-1997
08-MAY-2010
03-FEB-1997


DTE
----------
08-MAY-1997
08-MAY-1997
08-MAY-2010
03-FEB-1997
14-JUL-1910

ERROR:
ORA-01843: not a valid month


no rows selected

where dte > 2450450
            *
ERROR at line 4:
ORA-00932: inconsistent datatypes
```

DEBUG ALERT

The first example is an error because 01-JAN-1997 is not interpreted as a string at all, but as a column name—hence this particular error message.

Comparing a Row ID (rowid) and a Character String

In a comparison between a row ID (rowid) and a character string, the character string is converted to the rowid datatype if its format fits the rowid display for the server platform. Otherwise, an error may result, although the comparison is fairly forgiving. Listing 14.4 shows both cases. First, the rowid for the third record in pers1 is retrieved. That number is then inserted into the next two statements. The first one, where the rowid is not between single quotes, returns an error. The second one does an implicit conversion and works properly.

Listing 14.4. Using character and numeric representations to represent rowid.

```
--        Filename: 14squ04.sql
--         Purpose: Implicit conversion to rowid
--
select
    rowid
from pers1
where id = 3
;

select
    *
from pers1
where rowid > 00000158.0002.0002
;

select
    *
from pers1
where rowid > '00000158.0002.0002'
;
```

The statements return this output:

```
         ROWID
-----------------
00000158.0002.0002

where rowid > 00000158.0002.0002
                      *
ERROR at line 4:
ORA-00933: SQL command not properly ended


    ID LNAME          FMNAME          SSN         AGE S
--------- -------------- --------------- ---------- -------- -
     4 Kratochvil     Mary T.         969825711    48 F
     5 Melsheli       Joseph K.       000342222    14 M
```

> **NOTE**
>
> If you run this script on your machine, you need to set the active rowid for your system. To that end, run the first statement and then insert the rowid value into the second and third statements.

rowid value comparisons are fairly forgiving. A rowid string will be interpreted, even if a fourth number is added, if only the first two numbers are included and if leading zeroes are added or omitted. Only if an impossible value is included, such as a z (which has no hexadecimal meaning), will an error be returned. (See Listing 14.5.)

Listing 14.5. Converting to rowid.

```
--      Filename: 14squ05.sql
--       Purpose: Flexibility of conversions to rowid
--
select
    *
from pers1
where rowid > '00000000000158.000000002.00000002'
;

select
    *
from pers1
where rowid > '158.2.2'
;

select
    *
from pers1
where rowid >  '0000A158.0002.0002.003'
;

select
    *
from pers1
where rowid >  '0000G158.0002.0002.003'
;

select
    *
from pers1
where rowid >  '0000158.0002.'
;

select
    *
from pers1
where rowid <  '0000158.0002.'
;
```

This code returns the following:

```
    ID LNAME           FMNAME           SSN             AGE S
---------- --------------- --------------- --------- --------- -
     4 Kratochvil      Mary T.         969825711        48 F
     5 Melsheli        Joseph K.       000342222        14 M


    ID LNAME           FMNAME           SSN             AGE S
---------- --------------- --------------- --------- --------- -
     4 Kratochvil      Mary T.         969825711        48 F
     5 Melsheli        Joseph K.       000342222        14 M


no rows selected

ERROR:
ORA-01410: invalid ROWID


no rows selected


    ID LNAME           FMNAME           SSN             AGE S
---------- --------------- --------------- --------- --------- -
     1 Jones           David N.        895663453        34 M
     2 Martinelli      A. Emery        312331818        92 M
     3 Talavera        F. Espinosa     533932999        19 F
     4 Kratochvil      Mary T.         969825711        48 F
     5 Melsheli        Joseph K.       000342222        14 M


no rows selected
```

The first two examples add or eliminate leading zeroes. The output is not affected. The third statement include a `rowid` value that is a valid hexadecimal number by adding a leading A to the first number. Because no row has a `rowid` larger than this, no row is returned. The fourth statement include a `rowid` value that is not a valid hexadecimal number by adding a leading G to the first number. G is invalid because F is the highest hexadecimal digit allowed. An error is returned.

The last two examples include an incomplete `rowid` value. Every complete `rowid` value seems to be greater than an incomplete one.

Implicit Datatype Conversions in `insert` and `update` Statements

In `insert` and `update` statements, which are covered in Chapter 24, "Manipulating Single-Table Data," a value will be converted to the datatype of the column to be loaded, if necessary and possible. Listing 14.6 demonstrates this.

Listing 14.6. Inserting values with mismatched datatypes.

```
--          Filename: 14squ06.sql
--            Purpose: inserting with mismatched datatypes
--
insert into pers1 (id)
values ('15')
;

insert into pers1 (id, lname)
values ('16',67888888)
;

select
   *
from pers1
where id > 5
;
```

The first statement inserts a character string into a number. It is acceptable because the string contains a valid number. The second statement inserts a number into a string, which makes no sense but is acceptable to SQL because the number is in a valid format. The following is the output of these statements:

```
1 row created.


1 row created.


     ID LNAME           FMNAME           SSN        AGE S
-------- --------------- ---------------- --------- --------- -
     15
     16 67888888
```

The next statement updates age and fmname of the just-created columns, again using mismatched types. This statement makes no sense either, but is acceptable to SQL because the string contains a valid number, and the number can be expressed as a string. The next statement updates for the same reasons. At the end, everything is rolled back to return the table to its original state. (See Chapter 25, "Control Transactions," for more information.) Here's how it looks:

```
update pers1 set age = '99',
                 fmname = 902208420840
where id > 5
;

select
   *
from pers1
where id > 5
;


rollback;
```

The code returns the following output:

```
2 rows updated.


    ID LNAME           FMNAME          SSN           AGE S
--------- --------------- --------------- --------- ---------
    15                    902208420840                99
    16 67888888          902208420840                99


Rollback complete.
```

Explicit Datatype Conversion

Explicit datatype conversions have a number of advantages over the implicit ones:

- They can handle more sophisticated cases.
- They work consistently as a script is adapted, whereas implicit conversions might no longer work as statements become more complex.
- They work or can be made to work consistently across platforms or installations with different environmental parameters. Implicit conversions might not work after these parameters are changed.

Generally, in all but the most clear-cut cases, it is safer to use explicit conversions. On the other hand, when trying things out on the SQL interface, implicit conversions save a lot of typing and are certainly convenient.

A discussion of all conversion functions is included in the previous chapters. The emphasis thus far has been twofold: Either a value such as a date or number was to be converted to a string formatted to detailed specifications, or a string with simple or complex formatting was to be converted to its number or value equivalent. The last section of this chapter outlines the use of these functions strictly from the point of datatype conversions. Consult the previous chapters for examples of their use.

By far the most important conversions are between character strings and their equivalent values in other datatypes. Functions exist to convert character strings to and from numbers, dates, raw, long raw, and rowid values. The only conversion where character strings are not involved is between dates and integers via Julian dates.

Converting Between Character Strings and Numbers: to_number and to_char

The to_number and to_char functions provide number and character-string conversions, respectively. The implicit conversion between these datatypes works so well, however, that explicit functions are really not necessary except when formatting issues are a concern or where a "better safe than sorry" approach is taken. Listing 14.7 contains three pairs of statements, and

14

DATATYPE
CONVERSIONS
AND COMPARISONS

each pair returns the same output. The first statement in each pair uses an implicit conversion; the second uses an explicit one.

Listing 14.7. Using implicit and explicit number conversions.

```
--         Filename: 14squ07.sql
--         Purpose: implicit and explicit char/number conversions
--                  Takes substring of total income, and does some
--                  other calculations
--
select
   lname,
   age,
   interest + salary + profit + royalty income,
   substr(interest + salary + profit + royalty,1,2)
from
   pers3
;

select
   lname,
   age,
   interest + salary + profit + royalty income,
   substr(to_char(interest + salary + profit + royalty),1,2)
from
   pers3
;
```

SYBASE USE :
- SUBSTRING
- CONVERT

The code returns the same:

```
LNAME                 AGE    INCOME SU
----------------   --------   -------- --
Jones                  34     92200 92
Martinelli             92     92900 92
Talavera               19      4980 49
Kratochvil             48    188800 18
Melsheli               14        50 50
```

The substring function is used to get the two most significant digits of the income:

```
select
   lname,
   age,
   interest + salary + profit + royalty income,
   (interest + salary + profit + royalty) * 10 /
   substr(interest + salary + profit + royalty,1,2) modified_inc
from
   pers3
;

select
   lname,
   age,
   interest + salary + profit + royalty income,
   (interest + salary + profit + royalty) * 10 /
   to_number(substr(to_char
```

```
                 (interest + salary + profit + royalty),1,2)) modified_inc
from
    pers3
;
```

These statements divide the income by its two most significant digits and multiply by 10. They return the following:

```
LNAME                 AGE    INCOME MODIFIED_INC
----------------- --------- --------- ------------
Jones                  34     92200    10021.739
Martinelli             92     92900    10097.826
Talavera               19      4980    1016.3265
Kratochvil             48    188800    104888.89
Melsheli               14        50           10
```

The last two statements of the example state the income and calculate a hundredth of it:

```
select
    lname,
    age,
    interest + salary + profit + royalty income,
    (interest + salary + profit + royalty) / '100' hundredth
from
    pers3
;

select
    lname,
    age,
    interest + salary + profit + royalty income,
    (interest + salary + profit + royalty) / to_char('100') hundredth
from
    pers3
;
```

Both statements return

```
LNAME                 AGE    INCOME HUNDREDTH
----------------- --------- --------- ---------
Jones                  34     92200       922
Martinelli             92     92900       929
Talavera               19      4980      49.8
Kratochvil             48    188800      1888
Melsheli               14        50        .5
```

As you can see, a constant number expressed as a character can be included in a formula and will be implicitly converted, if necessary.

Converting Between Character Strings and Dates: to_date and to_char

The to_date and to_char functions provide conversions between dates and character strings. The implicit conversions between these datatypes do not work nearly as well as those with strings and numbers. It is, therefore, advisable to explicitly code conversions. The use of the to_char function to convert dates to strings is discussed extensively in Chapter 12, "Dates and Times: The date Datatype." Listing 14.8 includes a conversion of a date in a date calculation. It returns an error if the to_date function is not used.

Listing 14.8. Using implicit and explicit char/date conversions.

```
--         Filename: 14squ08.sql
--           Purpose: implicit and explicit char/date conversions
--
select
   trunc(dte - '01-JAN-1997') since1_1,
   trunc('31-DEC-1997' - dte) till31_12,
   trunc(dte - '01-JAN-0001') sinceyr1,
   trunc('01-JAN-2000'-dte)   tillyr2000
from dates1
;

select
   trunc(dte - to_date('01-JAN-1997')) since1_1,
   trunc(to_date('31-DEC-1997') - dte) till31_12,
   trunc(dte - to_date('01-JAN-0001')) sinceyr1,
   trunc(to_date('01-JAN-2000')-dte)   tillyr2000
from dates1
;
```

This code returns the following output:

```
trunc('01-JAN-2000'-dte)    tillyr2000
           *
ERROR at line 5:
ORA-00932: inconsistent datatypes
```

```
  SINCE1_1 TILL31_12  SINCEYR1 TILLYR2000
--------- --------- --------- ----------
      127       237    729153        968
      127       236    729153        967
     4875     -4511    733901      -3780
       33       330    729059       1061
   -31583     31947    697443      32678
 -1463417   1463781   -734391    1464512

6 rows selected.
```

Converting Between Character Strings and Row ID (rowid): rowidtochar and chartorowid

The rowidtochar and chartorowid functions, which explicitly convert rowid values to character strings, and vice versa, take only one argument: the rowid value or string to be converted. As you saw in the examples 14squ04.sql and 14squ05.sql, the implicit conversion works just fine. The statements in Listing 14.9 are equivalent to 14squ04.sql.

Listing 14.9. Converting to `rowid` explicitly.

```
--        Filename: 14squ09.sql
--        Purpose: explicit conversion to rowid
--
select
    *
from pers1
where rowid > chartorowid('00000158.0002.0002')
;

select
    *
from pers1
where rowidtochar(rowid) > '00000158.0002.0002'
;
```

They return the following output:

```
    ID LNAME           FMNAME          SSN         AGE S
--------- --------------- --------------- --------- --------- -
     4 Kratochvil      Mary T.         969825711    48 F
     5 Melsheli        Joseph K.       000342222    14 M


    ID LNAME           FMNAME          SSN         AGE S
--------- --------------- --------------- --------- --------- -
     4 Kratochvil      Mary T.         969825711    48 F
     5 Melsheli        Joseph K.       000342222    14 M
```

The comparison between these values returns the same two rows, whether compared as `rowid`s or as character-string representations. Comparing `rowid`s as character strings is not advisable because a `rowid` conversion and a string conversion are not necessarily equivalent. The last example returns an error—passing a `rowid` without single quotes into the `chartorowid` function still will not work:

```
select
    *
from pers1
where rowid > chartorowid(00000158.0002.0002)
```

It returns the following:

```
where rowid > chartorowid(00000158.0002.0002)
                                    *
ERROR at line 4:
ORA-00907: missing right parenthesis
```

Converting Between `raw` and `long raw` Values and Their Hexadecimal Digit String Equivalents: `rawtohex` and `hextoraw`

The `rawtohex` and `hextoraw` functions convert `raw` and `long raw` character strings to their hexadecimal digit representations, and vice versa.

Converting Between Dates and Their Julian Date Integer Values: `to_date` and `to_char`

The `to_date` and `to_char` functions, with the second parameter set to `'J'`, convert between dates and their Julian equivalents. Listing 14.10 demonstrates this.

Listing 14.10. Using Julian date conversions.

```
--         Filename: 14squ10.sql
--         Purpose: julian date conversions
--
--
select to_date(2400000,'J') from dual;

select to_char('01-DEC-1956','J') from dual;

select to_char(to_date('01-DEC-1956'),'J') from dual;
```

This code returns the following output:

```
TO_DATE(240
-----------
16-NOV-1858

ERROR:
ORA-01722: invalid number


no rows selected


TO_CHAR
-------
2435809
```

The second statement is another example where the implicit conversion of a string to a date does not work.

> **TIP**
>
> The use of a function called `to_char` to return a number is intuitively misleading. In the rare case that you ever will work with Julian dates, you may want to insert a comment in your script to point that out.

Summary

Although the same piece of information may be represented in several different formats, only values of the same datatype can be used in a calculation or comparison. If datatypes are not consistent, some or all values must be converted to make them so. While implicit conversions often work fine, explicit ones may be necessary or safer.

SQL will provide implicit conversions in the following cases:

- Character strings are converted to the number datatype in numeric expressions and in comparisons between numbers if their contents can be converted validly. The same holds for strings and dates, but a comparison between a date and a number results in an error.

- In a comparison between a row ID (rowid) and a character string, the character string is converted to the rowid datatype if its format is valid.

- In insert and update statements, a value will be converted to the datatype of the column to be loaded, if necessary and possible.

Explicit datatype conversions can handle more sophisticated cases. They work consistently as a script is adapted. The following functions are available:

- The to_number and to_char functions perform number/character-string conversions. The implicit conversion between these datatypes works very well, making the use of these functions less important.

- The to_date and to_char functions perform conversions between dates and character strings. They are frequently used because implicit conversions between these datatypes do not work well.

- The rowidtochar and chartorowid functions for string/rowid conversions are usually not necessary because the implicit conversions work well.

- Two functions, rawtohex and hextoraw, convert raw and long raw character strings to their hexadecimal digit representation, and vice versa.

- The to_date and to_char functions, with the second parameter set to 'J', convert between dates and their Julian equivalents.

14

DATATYPE CONVERSIONS AND COMPARISONS

Missing Data, Null, and Zero Values

CHAPTER 15

IN THIS CHAPTER

Building a computing system and processing data with it is an exercise in abstraction. It begins when someone cares enough about a given reality to spend time and resources to represent it. Examples of representative realities include the planets in the sky and their orbits, and customers of a business and their characteristics and actions. These entities and their *attributes*, as they are called in relational theory, can somehow be translated into tables and columns. Tables and columns must represent these realities closely enough that the system's purpose can be fulfilled. Eventually, these realities boil down to all zeroes and ones.

Decision rules and algorithms are necessary to translate a characteristic of an entity, such as a planet or person, into something meaningful in a table. If a set of decision rules and algorithms fails, missing values result. Missing values include unknown values, nonapplicable values, values too large or too small to handle (overflows and underflows), and so on. A *missing value* is not the same as zero. A bank account with a zero balance has no money in it; a bank account with a null balance might have a balance, the balance might be unknown, or the account might not exist at all, among other possibilities.

No matter the reason why a value is missing, SQL has only one way to express it: as a null value or token or, in short, a null. *Null* means no value. Using nulls has a few advantages and many disadvantages over alternatives. You can decide not to use nulls at all, but you must be certain that the data in tables with which you are working do not contain any. If you cannot be certain that they do not, it is helpful to know how nulls function:

- Null values in aggregate functions are ignored. This is the most important feature of nulls that ensures accurate results.
- Conditional statements are extended from a boolean two-valued `true`/`false` logic to a Lukasiewiczian three-valued `true`/`false`/unknown logic.
- All operators except ¦¦ return null if any of the operands are null.
- To test for null, use the comparison operators `is null` and `is not null`.
- A conversion function with `null` as an argument returns null.

This chapter starts by discussing the treatment of nulls in aggregate functions, which is where they are most useful. The next section includes the `nvl` function, which converts a null to a value passed as its second argument. Later sections explain and demonstrate the effect of `null` on other issues. Whether these effects are good or a kludge is in the eye of the beholder; it is still important to consider them.

 Run `crper8.sql`, which can be found on the CD-ROM accompanying this book, to create and load the table `pers8`. This table is similar to `pers4`, but it has 10 records with some nulls included in all but the `ID` column.

Nulls in Aggregate Functions

The biggest advantage of nulls is that aggregate functions ignore them in all calculations. Most affected by this feature are the `count` and `average` functions.

The Effect of Nulls on count

If the argument to count is a constant or a column without nulls, count will return the number of rows to which a certain condition or grouping applies. If the argument is a column that includes nulls, count will return the number of rows that are not null to which a certain condition or grouping applies.

If this feature of null were not available, the nonapplicable and missing values would have to be excluded through the where clause. Listing 15.1 shows the results of count against the pers8 table.

Listing 15.1. Counting over columns that contain nulls.

```
--        Filename: 15squ01.sql
--        Purpose: count over columns containing nulls
--
select
   count(1) c1,
   count(*) call,
   count(id) cid,
   count(interest) cint,
   count(salary) csal,
   count(profit) cpro,
   count(wealth) cwea,
   count((interest + salary + profit)/wealth) ciow
from pers8
;
```

This code returns the following output:

C1	CALL	CID	CINT	CSAL	CPRO	CWEA	CIOW
10	10	10	9	9	10	9	7

The columns C1, CALL, CID, and CPRO return the number of all rows. C1 counts a constant, and CALL *, CID, and CPRO count columns without nulls. The columns for interest, salary, and wealth have one null value each, but in different rows. Therefore, individually they return nine rows, but as a formula they return only seven. Whenever there is a null in a conversion formula, the result is null, as you can see from the upcoming example.

The behavior of count(*) is not dependent on nulls; it returns the same value as count(1), even if all values in a row or table are nulls. Listing 15.2 uses create view and create table statements (see Chapter 26, "Insertable Single-Table Views," and Chapter 28, "Creating Tables," for more on these statements). The pers8 view contains only the interest, salary, and wealth columns from pers8, each of which contains one null value in different rows.

Listing 15.2. Retrieving the value of count(*) in several null cases.

```
--        Filename: 15squ02.sql
--        Purpose: return value of count(*) in several null cases
```

continues

Listing 15.2. continued

```
--
create view pers8v
as
select
   interest,
   salary,
   wealth
from pers8
;

select count(*) from pers8v;

drop view pers8v;
```

This code returns the following output:

```
View created.


 COUNT(*)
---------
       10


View dropped.
```

The next part of the example creates a table called `nulltest`. Even if all values in all columns are nulls, `count(*)` returns all rows of the table, as follows:

```
create table nulltest (
    nt1   char(1),
    nt2   char(1),
    interest number(8));

insert into nulltest
select
   null,
   null,
   null
from pers1
;

select count(*) from nulltest;
```

This code returns

```
Table created.


5 rows created.


 COUNT(*)
---------
        5


Table truncated.
```

As this example demonstrates, there should never be a reason to use `count(*)`. Use `count(1)` instead.

The Effect of Nulls on `avg`

An *average* of a set of numbers equals the sum of the numbers divided by the number of elements in the set. If, however, some elements are null, meaning that their value is unknown or nonexistent, dividing by the number of all elements will result in an incorrect mean. For example, consider a set containing five children: Jakob, Charles, Anissa, Nicole, and Michael. Jakob is 54 inches tall, Charles is 43, Anissa is 55, and Nicole is 44. Michael, however, was sick when the children were measured, so his height is unknown. The sum of the heights is 196. If you want to know the average height of the children without knowing Michael's height, you have a few options:

- Wait a couple of days until Michael is better and can be measured.
- Decide that the average height cannot be determined at this time.
- Go with the numbers you have and adjust for the fact that Michael's height is not known.
- Treat Michael's height as if it were zero to err on the safe side.

The first two options are respectable but not always feasible. The third option is what SQL does—it simply calculates the average height of those children whose heights are known. It sums the heights to 196 and divides it by the count of nonnull values—4—for an average height of 49. Or, in generalized terms, the avg function calculates the average of all known values of a set of values.

But what should be done if it is important to know the true average of the heights of all five children and not just the four whose heights are known? Inferential statistics offers many methods for this purpose. In simplified terms, if the sample (the four kids whose heights are known) is representative of all the kids, the average height of the sample is the best estimate for Michael's height. Because adding 49 to the four other values and dividing the sum by 5 yields the same 49, 49 is also the best estimate for the average height of all five children. The fourth option, on the other hand, uses an extremely poor estimate for Michael's height—0—that then yields 39.2, almost 5 inches less than the lowest individual value.

> **NOTE**
>
> The first version of Lotus 1-2-3 was hampered by the same problem: If a range that was averaged contained nulls, the result was calculated by dividing the sum of the values by the total number of cells in the range, including the null cells. This approach understated the mean. In one of the earlier upgrades, the formula was changed to not include null cells in the denominator.

Listing 15.3 sums, counts, and averages columns from pers8. The average is first calculated by dividing the sum by the count and then using the avg function.

Listing 15.3. Calculating the average with columns containing nulls.

```
--        Filename: 15squ03.sql
--        Purpose: average over columns containing nulls
--
select
   sum(id)    sumid,
   count(id) cntid,
   sum(id)/count(id) avg1id,
   avg(id) avgid
from pers8
;

select
   sum(interest)    sumint,
   count(interest) cntint,
   sum(interest)/count(interest) avg1int,
   avg(interest) avgint
from pers8
;

select
   sum(salary)    sumsal,
   count(salary) cntsal,
   sum(salary)/count(salary) avg1sal,
   avg(salary) avgsal
from pers8
;

select
   sum(profit)    sumprofit,
   count(profit) cntprofit,
   sum(profit)/count(profit) avg1profit,
   avg(profit) avgprofit
from pers8
;

select
   sum(wealth)    sumwealth,
   count(wealth) cntwealth,
   sum(wealth)/count(wealth) avg1wealth,
   avg(wealth) avgwealth
from pers8
;

select
   sum((interest + salary + profit)/wealth)    sumiow,
   count((interest + salary + profit)/wealth) cntiow,
   sum((interest + salary + profit)/wealth)
          /count((interest + salary + profit)/wealth) avg1iow,
   avg((interest + salary + profit)/wealth) avgiow
from pers8
;
```

All calculations return correct values:

```
    SUMID     CNTID   AVG1ID    AVGID
--------- --------- --------- ---------
       55        10       5.5       5.5


   SUMINT    CNTINT  AVG1INT   AVGINT
--------- --------- --------- ---------
    51045         9 5671.6667 5671.6667


   SUMSAL    CNTSAL  AVG1SAL   AVGSAL
--------- --------- --------- ---------
   123307         9 13700.778 13700.778


SUMPROFIT CNTPROFIT AVG1PROFIT AVGPROFIT
--------- --------- ---------- ---------
   503748        10    50374.8   50374.8


SUMWEALTH CNTWEALTH AVG1WEALTH AVGWEALTH
--------- --------- ---------- ---------
  7134590         9 792732.22 792732.22


   SUMIOW    CNTIOW  AVG1IOW   AVGIOW
--------- --------- --------- ---------
18.635222         7 2.6621745 2.6621745
```

Replacing Null with Defined Values: nvl

The nvl function is a relative of the decode function. It takes two arguments: a value or column to be processed and the value to return in case the first value or column is null.

Listing 15.4 reworks parts of 15squ03.sql and 15squ02.sql by setting missing values to zeroes using the nvl function. Notice the wrong values for averages that are returned this way.

Listing 15.4. Using the nvl function.

```
--        Filename: 15squ04.sql
--         Purpose: average over columns containing nulls
--                  using nullvalue
--
select
   sum(interest)    sumint,
   sum(nvl(interest,0))   nsumint,
   count(interest) cntint,
   count(nvl(interest,0)) ncntint,
   avg(interest) avgint,
   avg(nvl(interest,0)) wrong
```

continues

Listing 15.4. continued

```
from pers8
;

select
   sum(salary)    sumsal,
   sum(nvl(salary,0))    nsumsal,
   count(salary) cntsal,
   count(nvl(salary,0)) ncntsal,
   avg(salary) avgsal,
  avg(nvl(salary,0)) wrong
from pers8
;
```

This code returns the following output:

SUMINT	NSUMINT	CNTINT	NCNTINT	AVGINT	WRONGAVG
51045	51045	9	10	5671.6667	5104.5

SUMSAL	NSUMSAL	CNTSAL	NCNTSAL	AVGSAL	WRONGAVG
123307	123307	9	10	13700.778	12330.7

As the output shows, null values are treated as if they were zero. Combining the avg function with the nvl function returns the wrong, understated result.

If a column has only nulls, aggregate functions return null as well. The following example shows this in the table nulltest. The select statement returns the sum, minimum, and count of a column with and without the use of nvl, as follows:

```
create table nulltest (
   nt1   char(1),
   nt2   char(1),
   interest number(8));

insert into nulltest
select
   null,
   null,
   null
from pers1
;

select
   sum(nt1) null_sum,
   sum(nvl(nt1,0)) nvl_sum,
   min(interest) null_min,
   min(nvl(interest,0)) nvl_min,
   count(nt1) null_cnt,
   count(nvl(nt1,0)) nvl_cnt
from nulltest
;

drop table nulltest;
```

This code returns

```
NULL_SUM   NVL_SUM  NULL_MIN   NVL_MIN  NULL_CNT   NVL_CNT
---------  -------- ---------  -------- ---------  -------
                 0                   0         0         5
```

Table dropped.

SQL-92's term for the function `nvl` is `coalesce`. It takes the same arguments and returns the same output as `nvl`.

ORACLE
vs SQL

Replacing a Value with Null: decode (nullif)

The SQL-92 standard includes the opposite of the `nvl` function, which is called `nullif`. If a column includes one or more values that indicate missing or nonapplicable values, averaging that column will not render correct results. By using `nullif`, such a value can be converted to a null. If missing values in the age column are coded as the value 9, `nullif(age,9)` will return an age in most cases, but will return 9 where it would otherwise return a null. Oracle does not have a `nullif` function, but `decode` can be used for that purpose: `decode(age,9,NULL,age)` is equivalent to `nullif(age,9)`. Listing 15.5 includes this subclause in a number of aggregations.

ORACLE
vs SQL

Listing 15.5. Using the decode function to produce nullif results.

```
--        Filename: 15squ05.sql
--        Purpose: faking nullif with decode
--
select
   sum(age)    sumage,
   sum(decode(age,9,NULL,age))   dcsumage,
   count(age) cntage,
   count(decode(age,9,NULL,age)) dccntage,
   avg(age) avgage,
   avg(decode(age,9,NULL,age)) dcavgage
from pers8
;
```

This code returns

```
 SUMAGE  DCSUMAGE   CNTAGE  DCCNTAGE   AVGAGE  DCAVGAGE
--------- --------- -------- --------- -------- ---------
     329       320        9         8 36.555556        40
```

Evaluating Three-Valued Conditional Statements

Conditional statements in the absence of nulls return one of two values: `true` or `false`. If nulls can occur in a column, a third value can be returned: `unknown`. In this revised scheme, the condition `where 2 = 2` evaluates as `true` and `where 2 = 4` evaluates as `false`, similar to a boolean scheme. The added option `where 2 = NULL` evaluates to unknown. The statement `where age = 43` would evaluate to `true` if the age were really 43, to `false` if the age were unequal to 43, and to unknown if the age were null. Therefore, now that null is included, SQL's processing of conditional statements is quite different from that of most other computer languages.

This three-valued logic has an impact on conditions and logical operators, as explained in the following sections.

Nulls in Conditions

If no nulls are possible in a condition, a condition and its opposite will retrieve all rows in a table or subset. If nulls are possible, a third statement is necessary—it retrieves just those rows where the value is null. Listing 15.6 first returns the number of records in `pers8` and then returns rows in three sets, where `sex` is male, female, or unknown.

Listing 15.6. Retrieving nulls in conditions.

```
--         Filename:  15squ06.sql
--          Purpose:  retrieve rows
--                    where sex equals male, female, or null
--
select count(1)
from pers8
;

select
   id,
   lname,
   sex,
   '##' || sex || '##' sxpad
from pers8
where sex = 'M'
;

select
   id,
   lname,
   sex,
   '##' || sex || '##' sxpad
from pers8
where sex = 'F'
;

select
   id,
   lname,
   sex,
   '##' || sex || '##' sxpad
from pers8
where sex is null
;
```

The statements return

```
COUNT(1)
---------
       10
```

```
        ID LNAME           S SXPAD
--------- --------------- - -----
         1 Jones           M ##M##
         2 Martinelli      M ##M##
         5 Melsheli        M ##M##
         8 Rochblatt       M ##M##
         9 Nungaray        M ##M##


        ID LNAME           S SXPAD
--------- --------------- - -----
         3                 F ##F##
         4 Kratochvil      F ##F##
         6 Robinson        F ##F##
        10 Oberstein       F ##F##


        ID LNAME           S SXPAD
--------- --------------- - -----
         7                   ####
```

> **TIP**
>
> sex is a fixed-length character string of length 1, meaning that a value would be blank-padded. One way to see whether such a column contains a null is to pad it between some character constants. If there is a blank between the constants, it is a blank value. If there is nothing between the pad characters, as in the last row, it is a null.

You can retrieve the same information simply by ordering the output by the sex column, which is done in Listing 15.7.

Listing 15.7. Using `order by` to retrieve nulls in conditions.

```
--        Filename: 15squ07.sql
--        Purpose: retrieve rows
--                 order by sex equals male, female, or null
--
break on sex skip 1

select
   id,
   lname,
   sex,
   '##' || sex || '##' sxpad
```

continues

15

MISSING DATA, NULL, AND ZERO VALUES

Listing 15.7. continued

```
from pers8
order by sex
;

clear breaks
```

This code returns

```
        ID LNAME            S SXPAD
--------- ---------------- - -----
         3                 F ##F##
         4 Kratochvil        ##F##
         6 Robinson          ##F##
        10 Oberstein         ##F##

         1 Jones           M ##M##
         8 Rochblatt         ##M##
         9 Nungaray          ##M##
         5 Melsheli          ##M##
         2 Martinelli        ##M##

         7                   ####
```

```
10 rows selected.
```

The Effect of Nulls on Logical Expressions

Chapter 10, "Compound Conditions and Logical Operators," discusses the use of the three logical operators: not, and, and or. All of these are affected by nulls.

Logical Not: not

When null is not used, the unary not operator reverses a true evaluation to false, and vice versa. A not null, however, still returns null. In other words, if the state is known, which means either true or false, not reverses it. If the state is unknown, meaning null, nothing can be said about the state; therefore, reversing it still keeps it unknown.

Figure 15.1 illustrates the effect of the not operator.

CAUTION

Using not in situations where null should be used is asking for trouble. If you see such a reversal in a script, it is very likely an error.

FIGURE 15.1.

Return value of three-valued not *operations.*

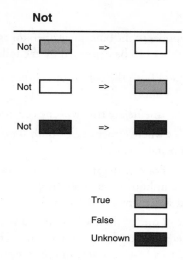

The not null case must be distinguished from the is not null condition, which is the opposite of is null. In essence, the use of is null and is not null leads to two-level logic. The top level distinguishes a value through is null or is not null, separating the known from the unknown values. The second level applies to the known values only, for which a comparative condition can return true or false. (See Listings 15.6 and 15.7 for examples.) Figure 15.2 illustrates this two-level logic as a block diagram.

FIGURE 15.2.

Two-level logic not *operations.*

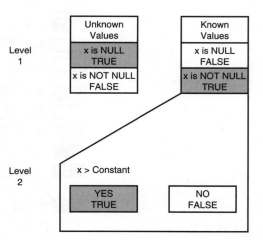

Logical And: and

The two-level logic applies to the binary and operator as well. The outcomes of both statements, of only one, or of neither can be discerned by the following criteria:

- If the outcomes of both the conditions compounded by the and operator are known, the boolean rules apply.
- Only if both statements are true will the compound statement be true.
- In all other cases where either one or both statements are false, the compound and statement will be false as well.
- If the outcome of one of the statements is unknown and the other statement is true, it matters that the unknown statement might be true as well. Therefore, the outcome of the compound statement is unknown.
- If the outcome of one of the statements is unknown and the other statement is false, it does not matter whether the unknown statement is true or false. One false statement suffices to lead to a false outcome of the compound condition.
- If the outcome of both statements is unknown, it is not possible to determine the outcome of the compound statement, which is therefore unknown as well.

Figure 15.3 summarizes the outcome of compound and conditions.

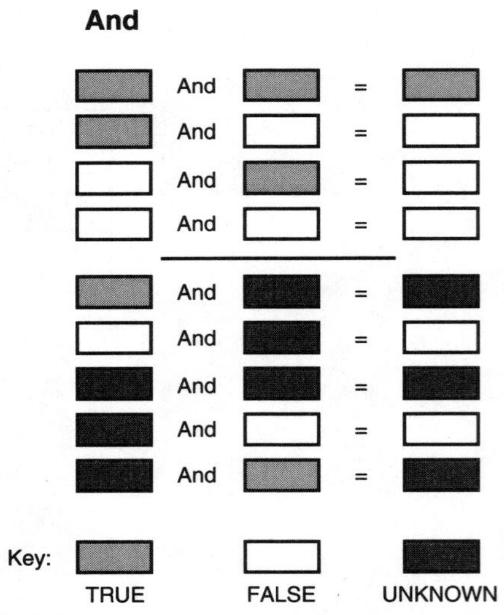

FIGURE 15.3.

Return value of valued compound and conditions.

And

Key: TRUE   FALSE   UNKNOWN

The approach in Listing 15.6 applies here as well, in essence separating the query for unknown values and the condition in question. The only rows returned are the ones where the compound condition is true. An is null condition has to be used to retrieve the unknown values.

Thus, the and condition retrieves all rows for which both conditions are true. A countervailing or condition retrieves all rows for which at least one condition is false. In that case it does not matter whether the other condition is true, false, or unknown; the compound outcome is false.

The last query retrieves the rows where the compound condition is unknown. This is a nested query where three compound and conditions are compounded by or:

- Both subcondition outcomes are unknown.
- The first subcondition outcome is unknown, and the other one is true.
- The first subcondition outcome is true, and the other one is unknown.

Listing 15.8, an adaptation of Listing 15.6 (`15squ06.sql`), shows these compound conditions.

Listing 15.8. Using compound conditions to retrieve data.

```
--        Filename: 15squ08.sql
--         Purpose: retrieve rows
--                  where sex equals male, female, or null
--                  and age > or < 36
--
select
   id,
   lname,
   sex,
   age
from pers8
where sex = 'M'
and age < 36
;

select
   id,
   lname,
   sex,
   age
from pers8
where sex = 'F'
or age >= 36
;

select
   id,
   lname,
   sex,
   age
from pers8
where (sex is null and age is null) or
      (sex = 'M'    and age is null) or
      (sex is null and age < 36    )
;
```

This code returns

```
    ID LNAME            S      AGE
--------- --------------- - ---------
     1 Jones            M       34
     5 Melsheli         M       14
     8 Rochblatt        M       32


    ID LNAME            S      AGE
--------- --------------- - ---------
     2 Martinelli       M       92
     3                  F       19
     4 Kratochvil       F       48
     6 Robinson         F
     9 Nungaray         M       58
    10 Oberstein        F        9

6 rows selected.


    ID LNAME            S      AGE
--------- --------------- - ---------
     7                           23
```

Logical Or: or

Complementary to the and operator with nulls present, the or operator also deals with the three situations where the outcomes of both statements, of only one, or of neither statement might be known. It does so in the following way:

- If the outcomes of both the conditions compounded by the and operator are known, the boolean rules apply.

- If at least one statement is true, the compound statement will be true.

- If both statements are false, the compound statement will be false as well.

- If the outcome of one of the statements is unknown and the other statement is true, it does not matter whether the unknown statement is true or false. One true statement suffices to lead to a true outcome of the compound or condition.

- If the outcome of one of the statements is unknown and the other statement is false, it does matter whether the unknown statement is true. Therefore, the outcome of the compound statement is unknown.

- Similar to the compound and statements, if the outcome of both statements is unknown, it is not possible to determine the outcome of the compound statement, which is therefore unknown as well.

Figure 15.4 summarizes the outcome of compound or conditions.

FIGURE 15.4.
Return value of three-valued compound or *conditions.*

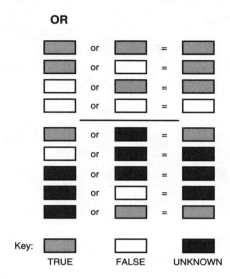

Three queries analogous to the compound and situation have to be used as well to retrieve all rows in mutually exclusive sets. The three possible outcomes of the compound statement are retrieved through three separate queries. The or condition retrieves all rows for which one or both conditions are true. In that case, it does not matter whether the other condition is true, false, or unknown; the compound outcome is true. A countervailing and condition retrieves all rows if neither condition is true.

The last query retrieves the rows where the compound condition is unknown. This is a nested query where three compound and conditions are compounded by or:

- Both subcondition outcomes are unknown.
- The first subcondition outcome is unknown and the other one is false.
- The first subcondition outcome is false and the other one is unknown.

As you will see, Listing 15.9 illustrates this approach and is a complementary example to 15squ08.sql (Listing 15.8). The listings are similar, but the conditions are slightly different.

Listing 15.9. Using the or operator to retrieve data.

```
--       Filename: 15squ09.sql
--        Purpose: retrieve rows
--                 where sex equals male, female, or null
--                 or age > 36
--
select
   id,
   lname,
   sex,
```

15

MISSING DATA, NULL, AND ZERO VALUES

continues

Listing 15.9. continued

```
    age
from pers8
where sex = 'M'
or age > 50
;

select
    id,
    lname,
    sex,
    age
from pers8
where sex = 'F'
and age <= 50
;

select
    id,
    lname,
    sex,
    age
from pers8
where (sex is null and age is null) or
      (sex = 'F'   and age is null) or
      (sex is null and age <= 50    )
;
```

This returns

```
       ID LNAME            S      AGE
--------- --------------- - ---------
        1 Jones            M       34
        2 Martinelli       M       92
        5 Melsheli         M       14
        8 Rochblatt        M       32
        9 Nungaray         M       58


       ID LNAME            S      AGE
--------- --------------- - ---------
        3                  F       19
        4 Kratochvil       F       48
       10 Oberstein        F        9


       ID LNAME            S      AGE
--------- --------------- - ---------
        6 Robinson         F
        7                          23
```

Nulls in Conversion Functions

A conversion function with null as an argument returns null. Listing 15.10, an adaptation of several examples in Chapter 5, "Single-Row Numerical Functions," shows such behavior.

Listing 15.10. Using a conversion function with null as an argument.

```
--        Filename: 15squ10.sql
--        Purpose: nulls as argument to functions
--
select
   abs(interest + salary + profit + royalty) absinc,
   sign(interest + salary + profit + royalty) signinc,
   (interest + salary + profit + royalty) / wealth incowea,
   ceil((interest + salary + profit + royalty) / wealth) ceiliow,
   floor((interest + salary + profit + royalty) / wealth) flooriow,
   mod((interest + salary + profit + royalty) / wealth, .5) remainp5
from pers8
;
```

This returns

ABSINC	SIGNINC	INCOWEA	CEILIOW	FLOORIOW	REMAINP5
92200	1	-.6447552	0	-1	-.1447552
92900	1	.14403101	1	0	.14403101
4980	1	.2075	1	0	.2075
188800	1	.078647	1	0	.078647
0	0	0	0	0	0
37700	1	18.85	19	18	.35
110791	1	.39288982	1	0	.39288982
0	0				

10 rows selected.

Notice the two zeroes in the last row. They stem from the fact that wealth, which is null in the last row, is not included in the first two expressions. The second part of the example shows the individual values:

```
select
   interest,
   salary,
   profit,
   royalty,
   wealth
from pers8
where id > 7
;
```

This returns

INTEREST	SALARY	PROFIT	ROYALTY	WEALTH
	4870	0	0	24000
3670		289000	0	3899200
0	0	0	0	

Nulls in Conversion Operations

All operators except ¦¦ return null if any of the operands are null. This is demonstrated in Listing 15.11, where such operations have a NULL operand. As a result, the whole conversion/calculation is deleted from the machine. The concatenation with null values is shown in Listing 15.7.

> **NOTE**
>
> Concurring with both Chris Date and Joe Celko (refer back to Chapter 1, "Introduction to SQL"), I recommend avoiding nulls as much as possible. I would allow nulls in columns designed to be aggregated to take advantage of the way SQL deals with nulls in counts and averages. In almost all other cases, especially in categorical values, nulls should not be allowed, and sets of predefined values should be used to indicate missing, nonapplicable, or otherwise unknown data.

Division by Zero

A witty person once wrote that the only original sin of mankind was division by zero. The problem with this operation is that mathematics has not defined its outcome. As a result, the computer does not know what to do, and processing stops with an error (or it should). Listing 15.11 demonstrates this problem.

Listing 15.11. Division by zero.

```
--       Filename: 15squ11.sql
--        Purpose: division by zero
--
select
   interest,
   salary,
   profit,
   royalty,
   interest + salary + profit + royalty total
from pers8
;
```

This returns

INTEREST	SALARY	PROFIT	ROYALTY	TOTAL
200	80000	12000	0	92200
24000	0	5000	63900	92900
110	4870	0	0	4980
4800	0	184000	0	188800
0	0	0	0	0
400	32000	5300	0	37700
17865	1567	8448	82911	110791

```
                  4870            0            0
         3670              289000            0
            0       0         0         0         0
```

```
10 rows selected.
```

Thus far everything has worked fine. However, a fairly typical report would list only the dollar values for the total and the percentages for the components that make up the total. The following statement attempts to do this:

```
col intpct format 99.99
col salpct format 99.99
col propct format 99.99
col roypct format 99.99

select
   interest + salary + profit + royalty total,
   interest*100/( interest + salary + profit + royalty) intpct,
   salary  *100/( interest + salary + profit + royalty) salpct,
   profit  *100/( interest + salary + profit + royalty) propct,
   royalty *100/( interest + salary + profit + royalty) roypct
from pers8
;

clear columns
```

It returns

```
ERROR:
ORA-01476: divisor is equal to zero

no rows selected
```

In the 5th and 10th row, the divisor is zero, indeed, because these two people have no income from any source.

The preferable way to deal with such a situation is to convert the mathematically undefined case to the unknown case in SQL using null. decode or nullif converts the divisor to a null if it is zero, as is done in Listing 15.12.

Listing 15.12. Avoiding division by zero using null.

```
--         Filename: 15squ12.sql
--          Purpose: avoid division by zero through null
--
col intpct format 99.99
col salpct format 99.99
col propct format 99.99
col roypct format 99.99

select
   interest + salary + profit + royalty total,
   interest*100/decode(interest + salary + profit + royalty,
                0,NULL,interest + salary + profit + royalty) intpct,
   salary  *100/decode(interest + salary + profit + royalty,
                0,NULL,interest + salary + profit + royalty) salpct,
```

continues

Listing 15.12. continued

```
    profit  *100/decode(interest + salary + profit + royalty,
                0,NULL,interest + salary + profit + royalty) propct,
    royalty *100/decode(interest + salary + profit + royalty,
                0,NULL,interest + salary + profit + royalty) roypct
from pers8
;

clear columns
```

This returns

```
   TOTAL INTPCT SALPCT PROPCT ROYPCT
---------- ------ ------ ------ ------
    92200    .22  86.77  13.02    .00
    92900  25.83    .00   5.38  68.78
     4980   2.21  97.79    .00    .00
   188800   2.54    .00  97.46    .00
        0
    37700   1.06  84.88  14.06    .00
   110791  16.12   1.41   7.63  74.84


        0

10 rows selected.
```

Assuming that a missing income component means zero, a few more rows could be reported on, as Listing 15.13 shows.

Listing 15.13. Avoiding division by zero using `null` and `nvl`.

```
--          Filename: 15squ13.sql
--           Purpose: avoid division by zero through NULL
--                    combine with nvl
--
col intpct format 999.99
col salpct format 999.99
col propct format 999.99
col roypct format 999.99

select
    nvl(interest,0) + nvl(salary,0) +
        nvl(profit,0) + nvl(royalty,0) total,
    interest*100/decode(nvl(interest,0) + nvl(salary,0) +
                    nvl(profit,0) + nvl(royalty,0),
                0,NULL,nvl(interest,0) + nvl(salary,0) +
                    nvl(profit,0) + nvl(royalty,0)) intpct,
    salary  *100/decode(nvl(interest,0) + nvl(salary,0) +
                    nvl(profit,0) + nvl(royalty,0),
                0,NULL,nvl(interest,0) + nvl(salary,0) +
                    nvl(profit,0) + nvl(royalty,0)) salpct,
    profit  *100/decode(nvl(interest,0) + nvl(salary,0) +
                    nvl(profit,0) + nvl(royalty,0),
                0,NULL,nvl(interest,0) + nvl(salary,0) +
                    nvl(profit,0) + nvl(royalty,0)) propct,
```

```
    royalty *100/decode(nvl(interest,0) + nvl(salary,0) +
                      nvl(profit,0) + nvl(royalty,0),
               0,NULL,nvl(interest,0) + nvl(salary,0) +
                      nvl(profit,0) + nvl(royalty,0)) roypct
from pers8
;

clear columns
```

This returns

```
   TOTAL  INTPCT  SALPCT  PROPCT  ROYPCT
---------- ------- ------- ------- -------
    92200     .22   86.77   13.02     .00
    92900   25.83     .00    5.38   68.78
     4980    2.21   97.79     .00     .00
   188800    2.54     .00   97.46     .00
        0
    37700    1.06   84.88   14.06     .00
   110791   16.12    1.41    7.63   74.84
     4870          100.00     .00     .00
   292670    1.25           98.75     .00
        0
```

10 rows selected.

For the purpose of reporting, the fact that the total is zero is obvious, and whether correct or not, we can live with all zeroes for the percentages in this case. One problem is that although all percentages ought to add up to 100, they will not with this approach. On the other hand, if any value were chosen for the total, 0 over that value is still 0.

This approach goes beyond SQL; it uses a user function called nulldiv, which returns the quotient if the division is unequal to zero and a zero if both numbers are zero. It will still return a zero division error if the numerator is unequal to zero but the divisor is not, which it should. Listing 15.14 demonstrates this.

Listing 15.14. Creating the nulldiv function.

```
--        Filename: 15squ14.sql
--        Purpose: nulldiv function
--
create or replace function nulldiv
          (numerator in number, denominator in number)
           RETURN number    is
    quotient number;
begin
    if numerator = 0 and denominator = 0 then
        quotient := 0;
    else
        quotient:= numerator/denominator;
    end if;
    return quotient;
end nulldiv;
/
```

This code returns

```
Function created.
```

The script then uses the nulldiv function as shown in Listing 15.15.

Listing 15.15. Using the nulldiv function.

```
--         Filename: 15squ15.sql
--          Purpose: use nulldiv function
--
col intpct format 999.99
col salpct format 999.99
col propct format 999.99
col roypct format 999.99

select
    nvl(interest,0) + nvl(salary,0) +
        nvl(profit,0) + nvl(royalty,0) total,
    nulldiv(interest*100, nvl(interest,0) + nvl(salary,0) +
                        nvl(profit,0) + nvl(royalty,0)) intpct,
    nulldiv(salary  *100, nvl(interest,0) + nvl(salary,0) +
                        nvl(profit,0) + nvl(royalty,0)) salpct,
    nulldiv(profit  *100,nvl(interest,0) + nvl(salary,0) +
                        nvl(profit,0) + nvl(royalty,0)) propct,
    nulldiv(royalty *100,nvl(interest,0) + nvl(salary,0) +
                        nvl(profit,0) + nvl(royalty,0)) roypct
from pers8
;

clear columns
```

This returns

```
    TOTAL   INTPCT  SALPCT  PROPCT  ROYPCT
--------- ------- ------- ------- -------
    92200      .22   86.77   13.02     .00
    92900    25.83     .00    5.38   68.78
     4980     2.21   97.79     .00     .00
   188800     2.54     .00   97.46     .00
        0      .00     .00     .00     .00
    37700     1.06   84.88   14.06     .00
   110791    16.12    1.41    7.63   74.84
     4870             100.00    .00     .00
   292670     1.25            98.75     .00
        0      .00     .00     .00     .00

10 rows selected.
```

The same result could be obtained by running 15squ14.sql, where intpct to roypct is passed into an nvl function. However, the approach using nulls is preferable.

Summary

SQL has only one way to express missing values: a null, which means that no value is available. Using nulls has a few advantages and many disadvantages over the alternatives.

Aggregate functions ignore nulls in all calculations. Most affected by this feature are the count and the average functions, which provide correct results because of this treatment of nulls.

Conditional statements are extended from a boolean two-valued true/false logic to a Lukasiewiczian three-valued true/false/unknown logic. Logical operators are impacted as follows:

- A not null still returns null; reversing an unknown state still keeps it unknown.

- and returns true only if both conditions are true. It returns false if at least one condition is known to be false. In all other cases, it returns unknown.

- or returns true if at least one condition is true. It returns false if both conditions are known to be false. In all other cases, it returns unknown.

All numerical operators return NULL if any of the operands are NULL.

To test for null, the comparison operators is null and is not null must be used.

Conversion functions with NULL as an argument return NULL.

A few functions deal with nulls:

- The nvl function, or coalesce in SQL-92, takes two arguments: a value or column to be processed, and the value to return in case the first value or column is null.

- The SQL-92 standard includes the opposite of the nvl function, which converts a number to null. In Oracle, you can use decode for this purpose.

It is advisable to avoid nulls as much as possible in cases not calling for aggregation.

Mathematics has not defined division by zero. As a result, the computer does not know what to do, and processing stops (or it should) with an error. The preferable way to deal with such a situation is to convert the mathematically undefined case to the unknown case in SQL using NULL. decode or nullif converts the divisor to null if it is zero. Another option is a user function that returns zero if both numerator and denominator are zero.

Multiple Tables

V

PART

CHAPTER 16

Retrieving Data from Multiple Tables

The first four parts of this book have given no consideration to the area where relational databases really shine—being able to combine information from different tables in a consistent, reliable, and efficient way. So far, all queries have retrieved information from one table only.

In a relational database, data that logically belongs to the same larger unit (referred to as an entity) is organized together in a database table. If necessary, several tables can be joined to create a larger, virtual table from which attributes of either table can be retrieved in one operation.

This chapter limits the discussion to the most frequent case: A parent record in one table is joined to one or more child records in another table. Chapter 17, "Joins," and Chapter 30, "Table Relationships and Entity Relationship Diagrams," include other options.

Redundant information, however, does not need to be maintained. If there is a table with some information on people, including a sex code, other information can be deduced from the value of that code. If the code is `'M'`, for example, the person who is characterized that way is likely to be addressed as Mr., while sex codes of `'F'` would translate to Ms. Those listed as `'M'` would not be women, and those listed as `'F'` would not be men. `'M'` would indicate a male, and `'F'` a female.

In a relational database, there is no need to maintain redundant attributes to hold values such as Mr./Ms., male/female, or man/women in the table with person information, as long as the basic codes `'M'` and `'F'` are maintained.

The `decode` function, which is explained in Chapter 4, "Operator Conversions and Value Decoding," takes advantage of this fact and converts sex codes accordingly. The other, more standard option to obtain the same result is to join the table containing the person information with a second table that has attributes for variables that are dependent on the sex code. The person table then references a static `sex` lookup table.

SQL Multiple-Table Approach

The same parent-child relationship can be seen from either end—start with the child record and look up information from the parent, or start with the parent and listing or aggregate information from the child records. The difference is mostly conceptual; as far as SQL and the RDBMS are concerned, the same steps are involved in either case. Another term for parent-child, which is used interchangeably throughout this book, is *master-detail*.

Selecting From Multiple Tables—Cartesian/Cross Joins

The `select` statements discussed so far have had only one table after the `from` keyword. To select from several tables, it is only necessary to extend that expression to a `from` comma list, similar to the `select` comma list that determines the columns to be retrieved.

If there are two tables in the `from` comma list, the RDBMS joins every row of the first table with every row of the second table. If there is a third table, each combined row resulting from the join of table 1 and table 2 is joined to each row of table 3, and so on.

Retrieving Data From Multiple Tables

CHAPTER 16

323

16

RETRIEVING DATA
FROM MULTIPLE
TABLES

This join is called a *cross join,* or *Cartesian join*, after the French mathematician and philosopher René Descartes, or Cartesius (1596–1650), who developed the underlying mathematical foundation. Thus, if table 1 has five rows and table 2 has two rows, the resulting cross table has 10 rows.

 Run the script `crsex1.sql`, which can be found on the accompanying CD-ROM, to create the `sex1` lookup table used in these examples, which is defined as follows:

```
SQL> desc sex1;

Name                             Null?    Type
-------------------------------- -------- ----
SXID                                      CHAR(1)
NOUN                                      VARCHAR2(6)
ATTR                                      VARCHAR2(6)
TITLE                                     VARCHAR2(3)
SALUTATION                                VARCHAR2(5)
```

This table has only two rows:

```
SQL> select * from sex1;

S NOUN   ATTR   TIT SALUT
- ------ ------ --- -----
M man    male   Mr. Sir
F woman  female Ms. Madam
```

If this table is joined with pers1, the output shown in Listing 16.1 results.

Listing 16.1. Retrieving rows from a cross join of two tables.

```
--        Filename: 16squ01.sql
--         Purpose: Retrieve rows from a cross join of pers1 and sex1
--
col id format 99
col age format 99
col lname format A10
col fmname format A11

select
    *
from
   pers1,
   sex1
;

clear columns
```

This code returns

```
ID LNAME      FMNAME      SSN        AGE S S NOUN   ATTR   TIT SALUT
--- ---------- ----------- ---------- --- - - ------ ------ --- -----
  1 Jones      David N.    895663453   34 M M man    male   Mr. Sir
  2 Martinelli A. Emery    312331818   92 M M man    male   Mr. Sir
  3 Talavera   F. Espinosa 533932999   19 F M man    male   Mr. Sir
```

```
4  Kratochvil  Mary T.      969825711   48  F  M  man     male    Mr.  Sir
5  Melsheli    Joseph K.    000342222   14  M  M  man     male    Mr.  Sir
1  Jones       David N.     895663453   34  M  F  woman   female  Ms.  Madam
2  Martinelli  A. Emery     312331818   92  M  F  woman   female  Ms.  Madam
3  Talavera    F. Espinosa  533932999   19  F  F  woman   female  Ms.  Madam
4  Kratochvil  Mary T.      969825711   48  F  F  woman   female  Ms.  Madam
5  Melsheli    Joseph K.    000342222   14  M  F  woman   female  Ms.  Madam
```

Figure 16.1 illustrates this behavior of cross joins. The set of combined rows results from combining each row of table 1 with each row of table 2.

Figure 16.1.

Cartesian (cross) join of two tables.

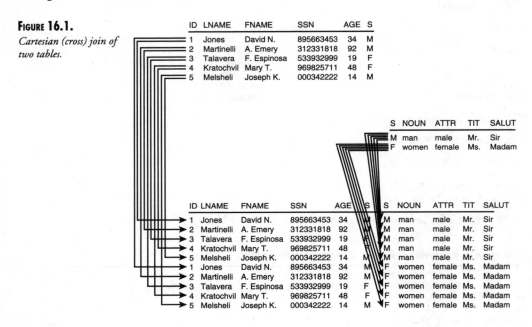

A `select` from two tables makes every column of both tables available for processing in

- The `select` comma list
- The `order by` comma list
- The `where` clauses
- Arguments to functions and operators

Obviously, the result of `16squ01.sql` does not make a whole lot of sense, a problem that will be fixed in the next section. There are only a few cases where a Cartesian join is useful. Nevertheless, the Cartesian join is the starting point of multi-table `select` statements.

Retrieving Data From Multiple Tables

CHAPTER 16

325

16

RETRIEVING DATA
FROM MULTIPLE
TABLES

Preventing Cartesian/Cross Joins Through Join Conditions

The problem of the Cartesian join is not that the resulting set of rows is wrong, but that it contains rows that are useless. All that you need to do to eliminate the unneeded rows is to use a `where` clause with an appropriate join condition, after which only the desired rows are printed. In this example, only those rows are desired where the `sex` column in `pers1` matches the `sxid` column in `sex1`. In SQL lingo, the tables are joined on these columns. Figure 16.2 illustrates this process.

FIGURE 16.2.

Eliminating non-matching rows.

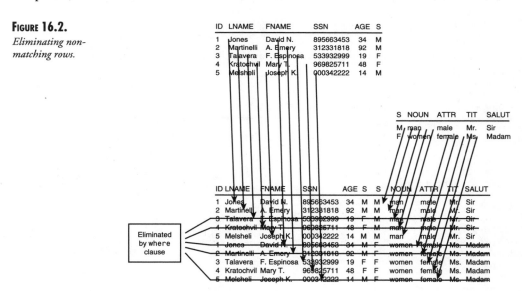

Listing 16.2 includes the necessary join condition `where sex = sxid`:

Listing 16.2. Retrieving rows from a cross join of two tables using a join condition.

```
--        Filename: 16squ02.sql
--        Purpose: Retrieve rows from a cross join of pers1 and sex1
--
col id format 99
col age format 99
col lname format A10
col fmname format A11

select
    *
from
    pers1,
    sex1
```

continues

Listing 16.2. continued

```
where sex = sxid
;

clear columns
```

It returns the desired rows:

```
 ID LNAME        FMNAME       SSN        AGE S S NOUN   ATTR    TIT SALUT
--- ---------    ----------   ---------- --- - - ------ ------  --- -----
  3 Talavera     F. Espinosa 533932999   19 F F woman  female  Ms. Madam
  4 Kratochvil   Mary T.     969825711   48 F F woman  female  Ms. Madam
  1 Jones        David N.    895663453   34 M M man    male    Mr. Sir
  5 Melsheli     Joseph K.   000342222   14 M M man    male    Mr. Sir
  2 Martinelli   A. Emery    312331818   92 M M man    male    Mr. Sir
```

From this set of columns, any desired output may be selected, as Listing 16.3—although somewhat impolite—shows.

Listing 16.3. Retrieving rows from a cross join of two tables.

```
--        Filename: 16squ03.sql
--        Purpose: Retrieve rows from a cross join of pers1 and sex1
--
col label      format A24
col salut      format A20
col statement  format A21

select
   title || ' ' || fmname || ' ' || lname   label,
   'Dear ' || title || ' ' || lname || ':'   salut,
   'You are ' || age || ' years old.'        statement
from
   pers1,
   sex1
where sex = sxid
;

clear columns
```

This code returns the following output:

```
LABEL                    SALUT                STATEMENT
-----------------------  -------------------  --------------------------------
Ms. F. Espinosa Talavera Dear Ms. Talavera:   You are female and 19 years old.
Ms. Mary T. Kratochvil   Dear Ms. Kratochvil: You are female and 48 years old.
Mr. David N. Jones       Dear Mr. Jones:      You are male and 34 years old.
Mr. Joseph K. Melsheli   Dear Mr. Melsheli:   You are male and 14 years old.
Mr. A. Emery Martinelli  Dear Mr. Martinelli: You are male and 92 years old.
```

Retrieving Data From Multiple Tables

CHAPTER 16

327

16

RETRIEVING DATA
FROM MULTIPLE
TABLES

DEBUG ALERT

Cartesian joins are one of the most frequent causes of why a statement might run forever and then ultimately not work.

If, for example, three tables of 1,000 rows each are joined without a where clause limiting the output to matching rows, a billion rows (1000×1000×1000) will be retrieved, a process that is likely to take a long time.

Therefore, a Cartesian join is the first thing to look for if a statement runs forever. More than one table in the from comma list without join conditions will return a full Cartesian join.

Almost as bad is a partial Cartesian join, which results from an incomplete join condition. If on the preceding three tables the join conditions only limit extraneous rows between table 1 and table 2, 1,000 compound rows will be valid. If these are joined to the 1,000 rows of table 3, still a million rows will be returned, which is a bit much. Therefore, a partial Cartesian join is the second thing to look for.

Partial Cartesian joins are easy to get when scripts are adapted. A script might start out with three tables and an appropriate join condition that results in an appropriate report. In one or more revisions, information from lookup tables might be included. At this point, it is easy to either forget to adapt the where clause as well, or the where clause gets complicated enough that an error is not immediately obvious. Therefore, make it a habit; whenever you change anything in the from comma list, go over the join condition as well.

All three expressions use columns from both tables. It is possible, however, to select only columns from one of the joined tables. This is inefficient if all selected columns are on the detail table—one of the examples where SQL allows inefficient programming to return a correct result. The following example results in twice the logical reads and table spans and two sort operations, when compared to its equivalent one-table statement:

```
select
    id,
    fmname,
    lname,
    age
from
    pers1,
    sex1
where sex = sxid
;
```

This code returns

```
     ID FMNAME          LNAME              AGE
-------- --------------- --------------- --------
      3 F. Espinosa     Talavera             19
      4 Mary T.         Kratochvil           48
      1 David N.        Jones                34
      5 Joseph K.       Melsheli             14
      2 A. Emery        Martinelli           92
```

However, if the selected columns are on the master table, as many applicable master rows will be printed as there are matching rows in the detail table, as shown in the following example:

```
select
   noun,
   attr,
   title,
   salutation
from
   pers1,
   sex1
where sex = sxid
;
```

This code returns

```
NOUN    ATTR    TIT SALUT
------  ------  --- -----
woman   female  Ms. Madam
woman   female  Ms. Madam
man     male    Mr. Sir
man     male    Mr. Sir
man     male    Mr. Sir
```

Some aggregation over these columns could yield some useful summary information, as shown in the following example:

```
select
   'There are ' s1,
   count(*)      s2,
   attr || 's.' s3
from
   pers1,
   sex1
where sex = sxid
group by
   attr || 's.'
;
```

This returns the following:

```
S1          S2 S3
----------  -- --------
There are    2 females.
There are    3 males.
```

REAL-WORLD EXPERIENCES

A friend and former student of mine, Tarmo Talts, reported the following story of a Cartesian join gone awry. He was the leader for a project that developed an ordering and billing system for a large primary goods corporation. A person on his staff who did not know SQL too well used some menu-driven facility to generate code and created something akin to the following statement:

```
select distinct
    attr
from
    pers1,
    sex1
;
```

Although this statement returns the desired result,

```
ATTR
------
female
male
```

it is inefficient—going through 10 rows in this case where two would suffice. This did not matter in the test system that had only fairly small tables. In production testing against large tables, however, it almost brought the system down, at which point the error got caught and fixed through this simple statement against the lookup table:

```
select
    attr
from
    sex1
;
```

The latter statement returns the same.

Table Aliases

The pers1 and sex1 tables are convenient because the column names across both tables are unique, meaning that no name is used twice. SQL requires that the columns within only one table be unique, which means that such convenience cannot be guaranteed. This case is demonstrated by joining pers1 with sex2, whose first column is called sex, just as in pers1. In reality, columns that contain the same kind of data (or *domain*, as this would be called in SQL-92) are usually given the same column name.

 Run the script crsex2.sql, which can be found on the accompanying CD-ROM, to create the sex2 lookup table.

If 16squ02.sql is run against pers1 and sex2, an error will result. (See Listing 16.4.)

Listing 16.4. Retrieving rows from a cross join using a table name and table alias.

```
--      Filename: 16squ04.sql
--       Purpose: Retrieve rows from a cross join of pers1 and sex2
--                Use table name and table alias
--
col id format 99
col age format 99
col lname format A10
col fmname format A11
```

continues

Listing 16.4. continued

```
select
    *
from
    pers1,
    sex2
where sex = sex
;
```

This code returns

```
where sex = sex
              *
ERROR at line 6:
ORA-00918: column ambiguously defined
```

What the error means is that SQL does not know what to make of sex. The same name could refer to a column in pers1 and in sex2. The error message does make sense, for a change, because this is an ambiguous definition. There are two ways to fix the situation: precede the column name with the table name or use table aliases. The following code illustrates preceding the column name with the table name:

```
select
    *
from
    pers1,
    sex2
where pers1.sex = sex2.sex
;
```

This example shows you how to use table aliases:

```
select
    *
from
    pers1 p,
    sex2  s
where p.sex = s.sex
;
```

```
clear columns
```

Both strategies return the same output:

```
ID LNAME      FMNAME       SSN        AGE S S NOUN   ATTR    TIT SALUT
--- ---------- ----------- ---------  --- - - ------ ------  --- -----
  3 Talavera   F. Espinosa 533932999   19 F F woman  female  Ms. Madam
  4 Kratochvil Mary T.     969825711   48 F F woman  female  Ms. Madam
  1 Jones      David N.    895663453   34 M M man    male    Mr. Sir
  5 Melsheli   Joseph K.   000342222   14 M M man    male    Mr. Sir
  2 Martinelli A. Emery    312331818   92 M M man    male    Mr. Sir
```

The alias is created the same way as a column alias, by inserting it after the table name but before the comma or the `where` keyword, as was done in `from pers1 p, sex2 s`. Now whenever necessary, the alias can be used to specify the table to which an ambiguously named column refers. Therefore, the clause `where p.sex = s.sex` means where the values of the `sex` column in `pers1` equal the values of the `sex` column in `sex2`.

> **TIP**
>
> In the examples so far, using the table name as a qualifier works the same as using an alias. In situations when the same table is listed more than once, as can happen when the same lookup is joined once each to two different columns of a table or in recursive joins where a table is joined to itself, using the table name will no longer work. Because aliases work in all situations, it is preferable to use aliasing for all statements.

Master-Detail Tables

The master-detail situation, where both tables are dynamic, is even more powerful than lookup tables. Lookup tables, such as `sex1` or `sex2`, are stable, meaning that it is unlikely that their contents change (much) over time. In a master-detail, or parent-child, relationship, both tables change all the time. In an order-processing system, there could be a customer table as a parent and an order table as a child. As new customers are entered or customer records are updated, the customer table changes. The order table will also be updated. The tables will be joined on a common column such as `customer ID`. In that situation, it is extremely important that all `customer ID` values in the detail table refer to a matching `customer ID` value in the customer table, and that the letters are unique. This requirement can be guaranteed through referential integrity constraints, which are discussed in Chapter 29, "Keys, Indexes, Constraints, and Table/Column Comments." Until then, referential integrity is assumed unless noted otherwise.

A master-detail relationship can be illustrated nicely by rearranging the income information of the `pers3` table. Instead of listing the four types of income in four separate columns, an income table could contain three columns, the person ID to which the line pertains, the income type, and the amount. This table can then be joined with `pers1` to return the same information as `pers3`.

Such an approach, where information from one table is broken up into several tables with like information, is in anticipation of the discussion in Chapter 38, "Optimizing SQL Statement Processing."

 Please run the script `crinc1.sql`, which can be found on the CD-ROM, to create the `inc1` detail table.

Because `inc1` is loaded from the values of `pers3`, the sums over the income sources ought to be the same. This is demonstrated in Listing 16.5.

Listing 16.5. Retrieving data from a master-detail table.

```
--          Filename: 16squ05.sql
--          Purpose: retrieval from master-detail table
--
select
   sum(interest),
   sum(salary),
   sum(profit),
   sum(royalty)
from pers3
;

select
   sum(decode(type,'I',1,0)*amount) interest,
   sum(decode(type,'S',1,0)*amount) salary,
   sum(decode(type,'P',1,0)*amount) profit,
   sum(decode(type,'R',1,0)*amount) royalty,
   count(1)
from inc1
;
```

Both statements return the same values:

SUM(INTEREST)	SUM(SALARY)	SUM(PROFIT)	SUM(ROYALTY)
29160	84870	201000	63900

INTEREST	SALARY	PROFIT	ROYALTY	COUNT(1)
29160	84870	201000	63900	11

However, because zero values are not stored, only 11 values are needed, rather than the 20 values that are the result of five rows at four columns in `pers3`. This approach is, therefore, potentially more efficient.

Calculating the total income of each person can now be done without any conversion operations. Type the following:

```
select
   lname,
   sum(amount)
from
   pers1 p,
   inc1  i
where p.id = i.id
group by lname
;
```

Retrieving Data From Multiple Tables

CHAPTER 16

333

16

RETRIEVING DATA
FROM MULTIPLE
TABLES

This code returns

```
LNAME            SUM(AMOUNT)
---------------  -----------
Jones                  92200
Kratochvil            188800
Martinelli             92900
Melsheli                  50
Talavera                4980
```

The same information broken down by income type is equally straightforward. It is only necessary to add the income type in the select comma list and the group by comma list. Instead of the type, however, the name column from inclu1 is used, which will display the information using a meaningful label for income type. This will require you to join inclu1 to inc1 by the mutual type column:

```
select
    lname,
    name inc_type,
    sum(amount)
from
    pers1  p,
    inc1   i,
    inclu1 l
where p.id   = i.id
and   i.type = l.type
group by
    lname,
    name
;
```

This returns the following:

```
LNAME            INC_TYPE   SUM(AMOUNT)
---------------  ---------  -----------
Jones            INTEREST           200
Jones            PROFIT           12000
Jones            SALARY           80000
Kratochvil       INTEREST          4800
Kratochvil       PROFIT          184000
Martinelli       INTEREST         24000
Martinelli       PROFIT            5000
Martinelli       ROYALTY          63900
Melsheli         INTEREST            50
Talavera         INTEREST           110
Talavera         SALARY            4870

11 rows selected.
```

CAUTION

If each join is on one common column only, the number of conditions in the where clause related to the join must be one less than the number of tables.

Finally, a slight variation (stripping out everything pertaining to pers1) aggregates the amounts per income type:

```
select
    name inc_type,
    sum(amount)
from
    inc1    i,
    inclu1 l
where i.type = l.type
group by
    name
;
```

This code returns the same values as the statements at the beginning of the example:

```
INC_TYPE   SUM(AMOUNT)
--------- -----------
INTEREST        29160
PROFIT         201000
ROYALTY         63900
SALARY          84870
```

The only blemish is that the output is not sorted the same way. However, the inclu1 table also has a column sort order through which that task can be accomplished, as shown in the following:

```
select
    name inc_type,
    sum(amount)
from
    inc1    i,
    inclu1 l
where i.type = l.type
group by
    sortorder,
    name
order by sortorder
;
```

This returns the rows in the desired order:

```
INC_TYPE   SUM(AMOUNT)
--------- -----------
INTEREST        29160
SALARY          84870
PROFIT         201000
ROYALTY         63900
```

This, incidentally, is a situation where the group by comma list contains a column that is not listed in the select comma list. The reason for this is that these columns are redundant, which means that no further breakdown into groups occurs through adding sort order. The column name fully describes the groups in the output.

NOTE

This example illustrates a fact of life with SQL: Many tasks are more straightforward, if you allow the project to be cast in the mold that SQL expects, which means having normalized data (see Chapter 39). The combination of the tables pers1 and inc1 is more normalized than the pers3 table, where the four income columns are essentially an array. Arrays violate the first normal form at least in spirit, if not in deed.

Lookup Tables Versus Parent-Child Tables

The difference of starting the analysis with a table and joining it to a parent lookup table, or working the other way around, where all detail records are retrieved for a master table, is conceptual only. For SQL proper, there is no difference. In either case, the record in all tables has to be retrieved and joined. The compound virtual table can then be used to either list out all the detail lines with some information from the master table, which retrieved 11 rows, or to aggregate over some master categories such as lname, which retrieved five rows.

Summary

Several tables can be joined to create a larger virtual table from which attributes of either table can be retrieved in one operation. For this purpose, it is only necessary to list all tables to be accessed in the from comma list. The RDBMS joins every row of the first table with every row of the second table and then each row of an additional table with each combined row, creating a cross join, or Cartesian join. Thus, if table 1 has three rows and table 2 has three rows, the resulting cross table has nine rows. If three tables with 1,000 rows each are joined, the resulting virtual table has a billion rows. A where clause with an appropriate join condition eliminates the unneeded rows.

All the columns of all the included tables can be used in the select comma list, the order by comma list, the where clause, and arguments to functions and operators. If, however, the column names in all included tables are not unique, spelling out a nonunique column name will return an error. The problem can be solved by preceding the columns in question with the table name and a period. Preferable to that is the use of table aliases, which are created by inserting the alias after the table name, but before the comma or where clause. The alias can now be used to specify the table to which an ambiguously named column refers. Aliases also work well in more complex situations where one table is listed more than once in the from comma list.

Joins

IN THIS CHAPTER

CHAPTER 17

The tables that were joined in Chapter 16, "Retrieving Data from Multiple Tables," all matched perfectly—all master or lookup records could be matched with at least one detail record, and all detail records referenced a master record. By default, SQL only retrieves matching rows, creating what is called an *inner join*. This approach creates a problem, however, if the unmatched rows are needed in the analysis—such as a query that asks for all master records without details or a query that needs to aggregate all details, even those where a master record cannot be found. In the latter cases, an operator has to be added, so that unmatched rows will be included as well.

This chapter deals with the most important join types: the inner join and the left or right outer join. The full outer join and a way to create it in absence of a dedicated operator are covered in Chapter 18, "Combining Output from Similar Tables Through Set and Pseudoset Operators."

The last section of the chapter shows you how to join tables that contain nulls in join columns.

 Run the script `crinc2.sql`, found on the CD, to create the `inc2` detail table and the `inclu2` lookup table, which will serve as a master table together with the `pers1` table for the following examples. Note that the contents of these tables are no longer consistent with that of the `pers3` table.

In this chapter, the `inc2` table contains income information. It references two other tables: `pers1`, which joins on `id`, and `inclu2`, which joins on `type`. The relationships are dotted throughout because they are optional on both ends, meaning that unmatched rows are allowed everywhere.

Joining Qualified Matches: Inner Join (Default)

SQL's default join type—the inner join—retrieves information only from those rows that can be matched to corresponding rows in the other table(s). This can lead to results that are less than desirable, as Listing 17.1 shows.

Listing 17.1. Retrieving data using the inner join.

```
--        Filename: 17squ01.sql
--        Purpose: retrieval from master-detail table
--
select
   sum(decode(type,'I',1,0)*amount) interest,
   sum(decode(type,'S',1,0)*amount) salary,
   sum(decode(type,'P',1,0)*amount) profit,
   sum(decode(type,'R',1,0)*amount) royalty,
   sum(decode(type,'R',1,0)*amount) annuity,
   count(1)
from inc2
;
```

This code returns the following:

INTEREST	SALARY	PROFIT	ROYALTY	ANNUITY	COUNT(1)
5938	180690	196000	45633	45633	14

An annuity income type has been added. The sum of annuities amounts to 45,633. In the next statement, pers1 is joined to inc2:

```
select
    p.id,
    lname,
    sum(amount)
from
    pers1 p,
    inc2  i
where p.id = i.id
group by
    p.id,
    lname
;
```

This code returns

```
    ID LNAME            SUM(AMOUNT)
---------- --------------- -----------
     1 Jones                 106889
     3 Talavera                9568
     4 Kratochvil            188800
     5 Melsheli               68983
```

Only four persons are included; the following code shows Martinelli, who is penniless in the sense that there are no matching rows in the inc2 table, is missing:

```
select
    id,
    lname
 from
    pers1 p
 where id not in(1,3,4,5)
;
```

```
        ID LNAME
---------- ---------------
         2 Martinelli
```

Looking at these two tables from the other way around, however, not all information in inc2 is included in the join. The sums of the first and second queries are not the same. The sum of the first is

```
select
    sum(amount)
from inc2
;
```

This first query returns the total of the amounts:

```
SUM(AMOUNT)
-----------
    516471
```

The total of the amounts when `inc2` and `pers1` are joined is less:

```
select
   sum(amount)
from
   pers1 p,
   inc2  i
where p.id = i.id
;
```

This query returns the following:

```
SUM(AMOUNT)
-----------
     374240
```

By creating a break-out report strictly against the `inc2` table, which groups by `id` values, the reason for the difference becomes obvious. This is shown here:

```
select
   id,
   sum(amount)
from inc2
group by
   id
;
```

This code returns

```
        ID SUM(AMOUNT)
--------- ------------
        1      106889
        3        9568
        4      188800
        5       68983
        6      142231
```

`ID 6`, which has an income listed as `142231`, has no matching row in `pers1`, which explains the difference of the two sums.

While in some situations the inner join is exactly what is needed, losing information due to unmatched rows is usually annoying and sometimes outright dangerous. There are, however, two ways to fix that problem:

- Ensure that all rows of interest have matching rows in the other table(s). Therefore, either the rows that can't be matched need to be deleted or the matching rows need to be inserted. The best way to do this is to rely on relational integrity constraints of the database, which eliminate the problem (see Chapter 29, "Keys, Indexes, Constraints, and Table/Column Comments").

- If that is not possible, it is necessary to test for the occurrence of unmatched rows and use outer join operators to adjust for these. This approach is explained in the following section.

> **CAUTION**
>
> Losing information due to unmatched rows in joins can have a devastating effect on the accuracy of reports. It is, therefore, necessary to ensure that this problem does not occur or else it is impossible to rely on the report. This problem is handled best through relational integrity or through testing and the use of outer join operators.

A similar problem exists between the tables inc2 and inclu2. inclu2 has a row G for government SSN income, which has no matching row in inc2. inc2 has several rows of type A for annuity, which are not matched by any row in inclu2. Listing 17.2 creates a break-out report of amount totals by type values.

Listing 17.2. Retrieving data using an inner join.

```
--       Filename: 17squ02.sql
--        Purpose: retrieval from master-detail table
--
select
   type,
   sum(amount)
from
   inc2   i
group by
   type
;
```

The preceding code returns five rows, as shown in the following:

```
T SUM(AMOUNT)
- -----------
A       88210
I        5938
P      196000
R       45633
S      180690
```

However, a join with inclu2 causes the first row to be dropped:

```
select
   name inc_type,
   sum(amount)
from
   inc2   i,
   inclu2 l
where i.type = l.type
group by
   sortorder,
   name
order by sortorder
;
```

This code returns

```
INC_TYPE   SUM(AMOUNT)
---------  -----------
INTEREST          5938
SALARY          180690
PROFIT          196000
ROYALTY          45633
```

Even more rows get dropped when inc2 gets joined to both pers1 and inclu2, as Listing 17.3 shows.

Listing 17.3. Retrieving data using an inner join.

```
--         Filename: 17squ03.sql
--         Purpose: retrieval from master-detail table and lookup
--
break on id skip 1

select
   id,
   type,
   sum(amount)
from
   inc2    i
group by
   id,
   type
order by id
;
```

This code returns the following 14 rows:

```
   ID T SUM(AMOUNT)
---------- - -----------
    1 A       14689
      I         200
      P       12000
      S       80000

    3 A        4588
      I         110
      S        4870

    4 I        4800
      P      184000

    5 A       68933
      I          50

    6 I         778
      R       45633
      S       95820


14 rows selected.
```

The following code returns only eight:

```
clear breaks
break on lname skip 1

select
    lname,
    name inc_type,
    sum(amount)
from
    pers1   p,
    inc2    i,
    inclu2 l
where p.id   = i.id
and    i.type = l.type
group by
    lname,
    name
;

clear breaks
```

Here are the eight rows that are returned:

```
LNAME            INC_TYPE  SUM(AMOUNT)
---------------  --------- -----------
Jones            INTEREST          200
                 PROFIT          12000
                 SALARY          80000

Kratochvil       INTEREST         4800
                 PROFIT         184000

Melsheli         INTEREST           50

Talavera         INTEREST          110
                 SALARY           4870


8 rows selected.
```

The rows that pertain to annuities or to the person whose ID entry equals 6 are not retrieved.

Including Unmatched Rows in One Table: Left/Right Outer Join

The outer join operator (+) directs SQL to join a row of one table with a null row of the table identified by it. Thus all rows of the table not marked by the join operator are retrieved.

The SQL-92 standard has a number of elaborate, convenient, and much-needed options for joins that use a set of keywords. Little of this is implemented at this point. The approach that Oracle has taken is implemented similarly by most vendors, except that vendors use different operators, such as *=.

ORACLE vs SQL

17

JOINS

Listing 17.4 adjusts for the fact that no row exists in the pers1 table that has an id value of 6 by including the outer join operator (+) after p.id in the where clause. As a result, every row in inc2 that cannot be matched with a row in pers1 is joined with a NULL row of that table. This results in a virtual row that can be processed further.

Listing 17.4. Retrieving data using left/right outer joins.

```
--        Filename: 17squ04.sql
--        Purpose: retrieval from master-detail table
--                 using left/right outer joins
--
select
   p.id,
   lname,
   sum(amount)
from
   pers1 p,
   inc2  i
where p.id (+) = i.id
group by
   p.id,
   lname
;
```

The resulting join is called a *left outer join* because the table to the left of the equal sign gets expanded. The statement now returns a sixth row in which the id and the sum(amount) columns are nulls:

```
    ID LNAME            SUM(AMOUNT)
--------- ---------------- -----------
     1 Jones                 106889
     3 Talavera                9568
     4 Kratochvil            188800
     5 Melsheli               68983
                             142231
```

The sum of the amount from inc2 is now the same as the sum of the amount of the combined rows, which results when using the left outer join. The following statements demonstrate that:

```
select
   sum(amount)
from inc2
;

select
   sum(amount)
from
   pers1 p,
   inc2  i
where p.id (+) = i.id
;
```

Both select statements return

```
SUM(AMOUNT)
-----------
     516471
```

> **NOTE**
>
> Other than for demonstration purposes, only the first statement should be used. The second one causes all the overhead of a join without any benefit.

If the first statement of this example gets changed to include a right outer join, such as in the following example, all rows of pers1 are printed, whether or not they have matching inc2 rows:

```
select
   p.id,
   lname,
   sum(amount)
from
   pers1 p,
   inc2  i
where p.id  = i.id (+)
group by
   p.id,
   lname
;
```

The preceding code returns all the rows of pers1, as shown here:

```
    ID LNAME              SUM(AMOUNT)
---------- --------------- -----------
     1 Jones                  106889
     2 Martinelli
     3 Talavera                 9568
     4 Kratochvil             188800
     5 Melsheli                68983
```

The row of poor, penniless Martinelli has a null in the SUM(AMOUNT) column.

Using a having clause, the previous statement can be adapted to answer a question such as "Which person does not have any income?" This is done in the following statement:

```
select
   p.id,
   lname,
   decode(sum(amount),NULL,'NULL',to_char(sum(amount))) Income
from
   pers1 p,
   inc2  i
where p.id  = i.id (+)
group by
   p.id,
   lname
having sum(amount) is null
;
```

This returns penniless Martinelli, as shown here:

```
    ID LNAME           INCOME
---------- --------------- ----------------------------------------
     2 Martinelli      NULL
```

Figure 17.1 illustrates the workings of the left outer join operator (+). Because it is attached to the column p.id, the pers1 table (on the left side of the join condition) gets logically expanded by one row that contains a null for each column. If a join column value from inc2 cannot be matched with a join column value of pers1, the inc2 column is joined with the NULL row of pers1. On the other hand, row 2 in pers1, which does not have matching rows in inc2, is not included in the combined output table.

FIGURE 17.1.

The effect of using the left outer join operator (+).

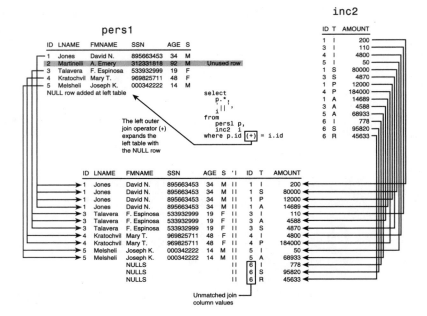

The workings of the right outer join operator (+), which are illustrated in Figure 17.2, are similar to the left outer join operator. Because the right outer join operator is attached to the column i.id, the inc2 table (which is on the right side of the join condition) gets logically expanded by one row that contains a null for each column. If a join column value from pers1 cannot be matched with a join column value of inc2, the pers1 column is joined with the NULL row of inc2. Now, three rows of inc2 are included in the combined output table, those whose ID value is 6.

FIGURE 17.2.

The effect of using the right outer join operator (+).

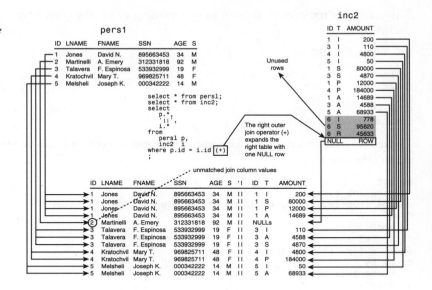

The same approach can be used for the lost rows when joining `inc2` and `inclu2`. This is shown in Listing 17.5.

Listing 17.5. Retrieving data the using left/right outer join.

```
--      Filename: 17squ05.sql
--      Purpose: retrieval from master-detail table
--               with left/right outer join

select
   decode(name,NULL,'UNKNOWN',name) inc_type,
   sum(amount)
from
   inc2  i,
   inclu2 l
where i.type = l.type (+)
group by
   sortorder,
   name
order by sortorder
;
```

This statement retrieves all amount rows, regardless of whether they have a matching row in inclu2:

```
INC_TYPE   SUM(AMOUNT)
--------   -----------
INTEREST          5938
SALARY          180690
PROFIT          196000
ROYALTY          45633
UNKNOWN          88210
```

The second statement retrieves all income types, regardless of whether there are amounts booked against them in inc2:

```
select
    name inc_type,
decode (sum(amount),NULL,'ZILCH',to_char(sum(amount))) total
from
    inc2   i,
    inclu2 l
where i.type (+) = l.type
group by
    sortorder,
    name
order by sortorder
;
```

The second statement returns the following output:

```
INC_TYPE   TOTAL
--------   ----------------------------------------
INTEREST   5938
SALARY     180690
PROFIT     196000
ROYALTY    45633
GVMT. SSN ZILCH
```

It is, finally, possible to combine several outer joins. This is done in Listing 17.6, where the query of 17squ03.sql is extended so that all rows of inc2 are retrieved, and information of matching rows in pers1 and inclu2 is inserted to the extent available.

Listing 17.6. Retrieving data using several outer joins.

```
--          Filename: 17squ06.sql
--          Purpose: retrieval from master-detail table and lookup
--                   using outer joins
--
break on lname skip 1

select
    lname,
    name inc_type,
    sum(amount)
from
    pers1  p,
    inc2   i,
    inclu2 l
```

```
where p.id (+)  = i.id
and    i.type = l.type (+)
group by
   lname,
   name
;

clear breaks
```

The statement returns

```
LNAME            INC_TYPE   SUM(AMOUNT)
---------------  ---------  -----------
Jones            INTEREST           200
                 PROFIT           12000
                 SALARY           80000
                                  14689

Kratochvil       INTEREST          4800
                 PROFIT          184000

Melsheli         INTEREST            50
                                  68933

Talavera         INTEREST           110
                 SALARY            4870
                                   4588

                 INTEREST           778
                 ROYALTY          45633
                 SALARY           95820
```

```
14 rows selected.
```

Limitations of the Outer Join Operator

The outer join operator cannot be used in a condition that is combined with another condition through the or logical operator. It also cannot be used with the in operator.

Full Outer Join

A full outer join prints all rows matched or unmatched from all tables. There is no one-shot approach to this query. The SQL-92 standard includes a way to specify a full outer join. A full outer join on example 17squ05.sql would be written as follows:

```
select
   decode(name,NULL,'UNKNOWN',name) inc_type,
   decode (sum(amount),NULL,'ZILCH',to_char(sum(amount))) total
from
   inc2 i FULL OUTER JOIN inclu2 l
   on(i.type = l.type)
group by
   sortorder,
   name
```

```
order by sortorder
;
```

This would retrieve the following:

```
INC_TYPE   TOTAL
--------   ----------------------------------------
INTEREST   5938
SALARY     180690
PROFIT     196000
ROYALTY    45633
GVMT. SSN  ZILCH
UNKNOWN    88210
```

Until this feature is implemented, a more cumbersome set operation has to be used for the same purpose. See Chapter 18 for the currently possible solution.

Redundant Rows in Referenced Tables

In a system without enforced integrity constraints, it is possible to have redundant values in the join columns of a master or lookup table. Under normal circumstances, this situation is highly undesirable because it leads to more combined rows than are appropriate to be retrieved.

 Run the script `crinc3.sql` to create the `inclu3` lookup table that is identical to `inclu2` except that one row has two redundant copies. `crinc3.sql` can be found on the CD-ROM attached to the back of this book.

This table has the following contents:

```
select * from inclu3;

T NAME          SORTORDER
- ------------- ---------
I INTEREST              1
S SALARY                2
P PROFIT                3
R ROYALTY               4
G GVMT. SSN             5
S SUPPLEMENTAL          6
S SALES INCOME          7

7 rows selected.
```

The value S in the column type is redundant.

Run the queries of `17squ05.sql` against `inc2` and `inclu3`, as in Listing 17.7.

Listing 17.7. Retrieving data from a detail and lookup table.

```
--       Filename: 17squ07.sql
--        Purpose: retrieval from detail and lookup table
--                 with left/right outer join
--                 lookup table has redundant join column values
--
select
   type,
   sum(amount)
```

```
from
   inc2    i
group by
   type
;

select
   decode(name,NULL,'UNKNOWN',name) inc_type,
   sum(amount)
from
   inc2    i,
   inclu3 l
where i.type = l.type (+)
group by
   sortorder,
   name
order by sortorder
;

select
   name inc_type,
   decode (sum(amount),NULL,'ZILCH',to_char(sum(amount))) total
from
   inc2    i,
   inclu3 l
where i.type (+) = l.type
group by
   sortorder,
   name
order by sortorder
;
```

This returns the following output:

```
T  SUM(AMOUNT)
-  -----------
A       88210
I        5938
P      196000
R       45633
S      180690


INC_TYPE      SUM(AMOUNT)
------------  -----------
INTEREST             5938
SALARY             180690
PROFIT             196000
ROYALTY             45633
SUPPLEMENTAL       180690
SALES INCOME       180690
UNKNOWN             88210

7 rows selected.


INC_TYPE      TOTAL
------------  ----------------------------------------
INTEREST      5938
```

```
SALARY       180690
PROFIT       196000
ROYALTY       45633
GVMT. SSN     ZILCH
SUPPLEMENTAL 180690
SALES INCOME 180690
```

```
7 rows selected.
```

Whether a left or right outer join is used, the sum of the amounts of type S is now listed three times: once as salary, once as supplemental, and once as sales income. This is obviously wrong.

Nulls in Join Columns

As is the case with nulls in general, nulls in join columns pose problems. These stem from the three-valued logic to which their introduction leads. Nulls can be used in join columns, but precautions must be taken. In practical terms, however, nulls should be avoided here as well.

 Run the script `crinc4.sql`, found on the CD attached to the back of this book, to create the `inclu4` lookup table, which is identical to `inclu2` except that it has one row with the type of NULL. Also created is the `inc4` table that has NULL values in both the type and ID columns.

Listing 17.8, which shows the issues involved with having nulls in join columns, is a variation of `17squ05.sql`.

Listing 17.8. Retrieving data with columns containing nulls.

```
--        Filename: 17squ08.sql
--        Purpose: retrieval from master-detail table
--                 with left/right outer join
--                 join columns contain NULLs
--
select
   type,
   sum(amount)
from
   inc4    i
group by
   type
;
```

This code returns the following output:

```
T SUM(AMOUNT)
- -----------
A       88210
I        5938
P      196000
R       45633
S      180690
       108762

6 rows selected.
```

The last row contains the sum of all amounts whose type is NULL.

The inclu4 table has one row of type NULL as well; this is illustrated here:

```
select
    *
from
    inclu4 l
;
```

This code returns the following:

```
T NAME        SORTORDER
- ---------- ----------
I INTEREST           1
S SALARY             2
P PROFIT             3
R ROYALTY            4
G GVMT. SSN          5
  UNKNOWN            6

6 rows selected.
```

An inner join does not include the rows with the join column values of NULL. The following statement shows this by joining inc4 with inclu4:

```
select
    decode(name,NULL,'NULL',name) inc_type,
    sum(amount)
from
    inc4    i,
    inclu4  l
where i.type = l.type
group by
    sortorder,
    name
order by sortorder
;
```

This returns just four rows, as shown here:

```
INC_TYPE   SUM(AMOUNT)
---------- -----------
INTEREST          5938
SALARY          180690
PROFIT          196000
ROYALTY          45633
```

Only those rows are returned that can be cleanly matched. By adapting the join condition, however, the matching NULL row can be retrieved. This is illustrated here:

```
select
    decode(name,NULL,'UNKNOWN',name) inc_type,
    sum(amount)
from
    inc4    i,
    inclu4  l
where (i.type = l.type ) or
      (i.type is null and l.type is null)
```

```
group by
   sortorder,
   name
order by sortorder
;
```

This code returns the following:

```
INC_TYPE    SUM(AMOUNT)
--------    -----------
INTEREST           5938
SALARY           180690
PROFIT           196000
ROYALTY           45633
UNKNOWN          108762
```

Combining this approach with an outer join operator (+) does not work because the outer join operator must not be used with an or or in expression. What does work, however, is to use the nvl function to convert the null to a character, preferably a weird one that is less likely to be used as a code in the future. The next statement utilizes this approach:

```
select
   decode(name,NULL,'NULL',name) inc_type,
   sum(amount)
from
   inc4   i,
   inclu4 l
where nvl(i.type,'^') = nvl(l.type (+),'^')
group by
   sortorder,
   name
order by sortorder
;
```

This returns all six rows:

```
INC_TYPE    SUM(AMOUNT)
--------    -----------
INTEREST           5938
SALARY           180690
PROFIT           196000
ROYALTY           45633
UNKNOWN          108762
NULL              88210
```

```
6 rows selected.
```

The same approach works for a left outer join:

```
select
   name inc_type,
   decode (sum(amount),NULL,'NULL',to_char(sum(amount))) total
from
   inc4   i,
   inclu4 l
where nvl(i.type (+),'^') = nvl(l.type,'^')
group by
   sortorder,
   name
```

```
order by sortorder
;
```

This code returns the following:

```
INC_TYPE   TOTAL
--------   ----------------------------------------
INTEREST   5938
SALARY     180690
PROFIT     196000
ROYALTY    45633
GVMT. SSN  NULL
UNKNOWN    108762

6 rows selected.
```

> **TIP**
>
> Using an arbitrary character for conversion from null poses the danger that at some future time that character might actually be used for a value. If the join columns are of a type character, some generally unused character can be used for that purpose. If it is a number column, which for key purposes is usually stocked with positive numbers, some negative number might do the trick.
>
> It is, however, preferable not to take chances through
>
> - Declaring the columns not `null`
> - Putting a check constraint on the column, which makes it impossible to store the character or negative number used to express nulls
> - Using appropriate foreign key referential integrity constraints.
>
> See Chapters 28, "Creating Tables," and 29, "Keys, Indexes, Constraints, and Table/Column Comments," for the use of these options.

Summary

By default, SQL retrieves only rows where matching join column values can be found, creating what is called an *inner join*. If the unmatched rows are needed in the analysis, an outer join operator (+) has to be included in the join condition, so that unmatched rows from one table will be joined with a NULL row of the table marked with the operator and included in the output as well. Depending on the side of the join condition at which the outer join operator is included, the resulting join is referred to as a *left* or *right outer join*. Rows in the expanded table that do not have matching rows in the other table are not included in the combined output table.

A full outer join prints all rows matched or unmatched from all tables. While the SQL-92 standard includes a way to specify a full outer join (`from inc2 i FULL OUTER JOIN nclu2 l on(i.type = l.type)`), this feature is not yet implemented; a more cumbersome set operation has to be used.

In multi-table queries, several outer joins may be combined. Whether used with two or more tables, however, the outer join operator cannot be used in a condition that is combined with another condition through the `or` logical or the `in` operator.

The outer join operator neither protects against a situation where join columns contain redundant values nor can it join on `NULL` values in the join columns. The prior is usually undesirable because it will retrieve an excessive number of combined rows. `NULL` value joins have to be handled with special coding.

If included in inner joins, an addition to the join condition similar to `or (i.type is null and l.type is null)` will do the trick. If included in an outer join, the `nvl` function can be used on both join columns to convert the null to a character or number.

It is preferable not to take any chances on join columns and to avoid the need for outer join operators and tricks to join `NULL` values, and to make sure that master and lookup tables do not contain any redundant join column values. In a safe approach

- Master or lookup tables must have values in join columns that match all values occurring in detail tables that reference them. Master or lookup tables also must not have redundant values in join columns. This is best done through relational integrity constraints (see Chapter 29).

- Nulls in join columns must be avoided by declaring them `not null` (see Chapter 28).

IN THIS PART

Multiple Table Accesses

PART

VI

CHAPTER 18

Combining Output from Similar Tables Through Set and Pseudoset Operators

IN THIS CHAPTER

While join operations combine tables in some horizontal fashion side to side, set and pseudoset operators allow you to combine the output of two or more queries end to end.

Set and pseudoset operators can combine only those query outputs that have identical layouts in terms of number and types of columns retrieved. Therefore, if the first query returns a number, a character, and a date column, the second query must return a number, a character, and a date column as well, or else an error will result.

This is the first time in this book that a SQL statement includes more than one query—an option that is explored in different ways in the next four chapters.

 Run `crper9.sql`, which can be found on the CD-ROM, to create and load the table `pers9`.

Most examples in this chapter use the `pers1` and the `pers9` tables. `pers9` is similar to `pers1`, except that it includes wealth data. It has five rows, two of which overlap with `pers1`. Listing 18.1 displays the contents for both `pers1` and `pers5`.

Listing 18.1. Displaying the contents of two tables.

```
--      Filename: 18squ01.sql
--       Purpose: display contents of pers1 and pers9 tables
--
col id      format 99
col lname   format a11
col fmname  format a12
col age     format 99

select * from pers1;

select * from pers9;

clear columns
```

This code returns

ID	LNAME	FMNAME	SSN	AGE	S
1	Jones	David N.	895663453	34	M
2	Martinelli	A. Emery	312331818	92	M
3	Talavera	F. Espinosa	533932999	19	F
4	Kratochvil	Mary T.	969825711	48	F
5	Melsheli	Joseph K.	000342222	14	M

ID	LNAME	FMNAME	SSN	AGE	S	WEALTH
1	Jones	David N.	895663453	34	M	-143000
2	Martinelli	A. Emery	312331818	92	M	645000
6	Robinson	Faye M.	966549339	31	F	2000
7	Kazen	M. Okechuku	854291872	23	F	281990
8	Rochblatt	Harold T.	290553810	32	M	24000

Input truncated to 13 characters

Set Operators

The three set operators behave like their mathematical counterparts and return elements of a set that are distinctly different from all other elements in the set. In other words, redundant rows are not allowed. Conforming with set theory, this section, therefore, uses the term *element* to denote a nonredundant row. Here are the three set operators:

- ■ `union` returns all elements of all queries.
- ■ `intersect` displays matching elements only.
- ■ `minus` selects those elements that exist in one table but not the other.

Returning All Elements: `union`

Two queries combined through a `union` operator return all elements of both queries. First, all rows are retrieved into the temporary tablespace that is used for sorting, and the distinct set of these is returned. Listing 18.2 shows a `union` operator joining two queries, `pers1` and `pers9`.

Listing 18.2. Using a `union` operator to join two queries.

```
--       Filename: 18squ02.sql
--       Purpose: union operator joining pers1 and pers9
--
col id      format 99
col lname   format a11
col fmname  format a12
col age     format 99

select
   id,
   lname,
   fmname,
   age,
   sex
from pers1
union
select
   id,
   lname,
   fmname,
   age,
   sex
from pers9
;

clear columns
```

This code returns

```
ID LNAME       FMNAME       AGE S
--- ----------- ------------ --- -
  1 Jones       David N.      34 M
  2 Martinelli  A. Emery      92 M
  3 Talavera    F. Espinosa   19 F
```

```
4 Kratochvil   Mary T.        48 F
5 Melsheli     Joseph K.      14 M
6 Robinson     Faye M.        31 F
7 Kazen        M. Okechuku    23 F
8 Rochblatt    Harold T.      32 M
```

8 rows selected.

Therefore, the rows with ID values of 1 or 2, which occur in both queries, are displayed only once.

> **NOTE**
>
> The combined query has only one semicolon. However, as many selects as there may be, a query combined as such is only one combined statement to SQL.

Figure 18.1 illustrates the behavior of the `union` operator in the standard set theory way. Two sets of elements are returned by the subquery. These sets overlap—in this case, the rows with the ID values 1 and 2 are represented in both sets. The query returns the elements that occur only in the first set, those that occur only in the second set, and those that occur in both.

FIGURE 18.1.

The union *set operator.*

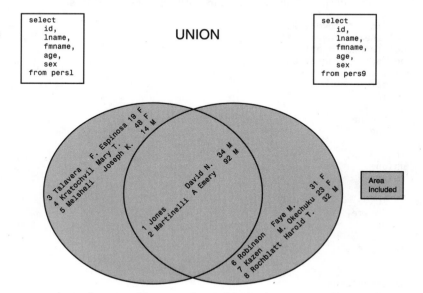

Even if the redundant rows originate in one table, the `union` operator will strip them out, just as a `select distinct` would. Listing 18.3 demonstrates this by inserting the rows with the IDs of 1 and 2 into the table `pers1` (see Chapter 24, "Manipulating Single-Table Data") and then reruns the query of the previous example. At the end, the insert is rolled back to revert `pers1` to its original state (see Chapter 25, "Control Transactions").

Listing 18.3. Using the union operator to join two queries with redundant rows.

```
--          Filename: 18squ03.sql
--           Purpose: union operator joining pers1 and pers9
--                    additional redundant rows
--
insert into pers1
   select * from pers1
   where id < 3
;

col id       format 99
col lname    format a11
col fmname   format a12
col age      format 99

select
   id,
   lname,
   fmname,
   age,
   sex
from pers1
union
select
   id,
   lname,
   fmname,
   age,
   sex
from pers9
;

clear columns

rollback;
```

This query returns the same output as 18squ02.sql.

Selecting Elements That Exist in One Table but Not the Other: minus

Note that Oracle happens to use the keyword minus for this purpose, whereas the SQL-92 standard would use except.

Two queries combined through a minus operator return all elements of the first query that do not occur in the second one. The minus operator strips out redundant rows of the first table as well.

Figure 18.2 illustrates the behavior of the minus operator in the standard set theory way. The query returns those elements that occur only in the first set. It doesn't return those that occur only in the second set or those that occur in both.

18

SET AND
PSEUDOSET
OPERATORS

ORACLE
vs. SQL

Figure 18.2.

The minus set operator.

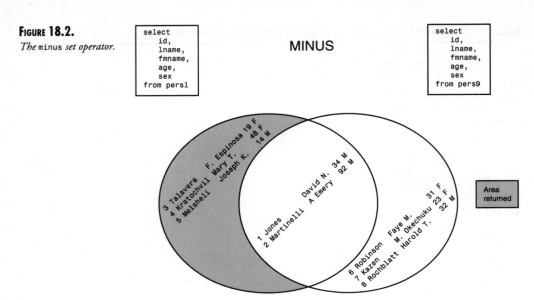

```
select
    id,
    lname,
    fmname,
    age,
    sex
from pers1
```

MINUS

```
select
    id,
    lname,
    fmname,
    age,
    sex
from pers9
```

Area returned

Listing 18.4 demonstrates the workings of the minus set operator. The 18squ04.sql script also contains the same example with redundant rows in the first table. A select of this table minus a select on pers9 returns the same rows.

Listing 18.4. Using the minus operator when joining queries.

```
--       Filename: 18squ04.sql
--        Purpose: minus operator joining pers1 and pers9
--                 additional redundant rows
--
select
    id,
    lname,
    fmname,
    age,
    sex
from pers1
minus
select
    id,
    lname,
    fmname,
    age,
    sex
from pers9
;

clear columns
```

This code returns

```
ID LNAME        FMNAME        AGE S
--- -----------  ------------  --- -
  3 Talavera     F. Espinosa    19 F
  4 Kratochvil   Mary T.        48 F
  5 Melsheli     Joseph K.      14 M
```

An Alternative to `minus` Through Outer Joins

There are other ways to obtain the same result, either through an outer join or through the use of a subquery. The next three chapters, especially Chapter 20, "Multiple-Value Subqueries," cover the use of a subquery to obtain the same result.

If the tables are joined on ID through a right outer join, meaning that the second table's ID in the `where` clause is marked with the join operator, each row in `pers1` that does not have a match in `pers9` is represented in a combined row where the `pers9` columns are all nulls. Thus, selecting the `pers1` columns of all rows where the `pers9` columns are nulls will return the same rows that a `minus` would. Listing 18.5 uses that approach to obtain the same result as `18squ04.sql`.

Listing 18.5. Using a right outer join to join queries.

```
--         Filename: 18squ05.sql
--          Purpose: same result as minus operator joining
--                   pers1 and pers9 through right outer join
--                   additional redundant rows
--
col id     format 99
col lname  format a11
col fmname format a12
col age    format 99

select
   a.id,
   a.lname,
   a.fmname,
   a.age,
   a.sex
from pers1 a, pers9 b
where a.id = b.id (+) and
      b.id is null
;
```

This code returns

```
ID LNAME        FMNAME        AGE S
--- -----------  ------------  --- -
  3 Talavera     F. Espinosa    19 F
  4 Kratochvil   Mary T.        48 F
  5 Melsheli     Joseph K.      14 M
```

18

SET AND
PSEUDOSET
OPERATORS

This is different from the `minus` set operator. Duplicate rows are printed if this approach is used, which the next part of the example shows:

```
insert into pers1
select * from pers1;

select
    a.id,
    a.lname,
    a.fmname,
    a.age,
    a.sex
from pers1 a, pers9 b
where a.id = b.id (+) and
      b.id is null
;
```

This code returns

```
ID LNAME        FMNAME        AGE S
--- -----------  -----------   --- -
  3 Talavera     F. Espinosa   19  F
  3 Talavera     F. Espinosa   19  F
  4 Kratochvil   Mary T.       48  F
  4 Kratochvil   Mary T.       48  F
  5 Melsheli     Joseph K.     14  M
  5 Melsheli     Joseph K.     14  M

6 rows selected.
```

Therefore, if redundant rows are a possibility, a `select distinct` has to be used, as shown here:

```
select distinct
    a.id,
    a.lname,
    a.fmname,
    a.age,
    a.sex
from pers1 a, pers9 b
where a.id = b.id (+) and
      b.id is null
;

clear columns

rollback;
```

This code returns the same as the very first statement in the example (`18squ04.sql`):

```
ID LNAME        FMNAME        AGE S
--- -----------  -----------   --- -
  3 Talavera     F. Espinosa   19  F
  4 Kratochvil   Mary T.       48  F
  5 Melsheli     Joseph K.     14  M
```

How fast each option runs depends on the way the database is set up. If you want to test the statements, you can do so as explained in Chapter 38, "Optimizing SQL Statement Processing." When I compared them, they were executed using a slightly different execution plan. They did take the identical amount of resources to execute, though.

Keeping Matching Rows Only: `intersect`

Two queries combined through an `intersect` operator return all elements of the first query that also occur in the second one. The `intersect` operator strips out redundant rows in the matching set as well.

Figure 18.3 illustrates that the query returns those elements that occur in both sets, as expressed by the overlapping area of the circles.

FIGURE 18.3.

The intersect *set operator.*

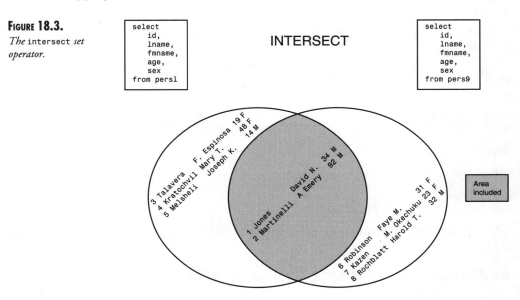

Listing 18.6 shows the effect of combining two queries through the `intersect` set operator.

Listing 18.6. Using the `intersect` operator to join two queries.

```
--        Filename: 18squ06.sql
--        Purpose: intersect operator joining pers1 and pers9
--                 additional redundant rows
--
insert into pers1
select * from pers1
;

insert into pers9
select * from pers9
where id < 3
;

col id     format 99
col lname  format a11
col fmname format a12
col age    format 99
```

continues

18

SET AND
PSEUDOSET
OPERATORS

Listing 18.6. continued

```
select
   id,
   lname,
   fmname,
   age,
   sex
from pers1
intersect
select
   id,
   lname,
   fmname,
   age,
   sex
from pers9
;

clear columns
```

This code returns

```
ID LNAME         FMNAME        AGE S
--- ----------   -----------   --- -
  1 Jones         David N.       34 M
  2 Martinelli    A. Emery       92 M
```

The example contains a second statement with redundant rows that returns the same output as the statement printed here.

An Alternative to `intersect` Through Inner Joins

As is the case with `minus`, the intersect results can be obtained through other ways as well. Besides a subquery, the discussion of which is delayed until Chapter 20, a `select distinct` on an inner join of the tables will work fine.

An inner join on ID will keep only the rows that have matches in both tables. Therefore, it is necessary to create only the inner join and to select all `pers1` columns from the qualifying rows. This is what Listing 18.7 does. Note that this example will work only if the `insert` statements at the very beginning of `18squ05.sql` have been run.

Listing 18.7. Using an inner join to join queries.

```
--      Filename: 18squ07.sql
--       Purpose: same result as intersect operator joining
--                pers1 and pers9 through inner join
--                additional redundant rows
--
col id     format 99
col lname  format a11
col fmname format a12
col age    format 99

select
```

```
        a.id,
        a.lname,
        a.fmname,
        a.age,
        a.sex
from pers1 a, pers9 b
where a.id = b.id
;
```

This code returns

```
ID LNAME       FMNAME       AGE S
--- ----------- ------------ --- -
  1 Jones       David N.      34 M
  2 Martinelli  A. Emery      92 M
```

Duplicate matching rows are printed if this approach is used, just as they are in with the preceding outer join example. The following statement shows that:

```
insert into pers1
select * from pers1
where id < 3
;

select
   a.id,
   a.lname,
   a.fmname,
   a.age,
   a.sex
from pers1 a, pers9 b
where a.id = b.id
;
```

This code returns

```
ID LNAME       FMNAME       AGE S
--- ----------- ------------ --- -
  1 Jones       David N.      34 M
  1 Jones       David N.      34 M
  2 Martinelli  A. Emery      92 M
  2 Martinelli  A. Emery      92 M
```

If, however, both tables have duplicate rows, each of these in one table is joined with each matching one in the other table, and many rows end up being returned, as the following statement demonstrates:

```
insert into pers9
select * from pers9
where id < 3;

select
    a.id,
    a.lname,
    a.fmname,
    a.age,
    a.sex
```

```
from pers1 a, pers9 b
where a.id = b.id
;
```

This code returns

```
 ID LNAME       FMNAME        AGE S
 -- ---------   -----------   --- -
  1 Jones       David N.       34 M
  1 Jones       David N.       34 M
  1 Jones       David N.       34 M
  1 Jones       David N.       34 M
  2 Martinelli  A. Emery       92 M
  2 Martinelli  A. Emery       92 M
  2 Martinelli  A. Emery       92 M
  2 Martinelli  A. Emery       92 M

8 rows selected.
```

Again, a `select distinct` takes care of duplicate rows. The last statement of the example uses the following:

```
select distinct
    a.id,
    a.lname,
    a.fmname,
    a.age,
    a.sex
from pers1 a, pers9 b
where a.id = b.id
;

clear columns

rollback;
```

This returns the same rows as the first `select` statement at the beginning of the example.

Keeping All Rows Retrieved by All Multiple Queries: union all

The `union all` pseudoset operator does not follow the mathematical rules of set theory because it returns rows of all queries whether they are redundant or not. It is, therefore, a *pseudoset operator*. It simply prints the output of the first query followed by the output of the second query. Listing 18.8 illustrates the use of the `union all` operator to join pers1 and pers9.

Listing 18.8. Using a union all to join queries.

```
--        Filename: 18squ08.sql
--        Purpose: union all operator joining pers1 and pers9
--
col id     format 99
col lname  format a11
col fmname format a12
col age    format 99

select
   id,
   lname,
   fmname,
   age,
   sex
from pers1
union all
select
   id,
   lname,
   fmname,
   age,
   sex
from pers9
;
```

This code returns

```
ID LNAME       FMNAME       AGE S
--- ----------- ------------ --- -
  1 Jones       David N.      34 M
  2 Martinelli  A. Emery      92 M
  3 Talavera    F. Espinosa   19 F
  4 Kratochvil  Mary T.       48 F
  5 Melsheli    Joseph K.     14 M
  1 Jones       David N.      34 M
  2 Martinelli  A. Emery      92 M
  6 Robinson    Faye M.       31 F
  7 Kazen       M. Okechuku   23 F
  8 Rochblatt   Harold T.     32 M

10 rows selected.
```

Figure 18.4 illustrates the workings of the union all operator in typical set graphics: The left square encloses the output of the first query, and the right square encloses the output of the second query. Because the overlapping lines are printed once for each query, they are repeated on the figure as well.

FIGURE 18.4.

The output of two queries combined with the union all *pseudoset operator.*

UNION ALL

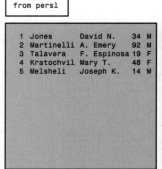

```
select
    id,
    lname,
    fmname,
    age,
    sex
from persl
```

1	Jones	David N.	34	M
2	Martinelli	A. Emery	92	M
3	Talavera	F. Espinosa	19	F
4	Kratochvil	Mary T.	48	F
5	Melsheli	Joseph K.	14	M

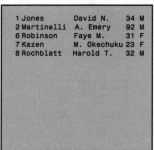

1	Jones	David N.	34	M
2	Martinelli	A. Emery	92	M
6	Robinson	Faye M.	31	F
7	Kazen	M. Okechuku	23	F
8	Rochblatt	Harold T.	32	M

Area included in output

Includes duplicate rows

Combining Set and Pseudoset Operators

Two kinds of operators are needed to create compound conditions: conditional operators for the conditions proper and logical operators to combine them. Set operators, however, can combine simple queries and compound queries alike. The queries may be enclosed between parentheses as applicable.

Exclusive Union

As is the case with the exclusive or, there is no corresponding exclusive union set operator either. An exclusive union contains all elements that are retrieved by the first query or the second query, but not both. Figure 18.5 shows the set or area of interest—all elements or the entire area covered by the combined set, with the exception of matching elements or the overlapping area.

If all nonmatching rows of both tables are to be selected, a compound statement has to be used. There are two straightforward ways to do that:

- By combining a union of the queries and an intersect of the queries through a (query1 union query2) minus (query2 intersect query1). The union operation returns the entire set, and the intersect operation returns only the matching set. By subtracting the latter from the former, the nonoverlapping portion remains.

- By combining a minus of the queries and a minus of the reversed queries through a union minus—(query1 minus query2) union (query2 minus query1). The first query minus the second query returns the portion of the overlapping area that pertains to the first query only. The second query minus the first returns the other portion. The two combined through the union return the nonoverlapping set.

FIGURE 18.5.

The output of two queries combined with an exclusive union.

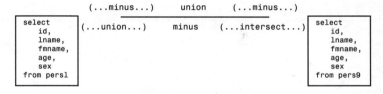

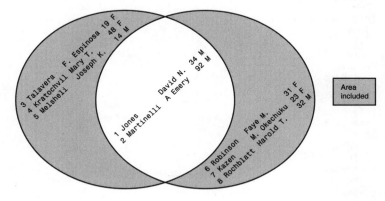

Listing 18.9 uses both approaches.

Listing 18.9. Using compound statements to join queries.

```
--          Filename: 18squ09.sql
--          Purpose: union minus intersect operator
--                   minus union minus    operator
--                   joining pers1 and pers9
--                   additional redundant rows
--
--
insert into pers1
select * from pers1
;

insert into pers9
select * from pers9
where id < 3
;

col id      format 99
col lname   format a11
col fmname  format a12
col age     format 99

(select
   id,
   lname,
   fmname,
   age,
   sex
from pers1
```

18

SET AND
PSEUDOSET
OPERATORS

continues

Listing 18.9. continued

```
union
select
    id,
    lname,
    fmname,
    age,
    sex
from pers9)
minus
(select
    id,
    lname,
    fmname,
    age,
    sex
from pers1
intersect
select
    id,
    lname,
    fmname,
    age,
    sex
from pers9)
;

(select
    id,
    lname,
    fmname,
    age,
    sex
from pers1
minus
select
    id,
    lname,
    fmname,
    age,
    sex
from pers9)
union
(select
    id,
    lname,
    fmname,
    age,
    sex
from pers9
minus
select
    id,
    lname,
    fmname,
    age,
    sex
```

```
from pers1)
;

rollback;
clear columns
```

Both queries return

```
 ID LNAME        FMNAME       AGE S
--- -----------  -----------  --- -
  3 Talavera     F. Espinosa   19 F
  4 Kratochvil   Mary T.       48 F
  5 Melsheli     Joseph K.     14 M
  6 Robinson     Faye M.       31 F
  7 Kazen        M. Okechuku   23 F
  8 Rochblatt    Harold T.     32 M
```

Full Outer Joins Through union all

As I said in Chapter 17, "Joins," for the time being Oracle allows only for a left or a right outer join, but not for a full one. If two tables are joined, an inner join returns all matching rows. Through an outer join, the nonmatching rows of one table can be retrieved and combined with a NULL row of the other, or vice versa.

The full outer join, however, would retrieve all three groups of rows:

■ The matching rows

■ The rows of the first table combined with the NULL row of the second

■ The rows of the second table combined with the NULL row of the first

The first two groups of rows can be retrieved through a right outer join. A left outer join retrieves the first and the third group. If one of these expressions uses the minus-through-outer-join approach to eliminate the matching rows (and a.id is NULL), which is demonstrated earlier in this chapter, all components are there. The union all operator can now retrieve everything. Listing 18.10 includes the necessary code.

Listing 18.10. Performing an outer join using union all.

```
--       Filename: 18squ10.sql
--        Purpose: retrieval from master-detail table
--                 full outer join through union all
--
select
   decode(name,NULL,'NULLTYPE',name) inc_type,
   to_char(sum(amount))              total
from
   inc2   i,
   inclu2 l
where i.type = l.type (+)
group by
```

continues

18

SET AND
PSEUDOSET
OPERATORS

Listing 18.10. continued

```
    sortorder,
    name
union all
select
    name inc_type,
    decode (sum(amount),NULL,'NULLAMT',to_char(sum(amount))) total
from
    inc2    i,
    inclu2 l
where i.type (+) = l.type and
      i.type is null
group by
    sortorder,
    name
;
```

This code returns

```
INC_TYPE   TOTAL
--------   ----------------------------------------
INTEREST   5938
SALARY     180690
PROFIT     196000
ROYALTY    45633
NULLTYPE   88210
GVMT. SSN  NULLAMT
6 rows selected.
```

Typical Errors Occurring with Set Operators

Set and pseudoset operators can combine only those query outputs that have identical layouts in terms of number and types of columns retrieved.

Unequal Number of Columns

If the queries do not return the same number of columns, an error will result, as shown in Listing 18.11.

Listing 18.11. Joining queries with an unequal number of columns.

```
--          Filename: 18squ11.sql
--          Purpose: union all operator joining pers1 and pers9
--                   inconsistent number of columns
--
col id      format 99
col lname   format a11
col fmname  format a12
col age     format 99

select
    *
from pers1
union all
```

```
select
    *
from pers9
;

clear columns
```

This code returns

```
select
*
ERROR at line 1:
ORA-01789: query block has incorrect number of result columns
```

The reason for the error is that pers1 and pers9 are not identical in their layout. pers9 has one more column, WEALTH:

```
SQL> desc pers1

Name                             Null?     Type
-------------------------------- --------- ----
ID                               NOT NULL  NUMBER(2)
LNAME                                      VARCHAR2(15)
FMNAME                                     VARCHAR2(15)
SSN                                        CHAR(9)
AGE                                        NUMBER(3)
SEX                                        CHAR(1)

SQL> desc pers9

Name                             Null?     Type
-------------------------------- --------- ----
ID                               NOT NULL  NUMBER(2)
LNAME                                      VARCHAR2(15)
FMNAME                                     VARCHAR2(15)
SSN                                        CHAR(9)
AGE                                        NUMBER(3)
SEX                                        CHAR(1)
WEALTH                                     NUMBER(9)
```

18

SET AND
PSEUDOSET
OPERATORS

Inconsistent Datatypes

An error will also result if the queries return the same number of columns but the datatypes of these columns are inconsistent across queries. Therefore, if the first query returns a number, a character, and a date column, the second query must return a number, a character, and a date column as well, or else an error will result. This requirement is actually quite forgiving; for its purposes, char datatypes match with varchar2, and any number datatype can be combined with the same or any other number datatype. The following example explores some unions with inconsistent datatypes. (See Listing 18.12.)

Listing 18.12. Joining queries with inconsistent datatypes.

```
--        Filename: 18squ12.sql
--        Purpose: union all operator joining pers1 and pers9
--                 inconsistent datatypes
--
col id      format 99
col lname   format a11
col fmname  format a12
col age     format 99

select
   id,
   lname,
   fmname,
   age,
   sex
from pers1
union all
select
   1,
   2,
   3,
   4,
   5
from dual
;
```

The statement returns an error because `lname` and `fmname` are `varchar2`, `sex` is `char`, but all five constants of the second query are numbers:

```
lname,
   *
ERROR at line 3:
ORA-01790: expression must have same datatype as corresponding expression
```

To fix that error, just enclose 2, 3, and 5 in single quotes:

```
select
   id,
   lname,
   fmname,
   age,
   sex
from pers1
union all
select
   1,
   '2',
   '3',
   4,
   '5'
from dual;
```

Doing so returns the following:

```
ID LNAME        FMNAME       AGE S
--- ----------- ------------ --- -
  1 Jones        David N.      34 M
  2 Martinelli   A. Emery      92 M
  3 Talavera     F. Espinosa   19 F
  4 Kratochvil   Mary T.       48 F
  5 Melsheli     Joseph K.     14 M
  1 2            3              4 5

6 rows selected.
```

The last line was generated from the second query.

Another issue is raised by null constants. The following statement of the example has a null constant in the column that corresponds to ID:

```
select
    id,
    lname,
    fmname,
    age,
    sex
from pers1
union all
select
    NULL,
    '2',
    '3',
    4,
    '5'
from dual
;
```

It returns an error:

```
lname,
    *
ERROR at line 3:
ORA-01790: expression must have same datatype as corresponding expression
```

This error can be fixed by typecasting the nulls through to_number and to_char functions. These functions still return nulls, but nulls of type number or type char, which suffices to create consistency of datatypes. This is shown in the following:

```
select
    id,
    lname,
    fmname,
    age,
    sex
from pers1
union all
select
    to_number(NULL),
    'ONE LINE FROM',
    'DUAL',
```

```
    to_number(NULL),
    to_char(NULL)
from dual
;
```

This code returns

```
ID LNAME             FMNAME         AGE S
--- --------------   ------------   --- -
  1 Jones            David N.        34 M
  2 Martinelli       A. Emery        92 M
  3 Talavera         F. Espinosa     19 F
  4 Kratochvil       Mary T.         48 F
  5 Melsheli         Joseph K.       14 M
    ONE LINE FROM    DUAL

6 rows selected.
```

The number datatype, on the other hand, is very forgiving. Numerical columns of any sort—integer, fixed point, or floating point—can be combined, which is shown in the final three parts of the example:

```
select id from pers1
union
select amount from inc2
;
```

ID is a two-digit integer, and amount is an eight-digit integer. The preceding statement returns

```
        ID
-----------
         1
         2
         3
         4
         5
        50
       110
       200
       778
     4,588
     4,800
     4,870
    12,000
    14,689
    45,633
    68,933
    80,000
    95,820
   184,000

19 rows selected.
```

Dividing amount by 1,000 (thus rendering a fixed-point number) and combining that with the two-digit integer ID works as well, as the following statement shows:

```
col id     format 99,999,999.999
```

```
select id from pers1
union
select amount/1000 from inc2
;
```

This code returns

```
              ID
- - - - - - - - - - - - - -
            .050
            .110
            .200
            .778
           1.000
           2.000
           3.000
           4.000
           4.588
           4.800
           4.870
           5.000
          12.000
          14.689
          45.633
          68.933
          80.000
          95.820
         184.000
```

19 rows selected.

Finally, a union with ft1 from float1 joins an integer to a floating-point number, as shown here:

```
col id      format 9.99999999EEEE

select id from pers1
union
select f1 from float1
;

clear columns
```

This code returns

```
               ID
- - - - - - - - - - - - - - -
-1.23456789E+125
-1.23456789E-127
 1.23456789E-127
 1.00000000E+00
 2.00000000E+00
 3.00000000E+00
 4.00000000E+00
 5.00000000E+00
 1.23456789E+125
```

9 rows selected.

Ordering Output Retrieved Through Set and Pseudoset Operators

Output combined through set and pseudoset operators can be ordered, but two limitations apply:

■ Only one order by subclause may be used for the entire statement.

■ The columns that are listed in the order by comma list *must be included in the* select *comma list*. This is different from a one-shot select where any column in any accessed table can be used for querying, whether included in the select comma list or not.

Ordering by Retrieved Columns

Listing 18.13 orders the output from 18squ03.sql by the second and third columns.

Listing 18.13. Ordering output when joining queries.

```
--       Filename: 18squ13.sql
--       Purpose: union operator joining pers1 and pers9
--                ordering output
--
col id     format 99
col lname  format a11
col fmname format a12
col age    format 99
select
   id,
   lname,
   fmname,
   age,
   sex
from pers1
union
select
   id,
   lname,
   fmname,
   age,
   sex
from pers9
order by 2, 3
;
```

This code returns

```
ID LNAME        FMNAME       AGE S
--- ----------- ------------ --- -
  1 Jones        David N.      34 M
  7 Kazen        M. Okechuku   23 F
```

```
     4 Kratochvil   Mary T.         48 F
     2 Martinelli   A. Emery        92 M
     5 Melsheli     Joseph K.       14 M
     6 Robinson     Faye M.         31 F
     8 Rochblatt    Harold T.       32 M
     3 Talavera     F. Espinosa     19 F
```

8 rows selected.

> **CAUTION**
>
> The positional order by syntax, such as `order by 2, 3`, must be used to order the output. Because only the datatypes of columns must be the same and not the names, a name does not always identify a column without ambiguity (because the name might be different in the queries, as was the case in the previous section with `id` and `ft1`). Naming order columns will not return an error, but it will not sort either, as the following example shows:
>
> ```
> select
>     id,
>     lname,
>     fmname,
>     age,
>     sex
> from pers1
> union
> select
>     id,
>     lname,
>     fmname,
>     age,
>     sex
> from pers9
> order by lname, fmname
> ;
> ```
>
> This code returns the following:
>
> ```
>  ID LNAME        FMNAME        AGE S
> --- ----------   -----------   --- -
>    1 Jones        David N.       34 M
>    2 Martinelli   A. Emery       92 M
>    3 Talavera     F. Espinosa    19 F
>    4 Kratochvil   Mary T.        48 F
>    5 Melsheli     Joseph K.      14 M
>    6 Robinson     Faye M.        31 F
>    7 Kazen        M. Okechuku    23 F
>    8 Rochblatt    Harold T.      32 M
>
> 8 rows selected.
> ```

If two `order by` clauses are used in one statement, as in Listing 18.14, an error will result.

Listing 18.14. Using two order by clauses in one statement.

```
--          Filename: 18squ14.sql
--          Purpose: union operator joining pers1 and pers9
--                   ordering output
--                   error on two order by clauses
--
col id     format 99
col lname  format a11
col fmname format a12
col age    format 99

select
   id,
   lname,
   fmname,
   age,
   sex
from pers1
order by 3,2
union
select
   id,
   lname,
   fmname,
   age,
   sex
from pers9
order by 2, 3
;

clear columns
```

This is the error that will result:

```
union
*
ERROR at line 9:
ORA-00933: SQL command not properly ended
```

This is not exactly a 4GL error message. What it means is that SQL expects the statement to end after the order by section and is therefore confused to see union rather than a semicolon.

Ordering by Nonretrieved Column(s)

If you recall, the columns in the order by comma list must be included in the select comma list. This is not really a problem. If it is desired to sort by a column that is not to be printed, the noprint option can be used in SQL*Plus. Corresponding options exist in other client tools. Oracle Reports, for example, allows you to specify a column in the data model, meaning that it will be retrieved, but not printed in the report. Listing 18.15 adapts 18squ15.sql to order by fmname without printing that column.

Listing 18.15. Ordering output by columns not retrieved.

```
--       Filename: 18squ15.sql
--       Purpose: union operator joining pers1 and pers9
--                ordering output by not printed column
--
col id      format 99
col lname   format a11
col fmname  noprint
col age     format 99

select
   id,
   lname,
   fmname,
   age,
   sex
from pers1
union
select
   id,
   lname,
   fmname,
   age,
   sex
from pers9
order by 3
;

clear columns
```

This code returns

```
ID LNAME        AGE S
--- ----------- --- -
  2 Martinelli   92 M
  1 Jones        34 M
  3 Talavera     19 F
  6 Robinson     31 F
  8 Rochblatt    32 M
  5 Melsheli     14 M
  7 Kazen        23 F
  4 Kratochvil   48 F

8 rows selected.
```

Ordering by Dummy Column(s)

Finally, it is possible to include a dummy column that is a different constant per query, set that column to noprint, and order by it. That way, the ordering by query in the statement can be assured. Listing 18.16 demonstrates this approach.

The first column is aliased as dummy to create a link with the noprint statement. It is referenced as the first column through the order by 1 subclause.

Listing 18.16. Ordering output by dummy columns.

```
--          Filename: 18squ16.sql
--           Purpose: union operator
--                    ordering output by dummy column
--
col dummy noprint
col statement a40

select 1 dummy, 'from first query' statement from dual
union
select 4 dummy, 'from second query' statement from dual
union
select 6 dummy, 'from third query' statement from dual
union
select 3 dummy, 'from fourth query' statement from dual
union
select 2 dummy, 'from fifth query' statement from dual
union
select 5 dummy, 'from sixth query' statement from dual
union
select 0 dummy, 'from seventh query' statement from dual
order by 1
;

clear columns
```

This code returns

```
STATEMENT
-----------------
from seventh query
from first query
from fifth query
from fourth query
from second query
from sixth query
from third query

7 rows selected.
```

TIP

If a different constant is included, two otherwise identical rows from two queries now are no longer identical—they differ by the constant. This approach, therefore, may retrieve different sets than the no-dummy-column version would.

Summary

Set and pseudoset operators allow you to combine the output of two or more queries end to end. These operators can combine only those query outputs that have identical layouts in terms of number and types of columns retrieved. Numerical columns of any sort—integer, fixed point, or floating point—can be combined. Output from char and varchar2 columns may be combined as well.

The three set operators behave like their mathematical counterparts and return elements of a set that are distinctly different from all other elements in the set (in other words, redundant rows are not allowed):

- union returns all elements of all queries.
- intersect displays matching elements only. The same results can be obtained through an inner join where the columns of only one table are included in the select comma list.
- minus selects those elements that exist in one table but not in the other. The same result can be obtained through a right outer join where only those rows of a table are selected that do not have a match in another table. Such rows can be identified as those combined rows where the second table's columns are all nulls.

The pseudoset operator union all does not follow the mathematical rules of set theory. It simply prints the output of the first query followed by the output of the second query.

Set operators can combine simple and compound queries alike. The queries may be enclosed between parentheses as applicable. Using such compound statements, exclusive union or full outer join output can be generated:

- The exclusive union is generated through the statement (query1 union query2) minus (query2 intersect query1) or through (query1 minus query2) union (query2 minus query1).
- The full outer join output can be generated through a union all combination of a left and right outer join, where one of these expressions uses the minus through outer join approach to eliminate the matching rows (and a.id is NULL).

Output combined through set and pseudoset operators can be ordered, but only one order by subclause must be used for the entire statement, and all order by columns must be included in the select comma list. It is possible, however, to include a column or a dummy variable in the select comma list and set that column to noprint in SQL*Plus, or suppress printing through methods available in other client tools.

CHAPTER 19

Single-Value Subqueries

IN THIS CHAPTER

Thus far, we have only issued one query at a time against one or more tables. Single queries are the typical case in data retrieval.

SQL allows for the use of subqueries, which provide a number of convenient, although not necessarily efficient, options for more complex tasks. This and the next three chapters will be devoted to subqueries. Three options are provided:

■ Subqueries are nested when a subquery is executed and its results are inserted into the where condition of the main query. This chapter starts with subqueries that return exactly one value. Chapter 20, "Multiple-Value Subqueries," provides information about queries that return multiple rows or columns.

■ Correlated subqueries present the opposite case, where the main query is executed first and a subquery is executed for every row retrieved by the main query. (See Chapter 21, "Correlated Subqueries," for more information.)

■ Hierarchical subqueries are specific to recursive relationships and the resulting trees. These statements can be recognized as subqueries only through the connect by and start with subclauses. (See Chapter 22, "Trees and Hierarchical Subqueries," for more information.)

Two-Stage Query Execution

Until this point, all conditions for the where or having subclauses have been static, such as where age > 30. If, however, the object were to find everybody who is older than the average person in the table, two queries are necessary: one to find the average age and the other to find all records where the age is greater than the average age. The following example shows that approach:

```
select avg(age) from pers1;
```

This code returns

```
 AVG(AGE)
---------
    41.4
```

This value is then inserted into the where clause of the second query to retrieve the desired rows, as follows:

```
select *
from pers1
where age > 41.4
;
```

This code returns

```
        ID LNAME           FMNAME           SSN              AGE S
--------- --------------- --------------- --------- --------- -
         2 Martinelli      A. Emery         312331818        92 M
         4 Kratochvil      Mary T.          969825711        48 F
```

The second query is the important one; it returns the information that was desired in the first place. The first query is subsidiary to it; it only retrieves a value that was necessary to fit into the second one—the average age.

Subqueries allow you to do exactly the same, but in a one-shot process. The statement begins with the outer query. The value 41.4 in the where subclause, however, is replaced by the subquery or inner query, which will return this value. The following statement does that:

```
select *
from pers1
where age >
    (select avg(age) from pers1)
;
```

This code returns the same output:

```
   ID LNAME           FMNAME          SSN          AGE S
-------- --------------- --------------- --------- --------- -
    2 Martinelli      A. Emery        312331818     92 M
    4 Kratochvil      Mary T.         969825711     48 F
```

Just as was the case with the initial example, the query is executed in two stages, except that now SQL does all the work. SQL executes the inner query first to find the average age. Then it executes the outer query, using the value returned by the inner query in the where subclause (see Figure 19.1).

FIGURE 19.1.
The execution order of a nested subquery.

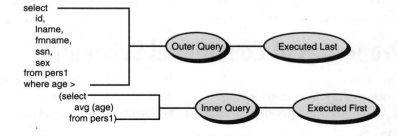

19

SINGLE-VALUE
SUBQUERIES

CAUTION

While SQL does all the work, you still need to make sure that your subquery returns exactly one value. If you are not absolutely sure, test it first.

The following statement includes a subquery that doesn't retrieve any rows:

```
SQL> select *
  2  from pers1
  3  where age >
  4      (select age from pers1 where id = 6)
  5  ;

no rows selected
```

The last-line is a SQL-style terse statement, which does not indicate an error. Go figure. No rows are selected because no rows fulfill the condition in the subquery. The next statement uses a subquery that returns too many values:

```
SQL>
SQL> select *
  2  from pers1
  3  where age >
  4      (select age from pers1 where age > 20)
  5  ;
ERROR:
ORA-01427: single-row subquery returns more than one row
no rows selected
```

The resulting error message is a no-brainer; SQL tells you exactly what's wrong.

The final statement uses a subquery that returns too many columns:

```
SQL> select *
  2  from pers1
  3  where age >
  4      (select min(age), max(age) from pers1)
  5  ;
   (select min(age), max(age) from pers1)
    *
ERROR at line 4:
ORA-00913: too many values
```

The last error message is not quite as clear, but mercifully, the offending line is printed as well, and it is the line that should be printed.

Properties of Conditional Subqueries

The preceding subqueries could have also been named conditional subqueries because what they return is subsequently inserted into a condition within the outer query. The inner queries of conditional subquery statements must have the following two conditions:

- They must be enclosed in parentheses.
- They must be on the right side of conditions.

The following example shows the errors that result if these rules are violated:

```
select *
from pers1
where (select avg(age) from pers1) < age
;
```

This code returns the following:

```
where (select avg(age) from pers1) < age
      *
ERROR at line 3:
ORA-00936: missing expression
```

This is another case where an error message returned by SQL is a bit terse. The same message results from omitting the parentheses:

```
SQL> select *
  2  from pers1
  3  where age >
  4     select avg(age) from pers1 where id = 6
  5  ;
   select avg(age) from pers1 where id = 6
   *
ERROR at line 4:
ORA-00936: missing expression
```

> **NOTE**
>
> Subqueries and the outer query may retrieve information from different tables or sets thereof.

Single-Row Comparison Operators

As their name says, single-row subqueries must return only one row. They can be used with the six comparison operators that compare exactly one value (expression) with another one shown in Table 19.1.

Table 19.1. Single-row comparison operators.

Operator	Meaning
=	Equal to
<>	Not equal to
>	Greater than
>=	Greater than or equal to
<	Less than
<=	Less than or equal to

The following example runs six sets of queries with subqueries, one set for each operator:

```
select '= ' op,
       id,
       lname,
       fmname,
       ssn,
       age,
       sex
from pers1
where age =
   (select avg(age) from pers1)
;
```

19

SINGLE-VALUE
SUBQUERIES

This returns the following:

```
no rows selected
```

It makes perfect sense that the query does not retrieve any row because no person in the table is exactly as old as the average. For the same reason, the not equal to (<>) condition returns all five rows:

```
select '<>' op,
       id,
       lname,
       fmname,
       ssn,
       age,
       sex
from pers1
where age <>
   (select avg(age) from pers1)
;
```

This code returns

```
OP       ID  LNAME           FMNAME           SSN        AGE       S
-- --------- --------------- ---------------- ---------- --------- -
<>        1  Jones           David N.         895663453  34        M
<>        2  Martinelli      A. Emery         312331818  92        M
<>        3  Talavera        F. Espinosa      533932999  19        F
<>        4  Kratochvil      Mary T.          969825711  48        F
<>        5  Melsheli        Joseph K.        000342222  14        M
```

The greater than condition (>) returns the same rows as the greater than or equal to condition (>=) because of the same reason:

```
select '> ' op,
       id,
       lname,
       fmname,
       ssn,
       age,
       sex
from pers1
where age >
   (select avg(age) from pers1)
;
```

This code returns the following output:

```
OP       ID LNAME            FMNAME           SSN        AGE       S
-- --------- --------------- ---------------- ---------- --------- -
>         2 Martinelli       A. Emery         312331818 92         M
>         4 Kratochvil       Mary T.          969825711 48         F
```

as does the following statement:

```
select '>=' op,
       id,
       lname,
       fmname,
       ssn,
       age,
       sex
from pers1
where age >=
   (select avg(age) from pers1)
;
```

OP	ID	LNAME	FMNAME	SSN	AGE	S
>=	2	Martinelli	A. Emery	312331818	92	M
>=	4	Kratochvil	Mary T.	969825711	48	F

Similarly, the less than condition (<) returns the same as the less than or equal to condition (<=). The following code illustrates this:

```
select '< ' op,
       id,
       lname,
       fmname,
       ssn,
       age,
       sex
from pers1
where age <
   (select avg(age) from pers1)
;
```

OP	ID	LNAME	FMNAME	SSN	AGE	S
<	1	Jones	David N.	895663453	34	M
<	3	Talavera	F. Espinosa	533932999	19	F
<	5	Melsheli	Joseph K.	000342222	14	M

```
select '<=' op,
       id,
       lname,
       fmname,
       ssn,
       age,
       sex
from pers1
where age <=
   (select avg(age) from pers1)
;
```

OP	ID	LNAME	FMNAME	SSN	AGE	S
<=	1	Jones	David N.	895663453	34	M
<=	3	Talavera	F. Espinosa	533932999	19	F
<=	5	Melsheli	Joseph K.	000342222	14	M

19

Parallel Subqueries

A further enhancement is the possibility to include more than one subquery into a statement. One possibility is to nest the query so that a main query is dependent on the results of a subquery, which in turn depends on the results of another one. A nested subquery is not limited to three levels.

> **TIP**
>
> Although it may be appealing, you are well advised to keep the complexity of expressions down. You may feel really smart and excited about that eight-level nested query with at least two parallel branches per level. These feelings will quickly subside if you, or worse, somebody else, must debug a tiny logical error of the statement a year later. Unless you have a major performance reason to do otherwise, keep it as simple as possible.

Further subqueries that are parallel to the first are much more frequent. The main query has a compound where clause, more than one component of which has subqueries attached.

The following query retrieves names, age, wealth, and income of every record in pers3 where the age, wealth, and income are greater than average. But first, let's recapitulate the averages for these three variables by themselves. To do this, type the following:

```
SQL> select avg(wealth) from pers3;

AVG(WEALTH)
----------
    622680
SQL>
SQL> select avg(interest + salary + profit + royalty) from pers3;

AVG(INTEREST+SALARY+PROFIT+ROYALTY)
-----------------------------------
                              75786
```

The query necessary to retrieve that information consists of a main or outer query whose where condition has three parts. Each of these has a subquery attached to it. These are parallel because they are executed at approximately the same time. The results are put into the respective places of the outer query, which is executed next (see Listing 19.1).

Listing 19.1. Using three subqueries against different tables.

```
--       Filename: 19squ01.sql
--        Purpose: three subqueries against different tables
--
select
   lname,
   fmname,
   age,
```

```
   wealth,
   (interest + salary + profit + royalty) income
from pers3
where age >
   (select avg(age) from pers1)
and   wealth >
   (select avg(wealth) from pers3)
and   (interest + salary + profit + royalty) >
   (select avg(interest + salary + profit + royalty) from pers3)
;
```

This code returns

```
LNAME              FMNAME               AGE     WEALTH    INCOME
--------------     ----------------     ------  --------  --------
Martinelli         A. Emery             92      645000    92900
Kratochvil         Mary T.              48      2400600   188800
```

Incidentally, the code outputs the same two people.

Figure 19.2 shows the execution order of this statement. The inner queries are executed first, followed by the outer query.

FIGURE 19.2.

The execution order of parallel subqueries.

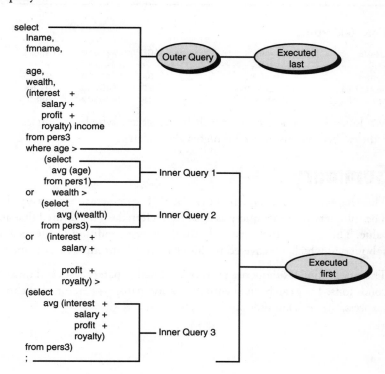

If, however, the boolean operators are set to or, a third row will be retrieved, as Listing 19.2 shows.

Listing 19.2. Using or when retrieving data from different tables.

```
--        Filename: 19squ02.sql
--          Purpose: three subqueries against different tables
--
select
   lname,
   fmname,
   age,
   wealth,
   (interest + salary + profit + royalty) income
from pers3
where age >
   (select avg(age) from pers1)
or   wealth >
   (select avg(wealth) from pers3)
or   (interest + salary + profit + royalty) >
   (select avg(interest + salary + profit + royalty) from pers3)
;
```

This code returns

LNAME	FMNAME	AGE	WEALTH	INCOME
Jones	David N.	34	43000	92200
Martinelli	A. Emery	92	645000	92900
Kratochvil	Mary T.	48	2400600	188800c

Mr. Jones, who is clearly younger than average and who has much less wealth, is retrieved nevertheless because his income is higher than average.

Summary

This chapter introduces the first cases of SQL statements that consist of more than one query. The subquery (or inner query as it is often referred to) is executed first and returns exactly one value. This value is then inserted into the where condition of the second query. Single-value subqueries, which are covered in this chapter, must return exactly one value.

These conditional subqueries must be enclosed in parentheses and must be on the right side of conditions. They can be used with the six comparison operators that compare exactly one value (expression) with another one: =, <>, >, >=, <, and <=.

CHAPTER 20

Multiple-Value Subqueries

IN THIS CHAPTER

Whereas Chapter 19, "Single-Value Subqueries," deals strictly with subqueries that return exactly one value, this chapter extends subqueries to retrieve more than one value. Two types of multiple-value subqueries exist:

■ Multiple-row subqueries return one or more rows that can be incorporated into the main query's where statement by means of special multiple-row comparison operators.

■ Multiple-column subqueries return matched sets of values that can then be compared with corresponding matched value sets in the main query.

This chapter discusses both cases. It also covers compound situations, in which a single-value subquery is nested within multiple-row subqueries, or where multiple-row and multiple-column subqueries are combined.

Multiple-Row Subqueries

Imagine a situation in which you need to list all lawyers from the `lawyer1` table who work in offices that yield a larger-than-average hourly rate (weighted by hour). The answer to this question could be found by executing three queries.

NOTE

All queries in this section are provided in the file `20squa.sql` on the CD-ROM that accompanies this book.

The first query finds the average hourly rate per lawyer:

```
SQL> select
  2      avg(bgross/bhrs)
  3  from lawyer1
  4  ;

AVG(BGROSS/BHRS)
----------------
        152.7733
```

The second query shows the average hourly rate per office in descending order:

```
SQL> select
  2      office,
  3      avg(bgross/bhrs)
  4  from lawyer1
  5  group by office
  6  order by office desc
  7  ;

OFFICE           AVG(BGROSS/BHRS)
---------------  ----------------
New York                201.52445
Los Angeles             155.55272
Houston                 110.55293
Boston                  107.26889
```

If you insert the first query as a subquery for the second, you can filter out the offices that average a higher billable rate than the average over all billed hours:

```
SQL> select
  2      office,
  3      avg(bgross/bhrs)
  4  from lawyer1
  5  having avg(bgross/bhrs) >
  6      (select
  7          avg(bgross/bhrs)
  8       from lawyer1)
  9  group by office
 10  order by avg(bgross/bhrs) desc
 11  ;

OFFICE          AVG(BGROSS/BHRS)
--------------- ----------------
New York             201.52445
Los Angeles          155.55272
```

Those offices, it turns out, are New York and Los Angeles. (Perhaps it's the two-word city names.) Finally, you can adapt the whole statement and insert it as a multi-row subquery to identify the lawyers in those cities and their average hourly earnings:

```
SQL> col rate format 999.99 heading 'Hourly¦ Rate'
SQL>
SQL> select
  2      office,
  3      name,
  4      bgross/bhrs rate
  5  from lawyer1
  6  where office in
  7      (select
  8          office
  9       from lawyer1
 10       having avg(bgross/bhrs) >
 11          (select
 12              avg(bgross/bhrs)
 13           from lawyer1)
 14       group by office)
 15  order by
 16      office,
 17      bgross/bhrs desc
 18  ;

                               Hourly
OFFICE          NAME             Rate
--------------- --------------- -------
Los Angeles     Easton          172.32
Los Angeles     Howe            163.60
Los Angeles     Miller          159.72
Los Angeles     Roll            155.51
Los Angeles     Martinez        151.74
Los Angeles     Ming            144.07
Los Angeles     Chandler        141.91
New York        Frankie         220.17
New York        Chatham         209.18
```

```
New York        Bonin           206.73
New York        Cheetham        200.60
New York        Earl            187.41
New York        Chabot          185.06

13 rows selected.

SQL>
SQL> clear columns

columns cleared
```

Note that Martinez, Ming, and Chandler made the list despite the fact that they made less than the average hourly rate—their offices made more, and that is the key criterion here.

Figure 20.1 illustrates the execution order of a multiple-row subquery combined with a nested subquery.

FIGURE 20.1.

The execution order of a multiple-row subquery combined with a nested subquery.

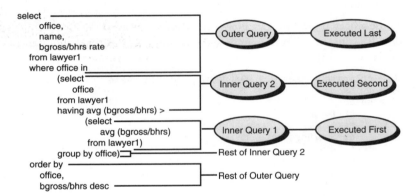

CAUTION

The caution in Chapter 19 applies here as well: Although SQL does all the work, you still need to make sure that your subqueries return what they are supposed to—exactly one value for inner query 1, which calculates the average `bgross/bhrs`, and exactly two values for inner query 2, which identifies the offices that do better than that average. If you are not absolutely sure, test.

Multiple-Row Comparison Operators

The example discussed in Chapter 19 showed the most frequent type of multiple-row subqueries. The inner query retrieves a set of values that is subsequently included by using the `in` operator in the `where` clause of the outer query. Other multiple-row comparison operators can be used as well. (See Table 20.1.)

Table 20.1. The multiple-row comparison operators.

Operator	Meaning
in	Equal to any value retrieved in an inner query.
not in	Unequal to any value retrieved in an inner query.
= any	Same as in; corresponds to logical or.
> any, >= any	Greater than or greater than or equal to any number retrieved. Equivalent to > or >= the smallest number retrieved.
< any, <= any	Less than or less than or equal to any number retrieved. Equivalent to < or <= to the largest number retrieved.
= all	Equal to all retrieved values. Equivalent to logical and. Likely to return no row at all.
> all, >= all	Greater than or greater than or equal to all numbers retrieved. Equivalent to > or >= the largest number retrieved.
< all, <= all	Less than or less than or equal to all numbers retrieved. Equivalent to < or <= the smallest number retrieved.

any

The any comparison operator must be used with a single-value comparison operator. When used with =, it is equivalent to in. Look at the following example.

Listing 20.1. Using the any comparison operator.

```
--      Filename: 20squ01.sql
--      Purpose: same as 20squa, but uses = any instead of in
--
col rate format 999.99 heading 'Hourly¦ Rate'

select
   office,
   name,
   bgross/bhrs rate
from lawyer1
where office = any
      (select
           office
        from lawyer1
        having avg(bgross/bhrs) >
              (select
                    avg(bgross/bhrs)
                 from lawyer1)
        group by office)
```

continues

Listing 20.1. continued

```
order by
    office,
    bgross/bhrs desc
;

clear columns
```

This statement returns the following, which is the same as what the original query returned:

```
                          Hourly
OFFICE          NAME        Rate
--------------- ----------- -------
Los Angeles     Easton      172.32
Los Angeles     Howe        163.60
Los Angeles     Miller      159.72
Los Angeles     Roll        155.51
Los Angeles     Martinez    151.74
Los Angeles     Ming        144.07
Los Angeles     Chandler    141.91
New York        Frankie     220.17
New York        Chatham     209.18
New York        Bonin       206.73
New York        Cheetham    200.60
New York        Earl        187.41
New York        Chabot      185.06

13 rows selected.

Columns cleared
```

DEBUG ALERT

Because the in operator is used all the time, it makes little sense to confuse yourself and others with an equivalent expression. Use in and save time trying to figure out six months down the road what you were thinking at the time.

The usefulness of the > any, >= any, < any, and <= any constructs, quite frankly, escapes me (except, perhaps, to flunk a hapless college student on a SQL exam). To say "where x is greater than the smallest number retrieved from a subquery" is even less intuitive than dragging a floppy-disk icon onto a Macintosh computer's trashcan icon to eject a floppy disk.

It is far preferable to rework that statement into a single-value subquery where the inner query yields the least of the values in question, similarly to the second example in the next section. Nevertheless, the aficionados of the obfuscated SQL contest could adapt the first example in the next section, which usually does not return any rows.

all

The `all` operator is at the same time better and worse than any. For starters, the expression = `all` is likely to indicate a logical error. This is shown by Listing 20.2.

Listing 20.2. Using the = `all` expression.

```
--      Filename: 20squ02.sql
--      Purpose: shows use of = all
--               returns nothing
--
col rate format 999.99 heading 'Hourly¦ Rate'

select
   office,
   name,
   bgross/bhrs rate
from lawyer1
where office = any
      (select
            office
       from lawyer1
       having avg(bgross/bhrs) = all
             (select
                   avg(bgross/bhrs)
              from lawyer1
              group by office)
       group by office)
order by
   office,
   bgross/bhrs desc
;
```

This code returns the following:

```
clear columns

no rows selected
```

There are only two situations in which this subquery will return rows:

- When exactly one row is retrieved
- When all rows retrieved return exactly the same value

To bank on either case is risky and counterintuitive.

DEBUG ALERT

Do yourself a favor and document it if you use such constructs. After all, you may very well have a legitimate reason, but in six months will you remember it?

As you can see in Listing 20.3, the only saving grace for `>` `all`, `>=` `all`, `<` `all`, and `<=` `all` is that they are not as counterintuitive as their any equivalents.

Listing 20.3. Using the `all` operator.

```
--        Filename: 20squ03.sql
--         Purpose: shows use of all
--
col rate format 999.99 heading 'Hourly¦ Rate'

select
   office,
   name,
   bgross/bhrs rate
from lawyer1
where office in
      (select
            office
       from lawyer1
       having avg(bgross/bhrs) >= all
              (select
                     avg(bgross/bhrs)
               from lawyer1
               group by office)
       group by office)
order by
   office,
   bgross/bhrs desc
;

clear columns
```

This code returns the following:

OFFICE	NAME	Hourly Rate
New York	Frankie	220.17
New York	Chatham	209.18
New York	Bonin	206.73
New York	Cheetham	200.60
New York	Earl	187.41
New York	Chabot	185.06

6 rows selected.

Because New York is the office with the highest average hourly rate, `>=` `all` returns only lawyers in that office. If the condition had been `>` `all`, it would not have returned any rows. It would be far preferable, however, to rewrite the `>=` `all` as a single-value subquery against the maximum average hourly rate. (See Listing 20.4.)

Listing 20.4. Using a single-value subquery.

```
--      Filename: 20squ04.sql
--      Purpose: reworks solution for 03 using max instead
--
col rate format 999.99 heading 'Hourly¦ Rate'

select
    office,
    name,
    bgross/bhrs rate
from lawyer1
where office = any
      (select
            office
       from lawyer1
       having avg(bgross/bhrs) >=
              (select
                    max(avg(bgross/bhrs))
               from lawyer1
               group by office)
       group by office)
order by
    office,
    bgross/bhrs desc
;

clear columns
```

This script returns the following output, which is the same as the query in `20squ03.sql` returned—all lawyers of the New York office.

```
                            Hourly
OFFICE          NAME          Rate
--------------- --------------- -------
New York        Frankie       220.17
New York        Chatham       209.18
New York        Bonin         206.73
New York        Cheetham      200.60
New York        Earl          187.41
New York        Chabot        185.06

6 rows selected.
```

Multiple-Column Subqueries

Thus far, all the outer-to-inner value comparisons have concerned only one column. Special syntax is required if the values across multiple columns are to be compared:

- The set of comparison columns is listed in the `where` clause, separated by commas.
- The subquery selects the corresponding columns.

This way, multiple where and subquery statements can be combined into one. Again, the usefulness of this feature is somewhat marginal. It will, however, answer queries such as "retrieve all lawyers that generate the same number of billable hours (rounded to thousands) and the same number of gross revenue (rounded to hundreds of thousands)." Listing 20.5 illustrates this.

Listing 20.5. Using multiple-column subqueries.

```
--         Filename: 20squ05.sql
--         Purpose: retrieve names of lawyers with the same hours
--                  and gross revenues as those occurring in Boston
--                  rounded to thousands and hundred thousands
--
select
   office,
   name,
   bgross,
   bhrs
from lawyer1
where (round(bgross,-5), round(bhrs,-3)) in
     (select
          round(bgross,-5),
          round(bhrs,-3)
      from lawyer1
      where office = 'Boston')
order by
   office,
   bhrs desc,
   bgross desc
;
```

This code returns

OFFICE	NAME	BGROSS	BHRS
Boston	Dewey	426800	2856
Boston	Greene	289435	2854
Boston	Wright	204133	2789
Boston	Cardinal	277952	2694
Boston	Paul	239855	2198
Houston	Clayton	190045	1789
Los Angeles	Chandler	423878	2987
Los Angeles	Martinez	403488	2659

8 rows selected.

I do not recall ever having a need to answer this kind of question, but SQL provides the options anyway.

The multi-column subquery construct appears to work with only the in and not in operators. If the in in the previous query is changed to not in, like this,

```
select
   office,
   name,
   bgross,
```

```
      bhrs
from lawyer1
where (round(bgross,-5), round(bhrs,-3)) not in
      (select
           round(bgross,-5),
           round(bhrs,-3)
       from lawyer1
       where office = 'Boston')
order by
    office,
    bhrs desc,
    bgross desc
;
```

the other 12 rows will be returned:

```
OFFICE          NAME              BGROSS      BHRS
-----------     ---------------   ---------   ---------
Houston         Roach             269844      2349
Los Angeles     Easton            654832      3800
Los Angeles     Howe              569338      3480
Los Angeles     Roll              498084      3203
Los Angeles     Miller            503582      3153
Los Angeles     Ming              359021      2492
New York        Earl              434801      2320
New York        Frankie           469843      2134
New York        Chatham           367944      1759
New York        Chabot            310897      1680
New York        Bonin             346892      1678
New York        Cheetham          280435      1398

12 rows selected.
```

Virtual Views by Subquery

Creating and working with views is discussed in depth in Chapters 26, "Insertable Single-Table Views," and 27, "Multi-Table, Distinct, and Aggregate Views." Views are database objects, which means they are created and dropped through separate SQL statements, and the Data Dictionary maintains information about them.

It is possible to create a virtual view through a subquery. This subquery can be used in the statement that includes it in the same way a real view could, but it is available only for the statement that includes the subquery and for the duration of that query's execution. Listing 20.6 calculates the average gross receipts of lawyers, broken out by the number of lawyers reporting them.

Listing 20.6. Retrieving data using recursive join and a subquery view.

```
--        Filename: 20squ06.sql
--        Purpose: retrieves avg gross receipts by number of reports
--                 uses recursive join and subquery view
--
col avggr heading 'Average¦Gross¦Receipts' format 999,999
col reps  heading 'Number¦of¦Reports'      format 9
```

continues

20

MULTIPLE-VALUE SUBQUERIES

Listing 20.6. continued

```
select
        m.id,
        count(e.name) reps,
        m.bgross
    from lawyer2 m, lawyer2 e
    where m.id = e.boss (+)
    group by m.id,
            m.bgross
;
```

It returns the following:

```
          Number
              of
      ID  Reports    BGROSS
---------  -------  --------
        1        2    426800
        2        0    280435
        3        1    569338
        4        0    190045
        5        1    269844
        6        1    498084
        7        5    654832
        8        1    346892
        9        2    469843
       10        1    289435
       11        0    277952
       12        0    423878
       13        0    403488
       14        2    434801
       15        0    204133
       16        0    310897
       17        1    503582
       18        1    359021
       19        0    367944
       20        1    239855

20 rows selected.
```

This, on the other hand,

```
select
    reps,
    avg(bgross) avggr
from
     (select
         m.id,
         count(e.name) reps,
         m.bgross
     from lawyer2 m, lawyer2 e
     where m.id = e.boss (+)
     group by m.id,
              m.bgross)
where reps > 0
group by reps
;
```

returns this:

```
Number  Average
    of    Gross
Reports Receipts
------- --------
     1  384,506
     2  443,815
     5  654,832
```

The first statement uses a recursive outer join from the BGROSS column to the ID column and creates the column named reps to hold the number of reports. This statement returns 20 rows, one per lawyer. The second statement uses the first statement as a subquery from which to break out the number of reports and the average salary. Note that this construct avoids the need for a having subclause.

For another example of using this feature, see Chapter 39, "Testing and Scrubbing Loaded Data."

Summary

This chapter discusses the very useful multiple-row subqueries, which return one or more rows and can then be incorporated into the main query's where statement by means of special multiple-row comparison operators. The most important of these are in and not in. The others are counterintuitive and can be replaced through single-value subqueries, which return a minimum or maximum value.

The second part of the chapter presents multiple-column subqueries that allow you to compare matched sets of values in the inner query with corresponding value sets in the outer query. There are few situations in which this feature is useful.

Correlated Subqueries

CHAPTER 21

Nested subqueries, which are discussed in Chapters 19, "Single-Value Subqueries," and 20, "Multiple-Value Subqueries," are executed first. The result is then used as part of the where clause of the statement that includes the subquery. Depending on this result, a row in the main (outer) query would or would not be retrieved.

Correlated subqueries employ the opposite approach, where the outer query retrieves all rows as candidate rows, which are then qualified through a subquery that is executed once per row of the outer query.

Correlated Subquery Execution

The correlated subquery execution is illustrated in Figure 21.1. It is processed as follows:

1. The outer query retrieves a candidate row.
2. For each candidate row, the correlated inner query is executed once.
3. The results of this query then are used to determine whether the candidate rows should be accepted and printed, or rejected and omitted.
4. The next row of the outer query is retrieved.

Revisiting Chapter 19, and returning to the lawyer1 table, a nested subquery could be used to find all lawyers who achieve a higher-than-average hourly rate. The solution to this question is in Listing 21.1.

Listing 21.1. Retrieving data using a nested subquery.

```
--      Filename: 21squ01.sql
--      Purpose: retrieve lawyers who achieve a higher
--               than average billable rate
--               uses nested subquery
--
col rate format 999.99 heading 'Hourly¦ Rate'
col avrate format 999.99 heading 'Average¦Hourly Rate'

select
   avg(bgross/bhrs) avrate
from lawyer1;
select
   office,
   name,
   bgross,
   bhrs,
   bgross/bhrs rate
from lawyer1
where bgross/bhrs >=
     (select
         avg(bgross/bhrs)
      from lawyer1)
order by bgross/bhrs desc
;

clear columns
```

FIGURE 21.1.
*The correlated subquery
execution order.*

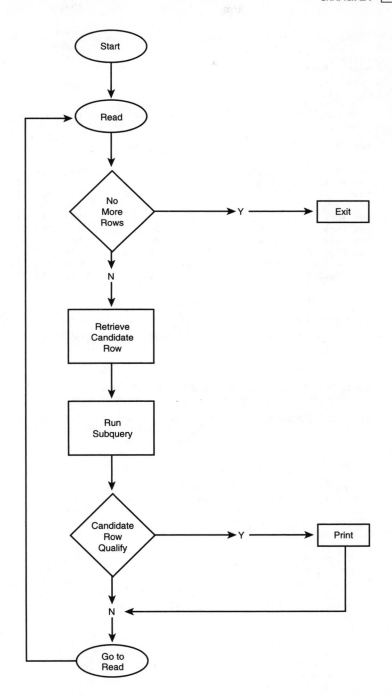

The inner query returns an average hourly rate of $152.77, as shown in the following code:

```
Average
Hourly Rate
-----------
     152.77
```

The second statement retrieves the 10 lawyers whose rates are above average:

OFFICE	NAME	BGROSS	BHRS	Hourly Rate
New York	Frankie	469843	2134	220.17
New York	Chatham	367944	1759	209.18
New York	Bonin	346892	1678	206.73
New York	Cheetham	280435	1398	200.60
New York	Earl	434801	2320	187.41
New York	Chabot	310897	1680	185.06
Los Angeles	Easton	654832	3800	172.32
Los Angeles	Howe	569338	3480	163.60
Los Angeles	Miller	503582	3153	159.72
Los Angeles	Roll	498084	3203	155.51

```
10 rows selected.
```

A correlated subquery comes into play when the question is slightly adapted, such as when you want to find lawyers who achieve a higher billable rate than the average rate for their office, as Listing 21.2 shows.

Listing 21.2. Retrieving data using a correlated subquery.

```
--          Filename: 21squ02.sql
--          Purpose: retrieve lawyers who achieve a higher
--                   than average billable rate of their office
--                   uses correlated subquery
--


col rate format 999.99 heading 'Hourly¦ Rate'
col avrate format 999.99 heading 'Average¦Hourly Rate'

select
    office,
    avg(bgross/bhrs) avrate
from lawyer1
group by office
order by office;

select
    office,
    name,
    bgross,
    bhrs,
    bgross/bhrs rate
from lawyer1 outer
where bgross/bhrs >=
     (select
```

```
            avg(bgross/bhrs)
        from lawyer1
        where office = outer.office)
order by
    office,
    bgross/bhrs desc
;

clear columns
```

The first query displays the average rates for all four offices, as shown here:

```
                    Average
OFFICE          Hourly Rate
--------------- -----------
Boston              107.27
Houston             110.55
Los Angeles         155.55
New York            201.52
```

The second query shows the high achievers per office:

```
                                            Hourly
OFFICE          NAME            BGROSS   BHRS   Rate
--------------- --------------- -------- ------ ------
Boston          Dewey            426800   2856  149.44
Boston          Paul             239855   2198  109.12
Houston         Roach            269844   2349  114.88
Los Angeles     Easton           654832   3800  172.32
Los Angeles     Howe             569338   3480  163.60
Los Angeles     Miller           503582   3153  159.72
New York        Frankie          469843   2134  220.17
New York        Chatham          367944   1759  209.18
New York        Bonin            346892   1678  206.73
```

9 rows selected.

NOTE

In most cases you will have to use an alias (such as outer in the example for the outer table). The only exception is the case when the outer and inner tables are different and use mutually exclusive column names. The default, where no table is specified, is the inner table.

All columns of the example can and should be fully qualified through table aliases, the same way as is explained in Chapter 17, "Joins." (See Listing 21.3.)

Listing 21.3. Retrieving data using a correlated subquery and alias for each column.

```
--      Filename: 21squ03.sql
--      Purpose: retrieve lawyers who achieve a higher
--               than average billable rate of their office
--               uses correlated subquery and alias for each column
--
```

continues

Listing 21.3. continued

```
col rate format 999.99 heading 'Hourly¦ Rate'
col avrate format 999.99 heading 'Average¦Hourly Rate'

select
    outer.office,
    outer.name,
    outer.bgross,
    outer.bhrs,
    outer.bgross/outer.bhrs rate
from lawyer1 outer
where outer.bgross/outer.bhrs >=
    (select
         avg(inner.bgross/inner.bhrs)
     from lawyer1 inner
     where inner.office = outer.office)
order by
    outer.office,
    outer.bgross/outer.bhrs desc
;

clear columns
```

The result is exactly the same as in 21squ02.sql. While aliasing in this case appears redundant and cluttered, it may help when more than two levels of queries are combined in a statement; however, even more complex statements will work with minimum aliasing. Listing 21.4 retrieves lawyers who achieve a higher-than-average billable rate by using a correlated subquery and minimum aliasing.

Listing 21.4. Retrieving data using correlated subquery and minimum aliasing.

```
--        Filename: 21squ04.sql
--         Purpose: retrieve lawyers who achieve a higher
--                  than average billable rate of their office
--                  uses correlated subquery and minimum aliasing
--
col rate format 999.99 heading 'Hourly¦ Rate'
col avgross format 999,999.99 heading 'Average¦Gross¦Receipts'
col avhrs format 9,999.99 heading 'Average¦Hours¦Billed'

select
    office,
    avg(bgross) avgross,
    avg(bhrs)   avhrs
from lawyer1
group by officeorder by office
;
```

The first query lists the average gross receipts and billable hours by office:

OFFICE	Average Gross Receipts	Average Hours Billed
Boston	287,635.00	2,678.20
Houston	229,944.50	2,069.00
Los Angeles	487,460.43	3,110.57
New York	368,468.67	1,828.17

The second query retrieves those lawyers who exceed *both* the average gross receipts *and* the average billable hours of their respective offices, as shown in the following:

```
select
   office,
   name,
   bgross,
   bhrs,
   bgross/bhrs rate
from lawyer1 outer
where bgross >=
    (select
        avg(bgross)
     from lawyer1
     where office = outer.office)
and bhrs >=
    (select
        avg(bhrs)
     from lawyer1
     where office = outer.office)
order by
   office,
   bgross/bhrs desc
;

clear columns
```

The second query returns the following output:

OFFICE	NAME	BGROSS	BHRS	Hourly Rate
Boston	Dewey	426800	2856	149.44
Boston	Greene	289435	2854	101.41
Houston	Roach	269844	2349	114.88
Los Angeles	Easton	654832	3800	172.32
Los Angeles	Howe	569338	3480	163.60
Los Angeles	Miller	503582	3153	159.72
Los Angeles	Roll	498084	3203	155.51
New York	Frankie	469843	2134	220.17
New York	Earl	434801	2320	187.41

```
9 rows selected.
```

 The fully aliased version of the second query is provided as `21squ04a.sql`, which can be found in the CD-ROM at the back of this book. It returns the same nine rows.

Correlated Subqueries Versus Temporary Views and Tables

Another approach—a temporary view or table that holds the averages per office—yields the same result as corresponding statements that include correlated subqueries. Views and tables are explained in detail in Chapter 26, "Insertable Single-Table Views," Chapter 27, "Multi-Table, Distinct, and Aggregate Views," and Chapter 28, "Creating Tables." This temporary view or table can then be joined to the original table (from which, in this case, it originates itself) and rows retrieved by simply using a `where` clause.

Listing 21.5 retrieves the same information as 21squ04.sql by using first a view, and then a temporary table.

Listing 21.5. Retrieving data using temporary views and tables.

```
--        Filename: 21squ05.sql
--         Purpose: retrieve lawyers who achieve a higher
--                  than average billable rate of their office
--                  uses temporary view
--                  then uses temporary table
--
col rate format 999.99 heading 'Hourly¦ Rate'
col avgross format 999,999.99 heading 'Average¦Gross¦Receipts'
col avhrs format 9,999.99 heading 'Average¦Hours¦Billed'
```

First, a view with average gross receipts, average hours billed, and average hourly rates is created, as shown in the following:

```
create or replace view avgoff as
select
   office,
   avg(bgross) avgross,
   avg(bhrs)   avhrs,
   avg(bgross/bhrs) avrate
from lawyer1
group by office
;
```

This code returns the output:

```
View created.
```

Next is a query against a join of the original table and the aggregate view just created. The `where` clause has three components, which limit the rows to those that

- Have a gross-receipt value larger than the average gross-receipt value for the office
- Have a billable-hours value larger than the average billable-hours value for the office
- Have matching office values for view and table

```
select
   l.office,
   l.name,
   l.bgross,
   l.bhrs,
   l.bgross/l.bhrs rate
from lawyer1 l, avgoff a
where
   l.bgross >= a.avgross and
   l.bhrs   >= a.avhrs   and
   l.office =  a.office
order by
   l.office,
   l.bgross/l.bhrs desc;
```

This query returns the following output:

OFFICE	NAME	BGROSS	BHRS	Hourly Rate
Boston	Dewey	426800	2856	149.44
Boston	Greene	289435	2854	101.41
Houston	Roach	269844	2349	114.88
Los Angeles	Easton	654832	3800	172.32
Los Angeles	Howe	569338	3480	163.60
Los Angeles	Miller	503582	3153	159.72
Los Angeles	Roll	498084	3203	155.51
New York	Frankie	469843	2134	220.17
New York	Earl	434801	2320	187.41

This is the familiar output of the correlated subquery. If a more permanent aggregate value table is desired, it can be created through the following statement:

```
create table avgofft as
select
   * from avgoff;
```

The query can then be run against the table instead the view, by exchanging the line

```
from lawyer1 l, avgoff a
```

with

```
from lawyer1 l, avgofft a
```

The output will be exactly the same.

Finally, it is advisable to drop both the view and the table through the statements:

```
drop table avgofft;
drop view avgoff;
```

These statements return the following:

```
Table dropped.
View dropped.
```

Performance Considerations

On a little table, such as the one used for these examples, there is no practical difference between the performance of any of the options. All the blocks of the table are likely in memory, which provides almost instant response.

The correlated query can be comparably efficient if

- Only relatively few rows are retrieved through the outer query, especially if the where clause, which limits the number of rows returned, can use an index.

- The correlated inner queries are performed through an index scan. This is especially important if the table(s) against which the inner query is performed is large and the index scan has to retrieve only a small portion of its rows.

Otherwise, views and tables are likely to be more efficient. The only way to say for certain, however, is to analyze the execution plan of a query and resources used by it. If you compare the statements in 21squ04.sql and 21squ05.sql using plan analyzer, you will find that the correlated subquery takes 89 logical reads and 23 full-table scans. The inner query takes only 10 logical reads and 2 full-table scans—about a tenth of the resources of the correlated subquery approach.

If the same aggregate view is used for a number of queries and if it's time consuming to generate, it is preferable to create a table, so that that portion of the project has to be done only once.

exists/not exists Operators

The exists operator and its counterpart not exists provide some subtle advantages over their closest relatives—in and not in—in terms of speed, and in cases where logic that includes null values is involved.

The exists operator provides the first example of a recursive relationship, where one row in a table contains a column which refers to another row of the same table. A typical situation is a manager column, which contains the ID of the person reported to in the same table. Because managing implies some creative, intelligent activity on the part of the manager, which cannot be necessarily assumed to be present, the lawyer2 table used here names this column boss, a word that does not imply anything except a reporting hierarchy.

Only one query is required to answer the question of to which person somebody reports as identified by the boss's own person ID value. To retrieve the name of the boss, a second query, or a join, is necessary. To answer the question of who has lawyers reporting to him or her requires a query with at least one join or subquery because the status of a boss is not included in the row of a lawyer; it has to be taken from all other rows.

The first query is the straightforward multiple-value subquery; generate a list of all boss ID values and insert the list into the where clause of the main query. This is done in Listing 21.6.

Listing 21.6. Using the `exists` operator.

```
--        Filename: 21squ06.sql
--        Purpose: retrieve lawyers who have at least one report
--                 uses exists operator
--
select
   name,
   office
from lawyer2
where id in
      (select distinct boss
       from lawyer2 )
order by
   office,
   name
;
```

The result of the preceding code would be

```
NAME            OFFICE
--------------- ---------------
Dewey           Boston
Greene          Boston
Paul            Boston
Roach           Houston
Easton          Los Angeles
Howe            Los Angeles
Miller          Los Angeles
Ming            Los Angeles
Roll            Los Angeles
Bonin           New York
Earl            New York
Frankie         New York

12 rows selected.
```

The next case is a correlated subquery that uses the `exists` operator. The main query retrieves candidate rows. For each candidate row, a subquery is executed. As soon as this subquery finds only one occurrence where the outer ID is used in the `boss` column, it stops execution and returns a `true` value to the outer query, which then qualifies the candidate row:

```
select
   name,
   office
from lawyer2 outer
where exists
      (select 1
       from lawyer2 inner
       where inner.boss = outer.id)
order by
   office,
   name
;
```

The output is the same as in the first statement of this example.

The last option, demonstrated in Listing 21.7, is to join the table to itself, which can then also easily return the number of employees who report to each boss.

Listing 21.7. Retrieving data using a recursive join.

```
--        Filename: 21squ07.sql
--        Purpose: retrieve lawyers who have at least one report
--                 uses recursive join

select
    m.name,
    m.office,
    count(e.name)
    from lawyer2 m, lawyer2 e
 where m.id = e.boss
 group by
    m.name,
    m.office
 order by
    m.office,
    m.name
;
```

This code returns the following output:

NAME	OFFICE	COUNT(E.NAME)
Dewey	Boston	2
Greene	Boston	1
Paul	Boston	1
Roach	Houston	1
Easton	Los Angeles	5
Howe	Los Angeles	1
Miller	Los Angeles	1
Ming	Los Angeles	1
Roll	Los Angeles	1
Bonin	New York	1
Earl	New York	2
Frankie	New York	2

12 rows selected.

Again, the preferred solution in most cases is the recursive join.

not exists Versus not in

The alternative question asks for all lawyers who are not bosses. Trying this with the not in operator returns an incorrect result because Easton in Los Angeles does not report to anybody. Hence the boss entry in his or her row is null. If the subquery retrieves at least one null value, the entire where condition evaluates to unknown. As a result, not a single row is returned, when in fact eight lawyers do not have reports. The first statement of Listing 21.8 illustrates this problem.

Listing 21.8. Using the not exists operator.

```
--       Filename: 21squ08.sql
--        Purpose: retrieve lawyers who do not have at least one report
--                 uses not exists operator

select
   name,
   office
from lawyer2
where id not in
      (select boss
        from lawyer2 )
order by
   office,
   name
;
```

The preceding code returns the following output:

```
no rows selected
```

The not exists operator as used in the next statement will remedy the problem. Note that in this example it is only important whether the query returns rows at all; what it returns is of no concern:

```
select
   name,
   office
from lawyer2 outer
where not exists
      (select 1
        from lawyer2
        where boss = outer.id )
order by
   office,
   name
;
```

This code returns

```
NAME             OFFICE
---------------  ---------------
Cardinal         Boston
Wright           Boston
Clayton          Houston
Chandler         Los Angeles
Martinez         Los Angeles
Chabot           New York
Chatham          New York
Cheetham         New York

8 rows selected.
```

Again there is a recursive join solution, which is demonstrated in the next example. The table is joined to itself by the boss field when looking at employees and the ID field when looking at bosses. The outer join indicator (+) after e.boss indicates that all the rows in the table aliased with e should be preserved even if no match in the other table can be found. From this joined set we select all boss names that don't have a single employee name entry.

> **TIP**
>
> In a situation where only the row count matters and not the content of a row, you can simply select a constant. A constant subquery will be more efficient.

Listing 21.9. Retrieving data using a recursive join.

```
--        Filename: 21squ09.sql
--        Purpose: retrieve lawyers who do not have a report
--                 uses recursive join
select
   m.name,
   m.office,
   count(e.name)
   from lawyer2 m, lawyer2 e
where m.id = e.boss (+)
having count(e.name) = 0
group by
   m.name,
   m.office
order by
   m.office,
   m.name
;
```

This code returns the same eight rows with a count of employees reporting to that person. This count would not be necessary to display because only those persons who are not bosses are selected in the query:

```
NAME            OFFICE           COUNT(E.NAME)
-----------     ---------------  -------------
Cardinal        Boston                       0
Wright          Boston                       0
Clayton         Houston                      0
Chandler        Los Angeles                  0
Martinez        Los Angeles                  0
Chabot          New York                     0
Chatham         New York                     0
Cheetham        New York                     0

8 rows selected.
```

Summary

Correlated subqueries retrieve all rows of the outer query as candidate rows to be qualified through one subquery each. Correlated subqueries are useful if the values of a column are to be compared with an aggregate value for a group of which that row is a part. Even then other, and often simpler, methods exist to achieve the same goal, most notably intermediate views or tables.

Correlated subqueries can take advantage of the exists operator, which qualifies an outer query row as soon as a single inner query that fulfills the condition is retrieved. The opposite operator, not exists, can be used to overcome the problem of the not in operator. The not in operator does not return any rows if a single value of the inner query compared in the where statement is null. Even here other options exist, such as a recursive outer join that will retrieve the same information.

CHAPTER 22

Trees and Hierarchical Subqueries

IN THIS CHAPTER

In Chapter 21, "Correlated Subqueries," you learned about correlated subqueries by working with a recursive table, `lawyer2`, which includes a column named `boss` that refers back to the `id` column in the same table.

These queries, then, were limited to two levels—a boss and a worker bee—without consideration of the fact that many bosses in turn work for another boss, and many worker bees are also bosses.

The purpose of the queries in this chapter is to retrieve information about the entire set of relationships, which is commonly referred to as a *tree*.

Tables That Are Joined to Themselves: Recursive Joins and N-Level Queries

A *hierarchical table* contains a column that references another column in the same table. An example is `lawyer2`, whose `boss` column references its own `id` column.

Listing 22.1. Displaying contents of a table using a two-level query.

```
--      Filename: 22squ01.sql
--       Purpose: display contents of lawyer2 table
--                two-level query
--
desc lawyer2
```

This returns

```
col id        format 99
col boss      format 9999
col office    format a11
col bee_name  format a10
col boss_name format a10
```

Two-Level Queries

Using this reference of the `boss` column to the `id` column and an outer join with an `nvl` function allows you to retrieve the worker-bee information on the left side of the vertical bar and the boss information on the right:

```
set pagesize 40
break on idb skip 1

select
   w.id,
   w.name bee_name,
   w.office,
   '|',
```

```
    b.id idb,
    nvl(b.name,'    NOBODY') boss_name,
    b.office
from
    lawyer2 w,
    lawyer2 b
where nvl(w.boss,-9) = b.id (+)
order by w.boss
;

clear columns
clear breaks
set pagesize 24
```

This returns the following:

```
ID BEE_NAME    OFFICE       ' IDB BOSS_NAME   OFFICE
-- --------    ----------   - --- ----------   ----------
10 Greene      Boston       |  1 Dewey        Boston
11 Cardinal    Boston       |    Dewey        Boston
 6 Roll        Los Angeles  |  3 Howe         Los Angeles
 4 Clayton     Houston      |  5 Roach        Houston
12 Chandler    Los Angeles  |  6 Roll         Los Angeles
 3 Howe        Los Angeles  |  7 Easton       Los Angeles
 9 Frankie     New York     |    Easton       Los Angeles
17 Miller      Los Angeles  |    Easton       Los Angeles
20 Paul        Boston       |    Easton       Los Angeles
 5 Roach       Houston      |    Easton       Los Angeles
 2 Cheetham    New York     |  8 Bonin        New York
 8 Bonin       New York     |  9 Frankie      New York
14 Earl        New York     |    Frankie      New York
15 Wright      Boston       | 10 Greene       Boston
16 Chabot      New York     | 14 Earl         New York
19 Chatham     New York     |    Earl         New York
18 Ming        Los Angeles  | 17 Miller       Los Angeles
13 Martinez    Los Angeles  | 18 Ming         Los Angeles
 1 Dewey       Boston       | 20 Paul         Boston
 7 Easton      Los Angeles  |       NOBODY
```

```
20 rows selected.
```

By using aggregate functions, you could create similar queries to return information such as the number of direct reports.

N-Level Queries

If you want to have more than two levels in your query, each level has to be covered with its own query, as Listing 22.2 shows. It first runs a three-level, and then a four-level, query.

Listing 22.2. Displaying contents of a table using multi-level queries.

```
--      Filename: 22squ02.sql
--      Purpose: display contents of lawyer2 table
--               three-level query and four-level query
--
col id        format 99
col idb       format 99
```

continues

Listing 22.2. continued

```
col office    format a11
col bee_name  format a10
col low_manag format a10
col mid_manag format a10
col boss_name format a10

set pagesize 40
break on idb skip 1

select
   w.id,
   w.name bee_name,
   '|',
   m.id,
   nvl(m.name,'    NOBODY') mid_manag,
   '|',
   b.id idb,
   nvl(b.name,'    NOBODY') boss_name
from
   lawyer2 w,
   lawyer2 m,
   lawyer2 b
where nvl(w.boss,-9) = m.id (+) and
      nvl(m.boss,-9) = b.id (+)
order by
   m.boss,
   w.boss
;
```

The three-level query returns

ID	BEE_NAME	'	ID	MID_MANAG	'	IDB	BOSS_NAME
15	Wright	|	10	Greene	|	1	Dewey
12	Chandler	|	6	Roll	|	3	Howe
6	Roll	|	3	Howe	|	7	Easton
4	Clayton	|	5	Roach	|		Easton
8	Bonin	|	9	Frankie	|		Easton
14	Earl	|	9	Frankie	|		Easton
18	Ming	|	17	Miller	|		Easton
1	Dewey	|	20	Paul	|		Easton
2	Cheetham	|	8	Bonin	|	9	Frankie
16	Chabot	|	14	Earl	|		Frankie
19	Chatham	|	14	Earl	|		Frankie
13	Martinez	|	18	Ming	|	17	Miller
10	Greene	|	1	Dewey	|	20	Paul
11	Cardinal	|	1	Dewey	|		Paul
3	Howe	|	7	Easton	|		NOBODY
17	Miller	|	7	Easton	|		NOBODY
20	Paul	|	7	Easton	|		NOBODY
5	Roach	|	7	Easton	|		NOBODY
9	Frankie	|	7	Easton	|		NOBODY
7	Easton	|		NOBODY	|		NOBODY

20 rows selected.

The next part extends the statement to four levels:

```
select
   w.id,
   w.name bee_name,
   '|',
   l.id,
   nvl(l.name,'    NOBODY') low_manag,
   '|',
   m.id,
   nvl(m.name,'    NOBODY') mid_manag,
   '|',
   b.id idb,
   nvl(b.name,'    NOBODY') boss_name
from
   lawyer2 w,
   lawyer2 l,
   lawyer2 m,
   lawyer2 b
where nvl(w.boss,-9) = l.id (+) and
      nvl(l.boss,-9) = m.id (+) and
      nvl(m.boss,-9) = b.id (+)
order by
   m.boss,
   l.boss,
   w.boss
;

clear columns
clear breaks
set pagesize 24
```

It returns the following:

ID	BEE_NAME	'	ID	LOW_MANAG	'	ID	MID_MANAG	'	IDB	BOSS_NAME
12	Chandler		6	Roll		3	Howe		7	Easton
2	Cheetham		8	Bonin		9	Frankie			Easton
16	Chabot		14	Earl		9	Frankie			Easton
19	Chatham		14	Earl		9	Frankie			Easton
13	Martinez		18	Ming		17	Miller			Easton
10	Greene		1	Dewey		20	Paul			Easton
11	Cardinal		1	Dewey		20	Paul			Easton
15	Wright		10	Greene		1	Dewey		20	Paul
6	Roll		3	Howe		7	Easton			NOBODY
4	Clayton		5	Roach		7	Easton			NOBODY
8	Bonin		9	Frankie		7	Easton			NOBODY
14	Earl		9	Frankie		7	Easton			NOBODY
18	Ming		17	Miller		7	Easton			NOBODY
1	Dewey		20	Paul		7	Easton			NOBODY
3	Howe		7	Easton			NOBODY			NOBODY
20	Paul		7	Easton			NOBODY			NOBODY
17	Miller		7	Easton			NOBODY			NOBODY
5	Roach		7	Easton			NOBODY			NOBODY
9	Frankie		7	Easton			NOBODY			NOBODY
7	Easton			NOBODY			NOBODY			NOBODY

20 rows selected.

Two more levels could be performed: The first one would show nobody as Easton's boss in the first seven rows, and Easton as Paul's boss in row 8. The last level would show nobody as Easton's boss in row 8 as well as in the first seven rows.

The Hierarchical `select` Statement: Using `connect by prior` and `start with`

ORACLE vs SQL

Oracle has its own approach to tree queries, using the keywords `connect by prior` and `start with`. These allow you to retrieve the entire tree structure in one query. The chapter will mostly work with that approach. Celko included an extensive discussion on tree issues in SQL-92, to which users of other SQL products are referred to.

Whereas the n-level queries in the previous section list the bosses and superbosses of all employees of a table side-by-side, the hierarchical `select` statement is used to answer similar questions with a slightly different tack:

- Who are the people who report to a person, or to anyone reporting to that person?
- Who are the people to whom a person reports and the people to whom those people report?

In other words, a hierarchical query allows you to choose one node in the hierarchy and to select from that node, up or down, to identify the entire subtree to which this node belongs.

The `connect by prior` keyword(s) replaces the join condition. In contrast to the join condition, the order of the columns following this keyword matter because they direct the query to go either upward or downward from the node identified with the `start with` keyword(s). Listing 22.3 first selects Greene, with the employee ID 10, and all people to whom he reports. Then it selects Greene and all people who report to him. The difference is that in the first case, the condition after `prior` is listed as `boss = id`; in the second, it is `id = boss`.

Listing 22.3. Displaying contents of a table using a hierarchical query.

```
--        Filename: 22squ03.sql
--         Purpose: display contents of lawyer2 table
--                  hierchical query
--
col id        format 99
col office    format a11
col name      format a10
col boss      format 99
set pagesize 40

select
   id,
   name,
   office,
   boss
from
```

```
      lawyer2
connect by prior boss = id
start with id=10
;

select
    id,
    name,
    office,
    boss
from
    lawyer2
connect by prior id = boss
start with id=10
;

clear columns
clear breaks
set pagesize 24
```

It returns the following:

```
ID NAME         OFFICE        BOSS
--- ----------   -----------   ----
 10 Greene       Boston           1
  1 Dewey        Boston          20
 20 Paul         Boston           7
  7 Easton       Los Angeles

ID NAME         OFFICE        BOSS
--- ----------   -----------   ----
 10 Greene       Boston           1
 15 Wright       Boston          10
```

Level of a Node in the Hierarchy: `level`

The `level` pseudocolumn returns the level of a node relative to the node listed after `start with`, which gets level 1. Every step away from that node adds 1 to `level`. Listing 22.4 includes `level` into the queries of `22squ03`. The query, however, starts with lawyer number 20, which leads to different rows being returned; for example, all subtrees reporting to Paul are now listed.

Listing 22.4. Displaying contents of a table using a hierarchical query displaying levels.

```
--       Filename: 22squ04.sql
--       Purpose: display contents of lawyer2 table
--                hierchical query displaying levels
--
col id       format 99
col office   format a11
col name     format a10
col boss     format 99
set pagesize 40

select
    level,
```

continues

Listing 22.4. continued

```
    id,
    name,
    office,
    boss
from
    lawyer2
connect by prior boss = id
start with id=20;
select
    level,
    id,
    name,
    office,
    boss
from
    lawyer2
connect by prior id = boss
start with id=20
;

clear columns
clear breaks
set pagesize 24
```

It returns this:

```
    LEVEL  ID NAME        OFFICE        BOSS
    -----  --- ---------- -----------   ----
        1  20 Paul        Boston           7
        2   7 Easton      Los Angeles

    LEVEL  ID NAME        OFFICE        BOSS
    -----  --- ---------- -----------   ----
        1  20 Paul        Boston           7
        2   1 Dewey       Boston          20
        3  10 Greene      Boston           1
        4  15 Wright      Boston          10
        3  11 Cardinal    Boston           1
```

A second subtree, consisting of Cardinal (who reports to Dewey), is now included.

Formatting Hierarchical Reports Using lpad

The lpad function (see Chapter 6, "Single-Row Character String Functions") usually has three arguments:

- The string to be padded.
- The display length of the output in characters.
- The *padset*, which is a string that will be repeated by the function until the specified display length is reached. If this argument is omitted, a single blank is used as default.

By using a calculated length that depends on level as the second argument, indentations by level can be created. The following examples use this approach, adapting 22squ04.sql.

Listing 22.5. Displaying a table using a hierarchical query displaying levels.

```
--          Filename: 22squ05.sql
--          Purpose: display contents of lawyer2 table
--                   hierchical query displaying levels
--
col id       format 99
col office   format a11
col name     format a10
col boss     format 99
col distance format a15
set pagesize 40

select
    lpad(level-1,level*4-3,'===>') distance,
    id,
    name,
    office,
    boss
from
    lawyer2
connect by prior boss = id
start with id=20
;

select
    lpad(level-1,level*4-3,'===>') distance,
    id,
    name,
    office,
    boss
from
    lawyer2
connect by prior id = boss
start with id=20
;

clear columns
clear breaks
set pagesize 24
```

It returns this:

```
DISTANCE         ID NAME        OFFICE        BOSS
---------------  --- ----------  -----------   ----
0                20 Paul        Boston           7
===>1             7 Easton      Los Angeles

DISTANCE         ID NAME        OFFICE        BOSS
---------------  --- ----------  -----------   ----
0                20 Paul        Boston           7
===>1             1 Dewey       Boston          20
===>===>2        10 Greene      Boston           1
===>===>===>3    15 Wright      Boston          10
===>===>2        11 Cardinal    Boston           1
```

The same trick can be used to create a stylized organizational chart that indents names according to reporting relationship and then lists level and office as is shown in Listing 22.6.

Listing 22.6. Displaying a stylized organizational chart.

```
--          Filename: 22squ06.sql
--          Purpose: display stylized organization chart
--
col office      format a11
col fake_chart format a35
col level       format 99 heading 'LV'
set pagesize 40

select
   lpad(' ',(level-1)*4) || name FAKE_CHART,
   level,
   office
from
   lawyer2
connect by prior id = boss
start with boss is NULL
;

clear columns
clear breaks
set pagesize 24
```

This script returns

```
FAKE_CHART                          LV OFFICE
----------------------------------- --- -----------
Easton                               1 Los Angeles
    Howe                             2 Los Angeles
        Roll                         3 Los Angeles
            Chandler                 4 Los Angeles
    Roach                            2 Houston
        Clayton                      3 Houston
    Frankie                          2 New York
        Bonin                        3 New York
            Cheetham                 4 New York
        Earl                         3 New York
            Chabot                   4 New York
            Chatham                  4 New York
    Miller                           2 Los Angeles
        Ming                         3 Los Angeles
            Martinez                 4 Los Angeles
    Paul                             2 Boston
        Dewey                        3 Boston
            Greene                   4 Boston
                Wright               5 Boston
            Cardinal                 4 Boston
20 rows selected.
```

The name FAKE_CHART is chosen to indicate that an organizational tree is usually represented in a graphically more pleasing fashion. On the other hand, retrieving the whole tree in a graphic approximation is actually a pretty nice feature.

Customized Ordering: Combining `level`, `lpad`, and `order by`

The output of a hierarchical query can be ordered through an `order by` subclause.

> **CAUTION**
>
> Relational theory has it that the ordering of rows in a database, and generally in output, is in no way facilitated or guaranteed. A hierarchical subquery with levels and indenting expresses meaning with the ordering of the rows, in particular that a node dependent on another node is indented in a row after the row it depends on, but before the next node on which it does not depend. Reordering might destroy that relationship.

In the `lawyer2` table, the reporting lines are consistent with office lines. It is, therefore, possible to order the output by office first, and then by level, which then provides organizational charts per office. This is done in Listing 22.7.

Listing 22.7. Displaying a stylized organizational chart using `order by`.

```
--        Filename: 22squ07.sql
--         Purpose: display stylized organization chart
--                  order by office
--
col office      format a11
col fake_chart  format a35
col level       format 99 heading 'LV'
col boss        format 99 heading 'BS'
col id          format 99

set pagesize 40
break on office skip 1

select
   office,
   lpad(' ',(level-1)*4) || name FAKE_CHART,
   level,
   id,
   boss
from
   lawyer2
connect by prior id = boss
start with boss is NULL
order by office, level
;

clear columns
clear breaks
set pagesize 24
```

This script returns

```
OFFICE        FAKE_CHART                      LV  ID  BS
------------  ------------------------------  --- --- ---
Boston        Paul                             2  20   7
                    Dewey                      3   1  20
                          Greene               4  10   1
                          Cardinal             4  11   1
                                Wright         5  15  10
Houston       Roach                            2   5   7
                    Clayton                    3   4   5
Los Angeles   Easton                           1   7
                    Howe                       2   3   7
              Miller                           2  17   7
                    Roll                       3   6   3
                    Ming                       3  18  17
                          Chandler             4  12   6
                          Martinez             4  13  18

New York      Frankie                          2   9   7
                    Bonin                      3   8   9
                    Earl                       3  14   9
                          Cheetham             4   2   8
                          Chabot               4  16  14
                          Chatham              4  19  14
```

TIP

If you reorder the output as shown here, always display the columns that establish the relationship—in this case, boss and id. The top line of each office reports to 7, or Easton. This indicates that the reordering has not compromised the information of levels and ordering.

Pruning Trees

The examples thus far have presented two possibilities:

- Displaying the entire tree
- Displaying a subtree

There are two more options for the partial representation of trees—eliminating whole branches, which is done through a second condition added to the connect by prior subclause, and eliminating single rows, which is done through a where subclause.

Eliminating Branches: Using connect by prior ... and

The connect by prior subclause allows for the use of logical and conditional operators beyond the join condition. In particular, combined with an and it can be used to include entire branches in the output or exclude them from it. You can use the previous example, which is already ordered by office, to demonstrate this. The first query will retrieve the East Coast offices, the second query the South(west)ern ones. Because everyone knows that Easton is the big boss, he will be eliminated from the query altogether, and the level indentations will be adjusted accordingly.

Listing 22.8. Displaying an organizational chart using order by and connect by

```
--          Filename: 22squ08.sql
--          Purpose: display stylized organization chart
--                   order by office, separate for East and South(west)
--                   eliminate Easton and adjust levels
--
col office     format a11
col fake_chart format a35
col level      format 99 heading 'LV'
col boss       format 99 heading 'BS'
col id         format 99

set pagesize 40
break on office skip 1

select
   office,
   lpad(' ',(level-2)*4) ¦¦ name FAKE_CHART,
   level,
   id,
   boss
from
   lawyer2
where name <> 'Easton'
connect by prior id = boss and
        office in ('Los Angeles','Houston')
start with boss is NULL
order by office, level
;

select
   office,
   lpad(' ',(level-2)*4) ¦¦ name FAKE_CHART,
   level,
   id,
   boss
from
   lawyer2
where name <> 'Easton'
connect by prior id = boss and
        office not in ('Los Angeles','Houston')
start with boss is NULL
order by office, level
;

clear columns
clear breaks
set pagesize 24
```

This script returns

```
OFFICE         FAKE_CHART                          LV  ID  BS
-----------    --------------------------------    --- --- ---
Houston        Roach                                2   5   7
                   Clayton                          3   4   5
Los Angeles    Howe                                 2   3   7
                   Miller                           2  17   7
                       Roll                         3   6   3
                       Ming                         3  18  17
                           Chandler                 4  12   6
                           Martinez                 4  13  18
```

8 rows selected.

```
OFFICE         FAKE_CHART                          LV  ID  BS
-----------    --------------------------------    --- --- ---
Boston         Paul                                 2  20   7
                   Dewey                            3   1  20
                       Greene                       4  10   1
                       Cardinal                     4  11   1
                           Wright                   5  15  10
New York       Frankie                              2   9   7
                   Bonin                            3   8   9
                   Earl                             3  14   9
                       Cheetham                     4   2   8
                       Chabot                       4  16  14
                       Chatham                      4  19  14
```

11 rows selected.

Summary

The purpose of hierarchical queries is to retrieve information about the entire set of relationships, which is commonly referred to as a tree.

Queries of two or more levels can be performed through one or more outer joins with nv1 functions, which allow you to retrieve the information about a node as well as information about the node(s) above it. With this approach, however, each level has to be covered with its own query.

ORACLE vs SQL Hierarchical queries, on the other hand, allow you to choose a node and to retrieve all information pertaining to a subtree above or below that node. Hierarchical queries in Oracle use the keywords connect by prior and start with.

The connect by prior keyword(s) replaces the join condition. Depending on the order of the columns, the query is directed either upward or downward from the node identified with the start with keyword(s).

Another useful feature of hierarchical subqueries is the `level` pseudocolumn, which indicates the level in the subtree, starting with 1 for the node listed after `start with`. You can use this to create indentations using the `lpad` function by passing a calculated length that depends on the level as the second argument into `lpad`.

The output of a hierarchical query can be ordered through an `order by` subclause. This, however, might destroy the inherent meaning of the ordering of the rows.

Finally, whole subtrees can be eliminated through a second condition added to the `connect by prior` subclause. Single nodes/rows can be omitted through a `where` subclause.

Generating SQL Statements Through SQL

IN THIS CHAPTER

CHAPTER 23

Because SQL is the only native tool that interacts with most relational databases, it is not only used for data retrieval but for data and database object manipulation and database administration as well. The first 22 chapters of this book show that SQL is fairly flexible when it comes to data retrieval, even if the methods used are not always efficient.

Nonretrieval tasks, on the other hand, are usually done one statement at a time. For example, it takes one statement

- To insert a new, original row into a table or view
- To create or alter a table
- To create or alter a user

To do those tasks, one statement at a time may be feasible and often necessary. In many cases, however, it is possible and preferable to generate a whole set of SQL statements from the database, spool these to a file, and execute them. This approach takes advantage of the fact that the Relational Database Management Systems (RDBMS) uses database tables and views to manage a database.

Rather than performing tasks one statement at a time, all statements necessary can be created through queries against these tables and views. In a second step, those statements are executed that perform the desired tasks.

Figure 23.1 illustrates this approach. SQL Statement 1 creates five SQL statements (numbered 2–6), which can then be executed to perform tasks.

FIGURE 23.1.

SQL generating a SQL two-step execution approach.

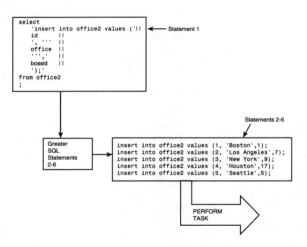

In a way, this chapter bridges the first two sections of the book. It retrieves information in a format usable to manipulate information and objects. For this reason, some of the examples retrieve statements that are explained in the next sections of the book.

The purpose of this chapter is to explain the method, not to provide an exhaustive overview of all system views and tables or all tasks necessary to administer the database.

Advantages of SQL Generating SQL

SQL generating SQL has five major advantages:

- It eliminates the need for excessive typing and/or editing of scripts.
- It eliminates the need to hard-code certain values in SQL scripts.
- It eliminates the errors that excessive typing and editing are likely to introduce into a script.
- It provides a means to create standardized scripts for repeated tasks.
- It provides a means to convert information about database objects and contents back to the scripts that are necessary to re-create them. This is another way to port the contents of a table, a schema, or an entire database to another database.

Including SQL Code as Constants

Chapter 4, "Operator Conversions and Value Decoding," introduced two features that are exploited for the creation of SQL statements through SQL:

- *Concatenation* is extensively used to string the statement together in the first place, enclose values in single quotes, and follow them with commas and semicolons.
- *Constants* are numbers or string values that remain the same for all rows retrieved and do not originate from the database proper. Any SQL command or stump thereof can be output by a query simply through inserting it as a string constant.

SQL generating SQL statements take advantage of two special constants: the single quote used as an escape character to print a single quote following it and the chr function with the argument 10, which prints a newline.

Single-Quote Constants

Single quotes are used in SQL statements to indicate string values. Therefore, a single quote is interpreted as the beginning or end of a string, and quotes used this way must come in pairs:

```
select 'string constant' from dual;
```

This returns the following output:

```
'STRINGCONSTANT
-------------
string constant
```

In this case, the first single quote is interpreted as the beginning of the string, and the second quote as the end.

Inside a string, it is possible to include a single quote by preceding it with another single quote—a method called *escaping*. Thus, four single quotes are necessary to print a single one:

- The first quote indicates the beginning of the string.
- The second quote escapes the third.
- The third is printed as a single quote.
- The fourth indicates the end of the string.

Here is an example of escaping:

```
select 'single quote ''' from dual;
```

This code returns

```
'SINGLEQUOTE''
--------------
single quote '
```

The words `single quote` were included in the string, but the single quotes without words could be printed just as easily, as shown here:

```
select '''' from dual;
```

This code would return

```
'
-
'
```

The last part of the example prints the words `string constant between quotes` between single quotes:

```
select '''string constant between quotes''' from dual;
```

This code returns

```
'''STRINGCONSTANTBETWEENQUOTES''
--------------------------------
'string constant between quotes'
```

Formatting Tricks—Hard Returns and Tabs

Chapter 3, "Readability and Formatting Issues," illustrates the importance of clean formatting to avoid stupid and unnecessary mistakes. The same applies for SQL generating SQL. You will benefit if the output of such a statement can be noticed quickly to discover glaring problems before that script is resubmitted. The entire formatting approach used here judiciously uses newlines and spaces.

Spaces can be introduced into string constants by typing them. Newlines and tabs can be included as well, or they can be inserted by using the `chr` function. `chr(9)` inserts a tab; `chr(10)` inserts a newline. Listing 23.1 shows an example of this.

Listing 23.1. Formatting using the chr function.

```
--          Filename: 23squ01.sql
--           Purpose: print a tab and a newline through
--                    chr(9) and chr(10)
--
--
select 'First Line
Next Line' from dual;
```

This code returns

```
'FIRSTLINENEXTLINE'
-------------------
First Line
Next Line
```

Using chr(10) has the same effect:

```
select 'Before Newline' || chr(10) || 'After Newline' from dual;
```

This returns

```
'BEFORENEWLINE'||CHR(10)||'A
----------------------------
Before Newline
After Newline
```

Tab characters work similarly by either inserting a tab in the code or using chr(9), as shown here:

```
select 'Before tab    After Tab' from dual;
```

```
select 'Before Tab' || chr(9) || 'after tab' from dual;
```

The statements return

```
'BEFORETABAFTERTAB'
-------------------
Before tab      After Tab
```

```
'BEFORETAB'||CHR(9)|
-------------------
Before Tab      after tab
```

All the tools necessary to create clean statements are now available.

Creating Extensive Single-Column Queries

This section uses these approaches to create a SQL statement from SQL. Listing 23.2 anticipates the insert statement that has been used in the create table scripts. See Chapter 24, "Manipulating Single-Table Data," for more information. The script creates the insert statements necessary to load the data of the office2 table. Such an approach would be useful if a column of this table were dropped and the table were reloaded. Listing 23.2 illustrates the office2 table structure.

Listing 23.2. Creating `insert` statements for a table.

```
--        Filename: 23squ02.sql
--         Purpose: create insert statements for office2
--
desc office2;
```

This returns

```
Name                             Null?    Type
------------------------------- -------- ----
ID                              NOT NULL NUMBER(2)
OFFICE                                   VARCHAR2(15)
BOSSID                                   NUMBER(2)
```

Its contents are

```
select * from office2;
```

This line of code returns the following output:

```
       ID OFFICE              BOSSID
--------- ---------------- --------
        1 Boston                  1
        2 Los Angeles             7
        3 New York                9
        4 Houston                17
        5 Seattle                 5
```

To load each record of the table, a statement like the following is necessary:

```
insert into office2 values (1,'Boston',1);
```

These statements are generated by the next part of the example:

```
select
    'insert into office2 values (' ||
    id ||
    ', ''' ||
    office ||
    ''', ' ||
    bossid ||
    ');'
from office2
;
```

This code returns

```
'INSERTINTOOFFICE2VALUES('||ID||','''||OFFICE||''','||BOSSID||');'
-------------------------------------------------------------------------------
-------
insert into office2 values (1, 'Boston',1);
insert into office2 values (2, 'Los Angeles',7);
insert into office2 values (3, 'New York',9);
insert into office2 values (4, 'Houston',17);
insert into office2 values (5, 'Seattle',5);
```

These statements then can be copied from SQL*Plus and pasted back at the command line.

Spooling Output to a File

Often, it is not practical or desirable to cut and paste statements. Another option is to spool the output to a file and call it up from there. A few steps are involved, each of which is performed through a SQL*Plus statement:

■ Suppress screen output, using `set termout off`, because a script thus generated could be many thousand lines long, which would take forever to scroll down the screen.

■ Suppress page breaks, using `set pagesize 0`. Otherwise, the page breaks may get inserted in an inappropriate spot and garble an otherwise good statement.

■ Suppress column headings using `set heading off`. Otherwise, column headings would be inserted into the output where they might create an error. In particular, they might render the first statement following the headings useless.

■ Suppress feedback using `set feedback off`. If you don't, feedback, such as *xx* `rows returned`, is inserted at the end of the output, where it might create an error or, at least, be a nuisance.

■ Specify a line size sufficiently long for the longest column, using `set linesize` *xx*. If possible, do not use excessively long lines; they can be painful to your eyes.

■ Specify a filename to spool the output by using `spool` *filename*.

Don't forget to reset all settings at the end. If you don't, they stay in effect for the remainder of the session.

> **CAUTION**
>
> Not resetting the screen output (`termout`) and heading will make the SQL session behave strangely for further processing. If the heading is set to off, no headings are displayed, whether the statement is issued on the command line or through the file. `termout` will only suppress terminal output of statements submitted through the file.

Listing 23.3 creates a file that contains the five `insert` statements returned in the last part of `23squ02.sql`.

Listing 23.3. Creating statements and spooling to a file.

```
--      Filename: 23squ03.sql
--       Purpose: create insert statements for office2
--                spooled to file 23squ03a.sql
--
set heading off
set pagesize 0
set feedback off
set termout off
--set the following line to an appropriate output directory
```

continues

Listing 23.3. continued

```
spool c:\squ\23or\23squ03a.sql

select
   'insert into office2 values (' ||
   id        ||
   ',  '''   ||
   office    ||
   ''','     ||
   bossid    ||
   ');'
from office2
;

spool off
set heading on
set termout on
set pagesize 24
set feedback on
set termout on
```

This creates the file `23squ03a.sql` with the following content:

```
insert into office2 values (1, 'Boston',1);
insert into office2 values (2, 'Los Angeles',7);
insert into office2 values (3, 'New York',9);
insert into office2 values (4, 'Houston',17);
insert into office2 values (5, 'Seattle',5);
```

Streamlining SQL Generating SQL Through the SQLCONST Table

The code used thus far was decidedly ugly, not quite worthy of the obfuscated SQL contest, but getting there if a longer table were used. If that bothers you, the SQLCONST table, which will be introduced in this section, offers an improvement.

The SQLCONST table contains only one row with a number of fields that contain frequently used combinations of single quotes, commas, newlines, and indentations.

This table can be joined with the table(s) used for the query. Selecting the short fieldnames has two advantages: A short and (hopefully) meaningful abbreviation can be used instead of the single quote combinations, and, because the columns already contain strings, the outermost pair of single quotes does not have to be used at all.

If the abbreviations used as fieldnames here appear unintuitive to you, you can make up your own. Mine have obviously been adversely affected by working with UNIX for too long.

Table 23.1 lists the column names and corresponding codes. The word *quote* indicates a single quote. Most fields come in sets of four, joining numerical or string columns with numerical or string columns.

Table 23.1. SQLCONST column names and contents.

Column name	Replaces	Description
NCN	',_'	Comma space
SCS	''', '''	Quote comma space quote
NCS	', '''	Comma space quote
SCN	'''_,'	Quote space comma
NRN	',<CR>'	Comma return
SRS	''', <CR>'''	Quote comma return quote
NRS	', <CR>'''	Comma return quote
SRN	''',<CR>'	Quote comma return
N3N	',<CR>___'	Comma return
S3S	''', <CR> '''	Quote comma return quote
N3S	', <CR> '''	Comma return quote
S3N	''', <CR> '	Quote comma return
N6N	',<CR> '	Comma return
S6S	''', <CR> '''	Quote comma return quote
N6S	', <CR> '''	Comma return quote
S6N	''', <CR> '	Quote comma return
N9N	',<CR> '	Comma return
S9S	''', <CR> '''	Quote comma return quote
N9S	', <CR> '''	Comma return quote
S9N	''', <CR> '	Quote comma return
NPE	');'	Parenthesis semicolon
SPE	''');'	Quote parenthesis semicolon
NE	';'	Semicolon
SE	''';'	Quote semicolon

Please run the script `crsqlco.sql` to create the `SQLCONST` table.

To create the `insert` statements for `lawyer2` is a straightforward task if the `SQLCONST` table is used, as shown in Listing 23.4.

Listing 23.4. Creating statements using a table.

```
--          Filename: 23squ04.sql
--           Purpose: create insert statements for lawyer2
--                    using sqlconst table
--                    spooled to file 23squ04a.sql
--
--
set heading off
set pagesize 0
set feedback off
set termout off
--set the following to an appropriate output directory
spool c:\squ\23or\23squ04a.sql

select
    'insert into lawyer2 values (' ||
    id       || ncn ||
    boss     || n3s ||
    name     || scs ||
    office   || scn ||
    bhrs     || ncn ||
    bgross   || npe
from lawyer2, sqlconst
;

spool off
set heading on
set termout on
set pagesize 24
set feedback on
set termout on
```

The statement creates the file 23squ04a.sql with the following contents:

```
insert into lawyer2 values (1, 20,
    'Dewey', 'Boston', 2856, 426800);


...
...
...
insert into lawyer2 values (20, 7,
    'Paul', 'Boston', 2198, 239855);
```

DEBUG ALERT

The ugly code necessary to create SQL generating SQL statements is a frequent source of confusion and small errors that are, nevertheless, cumbersome to debug. Therefore, good habits here are important to avoid code that does not work and the subsequent annoying debugging and recoding.

Inserting a Comment Section

A comment section can be included by simply selecting it as text from dual and then combining it with the statement proper through a `union all` set operator.

> **NOTE**
>
> Use a union all, not a union, because union all does not sort the output in any way.

Listing 23.5 includes a comment section with the statement of example `23squ05.sql`.

Listing 23.5. Including a comment section.

```
--      Filename: 23squ05.sql
--       Purpose: create insert statements for lawyer2
--                using sqlconst table
--                includes comment section
--                spooled to file 23squ05a.sql
--
set heading off
set pagesize 0
set feedback off
set termout off
--set the following to an appropriate output directory
spool c:\squ\23or\23squ05a.sql

select
'--      Filename: 23squ05a.sql
--       Purpose: insert statements for lawyer2
--                created by script 23squ05.sql
--
--      CAUTION
--      IF YOU ADAPT THIS SCRIPT DIRECTLY, YOU SHOULD SAVE IT
--      UNDER A DIFFERENT NAME. ANY CHANGES WILL BE WIPED OUT
--      SHOULD THE ORIGINAL SCRIPT BE RERUN.
--
--      Script has been run on ' || sysdate || ' by ' || user
from dual
union all
select
   'insert into lawyer2 values (' ||
   id        || ncn ||
   boss      || n3s ||
   name      || scs ||
   office    || scn ||
   bhrs      || ncn ||
   bgross    || npe
from lawyer2, sqlconst
;
```

continues

Listing 23.5. continued

```
spool off
set heading on
set termout on
set pagesize 24
set feedback on
set termout on
```

It returns

```
--         Filename: 23squ05.sql
--          Purpose: insert statements for lawyer2
--                   created by script 23squ05a.sql
--
--     CAUTION
--     IF YOU ADAPT THIS SCRIPT DIRECTLY, YOU SHOULD SAVE IT
--     UNDER A DIFFERENT NAME. ANY CHANGES WILL BE WIPED OUT
--     SHOULD THE ORIGINAL SCRIPT BE RERUN.
--
--     Script has been run on 28-MAY-1997 by HANS

insert into lawyer2 values (1, 20,
    'Dewey', 'Boston', 2856, 426800);

...

insert into lawyer2 values (20, 7,
    'Paul', 'Boston', 2198, 239855);
```

> **TIP**
>
> The most important comments in a SQL script that has been generated through SQL are a reference to the script that created it and a big CAUTION that any adaptations of these scripts might be wiped out by reruns of the originating scripts. Comments should also include when the script has been run and by whom.

If you like, you could get fancy here and include a few columns with standard text in the SQLCONST table, which would avoid much unnecessary copying and typing.

Typical Purposes

Although I have never seen official surveys, I would assume that many professional system administrators use SQL generating SQL extensively for their daily work. Why type everything?

Any SQL script that is used for administration qualifies as a candidate. These include

- Scripts that create a tablespace with exactly the same parameters as another tablespace (except for filenames, of course). A SQL statement would be generated for this purpose that reads system views to get the parameters of the model tablespace and creates a `create tablespace` script.

- ▪ Scripts that create a user with the same parameters as those of another user.
- ▪ Scripts that make database performance data more usable.

The many books on database administration include potential candidates. The following section just shows one example, a script that generates a script to re-create a table using Data Dictionary information.

> **NOTE**
>
> SQL Station, a test version of which is included, will create a similar script. Click the + signs next to the schema SQU, then Table, then the table for which you want create the script, and then on code. The statement will appear in the right pane. A tool such as SQL Station can generate many other such statements on-the-fly.

Chapter 28, "Creating Tables," includes a SQL generating SQL script that creates the start for a code lookup table from a data table.

Table Definition and Content Dumps

Almost the entire information necessary to tune databases is available through system tables and views. Several of these include information about database tables and columns. These will be used in the following example to piece together the script necessary to re-create the script. While this script looks convoluted and ugly, it can be used with minor modifications to unload the definitions of a large set of tables.

> **NOTE**
>
> If you use Oracle in real life, you would likely use the export/import utilities for the same task. If you port from Oracle to non-Oracle, or vice versa, such a script could do the trick quite nicely. But even then it is better to use a product such as Oracle Gateways, which allows you to copy data from one database directly to the other.

The script in the following example uses only one view, `all_tab_columns`, to create the column definitions. Other views would have to be used as well, such as `all_tables` for storage parameters and `all_constraints` and `all_cons_columns` for column constraints. The following is the structure of `all_tab_columns`:

```
SQL> desc all_tab_columns

 Name                          Null?    Type
 ----------------------------- -------- ----
 OWNER                         NOT NULL VARCHAR2(30)
 TABLE_NAME                    NOT NULL VARCHAR2(30)
 COLUMN_NAME                   NOT NULL VARCHAR2(30)
 DATA_TYPE                              VARCHAR2(9)
 DATA_LENGTH                   NOT NULL NUMBER
 DATA_PRECISION                         NUMBER
 DATA_SCALE                             NUMBER
 NULLABLE                               VARCHAR2(1)
 COLUMN_ID                     NOT NULL NUMBER
 DEFAULT_LENGTH                         NUMBER
 DATA_DEFAULT                           LONG
 NUM_DISTINCT                           NUMBER
 LOW_VALUE                              RAW(32)
 HIGH_VALUE                             RAW(32)
 DENSITY                                NUMBER
 NUM_NULLS                              NUMBER
 NUM_BUCKETS                            NUMBER
 LAST_ANALYZED                          DATE
 SAMPLE_SIZE                            NUMBER
```

The script uses only the columns from TABLE_NAME to NULLABLE.

As a first step, the contents of those columns are displayed for information only, which is done in Listing 23.6.

Listing 23.6. Re-creating a table.

```
--        Filename: 23squ06.sql
--         Purpose: create statements for re-creating the lawyer2 table
--                  spools to file 23squ06a.sql
--
select
   column_name,
   data_type,
   data_length,
   data_precision,
   data_scale,
   nullable
from all_tab_columns
where table_name  = 'LAWYER2'
;
```

This returns the following output:

COLUMN_NAME	DATA_TYPE	DATA_LENGTH	DATA_PRECISION	DATA_SCALE	N
ID	NUMBER	22	2	0	N
BOSS	NUMBER	22	2	0	Y
NAME	VARCHAR2	15			Y
OFFICE	VARCHAR2	15			Y

BHRS	NUMBER	22	4	0 Y
BGROSS	NUMBER	22	7	0 Y

```
6 rows selected.
```

The odd thing is that numbers are always listed as 22 bytes long; but numbers with shorter definitions such as a two-digit integer do not take up that much space. However, that also means that the column length has to be picked up from the `data_length` for `char` and `varchar2` columns and from the `data_precision` column for numerical columns.

The next part of the example consists of three `select` statements combined by `union alls`. The first enters the comments and the first line of the `create` statement. The second statement puts in one row for each column. The last statement enters the parentheses and semicolon:

```
set heading off
set pagesize 0
set feedback off
set termout off
;
--set the following to an appropriate output directory
spool c:\squ\23or\23squ06a.sql

select
'--      Filename: 23squ06a.sql
--       Purpose: creates table lawyer2
--               created by script 23squ06a.sql
--
--      CAUTION
--      IF YOU ADAPT THIS SCRIPT DIRECTLY, YOU SHOULD SAVE IT
--      UNDER A DIFFERENT NAME. ANY CHANGES WILL BE WIPED OUT
--      SHOULD THE ORIGINAL SCRIPT BE RERUN.
--
--      Script has been run on ' ¦¦ sysdate ¦¦ ' by ' ¦¦ user
from dual
union all
select
   'create table lawyer2 (' from dual
union all
select '        ' ¦¦
   rpad(column_name,20) ¦¦ ' ' ¦¦
   rpad(data_type,9) ¦¦
   decode (data_type, 'VARCHAR2', '(' ¦¦ data_length      ¦¦')',
                      'CHAR',     '(' ¦¦ data_length      ¦¦')',
                      'NUMBER',   '(' ¦¦ data_precision  ¦¦ ')',' ') ¦¦
   decode (nullable,'Y','  NULL','N','  NOT NULL') ¦¦ ','
from all_tab_columns
where table_name  = 'LAWYER2'
union all
select ');' from dual
;

spool off
set heading on
set termout on
set pagesize 24
set feedback on
set termout on
```

It returns

```
--        Filename: 23squ06a.sql
--         Purpose: creates table lawyer2
--                  created by script 23squ06a.sql
--
--      CAUTION
--      IF YOU ADAPT THIS SCRIPT DIRECTLY, YOU SHOULD SAVE IT
--      UNDER A DIFFERENT NAME. ANY CHANGES WILL BE WIPED OUT
--      SHOULD THE ORIGINAL SCRIPT BE RERUN.
--
--      Script has been run on 28-MAY-1997 by HANS

create table lawyer2 (
    ID                  NUMBER    (2)  NOT NULL,
    BOSS                NUMBER    (2)  NULL,
    NAME                VARCHAR2 (15)  NULL,
    OFFICE              VARCHAR2 (15)  NULL,
    BHRS                NUMBER    (4)  NULL,
    BGROSS              NUMBER    (7)  NULL,
);
```

The statement would create an error because the , in the second to last line is followed by a parenthesis. Thus, the comma needs to be deleted or a global search and replace needs to be performed if many tables are processed that way.

Please note that the script only deals with numbers of type integer. If fixed- or floating-point numbers need to be considered, a decode needs to be nested into the NUMBER line of the decode statement.

The content dump has already been demonstrated in 23squ05a.sql.

Summary

In the SQL generating SQL approach, one SQL statement creates other SQL statements, which, if executed, perform tasks. This approach takes advantage of the fact that the RDBMS manages itself through database tables and views.

SQL generating SQL eliminates the need for excessive typing and/or editing of scripts and for hard-coding of certain values in SQL scripts. It provides a means to create standardized scripts for repeated tasks and to convert information about database objects and contents back to the scripts that are necessary to re-create them.

The approach exploits two features: concatenation and string constants. The single quote also is used as an escape character to print a single quote following it and the chr function with the argument 10, which prints a newline.

The output of the SQL generating SQL statement can be cut and pasted back into SQL*Plus or spooled to a file and called up from there. A few steps must be performed through a SQL*Plus for that purpose:

- Suppress screen output using set termout off.
- Suppress page breaks using set pagesize 0.
- Suppress columns headings using set heading off.
- Suppress feedback using set feedback off.
- Specify a line size sufficiently long for the longest column using set linesize *xx*.
- Specify a filename to spool the output to using spool *filename*.

All settings should be reset at the end; otherwise, they stay in effect for the remainder of the session.

To avoid the ugly and unreadable SQL code that results from the excessive use of single quotes, the SQLCONST table offers an improvement. It contains only one row with a number of fields that contain frequently used combinations of single quotes, commas, newlines, and indentations. It can be joined with the table(s) used for the query.

A comment section can be included by simply selecting it as a multiline text column from the dual table and then combining it with the statement proper through a union all set operator.

Manipulating Information and Database Objects

B

SECTION

After having gone through all the options of retrieving information, Section B is concerned with manipulating information, manipulating the database objects through which information is accessed (views and tables), and the ways through which data and database objects can be kept secure.

The first part of this section covers the SQL data manipulation options—insert, delete, and update—and finalizing or reversing of data manipulations in the database through commit or rollback.

The second part of this section shows you how to customize the appearance of tables through views.

The third part includes four chapters on tables, which cover table creation options, keys, indexes, constraints, and relationships between tables.

The last part covers the security options available through SQL and Oracle's extensions: privileges, roles, the use of views to provide row-level security, and the ways to generate auditing information.

VII

PART

Manipulating Information

Manipulating Single-Table Data

CHAPTER 24

Data-manipulation statements in SQL are straightforward, and only three options are available:

- Inserting new rows into a table
- Deleting rows from a table
- Updating columns in a table

The latter two commands can affect an entire table or only those rows that are specified through a where clause. Queries and subqueries can be incorporated into these statements just as they can be into other queries. Subqueries can also be used to set values for updates and inserts.

CAUTION

SQL operates on sets—or more accurately, pseudo-sets, such as all rows in a table. It is, therefore, very easy to wipe out a whole table or to overwrite the values of an entire column with garbage values that, for all practical purposes, may very well have the same effect as wiping out the whole table.

Therefore, think twice before issuing any of these commands. Once issued and committed (see Chapter 25, "Control Transactions"), the changes cannot be undone short of restoring the table or entire database from a backup source.

Inserting New Rows into a Table: `insert`

The insert statement does two things:

- Creates a new row in the database table specified by it
- Loads the values listed into all columns, or those columns specified by it

The insert statement affects entire rows of tables. Even if not a single value is loaded (which is possible, if all columns are defined as null), a row is loaded anyway. Listing 24.1 demonstrates that with the pers1 table. First, the table definition is altered so that all columns can have null values. Then five rows with only null values are loaded. Finally, a row count is performed and everything is reset to where it was.

Listing 24.1. Inserting new rows into a table with null values.

```
--        Filename: 24squ01.sql
--        Purpose: alter the table definition to all nullable columns
--                 insert five rows with null values
--                 count rows and reset everything
--
select count(1) from pers1;

alter table pers1 modify (id null);
```

```
insert into pers1 values (NULL, NULL, NULL, NULL, NULL, NULL);
insert into pers1 values (NULL, NULL, NULL, NULL, NULL, NULL);
insert into pers1 values (NULL, NULL, NULL, NULL, NULL, NULL);
insert into pers1 values (NULL, NULL, NULL, NULL, NULL, NULL);
insert into pers1 values (NULL, NULL, NULL, NULL, NULL, NULL);

select count(1) from pers1;

rollback;

alter table pers1 modify (id not null);

select count(1) from pers1;
```

The script returns this:

```
 COUNT(1)
---------
        5

Table altered.

1 row created.
1 row created.
1 row created.
1 row created.
1 row created.

 COUNT(1)
---------
       10

Rollback complete.

Table altered.

 COUNT(1)
---------
        5
```

The most basic insert statement names the table to be affected and lists one value for each column. The previous example does that, inserting all NULL values. Listing 24.2 inserts "real" values.

Listing 24.2. Inserting rows into a table with real values.

```
--       Filename: 24squ02.sql
--        Purpose: insert rows through basic insert statement
--
insert into pers1 values (6, 'Thann', 'Karl H.', '881728371', 39, 'M');

select * from pers1;

rollback;
```

It returns this:

```
1 row created.
```

```
      ID LNAME           FMNAME          SSN             AGE S
-------- --------------- --------------- --------- --------- -
       1 Jones           David N.        895663453        34 M
       2 Martinelli      A. Emery        312331818        92 M
       3 Talavera        F. Espinosa     533932999        19 F
       4 Kratochvil      Mary T.         969825711        48 F
       5 Melsheli        Joseph K.       000342222        14 M
       6 Thann           Karl H.         881728371        39 M
```

```
6 rows selected.
```

```
Rollback complete.
```

The sixth row is inserted and retrieved just like all the other ones.

There are two conditions needed for the basic `insert` statement to work (other than the typical syntax requirements):

- Exactly the same number of values as the table has columns must be included.
- The datatypes of the values included must be compatible with the datatypes of the columns. In particular, string values must be between single quotes, and dates that do not follow the standard format must be converted using the `to_date` function.

The basic `insert` statement uses the position of the value within the set of values to match up each value with its column. The first value is loaded into the first column, the second into the second, and so on. Obviously, a syntactically correct statement can still load nonsense, if that is what is included in the *value* section of the `insert` statement.

Specifying Specific Columns to Insert

The example in `24squ01.sql` shows you that it is possible to insert rows where all columns are set to null, and that it is also possible to insert only some columns. You saw one way to do that in that example: Just include the word NULL in the position corresponding to the column(s) where no value should be loaded. This approach is referred to as positional notation.

The other option is to specifically name the columns that should be loaded. All others (assuming that they are not specified as `not null`) will simply insert NULLs.

Listing 24.3 uses this approach. Five new rows are loaded into the `pers1` table, but only values for the ID column are specified—the values 6–10.

Listing 24.3. Inserting rows using basic `insert` statements.

```
--      Filename: 24squ03.sql
--        Purpose: insert rows through basic insert statement
--
```

```
insert into pers1 (id) values (6);
insert into pers1 (id) values (7);
insert into pers1 (id) values (8);
insert into pers1 (id) values (9);
insert into pers1 (id) values (10);

select *
from pers1
where id > 5
;

rollback;
```

The script returns this:

```
1 row created.

1 row created.

1 row created.

1 row created.

1 row created.

        ID LNAME           FMNAME           SSN            AGE S
---------- --------------- ---------------- ---------- ---------- -
         6
         7
         8
         9
        10

Rollback complete.
```

In this case, all but the ID values are NULLs.

Using positional notation, the same goal can be reached by setting all but the ID values to NULL, which is shown in Listing 24.4.

Listing 24.4. Inserting rows using positional notation.

```
--       Filename: 24squ04.sql
--        Purpose: insert rows through basic insert statement
--                 using positional notation
--
insert into pers1 values (6,  NULL, NULL, NULL, NULL, NULL);
insert into pers1 values (7,  NULL, NULL, NULL, NULL, NULL);
insert into pers1 values (8,  NULL, NULL, NULL, NULL, NULL);
insert into pers1 values (9,  NULL, NULL, NULL, NULL, NULL);
insert into pers1 values (10, NULL, NULL, NULL, NULL, NULL);

select *
from pers1
where id > 5
;

rollback;
```

This returns the same as `24squ03.sql`.

Inserting Rows That Are Selected from Another Table Through a Subquery

Using the `insert` statement with a subquery allows you to load rows into one table using information from another table. All the examples here load information from a table in the same database, but it is possible to access tables located in other databases on the same or a different computer, provided the network pieces are in place.

Whereas the `insert` statement with a `values` clause adds exactly one row (if successful), the subquery `insert` statement adds as many rows to the table as the subquery retrieves.

In the subquery version of the `insert` statement, the first part is identical to the basic version. The part starting with the keyword `values` is replaced by a `select` statement. The number and type of columns returned by the subquery must match the number and type of the columns to be inserted.

> **TIP**
>
> This subquery is usually *not* enclosed between parentheses, although parentheses may be used.

Listing 24.5 uses information from the `pers8` table to insert rows 6–10 of the `pers8` table into `pers5`. The same result is accomplished by first naming the columns and then by using positional notation. For demonstration's sake, the first statement is then redone with parentheses.

Listing 24.5. Inserting rows using a subquery `insert` statement.

```
--        Filename: 24squ05.sql
--        Purpose: insert rows through subquery insert statement
--
insert into pers1
   (id, lname, fmname, ssn, age, sex)
select
   id,
   lname,
   fmname,
   ssn,
   age,
   sex
from pers8
where id > 5
;

rollback;
```

```
insert into pers1
select
    id,
    lname,
    fmname,
    ssn,
    age,
    sex
from pers8
where id > 5
;

select *
from pers1
where id > 5
;

rollback;

insert into pers1
    (id, lname, fmname, ssn, age, sex)
(select
    id,
    lname,
    fmname,
    ssn,
    age,
    sex
from pers8
where id > 5)
;

rollback;
```

The statements return

```
5 rows created.


Rollback complete.


5 rows created.


        ID LNAME           FMNAME          SSN             AGE S
---------- --------------- --------------- --------- ---------- -
         6 Robinson        Faye M.         966549339            F
         7                 M. Okechuku     854291872        23
         8 Rochblatt       Harold T.       290553810        32 M
         9 Nungaray        Dennis J.       944829477        58 M
        10 Oberstein       Florence L.     932840202         9 F


Rollback complete.

5 rows created.

Rollback complete.
```

All three versions create five rows that can be retrieved with the select statement, as is done after the second version.

Any valid subquery can be used in this context, whether it accesses one or many tables or selects single or grouped rows, as long as it returns the required number and types of columns. The insert statement with subquery is, therefore, a prime tool for any kind of data manipulation with intermediate storage.

Deleting Rows from a Table: delete and truncate

The opposite of inserting rows is deleting rows. The delete statement is very easy and very deadly because its simplest version—delete from *tablename*—wipes out all the rows in the table identified by *tablename*. Generally the important part of the delete statement is in the where clause, where the rows to be deleted are specified. (I would have written "the meat of the delete statement," but I am a vegetarian.)

Just as with the insert statement, the delete statement usually affects the row count. The only exceptions are when the where clause does not identify any row to delete or when the table contains no rows to start with.

Listing 24.6 shows the effect of the delete statement. The first part deletes all rows from pers1 through an unqualified delete. A rollback undoes the damage. The second part deletes all odd rows.

Listing 24.6. Deleting rows.

```
--        Filename: 24squ06.sql
--         Purpose: deleting rows
--
delete from pers1;

select *
from pers1
;

rollback;

delete from pers1
where mod(id,2) = 1
;

select *
from pers1
;

rollback;
```

It returns the following:

```
5 rows deleted.


no rows selected
```

An unqualified `delete` statement will wipe out all rows, indeed:

```
Rollback complete.


3 rows deleted.


        ID LNAME           FMNAME           SSN          AGE S
---------- --------------- --------------- ----------- -------- -
         2 Martinelli      A. Emery         312331818      92 M
         4 Kratochvil      Mary T.          969825711      48 F


Rollback complete.
```

The `where` clause may contain a subquery that references any accessible table(s). In Listing 24.7, every row in `pers8` is deleted where the corresponding income in `inc2` is less then $10,000 (which includes `NULL` incomes as well):

Listing 24.7. Deleting rows using a subquery.

```
--        Filename: 24squ07.sql
--        Purpose: deleting rows
--                 use subquery
--
select
   p.id,
   p.lname,
   p.fmname,
   sum(i.amount)
from pers8 p, inc2 i
where p.id = i.id(+)
group by
   p.id,
   p.lname,
   p.fmname
;
```

This returns the following:

```
ID LNAME           FMNAME           SUM(I.AMOUNT)
---------- --------------- --------------- -------------
         1 Jones           David N.               106889
         2 Martinelli      A. Emery
         3                 F. Espinosa              9568
         4 Kratochvil                             188800
         5 Melsheli        Joseph K.               68983
```

```
   6 Robinson        Faye M.                142231
   7                 M. Okechuku
   8 Rochblatt       Harold T.
   9 Nungaray        Dennis J.
  10 Oberstein       Florence L.
```

```
10 rows selected.
```

Only rows 1, 4, 5, and 6 qualify. Row 3 has too little income, and the remaining rows have none at all. In the next statement, a subquery is used to identify all persons with an income of $100,000 or more, and then deletes all persons who are not part of this group:

```
delete from pers8
where id not in
   (select
        id
    from inc2
    having sum(amount) >= 10000
    group by id)
;
```

This returns the following:

```
6 rows deleted.
```

The subquery is of interest also because the group function is only in the having statement and not in the select comma list, where it can't be because only one column may be returned to the delete statement. The same select statement as used in the previous example yields only the four remaining rows. A rollback, not shown here, reverses everything:

```
  ID LNAME           FMNAME          SUM(I.AMOUNT)
-------- --------------- --------------- -------------
   1 Jones           David N.               106889
   4 Kratochvil                             188800
   5 Melsheli        Joseph K.               68983
   6 Robinson        Faye M.                142231
```

Irreversibly Deleting All Rows in a Table: `truncate table`

As most of these examples have shown and as the next chapter explains in detail, a rollback can undo the changes of data-manipulation commands. This is possible because the database maintains information about the state of database tables before a change. From this information it is possible to piece things together and reverse the tables to their previous state.

The disadvantage of this approach is the need to write not only the changed information to the table, but also the old information to rollback space—dedicated storage for that purpose—which can take a long time if a large table is cleaned out.

The `truncate table` command speeds up this process by not writing pre-change information to rollback space. The downside is that the change cannot be reversed. This command is an indiscriminate reaper: All rows of a table disappear, and no `where` clause is possible. See Chapter 28, "Creating Tables," for an example of using `truncate table`.

Updating Existing Rows in a Table: update

The last of the data-manipulation commands is different from the other two because it *does not* affect the row count of the table. This command has three parts:

- ■ update *tablename*, which specifies the table to be updated
- ■ set commalist, which specifies the columns to be set and the values to which they are set
- ■ The where clause, which limits the rows affected

Thus, in a way, the update command uses a matrix approach—the set part identifies the columns, and the where clause specifies the rows affected. The update command also has commonalities with the select command—all columns in the active row can be used for formulas that derive the value for the column to be set.

update and delete share the same danger: If no where clause is included, all rows will be affected.

Listing 24.8 does a global update of pers1 and sets all first names to Leslie M. and all last names to Rocketon.

Listing 24.8. Performing a global update.

```
--        Filename: 24squ08.sql
--        Purpose: static update
--
update pers1
set fmname = 'Leslie M.',
    lname  = 'Rocketon'
;

select
    *
from pers1
;

rollback;
```

This returns the following:

```
5 rows updated.
```

ID	LNAME	FMNAME	SSN	AGE	S
1	Rocketon	Leslie M.	895663453	34	M
2	Rocketon	Leslie M.	312331818	92	M
3	Rocketon	Leslie M.	533932999	19	F
4	Rocketon	Leslie M.	969825711	48	F
5	Rocketon	Leslie M.	000342222	14	M

```
Rollback complete.
```

24

MANIPULATING
SINGLE-TABLE
DATA

Listing 24.9 uses information from several columns of the pers3 table to augment the value of the wealth column of pers3 by half of the income.

Listing 24.9. Updating values using data from other columns and calculations on the same column.

```
--          Filename: 24squ09.sql
--          Purpose: update using values of the same and other columns
--
select
   id,
   lname,
   wealth,
   interest,
   salary,
   profit,
   royalty
from pers3
;
```

It returns the contents of the table before the update:

ID	LNAME	WEALTH	INTEREST	SALARY	PROFIT	ROYALTY
1	Jones	43000	200	80000	12000	0
2	Martinelli	645000	24000	0	5000	63900
3	Talavera	24000	110	4870	0	0
4	Kratochvil	2400600	4800	0	184000	0
5	Melsheli	800	50	0	0	0

Then the wealth values are updated, and the information is retrieved again:

```
update pers3
set wealth = wealth + (interest + salary + profit + royalty)/2
;

select
   id,
   lname,
   wealth,
   interest,
   salary,
   profit,
   royalty
from pers3
;

rollback;
```

This returns the following:

```
5 rows updated.
```

ID	LNAME	WEALTH	INTEREST	SALARY	PROFIT	ROYALTY
1	Jones	89100	200	80000	12000	0
2	Martinelli	691450	24000	0	5000	63900
3	Talavera	26490	110	4870	0	0
4	Kratochvil	2495000	4800	0	184000	0
5	Melsheli	825	50	0	0	0

```
Rollback complete.
```

Qualifying Rows to Update

The rows to be updated are chosen the same way as they are for the `delete` statement—through the `where` clause that identifies the rows to be affected. Subqueries can be used as well. For example, if `24squ09.sql` were to be adapted such that the income's portion over $92,300 were added to wealth, but wealth would be unaffected by a lesser or no income, the formula and the `where` clause would have to be used together as shown in Listing 24.10.

Listing 24.10. Updating data using the where clause when qualifying rows.

```
--         Filename: 24squ10.sql
--          Purpose: update using values of the same and other columns
--                   includes where clause
--
update pers3
set wealth = wealth + (interest + salary + profit + royalty) - 92300
where  (interest + salary + profit + royalty) > 92300
;

select
   id,
   lname,
   wealth,
   interest,
   salary,
   profit,
   royalty
from pers3
;

rollback;
```

This returns the following:

```
2 rows updated.
```

ID	LNAME	WEALTH	INTEREST	SALARY	PROFIT	ROYALTY
1	Jones	43000	200	80000	12000	0
2	Martinelli	645600	24000	0	5000	63900
3	Talavera	24000	110	4870	0	0

24

MANIPULATING
SINGLE-TABLE
DATA

```
       4 Kratochvil      2497100      4800       0     184000        0
       5 Melsheli           800        50       0          0        0
```

Rollback complete.

Only rows 2 and 4 are now affected.

Updating with a Multiple-Column Subquery

The static update shown in `24squ08.sql` updated two columns in one run. This was not difficult because the values were static, and the set `lname='Rocketon'`, `fmname = 'Leslie'` did the
trick. A special syntax is provided for cases in which several values are to be updated through
one subquery. A set `commalist` between parentheses specifies the columns to be affected, and
the subquery returns the corresponding values. Listing 24.11 replaces the last name and first/
middle names of `pers1` with those of rows 6–10 of `pers8`. Note the use of aliasing for both
tables involved.

Listing 24.11. Updating with a multi-column subquery.

```
--       Filename: 24squ11.sql
--        Purpose: multi-column update through subquery
--
update pers1 a
set (lname, fmname) =
   (select
       lname,
       fmname
    from pers8 b
    where a.id = b.id - 5)
;

select * from pers1;

rollback;
```

This returns the following:

5 rows updated.

```
   ID LNAME           FMNAME           SSN          AGE S
-------- --------------- --------------- ---------- ---------- -
    1 Robinson        Faye M.          895663453     34 M
    2                 M. Okechuku      312331818     92 M
    3 Rochblatt       Harold T.        533932999     19 F
    4 Nungaray        Dennis J.        969825711     48 F
    5 Oberstein       Florence L.      000342222     14 M
```

Rollback complete.

REAL-WORLD EXPERIENCES

With update and insert statements, automatic type conversions are frequently performed, for example, when a character string is converted to a date. This feature is very convenient, but it is not without risks, especially when applications are ported.

I once prepared the porting of an application from one database to another. Before the port, all the data inserts worked just fine, but they didn't afterward. The problem was that the NLS_DEFAULT_DATE was set to a four-digit year in the test system but a two-digit year in the production system. In that situation, it was easy to change the parameters. In many other cases, the decision is that of the database administrator who needs to balance all applications, and such a quick fix might not be possible.

It is, therefore, preferable to not rely on automatic conversions in these statements, but to use explicit conversion functions with format masks. That way conversions will be performed that are completely independent of the default values.

Summary

SQL provides three data-manipulation commands to insert new rows into a table, to delete rows from a table, and to update columns in a table. Queries and subqueries can be incorporated into these statements just as they can into other queries. Subqueries can also be used to set values for updates and inserts.

Because these statements operate on pseudosets, it is very easy to wipe out a whole table or to overwrite the values of an entire column with garbage values.

The insert statement creates a new row in a database table and loads the values into its columns. The value/column match can be created through position, where the first value is loaded into the first column, the second into the second column, and so on, or through naming the columns explicitly. Using the insert statement with a subquery allows you to load rows into one table using information from another table from the same database or a different database. As many rows are added to the table as the subquery retrieves.

Two options are provided for deleting rows. The delete statement wipes out all rows of the table that are specified in its where clause. The truncate table command irrevocably sweeps a table clean and is, therefore, very fast.

The most versatile of the data-manipulation commands is update, which allows you to set certain columns to certain values. As is the case with the select command, all columns in the active row can be used for formulas that derive the value for the column to be set. A where clause can be used to specify rows to update. Subqueries can be used to determine values. They also can be used in the where clause. A special subquery syntax is available to update several columns through one subquery.

Control Transactions

CHAPTER 25

IN THIS CHAPTER

One of my son's favorite games is tricking me. He will do or say something semi-outlandish only to undo it with a "tricked you." You have probably figured out SQL's equivalent to "tricked you," `rollback`, which undoes most data manipulation steps. On the other extreme, `commit` finalizes the changes and it is pretty difficult, sometimes impossible, to undo these.

Between these all or nothing extremes, the `savepoint` feature allows you to commit or roll back transactions in steps.

Finalizing or Reversing Changes to a Database: commit and rollback

Storage is available to the Relational Database Management System (RDBMS) in blocks of usually 2 or 4KB. Whenever a row of data is manipulated, the block containing the row is retrieved from disk into a memory buffer (if it does not happen to be there already from a previous transaction). The information is then worked over in memory and eventually written back to disk. The blocks in their state before the change are also copied to rollback segments—storage objects maintained for that purpose. If for some reason the transaction needs to be undone, the RDBMS can be directed to do so through a `rollback` command. In this case, the blocks in the rollback segments overwrite the updated blocks in the database, and everything goes back to square one.

The `commit` statement, on the other hand, causes the RDBMS to flush the rollback segments and thus make the updated stage the permanent one.

 Run the script `crlaw8.sql`, which can be found on the CD accompanying this book, to create the `lawyer8` table that is laid out like `lawyer1` but doesn't contain rows. This table will be restocked from other tables as needed.

REAL-WORLD EXPERIENCES

For most people, an engagement is an important affair during which a couple decides to get married and then announces that decision. Usually, but not always, an engagement is followed by a wedding. By design and law, however, an engagement is fairly easy to break with hurt feelings and embarrassment being the most likely fallout. In many jurisdictions, it is impossible to enforce a promise to marry someone. This is a good thing because it provides a cushion in case something does not work out. A marriage, on the other hand, is final, and if at all, can be undone only with major legal, religious, personal, and financial commotions. Finally, a third party generally cannot undo the engagement of a couple.

SQL uses an approach similar to an engagement for its data manipulation. Like an engagement, a data transaction is usually intended to be serious. It can be fairly easily undone, however, with the only fallout being unnecessary milling through rollback segments, and another user or oneself being slowed down for a little while. Like a wedding, a `commit` is final, and if at all can be undone only with major commotions, such a recreating a table or restoring from a backup.

Listing 25.1 inserts the first lines into `lawyer8`, selects all rows, and commits.

Listing 25.1. Using `commit` and `rollback`.

```
--         Filename: 25squ01.sql
--         Purpose: commit and rollback
--
insert into lawyer8
select
   id,
   Name,
   Office,
   bhrs,
   bgross
from lawyer1
where mod(id,4) = 0
;

select * from lawyer8;

commit;
```

This code returns the following:

```
5 rows created.

        ID NAME           OFFICE            BHRS        BGROSS
--------- -------------- --------------- ---------- ---------
         4 Clayton        Houston           1789        190045
         8 Bonin          New York          1678        346892
        12 Chandler       Los Angeles       2987        423878
        16 Chabot         New York          1680        310897
        20 Paul           Boston            2198        239855

Commit complete.
```

Next, two rows are deleted, and the remaining rows are displayed, as shown here:

```
delete from lawyer8
where mod(id,8)= 0;

select * from lawyer8;
```

This returns

```
2 rows deleted.

        ID NAME           OFFICE            BHRS        BGROSS
--------- -------------- --------------- ---------- ---------
         4 Clayton        Houston           1789        190045
        12 Chandler       Los Angeles       2987        423878
        20 Paul           Boston            2198        239855
```

However, the changes were not permanent. A `rollback;` statement can undo them.

The following statement returns all five rows:

```
select * from lawyer8;
```

Here are the five rows that are returned:

```
    ID NAME        OFFICE           BHRS       BGROSS
---------- ----------- ---------------- --------- ---------
     4 Clayton     Houston          1789       190045
     8 Bonin       New York         1678       346892
    12 Chandler    Los Angeles      2987       423878
    16 Chabot      New York         1680       310897
    20 Paul        Boston           2198       239855
```

A rollback after a commit, however, has no effect. Here is an example of this:

```
delete from lawyer8
where mod(id,8)= 0;

commit;

rollback;

select * from lawyer8;
```

This returns the following output:

```
2 rows deleted.
```

```
Commit complete.
```

```
Rollback complete.
```

```
    ID NAME        OFFICE           BHRS       BGROSS
---------- ----------- ---------------- --------- ---------
     4 Clayton     Houston          1789       190045
    12 Chandler    Los Angeles      2987       423878
    20 Paul        Boston           2198       239855
```

The change cannot be undone.

Explicit and Implicit `commit` Commands

The examples here use the explicit commit command. There are, however, situations where transactions are autocommitted or where a transaction cannot be rolled back. The following are a few examples of such situations:

- Truncating a table—This cannot be undone, by design the whole rollback mechanism is disabled.

- Software that autocommits by default—The OLE driver for Oracle Server, for example, autocommits all transactions. This means that the rollback mechanism remains in place, but the commit is issued immediately after the transaction.

- Software that autocommits on logout or exit—SQL*Plus and many other tools autocommit all transactions upon logoff or exit. It is, therefore, not possible to issue a rollback at a later time.

However, an abnormal abortion of an application likely will not create an autocommit but will create a rollback. Thus, just shutting off the client machine when things go wrong may have unintended consequences.

Listing 25.2 shows the effects of truncate and autocommit, which results from logging off or exiting the program.

Listing 25.2. The effects of truncating and autocommitting.

```
--        Filename: 25squ02.sql
--        Purpose: auto commit and rollback
--
select * from lawyer8;
```

This code returns

```
     ID NAME         OFFICE          BHRS      BGROSS
--------- ----------- --------------- --------- ---------
      4 Clayton      Houston         1789      190045
     12 Chandler     Los Angeles     2987      423878
     20 Paul         Boston          2198      239855
```

Thus, three rows are still there. Next, the table is truncated and rolled back, and the contents are retrieved:

```
truncate table lawyer8;

rollback;

select * from lawyer8;
```

Because the truncate cannot be reversed, no rows are retrieved, as shown in the following:

```
Table truncated.

Rollback complete.

no rows selected
```

Truncate cannot be undone. The table is now restocked, and the transaction is committed—all five rows are there:

```
insert into lawyer8
select
   id,
   Name,
   Office,
   bhrs,
   bgross
from lawyer1
where mod(id,4) = 0
;

commit;
```

25

CONTROL
TRANSACTIONS

In the next statement, two rows are deleted from the table. If the transaction were rolled back, all five rows would still be there. However, by reconnecting to the database, an autocommit occurs:

```
delete from lawyer8
where mod(id,8)= 0;

connect username/password      -- change this to yours

select * from lawyer8;
```

This code returns

```
2 rows deleted.

Connected.

        ID NAME            OFFICE            BHRS       BGROSS
--------- ----------- ---------------- --------- ----------
         4 Clayton     Houston           1789       190045
        12 Chandler    Los Angeles       2987       423878
        20 Paul        Boston            2198       239855
```

As the next statement shows, a rollback has no effect in this situation because the logoff that resulted from issuing a reconnect autocommitted the transaction:

```
rollback;

select * from lawyer8;
```

This code returns

```
Rollback complete.

        ID NAME            OFFICE            BHRS       BGROSS
--------- ----------- ---------------- --------- ----------
         4 Clayton     Houston           1789       190045
        12 Chandler    Los Angeles       2987       423878
        20 Paul        Boston            2198       239855
```

These are the same three rows. The example now starts over by cleaning out the table and loading the five rows:

```
truncate table lawyer8;

insert into lawyer8
select
   id,
   Name,
   Office,
   bhrs,
   bgross
from lawyer1
where mod(id,4) = 0
;
```

```
commit;

delete from lawyer8
where mod(id,8)= 0;
```

The two rows are again deleted. Now if the session is ended without committing, the SQL session is closed:

```
Exit;
```

Listing 25.3 shows the effect of exiting and restarting SQL—it autocommits the transaction. You now need to restart SQL*Plus.

Listing 25.3. Autocommitting the transaction.

```
--      Filename: 25squ03.sql
--      Purpose: auto commit and rollback 2nd part
--
select * from lawyer8;

rollback;

select * from lawyer8;
```

This code returns the following output:

```
     ID NAME         OFFICE           BHRS      BGROSS
--------- ----------- --------------- --------- ---------
      4 Clayton      Houston          1789      190045
     12 Chandler     Los Angeles      2987      423878
     20 Paul         Boston           2198      239855

Rollback complete.

     ID NAME         OFFICE           BHRS      BGROSS
--------- ----------- --------------- --------- ---------
      4 Clayton      Houston          1789      190045
     12 Chandler     Los Angeles      2987      423878
     20 Paul         Boston           2198      239855
```

Again, the exiting of the session caused the transaction to be autocommitted.

The Effect of `commit` in Different Sessions

`commit` and `rollback` affect the transactions in the current section only. However, in a multi-user or multi-session situation, a transaction does not affect other users or sessions until it is committed.

Thus, the effect of a transaction can be immediately seen in the session in which the transaction occurs, and be undone through a rollback. To other sessions, the transaction is not even known until committed.

25

CONTROL
TRANSACTIONS

REAL-WORLD EXPERIENCES

Control statements in a multi-session environment compare to a secret engagement with a surprise wedding. The secret engagement is known only to the couple affected, just as the transaction is known only to the session in which it occurs. As the surprise wedding is announced, it is a done deal for everybody else, just as the `commit` creates a done deal for other sessions.

Listings 25.4 and 25.5 run in two separate SQL sessions to the visibility of transactions across sessions. The SQL session that is running will be referred to as Listing 25.4; the new, additional session will be known as Listing 25.5. If examples are printed on the left column, they pertain to Listing 25.4. If they are in the right column, they pertain to Listing 25.5.

Listing 25.4. Using `commit` and `rollback` on two sessions.

```
--       Filename: 25squ04.sql
--        Purpose: commit and rollback
--                 effect on two sessions
--
truncate table lawyer8;

select * from lawyer8;
```

This code returns

```
Table truncated.

no rows selected
```

Because `truncate` is beyond the `commit`/`rollback` scheme, the same is visible in Listing 25.5.

Listing 25.5. Using `commit` and `rollback` on two sessions.

```
--       Filename: 25squ05.sql
--        Purpose: commit and rollback
--                 effect on two sessions
--
select * from lawyer8;
```

This returns

```
no rows selected
```

Until `commit`, an insert in one session can be seen only there, not in the other one. This is illustrated in Listing 25.6.

Listing 25.6. Using commit and rollback on two sessions.

```
--          Filename: 25squ06.sql
--          Purpose: commit and rollback
--                   effect on two sessions
--
insert into lawyer8
select
   id,
   Name,
   Office,
   bhrs,
   bgross
from lawyer1
where mod(id,4) = 0
;

col id     format 99
col name   format a8
col office format a11
col bhrs   format 9999
col bgross format 999,999
select * from lawyer8;
```

This code returns

```
5 rows created.

ID NAME        OFFICE        BHRS    BGROSS
--- ----------- -------------- ------- --------
  4 Clayton     Houston       1789    190,045
  8 Bonin       New York      1678    346,892
 12 Chandler    Los Angeles   2987    423,878
 16 Chabot      New York      1680    310,897
 20 Paul        Boston        2198    239,855
```

Nothing can be seen in the session B, however, because the transaction is not committed. (See Listing 25.7.)

Listing 25.7. Using commit and rollback on two sessions.

```
--          Filename: 25squ07.sql
--          Purpose: commit and rollback
--                   effect on two sessions
--
col id     format 99
col name   format a8
col office format a11
col bhrs   format 9999
col bgross format 999,999

select * from lawyer8;
```

This code returns the following:

```
no rows selected
```

Even if session B issues a commit, session A still can't see anything, as the following statement shows. To use the wedding analogy, I cannot commit somebody else to a surprise wedding:

```
commit;
```

```
select * from lawyer8;
```

This code returns

```
Commit complete.
```

```
SQL>
SQL> select * from lawyer
```

```
no rows selected
```

However, a commit in one session will make it visible in the other session (see the following code):

```
SQL> commit;
```

```
Commit complete.
```

```
SQL> select * from lawyer

ID  NAME         OFFICE           BHRS     BGROSS
--- ------------ ---------------- -------  --------
  4 Clayton      Houston          1789     190,045
  8 Bonin        New York         1678     346,892
 12 Chandler     Los Angeles      2987     423,878
 16 Chabot       New York         1680     310,897
 20 Paul         Boston           2198     239,855
```

Stepwise Rollback/Commit Schemes: savepoint

The all or nothing approach of rollback and commit works fine for most transactions. A stepwise approach, however, can be quite useful where more complex transactions are involved. An example where a more refined approach would help is a bill represented as one record in a bills table and one record for each item on the bill in an items table. A bill without items is useless, and should therefore not be included in the bills table either. Therefore, it is desirable to insert one record in a master table and several related records in a detail table in one connected set of transactions.

If the insert on the detail table does not work out, the master record should not remain either. In this situation, it would be inconvenient to do a full rollback if the detail fails because on the next try the master record would have to be inserted again. On the other hand, a commit after the master record transaction would not be so great either because if the details could not be made to work out, the master transaction would have to be undone through a delete.

`savepoint` provides the functionality to handle such a situation efficiently. Figure 25.1 illustrates the approach as a block diagram.

FIGURE 25.1.

The stepwise `commit` *using* `savepoint`.

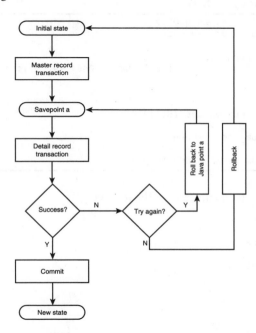

The process starts at some initial state, which is created through a fresh logon, a `commit`, or a `rollback` to a previously committed or freshly logged-on state. Next, the master record transaction, such as inserting a new bill record, is executed. An intermediate state is created with the command `savepoint a`. Now one or more detailed record transactions, such as inserts in the items table, are executed. If everything is fine, a final `commit`; commits both the master record and the client record transactions.

The situation may arise, however, where some client records are inserted only to have to be undone again. In our example, some items are available and inserted, but another item, without which the available items are useless to the customer, cannot be found. The detail record transactions are therefore a failure and need to be rolled back. However, the salesperson tries another combination to substitute. Therefore, the transaction is rolled back only to the `savepoint` a with the command `rollback to savepoint a`.

If a suitable combination of items can be found, these will be inserted in the items table, and the whole transaction will be committed, as above. If the substitution is not acceptable to the customer, however, a `rollback` reverts everything to the initial state.

Listing 25.8 includes the code for a gradual `commit`, using the `pers1` and the `inc1` table. It is desirable to add a sixth record to `pers1`, but only if matching detail records can be inserted into `inc1` as well.

Listing 25.8. Using `savepoint`.

```
--        Filename: 25squ08.sql
--         Purpose: savepoint
--
insert into pers1 values
   (6,'Franticek','Francis F.','302991048',44,'M');

savepoint a;

insert into inc1 values (6,'I',0);

select * from inc1  where id = 6;

select * from pers1 where id = 6;
```

Thus far, the statements return the following:

```
1 row created.

Savepoint created.

1 row created.

      ID T     AMOUNT
--------- - ----------
       6 I          0

      ID LNAME           FMNAME           SSN              AGE S
--------- --------------- --------------- ------------ --------- -
       6 Franticek       Francis F.       302991048       44 M
```

Both transactions are reflected in the output. Next, the second transaction is rolled back to savepoint a:

```
rollback to savepoint a;

select * from inc1  where id = 6;

select * from pers1 where id = 6;
```

Now only the master row is retrieved; the detail row has been undone through the rollback:

```
no rows selected

      ID LNAME           FMNAME           SSN              AGE S
--------- --------------- --------------- ------------ --------- -
       6 Franticek       Francis F.       302991048       44 M
```

Next, three rows are inserted, and everything is retrieved again:

```
insert into inc1 values (6,'I',1000);
insert into inc1 values (6,'S',48500);
insert into inc1 values (6,'R',64000);

select * from inc1  where id = 6;

select * from pers1 where id = 6;
```

This returns the following:

```
1 row created.

1 row created.

1 row created.

      ID T    AMOUNT
--------- - ---------
       6 I      1000
       6 S     48500
       6 R     64000

      ID LNAME          FMNAME          SSN            AGE S
--------- -------------- --------------- ------------- --------- -
       6 Franticek      Francis F.      302991048       44 M
```

Lo and behold, everything is there. A rollback, however, reverts everything to the initial state:

```
rollback;

select * from inc1  where id = 6;

select * from pers1 where id = 6;
```

This returns the following:

```
Rollback complete.

no rows selected

no rows selected
```

Because of the full rollback, everything is now gone. By means of the following statements, the values are re-created as above, including one rollback to savepoint a and the three inserts into the detail record:

```
insert into pers1 values
   (6,'Franticek','Francis F.','302991048',44,'M');

savepoint a;

insert into inc1 values (6,'I',0);

rollback to savepoint a;

insert into inc1 values (6,'I',1000);
insert into inc1 values (6,'S',48500);
insert into inc1 values (6,'R',64000);
```

```
commit;

rollback;

select * from inc1  where id = 6;

select * from pers1 where id = 6;
```

This returns the following:

```
1 row created.

Savepoint created.

1 row created.

Rollback complete.

1 row created.

1 row created.

1 row created.

Commit complete.

Rollback complete.
```

```
       ID T    AMOUNT
--------- - ---------
        6 I      1000
        6 S     48500
        6 R     64000


       ID LNAME           FMNAME           SSN              AGE S
--------- --------------- ---------------- ------------- --------- -
        6 Franticek       Francis F.       302991048           44 M
```

Thus, everything works as desired—the first detail transaction is rolled back, and the second three are still there. Once a commit is issued, a subsequent rollback has no effect—both the master and the detail transaction are committed. Because this is an easy example, the transactions can be undone through a delete and a subsequent commit, as shown here:

```
delete from inc1 where id = 6;

delete from pers1 where id = 6;

commit;
```

Summary

Whenever a row of data is manipulated, the blocks in its state before the change are copied to rollback segments. From there, the original state can be restored through a rollback command. In this case, the blocks in the rollback segments overwrite the updated blocks in the database.

The opposite of `rollback` is a `commit`, which causes the RDBMS to flush the `rollback` segments and thus make the updated stage the permanent one.

`rollback` and `commit` are usually done explicitly through commands. Some situations, however, cause an `autocommit` or an automatic rollback. Some software, such as the OLE driver for Oracle Server, autocommits by default. Most client software autocommits on logoff, disconnect, or exit, and rolls back the open transaction on abort. Truncating a table cannot be undone because the rollback mechanism is not used here.

Improving on the all or nothing approach of `rollback` and `commit`, `savepoint` provides for a stepwise functionality. `savepoint` is useful where more complex transactions are involved.

The process starts at some initial state created through a fresh logon, a `commit`, or a `rollback`. A master record transaction is executed, followed by a `savepoint` command. Now one or more detail record transactions are executed. If everything is fine, a final `commit`; commits both the master record and the client record transactions. However, it is also possible to roll back the transaction to the savepoint with only a `rollback to savepoint` *x*, or to the initial state with a simple `rollback`.

VIII

PART

Customizing the Appearance of Tables Through Views

Insertable Single-Table Views

IN THIS CHAPTER

CHAPTER 26

So far in this book, you have used the tables provided to select or manipulate information. Views, one of the most powerful features of SQL databases, add a new twist. Views allow you to customize the appearance of a table to the user:

- A view can limit the columns that a user can select from and insert into.
- A view can limit the rows that a user can select from and insert into.
- A view can include additional columns that are converted from other columns of a table.
- A view can include aggregations of rows in a table.

While it is possible to combine information from more than one table into a view, this chapter focuses on single-table views that can be inserted, deleted, and updated.

In most cases, views offer great convenience and an inkling of object-oriented features, although actions done through them could be completed just as well without but with more code or more repetitions. In a number of cases, views are hard or impossible to beat because they have

- Row-level security
- Intermediate steps for complex reports
- A complex layer between static objects, such as tables and report definitions

TIP

Just as the `select` statement is used more frequently than any other statement (by a factor of at least 10), you are likely to create and drop many more views than any other database object. Incidentally, a `select` statement is used to define a view. It is, therefore, definitely worth your while to be well versed in using `select` statements and views.

This chapter covers insertable views that must refer to one table only and must not contain a set operator, a group function, `group by`, or `distinct`. Chapter 27, "Multi-Table, Distinct, and Aggregate Views," covers complex views, which, as of now, cannot be inserted into or updated.

NOTE

While it is possible to insert, update, and delete rows through insertable single-table views, it is not possible to use `truncate`.

Basic Synonym Views

A synonym view is created through a `select` statement:

```
create view viewname as
select select_commalist from table
;
```

One issue that is a bit confusing is that a view that is mostly used for data manipulation is still defined with the `select` command, which is usually associated with data retrieval.

The creation or destruction of the view does not change in the table it references. Therefore, a view can be created with the `or replace` option. If a view with the same name exists already, it will be replaced with the new view. This is shown in the following example:

```
create or replace view viewname as
select select_commalist from table
;
```

This option saves an additional step for dropping the view first, and it cuts down on error messages. A view can also be dropped by issuing a `drop view viewname;` statement.

Table Synonym Views

The simplest view selects all rows and columns of a table, in essence having the same effect as a synonym, but being less efficient.

Listing 26.1 creates the view `pers8v` from `pers8`. It then inserts and deletes rows from the view and queries the table to show that every data manipulation affecting the view affects the table.

Listing 26.1. Creating a table synonym view.

```
--        Filename: 26squ01.sql
--         Purpose: table synonym view
--
truncate table lawyer8;

create or replace view law8v as
select * from lawyer8
;
```

This is the basic view creation command. The first statements return the following:

```
Table truncated.
View created.
```

Next, the table is loaded via the view, as shown here:

```
insert into law8v
select
   id,
   Name,
```

```
    Office,
    bhrs,
    bgross
from lawyer1
where mod(id,4) = 0
;

select * from lawyer8;

commit;
```

This returns the following output:

```
5 rows created.

        ID NAME             OFFICE            BHRS       BGROSS
--------- ---------------- ---------------- --------- ---------
        4 Clayton          Houston           1789       190045
        8 Bonin            New York          1678       346892
       12 Chandler         Los Angeles       2987       423878
       16 Chabot           New York          1680       310897
       20 Paul             Boston            2198       239855

Commit complete.
```

Note that `insert` was completed against the view, but the `select` was completed against the table. The next part of the example now does the same when deleting rows:

```
delete from law8v
where mod(id,8)= 0;

select * from lawyer8;

rollback;
```

This code returns the following:

```
2 rows deleted.

        ID NAME             OFFICE            BHRS       BGROSS
--------- ---------------- ---------------- --------- ---------
        4 Clayton          Houston           1789       190045
       12 Chandler         Los Angeles       2987       423878
       20 Paul             Boston            2198       239855

Rollback complete.
```

The last part demonstrates that `truncate` and views don't mix, but that a truncated table will not return rows through a view accessing it either:

```
truncate table law8v;

truncate view law8v;

truncate table lawyer8;

select * from law8v;
```

Insertable Single-Table Views

CHAPTER 26

505

26

INSERTABLE
SINGLE-TABLE
VIEWS

This returns the following code:

```
truncate table law8v
              *

ERROR at line 1:
ORA-01702: a view is not appropriate here

truncate view law8v
              *

ERROR at line 1:
ORA-03290: Invalid truncate command - missing CLUSTER or TABLE keyword

Table truncated.

no rows selected
```

TIP

Whenever you write an expression such as

```
create view viewname as select * from tablename;
```

you should seriously examine whether you should use a synonym instead. A synonym will give you the same benefit—a new name for the table—but it does not have the performance overhead that a view has. See Chapter 28, "Creating Tables," for more information.

Column Synonym Views

The second simplest view selects all rows and columns of a table, just like a table synonym view does. On top of that it takes column aliases in the table as the column names in the view.

A column synonym view provides an easy way to customize a generic table for user groups who insist on and/or need their own terminology.

Listing 26.2 demonstrates this approach, again using the lawyer1 table. Although deleting columns would work just as well here as it did with the table synonym, it is not demonstrated here. Both versions of creating column aliases are shown: one where the aliases are included with the select statement, and the other where they are specified between parentheses as a comma list after the view name.

Listing 26.2. Creating a column synonym view.

```
--        Filename: 26squ02.sql
--        Purpose: column synonym view
--
create or replace view law1v as
select
    id      id_no,
    Name    full_name,
```

continues

Listing 26.2. continued

```
    Office  Location,
    bhrs    hrs_work,
    bgross  gross_receipts
from lawyer1
;

create or replace view law1v
  (id_no,
   full_name,
   location,
   hrs_work,
   gross_receipts)
as
select
   id     ,
   Name   ,
   Office ,
   bhrs   ,
   bgross
from lawyer1
;

desc law1v
```

This code returns

```
View created.

Name                            Null?     Type
------------------------------- --------  ----
ID_NO                           NOT NULL  NUMBER(2)
FULL_NAME                                 VARCHAR2(15)
LOCATION                                  VARCHAR2(15)
HRS_WORK                                  NUMBER(4)
GROSS_RECEIPTS                            NUMBER(7)
```

Because the view columns take the name of the table column aliases, using the names of the table columns results in an error, which is shown in the following example:

```
select
   id,
   Name,
   Office,
   bhrs,
   bgross
from law1v
;
```

This code returns

```
   bgross
   *

ERROR at line 6:
ORA-00904: invalid column name
```

Insertable Single-Table Views

CHAPTER 26

507

26

INSERTABLE
SINGLE-TABLE
VIEWS

This is corrected by using the view column names:

```
select
    id_no,
    full_name,
    Location,
    hrs_work,
    gross_receipts
from law1v
where mod(id_no,3) = 2
;
```

This code returns

```
    ID_NO FULL_NAME       LOCATION        HRS_WORK  GROSS_RECEIPTS
--------- --------------- --------------- --------- ---------------
        2 Cheetham        New York        1398      280435
        5 Roach           Houston         2349      269844
        8 Bonin           New York        1678      346892
       11 Cardinal        Boston          2694      277952
       14 Earl            New York        2320      434801
       17 Miller          Los Angeles     3153      503582
       20 Paul            Boston          2198      239855

7 rows selected.
```

Masking Views

All the views in the previous section made a table and its columns accessible using different names for the table/view and the columns. Masking views go beyond that by restricting the columns or rows that can be accessed through the view.

Views That Mask Columns

While tables are intended to describe an entity with all attributes of interest for an application, not all of these attributes are intended to be seen by everyone. A frequent security feature is to allow some privileged users full access to the columns of a table and give all other users access to only some columns.

In the lawyer example, Easton decides that she could manipulate her underlings much easier if billing information were kept confidentially. Therefore, she has each lawyer sign a contract that should he ever divulge any such information, he will set himself on fire at the next company picnic. Then Easton sets out to ask her systems person to adapt the system so that nobody but she can see such information. The systems person does so through a view where the billing information columns are omitted. The view now acts as a mask to the table, covering up the billing information. This effect is illustrated in Listing 26.3. All you need to do is to select only those columns in a view that the user of the view is allowed to access.

Listing 26.3. Creating a column-masking view.

```
--          Filename: 26squ03.sql
--           Purpose: column masking view
--
truncate table lawyer8;

insert into lawyer8
select
    id,
    Name,
    Office,
    bhrs,
    bgross
from lawyer1
;

commit;
```

After re-creating the contents of `lawyer8`, the following example creates two views. The first includes only the ID, name, and office columns; the second also contains the billable hours information:

```
create or replace view law8v1 as
select
  id,
  name,
  office
from lawyer8
;

create or replace view law8v2 as
select
  id,
  name,
  office,
  bhrs
from lawyer8
;
```

This returns

```
View created.
View created.
```

Using `select` statements on both views return three and four columns, respectively. Figures 26.1 and 26.2 show the printouts:

```
select * from law8v1;

select * from law8v2;
```

Insertable Single-Table Views

CHAPTER 26

509

26

INSERTABLE
SINGLE-TABLE
VIEWS

FIGURE 26.1.

View law8v1 *masks two columns.*

```
 ID NAME        OFFICE          BHRS    BGROSS

  1 Dewey       Boston          2856    426800
  2 Cheetham    New York        1398    280435
  3 Howe        Los Angeles     3480    569338
  4 Clayton     Houston         1789    190045
  5 Roach       Houston         2349    269844
  6 Roll        Los Angeles     3203    498084
  7 Easton      Los Angeles     3800    654832
  8 Bonin       New York        1678    346892
  9 Frankie     New York        2134    469843
 10 Greene      Boston          2854    289435
 11 Cardinal    Boston          2694    277952
 12 Chandler    Los Angeles     2987    423878
 13 Martinez    Los Angeles     2659    403488
 14 Earl        New York        2320    434801
 15 Wright      Boston          2789    204133
 16 Chabot      New York        1680    310897
 17 Miller      Los Angeles     3153    503582
 18 Ming        Los Angeles     2492    359021
 19 Chatham     New York        1759    367944
 20 Paul        Boston          2198    239855

20 rows selected
```

FIGURE 26.2.

View law8v2 *masks one column.*

```
 ID NAME        OFFICE          BHRS    BGROSS

  1 Dewey       Boston          2856    426800
  2 Cheetham    New York        1398    280435
  3 Howe        Los Angeles     3480    569338
  4 Clayton     Houston         1789    190045
  5 Roach       Houston         2349    269844
  6 Roll        Los Angeles     3203    498084
  7 Easton      Los Angeles     3800    654832
  8 Bonin       New York        1678    346892
  9 Frankie     New York        2134    469843
 10 Greene      Boston          2854    289435
 11 Cardinal    Boston          2694    277952
 12 Chandler    Los Angeles     2987    423878
 13 Martinez    Los Angeles     2659    403488
 14 Earl        New York        2320    434801
 15 Wright      Boston          2789    204133
 16 Chabot      New York        1680    310897
 17 Miller      Los Angeles     3153    503582
 18 Ming        Los Angeles     2492    359021
 19 Chatham     New York        1759    367944
 20 Paul        Boston          2198    239855

20 rows selected
```

Inserts, Updates, and Deletes on Column-Masking Views

Selecting columns of a view has been straightforward—any column included in the view is available for selection. The same is true for updates; only the columns included in the view can be updated through the view as well.

`inserts` and `deletes`, on the other hand, function a little differently because an `insert` adds rows to the table whether or not there are values for the columns. The columns of the table that are not included in the view are either set to null or to the default values of these tables in the database definition.

Any `delete` removes rows from the table regardless of the values of the rows (except for the `where` clause, of course). Thus, even if a view can see only one column of a table, the entire row is deleted through the view. In both cases, then, the view can affect more on the table than can be seen through it.

> **CAUTION**
>
> This difference between being able to see only some columns but to be able to wipe out the entire row must be considered in multi-user systems. Typically, the rights of a limited user to delete rows through the view would be restricted by not granting the delete privileges (see Chapter 33, "Security Privileges").

Listing 26.4 demonstrates inserts, updates, and deletes through views and their impact on the table.

Listing 26.4. Deleting and inserting in a column-masking view.

```
--         Filename: 26squ04.sql
--          Purpose: delete from and insert into column-masking view
--
truncate table lawyer8;
insert into lawyer8
select
   id,
   Name,
   Office,
   bhrs,
   bgross
from lawyer1
;

commit;
```

The `lawyer8` table has just been restocked with 20 pristine rows. The next statement deletes 15 rows from the view:

```
delete from law8v1
where id > 5;
```

Insertable Single-Table Views

Chapter 26

511

26

INSERTABLE
SINGLE-TABLE
VIEWS

```
commit;

select * from lawyer8;
```

and therefore from the table, as the output shows:

```
15 rows deleted.

Commit complete.

       ID NAME          OFFICE          BHRS    BGROSS
--------- ------------- --------------- ------- ------
        1 Dewey         Boston          2856    426800
        2 Cheetham      New York        1398    280435
        3 Howe          Los Angeles     3480    569338
        4 Clayton       Houston         1789    190045
        5 Roach         Houston         2349    269844
```

An `insert` similarly affects the whole table, but the values of the columns not in the view are set to null (or the default, if defined), as the following example shows:

```
insert into law8v1 values
  (6,'Gabrieli','Boston');

commit;

select * from lawyer8;
```

Using this code, one row has been added and the last two columns are set to null, as shown here:

```
1 row created.

Commit complete.

       ID NAME          OFFICE          BHRS    BGROSS
--------- ------------- --------------- ------- ------
        1 Dewey         Boston          2856    426800
        2 Cheetham      New York        1398    280435
        3 Howe          Los Angeles     3480    569338
        4 Clayton       Houston         1789    190045
        5 Roach         Houston         2349    269844
        6 Gabrieli      Boston

6 rows selected.
```

All columns in the view can be updated through it, as the next part of the example shows:

```
update law8v1 set
     id      = id + 20,
     name    = 'unknown',
     office  = 'unknown';

commit;

select * from lawyer8;
```

This code returns

```
6 rows updated.

Commit complete.

        ID NAME        OFFICE      BHRS    BGROSS
--------- ---------- ---------- ------- -------
        21 unknown     unknown     2856    426800
        22 unknown     unknown     1398    280435
        23 unknown     unknown     3480    569338
        24 unknown     unknown     1789    190045
        25 unknown     unknown     2349    269844
        26 unknown     unknown

6 rows selected.
```

> **CAUTION**
>
> Inserting into a view that does not contain all not null columns of the table will result in an error because all columns not in the view will be set to null. The solution is to define the table columns with a default value, which will be used in this case, that eliminates the error.

Views That Mask Rows

Just as it has been possible to allow only some privileged users full access to the columns for a table and allow all other users access to only some columns, access to rows may be restricted through a view as well. To that end, the view needs to contain a condition in the where clause that limits the rows. Only those rows that fulfill the condition can be accessed through the view. It is possible to insert rows that fulfill these conditions through the view, yet afterwards it is not possible to retrieve them through it. This is a most interesting feature because now it is possible to have one table for many users, but to allow a user to see only those rows that pertain to him or her. However, the latter might be defined.

After Easton happily manipulated her underlings with abandon for a year, the bosses of the other offices (remember, being a boss does not imply being a manager), who together have a majority in the partnership, force the issue at the annual retreat, which this year happens to be a penguin-watching cruise to Antarctica. An agreement is forged into frozen air, under which the office bosses can see all the information pertaining to their offices. Upon returning, the systems person is asked to adapt the system accordingly.

The systems person now sets up a view for each boss, which shows only the rows pertaining to his office. The view acts as a mask to the table, covering up the rows of the other offices. This is illustrated in Figure 26.3 and Listing 26.5. Similar to the case of column-masking views, only those rows in a view, where the user of the view is allowed to access, must be specified through the where clause.

Insertable Single-Table Views

CHAPTER 26

513

26

INSERTABLE
SINGLE-TABLE
VIEWS

Listing 26.5. Creating a row-masking view.

```
--        Filename: 26squ05.sql
--         Purpose: row masking view
--
truncate table lawyer8;

insert into lawyer8
select
   id,
   Name,
   Office,
   bhrs,
   bgross
from lawyer1
;

commit;
```

After re-creating the contents of `lawyer8`, two views are created. The first includes only the rows pertaining to Boston; the second includes only those where the office is in New York. This is shown in the following example:

```
create or replace view law8v3 as
select *
from lawyer8
where office = 'Boston'
;

create or replace view law8v4 as
select *
from lawyer8
where office = 'New York'
;
```

This returns the following:

```
View created.
```

```
View created.
```

The `select` statements on both views return the Boston and New York rows respectively. Here are the `select` statements:

```
select * from law8v3;
```

```
select * from law8v4;
```

This code returns the Boston and New York rows, as shown here:

```
       ID NAME            OFFICE            BHRS      BGROSS
--------- --------------- ---------------  --------- ---------
        1 Dewey           Boston            2856      426800
       10 Greene          Boston            2854      289435
       11 Cardinal        Boston            2694      277952
       15 Wright          Boston            2789      204133
       20 Paul            Boston            2198      239855
```

```
        ID NAME         OFFICE       BHRS    BGROSS
--------- ------------ ------------ ------- ------
         2 Cheetham     New York      1398    280435
         8 Bonin        New York      1678    346892
         9 Frankie      New York      2134    469843
        14 Earl         New York      2320    434801
        16 Chabot       New York      1680    310897
        19 Chatham      New York      1759    367944

6 rows selected.
```

Figure 26.3 illustrates the masking of the first view.

Figure 26.3

View law8v3 *masks rows where the office is not in Boston.*

```
     ID  NAME         OFFICE            BHRS    BGROSS
      1  Dewey        Boston            2856    426800
     10  Greene       Boston            2854    289435
     11  Cardinal     Boston            2694    277952
     15  Wright       Boston            2789    204133
     20  Paul         Boston            2198    239855
```

5 rows remain visible through view

Inserts, Updates, and Deletes on Row-Masking Views

Any row included in the view is available for selection, updates, and deletes. Any row that is valid for the table can be inserted regardless of whether it is included in the view. Similarly, rows can be updated so that the altered row no longer fits the definition in the view. Thus, even if a view can see only certain rows of a table, other rows that can be seen through it can be created through the view.

Listing 26.6 demonstrates inserts, updates, and deletes through row-masking views, and their impact on the table and other row-masking views.

Listing 26.6. Deleting, inserting, and updating in a row-masking view.

```
--        Filename: 26squ06.sql
--         Purpose: delete from, insert into, and update of
--                  row masking view
--
truncate table lawyer8;

insert into lawyer8
select
   id,
   Name,
   Office,
   bhrs,
   bgross
from lawyer1
;

commit;
```

The `lawyer8` table has been restocked for yet another time. The next statement deletes all rows from the view where the `id` is greater than 5:

```
delete from law8v3
where id > 5;
commit;
select * from lawyer8
where id > 5
;
```

Only the rows that fit the where condition of the view are affected. All the rows that have an `id` greater than 5 and that do not pertain to Boston remain:

```
4 rows deleted.

Commit complete.

      ID NAME         OFFICE           BHRS     BGROSS
--------- ------------ ---------------  -------  ------
       6 Roll         Los Angeles       3203    498084
       7 Easton       Los Angeles       3800    654832
       8 Bonin        New York          1678    346892
       9 Frankie      New York          2134    469843
      12 Chandler     Los Angeles       2987    423878
      13 Martinez     Los Angeles       2659    403488
      14 Earl         New York          2320    434801
      16 Chabot       New York          1680    310897
      17 Miller       Los Angeles       3153    503582
      18 Ming         Los Angeles       2492    359021
      19 Chatham      New York          1759    367944

11 rows selected.
```

The next statements show how an insert into a view is possible, even if the resulting rows are not a part of the view. In the latter case, a view can create a row that subsequently it is not able to see:

```
insert into law8v3 values
  (6,'Gabrieli','Boston',2000,200000);

insert into law8v4 values
  (6,'Gabrieli','Boston',2000,200000);

commit;
```

The same row has been inserted twice, once through each view. Both rows can be seen in the Boston view but not in the New York view, even if one row has been created through the New York view:

```
1 row created.

1 row created.

Commit complete.
```

The two new rows can be seen in the view `law8v3` but not in `law8v4`. They can also be seen in the table proper:

```
select * from law8v3;

select * from law8v4;

select * from lawyer8
where id = 6
;
```

This returns

```
       ID NAME         OFFICE        BHRS     BGROSS
--------- -----------  -----------   -------  ------
        1 Dewey        Boston        2856     426800
        6 Gabrieli     Boston        2000     200000
        6 Gabrieli     Boston        2000     200000

       ID NAME         OFFICE        BHRS     BGROSS
--------- -----------  -----------   -------  ------
        2 Cheetham     New York      1398     280435
        8 Bonin        New York      1678     346892
        9 Frankie      New York      2134     469843
       14 Earl         New York      2320     434801
       16 Chabot       New York      1680     310897
       19 Chatham      New York      1759     367944

6 rows selected.

       ID NAME         OFFICE        BHRS     BGROSS
--------- -----------  -----------   -------  ------
        6 Roll         Los Angeles   3203     498084
        6 Gabrieli     Boston        2000     200000
        6 Gabrieli     Boston        2000     200000
```

Finally, both views are updated such that the resulting rows are no longer in the view, as shown here:

```
update law8v3 set
     office = 'unknown B';

update law8v4 set
     office = 'unknown N';

commit;

select * from lawyer8
where substr(office,1,6) = 'unknown'
;

select * from law8v3;

select * from law8v4;
```

This code returns the following:

```
    ID NAME         OFFICE         BHRS     BGROSS
--------- ------------ ------------ -------- ------
     1 Dewey        unknown B      2856     426800
     2 Cheetham     unknown N      1398     280435
     8 Bonin        unknown N      1678     346892
     9 Frankie      unknown N      2134     469843
     6 Gabrieli     unknown B      2000     200000
    14 Earl         unknown N      2320     434801
    16 Chabot       unknown N      1680     310897
    19 Chatham      unknown N      1759     367944
     6 Gabrieli     unknown B      2000     200000

9 rows selected.

no rows selected

no rows selected
```

Views with Special Options

A few special options are available when a view is created:

- ■ `force` covers the case where a view is to be defined before the base table to which it refers.
- ■ `with read only` prevents update, delete, and inserts.
- ■ `with check option` prevents the creation of rows through the view which cannot be selected through it.

Forcing Views Without Base Tables: `force`

A view provides another way to look at a base table. Without a special option, a view cannot be created if the base table does not exist. The `force` option, on the other hand, allows you to create the view, even if the base table does not exist.

Even if defined, manipulations are not possible without base table data. The advantage of using the `force` option is that a view can be defined before its base table. This might be convenient for development work.

The default and opposite of `force` is `noforce`.

Listing 26.7 creates a synonym view called `forcetest` against a nonexistent table, `nonlawyer`.

Listing 26.7. Using a view with the `force` option.

```
--      Filename: 26squ07.sql
--      Purpose: view with force option
--
create or replace view forcetest
as
select
   id    ,
   Name  ,
```

continues

Listing 26.7. continued

```
    Office ,
    bhrs   ,
    bgross
from nonlawyer
;
```

This returns an error because `nonlawyer` does not exist. This is shown here:

```
from nonlawyer
     *

ERROR at line 9:
ORA-00942: table or view does not exist
```

Using the `force` option circumvents the problem:

```
create or replace force view forcetest
as
select
    id     ,
    Name   ,
    Office ,
    bhrs   ,
    bgross
from nonlawyer
;
```

However, a warning is returned, which can be ignored:

```
Warning: View created with compilation errors.
```

As the next statement shows, operations on this view will return errors:

```
desc forcetest
select
    *
from forcetest
where mod(id,4) = 2
;
```

This returns the following:

```
ERROR:
ORA-04063: view "HANS.FORCETEST" has errors

from forcetest
     *

ERROR at line 3:
ORA-04063: view "HANS.FORCETEST" has errors
```

If now the table or, in this case, view on which the view is based is created, the operations will work:

```
create or replace view nonlawyer as
select * from lawyer1;
```

Insertable Single-Table Views

CHAPTER **26**

519

26

INSERTABLE
SINGLE-TABLE
VIEWS

```
select
    *
from forcetest
where mod(id,4) = 2
;
```

This returns the following:

```
View created.
```

```
        ID NAME         OFFICE       BHRS    BGROSS
--------- ------------ ------------ ------- ------
         2 Cheetham     New York     1398    280435
         6 Roll         Los Angeles  3203    498084
        10 Greene       Boston       2854    289435
        14 Earl         New York     2320    434801
        18 Ming         Los Angeles  2492    359021
```

Finally, the views are dropped, as shown here:

```
drop view nonlawyer;
```

```
drop view forcetest;
```

This code returns

```
View dropped.
```

```
View dropped.
```

Restricting Views to Query Only Use: `with read only`

The `with read only` option limits the use of a view to query only. Data manipulations are not possible.

Listing 26.8 creates a read-only view and demonstrates the error returned if a data manipulation is attempted.

Listing 26.8. Creating a read-only view.

```
--        Filename: 26squ08.sql
--         Purpose: with read only view
--
truncate table lawyer8;

insert into lawyer8
select
    id,
    Name,
    Office,
    bhrs,
    bgross
from lawyer1
;
```

continues

Listing 26.8. continued

```
commit;

create or replace view law8v5 as
select * from lawyer8
where id < 5
with read only
;

select * from law8v5;
```

The view is created and can be used for queries:

```
Table truncated.
```

```
20 rows created.
```

```
Commit complete.
```

```
View created.
```

```
        ID NAME        OFFICE       BHRS    BGROSS
--------- ----------- ----------- ------- ------
         1 Dewey       Boston       2856    426800
         2 Cheetham    New York     1398    280435
         3 Howe        Los Angeles  3480    569338
         4 Clayton     Houston      1789    190045
```

No data manipulation against this view is possible, although

```
delete from law8v5
where id = 1;

insert into law8v5 values
  (6,'Gabrieli','Boston',2000,200000);

update law8v5 set
      office = 'unknown';
```

returns

```
delete from law8v5
          *

ERROR at line 1:
ORA-01752: cannot delete from view without exactly one key-preserved table

insert into law8v5 values
*

ERROR at line 1:
ORA-01733: virtual column not allowed here

      office = 'unknown'
      *

ERROR at line 2:
ORA-01733: virtual column not allowed here
```

> **DEBUG ALERT**
>
> Note that the error messages are misleading, especially ORA 1733. The error has nothing to do with virtual columns but results from attempting to insert into or update a view that is defined with read only.

Allowing Only Those Data Manipulations That Fulfill the where Condition of the View: with check option

Defining a view with `with check option` enforces the `where` condition in its query for updates and inserts as well. It is no longer sufficient that the row is valid for the table, it must fit the definition in the view. Thus, through a `with check option` only those rows can be created that can be seen through it.

This option creates a database constraint that can be named with the `constraint` subcommand.

> **TIP**
>
> Whenever possible, give a meaningful name to constraints. Otherwise, the RDBMS will create its own with a weird combination of letters and names.

Listing 26.9 adapts `26squ06.sql` to demonstrate inserts, updates, and deletes on a `with check option` view.

Listing 26.9. Deleting, inserting, and updating in a `with check option` view.

```
--      Filename: 26squ09.sql

--      Purpose: delete from, insert into, and update on
--               with check option view
--
truncate table lawyer8;
insert into lawyer8
select
   id,
   Name,
   Office,
   bhrs,
   bgross
from lawyer1
;

commit;

create or replace view law8v3 as
select *
```

continues

Listing 26.9. continued

```
from lawyer8
where office = 'Boston'
with check option constraint CR_VW_BOSTON
;

create or replace view law8v4 as
select *
from lawyer8
where office = 'New York'
with check option constraint CR_VW_NEW_YORK
;
```

This code returns the following:

```
Table truncated.

20 rows created.

Commit complete.

View created.

View created.
```

Now the same row is submitted for `insert` into both rows:

```
insert into law8v3 values
  (6,'Gabrieli','Boston',2000,200000);

insert into law8v4 values
  (6,'Gabrieli','Boston',2000,200000);

commit;
```

This works on the first, but not on the second view:

```
1 row created.

insert into law8v4 values
             *

ERROR at line 1:
ORA-01402: view WITH CHECK OPTION where-clause violation

Commit complete.
```

Similarly, updates that violate the condition will be prevented, as shown in the next statement:

```
update law8v3 set
     office = 'unknown B';

update law8v4 set
     office = 'unknown N';

commit;
```

The preceding code returns errors, as shown here:

```
update law8v3 set
       *

ERROR at line 1:
ORA-01402: view WITH CHECK OPTION where-clause violation

update law8v4 set
       *

ERROR at line 1:
ORA-01402: view WITH CHECK OPTION where-clause violation

Commit complete.
```

Virtual Views Through Subqueries

Using views requires a two-stage process: First the view is defined through a create view with select statement, and then it is accessed. To obtain the benefit of views for transient purposes, it is possible to directly access the select statement without even creating a view. This approach also allows you to nest queries down several levels to accomplish tasks that are not possible with one single query. Chapter 22, "Trees and Hierarchical Subqueries," includes an example of that approach, which allows you to join a connect by query with another table, which is not possible by using just a single select statement.

Listing 26.10 demonstrates this approach. First, lawyer8 is repopulated.

Listing 26.10. Updating a virtual view through a subquery.

```
--         Filename: 26squ10.sql
--         Purpose: update virtual view through subquery
--
truncate table lawyer8;
insert into lawyer8
select
   id,
   Name,
   Office,
   bhrs,
   bgross
from lawyer1
;

commit;
```

The next two statements update the office column of a subquery that selects all Boston and New York rows of the lawyer8 table:

```
update (select *
        from lawyer8
        where office = 'Boston')
set office = 'unknown B';
```

```
update (select *
        from lawyer8
        where office = 'New York')
set office = 'unknown N';

commit;
```

They return the following:

```
5 rows updated.

6 rows updated.

Commit complete.
```

A select on lawyer8, again through an (unnecessary) subquery

```
select * from
    (select * from lawyer8);
```

shows that the updates have worked indeed and only affected the Boston and New York rows. This is illustrated here:

```
  ID NAME          OFFICE            BHRS    BGROSS
------- ------------- --------------- ------- ------
   1 Dewey         unknown B         2856    426800
   2 Cheetham      unknown N         1398    280435
   3 Howe          Los Angeles       3480    569338
   4 Clayton       Houston           1789    190045
   5 Roach         Houston           2349    269844
   6 Roll          Los Angeles       3203    498084
   7 Easton        Los Angeles       3800    654832
   8 Bonin         unknown N         1678    346892
   9 Frankie       unknown N         2134    469843
  10 Greene        unknown B         2854    289435
  11 Cardinal      unknown B         2694    277952
  12 Chandler      Los Angeles       2987    423878
  13 Martinez      Los Angeles       2659    403488
  14 Earl          unknown N         2320    434801
  15 Wright        unknown B         2789    204133
  16 Chabot        unknown N         1680    310897
  17 Miller        Los Angeles       3153    503582
  18 Ming          Los Angeles       2492    359021
  19 Chatham       unknown N         1759    367944
  20 Paul          unknown B         2198    239855

20 rows selected.
```

Comments on Views in the Data Dictionary: comment on

The comment on command allows you to create a comment—a string up to 2,000 characters long directly in the Data Dictionary. It is accessible through the all_tab_comments view.

Listing 26.11 creates a comment on the law8v3 view and retrieves it from all_tab_comments.

Listing 26.11. Creating comments on views.

```
--        Filename: 26squ11.sql
--        Purpose: view comments
--
--
comment on table law8v3 is
'This is the view law8v3';
commit;
```

Note that the statement reads `comment on table`. A view is treated as a table here. The statements return

```
Comment created.
Commit complete.
```

Now the comment is selected from the Data Dictionary, as shown here:

```
col table_type format a10 heading 'Type'
col comments    format a55

select
  table_type,
  comments
from all_tab_comments
where table_name = 'law8v3'
;

select
  table_type,
  comments
from all_tab_comments
where table_name = 'LAW8V3'
;

clear columns
```

The view name is stored in all uppercase; therefore, only the second query returns the comment, as shown here:

```
no rows selected

Type       COMMENTS
---------- -------------------------------------------------------
VIEW       This is the view law8v3
```

Similarly, comments on columns may be stored and retrieved from the `all_col_comments` view, as Listing 26.12 shows.

Listing 26.12. Viewing column comments.

```
--        Filename: 26squ12.sql
--        Purpose: view column comments
--
comment on column law8v3.id is
'Lawyer ID Number';
```

continues

Listing 26.12. continued

```
comment on column law8v3.name is
'Lawyer Last Name';

comment on column law8v3.office is
'Office Location';

commit;

col column_name format a10 heading 'Column'
col comments    format a55

select
  column_name,
  comments
from all_col_comments
where table_name = 'LAW8V3'
;

clear columns
```

Three column comments are created:

```
Comment created.

Comment created.

Comment created.

Commit complete.

Column     COMMENTS
---------- -------------------------------------------------------
ID         Lawyer ID Number
NAME       Lawyer Last Name
OFFICE     Office Location
BHRS
BGROSS
```

Note that the last two columns are included in the view but have only null comments.

Summary

One of the most powerful features of SQL databases allows you to customize the appearance of a base table to the user and limit either the rows, the columns that a user can select from and insert into, or both. Unless prevented through options, data can be manipulated through views just as the data can be manipulated on the base table proper.

A view is created using the statement `create or replace view viewname as select select_commalist from table`. The creation or destruction of the view does not affect the table it references.

In the easiest case, a view can serve to provide aliases for both the table name and the column names. On column-masking views, one or more columns of the table cannot be accessed through the views. A `delete` removes the entire row from the table, an `insert` puts nulls or column default values for the columns masked into the row.

On row-masking views, only a subset of rows can be accessed through the view. It is possible, however, to create a row through update or insert through a view, which subsequently cannot be seen via a `select` statment through the same view. The `with check option` prevents that, allowing updates and inserts only to values that can also be retrieved. The `with read only` option prevents all but selecting through the view. The `force` option allows you to create a view even if the base table or view underlying it does not yet exist. With the `comment` command, comments on views or columns can be inserted into the Data Dictionary from which they can be retrieved through the Data Dictionary views `all_tab_comments` and `all_col_comments`.

CHAPTER 27

Multi-Table, Distinct, and Aggregate Views

IN THIS CHAPTER

The views you saw in Chapter 26, "Insertable Single-Table Views," all had in common that they were defined against a single table or view, and that through these views, all data manipulations were possible. The only exception to the latter were the views defined with the `with read only` option, which explicitly prevents anything other than selecting through the view. These views thus serve as *interfaces* to tables on which they are based.

All views in this chapter allow `select` statements only because other data manipulations through them are either too complex or theoretically impossible and therefore cannot be implemented. These views, called *derived views*, keep a definition of a table operation or pre-aggregation in the Data Dictionary from which they can be conveniently accessed. Derived views thus are a powerful ingredient for any modular data-retrieval approach.

To review, every derived view is an interface, and every interface view is derived from a table or view. Interfacing is more important in the case of insertable single-table views, whereas maintaining derived definitions is the major purpose of derived views.

Limitations of the `select` Statement When Used to Create a View

Any legal `select` statement can be the basis of a derived view, with three limitations:

- There must not be an `order by` clause.
- There must not be a `for update` clause. `for update` locks the selected rows, which makes it impossible for other users to update or lock those rows until the transaction that includes this clause has finished.
- At most, 254 columns or column expressions may be included in the `select` comma list.

The first limitation results from the relational model, which specifies that the ordering of rows in a table is immaterial. There is also only one `order by` clause per retrieval statement allowed; it is applied after everything else is done.

Listing 27.1 shows the errors that are returned if a view is defined with `order by` or `for update`.

Listing 27.1. Using `order by` and `for update` to define a view.

```
--       Filename: 27squ01.sql
--        Purpose: ordered view and view for update
--                 returns errors
--
create or replace view law8o as
select * from lawyer1
order by name
;

create or replace view law8o as
select * from lawyer1
```

```
for update
;
```

Both statements return the same error:

```
order by name
*
ERROR at line 3:
ORA-00933: SQL command not properly ended


for update
*
ERROR at line 3:
ORA-00933: SQL command not properly ended
```

Aggregate Views

In a fully normalized database, no aggregate information on data that is available at a more detailed level is kept in tables. For example, in a master/detail relationship such as that between office2 and lawyer1, summary information pertaining to all the lawyers in an office is calculated anew every time it is needed. There is a good reason for that in a transactional database—the aggregate information has to be recalculated every time the detail information changes. That could be done through triggers, but then every transaction would cause one more processing step, something that has generally been avoided in the interest of performance. With cheaper and more powerful servers, however, that issue is probably less important now than it used to be—often it is possible to buy much more performance for a moderate sum. In a database that is used mostly for retrieval and analysis (such as a so-called data warehouse), pre-aggregated information is more often included either in an aggregate view or an aggregate table.

There are two purposes for pre-aggregation: convenience and speed of retrieval. Once the aggregate information is defined, all it takes to retrieve it is a select * on the view or table if maintained as a table. If the aggregate values are already available, a handful of records can return the same information for which a few million records might have to be aggregated otherwise. The entire multidimensional database industry is based on this fact.

An *aggregate view* is often the best compromise between convenience and currentness. Because it is only a definition, the information accessed through it is always up-to-date. There is no overhead at transaction time. To the user it looks like the aggregate table—except for speed, which in many cases does not matter. Batch processing done in a few minutes or even overnight is acceptable in many reporting situations.

Another huge advantage is that using an aggregate view allows for modularization of the reporting task. The view can be defined and debugged; at that point, all that goes into it can no longer foul up a report (assuming that everything has been done correctly). If a select based on the view does not work, only a fairly short statement has to be debugged and fixed. Divide and conquer.

Listing 27.2 defines an aggregate view that provides summary information by office, based on the `lawyer1` table.

Listing 27.2. Using an aggregate view.

```
--      Filename: 27squ02.sql
--      Purpose: aggregate view min and max functions
--
create or replace view offaggr
  (office,
   staff,
   tothrs,
   totrev)
as
select
   office,
   count(1),
   sum(bhrs),
   sum(bgross)
from lawyer1
group by office
;

desc offaggr
```

This code returns

```
View created.
```

Name	Null?	Type
OFFICE		VARCHAR2(15)
STAFF		NUMBER
TOTHRS		NUMBER
TOTREV		NUMBER

The view is now available and looks just like another table. This statement

```
select * from offaggr;
```

returns this:

OFFICE	STAFF	TOTHRS	TOTREV
Boston	5	13391	1438175
Houston	2	4138	459889
Los Angeles	7	21774	3412223
New York	6	10969	2210812

Distinct Views

Similar to aggregate views, a *distinct view* can be used to display the distinct values of one or more columns. Listing 27.3 illustrates this, using the location column only.

Listing 27.3. Using the distinct view.

```
--        Filename: 27squ03.sql
--         Purpose: distinct view
--
create or replace view offdist
as
select
   distinct office
from lawyer1
;

desc offdist

select * from offdist;
```

It returns the following:

```
View created.

Name                                Null?    Type
----------------------------------- -------- ----
OFFICE                                       VARCHAR2(15)


OFFICE
--------------
Boston
Houston
Los Angeles
New York
```

Multi-Table Views

A frequent use of views is to join tables to provide a larger, virtual table for reporting. This is an interesting approach that yields a number of advantages:

■ Because any database output that gets included in a report is a flat row of a table or virtual table, the intricacies of joining the tables are of little interest to the report design process proper. Oracle Reports, for example, distinguishes between the data model, which is based on a SQL statement and conversions, and the layout, which presents some or all of that information in specific format on the final report. Much of the data model can be created more conveniently through views.

■ Pre-joined lookup tables and base tables provide the best of both worlds for transactions that can use tight code schemes as well as reporting that gets several sets of meaningful labels right away, without complex join scripts in each report.

■ Ad hoc work can be made much safer through a modularized approach. If tested and reliable pre-joined views are available, it is much easier to complete a rather complex report in minimum time.

■ Pre-joined and tested views reduce errors related to incomplete or malformed join conditions—errors that subtly or obviously undermine the accuracy of reports, and thus the credibility and subsequently professional well-being of the people creating them.

The following examples pre-join the view of 27squ02.sql with the office2 table and the lawyer1 table, this time to get the name of the boss. Two approaches are used: The first is a one-step process and includes office2 in the original query, as shown in Listing 27.4; the second one joins the offaggr view with the table.

The result is the same. The first approach is likely to be slightly more efficient; the second approach is more modular, which has its advantages where readability and flexibility are concerned.

Listing 27.4. Using an aggregate view including a table join.

```
--      Filename: 27squ04.sql
--       Purpose: aggregate view including table join
--
create or replace view offagj
  (office,
   bossid,
   bossname,
   staff,
   tothrs,
   totrev)
as
select
   o.office,
   o.bossid,
   b.name,
   count(1),
   sum(l.bhrs),
   sum(l.bgross)
from lawyer1 l,
     office2 o,
     lawyer1 b
where
   l.office = o.office and
   o.bossid = b.id
group by o.office,
         o.bossid,
         b.name
;

desc offagj

select * from offagj;
```

The statements return

```
View created.
```

```
Name                             Null?      Type
------------------------------   --------   ----
OFFICE                                      VARCHAR2(15)
BOSSID                                      NUMBER(2)
BOSSNAME                                    VARCHAR2(15)
STAFF                                       NUMBER
TOTHRS                                      NUMBER
TOTREV                                      NUMBER
```

OFFICE	BOSSID	BOSSNAME	STAFF	TOTHRS	TOTREV
Boston	1	Dewey	5	13391	1438175
Houston	17	Miller	2	4138	459889
Los Angeles	7	Easton	7	21774	3412223
New York	9	Frankie	6	10969	2210812

Using the `offagj` view to join to `office2` and `lawyer1` eliminates the need for the `group by` and aggregate functions in the scripts because that part is already taken care of in the previous step, when the `offaggr` view was created in `27squ02.sql`. Listing 27.5 illustrates the aggregate view being joined to tables.

Listing 27.5. Using an aggregate view joined to tables.

```
--       Filename: 27squ05.sql
--       Purpose: aggregate view joined to tables
--
create or replace view offagj
  (office,
   bossid,
   bossname,
   staff,
   tothrs,
   totrev)
as
select
   o.office,
   o.bossid,
   b.name,
   a.staff,
   a.tothrs,
   a.totrev
from offaggr a,
     office2 o,
     lawyer1 b
where
   a.office = o.office and
   o.bossid = b.id
;

desc offagj

select * from offagj;
```

The output is identical to the previous example.

Hierarchical Views

A less frequent but powerful use of views is to get around the limitation of hierarchical `select` statements, which must include only one table in the `from` comma list. If the hierarchical query is encapsulated in the view, on the other hand, the columns in that view may be joined with columns of other tables and views.

> **CAUTION**
>
> Never use an `order` by if you depend on hierarchical ordering through a `connect` by to show the hierarchical relationships between records. The former is likely to destroy the effect of the latter, resulting in a report that is simply wrong.

The other advantages of hierarchical views are similar to those of views that join tables—convenience, modularity, safety, and tight tables combined with more meaningful labels through the view for reporting.

The following examples encapsulate a view by a subquery into a defined view. The first statement creates a view `org`, which is based on the hierarchical query. (See Listing 27.6.) The second statement creates another view, `orgoff`, which joins the office table to `org`, in order to include the state and division columns.

> **NOTE**
>
> If you get the error `"set pagesize 40" fails on execution; improper option,` try setting `pages 40` instead.

Listing 27.6. Creating a view based on a hierarchical query.

```
--        Filename: 27squ06.sql
--        Purpose: create hierarchical view
--                 display stylized organization chart
--
set pagesize 40
col office      format a11
col fake_chart format a35
col lv          format 99 heading 'LV'
col bs          format 99
col id          format 99

create or replace view org as
select
   office,
   lpad(' ',(level-1)*4) || name FAKE_CHART,
   level lv,
```

```
   id,
   boss bs
from
   lawyer2
connect by prior id = boss
start with boss is NULL
;

desc org

create or replace view orgoff as
select
   substr(c.fake_chart,1,35) fake_chart_short,
   c.lv,
   c.id,
   c.bs,
   c.office,
   o.division,
   o.state
from org c, office4 o
where c.office = o.office and
      o.year = 1
;

desc orgoff
```

This code returns

```
View created.
```

Name	Null?	Type
OFFICE		VARCHAR2(15)
FAKE_CHART		VARCHAR2(2000)
LV		NUMBER
ID	NOT NULL	NUMBER(2)
BS		NUMBER(2)

```
View created.
```

Name	Null?	Type
FAKE_CHART_SHORT		VARCHAR2(35)
LV		NUMBER
ID	NOT NULL	NUMBER(2)
BS		NUMBER(2)
OFFICE		VARCHAR2(15)
DIVISION		VARCHAR2(4)
STATE		CHAR(2)

Note that the SQL*Plus format specifications have no impact on the view—in the org view, FAKE_CHART is defined as up to 2,000 characters long. In orgoff, however, it can be no longer than 35 characters because the substring function, which has an impact on the SQL level, shortened it there, creating a new column, `fake_chart_short`. Selecting all columns from `orgoff` creates the full report, properly formatted and all:

```
select * from orgoff;

clear columns
clear breaks
set pagesize 24

drop view org;
```

This script returns

```
FAKE_CHART_SHORT                      LV  ID  BS OFFICE       DIVI ST
------------------------------------- --- --- --- ----------- ---- --
        Paul                           2  20   7 Boston       East MA
            Dewey                      3   1  20 Boston       East MA
                Greene                 4  10   1 Boston       East MA
                Cardinal               4  11   1 Boston       East MA
                    Wright             5  15  10 Boston       East MA
        Roach                          2   5   7 Houston      East TX
            Clayton                    3   4   5 Houston      East TX
Easton                                 1   7     Los Angeles West CA
    Howe                               2   3   7 Los Angeles West CA
    Miller                             2  17   7 Los Angeles West CA
        Roll                           3   6   3 Los Angeles West CA
            Chandler                   4  12   6 Los Angeles West CA
        Ming                           3  18  17 Los Angeles West CA
            Martinez                   4  13  18 Los Angeles West CA
    Frankie                            2   9   7 New York     East NY
        Bonin                          3   8   9 New York     East NY
            Cheetham                   4   2   8 New York     East NY
        Earl                           3  14   9 New York     East NY
            Chabot                     4  16  14 New York     East NY
            Chatham                    4  19  14 New York     East NY

20 rows selected.


View dropped.
```

This is an example of a chain of intermediate views.

If the hierarchical ordering within a sort column is to be preserved, then, within limitations (see Chapters 22 and 29), `rownum` can be used as an additional sort column. For that purpose, a `rownum` column has to be included in all views, as Listing 27.7 shows.

Listing 27.7. Creating a hierarchical view using `rownum`.

```
--       Filename: 27squ07.sql
--        Purpose: create hierarchical view
--                 display stylized organization chart
--                 order by office, use rownum to preserve order
--
set pagesize 40
col office     format a11
col fake_chart format a35
```

```
col lv          format 99 heading 'LV'
col bs          format 99
col id          format 99
col rn          format 99

create or replace view org as
select
   office,
   lpad(' ',(level-1)*4) || name FAKE_CHART,
   level lv,
   id,
   boss bs,
   rownum rn
from
   lawyer2
connect by prior id = boss
start with boss is NULL
;

desc org

create or replace view orgoff as
select
   substr(c.fake_chart,1,35) fake_chart_short,
   c.lv,
   c.rn,
   c.id,
   c.bs,
   c.office,
   o.division,
   o.state
from org c, office4 o
where c.office = o.office and
      o.year = 1
;

desc orgoff

break on office skip 1

select * from orgoff
order by office, rn;

clear columns
clear breaks
set pagesize 24

drop view org;
```

This script returns the rows ordered by office, and then within the office in proper hierarchical order:

```
OFFICE      FAKE_CHART                          LV  ID  BS
----------- ----------------------------------- --- --- ---
Boston          Paul                             2  20   7
                    Dewey                        3   1  20
                        Greene                   4  10   1
```

```
                Wright              5   15   10
                Cardinal            4   11    1

Houston      Roach                  2    5    7
                Clayton             3    4    5

Los Angeles Easton                  1    7
                Howe                2    3    7
                   Roll             3    6    3
                      Chandler      4   12    6
                Miller              2   17    7
                   Ming             3   18   17
                      Martinez      4   13   18

New York     Frankie                2    9    7
                Bonin               3    8    9
                   Cheetham         4    2    8
                Earl                3   14    9
                   Chabot           4   16   14
                   Chatham          4   19   14


20 rows selected.
```

Selecting the First *n* Rows as Ordered, Not as Retrieved

In Chapter 9, "Conditional Operands," the limitations of the rownum pseudocolumn have been demonstrated—it is unaffected by ordering. Therefore, rownum cannot be used for convenient purposes such as displaying the first *n* rows as sorted by an order by subclause. Through a view and the abuse of group functions, however, this limitation can be somewhat overcome, and a limited number of the rows can be retrieved by order. This approach takes advantage of the fact that a group by also orders the column by which it is grouped. This ordering is necessary because grouping groups by identical values of the group by columns is most easily determined by ordering. This approach is demonstrated in Listing 27.8.

Listing 27.8. Selecting rows as ordered.

```
--        Filename: 27squ08.sql
--        Purpose: select first 7 rows as ordered
--                 overcome limitation of rownum
--
create or replace view ordlaw as
select
   id,
   rownum rowsub,
   name,
   office
from lawyer1
group by name, id, office, rownum;

select id, rownum, rowsub, name
```

```
from ordlaw
where rownum < 8
;
```

This code returns

```
View created.

       ID    ROWNUM    ROWSUB NAME
--------- --------- --------- ---------------
        8         1         8 Bonin
       11         2        11 Cardinal
       16         3        16 Chabot
       12         4        12 Chandler
       19         5        19 Chatham
        2         6         2 Cheetham
        4         7         4 Clayton

7 rows selected.
```

Note that the row number of the full extract that was necessary for ordering the rows is preserved in the view column `rowsub`. `rownum` now limits the display of ordered rows to seven.

> **TIP**
>
> A `group by` is also a way to get around the limitation that `order by` must not be in a view definition. It should be used cautiously, though, because it is likely to have an adverse effect on performance when large tables are involved.

Views Based on (Pseudo-) Set Operators

Views can be based on queries that are combined through set or pseudoset operators (see Chapter 18, "Combining Output from Similar Tables Through Set and Pseudoset Operators"). Depending on the (pseudo-) set operator used, these views have similarities to distinct views (`union`, `minus`, and `intersect`) or to views that join tables (`union all`) except that the tables in this case are joined end to end and not side by side.

Listing 27.9 creates and displays the contents of a view based on an intersect.

Listing 27.9. Creating and displaying a view based on an intersect.

```
--       Filename: 27squ09.sql
--       Purpose: view with intersect joining pers1 and pers9
--
col id     format 99
col lname  format a11
col fmname format a12
col age    format 99
```

continues

27

OTHER VIEWS

Listing 27.9. continued

```
create view pers1i9
as
select
    id,
    lname,
    fmname,
    age,
    sex
from pers1
intersect
select
    id,
    lname,
    fmname,
    age,
    sex
from pers9
;

select
*
from pers1i9
;

clear columns
```

This script returns the following:

```
View created.


ID LNAME        FMNAME        AGE S
--- ----------- ------------- --- -
  1 Jones       David N.       34 M
  2 Martinelli  A. Emery       92 M
```

Set operators do not appear to be used extensively, yet they are useful. A good use would be a view that is based on a union all that combines a select on a current and a history table for reporting. An example would be two transaction tables—one including only the transactions of the previous month, and the other being a transaction history to the beginnings of time. All current transactions could be dealt with efficiently in a small table defined to be stored on a fast disk. If a multi-month or multi-year report is desired, on the other hand, it could be written against the union all view of these tables, thus creating a virtual table of both current and historical data. This method provides a way to partition large tables into more manageable chunks.

Virtual Views (Views by Subquery)

Virtual views (views by subquery) may be used in place of complex views as well. All caveats of that approach apply here as well, but virtual views do make sense in a reporting situation where views would have to be created and destroyed all the time. They also are handy on a multi-user system if you need a view but do not have the necessary database privileges to create one. Listing 27.10 uses a view by subquery.

Listing 27.10. Using a virtual view.

```
--        Filename: 27squ10.sql
--        Purpose: select first 7 rows as ordered
--                 use virtual view
--
select id, rownum, rowsub, name from
(select
   id,
   rownum rowsub,
   name,
   office
from lawyer1
group by name, id, office, rownum)
where rownum < 8
;
```

It returns the following:

```
     ID    ROWNUM    ROWSUB NAME
--------- --------- --------- --------------
      8        1         8 Bonin
     11        2        11 Cardinal
     16        3        16 Chabot
     12        4        12 Chandler
     19        5        19 Chatham
      2        6         2 Cheetham
      4        7         4 Clayton

7 rows selected.
```

Summary

Views based on select statements that include joins, (pseudo-) set operators, aggregations, or distinct rows are read only but are, nevertheless, powerful ingredients for any modular data-retrieval approach. Views can be defined and debugged individually.

Aggregate and distinct views maintain a definition of an aggregate select statement in the Data Dictionary. Once defined, aggregate information can be retrieved through the view by means of a simple select statement.

Views that join tables provide a convenient, larger, virtual table for reporting. Much of the complexities of reports can be hidden in a view, and meaningful value labels can be pre-attached. Ad hoc work can be made much safer and faster if tested and reliable pre-joined views are available. Pre-joined and tested views reduce errors.

A less frequent but powerful use of views is to get around the limitation of hierarchical `select` statements, which must include only one table in the `from` comma list. If the hierarchical query is encapsulated in the view, the columns in the view can be joined with columns of other tables and views.

Virtual views (views by subquery) may be used in place of complex views as well.

IX

PART

IN THIS PART

Tables

Creating Tables

IN THIS CHAPTER

CHAPTER 28

Whereas views are derived from one or more tables or from other views, tables are completely autonomous: They exist in the database as an independent means of storing information in an organized fashion—columns that define how data is structured, and one or more rows of data consistent with that structure. Tables and views have in common that they have a name by which they are defined, altered, deleted, and accessed.

A number of statements are used to manipulate tables:

- `create table` defines tables and columns
- `alter table` changes tables and columns
- `drop table` removes tables—definitions and contents alike
- `rename` renames tables

`create table` and `alter table` are also used to affect constraints, keys (which are covered in Chapter 29, "Keys, Indexes, Constraints, and Table/Column Comments"), and storage parameters that are an Oracle extension.

Creating New or Original Tables

You can create the simplest table with the statement `create table` *table_name* (*column_name1 datatype*);. The table `fakedual` was created with this simple statement. A table has to have at least one column.

A number of `create table` scripts have been provided for the sample tables of the previous chapters. To illustrate the behavior of the `create table`, a few scripts, such as `crper8.sql`, are reviewed here. See Listing 28.1.

Listing 28.1. Creating a table.

```
--      Filename: 28squ01.sql same as beginning of crper8.sql
--      Purpose: Creates and loads table pers8
--               which includes some income and wealth data.
--               includes negative, zero, and NULL values
--
create table pers8 (
   id       number(2) not null,
   LName    varchar2(15),
   FMName   varchar2(15),
   SSN      char(9),
   Age      number(3),
   Sex      char(1),
   interest number(8),
   salary   number(8),
   profit   number(8),
   royalty  number(8),
   wealth   number(9))
;
```

Because this table has been created already in the previous chapter, an error returns if the script is run:

```
create table pers8 (
                  *
ERROR at line 1:
ORA-00955: name is already used by an existing object
```

What the error shows is that the table name must be unique—technically unique—in a schema, which corresponds to database users. Therefore the statement `desc schema.pers8` will return as `desc pers8` assuming that the current user and the schema are identical. (See the section "Working with Database Schemas/Users: `create user`," later in this chapter.)

What the preceding explanation shows nicely, though, is the `column` comma list, which must have at least one column name unique within the table and a data definition per column. The `not null` after the id definition indicates that this column will not accept a null value. All non-numerical or categorical columns should be set to `not null`. You will learn more about this constraint in Chapter 29. Datatypes are covered in Chapters 2, 11, 12, and 13.

TIP

Two typical mistakes are frequently made when defining a fixed-point number:

- Using a period instead of commas between p and s. This results in an error.

- Not understanding "8,3" as eight digits before the point plus three decimal digits (rather than eight digits, of which three are decimal). The result is a number that has three digits too few.

Default Values: `default`

A default value for a column can be specified immediately after the datatype definition. If an `insert` statement does not include the value for a column, the default value is inserted, as is shown in Listing 28.2.

TIP

Default values are a great alternative to null values, especially where categorical columns are concerned. The standard non-numerical column should be specified as `not null` with a default value.

Listing 28.2. Using default values.

```
--         Filename: 28squ02.sql
--          Purpose: table with default values
--
create table t2802
  (id        number(2),
   name      varchar2(15) default 'Missing',
   cruser    varchar2(30) default user,
   crdate    date         default sysdate,
   age       number(3)    default 99,
   salary    number(8)    default -99)
;
```

This table sets a default value for each column except id. Each is specified as a text string, number, or pseudofunction. Note that currval, nextval, level, and rownum must not be used. Subsequently five rows are inserted, where only the id column is specified:

```
insert into t2802 (id) values (1);
insert into t2802 (id) values (2);
insert into t2802 (id) values (3);
insert into t2802 (id) values (4);
insert into t2802 (id) values (5);

commit;

col cruser format a8;

select * from t2802;

clear columns;
```

This script returns the following:

```
Table created.

1 row created.

1 row created.

1 row created.

1 row created.

1 row created.

Commit complete.


        ID NAME            CRUSER   CRDATE         AGE     SALARY
---------- --------------- -------- ----------- -------- --------
         1 Missing         HANS     05-JUN-1997       99      -99
         2 Missing         HANS     05-JUN-1997       99      -99
         3 Missing         HANS     05-JUN-1997       99      -99
         4 Missing         HANS     05-JUN-1997       99      -99
         5 Missing         HANS     05-JUN-1997       99      -99
```

As the example shows, the default values are inserted into the columns whose values weren't specified in the `insert` statements.

Affecting the Way the Table Is Stored: Space Directives and `storage`

Oracle's functionality described in this chapter exceeds that of standard SQL.

ORACLE vs SQL

A number of storage options can be specified in the `create table` statement. The fact of their availability violates the general notion that SQL should isolate the user from the nitty-gritty of data management. On the other hand, though, databases are scaleable from PC to supercomputer, and tables can range from one-row/one-column to unimaginably huge. Therefore, a one-size-fits-all storage specification is not sufficient, and a number of parameters can be specified. Space directives specify space usage within blocks, and the `storage` keyword specifies the storage characteristics of a table, which is especially important for large tables.

Space Directives

A block of data is the smallest operating-system unit of memory and storage with which a database works. If the blocksize parameter is set to `4K`, for example, whenever the RDBMS accesses one or more rows in a table, it moves the block that contains the row(s) into memory (if they aren't there already) and works with them there.

28

CREATING TABLES

The way that space within a block is used can have major performance ramifications. You use space directives to specify this.

Let's begin with the easiest one. `pctfree` sets the percentage in the block reserved for future row updates. It is necessary because rows are not necessarily all the same length—mainly because of the `varchar2` and `long` datatypes, which are variable by design. If a block is almost full, and a row is updated such that the added data exceeds the space still available in the block, the part that does not fit is put into another block, which results in a so-called chained row. In a separate step, the whole row can be migrated to a different block where it fits in entirely. In either case, the result is undesirable overhead.

If, on the other hand, `pctfree` is set to a sufficiently large percentage, that issue can be mostly eliminated. Oracle sets 10% as a default. `pctfree` should be set to a larger number if extensive updating that would extend the row length is expected. The equation 100–`pctfree` sets an upper threshold. Rows are not inserted if that insert would push the space usage beyond that threshold. The trade-off for setting `pctfree` is that you gain space usage while accepting the performance hit of the excessive chaining of rows.

The `pctused` directive specifies the minimum space usage the server maintains in a block. If usage falls below that percentage, the block becomes a candidate for row insertion. In reality, that means that the block is listed in the so-called *freelist*—a list of blocks that can be inserted into. The default for `pctused` is `40`. The sum of `pctfree` and `pctused` must not exceed 100.

The reason of having a value for `pctused` at all is that every time a block is listed or unlisted at the freelist, some processing cost results. If the usage of a block falls below the `pctused` setting, the block is listed in the freelist. It is then possible to keep inserting rows until an insert would reduce the `pctfree` so that it is under its set threshold. At this point the block is unlisted. Only if sufficient rows are deleted to make the usage less than `pctfree` will the block be listed again.

If the result of 100–*pctfree*–*pctused* is fairly large, a block does not get listed or unlisted often, which reduced overhead. However, on average, there will be more unused space in the block than in a situation where this number is close to zero.

How these values should be set is greatly elaborated in tuning guides. First, the values are used to optimize space usage while minimizing migrations. Suffice it to say that a read-only table that is never updated can set `pctfree` to `0` and `pctused` to `100`. In reality, it is better to leave a small percent in `pctfree` because in the end there might be a service upgrade on such a table after all.

REAL-WORLD EXPERIENCES

My father's house used to have its own well and pump. Somewhere in the basement was a pressure tank with a mercury switch that was operated by the level of the water in the tank. By means of a few spring-loaded screws, the switch could be adjusted to a high-water mark and a low-water mark setting.

If the water level fell below the low-water mark, the switch would engage, with the mercury flowing down through the vial over a couple electrical contacts, one of which was connected to the power, and the other to the pump. Then the pump came on and kept filling the tank until the high-water mark was reached. At this point, the vial was tilted sufficiently for the mercury to flow back, which interrupted the flow of electricity to the pump. In this case the levels had to be set so that the pump would not come on too often, that at the highest level there was still enough space for the compressed air in the tank, and that at the low-water mark there was still water flowing through the system.

`pctfree` can be thought of as the high-water mark at which the pump gets shut off, at which point no further rows can be pumped into the block. `pctused` is the low-water mark at which point the pump gets switched on, pumping (inserting) rows into the block. Just as the pump should not come on too often, the listing/unlisting process on the freelist should not happen too often either. Just as some space for air was necessary, some space for additional bytes from future updates should be kept. Just as there was always some water left in the tank, the utilization of a block should never fall under a certain level, which is determined by `pctused`.

The Oracle 7, Server Administrator's Guide, Release 7.3 recommends using a `pctfree` value of `20` and a `pctused` value of `40` in a situation when there are frequent upgrades that increase the size of rows. If there is little updating activity that results in longer rows, `pctfree` should be reduced to `5`, combined with a `pctused` of `60` for tables with frequent inserts, deletes, and updates or a `pctused` of `90` for very large tables with mostly read-only transactions.

The result of 100–*pctfree–pctused* should be larger than the percentage of an average row to the block size minus overhead. If the block size is 4,096 bytes, overhead is 200 bytes, and the average row is 390, the average row is 10% of the usable portion of a block. The result of 100–pctfree–pctused should then be at least 10.

Listing 28.3 includes the pctfree and pctused parameters.

Listing 28.3. Using pctfree and pctused parameters.

```
--        Filename: 28squ03.sql
--         Purpose: specify pctfree and pctused
--
create table t2803
  (id       number(2))
pctfree 20
pctused 50
;
```

As the example shows, these parameters are simply included after the parenthesis that closes the column comma list. The output is uneventful, and is therefore not included here.

Storage Characteristics: storage

As I explained in the beginning of this section, database tables can range in size from very small, certainly less than a block, to so huge that few people can imagine their size. In many situations it is, therefore, advantageous to tune the storage parameters. Otherwise, the table might run out of space as rows get inserted, space might be wasted without need, or performance might suffer.

Most of the storage clause is centered around *extents*. These are chunks of storage that are set aside for a table. When the table is created, an initial extent is set aside for it. As rows get inserted and exceed the first extent, another extent is used. Five parameters, all of them integers, control the size and number of extents used for a table:

- initial—The size of the initial extent used for the table. K or M can be used to indicate KB or MB, respectively. For purposes of reality checks, the extents should be multiples of the block size of the database. If the extent values are not such multiples, the value is automatically increased to the next block size increment.
- next—The size of the second extent.
- minextents—The minimum number of extents used, usually set to 1.
- maxextents—The maximum number of extents allowed.
- pctincrease—The percentage by which the size of the third-to-the-last extent is increased over the size of previous one. If set to 0, all extents after the second one are the same size. If set to 100, each of these extents is twice as large as the previous one. The default is 50.

28

CREATING TABLES

How exactly these values should be set is again an issue of database tuning and goes beyond the scope of this book. As a general rule, it is preferable to store a table in just a few extents rather than running toward the limit.

The default value for both the `initial` and `next` extents is five times the block size. The default block size of Personal Oracle is 2KB, or 2,048 bytes. The minimum values are twice the block size for initial and once the block size for next. Therefore, the smallest table that can be set up in this scenario has `4096` as `initial` and `2048` as next extent.

The `pctincrease` value is interesting because using just the default, the extents will quickly grow to a huge size, at which point the underlying tablespace, not the extents, will be the limiting factor. I generally prefer to set it to `0` and size the extents sufficiently large to start with.

REAL-WORLD EXPERIENCES

Do you remember the story about the person who invented the chess game? When he presented his brainchild to the court, the monarch in charge offered him a boon. The inventor asked for one grain of rice for the first field of the chess board, two for the second, four for the third, and so on. This would have made 9,223,372,036,854,780,000 grains of rice, or roughly a 1 followed by 19 zeroes. I have no idea how many grains of rice fit into a pound, but if it is 100,000, that amount would leave each inhabitant of the world today with roughly 9 short tons (2,000 pounds or about 900+ kg) of rice. The monarch realized that the whole world could not bring up that much rice, not to mention his empire.

A typical maximum number of extents is 121. If the next extent is set to 4K, and pctincrease is set to 50, as is the default, the 121st extent has a size of 3,438,111,093,617,970GB, which would take a pretty large machine to deal with.

The table definition in Listing 28.4 includes a `storage` clause.

Listing 28.4. Using the `storage` clause.

```
--        Filename: 28squ04.sql
--         Purpose: specify storage clause
--
create table t2804
  (id        number(2))
storage
  (initial 4K
   next     4K
   minextents 1
   maxextents 5
   pctincrease 0)
;
```

This sets storage parameters suitable for a small table that at the most can hold 24KB, including table and row overhead.

DEBUG ALERT

Because every other listing in SQL is done as a comma list, it is a bit confusing that the storage clause is done differently, just listing parameters and their values without commas. Take a look at the following `create table` statement:

```
drop table t2804;

create table t2804
  (id        number(2))
storage
  (initial 4K,
   next    4K,
   minextents 1,
   maxextents 5,
   pctincrease 0)
;
```

If this, which is identical to Listing 28.4, except for the commas, is run, an error results:

```
Table dropped.

  (initial 4K,
            *
ERROR at line 4:
ORA-02143: invalid STORAGE option
```

This error message actually puts the asterisk under the offending comma.

TIP

A tablespace, which is storage space available to the database, is defined with a `storage` clause that uses the same syntax. If any of the `storage` clause parameters are not included, the tablespace defaults for those parameters will be used.

Working with Database Schemas/Users: `create user`

A schema corresponds to database users. The name of the schema is set to a database user, which results in those objects being created under that user's schema.

As you saw in the example at the beginning of this chapter, a table is known to the database as *username.tablename*. An additional user is created with the create user command, which is also used to

- Set quotas on tablespaces for that user
- Set the default tablespace in which objects of that user are created
- Set a temporary tablespace that the RDBMS uses mostly for sorting intermediate jobs for that user

Listing 28.5 creates two users, called t1 and t2 and identified by those names, which means their passwords are the same as their usernames. Both are granted the roles connect and standard, which allows them to connect to the database and do a number of other things, such as creating tables.

Listing 28.5. Creating users.

```
--        Filename: 28squ05.sql
--        Purpose: create two more users
--
create user t1 identified by t1
   default tablespace user_data
   temporary tablespace temporary_data
   quota unlimited on user_data
   quota unlimited on temporary_data
;

create user t2 identified by t2
   default tablespace user_data
   temporary tablespace temporary_data
   quota unlimited on user_data
   quota unlimited on temporary_data
;

grant connect, standard to t1, t2;
```

This script returns

```
User created.

User created.

Grant succeeded.
```

> **NOTE**
>
> There is nothing that says a database user must be a physical person using the database. The two conditions are that any connection to a database is to a user, and that database objects can only be created under a schema that corresponds to a user as well.

There are benefits of having shared systems *not* created under the schema of a physical user:

■ What happens if that user moves on? Are all objects now moved to the successor, or is the username quietly maintained just to maintain the objects?

■ There are utilities that can export all objects in a schema to an operating-system file. If all objects of a system belong to one schema, that whole system can be easily imported or exported.

Both new users can now log on to the database. If you want to try out the scripts, start two more SQL*Plus sessions and log on as those users.

In the following section, three columns are used for displaying output—the first for the default user, the second for t1, and the third for t2.

Neither t1 nor t2 can see any of the objects created by the default user. Listing 28.6 demonstrates schemas.

Listing 28.6. Using schemas.

```
--          Filename: 28squ06.sql
--           Purpose: demonstrate schemas
--
connect t1/t1

select * from t2803;

select * from squ.t2803;
```

This script returns

```
Connected.
select * from t2803
              *
ERROR at line 1:
ORA-00942: table or view
  does not exist

        ID
----------
         1
         2
         3
         4
         5
```

Thus, if the *schemaname*. precedes the table name, user t1 can select from a table that belongs to the user squ. Without using a schema name, another user cannot see objects in another user's schema. In the next statement, t1 creates the table t2803 and inserts six rows:

```
create table t2803
  (id         number(2))
pctfree 20
pctused 50
;

insert into t2803 (id)
  values (8);
insert into t2803 (id)
  values (9);
insert into t2803 (id)
  values (10);
insert into t2803 (id)
  values (11);
insert into t2803 (id)
  values (12);

commit;

select * from t2803;
```

This script returns the following:

```
Table created.

1 row created.

1 row created.

1 row created.

1 row created.

1 row created.

Commit complete.


        ID
---------
        8
        9
       10
       11
       12
```

Now connect as user t2 and select three times from table t2803, first without schema (thus defaulting to t2), and then with schema squ and schema t1:

```
connect t2/t2

select * from t2803;

select * from squ.t2803;

select * from t1.t2803;
```

This returns the following:

```
Connected.
select * from t2803
               *
ERROR at line 1:
ORA-00942: table or view does
not exist


        ID
---------
         1
         2
         3
         4
         5


        ID
---------
         8
         9
        10
        11
        12
```

No such table is known in this schema. If schemas precede the table names, the respective tables are selected from.

Synonyms

In regular English, a *synonym* is a different word for the same meaning. In SQL, a synonym is a different name for the same object, similar to aliases, which are a different name for a column. Synonyms can be private, meaning that they are defined only for one user, or public, meaning that they are defined for all users.

Private Synonyms

A user can give a second name to objects that she has access to by creating a *private synonym*. This is called *private* because it is set for only one user, as opposed to a *public* synonym that is in effect for all users of a system. Often this only serves the purpose of renaming it within the schema. When working with an object in somebody else's schema, a frequent use is to strip out the schema name, thus making the table look the same for the owner and for another user.

A user can also create a private synonym for another user (provided he has the create any synonym privilege). This is routinely done in the same script that grants access to the object.

Private synonyms are mainly used in situations in which an object is shared among just a few users.

Listing 28.7 creates a few private synonyms—one within the schema and then a few between. The same three users as in the previous example will run sessions.

Listing 28.7. Using synonyms.

```
--        Filename: 28squ07.sql
--         Purpose: demonstrate synonyms
--
create synonym ht2803 for t2803;

select * from ht2803;

create synonym t1.ht2803 for t2803;

create synonym t2.ht2803 for t2803;
```

The script returns

```
Synonym created.

       ID
---------
        1
        2
        3
        4
        5

Synonym created.

Synonym created.
```

Both users t1 and t2 can now see the table under the name ht2803 in their own schemas, as is shown here:

```
connect t1/t1

select * from ht2803;
```

The script returns the following:

```
Connected

       ID
---------
        1
        2
        3
        4
        5
```

```
connect t2/t2

select * from ht2803;
```

This returns the following:

```
Connected
```

```
                          ID
                    ---------
                          1
                          2
                          3
                          4
                          5
```

In Listing 28.8, t1 and t2 attempt to create their own synonyms for the table squ.t2803 that eliminates the need to include the schema name.

Listing 28.8. Using synonyms.

```
--        Filename: 28squ08.sql
--        Purpose: demonstrate synonyms
--
connect t1/t1
create synonym t2803 for squ.t2803;
```

This returns

```
Connected.
create synonym t2803 for squ.t2803
                             *
ERROR at line 1:
ORA-00955: name is already used by an existing
object
```

t1 cannot create this synonym because he has already defined a table with the same name. t2, on the other hand, has no such conflict and can create the synonym:

```
connect t2/t2

create synonym t2803 for
squ.t2803;

select * from t2803;
```

It returns the following:

```
Connected.

Synonym created.

                    ID
              ---------
                    1
                    2
                    3
                    4
                    5
```

This works because t2 has no conflicting name in his schema.

28

CREATING TABLES

Removing Private Synonyms: drop synonym

A synonym is dropped through the drop synonym command. Listing 28.9 drops all synonyms created in the previous two examples (if you want to run this script, you need to connect as your *username/password* (squ/squ) to make the script work correctly).

Listing 28.9. Dropping synonyms.

```
--        Filename: 28squ09.sql
--        Purpose: drop synonyms
--
connect squ/squ

drop synonym ht2803;

drop synonym t1.ht2803;

drop  synonym t2.ht2803;
```

This returns the following:

```
Synonym dropped.

Synonym dropped.

Synonym dropped.
```

```
connect t2/t2

drop  synonym t2803;
```

This returns the following:

```
Connected.

Synonym dropped.
```

All synonyms are dropped now. Reconnect with user ID squ and password squ to go on, as shown here:

```
connect squ/squ
```

Public Synonyms

In a multi-user system, it is desirable that tables have the same name within all schemas. In other words, a table pers should be known to all users as pers and not as *some schema*.pers, such as comp.pers. To this effect, public synonyms can be created for tables. That way a table pers should be known to all users as pers and not as some schema.pers, such as comp.pers.

All it takes to make this work is to set the keyword public between create and synonym. The synonyms are dropped with the command drop public synonym.

Listing 28.10 creates a public synonym for table t2803. Users t1 and t2 select rows from table t2803 through this synonym. Then the synonym is dropped.

Listing 28.10. Creating, dropping, and selecting from public synonyms.

```
--        Filename: 28squ10.sql
--          Purpose: create, select from, and drop public synonyms
--
connect squ/sau;
create public synonym ht2803 for t2803;
```

It returns

```
Synonym created.
```

Both t1 and t2 can now select through this public synonym. The following

```
connect t1/t1

select * from ht2803;
```

returns this:

```
Connected.

      ID
---------
       1
       2
       3
       4
       5
```

```
connect t2/t2

select * from ht2803;
```

This returns

```
Connected.

      ID
---------
       1
       2
       3
       4
       5
```

Now the interface is reconnected to the original user and the synonym is dropped:

```
connect squ/squ
```

```
drop public synonym ht2803;
```

This script returns

```
Connected.
```

```
Synonym dropped.
```

Removing Tables and Their Contents from the Database: `drop table`

Tables and their contents are removed with the `drop table` command. For tables that are not referenced by any other foreign key, the table and its contents will disappear. There are a few options you can set for deleting from tables that are referenced, which will be covered later in this chapter.

Listing 28.11 drops the table `t2803` in the schemas for users `t1`, `t2`, and `t3`.

Listing 28.11. Dropping tables.

```
--        Filename: 28squ11.sql
--         Purpose: drop tables
--
connect squ/squ

drop table t2803;
```

It returns the following:

```
Connected.
```

```
Table dropped.
```

```
                          connect t1/t1

                          drop table t2803;
                          It returns

                          Connected.

                          Table dropped.
```

```
connect squ/squ
```

It returns this:

```
Connected.
```

Instant and Irreversible Deletion of Table Contents: `truncate table`

The `truncate table` command wipes out the contents of a table—irretrievably so, because the rollback mechanism is disabled for its execution. (Refer to Chapter 24, "Manipulating Single-Table Data," for details.)

> **CAUTION**
>
> Dropping a large table without truncating first might take a long time because every block deleted is copied into rollback space. Even if the execution of `drop table` is stopped after a while, it takes just as long to restore everything to as it was in the first place. Therefore, if you are about to wipe out a table, use `truncate table` first, and only then use `drop table`.

Changing Definitions of Existing Tables

It is unlikely that all table definitions fit over the life span of a system. Some new columns might have to be added, some columns might become obsolete, a new naming scheme might be implemented, and so on.

Depending on the task to be accomplished, different sets of commands have to be applied. Some of those are straightforward, such as adding a column; others require several steps. In this section, the table `lawyer8` is re-created and repopulated for these examples as needed. The parts of the examples that re-create that table will be included in the text only the first time, because repetitions of that portion would not add anything worthwhile.

Renaming Tables: `rename`

Renaming tables is the easiest change to make and can be done through the simple command `rename table old_table_name to new_table_name;`. Tables can be renamed only within the same schema, however, so it is not possible to move a table and its contents between schemas without re-creating it. Listing 28.12 starts with re-creating the `lawyer8` table and demonstrates renaming.

Listing 28.12. Renaming tables.

```
--       Filename: 28squ12.sql
--       Purpose: rename tables
--
drop table lawyer8;

create table lawyer8 (
   id       number(2) not null,
   Name     varchar2(15),
   Office   varchar2(15),
   bhrs     number(4),
   bgross   number(7))
;

insert into lawyer8
(select * from lawyer1);

commit;
```

This script returns

```
Table dropped.

Table created.

20 rows created.

Commit complete.
```

After blowing away and re-creating as well as repopulating the table, the rename can be executed. Before doing that, however, the total of the b gross column is calculated. This value will serve for comparison purposes later on:

```
select sum(bgross) from lawyer8;

rename lawyer8 to squ.renamed8;

rename lawyer8 to t1.lawyer8;
```

The script returns

```
SUM(BGROSS)
-----------
    7521099

rename lawyer8 to squ.renamed8
                    *
ERROR at line 1:
ORA-01765: specifying table's owner name is not allowed

rename lawyer8 to t1.lawyer8
                    *
ERROR at line 1:
ORA-01765: specifying table's owner name is not allowed
```

The previous two error messages simply state that one cannot specify the owner/schema name in this command. Renaming within the schema works fine, however, as the next statement shows:

```
rename lawyer8 to renamed8;

desc lawyer8

select sum(bgross) from renamed8;

rename renamed8 to lawyer8;
```

This script returns the following:

```
Table renamed.

Object does not exist.

SUM(BGROSS)
-----------
    7521099

Table renamed.
```

A rename within a schema works just fine. Afterward, the object under the old name no longer exists for the database. The select statement shows a sum of gross receipt that is the same as that of the previous select. In the end, the table was renamed to its old state.

Adding Columns: `alter table ... add`

Adding columns is done through the add option of the `alter table` command. This command is very versatile and is covered some more in Chapter 29. Adding columns does not affect the data in the existing columns.

Listing 28.13 adds a column for the first and middle names to the table `lawyer8`.

Listing 28.13. Adding columns to tables.

```
--       Filename: 28squ13.sql
--       Purpose: add columns to tables
--
alter table lawyer8 add (
   FMName      varchar2(15))
;

desc lawyer8

select sum(bgross) from lawyer8;
```

It returns

```
Table altered.

Name                            Null?     Type
------------------------------- --------- ----
ID                              NOT NULL  NUMBER(2)
NAME                                      VARCHAR2(15)
OFFICE                                    VARCHAR2(15)
BHRS                                      NUMBER(4)
BGROSS                                    NUMBER(7)
FMNAME                                    VARCHAR2(15)


SUM(BGROSS)
-----------
    7521099
```

This example demonstrates two facts:

- A column can be added without problems
- Existing data is not affected by the addition of a column

28

CREATING TABLES

Changing Column Definitions: `alter table ... modify`

With a number of limitations, four parts of the column definitions can be changed using the `modify` option of the `alter table` statement:

- A column can be changed to any valid datatype if is unpopulated, meaning that every row contains a NULL in this column. Otherwise, a varchar2 column can be changed to a char column of the same size, or vice versa. The following example shows that it can even be set to a larger size.

- An unpopulated column can be changed to any valid size/precision. The size/precision of a populated column must not be decreased.

- not null constraints may be added if there is not a single row that contains a NULL in that column. not null constraints may be removed as well.

- Default values may be altered.

Changes that are more drastic than these have to be handled through creating a new table with the desired characteristics and copying the contents of the old table to the new table.

Listing 28.14 demonstrates some successful and some unsuccessful attempts to modify columns. The beginning of the example creates a new `lawyer8` table, including the `FMName` column.

Listing 28.14. Modifying column definitions.

```
--      Filename: 28squ14.sql
--       Purpose: modify column definitions
--         Stage: production
--
drop table lawyer8;

create table lawyer8 (
   id       number(2) not null,
   Name     varchar2(15),
   Office   varchar2(15),
   bhrs     number(4),
   bgross   number(7))
;

insert into lawyer8
(select * from lawyer1);

commit;

alter table lawyer8 add (
   FMName      varchar2(15))
;

alter table lawyer8 modify (
  Name      varchar2(20))
;
```

```
desc lawyer8

alter table lawyer8 modify (
  Name     varchar2(5))
;
```

It returns

```
Table altered.
```

```
Name                              Null?     Type
------------------------------- -------- ----
ID                                NOT NULL NUMBER(2)
NAME                                       VARCHAR2(20)
OFFICE                                     VARCHAR2(15)
BHRS                                       NUMBER(4)
BGROSS                                     NUMBER(7)
FMNAME                                     VARCHAR2(15)


  Name     varchar2(5))
  *
ERROR at line 2:
ORA-01441: column to be modified must be empty to decrease column length
```

A populated column must not be decreased in length. An empty column, however, may be. The following

```
alter table lawyer8 modify (
  FMName     varchar2(5))
;
```

returns this:

```
Table altered.
```

A populated varchar column may be converted to a char column, and vice versa. This script

```
alter table lawyer8 modify (
  Name     char(20))
;

alter table lawyer8 modify (
  Name     varchar2(20))
;

alter table lawyer8 modify (
  Name     char(30))
;
```

returns this:

```
Table altered.

Table altered.

Table altered.
```

28

CREATING TABLES

Populated number columns may be increased but not decreased in precision:

```
alter table lawyer8 modify (
  bgross    number(12))
;

alter table lawyer8 modify (
  bgross    number(7))
;
```

This script is successful for the first, but not for the second statement. Here is the result:

```
Table altered.

  bgross    number(7))
       *
ERROR at line 2:
ORA-01440: column to be modified must be empty to decrease precision or scale
```

A populated integer number column can be modified to a floating-point number column. The following

```
alter table lawyer8 modify (
  bgross    number)
;
```

returns this:

```
Table altered.
```

A fixed-point column is then added and populated with the fraction of bgross over bhrs:

```
alter table lawyer8 add (
   fxpnt   number (6,3));

update lawyer8 set fxpnt = bgross/bhrs;

commit;

select fxpnt from lawyer8
where rownum < 5
;
```

This returns

```
Table altered.

20 rows updated.

Commit complete.

    FXPNT
----------
   149.44
  200.597
  163.603
   106.23
```

Three modifications are now attempted: one that decreases the scale (increases the number of digits after the period), one that does the same while also increasing the precision, and one that coverts the fixed point to a floating-point number:

```
alter table lawyer8 modify (
   fxpnt  number (6,5));

alter table lawyer8 modify (
   fxpnt  number (8,5));

alter table lawyer8 modify (
   fxpnt  number );
```

This returns the following:

```
fxpnt  number (6,5))
       *
ERROR at line 2:
ORA-01440: column to be modified must be empty to decrease precision or scale

Table altered.

Table altered.
```

Drastic Column Modifications or Removing Columns—Re-Creating Definitions and Copying Contents

Just as modify is limited to the cases described in the previous section, there is no direct way to drop a column from a table. The following steps have to be performed:

1. Create a new table with the desired definitions.
2. Copy the contents of the old table to the new table, perhaps after using some data conversions—in particular the substring function if a varchar2 column is reduced in size.
3. Rename the old table to some different name.
4. Rename the new table to the name of the old one.
5. Test whether the new table definitions work satisfactorily.
6. Truncate the old table.
7. Drop the old table.

Listing 28.15 illustrates these seven steps and creates a modified lawyer8 table that contains only the ID and NAME columns. The size of the NAME column is also reduced from 15 to 13 characters (the example starts from a clean lawyer8 table; the steps for creation are not shown here).

28

CREATING TABLES

Listing 28.15. Re-creating a table with dropped columns.

```
--          Filename: 28squ15.sql
--          Purpose: re-create lawyer8 with dropped/reduced columns

create table l8new (
    id          number(2) not null,
    Name        varchar2(13))
;

insert into l8new
select id, substr(name,1,13)
from lawyer8
;

commit;

rename lawyer8 to l8old;

rename l8new to lawyer8;
```

This returns

```
Table created.


20 rows created.


Commit complete.


Table renamed.


Table renamed.
```

At this point the change proper is done. The name `lawyer8` now refers to the new table. If that table tests out satisfactorily, it can be truncated and dropped, which is done in the following:

```
desc lawyer8;

select * from lawyer8;

truncate table l8old;

drop table l8old;
```

This returns

```
Name                            Null?    Type
------------------------------- -------- ----
ID                              NOT NULL NUMBER(2)
NAME                                     VARCHAR2(13)
```

```
       ID NAME
--------- -----------
        1 Dewey
        2 Cheetham
        3 Howe
...
...
       19 Chatham
       20 Paul

20 rows selected.

Table truncated.

Table dropped.
```

> **TIP**
>
> If you work in Oracleland, you can accomplish the same thing, probably more efficiently, through exporting the table, resetting the parameters, and importing it again.

One-Step Creation of Tables Whose Columns and Contents Are Derived from Other Tables

All tables thus far have been created by explicitly specifying column information. If a table is derived from a view or from another table using the as keyword and a query just as it is done for a creation of a view, the column specifications may be omitted because they are directly copied from the original table or view. This fact is very convenient for data-messaging projects. It is likely to be used less in production tables, because usually it is desirable to specify the difference between originating table or view and the derived table.

In Chapter 27, "Multi-Table, Distinct, and Aggregate Views," you created aggregate views, which are virtual tables that aggregate information from some other tables. This mechanism is automatically in sync because the aggregate information is a virtual derivation of the physical table.

If the original table is static or fairly static—the interpretation of "fairly" being determined by business needs—it might be preferable to keep the aggregate information in a separate table that is updated periodically. For example, if the aggregate table is accessed frequently and the original table has many millions of rows, scanning through this table every time is not very efficient.

Every create view statement can create an equivalent table by just replacing the word view with table. However, often tables take up space where views are only defined in the Data Dictionary. It is wise to consider that trade-off before getting carried away.

Listing 28.16 creates a table based on the view `offaggr`, which has been created in Chapter 27

Listing 28.16. Creating a table based on a view.

```
--       Filename: 28squ16.sql
--       Purpose: create a table as select from a view
--                uses view offaggr created in Chapter 27
--
desc offaggr

create table offaggrt as
select * from offaggr;

desc offaggrt

select * from offaggrt;
```

This returns

```
Name                                Null?     Type
-------------------------------- --------- ----
OFFICE                                      VARCHAR2(15)
STAFF                                       NUMBER
TOTHRS                                      NUMBER
TOTREV                                      NUMBER


Table created.

Name                                Null?     Type
-------------------------------- --------- ----
OFFICE                                      VARCHAR2(15)
STAFF                                       NUMBER
TOTHRS                                      NUMBER
TOTREV                                      NUMBER


OFFICE            STAFF    TOTHRS    TOTREV
---------------- -------- --------- ---------
Boston               5     13391    1438175
Houston              2      4138     459889
Los Angeles          7     21774    3412223
New York             6     10969    2210812
```

The table and view definitions are identical.

TIP

Oracle has a nice automated option for derived tables, which are called *snapshots* and are created with the `create snapshot` command. A *snapshot* is a derived table that can be automatically refreshed as determined by a refresh interval that is specified in the creation command. If the refresh interval has passed and the snapshot is accessed, it will be re-created at this point.

The Recoverable and Unrecoverable Options

One of the nice options of Oracle is archive log mode. As transactions are committed, information about them is recorded in *redo logs*, which are stored in sets of files independent of the database proper. If a database or disk on which (parts of) the database are located fails, the database can be restored from the last full backup, and all changes that occurred since that backup can be applied from the redo logs.

Although convenient, this option generates additional overhead that is not really desirable in a large transaction. Because derived tables can be redone again by applying the same script after the recovery, archive logging is not really necessary either. Therefore, it is possible to suspend it for a `create table` operation by adding the keyword `unrecoverable`. This keyword has an effect only on a database that uses archive logging and on a table creation that is derived from another table.

Listing 28.17 re-creates the `offaggrt` table while suspending archive logging.

Listing 28.17. Creating a table from a view using the unrecoverable option.

```
--          Filename: 28squ17.sql
--          Purpose: create a table as select from a view
--                   uses view offaggr created in Chapter 27
--                   uses unrecoverable option
--
drop table offaggrt;

create table offaggrt
   unrecoverable
as
select * from offaggr;
```

It returns

```
Table dropped.
```

```
Table created.
```

Moving a Table from One Schema to Another

As you learned in the "Renaming Tables" section, a schema name must not be included in the rename command. Therefore, if that operation is desired, a similar approach can be used, as described in the section "Drastic Column Modifications or Removing Columns—Re-Creating Definitions and Copying Contents."

28

CREATING TABLES

Listing 28.18 illustrates this approach (note that if you are in Oracleland, exporting and importing may be a better way to accomplish the same).

Listing 28.18. Moving a table from one schema to another.

```
--        Filename: 28squ18.sql
--        Purpose: move table lawyer8 to schema t1
--                 copy table and drop

connect squ/squ

drop table lawyer8;
drop table t1.lawyer8;
drop public synonym lawyer8;

create table lawyer8 (
    id        number(2) not null,
    Name      varchar2(15),
    Office    varchar2(15),
    bhrs      number(4),
    bgross    number(7))
;

insert into lawyer8
(select * from lawyer1);

commit;
```

At this point, lawyer8 is refurbished, and all objects with the names that will be used are dropped:

```
create table t1.lawyer8 as
select * from lawyer8;

drop table lawyer8;

create public synonym lawyer8 for t1.lawyer8;
```

This script returns

```
Table created.

Table dropped.

Synonym created.
```

Now the table is moved to schema t1. A public synonym exists so that all users can see the table without including the schema. The following shows how it looks to user t2:

```
connect t2/t2

select * from lawyer8;

select * from t2.lawyer8;
```

This script returns

```
Connected.

    ID NAME              OFFICE             BHRS     BGROSS
--------- --------------- ---------------- -------- --------
     1 Dewey             Boston             2856     426800
     2 Cheetham          New York           1398     280435
...
...
...
    19 Chatham           New York           1759     367944
    20 Paul              Boston             2198     239855

20 rows selected.

select * from t2.lawyer8
                *
ERROR at line 1:
ORA-00942: table or view does not exist
```

The second select shows that the object does not exist in the schema t2.

Creating Code Control and Lookup Tables (SQL Generating SQL)

When creating code control and lookup tables, one of the key issues is to make sure that all key values are included in the code table. A query such as the one used for the distinct view created in Chapter 27 is the basis for this script. The table sqlconst, created in Chapter 23, "Generating SQL Statements Through SQL," is used for the sake of convenience. Listing 28.19 illustrates the steps necessary to create the offlu8 code control table.

Listing 28.19. Generating SQL statements.

```
--        Filename: 28squ19.sql
--        Purpose: SQL generating SQL
--
connect squ/squ

create table offlu8 (
   Office    varchar2(15),
   City      varchar2(20),
   state     char(2),
   zip       char(5))
;

select distinct
   'insert into offlu8 values (''' ||
     office || SCS || SCS || SPE
from lawyer1, sqlconst
;
```

This code returns

```
Table created.

'INSERTINTOOFFLU8VALUES('''||OFFICE||SCS||SCS||SPE
--------------------------------------------------
insert into offlu8 values ('Boston', '', '');
insert into offlu8 values ('Houston', '', '');
insert into offlu8 values ('Los Angeles', '', '');
insert into offlu8 values ('New York', '', '');
```

The output can now be edited to include the additional values and is ready for an `insert`.

The cache Option

Oracle uses a *least recently used (LRU)* algorithm to determine which blocks of a table to keep in memory and which ones to let go of. This algorithm favors blocks that were updated over those that were read only. Within each category (updated versus read only) the least recently used blocks are overwritten first. In Oracle 7.2 or later, a `cache` option can be specified for a table, through which a read-only block gets the same priority as an updated block.

If `insert` and `update` statements use a lookup table extensively, the RDBMS will keep over-writing the blocks of this table with those of the inserted/updated table, which results in many unnecessary disk reads. Lookup tables should, therefore, be defined with the cache option that eliminates this problem. You can create a table using `cache` option of the `create table` script, as shown in Listing 28.20.

Listing 28.20. Creating and loading a table using the cache option.

```
--       Filename: croff3.sql
--        Purpose: Creates and loads table office3 code conversion table
--                 Uses Cache option
--
create table office3 (
   id        number(2) not null,
   Office    varchar2(15),
   NewOffice varchar2(15),
   ShOffice  char(2),
   State     char(2),
   bossid    number(2))
      cache
;
```

The RDBMS prioritizes the choice of data blocks to keep in memory.

Summary

Tables exist in the database as an independent means of storing information in an organized fashion—columns that define how data is structured, and one or more rows of data consistent with that structure. Tables are the ultimate storage object in a relational database. Through several SQL commands, tables can be created, have their definitions altered, be renamed, and be removed.

Besides the basic SQL functionality, Oracle provides a number of options to affect storage and tune performance.

A table can be created with the statement `create table table_name (column_name1 datatype);`. Even a simple table must have at least one column.

Table names must be unique among all the table and view names created under a user's schema. The column names must be unique within a table, and each column definition must include the datatype and the size as applicable. A `not null` constraint and a default value for a column can be specified immediately after the datatype definition as well.

As an extension to SQL, a number of storage options can be specified in the `create table` and `alter table` statements that allow for storage optimization depending on table size and predominant use.

Tables, and views for that matter, can only be created in a schema that is essentially a user ID. The `create user` command is used to define a new user to the database. A database user need not be a physical person using the database; typically, a system or system module is created under a user ID that does not correspond to a person.

The `create schema` command, on the other hand, allows you to create several tables and views in one statement.

A user can provide an alternate name for an object to which he or she has access by creating a private synonym. A user who has the `create any synonym` privilege can also create a private synonym for another user. Private synonyms are mainly used in situations where an object is shared just between a few users. A synonym is dropped through the `drop synonym` command. Through the `create public synonym` command, public synonyms can be created for these tables, at which point they are known to all users the same way.

Tables and their contents are removed with the `drop table` command. (Some additional options for when the table is referenced by any other foreign key are included in Chapter 29.) Usually it is preferable to truncate a table before dropping it to avoid unnecessary milling through rollback segments.

Tables can be renamed within the same schema through the `rename table old_table_name` to `new_table_name;` statement. Adding columns is done through the `add` option of the `alter table` command. This does not affect the data in the existing columns.

With a number of limitations, especially when the columns are populated, four parts of the column definitions can be changed using the `modify` option of the `alter table` statement— datatype, size/precision, `not null` constraints, and default values.

In all other cases, a new table with the desired definitions has to be created; the contents of the old table have to be copied over with modifications, as desired; the old table be renamed to some temporary name; and the new table is renamed to the old table name. If everything tests out, the old table can then be dropped.

A table may be derived from a view or another table using the as keyword and a query, just as it is done for the creation of a view. Every `create view` statement can create an equivalent table by just replacing the word `view` with `table`. In this case, the column specifications can be omitted because they are directly copied from the original table or view.

When creating a derived table, archive logging can be suspended by adding the keyword `unrecoverable` at the end of the `create table` statement.

Because tables can be renamed only within the same schema, a table can be moved to a different schema by creating a new table in the new schema based on a query from the old, and then deleting the old table. In Oracle, exporting and importing is usually preferable, though.

The first step of code control and lookup tables can be created through a SQL generating SQL script. The query of that script is based on a `select distinct` statement or on a distinct view. The output can then be edited to include additional values and is ready for an insert.

The next chapter, "Keys, Indexes, Constraints, and Table/Column Comments," covers the options with which table definitions can, and should, be greatly enhanced.

Keys, Indexes, Constraints, and Table/Column Comments

CHAPTER 29

Chapter 28, "Creating Tables," covered those facets of table creation that pertained to entire tables, with the exception of the not null constraint and the default keyword, which are inserted immediately with the column definition.

This chapter greatly expands on Chapter 28 and includes many of the very powerful table and column enhancements.

These enhancements have at least one of the following purposes:

■ They constrain the values that may be inserted into a column or a set of columns.

■ They speed or may speed retrieval of individual rows or sets of individual rows.

Constraints may be static, limiting the values or range of values that may be inserted (check, not null). They may be in relationship to all values of a column, limiting new rows to values that are not in certain columns or sets (unique, primary key). Also, constraints may be in relationship to another table, only allowing the insertion of a value that also occurs in another column in another (or the same) table (foreign key).

Indexes speed up data retrieval. Incidentally, indexes are also used to ensure unique values in a unique or primary key column.

This chapter begins with a discussion of static constraints, followed by options of naming, enabling, and disabling indexes, keys, and all constraints, static or otherwise. The next section deals with dynamic constraints on columns—the unique and primary key constraints—which is followed by a section on compound keys and determining suitable key values. A section on dynamic constraints between tables, foreign keys, and recursive foreign keys, follows. The next section covers indexes, and the final section comments on tables and columns in the Data Dictionary.

Constraints are among the most powerful features of an RDBMS. Static constraints ensure that inapplicable values cannot be entered. Dynamic constraints enforce relational integrity among tables, making sure that each detail row has one *and only one* master row.

Static Constraints

The purpose of *static constraints* is to make it impossible to insert inappropriate values into a table. Chapter 28 has included the most frequently used static constraint, not null, which prevents inserts of nulls in a row. The other constraint in this group is the check constraint, which limits the values that may be inserted in a row.

not null Constraints

The previous chapter introduced the not null constraint as part of the table definition. This section shows how to create a not null constraint and how to remove it after table creation.

not null constraints are special in the sense that they are *inline constraints*. This means they are part of the definition of the column to which they refer. Therefore, adding or removing a not null constraint requires *modifying* the column. This is done using the alter table *tablename* modify command.

> **NOTE**
>
> These examples all begin with dropping the tables before creating them. This creates a clean slate, but will return errors the first time, because the table is not there yet. Disregard this error.

Listing 29.1 creates the table tssn1 that contains three columns to hold social security numbers. The first one, assn, is defined as not null.

Listing 29.1. Adding and removing not null constraints.

```
--       Filename: 29squ01.sql
--          Purpose: adding and removing not null constraints
--
drop table tssn;

CREATE TABLE tssn (
 assn      CHAR(9)
    DEFAULT '.'
    NOT NULL,
 bssn      CHAR(9)
    DEFAULT '.',
 cssn      CHAR(9)
    default '.');

desc tssn
```

This code returns

```
drop table tssn1
          *
ERROR at line 1:
ORA-00942: table or view does not exist

Table created.
 Name                             Null?     Type
 ------------------------------   --------  ----
 ASSN                             NOT NULL  CHAR(9)
 BSSN                                       CHAR(9)
 CSSN                                       CHAR(9)
```

Because the table did not exist previously, an error occurs. The table is created, and a desc then shows that the first column indeed is defined as not null. Through the following alter table *tablename* `modify` statement, the last two columns are set to `not null`, and the first one is set to `null`. The keyword `null` is used for this purpose. Thus, `null` and `not null` act as toggles for modifying column definitions:

```
alter table tssn modify (
    bssn NOT NULL,
    cssn NOT NULL,
    assn NULL)
;

desc tssn
```

This returns the following code:

```
Table altered.

Name                            Null?    Type
------------------------------- -------- ----
ASSN                                     CHAR(9)
BSSN                            NOT NULL CHAR(9)
CSSN                            NOT NULL CHAR(9)
```

The constraints are now reversed.

> **CAUTION**
>
> The `tssn2` table, as well as the `zip1` table that will be used later in this chapter, include arrays of fictitious social security numbers and zip codes. This is done side by side to show how different constraints affect essentially the same columns. Generally, however, arrays should be avoided. True arrays with array indexes like `ssn[n]`, as they are available in programming languages such as C, are not supported in SQL. Arrays violate normalization rules—1st normal form in particular—which does not allow for repeating groups such as `test[1], test[2], test[3]`. A faked array that uses names such as `assn`, `bssn`, or `assn1`, `assn2` is not a good idea because there are no straightforward set operations available to deal with these arrays (such as indexing), and it leads to many data integrity and processing issues later on.

check Constraints

`check` constraints specify which value may be entered into a column, either as a range or as a list of values. There are several uses for `check` constraints:

- Categorical columns—Columns in tables that are categorical, such as job classifications, sex codes, ethnic codes, and the like: A `check` constraint on these columns can prevent the entering of values that are not defined. Therefore, it is impossible to enter invalid codes. The only possible error on such columns is to enter the wrong valid code. That's a major improvement.

- Valid ranges—Many, especially numerical, columns have only valid or plausible ranges. Salaries, for example, are usually not negative. Ages are not negative either, and a range of 0 to 150 is probably useful. Because ages are usually calculated from dates of birth, there would be conforming valid ranges for dates.

- Code ranges—There are types of codes, such as social security numbers or zip codes, that are really categorical in nature—you would not subtract one zip code from another—and also can start with leading zeroes that actually mean something (Maine zip codes start with 04, which is something different from a 4 with a leading zero). Similarly, a social security number issued in Maine starts with 00. Short of a categorical number datatype, which would be appropriate for such numbers, these codes can be defined as fixed char, such as `char(5)` for zip codes and `char(9)` for SSNs. A `check` constraint then can be used to specify a valid range of 00000 to 99999, or 000000000 to 999999999, plus a few letter-based codes such as 'M' and 'N/A' for *missing* and *not applicable*.

- Business rules—If there is a rule such as "no employee can make a higher salary than the president," then this rule can be enforced through `check` constraints as well.

The `check` constraint is defined using the subclause CHECK (*check_condition*) in either the `create table` or the `alter table` *tablename* add statement. The *check_condition* can include any column in the table, but no aggregate values or subqueries.

Listing 29.2 creates table `tssn2`, which includes a `check` constraint for `assn`.

CAUTION

This check constraint for valid SSNs catches some problems, such as letters in the beginning or end of the number, but not others, such as too few digits. For a complete constraint, see example `29squ05`.

29

KEYS, INDEXES,
AND
CONSTRAINTS

Listing 29.2. Creating check constraints.

```
--      Filename: 29squ02.sql
--      Purpose: creating check constraints
--
drop table tssn2;

CREATE TABLE tssn2 (
 assn      CHAR(9)
    DEFAULT '.' NOT NULL,
    CHECK ( assn IN ('         M' , '          N/A') OR
 assn BETWEEN '000000000' AND '999999999'),
 bssn      CHAR(9)
    DEFAULT '.' not null,
 cssn      CHAR(9)
    default '.' not null);
```

This code returns

```
Table dropped.
```

```
Table created.
```

The only way to see which check constraints are defined, other than violating the constraint and waiting for an error message, is to retrieve information about the constraint from Data Dictionary views. Listing 29.3 contains two scripts: one to list the constraints on a table, and the other one to list the constraints on columns.

Listing 29.3. A query for constraints.

```
--          Filename: 29squ03.sql
--          Purpose: query for constraints
--
set long            500
col constraint_name     format a15
col constraint_type     format a1    heading 'T'
col table_name          format a10
col column_name         format a10
col r_constraint_name   format a10
col Search_Condition    format a60
col status              format a1    heading 'S'

accept p_table   prompt 'Enter table name--UPPER CASE ONLY: '

select
    constraint_name,
    search_condition
from
    user_constraints
where table_name       = '&p_table' ;

select
    a.constraint_name,
    a.constraint_type,
    a.table_name,
    b.column_name,
    a.r_constraint_name,
    substr(a.status,1,1)
from
    user_constraints a,
    user_cons_columns b
where a.table_name       = '&p_table' and
      a.constraint_name = b.constraint_name
order by a.table_name;

set long            80

clear columns
```

This is an interactive script, and the whole dialog is shown. The script prompts for a table name and displays the constraints on the table specified. The first script yields constraint names and search conditions; the second script selects the columns concerned, the type of the constraint, and whether it is enabled. The following example uses `29squ03.sql` to display the constraints on the `tssn2` table:

```
Enter table name--UPPER CASE ONLY: TSSN2
old    6: where table_name    = '&p_table'
new    6: where table_name    = 'TSSN2'

CONSTRAINT_NAME SEARCH_CONDITION
--------------- ------------------------------------------------------------
SYS_C008742     ASSN IS NOT NULL
SYS_C008743     BSSN IS NOT NULL
SYS_C008744     CSSN IS NOT NULL
SYS_C008745      assn IN ('         M' , '      N/A') OR assn BETWEEN '000000
                 000' AND '999999999'
old   11: where a.table_name    = '&p_table' and
new   11: where a.table_name    = 'TSSN2' and

CONSTRAINT_NAME T TABLE_NAME COLUMN_NAM R_CONSTRAI S
--------------- - ---------- ---------- ---------- -
SYS_C008742     C TSSN2      ASSN                  E
SYS_C008743     C            BSSN                  E
SYS_C008744     C            CSSN                  E
SYS_C008745     C            ASSN                  E
```

The next script adds constraints to `bssn` and `cssn`. These constraints are identical to the ones already in force on `assn`. See Listing 29.4.

Listing 29.4. Creating `check` constraints using an `alter table` statement.

```
--      Filename: 29squ04.sql
--        Purpose: creating check constraints using alter table
--
--
alter table tssn2 add (
    check ( bssn IN
        ('         M' , '      N/A') OR bssn BETWEEN '000000000' AND '999999999'),
    check ( cssn IN
        ('         M' , '      N/A') OR cssn BETWEEN '000000000' AND '999999999'))
;
```

This code returns

```
Table altered.
```

Running `29squ03.sql` again shows that these changes are actually effective, as shown here:

```
old    6: where table_name    = '&p_table'
new    6: where table_name    = 'TSSN2'

CONSTRAINT_NAME SEARCH_CONDITION
--------------- ------------------------------------------------------------
SYS_C008742     ASSN IS NOT NULL
SYS_C008743     BSSN IS NOT NULL
SYS_C008744     CSSN IS NOT NULL
SYS_C008745      assn IN ('         M' , '      N/A') OR assn BETWEEN '000000
                 000' AND '999999999'
```

29

KEYS, INDEXES, AND CONSTRAINTS

```
SYS_C008746        bssn IN ('        M' , '        N/A') OR bssn BETWEEN '000000
                   000' AND '999999999'
SYS_C008747        cssn IN ('        M' , '        N/A') OR cssn BETWEEN '000000
                   000' AND '999999999'

6 rows selected.

old  11: where a.table_name      = '&p_table' and
new  11: where a.table_name      = 'TSSN2' and

CONSTRAINT_NAME T TABLE_NAME COLUMN_NAM R_CONSTRAI S
--------------- - ---------- ---------- ---------- -
SYS_C008742     C TSSN2      ASSN                  E
SYS_C008743     C            BSSN                  E
SYS_C008744     C            CSSN                  E
SYS_C008745     C            ASSN                  E
SYS_C008746     C            BSSN                  E
SYS_C008747     C            CSSN                  E

6 rows selected.
```

The constraints in the previous example were based on constant expressions. Any column in a row can be used in dynamic expressions as well. Listing 29.5 shows that it puts a check constraint on the bgross column in lawyer8, which limits bgross to 250 * bhrs. This constraint effectively enforces an hourly rate of less than $250.

Listing 29.5. Creating check constraints based on column values.

```
--       Filename: 29squ05.sql
--         Purpose: creating check constraints based on column values
--
drop table t1.lawyer8;

drop table lawyer8;

create table lawyer8 as
select * from lawyer1;

alter table lawyer8 add (
   check  (bgross < bhrs * 250 ))
;
```

This code returns

```
...
Table dropped.
Table created.
Table altered.
```

Inserting a bgross value higher than allowed produces an error:

```
insert into lawyer8 (id, bhrs, bgross) values (99,1000, 400000);
```

This code returns

```
insert into lawyer8 (id, bhrs, bgross) values (99,1000, 400000)
                 *
ERROR at line 1:
ORA-02290: check constraint (HANS.SYS_C008750) violated

alter table lawyer8 add
   ( check ( bgross < (select bgross from lawyer8 where id = 7))
;
```

This statement tries to base the constraint on a subquery, which is not allowed:

```
( check ( bgross < (select bgross from lawyer8 where id = 7))
                 *
ERROR at line 2:
ORA-02251: subquery not allowed here
```

REAL-WORLD EXPERIENCES

According to Celko, the ISO standard for sex codes has four values (ISO 5218— Representation of human sexes):

Code Value	Sex
0	Unknown
1	Male
2	Female
9	Not applicable

The FBI is purported to use seven values to code sex. Because everything there is secretive by design, I did not verify whether this is true and whether I got the code table right. I was afraid it would neither confirm nor deny. Oh well.

Code Value	Sex
1	Male
2	Female
3	Male, formerly female
4	Female, formerly male
5	Male, changing to female
6	Female, changing to male
7	Can't be determined

Combining the schemes to create the ISO-FBI scheme yields an improved system suitable for spy organizations:

continues

29

KEYS, INDEXES, AND CONSTRAINTS

continued

Code Value	Gender
0	Unknown
1	Male
2	Female
3	Male, formerly female
4	Female, formerly male
5	Male, changing to female
6	Female, changing to male
7	Can't be determined
9	Not applicable

The check constraints for these three schemes would be as follows:

```
create table sex
  (sexiso    char(1) not null
    check (sexiso in ('0','1','2','9')),
   sexfbi    char(1) not null
    check (sexiso in ('1','2','3','4','5','6','7'),
   sexisofbi char(1) not null
    check (sexiso in ('0','1','2','3','4','5','6','9'))
;
```

Now, if you wonder why this table is called sex and not gender, that is all Dawn's fault. Dawn, a lady close to retirement, was my secretary in the training center of a big six accounting firm. (Actually, *lady* is stretching it a bit. Come to think, *secretary* is stretching it a bit, too.) She always said, "People have a sex and nouns have a gender." At times she left out the articles in that sentence. So here you go, Dawn—I did not argue then, and I won't argue now.

Naming, Enabling, and Disabling Indexes, Keys, and Constraints

Rather than using the system-assigned names, constraints can be custom-named through the statement that creates them. A further convenience is the fact that a constraint can be deactivated or reactivated through enabling or disabling it.

Naming Constraints

Whenever a constraint is created, the RDBMS assigns a unique name to the constraint. In the previous example, the 29squ03.sql script retrieved the column names SYS_C008745 to SYS_C008750 from the user_constraints and user_cons_columns Data Dictionary views. The example before showed that when this constraint gets violated, the constraint name will be displayed in the error message.

In a production system, a name such as `SYS_C008745` is pretty meaningless. All the message does is put an asterisk under the table name to indicate that a `check` constraint has been violated (using the same message for `check` and for `not null`). If the name of the offended constraint made sense immediately, then it would not be necessary to issue another query just to find out what had gone wrong. Through a slightly changed syntax in the `create table` and the `alter table` statements, constraints can be given explicit names.

Listing 29.6 reworks example `29squ02.sql` to name all constraints. This example also introduces a lengthy `check` constraint, which is then tested with all sorts of invalid SSNs.

Listing 29.6. Naming constraints and testing large `check` constraints.

```
--       Filename: 29squ06.sql
--       Purpose: naming constraints; large check constraints
--
drop table tssn2;

CREATE TABLE tssn2 (
 assn     CHAR(9)
    DEFAULT '.'
    constraint a_nn NOT NULL,
    constraint a_chk CHECK (
(substr(assn,1,1) between '0' and '9' and
substr(assn,2,1) between '0' and '9' and
substr(assn,3,1) between '0' and '9' and
substr(assn,4,1) between '0' and '9' and
substr(assn,5,1) between '0' and '9' and
substr(assn,6,1) between '0' and '9' and
substr(assn,7,1) between '0' and '9' and
substr(assn,8,1) between '0' and '9' and
substr(assn,9,1) between '0' and '9' and
substr(assn,1,1) between '0' and '9') or
assn IN ('        M','       N/A')),
 bssn     CHAR(9)
    DEFAULT '.',
 cssn     CHAR(9)
    default '.');
alter table tssn2 modify (
    bssn constraint b_nn NOT NULL,
    cssn constraint c_nn NOT NULL)
;

alter table tssn2 add (
    constraint b_chk CHECK (
(substr(bssn,1,1) between '0' and '9' and
substr(bssn,2,1) between '0' and '9' and
substr(bssn,3,1) between '0' and '9' and
substr(bssn,4,1) between '0' and '9' and
substr(bssn,5,1) between '0' and '9' and
substr(bssn,6,1) between '0' and '9' and
substr(bssn,7,1) between '0' and '9' and
```

29

KEYS, INDEXES, AND CONSTRAINTS

continues

Listing 29.6. continued

```
substr(bssn,8,1) between '0' and '9' and
substr(bssn,9,1) between '0' and '9' and
substr(bssn,1,1) between '0' and '9') or
bssn IN ('       M','      N/A')),
    constraint c_chk CHECK (
(substr(cssn,1,1) between '0' and '9' and
substr(cssn,2,1) between '0' and '9' and
substr(cssn,3,1) between '0' and '9' and
substr(cssn,4,1) between '0' and '9' and
substr(cssn,5,1) between '0' and '9' and
substr(cssn,6,1) between '0' and '9' and
substr(cssn,7,1) between '0' and '9' and
substr(cssn,8,1) between '0' and '9' and
substr(cssn,9,1) between '0' and '9' and
substr(cssn,1,1) between '0' and '9') or
cssn IN ('       M','      N/A')))
;
```

Six constraints are now defined and can be seen in the `user_constraints` and `user_cons_columns` views:

```
Enter table name--UPPER CASE ONLY: TSSN2
old    6: where table_name      = '&p_table'
new    6: where table_name      = 'TSSN2'

CONSTRAINT_NAME SEARCH_CONDITION
--------------- ------------------------------------------------------------
A_NN            ASSN IS NOT NULL
A_CHK           (substr(assn,1,1) between '0' and '9' and substr(assn,2,1)
                between '0' and '9' and substr(assn,3,1) between '0' and '9'
                 and substr(assn,4,1) between '0' and '9' and substr(assn,5,
                1) between '0' and '9' and substr(assn,6,1) between '0' and
                '9' and substr(assn,7,1) between '0' and '9' and substr(assn
                ,8,1) between '0' and '9' and substr(assn,9,1) between '0' a
                nd '9' and substr(assn,1,1) between '0' and '9') or assn IN
                ('       M','      N/A')
B_NN            BSSN IS NOT NULL
C_NN            CSSN IS NOT NULL
B_CHK           (substr(bssn,1,1) between '0' and '9' and substr(bssn,2,1)
                between '0' and '9' and substr(bssn,3,1) between '0' and '9'
                 and substr(bssn,4,1) between '0' and '9' and substr(bssn,5,
                1) between '0' and '9' and substr(bssn,6,1) between '0' and
                '9' and substr(bssn,7,1) between '0' and '9' and substr(bssn
                ,8,1) between '0' and '9' and substr(bssn,9,1) between '0' a
                nd '9' and substr(bssn,1,1) between '0' and '9') or bssn IN
                ('       M','      N/A')
C_CHK           (substr(cssn,1,1) between '0' and '9' and substr(cssn,2,1)
                between '0' and '9' and substr(cssn,3,1) between '0' and '9'
                 and substr(cssn,4,1) between '0' and '9' and substr(cssn,5,
                1) between '0' and '9' and substr(cssn,6,1) between '0' and
                '9' and substr(cssn,7,1) between '0' and '9' and substr(cssn
                ,8,1) between '0' and '9' and substr(cssn,9,1) between '0' a
                nd '9' and substr(cssn,1,1) between '0' and '9') or cssn IN
                ('       M','      N/A')

6 rows selected.
```

```
old  11: where a.table_name    = '&p_table' and
new  11: where a.table_name    = 'TSSN2' and

CONSTRAINT_NAME T TABLE_NAME COLUMN_NAM R_CONSTRAI S
--------------- - ---------- ---------- ---------- -
A_NN            C TSSN2      ASSN                  E
A_CHK           C TSSN2      ASSN                  E
B_NN            C TSSN2      BSSN                  E
C_NN            C TSSN2      CSSN                  E
B_CHK           C TSSN2      BSSN                  E
C_CHK           C TSSN2      CSSN                  E

6 rows selected.
```

The output shows that there are six constraints on the table that are listed by constraint name. Type C indicates a check constraint that is used for both check and not null. The status code of E, listed under the heading S, indicates that all constraints are enabled.

> ### DEBUG ALERT
>
> The check constraints are stored in a long column exactly as typed in (with spaces, tabs, and so forth). Therefore, it is preferable to format without extraneous spaces because otherwise the printout from the search_condition field becomes almost unreadable.

Now a number of different insert statements are run against the table. The statements in the first set produce constraint violations. Only the output is printed here because the error message includes the offending statement anyway:

```
insert into tssn2 values ('00000099','303030303','281943822')
                *
ERROR at line 1:
ORA-02290: check constraint (HANS.A_CHK) violated

insert into tssn2 values ('000000999','03030303','281943822')
                *
ERROR at line 1:
ORA-02290: check constraint (HANS.B_CHK) violated

insert into tssn2 values ('000000999','303030303','81943822')
                *
ERROR at line 1:
ORA-02290: check constraint (HANS.C_CHK) violated

insert into tssn2 values (NULL,'303030303','281943822')
                *
ERROR at line 1:
ORA-01400: mandatory (NOT NULL) column is missing or NULL during insert

insert into tssn2 values ('000000999',NULL,'281943822')
                *
ERROR at line 1:
ORA-01400: mandatory (NOT NULL) column is missing or NULL during insert
```

29

KEYS, INDEXES, AND CONSTRAINTS

```
insert into tssn2 values ('000000999','303030303',NULL)
              *
ERROR at line 1:
ORA-01400: mandatory (NOT NULL) column is missing or NULL during insert

insert into tssn2 values ('AAAAA','303030303','81943822')
              *
ERROR at line 1:
ORA-02290: check constraint (HANS.C_CHK) violated

insert into tssn2 values ('A9','303030303','81943822')
              *
ERROR at line 1:
ORA-02290: check constraint (HANS.C_CHK) violated

insert into tssn2 values ('0A9','303030303','81943822')
              *
ERROR at line 1:
ORA-02290: check constraint (HANS.C_CHK) violated

insert into tssn2 values ('0A9','3B3','81943822')
              *
ERROR at line 1:
ORA-02290: check constraint (HANS.C_CHK) violated
```

Valid SSNs and valid missing or not applicable codes may be inserted, however, as shown here:

```
insert into tssn2 values ('000000999','303030303','281943822');
insert into tssn2 values ('        M','      N/A','819435822');
insert into tssn2 values ('000000999','        M','      N/A');
insert into tssn2 values ('000000999','      N/A','819435822');
insert into tssn2 values ('        M','000000999','819435822');
insert into tssn2 values ('        M','      N/A','819435822');

select * from tssn2;
```

This code returns

```
1 row created.
1 row created.
1 row created.
1 row created.
1 row created.
1 row created.

ASSN       BSSN       CSSN
---------  ---------  ---------
000000999  303030303  281943822
        M        N/A  819435822
000000999          M        N/A
000000999        N/A  819435822
        M  000000999  819435822
        M        N/A  819435822
6 rows selected.
```

Enabling and Disabling Constraints

When a constraint is defined, it is enabled by default. Constraints can then be disabled and re-enabled through an `alter table disable constraint` *constraint_name* statement, and can be re-enabled through the `alter table enable constraint` *constraint_name* statement. However, the re-enabling will only work if *all values in the column fulfill the* `check` *condition.*

Listing 29.7, an adaptation of `29squ06.sql`, disables all six constraints, reinserts the "illegal" lines, and then re-enables the constraints.

Listing 29.7. Disabling and re-enabling constraints.

```
--      Filename: 29squ07.sql
--      Purpose: disabling and re-enabling constraints
--
alter table tssn2
    disable constraint a_nn
    disable constraint b_nn
    disable constraint c_nn
    disable constraint a_chk
    disable constraint b_chk
    disable constraint c_chk
;
```

This code returns

```
Table altered.
```

The status in the `user_constraints` view is now set to disabled (D).

CONSTRAINT_NAME	T	TABLE_NAME	COLUMN_NAM	R_CONSTRAI	S
A_NN	C	TSSN2	ASSN		D
A_CHK	C	TSSN2	ASSN		D
B_NN	C	TSSN2	BSSN		D
C_NN	C	TSSN2	CSSN		D
B_CHK	C	TSSN2	BSSN		D
C_CHK	C	TSSN2	CSSN		D

Now all the statements that were previously illegal will work, as shown here:

```
insert into tssn2 values ('00000099','303030303','281943822');
insert into tssn2 values ('000000999','03030303','281943822');
insert into tssn2 values ('000000999','303030303','81943822');
insert into tssn2 values (NULL,'303030303','281943822');
insert into tssn2 values ('000000999',NULL,'281943822');
insert into tssn2 values ('000000999','303030303',NULL);
insert into tssn2 values ('AAAAA','303030303','81943822');
insert into tssn2 values ('A9','303030303','81943822');
insert into tssn2 values ('0A9','303030303','81943822');
insert into tssn2 values ('0A9','3B3','81943822');
insert into tssn2 values ('000000999','303030303','281943822');
insert into tssn2 values ('      M','      N/A','819435822');
insert into tssn2 values ('000000999','      M','      N/A');
insert into tssn2 values ('000000999','      N/A','819435822');
insert into tssn2 values ('      M','000000999','819435822');
insert into tssn2 values ('      M','      N/A','819435822');

select * from tssn2;
```

The following code is returned:

```
1 row created.
...
...

ASSN      BSSN       CSSN
--------- ---------- ---------
000000999 03030303   281943822
000000999 303030303  81943822
          303030303  281943822
000000999            281943822
000000999 303030303
AAAAA     303030303  81943822
A9        303030303  81943822
0A9       303030303  81943822
0A9       3B3        81943822
000000999 303030303  281943822
        M       N/A  819435822
000000999         M       N/A
000000999       N/A  819435822
        M 000000999  819435822
        M       N/A  819435822
000000999 303030303  281943822
        M       N/A  819435822
000000999         M       N/A
000000999       N/A  819435822
        M 000000999  819435822
        M       N/A  819435822
```

The next statements are intended to re-enable the constraints:

```
alter table tssn2
    enable constraint a_nn
    enable constraint b_nn
    enable constraint c_nn
    enable constraint a_chk
    enable constraint b_chk
    enable constraint c_chk
;
```

However, this does not work because of the values in the table that violate these constraints:

```
alter table tssn2
*
ERROR at line 1:
ORA-02293: cannot enable (HANS.C_CHK) - check constraint violated
```

Wiping out the table and restocking with the first six lines creates a situation where the constraints can be re-enabled:

```
delete from tssn2;
insert into tssn2 values ('000000999','303030303','281943822');
insert into tssn2 values ('        M','      N/A','819435822');
insert into tssn2 values ('000000999','        M','      N/A');
insert into tssn2 values ('000000999','      N/A','819435822');
insert into tssn2 values ('        M','000000999','819435822');
insert into tssn2 values ('        M','      N/A','819435822');
select * from tssn2;
```

```
alter table tssn2
    enable constraint a_nn
    enable constraint b_nn
    enable constraint c_nn
    enable constraint a_chk
    enable constraint b_chk
    enable constraint c_chk
;
```

This code returns

```
22 rows deleted.

1 row created.

1 row created.

1 row created.

1 row created.

1 row created.

ASSN       BSSN       CSSN
---------  ---------  ---------
000000999  303030303  281943822
        M        N/A  819435822
000000999          M        N/A
000000999        N/A  819435822
        M  000000999  819435822
        M        N/A  819435822

6 rows selected.

Table altered.
```

REAL-WORLD EXPERIENCES

I once worked for a university where all databases were run off a mainframe in a statewide data center. That approach worked fine most of the time, except for the primary registration period that was done during the same two days statewide. This overloaded the computer pretty badly. The data center simply disabled error checking during registration. Because some 80% of all registration records were created during these few days, the result was that error checking was off during the four days of the year when it was needed most and on the rest of the year when it was really not that useful. However, because the people who entered the data were quite competent, there were few errors.

Dynamic Constraints on Columns

The check and not null constraints are statically defined within a row. Dynamic constraints, on the other hand, can be based on

- An expression that uses constants and the values in the row
- Data stored in other tables (foreign key on other table)
- All other values in a column(s) of the table to be inserted or updated (unique, primary, and recursive keys)

Ensuring Unique Key Values: unique

The original relational theory developed by Dr. Codd required that all rows in a table be unique, in which case the rows in a table are sets in a mathematical sense. SQL proper has relaxed that requirement, but provides the option of unique and primary keys that ensure that all values in a column, or a set of columns, be unique. Listing 29.8 illustrates unique constraints.

Listing 29.8. unique constraints.

```
--        Filename: 29squ08.sql
--          Purpose: unique constraints
--
drop table tssn2;

CREATE TABLE tssn2 (
 assn      CHAR(9)
    DEFAULT '.'
    constraint a_nn NOT NULL,
    constraint a_uq unique(assn),
    constraint a_chk CHECK (
(substr(assn,1,1) between '0' and '9' and
substr(assn,2,1) between '0' and '9' and
substr(assn,3,1) between '0' and '9' and
substr(assn,4,1) between '0' and '9' and
substr(assn,5,1) between '0' and '9' and
substr(assn,6,1) between '0' and '9' and
substr(assn,7,1) between '0' and '9' and
substr(assn,8,1) between '0' and '9' and
substr(assn,9,1) between '0' and '9' and
substr(assn,1,1) between '0' and '9') or
assn IN ('         M','         N/A')),
 bssn      CHAR(9)
    DEFAULT '.',
 cssn      CHAR(9)
    default '.');
alter table tssn2 add (
    constraint b_uq unique (bssn),
    constraint c_uq unique (cssn))
;
```

In addition to some not null and check constraints, three unique constraints are defined, one for each column:

```
SQL> @29squ03a
Enter table name--UPPER CASE ONLY: TSSN2
old  11: where a.table_name    = '&p_table' and
new  11: where a.table_name    = 'TSSN2' and

CONSTRAINT_NAME T TABLE_NAME COLUMN_NAME      R_CONSTRAI STATUS
--------------- - ---------- ---------------  ---------- --------
A_NN            C TSSN2      ASSN                        ENABLED
A_UQ            U            ASSN                        ENABLED
A_CHK           C            ASSN                        ENABLED
B_UQ            U            BSSN                        ENABLED
C_UQ            U            CSSN                        ENABLED
```

The unique constraints are marked with the type U.

The next part of the example inserts rows that are not in violation of the constraint:

```
insert into tssn2 values ('000000999','303030303','281943822');
insert into tssn2 values ('      M','      N/A','819435822');
insert into tssn2 values ('000880999','      M','      N/A');
insert into tssn2 values ('855394888','000000999','819453322');
```

This code returns

```
1 row created.
1 row created.
1 row created.
1 row created.
```

The next insert statements violate unique constraints. Only the SQL output that contains the offending statements is shown:

```
insert into tssn2 values ('000330999','303030303','281943822')
            *
ERROR at line 1:
ORA-00001: unique constraint (HANS.B_UQ) violated

insert into tssn2 values ('      M','      N/A','819435822')
*
ERROR at line 1:
ORA-00001: unique constraint (HANS.A_UQ) violated

insert into tssn2 values ('303030303','855394888','819435822')
               *
ERROR at line 1:
ORA-00001: unique constraint (HANS.C_UQ) violated
```

unique and check Constraints with Nulls

Unique keys can be combined with null columns. In that case, to be inserted a value must be unique or NULL. In other words, it is possible to insert an unlimited number of nulls, but all non-null values must be unique.

If there is also a check constraint on the column, it is possible to insert an unlimited number of nulls. All non-null values must be fulfilling the check condition and must be unique.

Listing 29.9 illustrates this. The first column has the same SSN check constraint that you had in the previous examples and has a unique constraint. The second column has a unique constraint only.

Listing 29.9. unique constraints on null columns.

```
--        Filename: 29squ09.sql
--         Purpose: unique constraints on null columns
--
drop table tssn2;

CREATE TABLE tssn2 (
    assn       CHAR(9),
    constraint a_uq unique(assn),
    constraint a_chk CHECK (
(substr(assn,1,1) between '0' and '9' and
substr(assn,2,1) between '0' and '9' and
substr(assn,3,1) between '0' and '9' and
substr(assn,4,1) between '0' and '9' and
substr(assn,5,1) between '0' and '9' and
substr(assn,6,1) between '0' and '9' and
substr(assn,7,1) between '0' and '9' and
substr(assn,8,1) between '0' and '9' and
substr(assn,9,1) between '0' and '9' and
substr(assn,1,1) between '0' and '9') or
assn IN ('        M','        N/A')),
    bssn       CHAR(9),
    constraint b_uq unique (bssn))
;
```

When running the script 29squ03a.sql, three constraints on the tssn2 table are retrieved:

```
SQL> @29squ03a
Enter table name--UPPER CASE ONLY: TSSN2
old  11: where a.table_name      = '&p_table' and
new  11: where a.table_name      = 'TSSN2' and

CONSTRAINT_NAME T TABLE_NAME COLUMN_NAME      R_CONSTRAI STATUS
--------------- - ---------- ---------------  ---------- -------
A_UQ            U TSSN2      ASSN                        ENABLED
A_CHK           C            ASSN                        ENABLED
B_UQ            U            BSSN                        ENABLED
```

The next six rows can be inserted

```
insert into tssn2 values ('111111111','111111111');
insert into tssn2 values (NULL         , NULL      );
insert into tssn2 values (NULL         , NULL      );
insert into tssn2 values (NULL         , NULL      );
insert into tssn2 values (NULL         , NULL      );
insert into tssn2 values ('333333333','333333333');
```

but the next three violate one constraint each:

```
insert into tssn2 values ('Qeiiiido2','222222222')
                *
ERROR at line 1:
ORA-02290: check constraint (HANS.A_CHK) violated

insert into tssn2 values ('333333333','444444444')
                *
ERROR at line 1:
ORA-00001: unique constraint (HANS.A_UQ) violated

insert into tssn2 values ('444444444','333333333')
                *
ERROR at line 1:
ORA-00001: unique constraint (HANS.B_UQ) violated
```

TIP

Unless you have a really good reason, avoid the use of nulls as much as possible.

Primary Keys

Primary keys are special cases where a `unique` and `not null` constraint are combined. That combination of constraints has been included in previous examples such as `29squ08.sql`. Primary keys are special in several ways:

- There must be only one primary key per table.
- The primary key of a table is referenced by default by foreign keys.
- A row is identified by its primary key, although it may be accessed in different ways as well.

Listing 29.10 re-creates `tssn2` with a primary key defined on `assn`.

Listing 29.10. Primary keys.

```
--        Filename: 29squ10.sql
--         Purpose: primary keys
--
drop table tssn2;

CREATE TABLE tssn2 (
    assn        CHAR(9),
    constraint a_pk primary key (assn),
    constraint a_chk CHECK (
(substr(assn,1,1) between '0' and '9' and
substr(assn,2,1) between '0' and '9' and
substr(assn,3,1) between '0' and '9' and
substr(assn,4,1) between '0' and '9' and
substr(assn,5,1) between '0' and '9' and
```

continues

Listing 29.10. continued

```
substr(assn,6,1) between '0' and '9' and
substr(assn,7,1) between '0' and '9' and
substr(assn,8,1) between '0' and '9' and
substr(assn,9,1) between '0' and '9' and
substr(assn,1,1) between '0' and '9') or
assn IN ('        M','        N/A')),
    bssn       CHAR(9),
    constraint b_uq unique (bssn))
;
```

The constraints are now listed as follows:

```
SQL> @29squ03a
Enter table name--UPPER CASE ONLY: TSSN2
old   11: where a.table_name       = '&p_table' and
new   11: where a.table_name       = 'TSSN2' and

CONSTRAINT_NAME T TABLE_NAME COLUMN_NAME     R_CONSTRAI STATUS
--------------- - ---------- --------------- ---------- --------
A_PK            P TSSN2      ASSN                       ENABLED
A_CHK           C            ASSN                       ENABLED
B_UQ            U            BSSN                       ENABLED
```

The next four rows can be inserted:

```
insert into tssn2 values ('111111111','111111111');
insert into tssn2 values ('222222222', NULL     );
insert into tssn2 values ('555555555', NULL     );
insert into tssn2 values ('333333333','333333333');
```

The next five, however, violate constraints:

```
insert into tssn2 values (NULL        , NULL        )
                          *
ERROR at line 1:
ORA-01400: mandatory (NOT NULL) column is missing or NULL during insert

insert into tssn2 values (NULL        ,'666666666')
                          *
ERROR at line 1:
ORA-01400: mandatory (NOT NULL) column is missing or NULL during insert

insert into tssn2 values ('Qeiiiido2','222222222')
                          *
ERROR at line 1:
ORA-02290: check constraint (HANS.A_CHK) violated

insert into tssn2 values ('333333333','444444444')
                                       *
ERROR at line 1:
ORA-00001: unique constraint (HANS.A_PK) violated

insert into tssn2 values ('444444444','333333333')
                                       *
ERROR at line 1:
ORA-00001: unique constraint (HANS.B_UQ) violated
```

Unique and Primary Compound Keys

The unique and primary keys discussed so far have been all defined on one key only. It is also possible to define primary or unique keys that consist of more than one column. In this case, the entire set of values in the columns that make up the key has to be unique to fulfill the condition.

There are a few typical purposes to use that approach:

- In a master-detail relationship, it may be desirable to have a compound primary key on the detail table that consists of the foreign key referencing the primary key of the master table and a unique value within the parent.

- In a complex coding scheme such as Vehicle Identification Number (VIN), all elements of the number together give a unique value. The individual elements include additional information such as manufacturer, country of origin, and so on.

- Compound indexes, which need not be unique (see the section "Facilitating the Quick Retrieval of Rows Through Indexes" later in this chapter), provide some options for performance tuning.

The specification of a compound key is identical to that of unique or primary key constraints, except that a column comma list is put between the parentheses. Up to 16 columns may be contained in the comma list.

Nulls pose a separate issue with compound keys. Because, by design, primary keys must not contain null values, no special problem arises. unique constraints defined with not null behave the same. A compound unique constraint that allows nulls accepts several combinations of values:

- Any number rows where all compound values are nulls

- One row of any combination of a null and a valid value

Listing 29.11 creates a compound primary key and two compound unique constraints—one that allows nulls and one that does not.

Listing 29.11. Compound primary and unique keys.

```
--      Filename: 29squ11.sql
--          Purpose: compound primary and unique keys
--
drop table zip1;

CREATE TABLE zip1 (
    hzip        CHAR(5),
    hzext       char(4),
    wzip        char(5),
    wzext       char(4),
    szip        char(5) constraint wz_n not null,
    szext       char(4) constraint we_n not null,
    constraint h_p primary key (hzip, hzext),
    constraint w_u unique      (wzip, wzext),
    constraint s_u unique      (szip, szext))
;
```

The constraints are listed as follows:

```
SQL> @29squ03a
Enter table name--UPPER CASE ONLY: ZIP1
old  11: where a.table_name      = '&p_table' and
new  11: where a.table_name      = 'ZIP1' and

CONSTRAINT_NAME T TABLE_NAME COLUMN_NAME      R_CONSTRAI STATUS
--------------- - ---------- ---------------  ---------- --------
WZ_N            C ZIP1       SZIP                        ENABLED
WE_N            C            SZEXT                       ENABLED
H_P             P            HZIP                        ENABLED
H_P             P            HZEXT                       ENABLED
W_U             U            WZIP                        ENABLED
W_U             U            WZEXT                       ENABLED
S_U             U            SZIP                        ENABLED
S_U             U            SZEXT                       ENABLED
```

The first two constraints listed are single column. The other three are listed in two lines; each compound is two columns each.

The following `insert` statements create one row each. Please note the third and fourth rows, which illustrate that more than one null key value may be inserted. The last two lines insert nulls in the fourth column, which works because the other key column has different values in these cases:

```
insert into zip1 values ('11111','1111','11111','1111','11111','1111');
insert into zip1 values ('22222','2222','11111','2222','22222','2222');
insert into zip1 values ('44444','2222', NULL , NULL ,'44444','3333');
insert into zip1 values ('44444','3333', NULL , NULL ,'55555','3333');
insert into zip1 values ('33333','1111','33333', NULL ,'22222','3333');
insert into zip1 values ('33333','5555','11111', NULL ,'22222','5555');
```

Finally, another five rows violate the constraints and result in errors:

```
insert into zip1 values ('33333','1111','11111', NULL ,'22222','3333')
                   *
ERROR at line 1:
ORA-00001: unique constraint (HANS.H_P) violated
```

The primary key violation is picked up, yet the combination of '11111' and NULL exists already, and would create an error as well. The combination of '33333' and NULL which is attempted in the next statement exists already and returns an error:

```
insert into zip1 values ('44444','1111','33333', NULL ,'33333','3333')
                   *
ERROR at line 1:
ORA-00001: unique constraint (HANS.W_U) violated
```

The primary key must not be null, a violation that the following statement creates:

```
insert into zip1 values ( NULL  , NULL ,'44444','2222','66666','3333')
                   *
ERROR at line 1:
ORA-01400: mandatory (NOT NULL) column is missing or NULL during insert
```

The last two `insert` statements violate the `not null` constraints on `szip` and `szext`:

```
insert into zip1 values ('22222','1111','11111','2222', NULL  ,'2222')
                    *
ERROR at line 1:
ORA-01400: mandatory (NOT NULL) column is missing or NULL during insert
insert into zip1 values ('33333','3333','33333','3333','22222', NULL )
                    *
ERROR at line 1:
ORA-01400: mandatory (NOT NULL) column is missing or NULL during insert
```

Determining Suitable Key Values

As far as the database is concerned, key values must be unique within their own right or as a set in the case of compound keys. Three methods are generally used:

- Use generated unique number sequences. This is done by inserting a *sequence_name.nextval* for the value.
- Select a key value through a subquery.
- Select a sequence value for a key within a parent, also through a subquery.

Beyond that, there are keying systems that provide more information or intuitive meaning. Celko describes some of those.

Using Generated Unique Numbers or Sequences

Chapter 4, "Operator Conversions and Value Decoding," describes in great detail selecting sequence numbers using `nextval` and `currval`. In Oracle, a sequence is an object that returns a new number whenever accessed with *sequence_name.nextval*. If the row is inserted every time that *sequence_name.nextval* is accessed, key values will be distributed as a true sequence in equal steps. If, on the other hand, the sequence is accessed without an insert or a row is deleted, some numbers will be missing. Oracle is getting some heat for that fact. Perhaps, calling the feature *unique number generator* would be clearer.

The biggest advantage of using sequences is speed because no table needs to be accessed when generating them.

The most important options of the `create sequence` command are summarized in Table 29.1.

ORACLE vs SQL

29

KEYS, INDEXES, AND CONSTRAINTS

Table 29.1. Sequence generation options.

Option	Purpose
`increment by`	Sets the increment between adjacent values.
`start with`	Sets the start number of the first cycle.
`minvalue`	Sets the minimum value that the sequence can generate—is used on the first cycle if no `start with` value is listed and at the beginning of all further cycles.

continues

Table 29.1. continued

Option	Purpose
maxvalue	Maximum value the sequence can generate after which it recycles or stops generating.
nocycle	Once all sequence values are used up, the sequence cannot be reset back to the minimum value.
cycle	When the maximum value is reached, the sequence is reset back to the minimum value and a new cycle of generation begins.
cache	Number of sequence values cached in memory.
order	The order of sequence is guaranteed to be in the order of request. Only used for parallel server.
noorder	In a parallel server, order of sequence is not guaranteed to be in the order of request.

Listing 29.12 (re-)creates five sequences:

- step1 starts with 100 and increments by 1.
- step3 starts with 3 and increments by 3.
- default1 has no options specified; it starts with 1 and increments by 1.
- cycle1 starts with 9 and has a maximum value of 12, after which it resets to 3. This sequence increments by 3.
- sneg starts with -1 and increments by -1.

Listing 29.12. Creating a sequence and inserting sequence values.

```
--       Filename: 29squ12.sql
--        Purpose: creating a sequence and inserting sequence values
--
drop sequence step1;

CREATE SEQUENCE step1
   INCREMENT BY 1
    START WITH 100
    MINVALUE 1
    MAXVALUE 99999
;

drop sequence step3;

CREATE SEQUENCE step3
    INCREMENT BY 3
    MINVALUE 3
    MAXVALUE 99999
    CACHE 5
```

```
;

drop sequence default1;

CREATE SEQUENCE default1
;

drop sequence cycle1;

CREATE SEQUENCE cycle1
    INCREMENT BY 3
    START WITH 9
    MINVALUE 3
    MAXVALUE 12
    CYCLE
    CACHE 2
;

drop sequence sneg;

CREATE SEQUENCE sneg
 INCREMENT BY -1
;

drop table seq1;

CREATE TABLE seq1 (
    sprimkey    number(5),
    suniqkey    number(5),
    sdefault    number(5),
    scycle      number(5),
    snegative   number(5))
;

insert into seq1 values (step1.nextval,
    step3.nextval, default1.nextval, cycle1.nextval, sneg.nextval);
insert into seq1 values (step1.nextval,
    step3.nextval, default1.nextval, cycle1.nextval, sneg.nextval);
insert into seq1 values (step1.nextval,
    step3.nextval, default1.nextval, cycle1.nextval, sneg.nextval);
insert into seq1 values (step1.nextval,
    step3.nextval, default1.nextval, cycle1.nextval, sneg.nextval);
insert into seq1 values (step1.nextval,
    step3.nextval, default1.nextval, cycle1.nextval, sneg.nextval);
insert into seq1 values (step1.nextval,
    step3.nextval, default1.nextval, cycle1.nextval, sneg.nextval);

commit;

select * from seq1;
```

The following code is returned:

```
Sequence dropped.
Sequence created.
Sequence dropped.
Sequence created.
```

```
Sequence dropped.
Sequence created.
Sequence dropped.
Sequence created.
Sequence dropped.
Sequence created.

Table dropped.
Table created.

1 row created.
1 row created.
1 row created.
1 row created.
1 row created.
1 row created.

Commit complete.
```

SPRIMKEY	SUNIQKEY	SDEFAULT	SCYCLE	SNEGATIVE
100	3	1	9	-1
101	6	2	12	-2
102	9	3	3	-3
103	12	4	6	-4
104	15	5	9	-5
105	18	6	12	-6

```
6 rows selected.
```

Key Value by Subquery

There are situations where gaps in a sequence are simply not acceptable. Gaps in check numbers, which would make most accountants a bit nervous, are a typical example.

In such a situation, a key value can be generated by incrementing from the maximum or minimum value of a column.

The example in Listing 29.13 re-creates the information in example `29squ12.sql` using this approach.

Listing 29.13. Inserting sequence values.

```
--        Filename: 29squ13.sql
--        Purpose: inserting sequence values
--
drop table seq1;

CREATE TABLE seq1 (
    sprimkey    number(5),
    suniqkey    number(5),
    sdefault    number(5),
    scycle      number(5),
    snegative   number(5))
```

```
;

insert into seq1 values (100,3,1,9,-1);

insert into seq1 select max(sprimkey) + 1, max(suniqkey) + 3,
   max(sdefault) + 1, mod(max(scycle),12) + 3, min(snegative) - 1 from seq1;

insert into seq1 select max(sprimkey) + 1, max(suniqkey) + 3,
   max(sdefault) + 1, mod(max(scycle),12) + 3, min(snegative) - 1 from seq1;

commit;

insert into seq1 select max(sprimkey) + 1, max(suniqkey) + 3,
   max(sdefault) + 1, mod(max(scycle),12) + 3, min(snegative) - 1 from seq1;

commit;

insert into seq1 select max(sprimkey) + 1, max(suniqkey) + 3,
   max(sdefault) + 1, mod(max(scycle),12) + 3, min(snegative) - 1 from seq1;

commit;

select * from seq1;
```

The following code is returned:

```
Table dropped.
Table created.

1 row created.
1 row created.
1 row created.

Commit complete.

1 row created.

Commit complete.

1 row created.

Commit complete.

SPRIMKEY  SUNIQKEY  SDEFAULT    SCYCLE SNEGATIVE
--------- --------- --------- --------- ---------
      100         3         1         9        -1
      101         6         2        12        -2
      102         9         3         3        -3
      103        12         4         3        -4
      104        15         5         3        -5
```

Note the values in scycle. Because SQL works on pseudosets, a recycling sequence cannot be created with a max statement on the column in question. It can be generated using another column value, but that would require maintaining a separate column just for that purpose.

29

KEYS, INDEXES, AND CONSTRAINTS

Sequence in Parent

The last variant of the sequence topic is related to compound keys. If, in a master-detail relationship, there is a compound primary key on the detail table that consists of the foreign key referencing the primary key of the master table and a unique value within the parent, it is necessary to create the latter through a subquery.

Listing 29.14 creates a compound primary key that is then stocked with a compound key. Note the construct nvl(max(seqinpar),0) + 1. The null value has to be used because if there is no row with a certain parent key, the max function returns NULL. The construct, therefore, seeds the first sequence in parent value.

Listing 29.14. Generating sequences within parents.

```
--        Filename: 29squ14.sql
--         Purpose: generating sequences within parents
--
drop table seqinpar;

CREATE TABLE seqinpar (
    parkey        number(5),
    seqinpar      number(4),
    constraint  s_p primary key (parkey, seqinpar))
;

insert into seqinpar select
    1,
    nvl(max(seqinpar),0) + 1  from seqinpar where parkey = 1;

insert into seqinpar select
    2,
    nvl(max(seqinpar),0) + 1  from seqinpar where parkey = 2;

insert into seqinpar select
    3,
    nvl(max(seqinpar),0) + 1  from seqinpar where parkey = 3;

insert into seqinpar select
    4,
    nvl(max(seqinpar),0) + 1  from seqinpar where parkey = 4;

insert into seqinpar select
    5,
    nvl(max(seqinpar),0) + 1  from seqinpar where parkey = 5;
```

These five insert statements are run two more times:

```
select * from seqinpar
order by 1, 2
;
```

This code returns

```
    PARKEY  SEQINPAR
 ---------  --------
         1         1
         1         2
         1         3
         2         1
         2         2
         2         3
         3         1
         3         2
         3         3
         4         1
         4         2
         4         3
         5         1
         5         2
         5         3
```

15 rows selected.

Dynamic Constraints Between Tables—Foreign Keys

Dynamic constraints between tables are one of the most important features that define relational databases and ensure data integrity. In all the examples that joined tables in the previous chapters, join conditions indicated the columns in the parent and the child table that had to be the same so that particular rows of each table would be linked with the appropriate rows of the other table. The sample tables just happened to contain data that matched up properly, but the RDBMS did nothing to enforce this fact or enforce integrity, as this action is called in relational lingo.

Why does relational integrity matter?

It matters in two primary ways:

■ Orphaned rows in child tables cannot be made sense of using data within the database. That may not be such a big deal if the master table is only a lookup to the child and the column is not that important anyway. It is a very big deal in a true parent-child relationship between base tables. Imagine three levels of tables: a customer table is referenced by an order table that is in turn referenced by an order-item table. If the rows in the order table disappear, it is no longer possible to trace the orphaned order items back to the customer. The exception to this is if a compound foreign key in the order-item table includes the customer number. Even then, it is no longer possible to trace the order to which the items belong. It may be possible to piece that information back together, but it's a pain. Integrity constraints prevent this case by either making it impossible to delete a parent row where dependent child rows exist, or by deleting the child records with the deletion of the parent record (on `delete cascade` option).

29

KEYS, INDEXES, AND CONSTRAINTS

■ If integrity constraints are not enforced, the accuracy of a report that involves one or more joins cannot be guaranteed. Unless an outer join is used, orphaned detail rows are not included in the set of selected rows, which, in the case of aggregations, will understate results. If there are redundant rows in the parent table, redundant joined rows will be included in the results as well, which will result in overstated aggregates. With integrity constraints, on the other hand, the issue simply disappears because they ensure that the values in the referenced column are unique and that there are no orphaned detail rows.

The mechanism to enforce integrity is the combination of a primary or unique key on the parent table and a foreign key that references that primary or unique table on the child table. Parent and child tables may be identical, in which case a column or set thereof references a different column or set thereof, as could be done in some of the lawyer tables between the `bossid` and `id` columns.

Foreign Keys Between Tables

The *standard master-detail arrangement* joins the primary key column of the parent table to the foreign key column of the child table. These examples will use `lawyer9`, a variation of `lawyer8` that includes an office code in addition to the `officename` and `office2` enhanced with a primary key on `ID` and a unique key on the office code.

CAUTION

In a strictly normalized design, the columns office and office code together would not be permitted because these are redundant; if you know the office code, you know the office, and vice versa.

At times a denormalized design as the one here is used anyway. Joining tables creates a performance overhead, which can be avoided if columns of the parent table which are frequently accessed together with columns of the detail table are duplicated in the detail table. This denormalization, however, requires additional processing on inserts and updates. Therefore denormalization is a trade-off between performance hits on select versus performance hits on creation of data.

NOTE

Note the `cascade constraints` option after the `drop table` command. This option instructs the RDBMS to drop all rows in that table *and* all rows in the dependent child table that reference rows in this table. If this option is not used and there are dependent child rows, the following error will result:

```
drop table office2
          *
ERROR at line 1:
ORA-02266: unique/primary keys in table referenced by enabled foreign keys
```

Listing 29.15 re-creates `lawyer2` with a primary key on `id` and a unique key on `office`, and inserts some rows.

Listing 29.15. Foreign key referencing master table.

```
--        Filename: 29squ15.sql
--        Purpose: foreign key referencing master table
--
drop table office2 cascade constraints;

create table office2 (
   ID        number(2),
   Office    varchar2(15),
   bossid    number(2),
   constraint of2_p primary key (id),
   constraint of2_u unique (office))
;

insert into office2 values (1, 'Boston'     , 1);
insert into office2 values (2, 'Los Angeles', 7);
insert into office2 values (3, 'New York'   , 9);
insert into office2 values (4, 'Houston'    ,17);
insert into office2 values (5, 'Seattle'    , 5);
insert into office2 values (6, NULL         , 7);
insert into office2 values (7, NULL         , 7);
insert into office2 values (8, NULL         , 7);

commit;
```

Next, the `lawyer9` table that references `office2` is created. It is then loaded by selecting all rows from a join of `lawyer2` and `office2`. Then a few additional rows are inserted:

```
drop table lawyer9;

create table lawyer9 (
   id        number(2) not null,
   Name      varchar2(15),
   offid     number(2),
   Office    varchar2(15),
   boss      number(2),
   bhrs      number(4),
   bgross    number(7),
   constraint l9_p primary key (id),
   constraint l9_o2_f1 foreign key (offid)
         references office2,
   constraint l9_o2_f2 foreign key (office)
         references office2 (office))
;

insert into lawyer9
select
   l.id,
   l.name,
   o.id,
   l.office,
```

29

KEYS, INDEXES, AND CONSTRAINTS

```
    l.boss,
    l.bhrs,
    l.bgross
from lawyer2 l, office2 o
where l.office = o.office
;

insert into lawyer9 values(
21, 'Holocek',NULL,NULL,NULL,1400,84566);

insert into lawyer9 values(
22, 'Holocek',NULL,NULL,NULL,1400,84566);

insert into lawyer9 values(
23, 'Holocek',NULL,NULL,NULL,1400,84566);

insert into lawyer9 values(
24, 'Holocek',NULL,NULL,NULL,1400,84566);

commit;
```

The example returns the typical `table dropped`, `table created`, `row inserted`, and `commit complete` responses. The `lawyer9` table is now ready for use in the following examples.

Inserting Rows into a Table with Foreign Keys

Only those rows whose foreign key values are found in the corresponding column of the parent table, or where these values are null (provided the column is not defined as `not null`), as was the case in the last four rows inserted in Chapter 28, may be inserted into a table. Listing 29.16 attempts to insert four rows into `lawyer9`.

Listing 29.16. Inserting with foreign keys enabled.

```
--        Filename: 29squ16.sql
--        Purpose: inserting with foreign keys enabled
--
insert into lawyer9 values(
25, 'Alchuck',9,NULL,NULL,1850,232266);

insert into lawyer9 values(
25, 'Alchuck',NULL,'Las Vegas',NULL,1850,232266);

insert into lawyer9 values(
25, 'Alchuck',3,'New York',NULL,1850,232266);
```

The first two inserts will not work because 9 is not represented in the `ID` columns of `office2`, and `'Las Vegas'` is not in the `office` column of that table. The error messages include the key violated. The third statement works. The statements return the following:

```
ERROR at line 1:
ORA-02291: integrity constraint (HANS.L9_O2_F1) violated
          - parent key not found
insert into lawyer9 values(
        *
```

```
ERROR at line 1:
ORA-02291: integrity constraint (HANS.L9_02_F2) violated
            - parent key not found
1 row created.
```

The next statement, which works just as well, inserts a row it should not; the `office` with the id value 3 is combined with Boston, which should have the value 1. These are obviously data that should be corrected, but without some trigger in the database, that will not happen. This example illustrates one of the pitfalls of redundant data:

```
insert into lawyer9 values(
29, 'Gregory',3,'Boston',NULL,2136,315728);

commit;
```

Deleting Rows of a Referenced Table

A row in a parent table that has child rows cannot be attached unless all rows are removed through `drop table tablename` cascade constraints, as has been done in example `29squ15.sql`, or if the foreign key constraint is defined as on `cascade delete`. Listing 29.17 begins with attempting to delete a parent row with attached children.

Listing 29.17. Deleting rows of the parent table.

```
--       Filename: 29squ17.sql
--       Purpose: deleting rows of the parent table
--
@29squ15
```

The `29squ15.sql` script which has been listed previously is run first in order to re-create the `office2` and `lawyer9` tables. The next statement attempts to delete the `office2` record with the id value 2 which is not possible because some `lawyer9` records reference this `office2` record:

```
delete from office2 where id = 2;
```

The following error is returned:

```
delete from office2 where id = 2
                 *
ERROR at line 1:
ORA-02292: integrity constraint (HANS.L9_02_F2) violated - child record found
```

First the constraint is dropped, and then it is re-created with the on `delete cascade` option, as shown here:

```
alter table lawyer9
   drop constraint l9_o2_f1;

alter table lawyer9 add (
   constraint l9_o2_f1 foreign key (offid)
           references office2 on delete cascade);
```

The following code is returned:

```
Table altered.

Table altered.
```

The constraints are now defined as follows:

```
SQL> @29squ03b
Enter table name--UPPER CASE ONLY: LAWYER9
old  12: where a.table_name    = '&p_table' and
new  12: where a.table_name    = 'LAWYER9' and

CONSTRAINT_NAME  T TABLE_NAME COLUMN_NAME      R_CONSTRAI DR STATUS
---------------- - ---------- --------------- ---------- -- -------
SYS_C009003      C LAWYER9    ID                             ENABLED
L9_P             P            ID                             ENABLED
L9_O2_F1         R            OFFID           OF2_P      CA ENABLED
L9_O2_F2         R            OFFICE          OF2_U      NO ENABLED
```

The DR column stands for delete rule; it is a CA, short for cascade, or a NO for no action. Now it is possible to delete parent rows with children, which is demonstrated in the next few statements. The first statement returns the row count of the lawyer9 table. Then one record in office2 is deleted. Another count of lawyer9 rows shows that several rows in that table have been deleted as well. Finally everything is rolled back:

```
select count(1) from lawyer9;

delete from office2 where id = 2;

select * from lawyer9 where offid = 2;

select count(1) from lawyer9;

rollback;
```

This output is returned:

```
COUNT(1)
---------
       24

1 row deleted.

no rows selected

 COUNT(1)
---------
       17

Rollback complete.
```

Therefore, not only the one row in the parent table (office2) has been deleted, but also the seven child rows in the child table (lawyer9).

Joins Through Foreign Keys

The default situation in SQL is that a statement is parsed and the RDBMS creates an execution plan that is more or less optimized. Therefore, the statements necessary to join tables are identical whether or not a foreign key is defined. The foreign/primary key set, as defined here, prevents redundant rows in the master table. However, with or without a key, a join on null values still does not work.

Listing 29.18 shows this by calculating a breakout of bhrs and bgross by office. This is done first by using only lawyer9, then by means of a join of lawyer9 and office2. In the latter two cases, the rows in lawyer2, where either offid or office are null, are not included in the analysis.

Listing 29.18. Retrieval of data foreign keys joins.

```
--        Filename: 29squ18.sql
--         Purpose: retrieval of data foreign keys joins
--
select
office,
sum(bhrs),
sum (bgross)
from
lawyer9
group by office
;

elect
   o.office,
   sum(l.bhrs),
   sum(l.bgross)
from
lawyer9 l, office2 o
where l.offid = o.id
group by o.office
;
```

This code returns

```
OFFICE          SUM(BHRS) SUM(BGROSS)
--------------- --------- -----------
Boston              13391     1438175
Houston              4138      459889
Los Angeles         21774     3412223
New York            10969     2210812
                     5600      338264
```

The next two statements are based on joins:

```
select
   o.office,
   sum(l.bhrs),
   sum(l.bgross)from
```

```
lawyer9 l, office2 o
where l.office = o.office
group by o.office
;
```

The following code returns twice:

```
OFFICE          SUM(L.BHRS)  SUM(L.BGROSS)
--------------  -----------  -------------
Boston              13391          1438175
Houston              4138           459889
Los Angeles         21774          3412223
New York            10969          2210812
```

The `lawyer9` records that have nulls in `offid` in the first case or `office` in the second, which happen to be the same, are not included.

Therefore, to ensure accurate reports of data based on joined tables, the following conditions *must* be met:

- The referenced column(s) in the parent table (which may be a lookup table) must have a `unique` constraint, preferably with a `not null` constraint as well. This should, but need not, be the primary key. Even if it is defined as a null column, a null there does not make sense—see the next point.

- The child table must have a foreign key constraint.

- The foreign key column(s) of the child table must be defined as `not null`.

- If key values are redundant (which they normally aren't), appropriate triggers need to be defined to make sure that the redundant codes are in sync with the corresponding codes in the parent table.

If these constraints are in place, it is impossible to insert rows that create these integrity problems.

Recursive Foreign Keys

Much less frequent than a standard master-detail arrangement is a join of a column to the primary key column or a unique key column of the same table. Retrievals of data from such a table are shown in Chapter 22, "Trees and Hierarchical Subqueries."

Putting recursive foreign key constraints on a table has essentially the same benefits that a foreign key constraint between tables has—it ensures integrity.

There are two issues that must be considered with recursive keys:

- The order of row insertion matters. A referenced row in the parent table has to be loaded before a row in the child table that references it can be loaded. That may not be a big deal in a data entry situation; at best, operators need to know that the parent record has to be entered first, or the client application provides a seamless way to do that. In a bulk-loading situation, however, it can lead to many tripped up records. In that case, it is possible to disable the key and then re-enable it after the load.

■ The foreign key column must be defined as null because there is at least one top-level row in the hierarchy. Therefore, whenever a report is performed from a hierarchical join, care must be taken that *no* rows are lost. Unless a hierarchical query using `connect by` is used, an outer join is *necessary*.

Listing 29.19 redefines `lawyer9` with a recursive key from the `boss` column to the `id` column.

Listing 29.19. Recursive foreign key constraint.

```
--      Filename: 29squ19.sql
--      Purpose: recursive foreign key constraint
--
drop table lawyer9;

create table lawyer9 (
    id        number(2) not null,
    Name      varchar2(15),
    Office    varchar2(15),
    boss      number(2),
    bhrs      number(4),
    bgross    number(7),
    constraint l9_p primary key (id),
    constraint l9_r foreign key (boss)
            references lawyer9)
;

insert into lawyer9
select
    id,
    name,
    office,
    boss,
    bhrs,
    bgross
from lawyer2
;

commit;
```

The following code is returned:

```
Table dropped.

Table created.

Commit complete

20 rows created.
```

The constraints are listed as follows:

```
CONSTRAINT_NAME T TABLE_NAME COLUMN_NAME     R_CONSTRAI DR STATUS
--------------- - ---------- ------------    ---------- -- -------
SYS_C009008     C LAWYER9    ID                            ENABLED
L9_P            P            ID                            ENABLED
L9_R            R            BOSS            L9_P       NO ENABLED
```

The rows happened to be in a workable order, but inserting new rows out of the hierarchical order will not work. Three rows will be inserted twice. This is illustrated in Listing 29.20.

Listing 29.20. Inserting with recursive foreign key constraint.

```
--        Filename: 29squ20.sql
--        Purpose: inserting with recursive foreign key constraint
--
insert into lawyer9 values(
   21, 'Holocek',NULL,22,1400,84566);
insert into lawyer9 values(
   22, 'Alchuck','Boston',7,1850,232266);
insert into lawyer9 values(
   23, 'Gregory','Boston',22,2136,315728);

select * from lawyer9 where id > 20;

rollback;
```

This output is returned:

```
insert into lawyer9 values(
            *
ERROR at line 1:
ORA-02291: integrity constraint (HANS.L9_R) violated
           - parent key not found

1 row created.

1 row created.
```

ID NAME	OFFICE	BOSS	BHRS	BGROSS
22 Alchuck	Boston	7	1850	232266
23 Gregory	Boston	22	2136	315728

```
Rollback complete.
```

If, on the other hand, the constraint is disabled for the time being, all records can be inserted, as shown here:

```
alter table lawyer9
   disable constraint l9_r;
insert into lawyer9 values(
   21, 'Holocek',NULL,22,1400,84566);
insert into lawyer9 values(
   22, 'Alchuck','Boston',7,1850,232266);
insert into lawyer9 values(
   23, 'Gregory','Boston',22,2136,315728);

select * from lawyer9 where id > 20;

alter table lawyer9
   enable constraint l9_r;
```

This code returns

```
Table altered.

1 row created.

1 row created.

1 row created.
```

ID	NAME	OFFICE	BOSS	BHRS	BGROSS
21	Holocek		22	1400	84566
22	Alchuck	Boston	7	1850	232266
23	Gregory	Boston	22	2136	315728

```
Table altered.
```

Multi-Tier Parent-Child Tables

Tables may be layered in multiple levels where a child table of another table serves as the parent table of the third. In a situation like this, the foreign key of the bottom table is a compound key consisting of the primary key of the top table and the primary key of the second table.

In a multi-level situation it must be remembered that joins and keys that define a relationship between tables are between two tables only. In a three-level master-detail, you have the grandparents on the top, the parents in the middle, and the children at the bottom of the hierarchy. In this situation, the child table has a key to the parent table, which in turn has a key to the grandparent table. If compound keys are used, the foreign key of the parent table references the primary key of the top table. The foreign key of the child table is compound and references the foreign key of the parent table and the primary key of the parent table. Directly referencing the grandparent table from the bottom table is likely to lead to messy errors with design tools. This issue only matters for inserts and updates anyway; when retrieving, it is possible to jump a table in the join, as might be done when aggregating over some children values by grandparent categories.

A typical tri-level table definition is shown in Listing 29.21.

Listing 29.21. Three-level master-detail tables.

```sql
--       Filename: 29squ21.sql
--        Purpose: three-level master detail tables
--
drop table child;

drop table mama;

drop table granny;

create table granny (
    id      number(2) constraint gr_n not null,
    Name    varchar2(15),
    constraint gr_p primary key (id))
```

continues

Listing 29.21. continued

```
;

create table mama (
    id       number(2) constraint ma_n1   not null,
    ma       number(2) constraint ma_gr_n not null,
    sqinma   number(1) constraint ma_n2   not null,
    Name     varchar2(15),
    constraint ma_p primary key (id),
    constraint ma_u unique        (ma, sqinma),
    constraint ma_gr_f foreign key (ma)
            references granny)
;

create table child (
    id       number(2) constraint ch_n not null,
    ma       number(2) constraint ch_ma_n1 not null,
    gr       number(2) constraint ch_ma_n2 not null,
    sqinma   number(1) constraint ch_ma_n3 not null,
    Name     varchar2(15),
    constraint ch_p primary key (id),
    constraint ch_ma_f1 foreign key (ma)
            references mama,
    constraint ch_ma_f2 foreign key (gr, sqinma)
            references mama (ma, sqinma))
;

insert into granny values (1,'Gerda');
insert into granny values (2,'Greta');
insert into granny values (3,'Gertrud');
insert into granny values (4,'Gaby');
insert into mama values (1,1,1,'Maggie');
insert into mama values (2,1,2,'Margareth');
insert into mama values (3,1,3,'Mary');
insert into mama values (4,3,1,'Molly');
insert into mama values (5,4,1,'Minnie');
insert into mama values (6,4,2,'Marilyn');
insert into mama values (7,4,3,'Monica');
insert into mama values (8,2,1,'Morgan');
insert into mama values (9,2,2,'Martina');
insert into child values (1,1,1,1,'Jakob');
insert into child values (2,1,1,1,'Annissa');
insert into child values (3,2,1,2,'Ben');
insert into child values (4,2,1,2,'Eve');
insert into child values (5,3,1,3,'Julia');
insert into child values (6,3,1,3,'Charles');
insert into child values (7,3,1,3,'Alina');
insert into child values (8,4,3,1,'Nicole');
insert into child values (9,4,3,1,'Max');
insert into child values (0,4,3,1,'Azuree');
insert into child values (11,5,4,1,'Dana');
insert into child values (12,6,4,2,'Jaqueline');
insert into child values (13,7,4,3,'Ryan');
insert into child values (14,7,4,3,'Diana');
insert into child values (15,7,4,3,'Randy');
insert into child values (16,7,4,3,'Mary Beth');
```

```
insert into child values (17,8,2,1,'Ray');
insert into child values (18,8,2,1,'William');
insert into child values (19,9,2,2,'Christine');
insert into child values (20,9,2,2,'Lynn');
insert into child values (21,9,2,2,'Paul');
insert into child values (22,9,2,2,'Nathaniel');
insert into child values (23,9,2,2,'Kasha');
insert into child values (24,9,2,2,'Laurie');
insert into child values (25,9,2,2,'Anastasia');

commit;
```

The constraints for the tables are listed as follows:

CONSTRAINT_NAME	T	TABLE_NAME	COLUMN_NAME	R_CONSTRAI	DR	STATUS
GR_N	C	GRANNY	ID			ENABLED
GR_P	P		ID			ENABLED

CONSTRAINT_NAME	T	TABLE_NAME	COLUMN_NAME	R_CONSTRAI	DR	STATUS
MA_N1	C	MAMA	ID			ENABLED
MA_GR_N	C		MA			ENABLED
MA_N2	C		SQINMA			ENABLED
MA_P	P		ID			ENABLED
MA_U	U		MA			ENABLED
MA_U	U		SQINMA			ENABLED
MA_GR_F	R		MA	GR_P	NO	ENABLED

CONSTRAINT_NAME	T	TABLE_NAME	COLUMN_NAME	R_CONSTRAI	DR	STATUS
CH_N	C	CHILD	ID			ENABLED
CH_MA_N1	C		MA			ENABLED
CH_MA_N2	C		GR			ENABLED
CH_MA_N3	C		SQINMA			ENABLED
CH_P	P		ID			ENABLED
CH_MA_F1	R		MA	MA_P	NO	ENABLED
CH_MA_F2	R		GR	MA_U	NO	ENABLED
CH_MA_F2	R		SQINMA	MA_U	NO	ENABLED

Inserting into these tables has been shown in the examples in this chapter. If an illegal combination of mama and granny ID values is entered into the child table, an error will result. Therefore, the foreign key of child references the primary and foreign key of mama.

Retrieving data across tables can be done in several ways; some of which are demonstrated in the following examples.

First the family trees are shown with the names of grandmother, mother, and children, as shown in Listing 29.22. The first statement displays the data as a three-level hierarchy. The where clause connects the granny table with the mama table and the mama table with the child table. The outer join is used because otherwise a granny without mama or a mama without child would not be displayed.

29

Keys, Indexes, and Constraints

Listing 29.22. Retrieval from the three-level master-detail tables.

```
--          Filename: 29squ22.sql
--          Purpose: retrieval from three-level master detail tables
--
select
   g.name,
   m.name,
   c.name
from
   granny g,
   mama m,
   child c
where g.id = m.ma (+) and
      m.id = c.ma (+)
;
```

The code returns the following output:

GNAME	MNAME	NAME
Gerda	Maggie	Jakob
	Maggie	Annissa
	Margareth	Ben
	Margareth	Eve
	Mary	Julia
	Mary	Charles
	Mary	Alina
Gertrud	Molly	Nicole
	Molly	Max
	Molly	Azuree
Gaby	Minnie	Dana
	Marilyn	Jaqueline
	Monica	Ryan
	Monica	Diana
	Monica	Randy
	Monica	Mary Beth
Greta	Morgan	Ray
	Morgan	William
	Martina	Christine
	Martina	Lynn
	Martina	Paul
	Martina	Nathaniel
	Martina	Kasha
	Martina	Laurie
	Martina	Anastasia

The next two statements retrieve the same information—a count of children per grandmother:

```
select
   g.name,
   count(c.id) grandchildren
from
   granny g,
   mama m,
   child c
where g.id = m.ma (+) and
      m.id = c.ma (+)
```

```
group by g.name
;
......
where g.id =  c.gr
group by g.name
;
```

Both statements return the same:

```
NAME            GRANDCHILDREN
--------------- -------------
Gaby                        6
Gerda                       7
Gertrud                     3
Greta                       9
```

Facilitating the Quick Retrieval of Rows Through Indexes

Besides tables, indexes are the most important database objects. An index contains one or more columns and a `rowid` that points to a row in the table to which it belongs. Different than a table, an index is ordered using a method such as B-tree, which allows you to find the block that contains the index row with just a few accesses. Another access speed advantage stems from the fact that index rows are usually much shorter than rows of tables (usually only a key value and a `rowid` compared to a table row that may easily have a few hundred bytes, and possibly much more).

In a nonindexed table, if one particular row is to be found, all rows of the table have to be scanned until the desired row is located. If the `where` clause is based on nonunique values, the whole table has to be scanned, even if the desired rows are found right away. This is because SQL retrieves the set of rows that fulfills a condition that can only be done with a full table scan.

If rows are to be retrieved in a particular order, the contents of the table must be sorted into some temporary space first. If, on the other hand, the ordering of the index corresponds with the desired order of retrieval, the rows can be retrieved through the key that eliminates the sorting step.

If a row is to be located through an index, typically the following steps are performed:

1. The row or rows in the index that fulfill the conditions of the `where` clause are identified.

2. Using the `rowid` found in the index, the corresponding rows are retrieved from the table.

3. The retrieved information is re-sorted, and if necessary, aggregated, joined, and so on.

Both the primary and unique keys are implemented through indexes. Because in the previous `create index` examples no storage parameters were specified, defaults are used. Through brief extensions of the syntax, however, primary and unique indexes may be defined with explicit storage specifications. For the sole purpose of improving performance, it is also possible to specify indexes independently of these constraints. This section first works with the latter case and then deals with adding explicit storage clauses to unique and primary keys.

> **CAUTION**
>
> Indexes are not always more efficient. As a general rule, if a select statement retrieves more than a quarter of the columns in a table, a full table scan is more efficient.

Many factors affect the efficiency of an index, such as the distribution of index values or the physical layout of the database. In particular the indexes of a table should be stored on a disk drive different from that where the table proper is stored. This is done through the physical storage layout of tablespaces.

Indexed Columns: `create index`

Indexing columns pays most in cases in which the same column is used in many where clauses, in which many joins are worked out through such indexes, or in which the table is frequently accessed in a particular order. One frequent use is to index foreign keys on the referencing table that is intended to speed up the retrieval of all detail rows that belong to a particular master record. S-Designor, for example, a database modeling tool, puts in such an index by default.

Columns are indexed through the `create index` clause. This is a straightforward command with relatively few options (about half of which define the index proper and the other half set the way in which the index is stored).

Listing 29.23 creates an index on the `name` column in `lawyer9`, using the version created by `29squ15a.sql`.

Listing 29.23. Creating indexes.

```
--      Filename: 29squ23.sql
--       Purpose: creating indexes
--
set termout off

@29squ15a

set termout on

create index l9_name
on lawyer9(name);

create index l9_office
on lawyer9(office);
```

This returns

```
Index created.

Index created.
```

Because this feedback is a bit terse, it is to your advantage to query the related Data Dictionary views. The view `user_indexes` describes the indexes of a user while the view `user_ind_columns` describes the columns involved. These views are quite similar to `user_tables` and `user_tab_keys`.

Listing 29.24, which has been adapted from `29squ03b.sql`, contains scripts that retrieve the index information about a table which is accessible through the views `user_indexes` and `user_ind_columns`. It also includes storage information that is discussed later in this chapter in the section "Specifying Storage Parameters for Indexes, Primary Keys, and Unique Keys."

Listing 29.24. Query for indexes.

```
--        Filename: 29squ24.sql
--        Purpose: query for indexes
--
accept p_table   prompt 'Enter table name--UPPER CASE ONLY: '

col index_name          format a15    heading 'INDEX¦NAME'
col uniquen             format a1     heading 'U¦N'
col table_name          format a10    heading 'TABLE¦NAME'
col column_name         format a15    heading 'COLUMN¦NAME'
col column_position     format 999    heading 'COL¦POS'
col column_length       format 999    heading 'COL¦LEN'
col inkb                format 9,999  heading 'INIT.¦ KB'
col nekb                format 9,999  heading 'NEXT ¦ KB'
col min_extents         format 999    heading 'MIN¦EXT'
col max_extents         format 999    heading 'MAX¦EXT'
col pct_free            format 99     heading 'PCT¦FR.'

break on table_name skip 1

select
   a.table_name,
   a.index_name,
   substr(a.uniqueness,1,1) uniquen,
   c.constraint_type,
   b.column_name,
   b.column_position,
   b.column_length,
   a.initial_extent/1024 inkb,
   a.next_extent/1024 nekb,
   a.min_extents,
   a.max_extents,
   a.pct_free
from
   user_indexes      a,
   user_ind_columns b,
   user_constraints c
```

continues

Listing 29.24. continued

```
where a.table_name      = '&p_table' and
      a.index_name = b.index_name and
      a.index_name = c.constraint_name (+)
order by
   a.table_name,
   c.constraint_type,
   a.index_name,
   b.column_position,
   b.column_name
;

clear columns
clear breaks
```

If LAWYER9 is entered when prompted, the statement returns

TABLE NAME	INDEX NAME	U N	C T	COLUMN NAME	COL POS	COL LEN	INIT. KB	NEXT KB	MIN EXT	MAX EXT	PCT FR.
LAWYER9	L9_P	U	P	ID	1	22	10	10	1	121	10
	L9_NAME	N		NAME	1	15	10	10	1	121	10
	L9_OFFICE	N		OFFICE	1	15	10	10	1	121	10

The first two lines describe the indexes defined in 29squ23.sql. Neither of these lines are unique, therefore uniqueness (column UIN) is N. Neither are constraints, therefore the constraint type column (CIT) is null. The third index results from the original definition of the table in 29squ15.sql, where a primary key was defined. Both primary and unique keys are implemented through indexes. The remaining columns of output are discussed later in the chapter in the section "Specifying Storage Parameters for Indexes, Primary Keys, and Unique Keys."

There are indexes that are not constraints (nonunique), and there are constraints that are not indexes (check, not null, foreign key). Primary and unique keys are both indexes and constraints.

Indexes on Null Columns

An index only indexes non-null values, even on a column that allows nulls. This fact can be exploited in a situation where there is a large table that contains some rows that need to be accessed frequently while many other rows are only of intermittent interest. An example is a table that contains both active or inactive rows, or a long period's worth of data with a need to access only the most recent data frequently.

If there is a status flag that has a value for the frequently accessed rows and a null for the other rows, a select of all rows that have a valid status goes quickly through the index because the index is short and, through the index, can access the rows through rowid.

Compound Indexes

Compound indexes are allowed just as compound primary and unique keys were. These are useful for situations where rows are frequently selected or ordered on the basis of more than one column. The processes incurred when using these indexes are the same as those of a single-column index.

For access purpose, a compound index is also used to access or order rows of fewer columns, but in doing so the last column, two last columns, and so on, have to be omitted until only the first column is selected. For example, if an index uses four columns, it can access and sort by all four columns, by the first three ones, the first two, or only the first. No other combinations, such as the second column only, or the first and the third column, are allowed.

Listing 29.25 creates a compound index on `lawyer9`, using `office` and `name` as columns.

Listing 29.25. Creating indexes.

```
--       Filename: 29squ25.sql
--       Purpose: creating indexes
--
set termout off

@29squ14

set termout on

create index l9_off_name
on lawyer9(office, name);

@29squ23b
```

The following output is returned:

```
Index created.

Enter table name--UPPER CASE ONLY: LAWYER9
old  18: where a.table_name    = '&p_table' and
new  18: where a.table_name    = 'LAWYER9' and
```

TABLE NAME	INDEX NAME	U N	C T	COLUMN NAME	COL POS	COL LEN	INIT. KB	NEXT KB	MIN EXT	MAX EXT	PCT FR.
LAWYER9	L9_P	U	P	ID	1	22	10	10	1	121	10
	L9_OFF_NAME	N		OFFICE	1	15	10	10	1	121	10
	L9_OFF_NAME	N		NAME	2	15	10	10	1	121	10

Specifying Storage Parameters for Indexes, Primary Keys, and Unique Keys

Because indexes are database objects that are physically stored in the database, storage parameters can be set for indexes in the `create index` and `alter index` clauses, just as storage parameters could be set for tables in the `create table` and `alter table` clauses. The syntax can be slightly altered to explicitly set storage parameters where indexes are created through unique and primary key constraints.

ORACLE vs. SQL

Oracle's functionality, as described in this section, exceeds that of SQL-92.

As was the case with tables, space directives specify space usage within blocks, and storage specifies the storage characteristics of an index. This is especially important for large indexes on large tables.

Space Directive: `pctfree`

`pctfree` sets the percentage in the block reserved for future index value updates. This free space is necessary for indexes that contain `varchar2` columns; columns of `long` datatypes must not be used in indexes, anyway. A sufficiently large `pctfree` avoids unnecessary migrations of index rows. Oracle sets 10% as a default. It should be set larger if extensive updating and lengthening of `varchar2` columns in the index are expected.

`pctused` cannot be set on indexes.

Listing 29.26 includes the `pctfree` parameters for an index, a primary key, and a unique key constraint. The example adapts `29squ15.sql`, creating a `lawyer9` table definition that has a primary key, a unique key, and a nonunique index.

> **NOTE**
>
> If this example returns an error because `office2` cannot be found, run `29squ15.sql` first and then run `29squ26.sql` again.

Listing 29.26. Storage clauses for indexes, primary constraints, and unique constraints.

```
Filename: 29squ26.sql
--       Purpose: storage clauses for indexes, primary, and unique constraints
--
drop table lawyer9;

create table lawyer9 (
    id      number(2) constraint l9_id_n not null,
    Name    varchar2(15),
    offid   number(2),
    Office  varchar2(15),
    boss    number(2),
    bhrs    number(4),
    bgross  number(7),
    constraint l9_p primary key (id) using index pctfree 20,
    constraint l9_o2_f1 foreign key (offid)
            references office2,
    constraint l9_name_u unique (name) using index pctfree 20)
;
```

```
create index l9_off
on lawyer9(office)
pctfree 20;

@29squ23b
```

This code returns

```
Table dropped.
```

```
Table created.
```

```
Index created.
```

```
Enter table name--UPPER CASE ONLY: LAWYER9
old  18: where a.table_name      = '&p_table' and
new  18: where a.table_name      = 'LAWYER9' and
```

TABLE NAME	INDEX NAME	U N	C T	COLUMN NAME	COL POS	COL LEN	INIT. KB	NEXT KB	MIN EXT	MAX EXT	PCT FR.
LAWYER9	L9_P	U	P	ID	1	22	10	10	1	121	20
	L9_NAME_U	U	U	NAME	1	15	10	10	1	121	20
	L9_OFF	N		OFFICE	1	15	10	10	1	121	20

The `pctfree` entries are now all set to `20`. It does not appear that `pctfree` value can be changed except by re-creating the index. This is done in the next part of the example:

```
alter table lawyer9
drop primary key;

alter table lawyer9
drop constraint l9_name_u;

drop index l9_off;

alter table lawyer9 add(
    constraint l9_p primary key (id) using index pctfree 5,
    constraint l9_name_u unique (name) using index pctfree 5)
;

create index l9_off
on lawyer9(office)
pctfree 5;

@29squ23b
```

The following code is returned:

```
Table altered.
```

```
Table altered.
```

```
Index dropped.
```

```
Table altered.
```

```
Index created.
```

29

KEYS, INDEXES, AND CONSTRAINTS

```
Enter table name--UPPER CASE ONLY: LAWYER9
old  18: where a.table_name     = '&p_table' and
new  18: where a.table_name     = 'LAWYER9' and
```

TABLE NAME	INDEX NAME	U N	C T	COLUMN NAME	COL POS	COL LEN	INIT. KB	NEXT KB	MIN EXT	MAX EXT	PCT FR.
LAWYER9	L9_P	U	P	ID	1	22	10	10	1	121	5
	L9_NAME_U	U	U	NAME	1	15	10	10	1	121	5
	L9_OFF	N		OFFICE	1	15	10	10	1	121	5

CAUTION

Dropping and re-creating keys and indexes is no big deal for a small table, but it can take a while for large ones. Therefore, try to set the parameters so that changes are unlikely.

Storage Characteristics: `storage`

Just as database tables may range in size from very small to huge, related indexes may range from somewhat smaller to just as huge. Therefore, `storage` clauses can be specified in the same way as tables. (See Chapter 28 for explanations and rationales.) The same five parameters control the size and number of extents used for an index:

- `initial`—the size of the initial extent used for the index. `K` and `M` can be used to indicate KB and MB, respectively. For reality check purposes, the extents should be multiples of the block size of the database; if not, the value is automatically increased to the next block size increment. The default is five times the block size, and the minimum is twice the block size.

- `next`—The sizes of the second extent, default, and minimum are equal to the block size.

- `minextents`—The minimum number of extents used, usually set to 1. The default is 1.

- `maxextents`—The maximum number of extents allowed.

- `pctincrease`—The percentage by which the size of the third to the last extent is increased over the size of previous one. If set to 0, all extents after the second are the same size. If set to 100, each of these extents is twice as large as the previous one. The default is 50.

The rules for setting storage parameters for indexes are the same as the rules used to determine proper storage parameters for tables. (See Chapter 28.)

Listing 29.27 defines and alters `storage` clauses for indexes.

Listing 29.27. `storage` clauses for indexes, primary constraints, and unique constraints.

```
--      Filename: 29squ27.sql
--        Purpose: storage clauses for indexes, primary, and unique constraints
--
drop table lawyer9;
```

```
create table lawyer9 (
    id        number(2) constraint l9_id_n not null,
    Name      varchar2(15),
    offid     number(2),
    Office    varchar2(15),
    boss      number(2),
    bhrs      number(4),
    bgross    number(7),
    constraint l9_p primary key (id) using index pctfree 12
            storage (initial 2K next 2K minextents 1 maxextents 5),
    constraint l9_o2_f1 foreign key (offid)
            references office2,
    constraint l9_name_u unique (name) using index pctfree 12
            storage (initial 2K next 2K minextents 1 maxextents 5))
;

create index l9_off
on lawyer9(office)
    pctfree 12
    storage (initial 2K next 2K minextents 1 maxextents 5)
;

@29squ23b
```

This code returns

```
Table dropped.

Table created.

Index created.

Enter table name--UPPER CASE ONLY: LAWYER9
old  18: where a.table_name    = '&p_table' and
new  18: where a.table_name    = 'LAWYER9' and
```

TABLE NAME	INDEX NAME	U N	C T	COLUMN NAME	COL POS	COL LEN	INIT. KB	NEXT KB	MIN EXT	MAX EXT	PCT FR.
LAWYER9	L9_P	U	P	ID	1	22	4	2	1	5	12
	L9_NAME_U	U	U	NAME	1	15	4	2	1	5	12
	L9_OFF	N		OFFICE	1	15	4	2	1	5	12

Note that even though the initial extent had been specified as 2KB, it is set as 4KB because that is the minimum. The other values are set as specified.

Whether or not the indexes have been created through create index, through create table, or through alter table, its storage clause is changed through the alter index clause. Because the initial extent is set only once, when the index is created, initial cannot be set in alter index.

The following statements change the storage definitions for the primary key and the two indexes of the lawyer9 table:

```
alter index l9_p
    pctfree 5
    storage (next 4K minextents 1 maxextents 15)
```

29

KEYS, INDEXES, AND CONSTRAINTS

```
;

alter index l9_name_u
    pctfree 5
    storage (next 4K minextents 1 maxextents 15)
;

alter index l9_off
    pctfree 5
    storage (next 4K minextents 1 maxextents 15)
;

@29squ23b
```

The following code is returned:

```
Index altered.

Index altered.

Index altered.

Enter table name--UPPER CASE ONLY: LAWYER9
old   18: where a.table_name    = '&p_table' and
new   18: where a.table_name    = 'LAWYER9' and
```

TABLE NAME	INDEX NAME	U N	C T	COLUMN NAME	COL POS	COL LEN	INIT. KB	NEXT KB	MIN EXT	MAX EXT	PCT FR.
LAWYER9	L9_P	U	P	ID	1	22	4	4	1	15	12
	L9_NAME_U	U	U	NAME	1	15	4	4	1	15	12
	L9_OFF	N		OFFICE	1	15	4	4	1	15	12

The sizes of additional extents are now set to 4KB, and a maximum of 15 extents is allowed.

Comments on Tables and Columns

One of the sour spots of many software and system design projects is inadequate documentation. This problem is exacerbated in systems that are deployed in many different sites. Documentation may be available, but it is not accessible at a particular site where it might be needed. Finally, the network connection may support a database access but not access to, let's say, a file server where the documentation may be found.

If, on the other hand, some documentation is available as comments in the Data Dictionary, everybody who can connect to the database can also retrieve these comments. That is not likely to be sufficient to replace all documentation, but could certainly help out in a pinch.

ORACLE vs SQL The comment on statement is an Oracle extension to SQL. It allows you to add a comment on a table, view, or column directly in the Data Dictionary. Comments can then be retrieved through the views user_col_comments and user_tab_comments.

Comments are dropped through another comment statement with a null string (' ') after the is.

Listing 29.28 creates comments on the lawyer9 table and columns.

Listing 29.28. Comments on tables and columns.

```
--        Filename: 29squ28.sql
--        Purpose: comments on tables and columns
--
comment on table lawyer9 is
'Table is used to demonstrate constraints and indexes';
comment on column lawyer9.id is
'ID--Primary key';
comment on column lawyer9.name is
'Last Name';
comment on column lawyer9.offid is
'Office ID--foreign key of office2.id';
comment on column lawyer9.office is
'Office Name--denormalized from office2';
comment on column lawyer9.boss is
'Boss--recursive key to lawyer9.id';
comment on column lawyer9.bhrs is
'Hours billed in previous year';
comment on column lawyer9.bgross is
'Gross receipts of previous year';
```

The previous code returns the following output once for each statement:

Comment created.

Listing 29.29, which will be used again at the end of the next example, displays the comments.

Listing 29.29. Query for comments.

```
--        Filename: 29squ29.sql
--        Purpose: query for comments
--
accept p_table   prompt 'Enter table name--UPPER CASE ONLY: '
set long          500
col table_name          format a10
col ttype               format a1   heading 'TYPE'
col column_name         format a15
col comments            format a60

select
   table_name,
   substr(table_type,1,1) ttype,
   comments
from
   user_tab_comments
where table_name       = '&p_table' and
     comments <> ''
;

select
   column_name,
   comments
from
   user_col_comments
where table_name       = '&p_table' and
```

continues

Listing 29.29. continued

```
      comments <> ''
;

clear columns
set long        80
```

This code returns

```
Enter table name--UPPER CASE ONLY: LAWYER9
old   7: where table_name     = '&p_table'
new   7: where table_name     = 'LAWYER9'

TABLE_NAME T COMMENTS
---------- - -------------------------------------------------------------
LAWYER9    T Table is used to demonstrate constraints and indexes
old   6: where table_name     = '&p_table'
new   6: where table_name     = 'LAWYER9'

COLUMN_NAME     COMMENTS
--------------- -----------------------------------------------------------
ID              ID--Primary key
NAME            Last Name
OFFID           Office ID--foreign key of office2.id
OFFICE          Office Name--denormalized from office2
BOSS            Boss--recursive key to lawyer9.id
BHRS            Hours billed in previous year
BGROSS          Gross receipts of previous year

7 rows selected.
```

Listing 29.30 erases the comments by overwriting them with null strings.

Listing 29.30. Overwriting comments on tables and columns with null strings.

```
--        Filename: 29squ30.sql
--        Purpose: overwriting comments on tables and columns with
--                 null string
--
comment on table lawyer9 is '';
comment on column lawyer9.id is '';
comment on column lawyer9.name is '';
comment on column lawyer9.offid is '';
comment on column lawyer9.office is '';
comment on column lawyer9.boss is '';
comment on column lawyer9.bhrs is '';
comment on column lawyer9.bgross is '';
```

This code returns the following, once for each statement:

```
Comment created.
```

There are entries in the comments views, but because the `where` clause in `29squ29.sql` filters out NULL string comments, nothing is returned, as shown here:

```
no rows selected
```

```
no rows selected
```

Summary

Tables can be greatly enhanced by constraints, keys, and indexes. Constraints limit the values that may be inserted into a column or a set of columns:

- The `check` constraint specifies a list or a range of allowable values.
- The `not null` constraint prevents the insertion of null values.
- Unique and primary keys, which are implemented through indexes, limit new rows to values that are not in certain columns or sets.
- Foreign keys allow the insertion of only those values that are represented in another column in another or the same table.

Indexes are intended to speed up data retrieval.

Many options exist to naming, enabling, and disabling indexes, keys, and constraints and information about all of these can be retrieved from Data Dictionary views.

Comments on columns and tables can be maintained in the Data Dictionary. Comments are created through the statements `comment on table` *tablename* and `comment on column` *columnname*.

CHAPTER 30

Table Relationships and Entity Relationship Diagrams

IN THIS CHAPTER

Thus far in this book, tables that are related to one another in some way have been used in two ways:

- To join tables through a table join or a subquery
- As foreign key constraints from one table to another or from one table to itself

We have not given much consideration to the issue of how tables should be related to one another; the relationships were simply accepted as a given.

This chapter and Chapters 31 and 32 touch on the very basics of data modeling and how a data model relates to SQL. This chapter begins with the standard graphical way to express these relationships—entity relationship diagrams—and covers the most important typical arrangements, including code. Chapter 31, "The Optionality of Table Relationships," expands on these models and introduces optionality. Chapter 32, "Relational Database Design and Normalization," ends the section with normalization rules.

Entity Relationship Modeling

A full-blown database-design process is performed in several steps:

1. Real things or persons are mapped into *entities*—logical objects that correspond to them with attributes for each important piece of information about them. (What is "important" is a judgment call, which is made easier by the fact that each entity has to fulfill some functional purpose.) So, if a table is used for a personnel information system, it is likely to contain somewhat different attributes than if it is used for a spy organization, which again is likely to be different from the way attributes are laid out for a personal address database system.

2. Entities are related to one another through relationships. A relationship has two ends, one for each entity that relates through it. Relationship ends, in turn, are characterized through their cardinality and their optionality. Cardinality can either be one or many; optionality can be mandatory or optional. A typical parent-child relationship has a cardinality of one at the parent end and a cardinality of many at the child end. The parent end is usually optional, which means there may be parent records without associated child records. The child end is usually mandatory—child records must not exist without an associated parent record.

3. Entities, in turn, are mapped into tables, and attributes into columns. In simple systems, these mappings are one-to-one, but in complex ones, an entity might be broken into several tables, or several entities might be combined into one. Some entities that are not that important might not be mapped into tables at all. Although entities are not concerned about size and storage issues, they are usually included with the table definitions. Relationships between entities are mapped into foreign key constraints.

4. The table/column definitions are finally translated into SQL code and submitted to the RDBMS.

All CASE tools such as Oracle Designer/2000 and S-Designor support this approach.

Entity relationship (ER) diagrams are the standard way to express entities and their relationships. They are similar in appearance to diagrams for physical data models that include tables and views. However, while entities are shown with round corners, the corners of tables and views are square. Physical models also do not display the nature of table relationships in full detail.

Because all the examples in this chapter are fairly simple, they are expressed in typical ER style and will be directly translated to SQL. Because the `create table` statement is covered extensively in Chapter 29, "Keys, Indexes, Constraints, and Table/Column Comments," only those columns necessary to create the relationship are included in the examples. Because it would make little sense to run these against the database, they are not included as `.sql` scripts.

Entity Relationship Diagram Elements

An entity is expressed as a softbox—a rectangle with rounded corners. At the very least, an entity must have a name. It may also have a *synonym*, another name by which it is known. Figure 30.1 shows two entities, `lawyer` and `office`. `lawyer` is also known under the synonym `staff`, which is shown in parentheses.

FIGURE 30.1.
In this diagram, `office` *is an entity;* `lawyer` *is an entity with a synonym,* `staff`.

Office

Lawyer
(Staff)

A relationship between entities or an entity with itself is graphed through a line or a variation thereof. Each end of the line expresses the *cardinality* or *degree* of the relationship, which can be one of the following:

- One and only one—expressed through a line
- One or more—expressed through "crow's feet"

Figure 30.2 shows the two symbols that are used to express the cardinality of a relationship—the line and the crow's foot.

30

TABLE AND ENTITY RELATIONSHIPS

FIGURE 30.2.
These symbols are used to designate entity relationships.

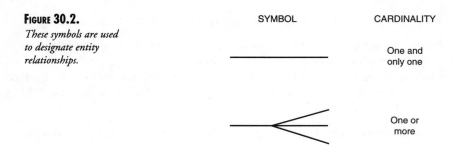

SYMBOL	CARDINALITY
	One and only one
	One or more

Because each relationship has two ends, four options can be expressed using these symbols:

- One to one
- One to many
- Many to one
- Many to many

The *one* means the somewhat stiff "one and only one"; the *many* means "one or many." Figure 30.3 shows the symbols for those four options.

FIGURE 30.3.
The four standard relationships are represented by these symbols.

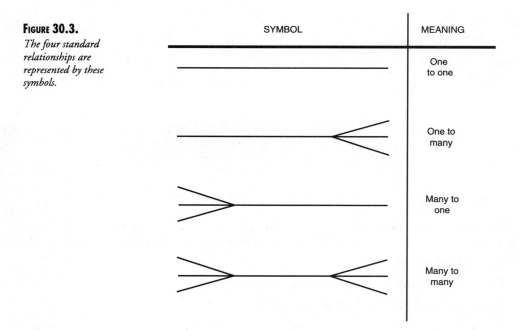

SYMBOL	MEANING
	One to one
	One to many
	Many to one
	Many to many

In this chapter, no further concern will be given to optionality, except that all examples will be mandatory for the referencing side and optional at the referenced side. Recursive relationships will be optional on both sides. As you will see in Chapter 31, these are the typical combinations of cardinality and optionality.

Mandatory ends of relationships are expressed through a solid line; optional ends are expressed with a dotted line. Chapter 31 explores some variations of this approach.

The attributes of an entity are usually listed under the name of the entity. The name of a synonym, if it exists, is put between the entity name and the attributes. As explained previously, only those attributes necessary to create the relationship are included in the examples here.

Finally, although a relationship is drawn with only one symbol, it describes two facets, one from the point of view of each end. Each of these is described through a brief comment.

Therefore, a typical relationship diagram has at least two entities (large data models may easily have a few hundred): a symbol that expresses the relationship and its cardinality at both ends, and two statements in plain English (or any other language in which the system happens to be built) that describe it from both ends. If an attribute serves also as a primary key, a # is put next to the attribute name to reflect that fact.

The following section and the next two chapters provide you with several examples of these diagrams.

Typical Entity Relationships

A few standard relationships are used quite frequently: one to many, recursive, one to one, many to many, and one to many to many. These are the standard building blocks of a system and are discussed here in detail.

One-to-Many Relationships

By far the most frequent relationship is one to many, where a child table references a parent table, and where the child end is mandatory and the parent end is optional. The example 29squ15.sql, which can be found on the CD and in Chapter 29, lays out such a relationship, except that the child end in that example is not mandatory.

Referring back to that example, this is how the situation would sound in real life:

There is a law firm that runs several offices across the United States. The rationale in the firm is that every lawyer working for it is assigned to an office. An office, on the other hand, need not have a lawyer associated to it—it might have just been started and lawyers have not yet been hired, or it might be ready to shut down and the lawyers are gone already.

This situation would be expressed as shown in Figure 30.4. This diagram contains two entities, lawyer and office. They are connected through a one-to-many relationship, with the many end pointing to lawyer and the one end pointing to office.

FIGURE 30.4.

The lawyer *and* office
*entities have a standard
one-to-many
relationship.*

Each lawyer
works in
one office

Lawyer

Office
ID

Each office
may house
one or more
lawyers

The essential parts of code, adapted from 29squ15.sql, are as follows:

```
create table office (
    ID       number(2),
    constraint of2_p primary key (id));
```

All that is necessary for a parent table is one key column defined either as a primary or unique key. There is no column that references a row in the child table. The child table, on the other hand, must have a not null column that references a primary or unique key at the parent table, like this:

```
create table lawyer (
    offid    number(2) constraint l_offid not null,
    constraint 19_o2_f2 foreign key (offid)
            references office);
```

Typically, at least two more things would be represented: a primary key for lawyer and an index for the office column. These are included in the following statement. Further attributes are of no concern for this discussion:

```
create table lawyer (
    id       number(2),
    offid    number(2) constraint l_offid not null,
    constraint 19_p primary key (id),
    constraint 19_o2_f1 foreign key (offid)
            references office)
;
```

One to Many in the Same Table: Recursive Joins

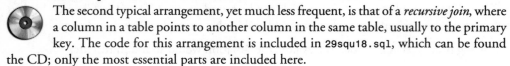 The second typical arrangement, yet much less frequent, is that of a *recursive join*, where a column in a table points to another column in the same table, usually to the primary key. The code for this arrangement is included in 29squ18.sql, which can be found the CD; only the most essential parts are included here.

Unless there is some procedural code included, this arrangement requires the foreign-key column to be defined as null. There must be at least one top-level row in the hierarchy.

An example of such a relationship is shown in Chapter 29 in 29squ18.sql. Each lawyer, except for Easton (who owns the entire outfit), has a boss. Each lawyer also may be the boss of one or more lawyers. The referenced column knows nothing about the relationship. That end is, therefore, optional by design. The foreign-key column, boss, must be defined as null.

In an ER diagram, this relationship is expressed as a so-called pig's ear—a dotted 270° circle around one corner of the table with a crow's foot on one end. Figure 30.5 illustrates a recursive relationship as it appears in an ER diagram.

FIGURE 30.5.
A standard recursive relationship is also known as a "pig's ear."

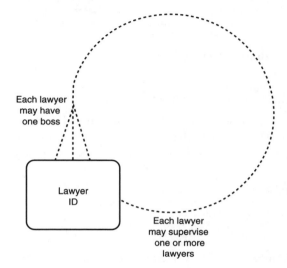

The essential parts of code, adapted from `29squ18.sql`, are as follows:

```
create table lawyer (
    id        number(2) not null,
    boss      number(2),
    constraint l9_p primary key (id),
    constraint l9_r foreign key (boss)
            references lawyer)
;
```

One-to-One Relationships

A one-to-one relationship joins a single row of one table to a single row of another table. This type of relationship is used in situations in which some attributes relate to all instances of an entity and others only to some attributes. For example, in many countries, a person may only have one spouse at a time—legally, that is. There could be a person table that is referenced by a spouse table. In many cases, the one-to-one relationship is similar to a one-to-many.

The relationship is defined as one-to-one because each person may be married to one spouse, and each spouse must be married to one person. Figure 30.6 shows the ER diagram for this arrangement.

FIGURE 30.6.

In this country, the spouse and person entities have a standard one-to-one relationship.

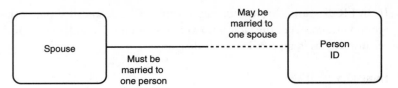

This relationship is coded as follows:

```
create table person (
    ID        number(2),
    constraint person_p primary key (id));
```

As with any other referenced column, the person ID must be defined as either a primary or unique key. The table with the mandatory end has a `not null` column that references that primary or unique key column. The code necessary to implement the one-to-one relationship follows:

```
create table spouse (
    persid    number(2) constraint s_persid not null,
    constraint s_persid_u unique (persid)
    constraint sp_pe_f foreign key (persid)
            references person);
```

This relationship could be worked out in a number of other ways:

- A person table with a few NULL columns for spouse information.

- A dependents table for spouse, children, and other dependents.

- A one-to-many table in which the current spouse is flagged with an active key and previous ones have beginning and ending dates. (Considering the fact that about 50% of marriages don't pan out as planned, this might be a reasonable idea.)

- A spouse column, just as there is a boss column, and a recursive key.

> **NOTE**
>
> A one-to-one relationship is very rare, but it might come in handy for that weird situation when nothing else works.

Multi-Level Relationships: One to Many to Many

The layered arrangement, in which a child table of a table serves as the parent table of a third, is quite frequent. As the Chapter 29 example `29squ20.sql` shows, this arrangement can be implemented by using a compound or an individual primary key in the middle table that is referenced by the bottom table. A multi-level arrangement need not be limited to just three levels, but becomes unwieldy quickly.

Expressed in typical ER modeling lingo, the relationships of `29squ20.sql` would be described as follows:

- Each granny may be the mother of one or more mothers.
- Each mother must be the daughter of one granny.
- Each mother may be the mother of one or more children
- Each child must be the offspring of one mother.

Figure 30.7 shows the ER diagram for a tri-level arrangement using compound keys—the primary key of the `mother` table includes the primary key of the `granny` table as a component, and the primary key of the `child` table includes them both.

> **NOTE**
>
> The fact that the primary ID of a table includes the primary ID of the referenced table is indicated through a little bar across the many end of the relationship.

FIGURE 30.7.
One type of a standard tri-level relationship uses compound keys.

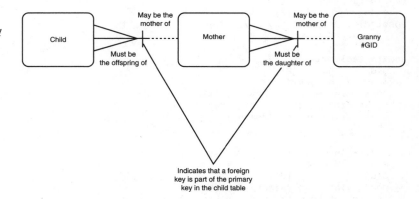

The minimum tri-level table definitions are as follows:

```
create table granny (
    gid      number(2),
constraint gr_p primary key (id))
;

create table mama (
    gid      number(2),
    mid      number(2),
    constraint ma_p primary key (gid, mid),
    constraint ma_gr_f foreign key (gid)
            references granny)
;

create table child (
```

```
    gid        number(2),
    mid        number(2),
    cid        number(2),
    constraint ch_p primary key (gid, mid, cid),
    constraint ch_ma_f1 foreign key (gid,mid)
            references mama)
;
```

The other method of implementing a one-to-many-to-many relationship, using individual keys, is shown in Figure 30.8. Inserts and reporting options for both versions are shown in Chapter 29.

FIGURE 30.8.

The other method of implementing a standard tri-level relationship uses individual primary keys.

The minimum tri-level table definitions are as follows:

```
create table granny (
    gid        number(2),
constraint gr_p primary key (id))
;

create table mama (
    gid        number(2),
    mid        number(4),
    constraint ma_p primary key (mid),
    constraint ma_gr_f foreign key (gid)
            references granny)
;

create table child (
    mid        number(4),
    cid        number(6),
    constraint ch_p primary key (cid),
    constraint ch_ma_f1 foreign key (mid)
            references mama)
;
```

Many-to-Many Relationships and Intersect Tables

Although there is a symbol for a many-to-many relationship in ER diagramming, there is no such thing as a direct many-to-many relationship between two tables on the database level because this construct is theoretically impossible. Instead, this relationship has to be resolved through an *intersect table*.

I'll use the lawyer table to illustrate the issue. Assume a lawyer and a client table. Each lawyer may serve one or more clients, and each client may be served by one or more lawyers. See Figure 30.9 for the ER diagram of this.

FIGURE 30.9.

An ER diagram of a many-to-many relationship.

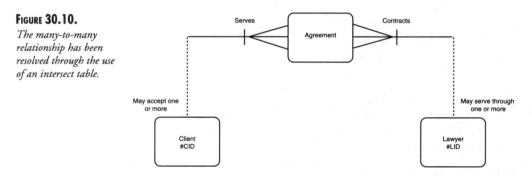

If this were a one-to-one relationship, a foreign key would have to be put into one of the tables, and that would be the end of it. The many-to-many case cannot be implemented in SQL, however. To resolve this problem, a third—intersect—table must be included. Most CASE tools do this automatically. Taking advantage of this, however, is not advisable because the tools tend to give some weird name to the intersect table. Furthermore, it is often desirable to add information such as to and from dates, the nature of the relationship, and the outcome. In this example, the intersect table is named `agreement`.

Four relationship descriptions are now necessary:

- Each lawyer may serve through one or more agreement.
- Each agreement contracts one lawyer.
- Each client may accept one or more agreements.
- Each agreement serves one client.

Figure 30.10 shows the revised ER diagram.

FIGURE 30.10.

The many-to-many relationship has been resolved through the use of an intersect table.

The minimum table definitions are as follows:

```
create table client (
    cid        number(2),
    constraint client_p primary key (cid))
;

create table lawyer (
    lid        number(2),
    constraint lawyer_p primary key (lid))
;
```

30

TABLE AND ENTITY RELATIONSHIPS

```
create table agreement (
   cid      number(2),
   lid      number(2),
   constraint agreement_p primary key (lid, cid)),
   constraint ag_cl_f foreign key (cid)
            references client),
   constraint ag_la_f foreign key (lid)
            references lawyer)
;
```

Other Combinations

The examples thus far have been tiny building blocks that would be used in much larger diagrams and, eventually, in systems. A full data model for a university, for example, could easily have over 500 tables. A small project is considered one with no more than 50 tables. ER modeling allows you to perform this task.

The last example in this chapter extends the previous example to include the office table to which both lawyers and clients are assigned, identical to the first example of the chapter. It will also add two tables below agreement: lcase and billing.

The additional business rules for the office table are as follows:

- Each lawyer is assigned to an office.
- Offices may be assigned one or more lawyers.
- Each client is assigned to an office.
- Offices may be assigned one or more clients.

The business rules for cases are as follows:

- Each case stems from an agreement.
- Each agreement may involve cases.

The business rules for billings are as follows:

- Each billing is charged for a case.
- Each case may incur billable time.

Figure 30.11 presents the revised and enhanced ER diagram.

FIGURE 30.11.

The multi-table relationship has been enhanced by more information.

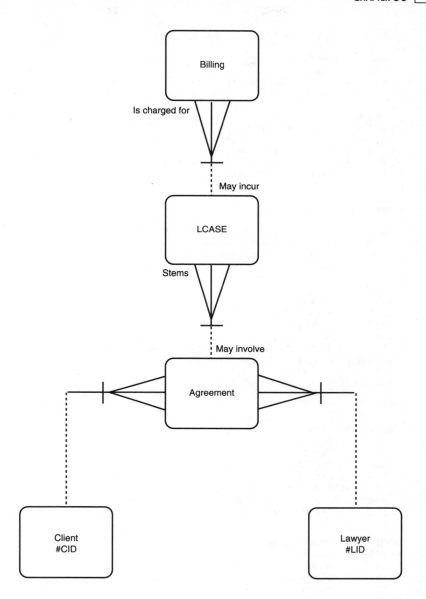

The minimum table definitions are as follows:

```
create table office (
    ID          number(2),
    constraint of2_p primary key (id))
;

create table client (
    cid         number(2),
    offid       number(2) constraint l_offid not null,
    constraint client_p primary key (cid),
    constraint cl_of_f foreign key (offid)
            references office)
;

create table lawyer (
    lid         number(2),
    offid       number(2) constraint l_offid not null,
    constraint lawyer_p primary key (lid)),
    constraint cl_of_f foreign key (offid)
            references office)
;

create table agreement (
    cid         number(2),
    lid         number(2),
    aid         number(2),
    constraint agreement_p primary key (lid, cid, aid)),
    constraint ag_cl_f foreign key (cid)
            references client),
    constraint ag_la_f foreign key (lid)
            references lawyer)
;

create table lcase (
    cid         number(2),
    lid         number(2),
    aid         number(2),
    bid         number(2),
    constraint case_p primary key (lid, cid, aid, bid)),
    constraint lc_ag_f foreign key (lid, cid, aid)
            references agreement)
;

create table billing (
    cid         number(2),
    lid         number(2),
    aid         number(2),
    bid         number(2),
    fid         number(2),
    constraint case_p primary key (lid, cid, aid, bid, fid)),
    constraint lc_ag_f foreign key (lid, cid, aid, bid)
            references lcase)
;
```

Summary

Tables are related to one another through relationships whose ends are described through their cardinality (one or many) and optionality (optional or mandatory). The most frequent relationship—one to many or many to one—has a one/optional end at the parent table and a many/mandatory end at the child table. A less-frequent variation of a one-to-many relationship is a recursive relationship, where a column in a table points to another column in the same table, usually to the primary key. A one-to-one relationship, which is rare, joins a single row of one table to a single row of another table.

Quite frequently, three tables are arranged in a one-to-many-to-many arrangement that can be implemented through a compound primary key or single-column primary keys. Although many-to-many relationships can be expressed in ER diagrams, they have to be resolved by means of an intersect table that is related to the original tables by one-to-many relationships.

The Optionality of Table Relationships

CHAPTER 31

You covered the cardinality of relationships in Chapter 30, "Table Relationships and Entity Relationship Diagrams." Cardinality can either be one or many. In a typical parent/child relationship, the parent end has a cardinality of one and the child end has a cardinality of many. Optionality refers to the requirement whether records must or must not have associated records in the other table. To refresh your memory from Chapter 30, the parent end is usually optional, which means that there may be parent records without associated child records. The child end is usually mandatory—child records must not exist without an associated parent record. No further consideration was given to the optionality of relations, but the most frequent and useful cases were assumed: a mandatory end for the referencing side and an optional end at the referenced side, except for recursive relationships that are optional on both sides.

Optionality is expressed as follows: Mandatory ends of relationships are solid lines and optional ends are dotted.

This chapter explores other combinations of cardinality and optionality, the caveat being that nonstandard options tend to make less sense and create more problems. Therefore, the purpose of this chapter is to address the pitfalls of these (of which there are many), more than the benefits (of which there are few).

The examples of this chapter build on those of Chapter 30.

> **NOTE**
>
> Throughout the chapter, only single-column constraints will be used, except for the multi-level design. All examples will also work with compound keys.

Mandatory and Optional Relationships

Whether a relationship end is mandatory or optional, cardinality of one or many is specified in three factors of the referencing table:

- A foreign key that specifies the many end (which may then be reduced to a one end).
- A not null constraint on the referencing table that specifies the end is mandatory—If the value must be not null and it must reference a valid value on the referenced table, a mandatory end results by default.
- A unique constraint that determines the cardinality—If the foreign key column is unique, the cardinality is one because only one reference value may be in the table.

On the referenced table, the reference column must be a primary or unique key. Therefore, a cardinality of one is a given.

A relationship that is mandatory on both ends has to be set up with two foreign keys, which can be implemented only through procedural code or through disabling and re-enabling constraints. Generally, that approach is a bad idea.

TIP

Using nonstandard relationships is asking for trouble. If you are tempted to do so anyway, make sure that there is not a better workaround, whether the nonstandard version is really necessary, and, if you do use it after all, whether your database and client tools support nonstandard relationships properly. This means testing all the way to screen generation. Just because a tool can create SQL DDL does not mean that everything else will work, too.

If at all possible, limit your design to standard options and to all optional options. Everything else is bound to snag either in the database or with client tools.

REAL-WORLD EXPERIENCES

During my Ph.D. training, I took a lot of research and statistics courses of the multivariate and more complex kind. Statistical analysis models a reality into variables that can be related to one another through methods and formulas. While a more complex model may be intellectually more appealing and theoretically more powerful, the huge cost of adding variables to the model is reduced statistical significance. As a result, a much larger sample size is needed; this usually drives expenses through the sky. Therefore, the best models have as many variables as are absolutely necessary to explain the phenomenon of interest but no more.

When modeling entities and data, the cost of overly complex solutions is poor performance, excessive cost for developing modules, and tools that ultimately cannot deal with the design without extensive tweaking and rework. Therefore, parsimony is a desirable goal here as well. A tight, efficient design that most people can understand is preferable to the "grandmother of all data models" with hundreds of tables whose purpose few people understand.

If you use overly complex or nonstandard designs, you will pay the price.

The Mandatory Many-to-Optional One Relationship

As a starting point, the mandatory many-to-optional one relationship is essentially the same situation that has been presented in the one-to-many relationship in Chapter 30. A mandatory many end of a relationship must have exactly one matching row in the other table. A mandatory end is enforced through a foreign key on a `not null` column. Figure 31.1 illustrates this implementation. There are two tables, called parent and child. The parent, in the SQL sense meaning that it can be a parent even without a child, is an oxymoron, yet that's how the data modeling lingo uses it. The child end, which is the relationship end of interest, is mandatory and of cardinality many.

FIGURE 31.1.

The implementation of the mandatory one-to-optional many relationship.

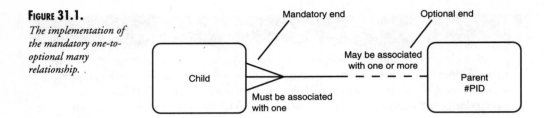

The minimum code to create this relationship is as follows:

```
create table parent (
   pid          number(2),
   constraint par_p primary key (pid));
```

A one-key column defined either as a primary or unique key is the only thing necessary for a parent table. This fact guarantees that on the parent side of the relationship there is exactly one matching row. *The foreign key constraint is implemented on the other table.* The following example shows the code necessary to implement a mandatory many end on the child table:

```
create table child (
   pid    number(2) constraint ch_pa_n not null,
   constraint ch_pa_f foreign key (pid)
          references parent);
```

The foreign key `ch_pa_f` enforces that the `pid` in the child table is either null or identical to exactly one parent row. The `not null` constraint makes the child end mandatory.

The Optional Many-to-Optional One Relationship

The optional many-to-optional one relationship is the same relationship as the previous one, except that the `not null` constraint of the foreign key column is dropped. This column may now either have a null value, which means it is no longer linked to the parent table, or a value represented in the referenced column. Figure 31.2 illustrates this implementation.

FIGURE 31.2.

The implementation of the optional one-to-optional many relationship.

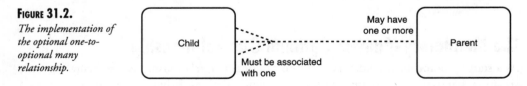

The minimum code to create this relationship is like the previous example, except that the `ch_pa_n not null` constraint is no longer in force:

```
create table child (
   pid    number(2)
  ...
```

The Optionality of Table Relationships

CHAPTER 31

659

31

THE OPTIONALITY
OF TABLE
RELATIONSHIPS

The Optional One-to-Optional One Relationship

You saw in Chapter 30 that the mandatory one-to-optional one relationship is a fairly typical standard. Just as with the optional many-to-optional one relationship, you just need to remove the `not null` constraint from the foreign key column to change this to optional both ways.

Conceptually this is a funny case unless one table is still considered a parent or reference table. The entities may exist by themselves or they may be joined as one on one. An example could be a license(s) that is preprinted and sitting in some vault until assigned and where a person may hold only one current copy. There would be no requirement on the person table, other than a suitable primary or unique key.

In entity relationship (ER) modeling lingo, each person may carry no or only one license, and each license may be assigned to zero or one person. The ER diagram for this arrangement is illustrated in Figure 31.3.

FIGURE 31.3.
The optional one-to-optional one relationship.

This relationship is coded as follows:

```
create table person (
    ID        number(2),
    constraint person_p primary key (id));
```

As with any other referenced column, the person ID must be defined either as a primary or unique key. The other table, `license`, is created through the following statement:

```
create table license (
    persid    number(2),
    constraint l_persid_u unique (persid)
    constraint li_pe_f foreign key (persid)
            references person);
```

The Mandatory One-to-Mandatory One Relationship

The mandatory one-to-mandatory one relationship is the other extreme, where one line of a table is always joined with another line from another table. Its use is limited and the relationship is cumbersome to deal with. In practical terms, such a relationship is not really implemented feasibly because constraints have to be disabled for inserts and re-enabled afterwards. Obviously, that would be a rather unsatisfactory workaround. If it is really desired, it is preferable to use procedural extensions and triggers instead.

The example starts with the mandatory one-to-optional relationship, which has been illustrated in Figure 30.6. Instead of stripping out the not null constraint, as has happened previously, a second foreign key is put in from the previously referenced table to the referencing one. In essence, now the tables keep each other in check. This makes it impossible to enter a row into either table without temporarily disabling at least one constraint.

This is now the totalitarian state where each person must carry exactly one license and each license must be assigned to exactly one person. The ER diagram for this arrangement is illustrated in Figure 31.4.

FIGURE 31.4.

A mandatory one-to-mandatory one relationship.

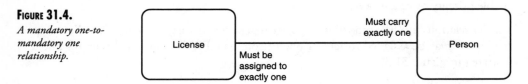

Because a foreign key constraint needs a valid referenced column, the mandatory one-to-mandatory one relationship needs to be established in a three-step process:

1. Create one table without foreign key constraint.
2. Create the other table with all constraints.
3. Add the foreign key to the first table.

The following example demonstrates this three-step process. First the person table is dropped and re-created:

```
drop table person;

create table person (
   id        number(2),
   constraint person_p primary key (id);
```

This code returns

```
Table dropped.
Table created.
```

Then the license table is dropped and re-created. The constraints for both tables are retrieved from Data Dictionary views:

```
drop table license cascade constraints;

create table license (
   id    number(2),
   constraint license_p primary key (id),
   constraint li_pe_f foreign key (id)
           references person);
alter table person add (
  constraint pe_li_f foreign key (id)
           references license)
;
```

```
@29squ03b
@29squ03b
```

This code returns

```
Table dropped.
Table created.
Table dropped.
Table created.
Table altered.

Enter table name--UPPER CASE ONLY: PERSON
old  12: where a.table_name      = '&p_table' and
new  12: where a.table_name      = 'PERSON' and

CONSTRAINT_NAME T TABLE_NAME COLUMN_NAME      R_CONSTRAI DR STATUS
--------------- - ---------- ---------------  ---------- -- -------
PERSON_P        P PERSON     ID                             ENABLED
PE_LI_F         R            ID               LICENSE_P  NO ENABLED

Enter table name--UPPER CASE ONLY: LICENSE
old  12: where a.table_name      = '&p_table' and
new  12: where a.table_name      = 'LICENSE' and

CONSTRAINT_NAME T TABLE_NAME COLUMN_NAME      R_CONSTRAI DR STATUS
--------------- - ---------- ---------------  ---------- -- -------
LICENSE_P       P LICENSE    ID                             ENABLED
LI_PE_F         R            ID               PERSON_P   NO ENABLED
```

Thus, to implement the mandatory one-to-mandatory one relationship takes two constraints and one matching column per table, not including the not nulls that are thrown in by the primary key.

Inserting any row into either table returns errors, as Listing 31.1 shows.

Listing 31.1. Inserting a mandatory one-to-one relationship.

```
--       Filename: 31squ01.sql
--        Purpose: inserting mandatory one on one relationship
--                 returns errors
--
insert into person  values (1);
insert into license values (1);
```

This code returns

```
insert into person  values (1)
           *
ERROR at line 1:
ORA-02291: integrity constraint (HANS.PE_LI_F) violated - parent key not found

insert into license values (1)
           *
ERROR at line 1:
ORA-02291: integrity constraint (HANS.LI_PE_F) violated - parent key not found
```

Therefore, you must disable one of the foreign key constraints, load the data in proper order, and then re-enable the constraint. Listing 31.2 illustrates this procedure.

Listing 31.2. Inserting a mandatory one-to-one relationship and disabling the foreign key.

```
--        Filename: 31squ02.sql
--         Purpose: inserting mandatory one on one relationship
--                  temporarily disabling foreign key to avoid errors
--
alter table license
   disable constraint li_pe_f;

@29squ03b
```

This code returns

```
Table altered.

Enter table name--UPPER CASE ONLY: LICENSE
old  12: where a.table_name     = '&p_table' and
new  12: where a.table_name     = 'LICENSE' and

CONSTRAINT_NAME T TABLE_NAME COLUMN_NAME     R_CONSTRAI DR STATUS
--------------- - ---------- --------------- ---------- -- -------
LICENSE_P       P LICENSE    ID                            ENABLED
LI_PE_F         R            ID              PERSON_P   NO DISABLED
```

The foreign key is there; it's just not enabled. If the `license` row is inserted first, the matching person row may be inserted as well. However, the other way around, as shown in the following example, leads to an error.

```
insert into license values (1);
insert into person  values (1);
insert into person  values (2);
insert into license values (2);
insert into license values (3);
insert into person  values (3);
```

This code returns

```
1 row created.

1 row created.

insert into person  values (2)
                *
ERROR at line 1:
ORA-02291: integrity constraint (HANS.PE_LI_F) violated - parent key not found

1 row created.

1 row created.

1 row created.
```

As a result, the `person` table has one row less than the `license` table, which is shown through the next two statements:

```
select * from license;

select * from person;
```

This code returns

```
       ID
---------
        1
        2
        3

       ID
---------
        1
        3
```

Because of this discrepancy, the foreign key cannot be re-enabled. This is illustrated through the following statement:

```
alter table license
   enable constraint li_pe_f;
```

It returns

```
alter table license
*
ERROR at line 1:
ORA-02298: cannot enable (HANS.LI_PE_F) - parent keys not found
```

The problem is eliminated by reinserting the missing row; this is done in the next statement. This works now because the matching license row was created in the first run:

```
insert into person  values (2);

alter table license
   enable constraint li_pe_f;
```

```
@29squ03b
```

This code returns

```
1 row created.

Table altered.

Enter table name--UPPER CASE ONLY: LICENSE
old  12: where a.table_name     = '&p_table' and
new  12: where a.table_name     = 'LICENSE' and
```

CONSTRAINT_NAME	T	TABLE_NAME	COLUMN_NAME	R_CONSTRAI	DR	STATUS
LICENSE_P	P	LICENSE	ID			ENABLED
LI_PE_F	R		ID	PERSON_P	NO	ENABLED

Now the rows are loaded and the constraints are enforced.

CAUTION

If both tables are fully defined right away, rather than adding the foreign key constraint of the first table after defining the second, the key is created, listed as enabled, but not consistently enforced. Therefore, person values may be entered as long as the primary key constraint is not violated. License values may be entered only if the primary key constraint is not violated and the value is found in the person table. The following illustrates this behavior:

```
--      Filename: 31squ02a.sql
--       Purpose: mandatory one on one relationship
--                not enforced
--
insert into person  values (1);
insert into license values (1);
insert into license values (1);
insert into person  values (1);
```

This returns this output:

```
1 row created.

1 row created.

insert into license values (1)
*
ERROR at line 1:
ORA-00001: unique constraint (HANS.LICENSE_P) violated

insert into person  values (1)
*
ERROR at line 1:
ORA-00001: unique constraint (HANS.PERSON_P) violated
```

The first two insert statements should have resulted in foreign key violations, but did not. Both of the errors in the output listing result from primary key violations. The next statement first attempts to load a license record that has no matching person record. This results in an error, which it should. The next three statements should return errors but do not:

```
insert into license values (2);
insert into person  values (2);
insert into person  values (3);
insert into license values (3);
```

The statements return the following:

```
insert into license values (2)
            *
ERROR at line 1:
ORA-02291: integrity constraint (HANS.LI_PE_F) violated - parent key not found

1 row created.

1 row created.

1 row created.
```

This switch on/switch off approach may be fine for static data or lookup tables that don't change much but are risky in a transactional system if another user can enter data into the tables while the constraint is disabled. There are workarounds, but complexity increases when workarounds are implemented.

In most cases, it is preferable to avoid this relationship altogether because

- One side may turn out not to be mandatory after all.
- One table could handle the attributes of both. This is the preferred solution.
- If this relationship has to be used, a procedural Application Programmer's Interface (API) should be built to support it. While the subject of procedural APIs goes beyond the scope of this book, in essence the tables are set so that nobody can directly insert records. The insert is then done in procedural code that ensures that the matching values are there. Users with a need to insert are granted access to that procedure, which provides a tightly controlled method.

The Mandatory Master and Optional Detail Relationship

Earlier in this chapter, it was fairly easy to drop the mandatory detail end down to an optional detail end. All it took was the elimination of a few constraints. Working from that relaxed model, the next example attempts to make the master end mandatory.

The standard one mandatory-to-many optional parent-child relationship is an oxymoron when applied to the reality of parents and children. A parent is defined as a person who has at least one live child. As the case of orphans illustrates, somebody can be a child without having live parents. Thus, the parent end is of cardinality one and mandatory; the child end is of cardinality many and optional. Figure 31.5 illustrates this implementation.

FIGURE 31.5.

The implementation of the mandatory one-to-optional many relationship.

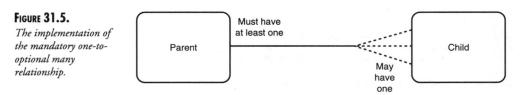

The minimum code to create this relationship starts out with the doubly optional case, adding a constraint in the parent as a third step. The necessary code is presented in Listing 31.3.

Listing 31.3. Mandatory one-to-optional many relationship.

```
--        Filename: 31squ03.sql
--         Purpose: mandatory one to optional many relationship
--
drop table parent cascade constraints;

drop table child  cascade constraints;
```

continues

Listing 31.3. continued

```
create table parent (
    pid         number(2),
    constraint par_p primary key (pid),
    cid         number(2) constraint p_cid_n not null)
;

create table child (
    cid     number(2),
    constraint chi_p primary key (cid),
    pid     number(2),
    constraint ch_pa_f foreign key (pid)
        references parent,
    constraint ch_p_c_u unique (pid, cid))
;

alter table parent add (
  constraint pa_ch_f foreign key (pid,cid)
          references child(pid, cid))
;

@29squ03b
@29squ03b
```

This code returns

```
Table dropped.

Table dropped.

Table created.

Table created.

Table altered.

Enter table name--UPPER CASE ONLY: PARENT
old  12: where a.table_name     = '&p_table' and
new  12: where a.table_name     = 'PARENT' and
```

CONSTRAINT_NAME	T	TABLE_NAME	COLUMN_NAME	R_CONSTRAI	DR	STATUS
P_CID_N	C	PARENT	CID			ENABLED
PAR_P	P		PID			ENABLED
PA_CH_F	R		PID	CH_P_C_U	NO	ENABLED
PA_CH_F	R		CID	CH_P_C_U	NO	ENABLED

```
Enter table name—UPPER CASE ONLY: CHILD
old  12: where a.table_name     = '&p_table' and
new  12: where a.table_name     = 'CHILD' and
```

CONSTRAINT_NAME	T	TABLE_NAME	COLUMN_NAME	R_CONSTRAI	DR	STATUS
CHI_P	P	CHILD	CID			ENABLED
CH_P_C_U	U		CID			ENABLED

| CH_P_C_U | U | PID | | ENABLED |
| CH_PA_F | R | PID | PAR_P | NO ENABLED |

The next script attempts to insert rows into both tables.

Listing 31.4. Inserting into a mandatory one-to-optional many relationship.

```
--       Filename: 31squ04.sql
--        Purpose: inserting into
--                 mandatory one to optional many relationship
--
insert into child values (1,NULL);
insert into child values (2,NULL);
insert into child values (3,NULL);
insert into child values (4,NULL);
insert into child values (5,NULL);
insert into child values (6,NULL);
```

Thus far things work fine; six rows are inserted (no output listed). The problem starts with the next three statements because the combination of child and parent values is a compound key in parent:

```
insert into parent values (1,1);
insert into parent values (2,3);
insert into parent values (3,4);
```

The following error is returned for each row with minor modifications:

```
insert into parent values (1,1)
                *
ERROR at line 1:
ORA-02291: integrity constraint (HANS.PA_CH_F) violated - parent key not found
```

Therefore, an update of child to appropriate parent values, as shown in the next example, does not work either:

```
update child set pid = 1 where cid = 1;
update child set pid = 2 where cid = 3;
update child set pid = 3 where cid = 4;
update child set pid = 3 where cid = 5;
update child set pid = 1 where cid = 6;
```

This returns the following code five times with modifications:

```
update child set pid = 1 where cid = 6
            *
ERROR at line 1:
ORA-02291: integrity constraint (HANS.CH_PA_F) violated - parent key not found
```

Therefore, the initially loaded rows are rolled back.

```
rollback;
```

Listing 31.5 gets around the limitations by disabling a foreign key, loading, and then re-enabling the key.

Listing 31.5. Inserting into a mandatory one-to-optional many relationship.

```
--          Filename: 31squ05.sql
--           Purpose: inserting into
--                    mandatory one to optional many relationship
--
alter table parent disable constraint pa_ch_f;

insert into parent values (1,1);
insert into parent values (2,3);
insert into parent values (3,4);
insert into child values (1,1);
insert into child values (2,NULL);
insert into child values (3,2);
insert into child values (4,3);
insert into child values (5,3);
insert into child values (6,1);

alter table parent enable constraint pa_ch_f;
```

This code returns

```
Table altered.
1 row created.
...
1 row created.

Table altered.
```

The alternatives described for resolving mandatory one-to-mandatory one relationships apply here as well:

- Consider whether the mandatory end could not be optional.

- If this relationship absolutely has to be used, a procedural API should be built to support it.

REAL-WORLD EXPERIENCES

I use Oracle Designer/2000 a lot. One of its nice features is a list of values (LOV) form (client screen application), which can be called from another form to provide a lookup value, return that value into the calling form, and then disappear into cyberspace. This feature requires a defined foreign key from the base table of the calling form to the lookup table on which the LOV form is based.

Once I tried to use the LOV feature but happened to have a compound foreign key involved (see Chapter 29, "Keys, Indexes, Constraints, and Table/Column Comments"). Too bad the LOV feature works only with a single-column foreign key. I had to use a workaround—a surrogate primary key combined with some code that copied the compound column values from one table to the other.

Summary

This chapter outlines standard table relationships. It presents other combinations of cardinality and optionality. Some of these are easy to implement. Examples are optional one-to-optional one, or optional one-to-optional many relationships. For both of these, it is only necessary to drop the not null constraint on the foreign key field of the referencing table.

The other, nonstandard options, which were shown here, tend to make less sense and create more problems. A relationship that is mandatory on both ends has to be set up with two foreign keys, which can be implemented only through procedural code or through disabling and re-enabling constraints. The mandatory master and optional detail relationship requires procedural code or the disabling and re-enabling of the constraints approach.

CHAPTER 32

Relational Database Design and Normalization

IN THIS CHAPTER

Many tables have been used in the discussion thus far, and all of them were provided and were more or less taken as givens. The previous chapters described the mechanics and the options of table creation, but there was no concern about how a database, its tables, and their columns should be laid out in the first place. Chapters 30, "Table Relationships and Entity Relationship Diagrams," and 31, "The Optionality of Table Relationships," present ways that entities (and subsequently, tables) can be related to one another—standard ways, possible ways, and cumbersome ways. This chapter deals with the most important principles of database design. Because this is a book about the SQL language, this chapter can provide only a cursory treatment of design topics.

Database Design Steps

The formal models of database-systems design use a three-step approach:

1. The logical design—entity relationship models with softboxes and relationship symbols that relate some real-life entities and their attributes of interest to one another—is created.

2. The logical design is then translated into the physical design, which changes the logical model into tables, columns, and constraints.

3. The physical design is converted to the SQL code that is necessary to create tables, columns, and constraints in the database.

There is a good reason for having both a logical and a physical step. The logical model attempts to create a methodologically clean way to represent a reality of interest in a data model. The physical model takes necessary trade-offs in consideration—trade-offs motivated by estimated table size, predominant use (transactional processing versus query performance), and acceptable complexity. The SQL data-definition statements are usually a very close translation of the physical model, except that some constructs require the use of procedural code that goes beyond SQL proper in order to work properly.

REAL-WORLD EXPERIENCES

In a previous life, I studied economics at the University of Vienna in Austria. Once we got into economic modeling, we quickly got used to the phrase "everything else being equal." That being the case, some variation in one variable would produce a related variation in another variable. This is a *logical model.* The problem of that approach is that in real life, everything else usually is not equal. To deal with that fact requires a much more complex approach. Often, data about certain phenomena is not directly available, and an empirical test of a model has to make do with surrogates. That reality corresponds to a *physical model.*

In the entity-relationship step, it is (or should be) attempted to achieve a theoretically clean model, also referred to as a *fully normalized model.* Such a model fulfills all the mandates of the normalization approach.

In the physical modeling step, the entity model may be denormalized, which is done for the purpose of making things simpler (which backfires quite often) or speeding up processing, especially where heavy-duty queries are involved.

The Aesthetics of Database Design

The people who compose great music or create great works of art tend to have a great deal of knowledge and experience that lays the foundation on which their creativity, artistry, and intuition can construct a whole. Once all is done, a ton of critics and otherwise initiated individuals will analyze and explain whether or why the outcome is great or faulty.

On the other end of the spectrum (engineering, hard-core science, or mathematics), the situation is still the same—creativity, artistry, and intuition working on a foundation of knowledge and experience. An example of this is how Watson and Crick figured out the double-helix shape of DNA. Therefore, it is not surprising how many artists and musicians can be found in mathematics, engineering, and computing, and how many mathematicians, engineers, and computer or software professionals are artists or musicians.

Relational database design is no different, combining artistry and analysis. The more formal, analytical aspects are covered in the section "Data Normalization," later in this chapter. The next few sections outline the artistic criteria.

Parsimony and Effectiveness

If you have something that can be modeled with a few tables, using many more for a tiny gain of functionality or no gain at all would be a much worse model. A model should use as many entities as are needed and no more. What is needed can be gleaned from a good analysis of the situation to be modeled. Not all aspects of this situation are important, though, and things change. Efficient design focuses on the important aspects and provides at least the flexibility for future growth. This is a matter of understanding priorities, current and future, and having them represented in the model.

By looking at existing systems, records, and other information stores, an expert in a field—be it hard goods, financials, software, or human resources—should be able to come up with a meaningful set of entities and tables, at least if properly prodded by a modeler who has sufficient people skills to find out what really matters to the expert.

Short of revolutionary change, such an expert should not be too surprised about the development of his or her field in the course of a few years. A good data modeler needs to be able to work with such a professional in order to formulate features and sort out priorities.

> **NOTE**
>
> The formal normalization rules do not deal with this issue at all. Instead, the information to be included in entities and attributes is simply considered a given. Other methods do try to provide help in this context; some CASE tools such as Oracle Designer/2000 have a business-process modeling step that tries to capture all important parts. Other methods, such as business-process reengineering, try to optimize the process and the system aspects at the same time—besides, of course, giving a handy excuse for massive firings. Where existing systems are to be reengineered, metrics about these systems can help indicate relative priorities.

Simplicity and Efficiency

Complexities are the stuff bureaucracies are made of, and sometimes complexities seem to be their only purpose. Just look at all the small-print legalese you have seen in the course of your life—the average tax return, the laws of most countries, or the purchase order forms of most organizations. There seems to be a real fascination with complexities, and most organizations keep developing them as they grow.

Complexities also come with an incredible price tag. That's what the U.S. military's $500 screwdrivers and toilet seats are all about. A commercial example of unnecessary complexity are bank accounts in this country. A creditor sends me a bill. I mail a check to him. He submits the check to his bank, which eventually credits his account. His bank sends the check to my bank, presumably through some routing or clearance service. My bank pays his bank. If, however, my account has insufficient funds, the check is rejected. It eventually gets back to his bank, which then notifies him—a process that is not stopped even if the funds to cover it become available one second after my bank has rejected the claim. A more complex and idiotic system is hard to imagine, yet that's what the largest economic might in the world uses.

In continental Europe, the original bill comes with a deposit slip with all the creditor's information—account number, name, reference number, and so on. All I need to do is sign it and submit it to my bank, which then will pay his account (again, through some clearinghouse). If there is no money in the account or the credit limit is exceeded, either I am informed on the spot or everything is returned to me at once so that I can deal with it before further problems arise. This system does the same as the U.S. system (routes funds to creditors), but it does so with much less complexity, with superior error handling, and without the need for me to balance my account myself. Obviously, it is far superior.

In database design, complexities result from

- Poor design in its own right, not motivated by other issues.
- Workarounds for inappropriate other systems or because of resource limitations.

■ Inability to reduce overly complex semantics to their basis. Organizations that can't say no to pressures from within, such as universities, thrive on this and end up with a proliferation of majors, options, electives, tracks, and whatever other name a department might think about in order to get a program going that might attract a handful of students in the course of a few years. If now each department chooses its own terminology for the same set of things, it is almost impossible to model without some up-front streamlining. Otherwise, you end up with an unwieldy hierarchical structure or with many levels of tables where a couple might have been sufficient.

■ Effort to be everything to all people. The 80/20 rule applies to database design as well, and often I wonder whether this is not a 90/10 rule. This is the effectiveness revisited inside a system. Even if the total scope is set, there are tons of little design decisions that can be handled with more or less complexity.

■ Overly generalized data models aimed at handling just about any situation that might arise for an application. This is the systematic way to be all things to all people, resulting in a data model that is all normalized and clean but so huge that few people can fully understand it. At least one large vendor sells one of these, and smaller vendors do the same with vertical markets. A model with some 600 or 1,000 tables might be acceptable if it covers the entire business, but would be a bit much for handling just one major function.

An example would be a universal data model for ways to reach people or organizations, consisting of about eight tables and being able to hold information about any possible way to reach a person or organization, present and future. That does sound good, but it might be just as good to have one table for addresses, one for phones, one for fax, one for a pager, and so on, and perhaps one for e-mail and Web addresses. If only three tables are needed, why bother with eight?

Other Dimensions

Other aesthetic elements, such as form and structure, balance, blend, unity, elegance, and expression have their counterpoints in systems design as well. They are well described in Steve McConnell's *Code Complete* (Microsoft Press, 1993).

As a southeastern senator once said: "I can't define what pornography is, but when I see it, I know it." Begging the question of what the good senator is doing in his spare time in order to have developed that competency, he is correct in the sense that many issues cannot be decided on the basis of hard rules alone.

Data Normalization

The rules of data normalization supply formal tests for a model. According to Richard Barker (*CASE*Method Entity Relationship Modelling*, Addison Wesley, 1989), the normalization procedure enforces some useful standards for the data model that avoid data redundancy and allow the model to be mapped to many different physical database designs. The logical model should, therefore, always be fully normalized.

Having a fully normalized design avoids so-called anomalies, problems that will otherwise beset the quality of information. Nevertheless, it is frequently decided to denormalize a model in a trade-off between performance and problems. Denormalization is an obvious trick of the trade that requires good understanding about what is won or lost, or else it is an unpredictable gamble. Starting out with a non-normalized design is even more dangerous because now the trade-off is implicit and one soon loses track of what it was in the first place. Good gamblers know the odds and know whether they are gambling, and good analysts understand the trade-offs and know whether they are engaging in one. This section, therefore, illustrates the steps of normalization using several variations of an example.

Normalization is done within the framework of five normal forms (numbered from first to fifth). Most designs conform to at least the third normal form. It is fair to say that models that do not are likely to cause a lot of problems later on. A variation of the third normal form is the Boyce-Codd normal form, which is not discussed here because it is beyond the scope of this book. The fourth and fifth form are less frequently implemented and even less frequently explained.

First Normal Form: No Repeating Groups

The most painful change for anyone who is moving from a procedural language such as C or Pascal to SQL is the absence of arrays. Arrays offer a very convenient way to deal with repeating sets of data and work through them with an indexed loop. SQL giveth and SQL taketh away—you can think of indexed tables as arrays of structures that are so flexible that you do not have to know the size of the array up front. On the other hand, indexed arrays within records are not implemented and, as of the first normal form, are verboten.

The industry trend toward object-oriented extensions will change this by implementing arrays. Although it is nice to have such extensions available, it is advisable to use them sparingly. Even if extended versions of SQL and the RDBMS can deal with them, third-party client tools might not be able to.

A typical example of an array is the way that student records are often represented in a flat file system:

```
ssn
name
...
course1
credits1
grade1
course2
credits2
grade2
...
course15
```

```
credits15
grade15
```

Figure 32.1 illustrates such a table—so wide that it cannot be represented on a single line, instead taking up several.

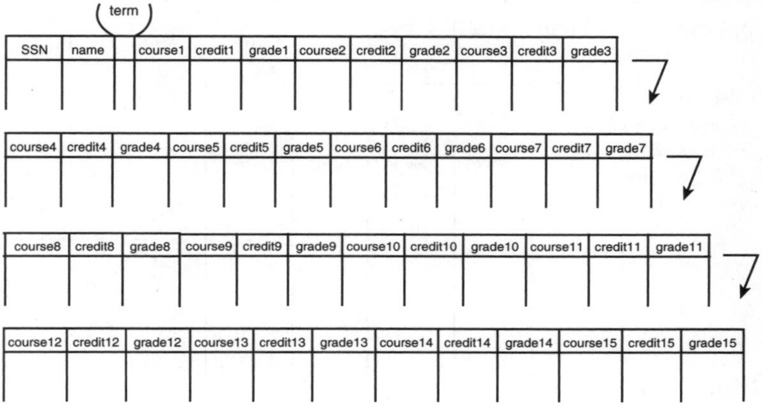

FIGURE 32.1.

This students *table, including the enrollment array, is quite unwieldy.*

This is the good old COBOL-with-flatfile way that causes a number of problems:

- It is a waste of space because most students take only a handful of courses, leaving the remaining slots unused.

- Unless every student is made to take 15 courses, nulls have to be used for the remaining ones, with all the problems that those bring.

- It cannot accommodate the student who tries to load up as much as possible in one semester. At the University of Illinois, for example, graduate students may take a full load of graduate courses *and* a full load of undergraduate courses. If some of these are for lab or activity classes, 15 slots are not sufficient to represent such a pattern.

- It is a pain to summarize across the array using SQL. To get the total credit or the grade point average requires calculations on 15 or 30 columns. A procedural language could do that with a simple loop expression.

- If the array values are to be joined to another table, such as a course lookup table, a join has to be performed for all 15 columns (course1...course15), which is unwieldy and error prone.

- Subtleties such as adding or dropping courses are hard to represent in this structure. At some schools, academic regulations have it that dropping within a few weeks results in the record of having been enrolled being eliminated. That means finding the structure with the offending course and, usually, moving the contents of the subsequent structures up a slot to prevent a hole in the row.

■ If the student record is the only place where course information is stored, courses that are offered but not taken cease to exist. This problem is not resolved by conforming to the first normal form alone, however.

The proper way to remodel this array is to use two tables, one for students and one for enrollments, that are joined by SSN. Then each student may have as few or as many enrollments as applicable. (See Figure 32.2.)

FIGURE 32.2.

The students *and* enrollment *tables, fulfilling the first normal form.*

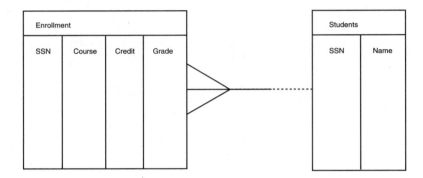

Second Normal Form: Dependency of All Attributes on the Entire Unique Identifier

The second normal form is explained on the basis of two concepts: functional dependency and unique identifier (UID).

An attribute (A) is functionally dependent on another attribute (B) if for each value of attribute B there exists only one value of attribute A. For example, short of someone changing his or her gender or falsifying his or her Social Security card, gender is functionally dependent on Social Security number. The SSN determines the person, whose gender remains the same.

If there is a table with either a primary key or a unique key defined as not null, by knowing this key, it is possible to uniquely identify and retrieve the row associated with that key. In relational lingo, you can say the following:

■ Such a key is a unique identifier for the row. If this identifier is known, exactly that row and no other row can be retrieved with the statement select * from *table* where *uid = value*;.

■ The key is termed a determinant of all row values because they can be determined by looking them up in the row retrieved through the key. Therefore, all other row values depend on the key.

The second normal form applies only to tables with a compound unique key. The enrollments table is likely to contain a compound unique identifier, made up of the SSN column and a sequence within the parent sub id column. That being the case, enrollments must not contain an attribute that is determined by any of these columns alone. This means that enrollments must not contain any information pertaining to a student without regard to the sub id value. Figure 32.3 illustrates a model in violation of this rule. The enrollments table now contains an additional column, called student_level, that shows whether the student is a freshman, sophomore, junior, or senior.

FIGURE 32.3.

An attribute depending on a partial key is a violation of second normal form.

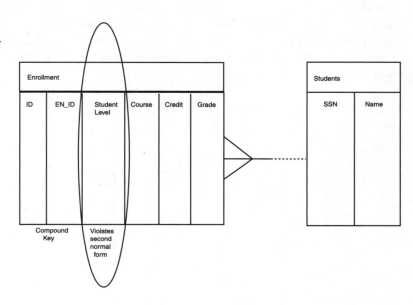

The problem is easily resolved by moving the offending column to the students table, as has been done in Figure 32.4. The student level, which depends on the student UID, is now placed in that table.

FIGURE 32.4.

Having an attribute depending on a full UID-only key resolves the violation.

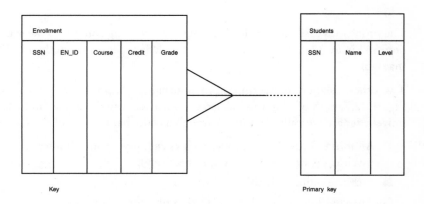

Third Normal Form: No Non-Key Attribute Depends on Another Non-Key Attribute

The issue addressed in the third normal form is either one of redundancy or one of information being put into the wrong spot. As a condition, the third normal form requires that the value of a non-key attribute must not determine the value of another non-key attribute. A typical example is a short-name/long-name set of columns, or a value/derived value set. If, in the example shown in Figure 32.3, SSN were not part of the primary key but was just a foreign key to SSN, this would violate the third rather than the second normal form. This violation is illustrated in Figure 32.5 and resolved in Figure 32.6.

FIGURE 32.5.

Having a non-key attribute depending on another non-key attribute is a violation of third normal form.

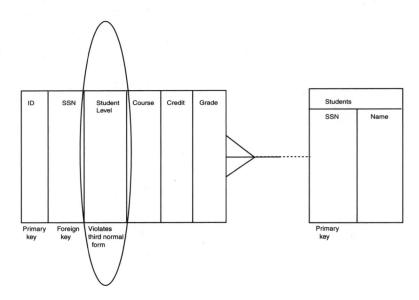

The problem is easily resolved by moving the offending column to the students table, as was done in Figure 32.4. The student's level, which depends on the student UID, is now placed in that table.

Two other violations of the third normal form just within the enrollments table are shown in Figure 32.7, both of which are related to course identifiers. Courses in most U.S. colleges and universities are typically identified through a code that consists of three or four parts:

- A subject or department code, such as eng, psy, or mus (indicating an engineering, a psychology, or a music course, respectively).
- A course number, such as 100 or 635.
- An extension, such as L for a lab class or S for a seminar.
- A serial number that allows you to distinguish between two sections of an otherwise identical course.

FIGURE 32.6.

Having the attribute depend only on a primary key resolves the violation.

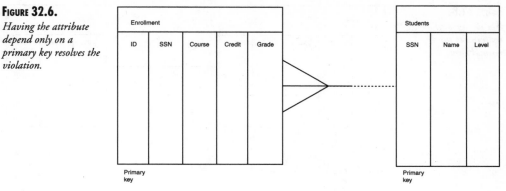

In good old mainframe style, the last two parts are often meshed into one code, which is not good because the meaning can become quite ambiguous.

What is already interesting here is the distinction of course and course section, which is an instance of type course but now has a room, time, and professor associated with it. This distinction, however, will be neglected for the time being.

The subject code determines the subject; the course number determines the level, such as freshman, sophomore, junior, senior, master's level, and doctoral level or lower division, upper division, and graduate. Such a level code, which depends on a part of the key (the course number), is often included only in the table, however, *which violates the third normal form.* The same is the case if a plain-English subject column is included, because the subject is known from the subject code, which is the other part of the key (see Figure 32.7).

FIGURE 32.7.

Having non-key attributes depending on another non-key attribute or on a partial key violates third normal form.

Enrollment

ID	SSN	Course level	Subject	Course	Credit	Grade

These violations are resolved by decomposing this enrollment table into two separate ones: one for enrollments and one for courses. (See Figure 32.8.)

FIGURE 32.8.
The decomposed model conforms to third normal form.

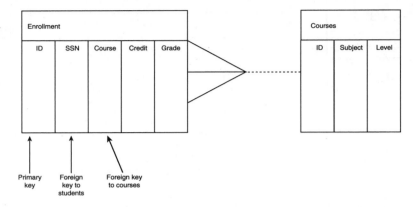

Denormalization

Denormalization introduces a controlled redundancy into the design with the purpose to avoid join operations. In addition to the foreign key in the child table that references the primary key of the parent table, the columns of the parent table that are most frequently used together with the child table are copied into the child table as well.

If a query needs only those columns of the master table that are doubled up anyway, the join is not necessary. On the other hand, on an insert or update, both tables are affected. If a value in the denormalized column changes, all instances have to be updated, not just the one row in the parent table.

In this example, if queries against the `enrollments` table frequently include the student name, having a redundant student name column in `enrollments` would make sense. These columns are *synchronized*, meaning that a change in one of its values in the parent table must trigger a change in the detail table. Figure 32.9 illustrates this approach.

FIGURE 32.9.

This denormalized model now has a redundant, synchro- nized name column in the enrollment *table.*

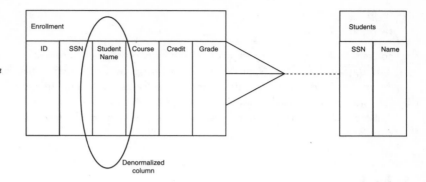

In transactional systems, denormalization should be used sparingly if at all. In informational systems for decision support or analysis, denormalization can be used much more and can have enormous advantages. Because informational systems are mostly read-only, their overhead for inserts or updates is negligible anyway.

Manipulating Denormalized Tables with Synchronized Columns

If the denormalized columns are in sync, selecting from them is no problem; choosing from either one should return the same results. Often, however, a join can be avoided, and that means, usually, performance gains.

When inserting or updating the affected tables, additional code is necessary to keep the values synchronized. This cannot be done automatically in SQL, but is in reality not much of a prob- lem either, because two mechanisms exist to take care of it:

- The typical client application keeps parent and child records that belong to each other in memory. Therefore, whenever the client record is inserted or updated, the redun- dant value can be copied in from the block of the parent, and the client program will keep the two in sync.

- Strictly on the database level, and going beyond SQL, are database triggers that can be set to fire whenever a certain event occurs. One post insert or post update trigger would have to be set on the child table, which then would direct the RDBMS to find the appropriate value in the parent table and insert it in the client table. Another post update trigger would have to be placed in the parent table to update all values in the child column if the synchronized parent column value changes.

TIP

In my own designs, I tend to not denormalize transactional systems at all, but resort instead to a liberal use of keys and indexes to facilitate joins. The only exceptions are redundant

continues

32

DATABASE DESIGN AND NORMALIZATION

> *continued*
>
> columns that hold what would have been a compound key where a surrogate primary key is used. (See the section "Conversion Using Surrogate Keys," later in this chapter, which includes a design example with surrogate keys for an illustration.) In informational systems, I still start out from a fully normalized design, to which I add redundant, flattened-out tables that are derived from the normalized ones. That gives me all the flexibility I need and also prejoins tables for fast reporting.

Fake Arrays

The first normal form requires that repeating groups be prohibited. To remedy a violation of the first normal form, the 15 repeated columns with course information in the enrollments table have to be reorganized into their own separate table.

As with most fun things in life, what does and does not constitute a repeating group may be subject to interpretation—often determined, as are many not-so-fun things in life, by policies and business rules.

In a university setting, a good example is prerequisite test scores. It used to be, at least purportedly so, that a school would accept either an ACT or SAT score. Therefore, obligingly, the flatfilesmith at IT inserted an SAT or ACT field into the design and that was that. Then, however, some of the professors thought that either the math or the English subscore in itself was more meaningful, and then the total score was broken out into two subscores and a total.

Now, however, the university finds itself in a plight for recruiting students (read the Walden college subseries in *Dilbert*, if you wonder why) and decides to be a little bit more student-centered. Real change is out of the question, of course, so a meaningless, yet good-looking measure is adopted: The university will now accept either ACT or SAT scores. On top of that, graduate student administration is now rolled into the system as well, with a proliferation of GRE, GMAT, LSAT, and other specialized tests. What started out as no big deal is now a real mess, and now it is quite obvious that a subtable is really needed. If you think now that the stupid flatfilesmith should have thought about that in the first place, consider again that he might not have been stupid at all but was forced into frugal space allocation, and that he is no more guilty than is the entire computer/software industry of the equally stupid Year 2000 problem.

What it really boils down to is that this is not a matter of being stupid, but often a matter of a judgment call. If a subtable has only a few rows, and they always have the same subindex, a fake array is probably okay. If only one entrance test is required and accepted, one set of test columns is probably okay as well, combined with a test lookup table that indicates what all these subtests mean (including maximum, minimum, average scores, percentile ranges, and the like). Figure 32.10 shows this approach, which is in violation of the first normal form—it has repeating groups in both tables.

FIGURE 32.10.

*This fake array of
denormalized test scores
violates the first normal
form.*

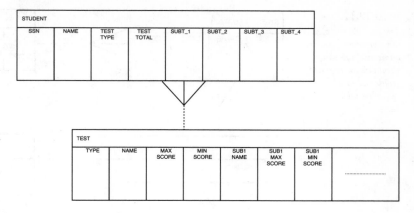

If the organization wants to be flexible about things, though, a subtable is preferable even though
that table is likely to violate the first normal form by having a repeating group for, let's say, up
to five subtests and a total score. That would be acceptable in this case because generally there
is no need to sum the scores across the columns—the total column is already there. Even if this
total needs to be calculated, the formula consists of only a few elements. In essence, the total
column contains the most-often used information, and the subscores are available as well, in
case anybody needs to see them. This model is illustrated in Figure 32.11.

FIGURE 32.11.

*The test score subtable
now has a
denormalized subtest
score fake array.*

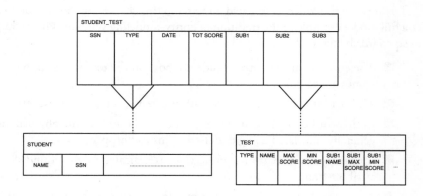

The fully decomposed model is shown in Figure 32.12. An additional table for student subtest
scores eliminates the repeating group in a student test. The `testtype` table is also broken into
two tables to accommodate subtest types.

Figure 32.12.

The fully decomposed test score model has an additional table to eliminate the repeating group and breaks the testtype *table into two parts.*

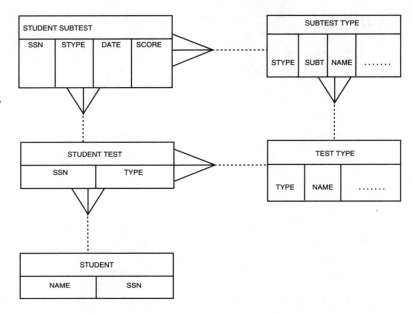

A Full Model Example

To illustrate the concepts touched on so far in this chapter, in this section I lay out and discuss a full model example in the tradition of entity-modeling symbols. Figure 32.13 introduces the standards being used:

- ■ The entity name is written inside the box, on the top line, in uppercase letters. Entity names are singular.

- ■ The attributes are listed underneath the name, using lowercase letters.

- ■ Multi-word entity and attribute names are allowed (in the physical model, these are generally translated using underscores instead of spaces).

- ■ A primary key or part of a primary key is indicated by the pound sign in front of the attribute name.

- ■ An optional column is indicated by a lowercase · in front of the attribute name; a not null column is the default and is therefore not marked with any symbol.

- ■ A foreign-key column that necessary is to implement a relation is not listed among the attributes.

- ■ If a foreign-key column is part of a primary key, that is indicated through a short bar across the relationship end.

- ■ The relationship symbols shown in the previous chapter are used.

FIGURE 32.13.

The full model example in this section is based on these entity relationship (ER) modeling standards.

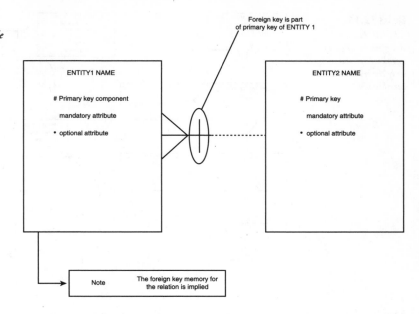

Entities and Relationships

A system or subsystem designed to handle enrollments brings together a few core entities:

- People who end up being either students or teachers
- Students—The people for whom the whole enterprise exists in the first place
- Teachers who deliver the goodies
- Departments that employ professors and offer majors and courses
- Majors—More-or-less defined programs of study leading to a degree
- Student major—An intersect between the `student` and `major` entities that shows from when to when the student was intending to get a certain major, and which degree he or she earned, if any.
- Course—A defined type of an instructional unit, described with a title, a syllabus, and (one would hope) fitting into a curriculum.
- Term—The period of time during the school year when instruction is regularly given to students
- Registration of a student during a term
- Course sections—instances of courses delivered during a term
- Enrollments of students in course sections.

Figure 32.14 pulls these together in an entity relationship (ER) diagram. Note that this diagram includes only the most essential attributes, which are usually the unique identifiers of their entities.

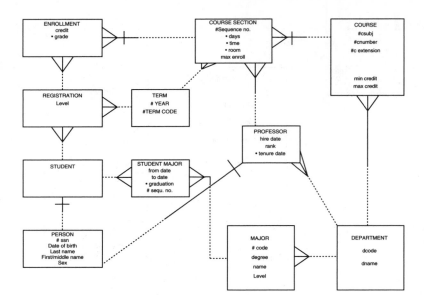

FIGURE 32.14.

The ER skeleton diagram for student enrollments, showing only the most essential attributes.

Much information is packed into the relationships among the entities:

■ person, department, term, and, in a way, course are the reference entities. All other entities are children to at least one of these reference entities.

■ A person may be a student or a professor, or both. This is implemented as two relationships, one between person and student and one between person and professor. Both are one-to-one, with an optional end pointing to student and a mandatory end that includes a unique identifier bar indicating that the SSN column is the UID of all three entities.

At the left side of the diagram is the student set of entities:

■ A student registers for one term at a time, which is recorded in the registration entity. The UID is now compound, consisting of the UIDs of student (SSN) and term (year and term code).

■ For each registration, the student enrolls in one or more course sections. The compound UID of the course section contains the UID of registration combined with the UID of the course section.

At the top row of the diagram is the course set of tables:

■ Each course may have one or more course sections that are also an intersect to term and inherit the UIDs of both.

■ Each course section is taught by a professor, represented as an optional one-to-mandatory many relationship. In reality, to accommodate approaches such as team teaching or supervision courses, this would more likely be modeled as a many-to-many relationship to be resolved with an intersect table. For now, however, assume that only one professor is assigned to a course section.

■ Because the same course may be taught in several sections per term, an additional key component—sequence number—is necessary.

■ Each course section may be enrolled in by one or more students, which is reflected in the registration entity.

The department entity affects three other entities:

■ Professors are assigned to departments.

■ Departments offer majors.

■ Departments offer courses.

It is not surprising that some writers on higher education treat the department as the most important unit within a university. Departments in turn are parts of larger units such as schools, colleges, divisions, and so on, but for this model that fact is not important.

Finally, the major component warrants some discussion:

■ As mentioned, majors are offered by departments. As modeled here, this is a one-to-many relationship, but two or more departments might be involved. More than two is rare, though, and one usually takes the lead; hence, it might be feasible to treat this through a primary department/secondary department column and the necessary foreign keys.

■ In most universities a student can take courses before declaring a major. Eventually, the students will declare at least one—hence the optional one-to-mandatory many relationship from the student to the student major intersect entity.

In a more abstract diagram, the two intersect entities—student major and registration—would be treated as optional many-to-many relationships, at least as long as they didn't have attributes of their own. (See Figure 32.15 for this subdiagram.)

Showing the intersect tables explicitly is preferable. There is likely to be at least one attribute of interest, so the table is needed in its own right. Secondly, if you use CASE tools, they will resolve the many-to-many relationships to the intersect table automatically and provide an incomprehensible and meaningless table name in the process. Putting in the interface entity right away keeps entities and tables in sync.

Converting ER Models to Physical Models

The previously described ER model is fairly small, and is laid out so that it lends itself to a one-to-one conversion to a physical model. I'll show you that one-on-one conversion in this section. The only potential problem is that some tools do not deal well with the compound foreign keys that result from such a direct translation. Therefore, I will also show you a second conversion that uses surrogate primary keys, thus avoiding the need to use compound foreign keys.

FIGURE 32.15.
This abstract diagram reduces the intersect tables to many-to-many relationships.

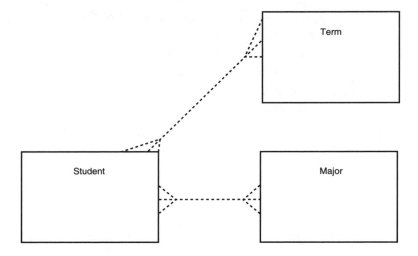

One-to-One Conversion

In a direct translation from the ER model to the physical model, the following rules apply:

- Each entity is mapped into a table. Standard convention has it that entities use singular nouns, and tables use their plurals. Some CASE tools even "know" the irregular plural forms of certain nouns.
- Each attribute is mapped into a column.
- Each relationship is mapped into a foreign key at the mandatory end. In a one-to-one relationship, this foreign key also gets a unique constraint.
- Each UID bar causes the corresponding foreign key to be included in the UID of the table.

Figure 32.16 shows the physical model that results from a one-to-one translation of the ER diagram.

What becomes immediately obvious is that where the ER diagram had just a few attributes, the physical model has about three times as many columns; this is a result of the many compound foreign keys. A violation of the third normal form remains in the majors table, though—if one knows the degree, one knows the level of the major, so these are redundant. Because this table is essentially a lookup table, however, this does not matter.

A similar problem remains in the course_sections table—the size of the room may determine the maximum enrollment. Furthermore, a room-scheduling subset of tables is needed to resolve issues so that a time slot in a room could be used for only one course.

Translated into SQL, the following scripts, presented in Listing 32.1, would be necessary to define this physical model in the database.

FIGURE 32.16.
*The physical model of
the student enrollments
example, resulting from
a one-to-one translation
of the ER skeleton
diagram.*

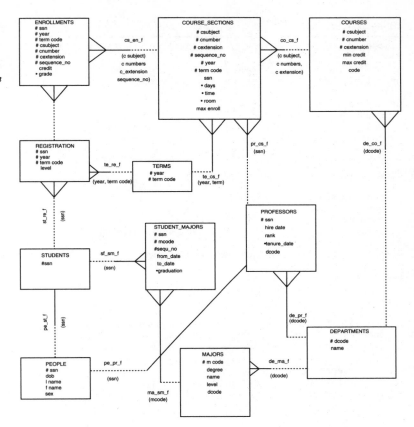

Listing 32.1. Creating enrollment tables.

```
--        Filename: 32squ01.sql
--        Purpose: Creates enrollment tables
--
drop table people cascade constraints;

create table people (
   Ssn        number(9),
   Lname      varchar2(15) constraint pe_ln_n not null,
   Fmname     varchar2(15) constraint pe_fm_n not null,
   dob        date         constraint pe_do_n not null,
   sex        char(1)      constraint pe_sx_n not null,
   constraint people_p    primary key (ssn))
;

drop table students1 cascade constraints;

create table students1 (
   Ssn        number(9),
   constraint students_p     primary key (ssn),
```

continues

Listing 32.1. continued

```
        constraint pe_st_f foreign key (ssn) references people)
;

drop table departments cascade constraints;

create table departments (
    Dcode       char(4),
    Dname       varchar2(15) constraint de_na_n not null,
    constraint departments_p    primary key (dcode))
;

drop table terms cascade constraints;

create table terms (
    year        number(4),
    termcode    number(1),
    constraint terms_p      primary key (year, termcode))
;
drop table registrations cascade constraints;

create table registrations (
    Ssn         char(9),
    year        number(4),
    termcode    number(1),
    rlevel      number(1)           constraint re_rl_n not null,
    constraint  registrations_p     primary key
        (ssn, year, termcode),
    constraint st_re_f foreign key (ssn)
        references students,
    constraint te_re_f foreign key (year, termcode)
        references terms)
;

drop table professors cascade constraints;

create table professors (
    Ssn         number(9),
    hired       date            constraint pr_hd_n not null,
    rank        char(1)         constraint pr_rk_n not null,
    tenured     date,
    Dcode       char(4)         constraint pr_dc_n not null,
    constraint professors_p     primary key (ssn),
    constraint pe_pr_f foreign key (ssn) references people,
    constraint de_pr_f foreign key (dcode) references departments)
;

drop table courses cascade constraints;

create table courses (
    csubject    char(4),
    cnumber     number(3),
    cextension  varchar2(3),
    mincredit   number(3,1) constraint co_mi_n not null,
    maxcredit   number(3,1) constraint co_ma_n not null,
    Dcode       char(4)         constraint co_dc_n not null,
    constraint courses_p    primary key (csubject, cnumber, cextension),
```

```
        constraint de_co_f foreign key (dcode) references departments)
;

drop table course_sections cascade constraints;

create table course_sections (
    csubject    char(4),
    cnumber     number(3),
    cextension  varchar2(3),
    cs_seq_no   number(2),
    year        number(4),
    termcode    number(1),
    Ssn         number(9)       constraint cs_sn_n not null,
    days        varchar2(7),
    times       varchar2(9),
    room        char(9),
    maxenroll   number(3)       constraint cs_ma_n not null,
    constraint  course_sections_p    primary key
        (csubject, cnumber, cextension, cs_seq_no, year, termcode),
    constraint co_cs_f foreign key (csubject, cnumber, cextension)
        references courses,
    constraint pr_cs_f foreign key (ssn)
        references professors,
    constraint te_co_f foreign key (year, termcode)
        references terms)
;

drop table enrollments cascade constraints;

create table enrollments (
    Ssn         char(9),
    year        number(4),
    termcode    number(1),
    csubject    char(4),
    cnumber     number(3),
    cextension  varchar2(3),
    cs_seq_no   number(2),
    credit      number(3,1)     constraint en_cr_n not null,
    grade       char(3)         constraint en_gr_n not null,
    constraint  enrollments_p    primary key
        (csubject, cnumber, cextension, cs_seq_no, year, termcode, ssn),
    constraint cs_en_f foreign key
        (csubject, cnumber, cextension, cs_seq_no, year, termcode)
        references course_sections,
    constraint re_en_f foreign key (ssn, year, termcode)
        references registrations)
;

drop table majors cascade constraints;

create table majors (
    Mcode       char(4),
    Mname       varchar2(15) constraint ma_na_n not null,
    degree      varchar2(10) constraint ma_de_n not null,
    Mlevel      number(1)    constraint ma_lv_n not null,
    dcode       char(4)      constraint ma_dp_n not null,
    constraint majors_p       primary key (mcode),
```

continues

Listing 32.1. continued

```
    constraint de_ma_f foreign key (dcode) references departments)
;

drop table student_majors cascade constraints;

create table student_majors (
    Ssn         char(9),
    Mcode       char(4),
    Smsequ_no   number(2),
    from_dt     date  constraint sm_fr_n not null,
    to_dt       date  constraint sm_to_n not null,
    graduation date,
    constraint student_majors_p      primary key (ssn, mcode, smsequ_no),
    constraint ma_sm_f foreign key (mcode) references majors,
    constraint st_sm_f foreign key (ssn)   references students)
;
```

Two things come to mind when looking over this script:

■ Primary keys made up of six components get a bit murky and unwieldy to work with. Once a key gets too convoluted, it is time to look into surrogate primary keys.

■ Even this fairly small model is laced with constraints where the chance for missing something is fairly large. Furthermore, new submodules are likely to be added over time, and what starts as a small model may end up at least midsized. Therefore, this model may very well be around the break-even point where a modeling or CASE tool should be used.

Conversion Using Surrogate Keys

To avoid overly convoluted compound primary keys, a column can be added that serves as a single-column primary key—the surrogate primary key. Then all joins can be done via that single column. The surrogate key translation essentially ignores most UID bars of the relationships in the ER model and adds its own key. Some of the original primary key columns remain, because they also are part of foreign keys. It would, however, be possible to slightly denormalize and to keep some or all of the eliminated columns for fast retrieval's sake.

Figure 32.17 presents the physical model that results from this approach. The model and the scripts shown here are (mostly) normalized.

The revised code is shown in Listing 32.2. The `registrations`, `courses`, `course_sections`, and `enrollments` tables were changed.

FIGURE 32.17.

Here, the student enrollment physical model includes surrogate primary keys.

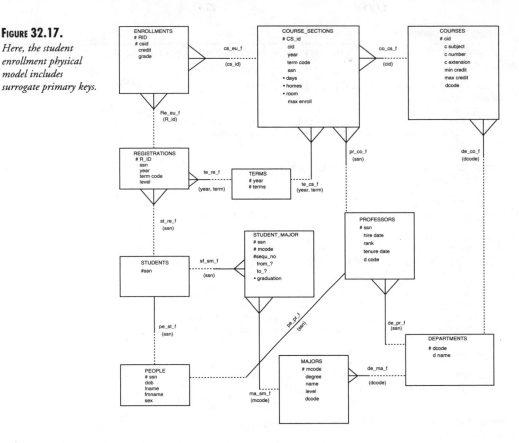

32

DATABASE DESIGN
AND
NORMALIZATION

Listing 32.2. Creating enrollment tables that include surrogate keys.

```
--        Filename: 32squ02.sql
--          Purpose: Creates enrollment tables including surrogate keys
--
drop table people cascade constraints;

create table people (
   Ssn        number(9),
   Lname      varchar2(15) constraint pe_ln_n not null,
   Fmname     varchar2(15) constraint pe_fm_n not null,
   dob        date         constraint pe_do_n not null,
   sex        char(1)      constraint pe_sx_n not null,
   constraint people_p    primary key (ssn))
;

drop table students1 cascade constraints;

create table students1 (
   Ssn        number(9),
   constraint students_p    primary key (ssn),
```

continues

Listing 32.2. continued

```
    constraint pe_st_f foreign key (ssn) references people)
;

drop table departments cascade constraints;
create table departments (
    Dcode       char(4),
    Dname       varchar2(15) constraint de_na_n not null,
    constraint departments_p    primary key (dcode))
;

drop table terms cascade constraints;
create table terms (
    year        number(4),
    termcode    number(1),
    constraint terms_p      primary key (year, termcode))
;

drop table registrations cascade constraints;
create table registrations (
    rid         number(8),
    Ssn         char(9),
    year        number(4),
    termcode    number(1),
    rlevel      number(1)       constraint re_rl_n not null,
    constraint  registrations_p    primary key
        (rid),
    constraint st_re_f foreign key (ssn)
        references students,
    constraint te_re_f foreign key (year, termcode)
        references terms)
;

drop table professors cascade constraints;
create table professors (
    Ssn         number(9),
    hired       date            constraint pr_hd_n not null,
    rank        char(1)         constraint pr_rk_n not null,
    tenured     date,
    Dcode       char(4)         constraint pr_dc_n not null,
    constraint professors_p     primary key (ssn),
    constraint pe_pr_f foreign key (ssn) references people,
    constraint de_pr_f foreign key (dcode) references departments)
;

drop table courses cascade constraints;
create table courses (
    cid         number(8),
    csubject    char(4),
    cnumber     number(3),
    cextension  varchar2(3),
    mincredit   number(3,1) constraint co_mi_n not null,
    maxcredit   number(3,1) constraint co_ma_n not null,
    Dcode       char(4)         constraint co_dc_n not null,
    constraint courses_p     primary key (cid),
    constraint de_co_f foreign key (dcode) references departments)
;
```

```
drop table course_sections cascade constraints;

create table course_sections (
   csid          number(8),
   cid           number(8),
   year          number(4),
   termcode      number(1),
   Ssn           number(9)        constraint cs_sn_n not null,
   days          varchar2(7),
   times         varchar2(9),
   room          char(9),
   maxenroll     number(3)        constraint cs_ma_n not null,
   constraint   course_sections_p    primary key
      (csid),
   constraint co_cs_f foreign key (cid)
       references courses,
   constraint pr_cs_f foreign key (ssn)
       references professors,
   constraint te_co_f foreign key (year, termcode)
       references terms)
;

drop table enrollments cascade constraints;

create table enrollments (
   rid           number(8),
   csid          number(8),
   credit        number(3,1)      constraint en_cr_n not null,
   grade         char(3)          constraint en_gr_n not null,
   constraint   enrollments_p    primary key
      (rid, csid),
   constraint cs_en_f foreign key (csid)
       references course_sections,
   constraint re_en_f foreign key (rid)
       references registrations)
;

drop table majors cascade constraints;

create table majors (
   Mcode         char(4),
   Mname         varchar2(15) constraint ma_na_n not null,
   degree        varchar2(10) constraint ma_de_n not null,
   Mlevel        number(1)    constraint ma_lv_n not null,
   dcode         char(4)      constraint ma_dp_n not null,
   constraint majors_p      primary key (mcode),
   constraint de_ma_f foreign key (dcode) references departments)
;

drop table student_majors cascade constraints;

create table student_majors (
   Ssn           char(9),
   Mcode         char(4),
   Smsequ_no     number(2),
   from_dt       date  constraint sm_fr_n not null,
   to_dt         date  constraint sm_to_n not null,
```

32

DATABASE DESIGN
AND
NORMALIZATION

continues

Listing 32.2. continued

```
    graduation date,
    constraint student_majors_p      primary key (ssn, mcode, smsequ_no),
    constraint ma_sm_f foreign key (mcode) references majors,
    constraint st_sm_f foreign key (ssn)   references students)
;
```

Summary

This chapter presents the most important principles of database design. In a typical three-step approach, first a logical ER model is produced that models entities, their attributes, and the relationships between entities. The ER model is then translated to a physical design, where database- and implementation-specific changes are performed. The physical model is then converted to the SQL code necessary to create all the objects it contains.

The chapter also touches on data normalization, which provides formal rules that can be used to analyze the quality of an ER model. For the sake of specific performance gains, the physical model can be denormalized. Examples are the adding of redundant columns, which eliminates the need for join operations on certain queries, and the adding of fake arrays, which provide a way to get around the no-repeating-groups rule of the first normal form. To avoid compound keys that contain many columns, a surrogate primary key can be added on a table through which join operations can be performed.

X

PART

IN THIS PART

Security

Security Privileges

IN THIS CHAPTER

In multi-user operating systems, security is generally handled in a fairly straightforward way, where users are either the owners of resources or get access to them to read, write/update, or execute. In some cases, add-ons or third-party tools exist to provide a richer functionality. There also might be some auditing function that keeps track of who does what, as well as some resource metering that prevents users from using more space or processing than they are authorized to, and that may be used for chargebacks.

SQL proper uses a similar approach by defining users who get access to resources that in turn allow them to create database objects, run certain operations, and, if specifically authorized to do so, grant access to the resources to others.

ORACLE vs. SQL Oracle implements the standard SQL security features using its own command set, except for the basic grant command. On top of that, Oracle provides some specific security options, and others that can be used to implement security:

- Rather than providing individual privileges to individual users, a role may be defined and granted the privileges in question. The role in turn is granted to users.

- Using the set role command, only one role may be active at a time, which avoids risking that someone who has access to several roles will end up with an unexpected superrole that combines the rights of all. This approach is especially useful in combination with client applications that are capable of enforcing their own security.

- Views have definite security purposes: A view defined with check option can limit the type of rows that a user may insert or update.

- If access to the columns of a table is to be restricted, it can be done through specific grants as well.

- Access to resources is provided through options of the create user and alter user commands.

- Last but not least, and going beyond the scope of this book, access to objects may be given only through database procedures that set what can and must not be done with it. The result is an API that can be set up to enforce an elaborate security scheme.

This chapter first covers the standard SQL way of security on the basis of users and grants. It then goes on to roles and the ways to work with them. Finally, using views for row-level access is illustrated.

Database Users

Anyone accessing a database is known to it as a *user*. A user can reflect a real person or a pseudo-person. The latter, in fact, might be a sort of superuser who is the owner of record of a large system, or an anonymous username through which others may access the database. Without logging on to the database as a user who is known by it, it is not possible for you to do any SQL work.

A user is defined using the following command:

```
create user user_name identified by password;
```

Now the user is known to the database, but he or she cannot do anything, as shown in Listing 33.1.

Listing 33.1. Creating users.

```
--          Filename: 33squ01.sql
--          Purpose: creating users
--

drop user t1 cascade;

create user t1 identified by t1;
```

The first statement drops the user t1, first deleting all objects in his schema because of the cascade option. The second statement re-creates user t1. However, that user cannot do anything—not even log on:

```
Connect t1/t1
```

This code returns

```
ERROR: ORA-01045: user T1 lacks CREATE SESSION privilege; logon denied
```

```
Warning: You are no longer connected to ORACLE.
```

After reconnecting as the original user, this privilege can be granted:

```
Connect squ/squ
```

```
Connected.
```

```
grant create session to t1;
```

```
Grant succeeded.
```

```
connect t1/t1
Connected.
```

At this point, t1 is allowed to connect to the database, but still cannot do much else. From this point, one or both of the following paths can be taken:

- Provide the resources and privileges to the user so that he can create his own tables and views.
- Grant the user access to other users' objects.

This discussion starts with the second path, which is intended to allow users access to predefined tables and views, but nothing else. The script `privs.sql` can be used to display a user's privileges. (See Listing 33.2.)

Listing 33.2. Displaying privileges of a user.

```
--        Filename: privs.sql
--         Purpose: display privileges of a user
--
accept p_user  prompt 'Enter user name—UPPER CASE ONLY: '

col PRIVILEGE        FORMAT A40

select
    *
from
dba_sys_privs
where grantee = '&p_user'
;

clear columns
```

The script is run interactively:

```
SQL> @privs
Enter user name—UPPER CASE ONLY: T1
old    5: where grantee = '&p_user'
new    5: where grantee = 'T1'

GRANTEE                          PRIVILEGE                                ADM
-------------------------------  ---------------------------------------  ---
T1                               CREATE SESSION                           NO
```

Protecting Database Objects and Data

A user who has created a table or view in his schema can access that table himself. He also can make this table available to other users—for update, insert, delete, or all of these. Finally, such access may be limited to some columns only—either through views or specific grants on these columns.

The following examples use two users. t2, who can do just about everything and who is defined in Chapter 28, "Creating Tables," is redefined here with the same parameters (see Listing 33.3). The explanation of the commands used in the listing is provided in a later part of this chapter. t1, as defined in Listing 33.1, is the other user.

Listing 33.3. Creating a user with a lot of privileges.

```
--        Filename: 33squ03.sql
--         Purpose: re-create user t2
--
drop user t2;

create user t2 identified by t2
   default tablespace user_data
   temporary tablespace temporary_data
   quota unlimited on user_data
   quota unlimited on temporary_data
;

grant connect, standard to t2;
```

This returns

```
User dropped.
```

```
User created.
```

```
Grant succeeded.
```

First, t2 re-creates the table t1pers in his schema. (See Listing 33.4.) This table is identical to pers1.

Listing 33.4. Creating and loading a table in a user's schema.

```
--        Filename:      33squ04.sql
--        Purpose:       creating and loading
--                       table t2pers in the
--                       schema of t2
--
connect t2/t2;

create table t2pers (
            id       number(2) not null,
          LName      varchar2(15),
         FMName      varchar2(15),
            SSN      char(9),
            Age      number(3),
            Sex      char(1))
;

insert into t2pers values (
1, 'Jones',          '       David N.',   '895663453',34, 'M');
insert into t2pers values (
2, 'Martinelli', 'A. Emery',    '312331818',92, 'M');
insert into t2pers values (
3, 'Talavera',    'F. Espinosa','533932999',19, 'F');
insert into t2pers values (
4, 'Kratochvil', 'Mary T.',     '969825711',48, 'F');
insert into t2pers values (
5, 'Melsheli',    'Joseph K.',   '000342222',14, 'M');

commit;
```

It returns the following:

```
Connected.
```

```
Table created.
```

```
1 row created.
```

```
1 row created.
```

```
1 row created.
```

```
1 row created.
```

```
1 row created.
```

Commit complete.

t2 now can select from this table. (See Listing 33.5.)

Listing 33.5. Accessing a table.

```
--        Filename: 33squ05.sql
--         Purpose: accessing
--                  table t2pers
--
select * from t2pers;
```

This returns the following:

```
    ID LNAME          FMNAME          SSN              AGE S
------- -------------- --------------- ---------- --------- -
     1 Jones          David N.        895663453         34 M
     2 Martinelli     A. Emery        312331818         92 M
     3 Talavera       F. Espinosa     533932999         19 F
     4 Kratochvil     Mary T.         969825711         48 F
     5 Melsheli       Joseph K.       000342222         14 M
```

But t1 cannot select. This code

```
connect t1/t1;

select * from t2pers;

select * from t2.t2pers;
```

returns this:

```
Connected.
select * from t2pers
                *
ERROR at line 1:
ORA-00942: table or view does not exist


select * from t2.t2pers
                   *
ERROR at line 1:
ORA-00942: table or view does not exist
```

DEBUG ALERT

Note that the same error message results regardless of whether the schema name is used. In either case, the message says that the table does not exist, when in fact it is just not accessible to the user. This is another example of cryptic (or better, misleading) error messages. What it really ought to say is something like this:

```
ERROR at line 1:
ORA-00942A: Sorry buddy, but you have no access privileges to this table
```

Short of meaningful error messages, therefore, check the access grants if you get that message.

Now the session reconnects to t2, who in turn issues `select` privileges on the table to t1. t1 subsequently can access the table, but only by preceding the table name with the schema name:

```
connect t2/t2;

grant select on t2pers to t1;

        connect t1/t1;

        select * from t2pers;

        select * from t2.t2pers;
```

This script returns the following:

```
Connected.

Grant succeeded.

        Connected.

        select * from t2pers
                      *
        ERROR at line 1:
        ORA-00942: table or view does not exist


            ID LNAME        FMNAME          SSN        AGE S
        -------- ------------ --------------- --------- -------- -
             1 Jones        David N.        895663453   34 M
             2 Martinelli   A. Emery        312331818   92 M
             3 Talavera     F. Espinosa     533932999   19 F
             4 Kratochvil   Mary T.         969825711   48 F
             5 Melsheli     Joseph K.       000342222   14 M
```

However, because only `select` privileges have been granted, inserts, updates, or deletes are still not possible for t1. The following script

```
delete from t2.t2pers;

insert into t2.t2pers values (
6, 'Jackers','Goliath M.','655993933',64, 'M');

update t2.t2pers set fmname = 'FORGOTTEN'
where ID < 3;
```

returns this:

```
delete from t2.t2pers
                 *
ERROR at line 1:
ORA-01031: insufficient privileges


insert into t2.t2pers values (
                             *
ERROR at line 1:
ORA-01031: insufficient privileges


update t2.t2pers set fmname = 'FORGOTTEN'
                 *
ERROR at line 1:
ORA-01031: insufficient privileges
```

The same options do work, however, if `insert`, `update`, and `delete` privileges are granted:

```
connect t2/t2
```

```
grant insert, update, delete on t2.t2pers to t1;
```

```
connect t1/t1

insert into t2.t2pers values (
6, 'Jackers','Goliath M.','655993933',64, 'M');

commit;

update t2.t2pers set fmname = 'FORGOTTEN'
where ID < 3;
```

This time, it returns this:

```
Connected.
```

```
Grant succeeded.
```

```
Connected.

1 row created.


Commit complete.

2 rows updated.
```

t2 can see all changes. The following

```
connect t2/t2
```

```
select * from t2pers;
```

returns this:

```
Connected.

     ID LNAME           FMNAME          SSN              AGE S
-------- --------------- --------------- --------- --------- -
      1 Jones           FORGOTTEN       895663453        34 M
      2 Martinelli      FORGOTTEN       312331818        92 M
      3 Talavera        F. Espinosa     533932999        19 F
      4 Kratochvil      Mary T.         969825711        48 F
      5 Melsheli        Joseph K.       000342222        14 M
      6 Jackers         Goliath M.      655993933        64 M

6 rows selected.
```

t1 may also delete rows. If he writes the following,

```
connect t1/t1

delete from t2.t2pers;

select * from t2.t2pers;

rollback;
```

it returns this:

```
6 rows deleted.

no rows selected

Rollback complete.
```

The script `tgrants.sql` shows the table grants that a user has received. `tgrants_.sql` is the same except that the username is passed in as the first argument and the table name as the second. (See Listing 33.6.)

Listing 33.6. Displaying table privileges granted to a user.

```
--        Filename: tgrants.sql
--         Purpose: display table privileges
--                  granted to a user
--
accept p_user  prompt 'Enter user name--UPPER CASE ONLY: '

COL OWNER           FORMAT A12
COL TABLE_NAME      FORMAT A25
col GRANTOR         FORMAT A12
col PRIVILEGE       FORMAT A15
col G_O             FORMAT A3
```

continues

Listing 33.6. continued

```
select
   OWNER,
   TABLE_NAME,
   GRANTOR,
   PRIVILEGE,
   GRANTABLE G_O
from
dba_tab_privs
where grantee = '&p_user'
;

clear columns
```

Interactively run, the script returns this:

```
SQL> @tgrants
Enter user name--UPPER CASE ONLY: T1
old   9: where grantee = '&p_user'
new   9: where grantee = 'T1'


OWNER           TABLE_NAME                    GRANTOR         PRIVILEGE         G_O
-----------     ----------------------------  ------------    ----------------  ---
T2              T2PERS                        T2              DELETE            NO
T2              T2PERS                        T2              INSERT            NO
T2              T2PERS                        T2              UPDATE            NO
T2              T2PERS                        T2              SELECT            NO
```

The G_O column indicates whether the grantee has the right to grant access to the object to yet another user. This is a useful feature where the table is owned by some pseudouser, but an applications administrator provides access to users as needed. The administrator receives the privilege with admin option and can then grant it to other users.

Other Object Privileges: all (privileges), alter, index, references, and execute

The object privileges in Listing 33.5 are limited to data manipulation. Three more are available on tables:

- alter—Allows the grantee to use the alter table command to change the table definition.
- index—Allows the grantee to create an index against the table.
- references—Allows the grantee to create a foreign key on another table that references the table on which the privilege is granted.

The execute privilege allows the grantee to execute a procedure, execute a function (whether packaged or standalone), and access program objects declared in a package specification. This privilege applies to procedural code only.

It is also possible to grant all allowable privileges on an object using the statement `grant all on object to user_name`; or `grant all privileges on object to user_name`;.

Types of Privileges That May Be Assigned on Objects

On both views and tables, the `insert`, `delete`, `update`, and `select` privileges may be granted; in addition, the `alter`, `index`, and `references` privileges may be granted on tables.

For sequences, only the `alter` and `select` privileges may be assigned; and for functions, procedures, and packages, only `execute` is valid.

Granting Column-Level Access to Objects

The example in Listing 33.5 provides privileges on entire tables and views. Using a slight variation of the same statements, the privileges can be limited to columns only. The syntax of the Oracle Server SQL Reference is as follows:

```
grant privilege (column commalist) on table/view_name to user_name;
```

In reality, however, columns can be specified only for the `insert`, `update`, and `references` privileges, at least in version 7.3.2. of Personal Oracle.

This makes sense for `delete`, because a whole row is deleted anyway, and column access is meaningless in this context. It makes some sense for `alter`, because that affects mostly the table as a whole. `index` is in the same category, although limiting the rows on which an index could be would make sense as well. Why the `select` can't be limited is anybody's guess.

Limiting the rows that can be updated has the side effect that the column names must be specified in the `insert` statement after the table name. This is so because the privilege grant does not create a view. Therefore, if the column names are not specified, the RDBMS sees fewer variables in the `values` list than are listed for the table in the Data Dictionary, and an error results. In reality, this is no big deal because the client tools tend to use the `insert` statement with fully specified column names anyway.

All privileges on a table may be granted in one statement using a `privilege` comma list. The same privileges may be granted to more than one user, all of whom must be included in a `user` comma list.

CAUTION

The statement structural diagram for grant in the Oracle Server SQL Reference has a user list rather than a user comma list. If the comma is not there, an error will result:

```
SQL> grant select on lawyer1 to t1 t2
  2 ;
```

continues

```
continued

grant select on lawyer1 to t1 t2
                              *
ERROR at line 1:
ORA-00933: SQL command not properly ended


SQL> grant select on lawyer1 to t1, t2;

Grant succeeded.
```
The same is the case for revoke:
```
SQL> revoke select on lawyer1 from t1, t2;

Revoke succeeded.
```

The script in Listing 33.7 first strips t1 of most privileges and then grants or attempts to grant column privileges.

Listing 33.7. Accessing a table's columns and column-level grants.

```
--        Filename: 33squ07.sql
--         Purpose: accessing
--                  table t2pers columns
--                  column level grants
--
@33squ03

revoke all on t2pers from t1;

revoke
    alter any table,
    comment any table,
    create any table,
    create any view ,
    drop any table from t1;

@grants
```

First, 33squ03.sql is called to re-create the t2pers table. Then most grants to t1 are revoked, and the current state of grants to t1 are displayed by querying the Data Dictionary:

```
Connected.

Table dropped.
Table created.

....
Commit complete.
```

```
Revoke succeeded.

revoke
*
ERROR at line 1:
ORA-01952: system privileges not granted to 'T1'
```

t1 happens to have none of these privileges. Otherwise, the command would return this:

```
Revoke succeeded.b

Enter user name--UPPER CASE ONLY: T1
old    5: where grantee = '&p_user'
new    5: where grantee = 'T1'

GRANTEE                            PRIVILEGE                   ADM
------------------------------     ------------------------    ---
T1                                 CREATE SESSION              NO
T1                                 CREATE TABLE                NO
T1                                 CREATE VIEW                 NO

old    5: where grantee = '&p_user'
new    5: where grantee = 'T1'

no rows selected
```

Now a number of invalid grant statements are submitted:

```
grant select (id, lname, fmname, ssn) on t2pers to t1;
grant delete (id)  on t2pers to t1;
grant alter  (id)  on t2pers to t1;
grant index  (id)  on t2pers to t1;
```

The same error results from all of these:

```
grant select (id, lname, fmname, ssn) on t2pers to t1
             *
ERROR at line 1:
ORA-00969: missing ON keyword

grant delete (id)  on t2pers to t1
             *
ERROR at line 1:
ORA-00969: missing ON keyword

grant alter  (id)  on t2pers to t1
             *
ERROR at line 1:
ORA-00969: missing ON keyword

grant index  (id)  on t2pers to t1
             *
ERROR at line 1:
ORA-00969: missing ON keyword
```

These statements are then resubmitted, but without the column references:

```
grant select on t2pers to t1;
grant delete on t2pers to t1;
grant alter  on t2pers to t1;
grant index  on t2pers to t1;
```

Now they work:

```
Grant succeeded.

Grant succeeded.

Grant succeeded.

Grant succeeded.
```

Next are three valid statements that give specific access to columns, Grants are again queried from Data Dictionary views. (The cgrants script is shown after this example, in the "Querying Column Privileges from the Data Dictionary" section.) The following script

```
grant update (lname, fmname) on t2pers to t1;
grant insert (id)            on t2pers to t1;
grant references (id)        on t2pers to t1;

@tgrants
@cgrants
```

returns this:

```
Grant succeeded.

Grant succeeded.

Grant succeeded.

Enter user name--UPPER CASE ONLY: T1
old   9: where grantee = '&p_user'
new   9: where grantee = 'T1'
```

OWNER	TABLE_NAME	GRANTOR	PRIVILEGE	G_O
T2	T2PERS	T2	DELETE	NO
T2	T2PERS	T2	ALTER	NO
T2	T2PERS	T2	INDEX	NO
T2	T2PERS	T2	SELECT	NO

```
Enter user name—UPPER CASE ONLY: T1
old  10: where grantee = '&p_user'
new  10: where grantee = 'T1'
```

OWNER	TABLE_NAME	COLUMN_NAME	GRANTOR	PRIVILEGE	G_O
T2	T2PERS	ID	T2	INSERT	NO
T2	T2PERS	ID	T2	REFERENCES	NO
T2	T2PERS	LNAME	T2	UPDATE	NO
T2	T2PERS	FMNAME	T2	UPDATE	NO

The privileges are again revoked and then re-granted, all in one statement:

```
revoke all on t2pers from t1;

grant
   select,
   delete,
```

```
    alter,
    index,
    update (lname, fmname),
    insert (id),
    references (id)
on t2pers to t1
;

@tgrants
@cgrants
```

It returns this:

```
Revoke succeeded.

Grant succeeded.
```

The Data Dictionary views contain exactly the same privilege information as in the preceding example.

The script in Listing 33.8 tests column privileges. All of it is run as user t1; therefore, no indentation will be used when displaying it.

Listing 33.8. Testing column privileges.

```
--        Filename: 33squ08.sql
--         Purpose: accessing
--                  table t2pers columns
--                  column level grants
--
connect t1/t1;

select * from t2.t2pers;

delete from t2.t2pers;

rollback;
```

This returns

```
Connected.

        ID LNAME         FMNAME         SSN         AGE S
---------- ------------- -------------- ---------- ---------- -
         1 Jones         David N.       895663453          34 M
         2 Martinelli    A. Emery       312331818          92 M
         3 Talavera      F. Espinosa    533932999          19 F
         4 Kratochvil    Mary T.        969825711          48 F
         5 Melsheli      Joseph K.      000342222          14 M

5 rows deleted.

Rollback complete.
```

All the statements of the first part of Listing 33.8 work because proper privileges are in place.

Of the next three statements, the first one does not work because insert privileges are provided for ID only. The second one fails because the RDBMS expects six values for an insert into that table, because that's the number of columns that the Data Dictionary contains for this table, yet only one is included. The third statement, which specifies the column, works like this:

```
insert into t2.t2pers values (
6, 'Jackers','Goliath M.','655993933',64, 'M');

insert into t2.t2pers values (16);

insert into t2.t2pers (id) values (16);
```

The statements return

```
insert into t2.t2pers values (
                             *
ERROR at line 1:
ORA-01031: insufficient privileges


insert into t2.t2pers values (16)
                            *
ERROR at line 1:
ORA-00947: not enough values


1 row created.
```

Next, two updates are attempted. The first one fails because it has no privileges to update the id column. The second one works because the proper privileges are in place. Finally, everything is rolled back, and the session is connected back to t2:

```
update t2.t2pers set id = 0
where ID < 3;

update t2.t2pers set fmname = 'FORGOTTEN'
where ID < 3;

rollback;

connect t2/t2
```

It returns the following:

```
update t2.t2pers set id = 0
                     *
ERROR at line 1:
ORA-01031: insufficient privileges


2 rows updated.


Rollback complete.

Connected.
```

Querying Column Privileges from the Data Dictionary

The script cgrants.sql (see Listing 33.9) asks for a username and displays all column privilege grants for that user.

Listing 33.9. Displaying column privileges granted to a user.

```
--        Filename: cgrants.sql
--         Purpose: display column privileges
--                  granted to a user
--
accept p_user  prompt 'Enter user name—UPPER CASE ONLY: '

COL OWNER            FORMAT A10
COL TABLE_NAME       FORMAT A15
col column_name      format A15
col GRANTOR          FORMAT A12
col PRIVILEGE        FORMAT A15
col G_O              FORMAT A3

select
   OWNER,
   TABLE_NAME,
   COLUMN_NAME,
   GRANTOR,
   PRIVILEGE,
   GRANTABLE G_O
from
dba_col_privs
where grantee = '&p_user'
;

clear columns
```

The output of this script is shown in example 33squ10.sql. (See Listing 33.10.)

Changing User Characteristics and Providing Database Resources

In the previous session, t1 received the create session privilege, which was necessary so that he could log on to the database in the first place. As far as privileges are concerned, t1 cannot do much more than access those objects of other users to which he has been granted access. To create a table, a user must have the create table privilege, have a sufficiently large quota on a tablespace, and name this tablespace in the create table statement or have it set as a default.

Granting the create table Privilege

Anticipating the next section of this chapter, t1 will next receive the create table privilege. He still can't do anything more, because he does not have a quota on any database resource. (See Listing 33.10.)

Listing 33.10. Creating table privileges and tablespace quotas.

```
--        Filename: 33squ10.sql
--         Purpose: create table privilege;
--                  tablespace quotas
--
connect t2/t2

grant create table to t1;

@privs

     connect t1/t1

create table test (test number);
```

This script returns

```
Connected.

Grant succeeded.

Enter user name—UPPER CASE ONLY: T1
old    5: where grantee = '&p_user'
new    5: where grantee = 'T1'

GRANTEE                          PRIVILEGE                                ADM
-------------------------------- ---------------------------------------- ---
T1                               CREATE SESSION                           NO
T1                               CREATE TABLE                             NO

     Connected.
     create table test (test number)
     *
     ERROR at line 1:
     ORA-01950: no privileges on tablespace 'SYSTEM'
```

The problem is that t1 may create tables, but he has no resources to do so.

Default Tablespaces and Quotas

When a user is created, default tablespace, temporary tablespace, and quotas on both can be set. If nothing is indicated, both are simply set to SYSTEM, and no quota is assigned. That is the case for the user t1. The rusers.sql script, shown in Listing 33.11, can be used to display resource quotas of a user.

Listing 33.11. Displaying resource grants of a user.

```
--        Filename: rusers.sql
--         Purpose: display resource grants of a user
--
accept p_user  prompt 'Enter user name—UPPER CASE ONLY: '

col USERNAME             format A10      heading 'User¦Name'
col USER_ID              format 9999     heading 'User¦Id'
col DEFAULT_TABLESPACE   format A14      heading 'Default¦Tablespace'
```

```
col TEMPORARY_TABLESPACE  format A14      heading 'Temporary¦Tablespace'
col TABLESPACE_NAME       format A20      heading 'Temporary¦Tablespace'
col CREATED               format A11      heading 'Date¦Created'
col PROFILE               format A10      heading '¦Profile'
col kbytes                format 999,999  heading 'KILO¦BYTES'
col mbytes                format A10      heading 'MAXIMUM¦  KB'
col blocks                format 999,999  heading 'DATABASE¦BLOCKS'
col mblocks               format A10      heading 'MAXIMUM¦DB BLOCKS'

select
   username,
   user_id,
   default_tablespace,
   temporary_tablespace,
   created,
   profile
from dba_users
where username = '&p_user'
;
```

Note that t1 does not have access to the underlying Data Dictionary view; therefore, it is necessary to connect to t2 first:

```
connect t2/t2
```

```
@rusers
```

This script returns

```
Connected.
Enter user name—UPPER CASE ONLY: T1
old   9: where username = '&p_user'
new   9: where username = 'T1'
```

User Name	User Id	Default Tablespace	Temporary Tablespace	Date Created	Profile
T1	51	SYSTEM	SYSTEM	23-JUN-1997	DEFAULT

In plain English, t1 has the database ID of 51; the default tablespace in which any of his database objects will go if t1 does not specify a tablespace is SYSTEM; and the temporary tablespace, which is used for pre-sorting of output and intermediate storage of joined rows, is SYSTEM as well. Date created is self-explanatory. The profile is a named set of resource limits—such as number of sessions per user, connect time, idle time, and so on—that can be set with the create profile and alter profile commands. This feature is not further explained here; please consult your Oracle Server SQL Reference for all options.

The second part of the script shows the quotas on tablespaces (provided any have been defined):

```
select
   tablespace_name,
   trunc(bytes/1024) kbytes,
   decode(max_bytes,-1,'UNLIMITED',
            to_char(trunc(max_bytes/1024),'9,999,999')) mbytes,
```

```
    blocks,
    decode(max_blocks,-1,'UNLIMITED',
            to_char(max_blocks,'9,999,999')) mblocks
from dba_ts_quotas
where username = '&p_user'
;
```

No row is returned for t1.

For comparison's sake, the output of rusers for t2 is as follows:

User Name	User Id	Default Tablespace	Temporary Tablespace	Date Created	Profile
T2	53	USER_DATA	TEMPORARY_DATA	24-JUN-1997	DEFAULT

Temporary Tablespace	KILO BYTES	MAXIMUM KB	DATABASE BLOCKS	MAXIMUM DB BLOCKS
TEMPORARY_DATA	0	UNLIMITED	0	UNLIMITED
USER_DATA	4	UNLIMITED	2	UNLIMITED

What therefore emerges is that three things need to be in place before a user can create tables:

- He must have the create table privilege.
- He must have a quota on a tablespace in which to create the table.
- Either a default tablespace must be set in which he has a quota, or such tablespace must be included in the create table command using the tablespace *tablespace_name* subclause.

If any one, two, or all are missing, various errors will result if the user attempts to create a table.

Setting Defaults and Temporary Tablespaces as well as Quotas

Default and temporary tablespaces, as well as quotas on them, can be set with either the create user or alter user command. (See Listing 33.12.) These commands can also be used to assign quotas on additional tablespaces.

Listing 33.12. Setting default tablespaces and tablespace quotas.

```
--       Filename: 33squ12.sql
--       Purpose: set default tablespaces
--                and tablespace quotas
--
connect t2/t2

alter user t1
    default tablespace user_data
    temporary tablespace temporary_data
    quota 500 K on user_data
    quota unlimited on temporary_data
;

@rusers
```

```
connect t1/t1

create table test (test number);
```

It returns the following:

```
Connected.

User altered.

Enter user name—UPPER CASE ONLY: T1
old    9: where username = '&p_user'
new    9: where username = 'T1'

User          User Default         Temporary      Date
Name            Id Tablespace      Tablespace     Created     Profile
...........   .... ..............  ............   .........   ...........
T1             51 USER_DATA        TEMPORARY_DATA 23-JUN-1997 DEFAULT

Temporary                  KILO MAXIMUM    DATABASE MAXIMUM
Tablespace                 BYTES KB         BLOCKS DB BLOCKS
..................         ......... .......... ........ ..........
TEMPORARY_DATA                 0 UNLIMITED        0 UNLIMITED
USER_DATA                      4       500        2       250

    Connected.

    Table created.
```

Now the three conditions are met, and the test table could be created, indeed. Note that any number of quote *quote_size* on *tablespace* substatement may be included. The substatements shown here can also be included right away in the create table statement, as is done when t2 is created in 33squ04.sql. (Refer to Listing 33.4.)

TIP

There is no quick way to change any of these parameters for a whole set of users. The best solution is to write a SQL generating SQL script against the Data Dictionary.

Granting Further Privileges

In the previous sections, t1 received the create session and create table privileges that were necessary so that he could log on to the database in the first place and create a table (provided a quota in a suitable tablespace was available). There are many other privileges that can be granted to a user. They come in groups and are named the same as the SQL command that they allow a user to issue (or are the same modified with the keyword any).

- The create ... privileges generally allow users to create, alter, or delete objects in their own schema.
- The create any ..., alter any ..., and drop any ... privileges allow a user to issue commands that affect anybody's objects.
- A number of privileges are intended for database administrators.

Privileges Affecting a User's Work on His or Her Own Schema

Most of the create ... privileges allow users to create objects in their own schema. It also allows users to alter or delete the same objects. The following briefly describes these privileges.

create session and create table allow a user to connect to the database and to create, alter, and delete a table. create table does not include the right to create a view, even on a table in one's own schema—the create view privilege is necessary for that. Whereas most create ... statements include the rights to alter and drop the object in question, create session does not. This makes sense, because it is intended to only allow logon without any further customization. For the latter, an additional privilege, alter session, is provided that gives the grantee the right to customize the session, such as choosing a different NLS_DATE_FORMAT.

unlimited tablespace allows a user to use up the entire available space in any tablespace. In that regard it would be equivalent to issuing alter user quota unlimited on ... statements for each single tablespace. The difference is that unlimited tablespace overrides those quotas as long as it is in effect. Once it is revoked, however, they become effective again. Therefore, it is preferable to assign quotas and use unlimited tablespace for specific tasks only.

Listing 33.13 demonstrates the options that the create table and create view privileges provide.

Listing 33.13. Using create table and create view privileges.

```
--      Filename: 33squ13.sql
--       Purpose: alter and drop table
--                using create table privilege
--                create view privilege
--
    connect t1/t1

    create or replace view vtest
    as select * from test;
```

In this situation, t1 may not create a view because that requires a separate privilege:

```
Connected.
create or replace view vtest
                     *
ERROR at line 1:
ORA-01031: insufficient privileges
```

He may, however, alter, comment on, drop, and re-create his table. This script

```
alter table test add
(test2 number);

comment on table test is 'Test table of T1';.

drop table test;

create table test (test number);
```

returns the following:

```
Table altered.

Comment created

Table dropped.

Table created.
```

Next he is granted the `create view` privilege and is then able to create the view. This script

```
connect t2/t2

grant create view to t1;

connect t1/t1

create or replace view vtest
as select * from test;
```

now returns this:

```
Connected.

Grant succeeded.

Connected.

View created.
```

Two more privileges should be fairly self-explanatory. `create sequence` and `create synonym` allow you to do just as they say. The next two privileges, `create procedure` and `create trigger`, are necessary if a user is to take advantage of the procedural extensions of SQL. The last three, `create cluster`, `create database link`, and `create snapshot`, relate to database features that this book does not discuss further. Briefly, a *cluster* is a special way to store detail table rows together with the master table rows to which they belong, a *database link* allows access to remote databases or allows a read-only mount on secondary databases, and a *snapshot* is a copy of a table that is refreshed at pre-set intervals. (For more, see your Oracle Server SQL Reference.)

Privileges Affecting Anybody's Schema

Mirroring the functionality of the previously discussed privileges, the `create any ...`, `alter any ...`, and `drop any ...` privileges allow a user to issue commands that affect anybody's objects. These privileges are usually assigned to a database administrator or a subadministrator.

The most important privileges are those affecting tables. `create any table` allows a user to create any table in anyone else's schema; `alter any table`, `drop any table`, and `comment any table` allow him to alter, drop, and comment on others' schemas. `delete any table` allows him to delete rows or truncate tables in any schema, and `insert any table` allows him to insert records into any table. The `lock any table` privilege allows him to lock any table or view, which means that for the duration of the lock, other users can only see the information in the locked row or table; they cannot insert, update, or delete anything. The `select any table` and `update any table` privileges are self-explanatory.

Listing 33.14 shows this by giving t1 these privileges and then having him create, alter, comment on, and drop a table in t2's schema. Note that `alter any view`, `create any view`, and `drop any view` are similar, affecting views only.

Listing 33.14. Using any table privileges to alter, create, and drop any view.

```
--      Filename: 33squ14.sql
--       Purpose: alter, drop, ...  table
--               using .... any table privileges
--
 connect t2/t2

grant
  create any table,
  alter   any table,
  drop    any table,
  comment any table
to t1
;
```

It returns this:

```
Connected.

Grant succeeded.
```

t1 may now create, alter, drop, and comment on a table in anybody else's schema. For example, the following script

```
connect t1/t1

create table t2.test (test number);

alter table t2.test add
(test2 number);

comment on table t2.test is 'Test table of T1';
```

returns this:

```
Table created.


Table altered.
```

```
Comment created.
```

t2 can see the table, because it is in his schema. This script

```
connect t2/t2
```

```
desc test
```

returns this:

```
Connected.
```

```
Name                            Null?    Type
------------------------------- -------- -----
TEST                                     NUMBER
TEST2                                    NUMBER
```

Now, t1 drops and re-creates the table and attempts to create a view in t2's schema:

```
connect t1/t1

drop table t2.test;

create table t2.test (
    test number,
    test2 number)
;

create or replace view t2.vtest
as select * from test
;
```

The script returns this:

```
Table dropped.


Table created.

create or replace view t2.vtest
                      *
ERROR at line 1:
ORA-01031: insufficient privileges.
```

Again, the create any table privilege does not include the creation of views. Therefore, t1 is granted the create any view privilege:

```
connect t2/t2
```

```
grant create any view to t1;
```

```
connect t1/t1

create or replace view t2.vtest
as select * from test
;
```

Now the view can be created by t1:

```
View created.
```

t2 can see it, which is shown through a `desc` issued by him:

```
connect t2/t2

desc vtest
```

returns this:

```
Connected.
 Name                           Null?    Type
 ------------------------------ -------- -----
 TEST                                    NUMBER
 TEST2                                   NUMBER
```

Indexes and sequences have their own sets of three commands each—`create any index`, `alter any index`, and `drop any index` and `create any sequence`, `alter any sequence`, and `drop any sequence`, respectively. `select any sequence` allows the grantee to call up the current and the next value of any sequence. Synonyms can only be created and dropped; hence there are only two associated privileges each—`create any synonym` and `drop any synonym` for private synonyms, and `create public synonym` and `drop public synonym` for public ones (see Chapter 28).

A total of seven privileges are associated with the procedural extensions: `create any trigger`, `alter any trigger`, and `drop any trigger` on the one hand, and `create any procedure`, `alter any procedure`, and `drop any procedure` on the other. The privilege `execute any procedure` allows the grantee to execute standalone or packaged procedures and functions and to reference public package variables.

The all-out equivalents for `create cluster` and `create snapshot` are not surprising either—`create any cluster`, `alter any cluster`, and `drop any cluster` and `create any snapshot`, `alter any snapshot`, and `drop any snapshot`. Database links are different in the sense that they can only be created/altered/dropped in one's own schema (which is permitted under the `create database link` privilege) or as public links for which three privileges are provided—`create public database link`, `alter public database link`, and `drop public database link`.

Database Administration Privileges

In RDBMS lingo, the database administrator is the superuser of the database who can deploy resources and set the parameters within which other users perform their work. There may be a whole set of administrators with subsets of responsibilities and concomitant privileges, most of which can be granted to an individual for his or her own use or with the `grant` option with the intent to bestow it on others as well. Most database administrators have all the privileges that allow them to affect anyone's schema. An additional set of privileges allows them to perform typical administration tasks.

Related to user administration, `create user`, `alter user`, `drop user`, `grant any privilege`, `grant any role`, and `create role` are self-explanatory. You simply need to have these privileges if you want to do related tasks. Three more privileges that correspond to the commands with the same names allow the grantee to institute resource metering and limiting—`create profile`, `alter profile`, and `alter resource cost`.

`backup any table` and `become user` are necessary for importing and exporting databases. They are usually provided through the predefined roles `exp_full_database` and `imp_full_database`, which are explained further in Chapter 34, "Database Roles."

For the purposes of database storage management, the `create tablespace`, `alter tablespace`, and `drop tablespace` privileges are available. `manage tablespace` allows the administrator to take tablespaces online or offline and to begin or end backups of tablespaces. The `create rollback segment`, `drop rollback segment`, and `alter rollback segment` privileges allow him to use the commands with the identical names, as do the `alter database` and `alter system` privileges.

The `restricted session` privilege can be used to create two classes of users. Using the `alter system enable restricted session` statement limits the logon of users to those who have that privilege.

`force any transaction` and `force transaction` allow the grantee to commit or roll back all distributed transactions that are in doubt, or only those started by the grantee. This is of concern only for distributed databases with a two-stage commit process.

The `analyze any` privilege allows the grantee to issue `analyze` statements against any table, index, or cluster. This command will be used for optimization purposes.

Finally, two privileges relate to auditing: `audit any` allows the grantee to audit any database object; `audit system` allows him to audit SQL statements.

Typical Administrative Structures

Although in most cases there are one or more database administrator(s) who has/have just about all privileges, the detailed breakdown of privileges allows for the implementing of a refined administration structure where some users handle the database side, some manage the user side, and others focus on applications.

There is at least one superuser on the machine at which the database is implemented. This person has access to the root password and controls all resources on that machine. This superuser needs to define some of the following users as operating system users and needs to set up a group to whom system resources can be granted. There also needs to be a user account under which the database is run.

There needs to be at least one database superuser who ultimately controls all resources and grants. This user also needs access to operating system resources—files or filesystems and CPU time if these resources are not already available to users. This superuser has all privileges.

One distinct function of the superuser is managing database storage administration—tablespaces, rollback segments, and their mapping to operating system files or devices. This person is likely to be responsible for backup and recovery of the database, and for exports and imports, if applicable. Generally, root-level access to the host machine is necessary for these functions.

Another distinct function of the superuser is performance tuning of the database, which requires the `analyze` privilege. Some of this work requires access to host files.

The last two functions deal with user administration—using `create user`, `alter user`, `drop user`; granting users resources and privileges; and auditing critical database objects and SQL statements.

Revoking Privileges

Any privilege that can be granted can be revoked through the `revoke privilege from user_name;` command. All privileges not revoked remain granted to the user. (See Listing 33.7, which contains some examples of the use of this statement.)

Summary

SQL's approach to security is similar to most multi-user operating systems, where there are either the owners of resources or those who get access to them to read, write/update, or execute. Database users get access to resources through privileges that in turn allow them to create database objects, run certain operations, and, if specifically authorized to do so, grant access to the resources to others.

Object privileges allow access to tables or views. Other privileges allow the grantee to use database resources, to affect objects in somebody else's schema, and to administer a database and its users in general. Most privileges can be granted with `grant option`, which allows the grantee to grant them to another user. Privileges are revoked through the `revoke` command.

The next chapter expands on the functionality of privileges by introducing roles.

Database Roles

IN THIS CHAPTER

ORACLE vs SQL

Database roles are an Oracle extension to SQL. They serve two purposes:

- They create sets of privileges that can be granted or revoked from a single user in one statement.
- They activate and deactivate sets of privileges so that a user has only one active set.

The first point is a matter of convenience, especially in systems with many users. The second point is a powerful means to avoid a dangerous security hole.

Creating and assigning roles is a four-step process:

1. The role is created using the `create role` statement.
2. Privileges are granted to the role through the `grant` statement.
3. The role is granted to users through the `grant` statement.
4. The role is activated through the `set role` statement or is automatically activated through a listing as a default role of the user.

Creating Roles and Assigning Privileges to Roles

Roles are created using the `create role` statement. Privileges are assigned to roles through `grant` statements just as is the case with grants to individual users.

> **CAUTION**
>
> Not all privileges may be granted to roles.

The `create role` statement has only a few options, namely

- `not identified`, meaning that the user can enable the role without specifying a password
- `identified by password`, which specifies a password that has to be provided when enabling the role
- `identified externally`, which specifies that the user enabling the role has to be verified through the operating system

The last option makes sense only if the user is defined the same way on the host, at which point the Relational Database Management System (RDBMS) relies on host computer security mechanisms.

> **TIP**
>
> Do not use the `identified externally` option. It only makes sense in a host-based environment, where the user is defined in the host system as well. In this day and age when most sessions are provided through client/server or three/multi-tier approaches, database users are generally *not* known to the host computer on which the database is housed.

Generally, `identified by password` is the way to go.

The identification method can be changed using the `alter role` statement. Its options are the same as those of the `create role` statement. Finally, a role is unceremoniously dropped using the command `drop role role_name;`.

Listing 34.1 creates a role t2prole, which receives the same privileges that have been granted to t1 in Chapter 33, "Security Privileges."

Listing 34.1. Creating and granting privileges to roles.

```
--        Filename: 34squ01.sql
--        Purpose: creating role and granting privileges to it.
--                 table t2pers columns
--                 column level grants
--
connect t2/t2

set echo off
set feedback off
@33squ04
set feedback on
set echo on

drop role t2prole;

create role t2prole identified by rolepw;

alter role t2prole not identified;
```

After re-creating the table, the example starts out with all three role statements, each of which succeeds, assuming the role had been defined previously:

```
Role dropped.

Role created.

Role altered.
```

Now the same `grant` statement that was used in Chapter 33 is used:

```
grant
   select,
   delete,
   alter,
   index,
   update (lname, fmname),
   insert (id),
   references (id)
on t2pers to t2prole
;
```

but the statement fails:

```
grant
*
ERROR at line 1:
ORA-01931: cannot grant REFERENCES to a role
```

The reason why it fails it because neither the `index` nor the `references` privilege may be granted to roles. Therefore, the statement is revised accordingly and the privileges granted to the role are displayed as shown in the following part of the example:

```
grant
   select,
   delete,
   alter,
   update (lname, fmname),
   insert (id)
on t2pers to t2prole
;

@tgrants _ T2PROLE T2PERS
@cgrants _ T2PROLE T2PERS
```

Now the statements work, as shown here:

```
Grant succeeded.

old   9: where grantee = '&1'
new   9: where grantee = 'T2PROLE'
old  10: and table_name = '&2'
new  10: and table_name = 'T2PERS'
```

OWNER	TABLE_NAME	GRANTOR	PRIVILEGE	G_O
T2	T2PERS	T2	ALTER	NO
T2	T2PERS	T2	DELETE	NO
T2	T2PERS	T2	SELECT	NO

OWNER	TABLE_NAME	COLUMN_NAME	GRANTOR	PRIVILEGE	G_O
T2	T2PERS	ID	T2	INSERT	NO
T2	T2PERS	LNAME	T2	UPDATE	NO
T2	T2PERS	FMNAME	T2	UPDATE	NO

Assigning Roles to Users, Activating Roles, and Setting Default Roles

A role is assigned to a user through the statement

```
grant role_name to user_name;
```

Whether this role is activated depends on the default role setting of the user. By default, all roles granted to a user are activated automatically at logon without password verification. In this case, the role password is used only if the user is assigned that role while logged on to the database and needs to activate the role right away.

The default roles and activating or deactivating roles approaches avoid the possibility that a user with access to several applications, and thus roles, ends up with a combined set of privileges that allows him to do much more than intended. It also allows him to switch off and on roles from within an application, which might provide tight control of the application through its own logic.

Through the `default role` option of the `alter user` command, default roles may be explicitly set. This option is the rare example of a feature that is available in an `alter ...` statement but not the corresponding `create ...` statement. The `default role` option can be set as follows:

- `none`—No role granted is a default role.
- `all`—All roles are in the default role set. This is the default.
- `role commalist`—A comma list that specifically states which roles are active at connect.
- `all except`—All roles granted except the ones listed.

> **CAUTION**
>
> Generally at the most one role should be in the default set, otherwise the security that is provided by activating or deactivating is lost.

Listing 34.2 assigns the `t2prole` to `t1` and sets it as a default role. `t1` then accesses the table `t2pers` using the privileges granted through the role.

Listing 34.2. Activating and deactivating roles.

```
--      Filename: 34squ02.sql
--      Purpose: activating and deactivating roles
--
connect t2/t2

revoke all on t2pers from t1;
```

continues

34

Database Roles

Listing 34.2. continued

```
revoke t2prole from t1;
@tgrants_ T1 T2PERS
@tgrants_ T1 T2PERS
```

This code returns

```
Connected.

Revoke succeeded.

Revoke succeeded.

old   9: where grantee = '&1'
new   9: where grantee = 'T1'
old  10: and table_name = '&2'
new  10: and table_name = 'T2PERS'

no rows selected

SQL> @tgrants_ T1 T2PERS
SQL> SET ECHO OFF
old   9: where grantee = '&1'
new   9: where grantee = 'T1'
old  10: and table_name = '&2'
new  10: and table_name = 'T2PERS'

no rows selected
```

First, the attempt is made to set the role t2prole as t1's default role, as shown here:

```
alter user t1 default role t2prole;
```

This does not work, however, because the role first has to be granted to the user:

```
alter user t1 default role t2prole
*
ERROR at line 1:
ORA-01955: DEFAULT ROLE 'T2PROLE' not granted to user
```

Granting the role and then assigning it to the default role set does work, however, as shown here:

```
grant t2prole to t1;

@UROLES

alter user t1 default role t2prole;

@UROLES
```

This code returns

```
Grant succeeded.

old   8: where grantee = '&1' and
new   8: where grantee = 'T1' and
```

```
ROLE          G_O DEF PW
-----------   --- --- --
T2PROLE        NO  NO  NO
```

```
User altered.
```

```
old   8: where grantee = '&1' and
new   8: where grantee = 'T1' and
```

```
ROLE          G_O DEF PW
-----------   --- --- --
T2PROLE        NO YES NO
```
```
1 row selected.
```

Using the role grant, Listing 34.3 shows the use of default rows as well as the activating and deactivating of roles.

Because t1 has been granted the role and has it in his default role set, he should be able to access the table through the role privileges.

Listing 34.3. Activating and deactivating roles.

```
--       Filename: 34squ03.sql
--        Purpose: activating and deactivating roles
--
--
    connect t1/t1;

select * from t2.t2pers;
```

This code returns

```
Connected.
        ID LNAME         FMNAME         SSN           AGE S
--------- ------------- -------------- ------------ ------- -
         1 Jones         David N.       895663453      34 M
         2 Martinelli    A. Emery       312331818      92 M
         3 Talavera      F. Espinosa    533932999      19 F
         4 Kratochvil    Mary T.        969825711      48 F
         5 Melsheli      Joseph K.      000342222      14 M

        5 rows selected.
```

With the next statement, the role is removed from t1's default role set:

```
connect t2/t2

alter user t1 default role none;
```

This code returns

```
Connected.
```

```
User altered.
```

t1 now can no longer access the table, although he has the privilege, because the privilege is not activated. The next statement in which t1 tries to access the table fails:

```
connect t1/t1;

select * from t2.t2pers;
```

This code returns the following error:

```
Connected.
select * from t2.t2pers
                *
ERROR at line 1:
ORA-00942: table or view does not exist
```

If, however, t2prole is set by t1, all the privileges can be exercised again, as shown here:

```
set role t2prole;

select * from t2.t2pers;

delete from t2.t2pers;

rollback;
```

This code returns

```
Role set.
```

ID	LNAME	FMNAME	SSN	AGE	S
1	Jones	David N.	895663453	34	M
2	Martinelli	A. Emery	312331818	92	M
3	Talavera	F. Espinosa	533932999	19	F
4	Kratochvil	Mary T.	969825711	48	F
5	Melsheli	Joseph K.	000342222	14	M

```
5 rows selected.

5 rows deleted.

Rollback complete.
```

The insert statement still needs a column (comma list) specified, and inserts into columns that are not granted still do not work, as they should not. This is illustrated here:

```
insert into t2.t2pers values (16);

insert into t2.t2pers (id) values (16);

update t2.t2pers set id = 0
where ID < 3;

update t2.t2pers set fmname = 'FORGOTTEN'
where ID < 3;

rollback;
```

This code returns

```
insert into t2.t2pers values (16)
                *
ERROR at line 1:
ORA-00947: not enough values

1 row created.

update t2.t2pers set id = 0
                *
ERROR at line 1:
ORA-01031: insufficient privileges

2 rows updated.

Rollback complete.
```

Setting the active role to none makes accesses impossible again:

```
set role none;
```

```
insert into t2.t2pers (id) values (16);
```

This code returns

```
Role set.
```

```
insert into t2.t2pers (id) values (16)
                  *
ERROR at line 1:
ORA-00942: table or view does not exist
```

Other set role and default role Options

Both the set role and the default role subclauses of the alter user statement have a few more options; some are necessary, while others greatly enhance the power of these subclauses.

Most importantly, both statements may include more than one role, which means a whole set may be activated at a time. There is also an all option, which enables all roles; a none option, which disables all roles; and an all except option, which enables all roles but the listed ones.

All roles in the default role set are enabled the next time the user logs on or connects. The passwords of roles in the default role set are *not* enforced.

Roles with passwords affect the set role statement as follows:

- The password has to be included in the role comma list using the identified by *password* syntax.
- Specifying all roles through the all keyword works only if no role has a password.
- When the all except specification is used, none of the remaining roles must have a password.

34

DATABASE ROLES

> **NOTE**
>
> Roles that are granted through roles or that are managed by the operating system cannot be included in the default role set.

The following section offers examples that use these features.

Implementing Security Through Roles and Activation Approaches

When implementing security through roles and role activation/deactivation features, a few key objectives need to be accomplished:

- A session that performs a task should have exactly the system and object privileges that are necessary to perform that task. If too few are provided, errors will result (and many of the error messages will not make sense). If too many are there, some unexpected destructive action may be possible.
- Role setting and unsetting should be done in the background and hidden from users. Otherwise, users can set roles and combinations to their hearts' desire, which makes the whole approach useless.
- All rows that provide object privileges should be password protected.

In a production setting, such as a database with a screen client/server system, the user never sees a SQL statement and does not even need to know that SQL is involved. For each module in the system, a set of necessary privileges is assigned to a password-protected role.

Each user is granted the roles that they need in order to run all modules that they are supposed to run. None of these roles must be in their active set. Each module now must enable the role necessary to run it upon startup and reset the role set to none when exiting. This part of code must be hidden from the user, which is best done through the use of compiled screen modules.

The result is that a user can never activate any of the access roles by himself when accessing the database through a general purpose tool such as SQL*Plus or one of the many browsers available. The modules activate and deactivate the roles as needed. Because the active role set is only in force for the session, a user cannot enable all roles by starting all modules and then going into the system through a general purpose tool at the same time and taking advantage of the combined role set.

If your client software cannot hide the role password from the user, other security options should be considered.

Listing 34.4 shows how roles and role sets are switched on and off through repeated use of set role.

Listing 34.4. Setting role options.

```
--          Filename: 34squ04.sql
--          Purpose: set role options
--
connect t1/t1

set role t2prole identified by t2pw;

select count(1) from t2.t2pers;

insert into t2.t2pers (lname) values ('newname');
```

The role t2prole, which has been created in Listing 34.1, is set in the following statement. It allows you to count the rows but not to insert into the lname column:

```
Connected.

Role set.


  COUNT(1)
---------
       10

1 row selected.

insert into t2.t2pers (lname) values ('newname')
                 *
ERROR at line 1:
ORA-01031: insufficient privileges
```

Now all three roles are set. t2prole allows you to insert the ID, t2names allows you to insert lname and fmname, and t2dat allows you to insert the rest, as shown here:

```
set role
    t2prole identified by t2pw,
    t2names identified by t2namespw,
    t2dat identified by t2datpw;

insert into t2.t2pers values
    (23,'Allan','Timothy','883449399',54,'M');

rollback;
```

Thanks to the combined roles, a full line may be inserted:

```
Role set.


1 row created.


Rollback complete.
```

Listing 34.5 unsets the role t2dat through a new set role statement that only sets the other roles. Remember, that set role unsets all roles that are not explicitly set.

34

DATABASE ROLES

Listing 34.5. Resetting role options.

```
--        Filename: 34squ05.sql
--         Purpose: reset role options
--
set role
   t2names identified by t2namespw,
   t2prole identified by t2pw
;

insert into t2.t2pers values
   (24,'Molterer','Melchior','499204781',99,'M');

insert into t2.t2pers (id, lname, fmname) values
   (24,'Molterer','Melchior');

set role none;
```

The first insert fails because the last three columns are not covered under any insert privilege. The second one matches the privileges and succeeds, as shown here:

```
Role set.

insert into t2.t2pers values
                 *
ERROR at line 1:
ORA-01031: insufficient privileges

1 row created.

Role set.
```

Granting Privileges to public

Privileges can also be granted to public, at which time they are available to all database users without any further grants. public privileges can also be revoked. The syntax in either case is the same; however, the word public is used instead of the username or role name. If a privilege is to be granted permanently to all users, granting it to public is the way to do it. In most cases, it is a bad idea.

All users could have a create session privilege with the rationale that if they can't log on, what good is the user definition. However, there are pseudo-users that own whole application system components. These users do not exist and they never do any work on the system. Their only purpose is to own a schema under which database objects such as tables, views, and so on can be created. Quite likely, a real user with the necessary privileges, such as create any table, would create these objects in the pseudoschema.

There could be some tables or views available to all users, such as tables used for messaging or for some application system global variables. These could have public permissions set. However, at a later point another class of users might be defined, for whom these tables don't apply. The public grant would then become inappropriate.

Therefore, think twice before using grants to public.

Listing 34.6 grants rights to public.

Listing 34.6. Granting privileges to public.

```
--          Filename: 34squ06.sql
--          Purpose: granting privileges on
--                   table t2pers columns to public
--                   column level grants
--
set feedback off
@33squ03
set feedback on

connect t2/t2

revoke all on t2pers from public;

grant
   select,
   delete,
   alter,
   index,
   update (lname, fmname),
   insert (id),
   references (id)
on t2pers to public
;

@tgrants_ PUBLIC T2PERS
@cgrants_ PUBLIC T2PERS
```

This code returns

```
Connected.

Revoke succeeded.

Grant succeeded.

old    9: where grantee = '&1'
new    9: where grantee = 'PUBLIC'
old   10: and table_name = '&2'
new   10: and table_name = 'T2PERS'

OWNER        TABLE_NAME                  GRANTOR       PRIVILEGE        G_O
------------ --------------------------- ------------- ---------------- ---
T2           T2PERS                      T2            DELETE           NO
T2           T2PERS                      T2            INDEX            NO
T2           T2PERS                      T2            SELECT           NO
T2           T2PERS                      T2            ALTER            NO

4 rows selected.
```

34

DATABASE ROLES

```
old  10: where grantee = '&1'
new  10: where grantee = 'PUBLIC'
old  11: and table_name = '&2'
new  11: and table_name = 'T2PERS'
```

OWNER	TABLE_NAME	COLUMN_NAME	GRANTOR	PRIVILEGE	G_O
T2	T2PERS	ID	T2	INSERT	NO
T2	T2PERS	ID	T2	REFERENCES	NO
T2	T2PERS	LNAME	T2	UPDATE	NO
T2	T2PERS	FMNAME	T2	UPDATE	NO

```
4 rows selected.
```

Now, every user should have access to the object. In Listing 34.7, t2 will first revoke the object privileges *directly* granted to t1. t1 will then be able to access the table anyway because the privileges are granted to public.

Listing 34.7. Working through public object privileges.

```
--        Filename: 34squ07.sql
--         Purpose: working through public object privileges
--
connect t2/t2

revoke all on t2pers from t1;
revoke t2prole from t1;
```

Now t1 has no privileges on t2pers either granted directly or through roles, as shown here:

```
Connected.

Revoke succeeded.

Revoke succeeded.
```

However, because the privileges have been granted to public, he can do the covered operations anyway:

```
connect t1/t1;

select * from t2.t2pers;

delete from t2.t2pers;

insert into t2.t2pers (id) values (16);

update t2.t2pers set id = 0
where ID < 3;

update t2.t2pers set fmname = 'FORGOTTEN'
where ID < 3;

rollback;
```

This code returns

```
Connected.

        ID LNAME          FMNAME            SSN           AGE S
---------- -------------- ---------------- ----------- -------- -
         1 Jones          David N.         895663453        34 M
         2 Martinelli     A. Emery         312331818        92 M
         3 Talavera       F. Espinosa      533932999        19 F
         4 Kratochvil     Mary T.          969825711        48 F
         5 Melsheli       Joseph K.        000342222        14 M

5 rows selected.

5 rows deleted.

1 row created.

update t2.t2pers set id = 0
              *
ERROR at line 1:
ORA-01031: insufficient privileges

0 rows updated.

Rollback complete.
```

Predefined Roles

For convenience's sake, five roles are predefined and include the privileges usually associated with such a role. The Oracle Server SQL reference manual includes a stern warning that these roles may not be included with future releases. The manual also states that these roles should be customized for each installation.

Earlier in this chapter you saw that all a user needs to access objects in somebody else's schema are the `create session` privilege and object privileges to these objects. A predefined role for such users makes no sense, and therefore is not provided.

Two rules are provided for application developers—`connect` and `resource`.

`connect` allows a user to log on to customize a session, and create database objects such as tables or views. Running the `grants.sql` script and entering the word CONNECT as the username shows the privileges granted to the connect role:

```
SQL> @GRANTS
Enter user name—UPPER CASE ONLY: CONNECT
old    5: where grantee = '&p_user'
new    5: where grantee = 'CONNECT'

GRANTEE                      PRIVILEGE                  ADM
--------------------------   ------------------------   ---
CONNECT                      ALTER SESSION              NO
CONNECT                      CREATE CLUSTER             NO
CONNECT                      CREATE DATABASE LINK       NO
CONNECT                      CREATE SEQUENCE            NO
```

```
CONNECT                        CREATE SESSION              NO
CONNECT                        CREATE SYNONYM              NO
CONNECT                        CREATE TABLE                NO
CONNECT                        CREATE VIEW                 NO
```

resource provides the privileges necessary for the development of procedural codes as running the grants.sql script and entering the word RESOURCE shows:

```
SQL> @grants
Enter user name—UPPER CASE ONLY: RESOURCE
old    5: where grantee = '&p_user'
new    5: where grantee = 'RESOURCE'

GRANTEE                        PRIVILEGE                   ADM
------------------------------ --------------------------- ---
RESOURCE                       CREATE CLUSTER              NO
RESOURCE                       CREATE PROCEDURE            NO
RESOURCE                       CREATE SEQUENCE             NO
RESOURCE                       CREATE TABLE                NO
RESOURCE                       CREATE TRIGGER              NO
```

What goes into which role is a bit arbitrary, and Oracle's suggestion to customize makes a lot of sense.

Another two roles are provided for importing and exporting of databases—imp_full_database and exp_full_database. Their respective privileges are as follows:

```
SQL> @grants
Enter user name—UPPER CASE ONLY: IMP_FULL_DATABASE
old    5: where grantee = '&p_user'
new    5: where grantee = 'IMP_FULL_DATABASE'

GRANTEE                        PRIVILEGE                   ADM
------------------------------ --------------------------- ---
IMP_FULL_DATABASE              ALTER ANY TABLE             NO
IMP_FULL_DATABASE              AUDIT ANY                   NO
IMP_FULL_DATABASE              BECOME USER                 NO
IMP_FULL_DATABASE              COMMENT ANY TABLE           NO
IMP_FULL_DATABASE              CREATE ANY CLUSTER          NO
IMP_FULL_DATABASE              CREATE ANY INDEX            NO
IMP_FULL_DATABASE              CREATE ANY PROCEDURE        NO
IMP_FULL_DATABASE              CREATE ANY SEQUENCE         NO
IMP_FULL_DATABASE              CREATE ANY SNAPSHOT         NO
IMP_FULL_DATABASE              CREATE ANY SYNONYM          NO
IMP_FULL_DATABASE              CREATE ANY TABLE            NO
IMP_FULL_DATABASE              CREATE ANY TRIGGER          NO
IMP_FULL_DATABASE              CREATE ANY VIEW             NO
IMP_FULL_DATABASE              CREATE DATABASE LINK        NO
IMP_FULL_DATABASE              CREATE PROFILE              NO
IMP_FULL_DATABASE              CREATE PUBLIC DATABASE LINK NO
IMP_FULL_DATABASE              CREATE PUBLIC SYNONYM       NO
IMP_FULL_DATABASE              CREATE ROLE                 NO
IMP_FULL_DATABASE              CREATE ROLLBACK SEGMENT     NO
IMP_FULL_DATABASE              CREATE TABLESPACE           NO
IMP_FULL_DATABASE              CREATE USER                 NO
IMP_FULL_DATABASE              DROP ANY CLUSTER            NO
IMP_FULL_DATABASE              DROP ANY INDEX              NO
IMP_FULL_DATABASE              DROP ANY PROCEDURE          NO
```

```
IMP_FULL_DATABASE              DROP  ANY  ROLE              NO
IMP_FULL_DATABASE              DROP  ANY  SEQUENCE          NO
IMP_FULL_DATABASE              DROP  ANY  SNAPSHOT          NO
IMP_FULL_DATABASE              DROP  ANY  SYNONYM           NO
IMP_FULL_DATABASE              DROP  ANY  TABLE             NO
IMP_FULL_DATABASE              DROP  ANY  TRIGGER           NO
IMP_FULL_DATABASE              DROP  ANY  VIEW              NO
IMP_FULL_DATABASE              DROP  PROFILE                NO
IMP_FULL_DATABASE              DROP  PUBLIC  DATABASE  LINK  NO
IMP_FULL_DATABASE              DROP  PUBLIC  SYNONYM        NO
IMP_FULL_DATABASE              DROP  ROLLBACK  SEGMENT      NO
IMP_FULL_DATABASE              DROP  TABLESPACE             NO
IMP_FULL_DATABASE              DROP  USER                   NO
IMP_FULL_DATABASE              EXECUTE  ANY  PROCEDURE      NO
IMP_FULL_DATABASE              INSERT  ANY  TABLE           NO
IMP_FULL_DATABASE              SELECT  ANY  TABLE           NO
```

In essence, a user who needs to import a database has to be able to create, alter, and drop just about any database object. This makes sense because those objects that need to be created depend on the application being imported. Exporting, on the other hand, only requires access to some tables and views:

```
GRANTEE                        PRIVILEGE                    ADM
------------------------------ ---------------------------- ---
EXP_FULL_DATABASE              BACKUP  ANY  TABLE           NO
EXP_FULL_DATABASE              EXECUTE  ANY  PROCEDURE      NO
EXP_FULL_DATABASE              SELECT  ANY  TABLE           NO

old    5: where grantee = '&p_user'
new    5: where grantee = 'EXP_FULL_DATABASE'

no rows selected

old    9: where grantee = '&p_user'
new    9: where grantee = 'EXP_FULL_DATABASE'
```

```
OWNER          TABLE_NAME                GRANTOR       PRIVILEGE       G_O
-------------- ------------------------- ------------- --------------- ---
SYS            INCEXP                    SYS           DELETE          NO
SYS            INCEXP                    SYS           INSERT          NO
SYS            INCEXP                    SYS           UPDATE          NO
SYS            INCVID                    SYS           DELETE          NO
SYS            INCVID                    SYS           INSERT          NO
SYS            INCVID                    SYS           UPDATE          NO
SYS            INCFIL                    SYS           DELETE          NO
SYS            INCFIL                    SYS           INSERT          NO
SYS            INCFIL                    SYS           UPDATE          NO
```

The DBA role provides every single existing database privilege with `admin option` and two additional roles—`imp_full_database` and `exp_full_database`. The following output lists these privileges and roles:

```
SQL> @grants
Enter user name—UPPER CASE ONLY: DBA
old    5: where grantee = '&p_user'
new    5: where grantee = 'DBA'
```

GRANTEE	PRIVILEGE	ADM
DBA	ALTER ANY CLUSTER	YES
DBA	ALTER ANY INDEX	YES
DBA	ALTER ANY PROCEDURE	YES
DBA	ALTER ANY ROLE	YES
DBA	ALTER ANY SEQUENCE	YES
DBA	ALTER ANY SNAPSHOT	YES
DBA	ALTER ANY TABLE	YES
DBA	ALTER ANY TRIGGER	YES
DBA	ALTER DATABASE	YES
DBA	ALTER PROFILE	YES
DBA	ALTER RESOURCE COST	YES
DBA	ALTER ROLLBACK SEGMENT	YES
DBA	ALTER SESSION	YES
DBA	ALTER SYSTEM	YES
DBA	ALTER TABLESPACE	YES
DBA	ALTER USER	YES
DBA	ANALYZE ANY	YES
DBA	AUDIT ANY	YES
DBA	AUDIT SYSTEM	YES
DBA	BACKUP ANY TABLE	YES
DBA	BECOME USER	YES
DBA	COMMENT ANY TABLE	YES
DBA	CREATE ANY CLUSTER	YES
DBA	CREATE ANY INDEX	YES
DBA	CREATE ANY PROCEDURE	YES
DBA	CREATE ANY SEQUENCE	YES
DBA	CREATE ANY SNAPSHOT	YES
DBA	CREATE ANY SYNONYM	YES
DBA	CREATE ANY TABLE	YES
DBA	CREATE ANY TRIGGER	YES
DBA	CREATE ANY VIEW	YES
DBA	CREATE CLUSTER	YES
DBA	CREATE DATABASE LINK	YES
DBA	CREATE PROCEDURE	YES
DBA	CREATE PROFILE	YES
DBA	CREATE PUBLIC DATABASE LINK	YES
DBA	CREATE PUBLIC SYNONYM	YES
DBA	CREATE ROLE	YES
DBA	CREATE ROLLBACK SEGMENT	YES
DBA	CREATE SEQUENCE	YES
DBA	CREATE SESSION	YES
DBA	CREATE SNAPSHOT	YES
DBA	CREATE SYNONYM	YES
DBA	CREATE TABLE	YES
DBA	CREATE TABLESPACE	YES
DBA	CREATE TRIGGER	YES
DBA	CREATE USER	YES
DBA	CREATE VIEW	YES
DBA	DELETE ANY TABLE	YES
DBA	DROP ANY CLUSTER	YES
DBA	DROP ANY INDEX	YES
DBA	DROP ANY PROCEDURE	YES
DBA	DROP ANY ROLE	YES
DBA	DROP ANY SEQUENCE	YES
DBA	DROP ANY SNAPSHOT	YES
DBA	DROP ANY SYNONYM	YES
DBA	DROP ANY TABLE	YES

```
DBA                          DROP ANY TRIGGER              YES
DBA                          DROP ANY VIEW                 YES
DBA                          DROP PROFILE                  YES
DBA                          DROP PUBLIC DATABASE LINK     YES
DBA                          DROP PUBLIC SYNONYM           YES
DBA                          DROP ROLLBACK SEGMENT         YES
DBA                          DROP TABLESPACE               YES
DBA                          DROP USER                     YES
DBA                          EXECUTE ANY PROCEDURE         YES
DBA                          FORCE ANY TRANSACTION         YES
DBA                          FORCE TRANSACTION             YES
DBA                          GRANT ANY PRIVILEGE           YES
DBA                          GRANT ANY ROLE                YES
DBA                          INSERT ANY TABLE              YES
DBA                          LOCK ANY TABLE                YES
DBA                          MANAGE TABLESPACE             YES
DBA                          RESTRICTED SESSION            YES
DBA                          SELECT ANY SEQUENCE           YES
DBA                          SELECT ANY TABLE              YES
DBA                          UPDATE ANY TABLE              YES

77 rows selected.

old    5: where grantee = '&p_user'
new    5: where grantee = 'DBA'

GRANTEE                      GRANTED_ROLE                  ADM DEF
---------------------------- ----------------------------- --- ---
DBA                          EXP_FULL_DATABASE             NO  YES
DBA                          IMP_FULL_DATABASE             NO  YES

old    9: where grantee = '&p_user'
new    9: where grantee = 'DBA'

no rows selected
```

Summary

Rather than providing individual privileges to individual users, a role may be defined and granted the privileges in question. The role in turn is granted to users. Privileges can also be granted to all database users by granting them to public.

If a user has been granted at least one role, the set role command can be used to activate or deactivate some or all of these roles for a user session. This mechanism can be used to avoid the risk that someone who has access to several roles will end up with an unexpected superrole that combines the rights of all. This approach is especially useful in combination with client applications that are capable of enforcing their own security.

ORACLE
vs.SQL

34

DATABASE ROLES

Providing and Controlling Access to Database Objects Through Views

IN THIS CHAPTER

Single-table views can be used to control access to table columns or table rows, as you might recall from Chapter 26, "Insertable Single-Table Views." If the view is defined using the with check option, a user who accesses a table through it cannot insert or update records that violate the definition of the view.

Controlling Row Access Through Views

A view provides row-level access control that privileges do not accommodate. Highly distinctive column access control through the view alone is not possible. However, column access privileges may be set on the view columns just as they are set on table columns. By combining a view that controls row access with a set of privileges that controls column access in detail, a sophisticated security scheme can be worked out.

This approach is demonstrated in the following set of examples.

Creating Row Access Control Views

Let's first look at a variation of t2pers, which has creator and crdate columns added, as shown in Listing 35.1. The new columns have default values of user and sysdate.

Listing 35.1. Adding creator and crdate columns.

```
--        Filename: 35squ01.sql
--         Purpose: creating and loading
--                  table t3pers in the
--                  schema of t2 includes creator column
--
connect t2/t2;

drop table t3pers;

create table t3pers (
    id        number(2) not null,
    LName     varchar2(15),
    FMName    varchar2(15),
    SSN       char(9),
    Age       number(3),
    Sex       char(1),
    creator   varchar2(30) default user,
    crdate    date         default sysdate)
;

insert into t3pers values (
1, 'Jones',      'David N.',    '895663453',34, 'M', user, sysdate);
insert into t3pers values (
2, 'Martinelli', 'A. Emery',    '312331818',92, 'M', user, sysdate);
insert into t3pers values (
3, 'Talavera',   'F. Espinosa','533932999',19, 'F', user, sysdate);
insert into t3pers values (
4, 'Kratochvil', 'Mary T.',     '969825711',48, 'F', user, sysdate);
insert into t3pers values (
5, 'Melsheli',   'Joseph K.',   '000342222',14, 'M', user, sysdate);
```

```
commit;

col creator format a8
col id      format 999

select * from t3pers;

clear columns
```

These statements return

```
Connected.

Table dropped.

Table created.
.....

 ID LNAME           FMNAME          SSN           AGE S CREATOR  CRDATE
 --- --------------- --------------- --------- --- - -------- -----------
  1 Jones           David N.        895663453      34 M T2       28-JUN-1997
  2 Martinelli      A. Emery        312331818      92 M T2       28-JUN-1997
  3 Talavera        F. Espinosa     533932999      19 F T2       28-JUN-1997
  4 Kratochvil      Mary T.         969825711      48 F T2       28-JUN-1997
  5 Melsheli        Joseph K.       000342222      14 M T2       28-JUN-1997
```

Listing 35.2 creates a view that restricts rows to those that were created by the current user.

Listing 35.2. Restricting access to those rows created by current users.

```
--      Filename: 35squ02.sql
--      Purpose: creating view v3pers
--               restricts rows to those created by current user
--
connect t2/t2;

drop view v3pers;

create view v3pers as
select
   id,
   LName,
   FMName,
   SSN,
   Age,
   Sex
from t3pers
where creator = user
with check option;
```

The following code is returned:

```
Connected.

View dropped.

View created.
```

Next, all privileges to t1 and public on t3pers are revoked:

```
revoke all on t3pers from t1, public;
```

This code returns

```
Revoke succeeded.
```

In the following, privileges on the view are granted to t1. Note that t1 does not have insert, update, or delete rights to the creator and crdate. On an insert, the RDBMS inserts the current user and the current date because these are set as defaults:

```
grant
    select,
    delete,
    update (lname, fmname),
    insert (id,lname,fmname,ssn,age,sex)
on t2.v3pers to t1
;

@tgrants_ T1 V3PERS
@cgrants_ T1 V3PERS
```

Now all permissions are set properly:

```
Grant succeeded.

old   9: where grantee = '&1'
new   9: where grantee = 'T1'
old  10: and table_name = '&2'
new  10: and table_name = 'V3PERS'
```

OWNER	TABLE_NAME	GRANTOR	PRIVILEGE	G_O
T2	V3PERS	T2	SELECT	NO
T2	V3PERS	T2	DELETE	NO

```
old  10: where grantee = '&1'
new  10: where grantee = 'T1'
old  11: and table_name = '&2'
new  11: and table_name = 'V3PERS'
```

OWNER	TABLE_NAME	COLUMN_NAME	GRANTOR	PRIVILEGE	G_O
T2	V3PERS	ID	T2	INSERT	NO
T2	V3PERS	LNAME	T2	INSERT	NO
T2	V3PERS	FMNAME	T2	INSERT	NO
T2	V3PERS	SSN	T2	INSERT	NO
T2	V3PERS	SEX	T2	INSERT	NO
T2	V3PERS	AGE	T2	INSERT	NO
T2	V3PERS	LNAME	T2	UPDATE	NO
T2	V3PERS	FMNAME	T2	UPDATE	NO

Accessing Rows Through Row Access Control Views

In the third script of this example, t1 inserts rows through the view, and then updates and selects from them (see Listing 35.3).

Listing 35.3. Inserting rows through the control view.

```
--        Filename: 35squ03.sql
--        Purpose: accessing through row controlling view and
--                 detailed column privileges.
--
                                      connect t1/t1;

                                      select * from t2.v3pers;
```

t1 can't see a thing because there is no row in the table that fulfills the view condition that the creator must be the current user:

```
                          Connected.

                          no rows selected
```

t1 can insert into the view to his hearts desire; he has insert privileges to all view columns, and the last two columns of the table are automatically set to the default—the current user and the current system date. This makes it impossible to insert a value that violates the view condition. He can also update the lname and fmname columns as shown here:

```
insert into t2.v3pers values (
6, 'Robinson',         'Faye M.' ,   '966549339',NULL, 'F');
insert into t2.v3pers values (
7, NULL       ,        'M. Okechuku' ,   '854291872',23, NULL);
insert into t2.v3pers values (
8, 'Rochblatt',        'Harold T.','290553810',32, 'M');
insert into t2.v3pers values (
9, 'Nungaray',         'Dennis J.',    '944829477',58, 'M');
insert into t2.v3pers values (
10, 'Oberstein',       'Florence L.', '932840202',9, 'F');

update t2.v3pers set lname = 'Borghese'
where id = 7;
```

This code returns

```
1 row created.

1 row created.

1 row created.

1 row created.

1 row created.

1 row updated.

1 row updated.
```

t1 cannot select from the table t3pers because he has no privileges to it. He can select his own rows from v3pers:

```
col creator format a8
col id       format 999

select * from t2.t3pers;

select * from t2.v3pers;
```

The following code is returned:

```
select * from t2.t3pers
              *
ERROR at line 1:
ORA-00942: table or view does not exist
```

ID	LNAME	FMNAME	SSN	AGE	S
6	Robinson	Faye M.	966549339		F
7	Borghese	M. Okechuku	854291872	23	
8	Rochblatt	Harold T.	290553810	32	M
9	Nungaray	Dennis J.	944829477	58	M
10	Oberstein	Florence L.	932840202	9	F

t2, on the other hand, can select his own rows through the view and all rows through the table, as shown here:

```
connect t2/t2

select * from t2.v3pers;

select * from t2.t3pers;

clear columns
```

This code returns

```
Connected.
```

ID	LNAME	FMNAME	SSN	AGE	S
1	Jones	David N.	895663453	34	M
2	Martinelli	A. Emery	312331818	92	M
3	Talavera	F. Espinosa	533932999	19	F
4	Kratochvil	Mary T.	969825711	48	F
5	Melsheli	Joseph K.	000342222	14	M

```
ID LNAME            FMNAME           SSN         AGE S CREATOR  CRDATE
-- ---------------- ---------------- ---------   --------- - -------- -----------
 1 Jones            David N.         895663453    34 M T2       28-JUN-1997
 2 Martinelli       A. Emery         312331818    92 M T2       28-JUN-1997
 3 Talavera         F. Espinosa      533932999    19 F T2       28-JUN-1997
 4 Kratochvil       Mary T.          969825711    48 F T2       28-JUN-1997
 5 Melsheli         Joseph K.        000342222    14 M T2       28-JUN-1997
 6 Robinson         Faye M.          966549339       F T1       28-JUN-1997
 7 Borghese         M. Okechuku      854291872    23   T1       28-JUN-1997
 8 Rochblatt        Harold T.        290553810    32 M T1       28-JUN-1997
 9 Nungaray         Dennis J.        944829477    58 M T1       28-JUN-1997
10 Oberstein        Florence L.      932840202     9 F T1       28-JUN-1997

10 rows selected.
```

> **NOTE**
>
> You might have realized that t2 can see t1's entries despite the fact that t1 has not issued a commit statement. The reason is that every time the connect command is issued, the session commits. If you run the same example interactively on two independent sessions, t2 can see only the original five rows.

Summary

Single-table views defined with the check option can be used to control access to table columns or table rows. A user who accesses a table through such a view cannot insert or update records that violate the definition of the view. Row-level access control is not accommodated by privileges, and detailed column access control is not accommodated by views. A sophisticated security scheme can be implemented by combining a view that controls row access with a set of privileges that controls column access in detail.

35

ACCESS THROUGH VIEWS

Auditing

IN THIS CHAPTER

All the security features and mechanisms discussed so far are set up to prevent undesired events. History is replete with cases, however, in which nuclear power plants blow up, safe encryption schemes are cracked, or unsinkable ships are sunk by icebergs; supposedly secure systems were not that secure after all. The danger is worse with computer systems because the complexity of the hardware and software provides an inherent security hole.

Preventing such loss is where auditing comes in. Auditing collects data about transactions on an ongoing basis. You can use these data for a number of purposes:

- If a security breach is detected and you have a trail of the system's transactions, you at least have a chance to retroactively piece together what happened. Using that knowledge, you can take corrective action aimed at either systems or individuals.

- Even if everything appears to be fine, routine audits can surface suspicious activity.

- In some systems, it is desirable to keep information on all database transactions as well as a current state of information. With such complete information, you can choose a certain day and time and retrieve the status of the database at that moment.

The discussion of auditing is also a bridge to the next set of topics in this book. Auditing your system delivers some of the statistics necessary for performance tuning.

The easiest (and most incomplete) option is to include four columns with your database tables: creator, date created, person who updated the table, and date updated. With that information, you can know who created the row in the first place and who is responsible for the most recent update.

The more complex version of this method is to maintain a separate transaction log table. Whenever a row in the original table is deleted or updated, a copy of the row before the change or deletion is included in the audit table.

ORACLE vs SQL Oracle provides a number of auditing mechanisms that let you audit statements, privileges, and objects.

Including Creation and Update Fields

The mechanism for automatically inserting the creator and the create date was already shown on the t3pers table in the code examples from Chapter 35, "Providing and Controlling Access to Database Objects Through Views." That part does not take much effort; you add a Creator field with the default set to user and a create_date or Crdate field with the default set to sysdate. You perform inserts either through a view that does not include these columns or through the table using a comma-separated list that does not contain these columns, or you include user and sysdate in the insert statement.

Incorporating the second part of the information in your table is a little more cumbersome. You need to include two more columns: one for the person who updated the table and one for update_date. If all updates are performed through a client tool, you can attach some code that will update those two fields as well. You can set up a post-update trigger in the module to copy the current user and date values into the respective fields. When the changes in the module are saved, those values are inserted into the database. Another possible method is to modify the `insert` statement to take care of these columns.

Database Triggers

Another, and usually better, option is to create a database trigger that maintains the update columns directly.

Database triggers are an extension to SQL. Whenever the triggering event occurs, the PL/SQL module defined through the `create trigger` statement executes. For the example here, the trigger is set to fire before any update of any of the table's row. The module copies the current user and current date into the respective fields. When the update occurs, these values are saved.

ORACLE vs. SQL

The following code examples implement this approach. First, in Listing 36.1, table `t4pers` is created to be identical to `t3pers` from Chapter 35 but adds two columns, one for the username of the person updating a row and one for the date.

Listing 36.1. Creating and loading a table.

```
--        Filename: 36squ01.sql
--         Purpose: creating and loading
--                  table t4pers in the
--                  schema of t2
--                  includes creator/create date and
--                  updated/update date columns
--
connect t2/t2;

drop table t4pers;

create table t4pers (
    id       number(2) not null,
    LName    varchar2(15),
    FMName   varchar2(15),
    SSN      char(9),
    Age      number(3),
    Sex      char(1),
    creator  varchar2(30) default user,
    crdate   date         default sysdate,
    updated  varchar2(30),
    up_date  date)
;

insert into t4pers (id, lname, fmname, ssn, age, sex) values (
1, 'Jones',     'David N.',   '895663453',34, 'M');
insert into t4pers (id, lname, fmname, ssn, age, sex)  values (
2, 'Martinelli', 'A. Emery',   '312331818',92, 'M');
insert into t4pers (id, lname, fmname, ssn, age, sex)  values (
3, 'Talavera',   'F. Espinosa','533932999',19, 'F');
insert into t4pers (id, lname, fmname, ssn, age, sex)  values (
```

continues

Listing 36.1. continued

```
4, 'Kratochvil', 'Mary T.',     '969825711',48, 'F');
insert into t4pers (id, lname, fmname, ssn, age, sex)  values (
5, 'Melsheli',   'Joseph K.',  '000342222',14, 'M');

commit;

col creator format a4
col id        format 999
col age       format 999
col updated format a4
col lname     format a12
col fmname    format a12

select * from t4pers;

clear columns
```

These statements return the following output:

```
Connected.

Table dropped.

...
Commit complete.


  ID LNAME        FMNAME        SSN       AGE S CREA CRDATE      UPDA UP_DATE
---- ------------ ------------- --------  --- - ---- ----------- ---- --------
   1 Jones        David N.      895663453  34 M T2   28-JUN-1997
   2 Martinelli   A. Emery      312331818  92 M T2   28-JUN-1997
   3 Talavera     F. Espinosa   533932999  19 F T2   28-JUN-1997
   4 Kratochvil   Mary T.       969825711  48 F T2   28-JUN-1997
   5 Melsheli     Joseph K.     000342222  14 M T2   28-JUN-1997
```

The next step, as shown in Listing 36.2, is to define a `before update` trigger on that table and to grant access to user t1.

Listing 36.2. Defining a `before update` trigger to load.

```
--        Filename: 36squ02.sql
--         Purpose: creating before update trigger to load
--                  updated/update date columns
--
--
create or replace trigger updt4pers
before update on t4pers
for each row
begin
   :new.updated := user;
   :new.up_date := sysdate;
end;
/

grant select, insert, update on t4pers to t1;
```

These statements return the following output:

```
Trigger created.
```

```
Grant succeeded.
```

Now the mechanism is in place so that the updated/date columns are automatically maintained. The user t1 can now load rows into the table. User t1 first loads five rows, as shown in Listing 36.3.

Listing 36.3. Loading rows.

```
connect t1/t1;


insert into t2.t4pers (id, lname, fmname, ssn, age, sex)  values (
6, 'Robinson',         'Faye M.' ,  '966549339',NULL, 'F');
insert into t2.t4pers (id, lname, fmname, ssn, age, sex)  values (
7, NULL        ,       'M. Okechuku'  ,  '854291872',23, NULL);
insert into t2.t4pers (id, lname, fmname, ssn, age, sex)  values (
8, 'Rochblatt',        'Harold T.','290553810',32, 'M');
insert into t2.t4pers (id, lname, fmname, ssn, age, sex)  values (
9, 'Nungaray',       'Dennis J.',   '944829477',58, 'M');
insert into t2.t4pers (id, lname, fmname, ssn, age, sex)  values (
10, 'Oberstein',        'Florence L.',  '932840202',9, 'F');
```

These statements return the following output:

```
Connected.
...
5 rows created.
```

The next code updates a few rows, some created by user t2 and one created by user t1:

```
update t2.t4pers set
    lname = 'FORGOT',
    fmname = 'IT'
where id in (1,2,4)
;

update t2.t4pers set lname = 'Borghese'
where id = 7;
```

These update statements return the following output:

```
3 rows updated.
```

```
1 row updated.
```

Now the session reconnects to user t2, who also updates a few rows and commits:

```
connect t2/t2

update t4pers set
    lname  = '    ERASED',
    fmname = '    IT'
```

```
where id in (3,6,8,10)
;

commit;
```

The statements return the following:

```
Connected.

4 rows updated.

Commit complete.
```

Finally, a full select of the table reveals some of its history:

```
clear columns

col creator format a4
col id      format 999
col age     format 999
col updated format a4
col lname   format a12
col fmname  format a12

select * from t2.t4pers;

clear columns
```

These statements return the following output:

ID	LNAME	FMNAME	SSN	AGE	S	CREA	CRDATE	UPDA	UP_DATE
1	FORGOT	IT	895663453	34	M	t2	29-JUN-1997	T1	29-JUN-1997
2	FORGOT	IT	312331818	92	M	t2	29-JUN-1997	T1	29-JUN-1997
3	ERASED	IT	533932999	19	F	t2	29-JUN-1997	T2	29-JUN-1997
4	FORGOT	IT	969825711	48	F	t2	29-JUN-1997	T1	29-JUN-1997
5	Melsheli	Joseph K.	000342222	14	M	t2	29-JUN-1997		
6	ERASED	IT	966549339		F	t1	29-JUN-1997	T2	29-JUN-1997
7	Borghese	M. Okechuku	854291872	23		t1	29-JUN-1997	T1	29-JUN-1997
8	ERASED	IT	290553810	32	M	t1	29-JUN-1997	T2	29-JUN-1997
9	Nungaray	Dennis J.	944829477	58	M	t1	29-JUN-1997		
10	ERASED	IT	932840202	9	F	t1	29-JUN-1997	T2	29-JUN-1997

```
10 rows selected.
```

TIP

If you do not have triggers available, make sure that updated and up_date are set in each update statement as well. Following is a revision of the first update statement in the previous example that incorporates these columns:

```
update t2.t4pers set
    lname  = 'FORGOT',
    fmname = 'IT',
```

```
    updated = user,
    up_date = sysdate
where id in (1,2,4)
;
```

Transaction Log Tables

Most databases are set up to keep information up to date. An example is address information; most businesses are interested only in the current address for mailing things. What the address happened to be a year ago is not usually a concern. The information of such a database is permanently in flux, and updates or deletes of records destroy previously maintained information for good.

Auditing, on the other hand, is as much interested in the transactions that led to the current state as it is in the current state. For that purpose, the database tables must be designed somewhat differently:

- You can set up the table to maintain records with a from date and a to date. Only those records with a to date of NULL are considered active.

- You can set up a table that is kept current plus a transaction log table for each entity. Before a record in the current table is updated or deleted, a record of the state before the update or delete is copied into the transaction log table.

- Combining the first two approaches, you can set up a current table and a table that maintains current and previous states. That approach offers the advantage of immediately using the log table for historical queries.

This section focuses on the second approach.

The transaction log table should contain the columns of the current table to be logged plus six columns (four of which are somewhat familiar from previous examples):

- Creator
- Creation date
- Creation type: A code for the action that led to creation of the row in the first place (insert = I, update = U)
- Destroyer
- Destroy date
- A code for the action that led to destruction of the row

The current table must contain the first three columns as well. The defaults are set so that the creator is the user, the create date is the sysdate, and the create type is I for insert.

Whenever a row is updated from the current table, the existing row is first copied into the transaction log table, and the username is inserted into the destroyer column, the date into the destroy date, and a U into the action column. The same happens for a row to be deleted, but the action code is a D. The best way to make these changes, which is shown in the following example, is through a trigger. If that is not possible, you must issue a set of SQL statements for the same effect through the client tool.

The first part of the example, shown in Listing 36.4, creates the tables t5pers and t5perslog. It also loads the same rows that were loaded by users t2 and t1 into t4pers.

Listing 36.4. Creating transaction log tables.

```
--          Filename: 36squ04.sql
--           Purpose: creating and loading
--                    table t5pers in  the schema of t2
--                    includes creator/create date/create type columns
--                    creating t5perslog table which also includes
--                    destroyer/destroy date/destroy type columns
--
--
connect t2/t2;

drop table t5pers;

create table t5pers (
    id        number(2) not null,
    LName     varchar2(15),
    FMName    varchar2(15),
    SSN       char(9),
    Age       number(3),
    Sex       char(1),
    creator   varchar2(30) default user,
    crdate    date         default sysdate,
    cract     char(1)      default 'C')
;

grant all on t5pers to t1;

drop table t5perslog;

create table t5perslog (
    id        number(2) not null,
    LName     varchar2(15),
    FMName    varchar2(15),
    SSN       char(9),
    Age       number(3),
    Sex       char(1),
    creator   varchar2(30),
    crdate    date,
    cract     char(1),
    destroyer varchar2(30),
    desdate   date,
    desact    char(1))
;
```

```
--... insert statements ...see 36squ01.sql

connect t1/t1;
--... insert statements ...see 36squ02.sql

connect t2/t2;

col creator format a4
col id      format 999
col age     format 999
col updated format a4
col lname   format a12
col fmname  format a12

select * from t5pers;

clear columns
```

These statements return the following output:

```
Connected.

....

ID  LNAME        FMNAME        SSN        AGE S CREA CRDATE       C
--- ------------ ------------  ---------  --- - ---- ----------- -
  1 Jones        David N.      895663453   34 M T2   29-JUN-1997 C
  2 Martinelli   A. Emery      312331818   92 M T2   29-JUN-1997 C
  3 Talavera     F. Espinosa   533932999   19 F T2   29-JUN-1997 C
  4 Kratochvil   Mary T.       969825711   48 F T2   29-JUN-1997 C
  5 Melsheli     Joseph K.     000342222   14 M T2   29-JUN-1997 C
  6 Robinson     Faye M.       966549339      F T1   29-JUN-1997 C
  7              M. Okechuku   854291872   23   T1   29-JUN-1997 C
  8 Rochblatt    Harold T.     290553810   32 M T1   29-JUN-1997 C
  9 Nungaray     Dennis J.     944829477   58 M T1   29-JUN-1997 C
 10 Oberstein    Florence L.   932840202    9 F T1   29-JUN-1997 C

10 rows selected.
```

The next part of the example, shown in Listing 36.5, creates an `after update or delete` trigger on t5pers that performs the required copying of the old records of t5pers into the log file. Because this is a trigger on t5pers, the two records called old and new are already available for use without any further coding.

Listing 36.5. Creating an `after update or delete` trigger.

```
--      Filename: 36squ05.sql
--       Purpose: creating after update or delete trigger to load
--                t5perslog table
--
--
create or replace trigger upde5pers
after update or delete on t5pers
for each row
declare
```

continues

Listing 36.5. continued

```
   destr_action    char(1);
begin
   if updating then destr_action := 'U';
   else             destr_action := 'D';
   end if;

   insert into t5perslog values (
     :old.id,
     :old.lname,
     :old.fmname,
     :old.ssn,
     :old.age,
     :old.sex,
     :old.creator,
     :old.crdate,
     :old.cract ,
     user,
     sysdate,
     destr_action);

end;
/
```

Successful creation of the trigger is reported through

```
Trigger created.
```

Finally, some update and delete statements are performed on t5pers, as shown in Listing 36.6. The user t1 updates a few rows and deletes one row from t5pers.

Listing 36.6. Deleting and updating from a table.

```
--       Filename: 36squ06.sql
--        Purpose: deleting from and updating t5pers
--

                         connect t1/t1

                         update t2.t5pers set
                            lname  = 'FORGOT',
                            fmname = 'IT'
                         where id in (1,2,4)
                         ;

                         update t2.t5pers set lname = 'Borghese'
                         where id = 7;

                         delete from t2.t5pers where id = 9;
```

The statements return:

```
3 rows updated.

1 row updated.

1 row deleted.
```

The user t2 also updates a few columns and deletes a few rows from t5pers:

```
connect t2/t2

update t5pers set
    lname  = '    ERASED',
    fmname = '    IT'
where id in (3,6,8,10)
;

delete from t5pers where id in (1,6,7);

commit;
```

The statements return

```
Connected.

4 rows updated.

3 rows deleted.

Commit complete.
```

Only six rows remain in t5pers:

```
col creator   format a4
col cract     format a1    heading 'C'
col desact    format a1    heading 'C'
col id        format 999
col age       format 999
col destroyer format a4
col lname     format a12
col fmname    format a12

select * from t2.t5pers;
```

This returns

```
ID  LNAME         FMNAME        SSN         AGE S CREA CRDATE        C
--- ------------- ------------- ----------- --- - ---- ------------- -
  2 FORGOT        IT            312331818    92 M T2   29-JUN-1997   C
  3     ERASED        IT        533932999    19 F T2   29-JUN-1997   C
  4 FORGOT        IT            969825711    48 F T2   29-JUN-1997   C
  5 Melsheli      Joseph K.     000342222    14 M T2   29-JUN-1997   C
  8     ERASED        IT        290553810    32 M T1   29-JUN-1997   C
 10     ERASED        IT        932840202     9 F T1   29-JUN-1997   C

6 rows selected.
```

T5perslog ends up with twice as many rows because every time a t5pers row is updated or deleted, a t5perslog row is written:

```
select * from t2.t5perslog
order by id, crdate;

clear columns
```

These statements return the following output:

```
ID LNAME        FMNAME       SSN        AGE S CREA CRDATE       C DEST DESDATE      C
-- ----------   -----------  ---------- --- - ---- -----------  - ---- -----------  -
 1 Jones        David N.     895663453   34 M T2   29-JUN-1997  C T1   29-JUN-1997  U
 1 FORGOT       IT           895663453   34 M T2   29-JUN-1997  C T2   29-JUN-1997  D
 2 Martinelli   A. Emery     312331818   92 M T2   29-JUN-1997  C T1   29-JUN-1997  U
 3 Talavera     F. Espinosa  533932999   19 F T2   29-JUN-1997  C T2   29-JUN-1997  U
 4 Kratochvil   Mary T.      969825711   48 F T2   29-JUN-1997  C T1   29-JUN-1997  U
 6 Robinson     Faye M.      966549339      F T1   29-JUN-1997  C T2   29-JUN-1997  U
 6 ERASED       IT           966549339      F T1   29-JUN-1997  C T2   29-JUN-1997  D
 7              M. Okechuku  854291872   23   T1   29-JUN-1997  C T1   29-JUN-1997  U
 7 Borghese     M. Okechuku  854291872   23   T1   29-JUN-1997  C T2   29-JUN-1997  D
 8 Rochblatt    Harold T.    290553810   32 M T1   29-JUN-1997  C T2   29-JUN-1997  U
 9 Nungaray     Dennis J.    944829477   58 M T1   29-JUN-1997  C T1   29-JUN-1997  D
10 Oberstein    Florence L.  932840202    9 F T1   29-JUN-1997  C T2   29-JUN-1997  U

12 rows selected.
```

NOTE

No one needs permissions on t5perslog. The inserts on this table are done through a procedural object, a trigger, which is in user t2's schema. The t5perslog table is loaded by that trigger using user t2's privileges.

Using Built-in RDBMS Auditing Features

Using log tables can capture other actions as well, such as selecting from tables. However, statements that do not involve tables, views, or privileges cannot be audited that way.

ORACLE vs SQL

Oracle Server provides built-in auditing features that can handle all three of these options. These features support three kinds of auditing:

- Object auditing generates logs on the use of specific statements on specific objects. Object auditing is active for all users of the database.
- Privilege auditing generates logs on the use of a specific system privilege. It can be activated for all users or a list of specific users.
- Statement auditing generates logs on the use of specific SQL statements. It can be activated for all users or a list of specific users.

These features require the installation of audit views, the setting and unsetting of audit options using the audit and noaudit commands, truncating the sys.aud$ table when the information is no longer needed, protecting the audit trail by granting the delete any table privilege only to security administrators (who may or may not be the database administrator), and retrieving information from the audit trail through the audit views.

You can find information on these features in the *Oracle Server Administrator's Guide* and the *Oracle Concepts Manual.*

Summary

Auditing collects data about transactions on an ongoing basis. Auditing data can be used to trace security breaches, to identify suspicious activity, and to keep full information about the state of the database or a few key tables at any given time.

Three basic auditing options can be implemented:

- Include four auditing columns in database tables: creator, date created, person who updated the table, and date updated.
- Maintain separate transaction log tables that hold copies of the row before the change or deletion.
- Implement the auditing mechanisms that let you audit statements, privileges, and objects.

Optimizing and Data Quality Issues

C
Section

The final section of this book focuses on two issues on which good database systems depend, yet that are not talked about much—optimization and data quality.

The goal of optimization is to get the same SQL statement processing accomplished with much fewer resources. Optimization aims at reducing the number of times that a SQL statement has to be parsed, and at determining the most efficient execution plan.

Last but not least, if the data in a system is garbage, the system itself is pretty useless, too. This is especially a problem if data is loaded from sources in somebody else's control. For this purpose, the second part of this section presents a methodology that can be used to test and scrub data.

Optimization

Optimizing the Statement Processing Performance: Parsing Phase

CHAPTER 37

The idea behind a higher-generation language such as SQL is to insulate the user from the nuts and bolts of the action to be performed. Simply put, the user specifies what he wants to accomplish, and the RDBMS determines and executes the best way to do it.

This idea is implemented through an *optimizer*, which analyzes a SQL statement and, if applicable, attempts to convert it to an equivalent statement that can be executed using fewer resources. The optimizer, however, is not always that effective.

Therefore, the basic assumption that SQL and the optimizer perform all low-level tasks no longer holds. It becomes important to look at what a statement is doing on a lower level. Performance tuning still does not approach low-level programming, just smart tweaking of the system.

The potential rewards of optimizing SQL are huge: Guy Harrison, in *Oracle SQL High Performance Tuning*, (published by Prentice Hall) claims performance gains of 100 percent or more due to SQL tuning without any associated hardware or software upgrades. He also argues that once SQL code is implemented, it tends not to be improved at a later time either because there is nobody there to do it or because improving it might have prohibitive costs in a production environment (especially where the data model is affected). Therefore, code should be optimized at design time, which has the added advantage of requiring testing only once.

The optimization effort is focused on three areas:

- Facilitating efficient statement processing
- Affecting the optimizer to execute statements in the most efficient manner
- Adapting the database design to improve performance, especially through the use of indexes

SQL Query Processing

Oracle vs SQL

This chapter covers the way Oracle executes SQL. Because the method of execution is left to the manufacturer of the software, its optimization is by definition not included in the standard.

SQL statements are processed through a series of steps. Some of these steps apply only to query processing, and others may be skipped altogether. In its simplest variation, four steps are performed:

1. A cursor is opened.
2. The statement is parsed.
3. The statement is executed.
4. The cursor is closed.

This simple variation applies only to data-manipulation statements (`update`, `insert`, and `delete`) that do not use bind variables.

Cursors

Cursors are memory structures that are usually created automatically by client programs in anticipation of a SQL statement. Some programs, however, require the explicit creation of a cursor (for example, Oracle Call interfaces such as `pro*C` or `pro*Cobol`).

Cursors contain

- Two representations of the SQL statement—parsed and unparsed (see the "Parsing" section later in this chapter.)
- A list of the database objects referenced by the statement
- The execution plan for the statement
- A pointer to the current row

Because cursors are memory objects, they must reside in memory available to the RDBMS. Memory is allocated to a database through a set of initialization parameters in the `init`*sid*`.ora` file, which is read every time the database is started. If you run Personal Oracle on Windows 95 using the default database installation, this file is most likely called `c:\orawin95\database\initorcl.ora`, in Oracle V7.3 for NT Server, it is `c:\orant\database\initorcl.ora`. The initialization parameter that matters for cursors is the `shared_pool_size`. The shared pool contains the dictionary and library caches, also known as the shared SQL area. Cursors are maintained there. As the space is used, the cursor that has not been used for the longest time is released so that a new cursor can be put there.

Parsing

During the parsing phase, the Relational Database Management System (RDBMS) checks the syntax of the statement. If there is a syntax error, an error message is returned. The next step is to look in the shared SQL area to determine whether an identical statement that uses the identical database objects is already there. If so, the cursor for the already-existing statement is used. The benefit of this is that the parse phase can be concluded at this point and the execution phase can start.

If no existing cursor can be used, three more steps are performed after the Data Dictionary is queried:

1. A semantic check is performed. All references to database objects, such as tables, views, and columns, are resolved. An error is returned if this cannot be accomplished. Hopefully, all that information can be found in the Data Dictionary cache. If not, a so-called recursive SQL statement is issued by the RDBMS to retrieve the information from the Data Dictionary.
2. It is verified whether the user has all the necessary system and object privileges to perform the desired action. If not, an error is returned.
3. The most effective search path is determined.

The next step, which is one of the most important ones, is to determine an execution plan, which describes the steps the RDBMS will take to perform the desired action. Refer to Chapter 35, "Providing and Controlling Access to Database Objects Through Views," for ways to affect and optimize the execution plan.

Execution

The statement is now ready to be executed. This process is performed in the manner established in the execution plan. At this point, the RDBMS brings about the necessary physical and logical read and write operations. This step is more complicated, and is accompanied by an additional fetch step for queries (see the "Execution" section later in this chapter).

Closing of the Cursor

The cursor is now closed, but remains in memory unless it is not used for a certain period of time. Once all storage space is used up for SQL statements, the least recently used cursor is overwritten.

Affecting the Re-use of Cursors

The first tuning objective is to optimize the probability that cursors can be re-used or concurrently used for subsequent statements. If so, processing can take the parsing shortcut, which eliminates the semantic check, the privilege check, and the creation of the execution plan. For this to happen, a new statement must be identical to one in the cache. The only exception to this is that bind variables can be used.

Re-using cursors can provide enormous performance gains. At the very least, the time, effort, and resources necessary for reparsing need not be spent. If there is plenty of memory and if all necessary information is already in the library cache, reparsing is not such a big problem. If there is inadequate memory or if information is missing from the library cache, some disk I/O is incurred in the reparsing process.

If all the available space in memory is used for other cursors, the cursor used least recently is destroyed to make room for the new one that comes with the statement. This might affect the performance of a subsequent statement if the destroyed cursor could have serviced it. In itself, this is not such a big issue either, but if it happens a lot, it will have a pretty nasty performance effect.

To compensate for these unnecessary cursors and to achieve acceptable performance, it might be necessary to set aside a bigger shared pool. The memory taken up for that larger shared pool might have been advantageously used elsewhere, such as for more buffers or for keeping more objects in memory.

Oracle uses internal locks and latches. Latches protect shared memory structures in the System Global area, part of which is the shared pool used for the library and dictionary caches. A latch must be acquired each time a new statement is put into memory. A dictionary lock on the objects that are referenced in the query is acquired during parsing of the statement to make sure that the referenced dictionary information does not change during the parsing phase. If no more latches are available, this process has to wait until a latch of another statement becomes free— a problem called *latch contention*. If that happens, performance will suffer even if sufficient memory is available.

Getting Identical Statements

When a statement is parsed, a hashing algorithm is applied, which converts that statement into a number guaranteed to be unique. This number is maintained with the cursor. If another statement is parsed, its hash value is calculated. Then it is necessary only to compare the hashed values to determine whether one of the cached cursors contains an identical SQL statement.

To be hashed to the same value, the text of a SQL statement must be identical in every regard except for bind variables, which are covered in the next section.

This includes the case of all letters; SQL proper is not case sensitive, and any combination of uppercase and lowercase letters in a statement will give the same results (the only exception being characters and character strings). The SQL-89 standard also requires column names to be capitalized, but that is not implemented. To evaluate to the same hash value, however, uppercase and lowercase letters must be used in the same way in both statements. Use of white space (spaces, tabs, and newlines) must be identical as well, as is the case with comments.

The referenced objects, such as tables, views, or columns, must be the same. In this context, identically named objects in different schemas are not the same. For example, if t1 creates a table called test and t2 does the same, t1 selecting from its test table does not evaluate to the same hash value as t2 selecting from its test table because different objects are accessed.

Bind Variables

Constants can be used in SQL for columns that always retrieve the same value. Constants are unrelated to any value in a table or are the result of expressions. By far, the most important use of constants is in conditional expressions, such as where id = 1, where salary < 15000, where name like 'Ham%', or having max(income) > 200000.

Such a constant might be specified as a literal value, as has been done in this book so far, or as a *bind variable*. The major problem of using literal values is caused by the need to reparse otherwise identical statements only because the literal value has changed. As has been described, this might adversely affect performance.

A bind variable, on the other hand, is defined in the session, which can be set to a new value every time the statement is reprocessed. As long as the bind variable has the same datatype (in Oracle 7.3 or later) or the same type and name (previous versions), the statement will be parsed as identical and the parsing shortcut can be used.

The disadvantage of using bind variables is that they prevent the cost-based optimizer from using a histogram of index values to decide whether an index or a table scan is the best execution approach. There might, therefore, be a performance trade-off to bind variables.

Using Bind Variables

For comparison's sake, the use of bind variables is shown in an example that selects lawyers from the `lawyer1` table using ranges from < 1500 billable hours to > 3500 billable hours in increments of 200. If your purpose is to display range information, Listing 37.1 is not the one to follow; it is inefficient and inelegant. You could use a range lookup table or use some formula or formula/decode combination. In any case, the comparison example that follows uses 11 single statements for the same purpose.

Listing 37.1. Retrieving bhrs ranges.

```
--        Filename: 37squ01.sql
--         Purpose: retrieve bhrs ranges
--
select
   id,
   name,
   office,
   bhrs,
   bgross
from lawyer1
where
   bhrs < 1500
;

select
   id,
   name,
   office,
   bhrs,
   bgross
from lawyer1
where
   bhrs >= 1500 and
   bhrs <= 1700
;

select
   id,
   name,
   office,
   bhrs,
   bgross
from lawyer1
where
   bhrs >= 1700 and
   bhrs <= 1900
;

...
```

```
...

select
   id,
   name,
   office,
   bhrs,
   bgross
from lawyer1
where
   bhrs >= 3500;
```

These statements are essentially identical except for the where clause and the values in the where clause.

The statements return

ID	NAME	OFFICE	BHRS	BGROSS
2	Cheetham	New York	1398	280435

ID	NAME	OFFICE	BHRS	BGROSS
8	Bonin	New York	1678	346892
16	Chabot	New York	1680	310897

ID	NAME	OFFICE	BHRS	BGROSS
4	Clayton	Houston	1789	190045
19	Chatham	New York	1759	367944

no rows selected

ID	NAME	OFFICE	BHRS	BGROSS
9	Frankie	New York	2134	469843
20	Paul	Boston	2198	239855

ID	NAME	OFFICE	BHRS	BGROSS
5	Roach	Houston	2349	269844
14	Earl	New York	2320	434801
18	Ming	Los Angeles	2492	359021

ID	NAME	OFFICE	BHRS	BGROSS
11	Cardinal	Boston	2694	277952
13	Martinez	Los Angeles	2659	403488

ID	NAME	OFFICE	BHRS	BGROSS
1	Dewey	Boston	2856	426800
10	Greene	Boston	2854	289435
15	Wright	Boston	2789	204133

```
    ID NAME             OFFICE            BHRS     BGROSS
--------- ---------------- ------------ ----------- --------
    12 Chandler         Los Angeles        2987     423878

    ID NAME             OFFICE            BHRS     BGROSS
--------- ---------------- ------------ ----------- --------
     6 Roll             Los Angeles        3203     498084
    17 Miller           Los Angeles        3153     503582

    ID NAME             OFFICE            BHRS     BGROSS
--------- ---------------- ------------ ----------- --------
     7 Easton           Los Angeles        3800     654832
```

The main purpose of bind variables seems to be to serve as a mechanism through which PL/SQL and SQL*Plus can exchange data. This works as follows:

1. The variable is defined using the variable *variable_name variable_type* syntax.

2. A small PL/SQL procedure is created, which assigns values to the variables.

3. The procedure is run using the /.

4. In the where clause, the bind variable, preceded by a colon, is used instead of the literal constant.

Listing 37.2 shows this approach. The select statements could be run within a loop, using either PL/SQL or an interface to a procedural language. In this example, the SQL statements are identical; only the values of the bind variables change.

Listing 37.2. Retrieving bhrs ranges using bind variables.

```
--        Filename: 37squ02.sql
--        Purpose: retrieve bhrs ranges
--                 using bind variables
--
variable range_l number
variable range_h number

begin
:range_l := 0;
:range_h := 1500;
end;
/

select
   id,
   name,
   office,
   bhrs,
   bgross
from lawyer1
where
   bhrs >= :range_l and
   bhrs <= :range_h
;

begin
:range_l := 1500;
```

Optimizing the Statement Processing Performance: Parsing Phase

CHAPTER 37

783

37

OPTIMIZING
STATEMENT
PROCESSING

```
:range_h := 1700;
end;
/

select
   id,
   name,
   office,
   bhrs,
   bgross
from lawyer1
where
   bhrs >= :range_l and
   bhrs <= :range_h
;

....
....

begin
:range_l := 3500;
:range_h := 100000;
end;
/

select
   id,
   name,
   office,
   bhrs,
   bgross
from lawyer1
where
   bhrs >= :range_l and
   bhrs <= :range_h
;
```

The output is almost identical to the previous code except for some feedback concerning the procedures. Here is the output:

```
PL/SQL procedure successfully completed.


       ID NAME             OFFICE            BHRS    BGROSS
--------- ---------------- --------------- -------- ---------
        2 Cheetham         New York          1398    280435

....
....

PL/SQL procedure successfully completed.

       ID NAME             OFFICE            BHRS    BGROSS
--------- ---------------- --------------- -------- ---------
        7 Easton           Los Angeles       3800    654832
```

The first version, however, runs through all the parse steps 11 times; the second version runs through the steps only once.

Examining the Data Dictionary for SQL Statement Statistics

Listing 37.3, which extracts statistics about the processing of statements, shows how often the different version of the SQL statements have been parsed since the most recent startup of the database.

Listing 37.3. Checking for parsing execution statistics.

```
--          Filename: 37squ03.sql
--           Purpose: checking for parsing execution statistics.
--
-
--             Stage: production
col sql_text        format a50 heading 'SQL STATEMENT'
col version_count   format 999 heading 'VER-|SION|CNT.'
col loads           format 999 heading '# OF|LOAD| S '
col invalidations   format 999 heading 'IN- |VAL-|IDS '
col parse_calls     format 999 heading 'PAR-|SE |CLLS'
col version_counts  format 999 heading 'VER-|SION|CTS.'
col executions      format 999 heading 'EXE-|CUT-|IONS'
col command_type    format 999 heading 'COM-|MAND|TYPE'

variable sqltxt varchar2(1000);

begin
:sqltxt := '&1';
end;
/

select
   sql_text,
   parse_calls,
   executions,
   version_count,
   loads,
   invalidations
from v$sqlarea
where instr(sql_text,:sqltxt) > 0 and
   command_type in (2,3,6,7)
;

clear columns
```

This script displays the statistics for each SQL statement that has a substring identical to the one passed in as the first argument. However, the string passed in must be correct in terms of white space; otherwise, the condition will not retrieve the desired statement.

The script is written against the v$sqlarea view, which can access every single SQL statement since startup of the database instance. To obtain the same results, it is necessary to shut down the instance, bring it back up, create a clean slate, and run the script 37squ04.sql, which is shown in Listing 37.4. This script runs 37squ01.sql and 37squ02.sql 10 times each.

37

Listing 37.4. Running the scripts 37squ01.sql and 37squ02.sql 10 times each.

```
--       Filename: 37squ04.sql
--        Purpose: runs the scripts 37squ01.sql
--                 and 37squ02.sql ten times each.
--
set termout off
@@37squ01
...
...
...
@@37squ02

set termout on

@37squ03
```
➡ 'select   id,   name,   office,   bhrs,   bgross from lawyer1 where'

This code returns

```
old   2: :sqltxt := '&1';
new   2: :sqltxt :=
```
➡ 'select   id,   name,   office,   bhrs,   bgross from lawyer1 where';

```
PL/SQL procedure successfully completed.
```

SQL STATEMENT	PAR-SE CLLS	EXE-CUT-IONS	VER-SION CNT.	# OF LOADS	IN-VAL-IDS
select id, name, office, bhrs, bgro ss from lawyer1 where bhrs < 1500	10	10	1	1	0
select id, name, office, bhrs, bgro ss from lawyer1 where bhrs >= 1500 and bhrs <= 1700	10	10	1	1	0
... ...					
select id, name, office, bhrs, bgro ss from lawyer1 where bhrs >= 3500	10	10	1	1	0
select id, name, office, bhrs, bgro ss from lawyer1 where bhrs >= :range_l and b hrs <= :range_h	130	130	1	1	0

```
12 rows selected.
```

Each statement in 37squ01.sql was called and executed 10 times. Only one version of each statement was submitted; each statement was loaded only once. None of the statements was invalid.

The last section of data shows the entire parsing activity necessary for running the script `37squ02.sql` 10 times. One single statement was submitted and executed 130 times, but had to be loaded and fully parsed only one time. Only one version of the statement exists, and no invalid statements were submitted.

Note that `37squ03.sql` uses a bind variable for its own processing.

Bind Variables with Different Names

Until version 7.2, bind variables had to be identical in name and type so that the statements using them would have to complete parsing only once. Starting with version 7.2, only the datatype has to match. Thus, the two statements in Listing 37.5 (in which only the names of the bind variables differ) should be treated as the same.

Listing 37.5. Using bind variables with different names.

```
--        Filename: 37squ05.sql
--         Purpose: retrieve bhrs ranges
--                  using bind variables with different names
--
variable range_l1 number
variable range_h1 number
variable range_l2 number
variable range_h2 number

begin
:range_l1 := 1500;
:range_h1 := 1700;
end;
/

select
    id,
    name,
    office,
    bhrs,
    bgross
from lawyer1
where
    bhrs >= :range_l1 and
    bhrs <= :range_h1
;

begin
:range_l2 := 1700;
:range_h2 := 1900;
end;
/

select
    id,
    name,
    office,
    bhrs,
    bgross
```

```
from lawyer1
where
   bhrs >= :range_12 and
   bhrs <= :range_h2
;

@37squ03
➥ 'select    id,    name,    office,    bhrs,    bgross from lawyer1 where'
```

With this version of Personal Oracle (7.3.3), it appears that the datatype still has to match. The two statements in Listing 37.5 (in which only the names of the bind variables differ) are still treated as though they are different. The following output shows that

```
PL/SQL procedure successfully completed.


      ID NAME            OFFICE           BHRS    BGROSS
--------- --------------- ------------    ----------- ---------
       8 Bonin           New York          1678    346892
      16 Chabot          New York          1680    310897


PL/SQL procedure successfully completed.


      ID NAME            OFFICE           BHRS    BGROSS
--------- --------------- ------------    ----------- ---------
       4 Clayton         Houston           1789    190045
      19 Chatham         New York          1759    367944

old   2: :sqltxt := '&1';
new   2: :sqltxt :=
➥'select    id,    name,    office,    bhrs,    bgross from lawyer1 where';

PL/SQL procedure successfully completed.
```

SQL STATEMENT	PAR-SE CLLS	EXE-CUT-IONS	VER-SION CNT.	# OF LOADS	IN-VAL-IDS
select id, name, office, bhrs, bgro ss from lawyer1 where bhrs >= :range_l1 and bhrs <= :range_h1	1	1	1	1	0
select id, name, office, bhrs, bgro ss from lawyer1 where bhrs >= :range_l2 and bhrs <= :range_h2	1	1	1	1	0

White Space

The white space (spaces, tabs, and returns) used in statements must be identical for the statements to be parsed only once. Listing 37.6 formats the same statement in four different ways—the first is the original statement, the second flattens the select comma list, the third replaces some hard returns with spaces, and the fourth replaces some spaces in the second statement with tabs.

Listing 37.6. Dealing with white space.

```
--        Filename: 37squ06.sql
--        Purpose: retrieve bhrs ranges
--                 dealing with white space
--
variable range_l number
variable range_h number

begin
:range_l := 1500;
:range_h := 1700;
end;
/

select
    id,
    name,
    office,
    bhrs,
    bgross
from lawyer1
where
    bhrs >= :range_l and
    bhrs <= :range_h
;

select id, name, office, bhrs, bgross
from lawyer1
where bhrs >= :range_l and bhrs <= :range_h
;

select
    id,     name,     office,     bhrs,     bgross
from lawyer1
where
    bhrs >= :range_l and      bhrs <= :range_h
;

select id,     name,     office,     bhrs,     bgross
from lawyer1
where bhrs >= :range_l and bhrs <= :range_h
;

@37squ03 'from lawyer1 where'
```

For parsing purposes, these are treated as four different statements, as shown here:

```
PL/SQL procedure successfully completed.

        ID NAME            OFFICE           BHRS    BGROSS
---------- --------------- --------------- ---------- ---------
         8 Bonin           New York           1678    346892
        16 Chabot          New York           1680    310897

... same three times more ...
```

```
old   2: :sqltxt := '&1';
new   2: :sqltxt := 'from lawyer1 where';

PL/SQL procedure successfully completed.
```

SQL STATEMENT	PAR-SE CLLS	EXE-CUT-IONS	VER-SION CNT.	# OF LOADS	IN-VAL-IDS
select id, name, office, bhrs, bgro ss from lawyer1 where bhrs >= :range_l and b hrs <= :range_h	1	1	1	1	0
select id, name, office, bhrs, bgro ss from lawyer1 where bhrs >= :range_l and b hrs <= :range_h	1	1	1	1	0
select id, name, office, bhrs, bgross from lawyer1 where bhrs >= :range_l and bhrs <= :range_h	1	1	1	1	0
select id, name, office, bhrs, bgross from lawyer1 where bhrs >= :range_l and bhrs <= :range_h	1	1	1	1	0

Therefore, identical formatting standards need to be enforced within a database and, preferably, within an organization.

> **NOTE**
>
> The table(s) on which the v$sqlarea view is based contains information about all SQL statements since the most recent startup of the database. If statements are repeatedly submitted, the numbers will increase accordingly. For the examples in this chapter, the database was shut down and restarted to reset these tables.
>
> For the purpose of specifying the statement in v$sqlarea, and thus the 37squ03.sql utility, tabs and returns are converted to spaces. For the purpose of parsing, these are treated as different.

Comments in SQL Text

Comments affect parsing the same way that differences in white space do. The comment text is kept with the statement, and otherwise identical statements that differ in their use of comments are treated as different, as Listing 37.7 shows.

Listing 37.7. Dealing with comments.

```
--        Filename: 37squ07.sql
--         Purpose: retrieve bhrs ranges
--                  dealing with comments
--
variable range_l number
variable range_h number
```

continues

Listing 37.7. continued

```
begin
:range_l := 1500;
:range_h := 1700;
end;
/

select
    id,
    name,
    office,
    bhrs,
    bgross
from lawyer1
where      .
    bhrs >= :range_l and
    bhrs <= :range_h
;

select
    id,
    name,
    office,
    bhrs,
    bgross
from lawyer1
-- comment for comment's sake
where
    bhrs >= :range_l and
    bhrs <= :range_h
;


@37squ03 'from lawyer1'
```

As the output shows, these statements, which are essentially the same and return the same results, are parsed as not identical:

```
PL/SQL procedure successfully completed.

        ID NAME             OFFICE           BHRS     BGROSS
--------- ---------------- ------------ ---------- ---------
        8 Bonin            New York           1678    346892
       16 Chabot           New York           1680    310897

        ID NAME             OFFICE           BHRS     BGROSS
--------- ---------------- ------------ ---------- ---------
        8 Bonin            New York           1678    346892
       16 Chabot           New York           1680    310897
```

```
Input truncated to 23 characters
old    2: :sqltxt := '&1';
new    2: :sqltxt := 'from lawyer1';

PL/SQL procedure successfully completed.
```

SQL STATEMENT	PAR- SE CLLS	EXE- CUT- IONS	VER- SION CNT.	# OF LOAD S	IN- VAL- IDS
select id, name, office, bhrs, bgro ss from lawyer1 -- comment for comment's sake wher e bhrs >= :range_l and bhrs <= :range_h	1	1	1	1	0
select id, name, office, bhrs, bgro ss from lawyer1 where bhrs >= :range_l and b hrs <= :range_h	1	1	1	1	0

A Reality Check

The issues covered in this chapter are most important when SQL code is executed from within procedural code. In that case, the programmer has control over the formatting of the statements and the use of bind variables. Obviously, these should be consistent across the program. The same care should be exercised when SQL scripts are created, especially if these are to be used by many people.

Client tools that create and execute SQL statements do so in a consistent way—a selection from the same tables and columns results in an identical SQL statement. Many also use bind variables.

When issuing SQL statements in an ad-hoc fashion through a SQL interface (which is reasonably inefficient to start with), whether the statement must be parsed again is probably unimportant.

Summary

Optimizing SQL processing can yield huge rewards. Major performance gains can be achieved with little if any additional cost for hardware and software. In order to shed light on the performance tuning process, this chapter starts a lower-level look at how SQL statements are executed.

When a SQL statement is submitted, most execution steps can be avoided if an identical statement from a previous submit can be found already loaded in memory. This chapter presented the means to ensure that essentially identical SQL statements have to be parsed only once. Re-parsing can be avoided if statements are identical in all regards—the text of the statement proper, white space, and comments. Statements that are identical except for constant values can be made to look identical for parsing purposes by means of bind variables.

Optimizing SQL Statement Processing

IN THIS CHAPTER

This chapter continues the optimizing process and looks closely at the workings of the optimizer. The optimizer analyzes a SQL statement and, if applicable, attempts to convert it to an equivalent statement that can be executed using fewer resources. Then it attempts to determine the most efficient execution plan. The optimizer, however, is not always that effective.

Optimizing the workings of the optimizer is an iterative process between analyzing and affecting performance with appropriate actions.

 This chapter covers the way Oracle executes SQL. Because the method of execution is left to the manufacturer of the software, its optimization is by definition not included in the standard.

Oracle Performance Tuning Utilities

Oracle provides a few utilities that allow for rudimentary performance analysis. These include `explain plan`, SQL trace, and tkprof.

`explain plan` loads an execution plan of a statement into a plan table, from which it can be retrieved with a recursive SQL statement. `explain plan` is a command issued in SQL and requires running the `utlxplan.sql` script, which creates the `plan_table` where its results are loaded. You can find this script in `c:\orawin95\rdbms73\admin` or its equivalent directory, depending on where the software is installed. `explain plan` loads the execution plan into the plan table, where you can retrieve it using a hierarchical query with the following approach:

1. From SQL, run `@c:\orawin95\rdbms73\admin\utlxplan.sql`, which creates the `plan_table` in your schema. You can edit that script and create an identical table with a different name.

2. Issue the statement `explain plan for` *sql_statement*`;`. This loads the plan into the plan table. If you want to use your own table, adapt the statement as follows: `explain plan into` *your_table* `for` *sql_statement*`;`.

3. Retrieve the information using a hierarchical query such as the following:

```
select
    lpad(' ', 2*level) || operation,
    options,
    object_name,
from plan_table
connect by prior id=parent_id
start with id=0;
```

The SQL trace facility gathers trace statistics about the resources used for executing a statement. SQL trace is set either in *init*`sid`*.ora* for the entire database or through an `alter session` statement for the current session only.

In the first case, open your *init*`sid`*.ora* file that sets the parameters for your installation. Using Personal Oracle in Windows 95 with everything installed on C:, start Notepad and open the file `c:\orawin95\Database\initorcl.ora`. In Windows NT, replace `orawin95` with `orant`. In this file, find the line that starts with `# timed_statistics = true`. Delete the `#` and the space. Click OK. As soon as you shut down and restart the database, SQL trace operates as well.

In either case, there are two more parameters in the init*sid*.ora file, MAX_DUMP_FILE_SIZE and USER_DUMP_DEST. The first sets the maximum size of that file (default 500), and the latter sets the directory into which it is loaded. Sample settings follow:

```
timed_statistics = true
max_dump_file_size = 10240
user_dump_dest=%RDBMS73%\trace
```

Upon startup, issue the statement alter session set sql_trace = true;. From this point, a trace file is written for the session. If the Registry entry for RDBMS73 is c:\orawin95\rdbms73, you can find the trace files in c:\orawin95\rdbms73\trace.

The tkprof utility formats the output of SQL trace so the statistics can be displayed. To run tkprof, you first need to figure out which trace file was written. Look into the trace directory for the most recent file called something like ora*xxxxx*.trc, where *xxxxx* stands for a five-digit number. Then run tkprof using the MS-DOS command-line window.

For a standard Windows 95 installation, go to the Start Menu and select Programs | MSDOS. Change the directory (cd) to c:\orawin95\bin and type

```
tkprof c:\orawin95\rdbms73\trace\ora03671.trc trcout.txt
```

Note that you must use a trace file that can be found in that directory. Trcout.txt contains something similar to the following:

```
TKPROF: Release 7.3.3.0.0 - Production on Sat Jul 05 22:14:09 1997

Copyright (c) Oracle Corporation 1979, 1996.  All rights reserved.

Trace file: c:\orawin95\rdbms73\trace\ora58607.trc
Sort options: default

*****************************************************************************
count   = number of times OCI procedure was executed
cpu     = cpu time in seconds executing
elapsed = elapsed time in seconds executing
disk    = number of physical reads of buffers from disk
query   = number of buffers gotten for consistent read
current = number of buffers gotten in current mode (usually for update)
rows    = number of rows processed by the fetch or execute call
*****************************************************************************
```

The following statements encountered an error during parse:

```
alter view browser_a ...
STAT #2 id=1 cnt=0 pid=0
Error encountered: ORA-00942
-------------------------------------------------------------------------

....

select object_name, object_type from dba_objects
where status = 'INVALID' and
owner in ('SYS','SYSTEM')
```

38

OPTIMIZING SQL
STATEMENT
PROCESSING

```
call       count       cpu    elapsed        disk       query     current        rows
------   -------   -------   --------   --------   ---------   ---------   ---------
Parse         1      0.02       0.04          0           0           0           0
Execute       1      0.09       0.18          0           0           0           0
Fetch         1      2.24       6.43         52         824           0           6
------   -------   -------   --------   --------   ---------   ---------   ---------
total         3      2.35       6.65         52         824           0           6

Misses in library cache during parse: 1
Optimizer goal: CHOOSE
Parsing user id: SYS
*******************************************************************************
```

For each statement that was executed, the statement is listed, followed by a table that reports statistics separately for the parse, the execute, and the fetch phases. The fetch phase only applies for queries; one or more rows are retrieved during the fetch phase. The following statistics are reported:

- count—The number of times the statement was parsed or executed or the number of fetch calls (which can be batched) issued.
- CPU—Processing time.
- elapsed—Elapsed time.
- disk—Number of physical data blocks read from database files.
- query—Number of logical buffers retrieved for consistent read.
- current—Number of logical buffers retrieved in current mode.
- rows—Number of rows processed, not including subqueries.

These utilities are explained in the *Application Developer's Guide* and the *Server Concepts Manual*. An exhaustive treatment of the topic is Guy Harrison's *Oracle SQL High Performance Tuning*. Although these utilities yield all the information necessary to properly tune a statement, they are not exactly convenient to use. The remaining part of this chapter will therefore use an integrated tool for this purpose, Platinum Plan Analyzer, which is part of SQL Station.

Installing SQL Station

 A trial copy of Platinum Plan Analyzer and Platinum SQL Station is included in the CD attached to this book.

> **TIP**
>
> The full installation of SQL Station takes about 50MB. This might be a good time to clean out those old programs and files you haven't used for a year and free some space.

To install SQL Station, do the following:

1. Put the CD into the drive. Select Start | Run.

2. Enter `d:\3rd party\platinum\setup`, and then choose the SQL Station directory assuming that D is the drive letter of your CD-ROM drive. Ignore the message box with the Install Wizard.

3. You see a User Information dialog like the one shown in Figure 38.1.

FIGURE 38.1.
The User Information dialog.

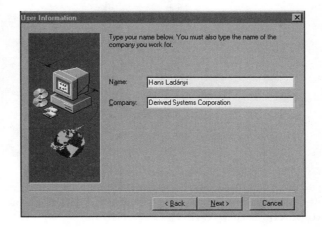

4. Enter your name and company information. Click Next.

5. A component selection dialog appears. (See Figure 38.2.) The only part that you will not use in this book is the Debugger, which is used for PL/SQL. If there is a chance that you will use that module, install it; it takes less than 4MB.

FIGURE 38.2.
The component selection dialog.

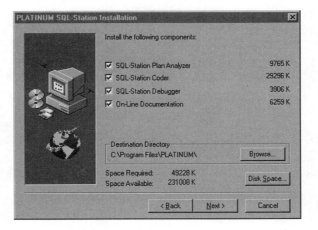

6. Check the boxes for the components to install. You can select a different drive and destination by clicking the Browse button. Click Next when you are done.

7. Another screen appears; click Next if the file destination is okay. (See Figure 38.3.)

FIGURE 38.3.
The Common Files Path dialog.

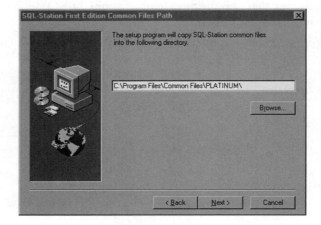

8. The license number screen appears. (See Figure 38.4.) If you use SQL Station on the 30-day evaluation license, which is provided with the product on the companion CD-ROM, simply click Next. The screen returns twice more; just keep clicking Next.

FIGURE 38.4.
The license dialog box.

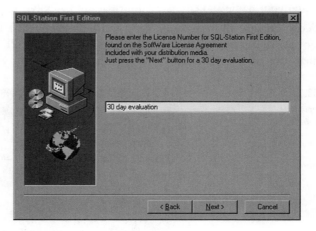

9. You see another file destination dialog. (See Figure 38.5.) Click the Next button.

FIGURE 38.5.

The Destination Path dialog box.

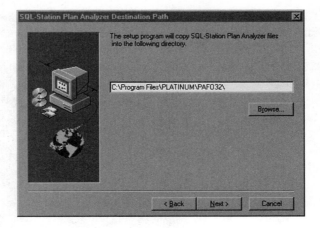

10. Next comes a dialog that asks whether you want a full install or a network install, which uses the installation on a server and installs only icons and program groups on your local machine. You should check Typical.

TIP

Client tools for databases, especially those for design, tend to be fairly substantial. Unless you only occasionally use these client tools or you have a very fast network connection and a very fast file server, you should subscribe to the "very fat client" concept, where you install all the programs on the client machine. Progress in networking might change that in due time. At this point, you might not want to wait forever until modules of programs load.

11. Choose the appropriate folder from the Select Program Folder dialog (see Figure 38.6). Click Next when finished.

FIGURE 38.6.

The Select Program Folder dialog.

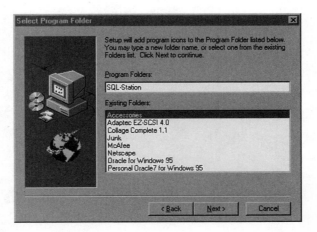

12. The Start Copying Files dialog lists the current folders where the files will install. Click Next to continue if the settings are correct.

FIGURE 38.7.

The Start Copying Files dialog box.

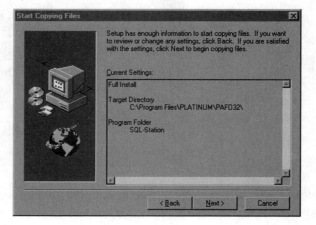

13. Click OK when the copying is done.

14. At this point, you can choose to continue with the installation of two more products, Coder and Debugger. Continue installing these if you want by following the directions on the dialog boxes.

15. If you stop here, you see two icons in a SQL Station window. (See Figure 38.8.) Proceed to the last step of this list if you want to customize your Start Menu. You must also install server-side objects for Plan Analyzer, which is described in the next list.

FIGURE 38.8.

The SQL Station Plan Analyzer program icons window.

16. Next you see a dialog box that asks for Coder install options. (See Figure 38.9.) Typical is a full install of options, and Network uses the installation on a server and installs only icons and program groups on your local machine. As you did in step 10, you should probably check Typical.

FIGURE 38.9.
The Coder Setup Type dialog.

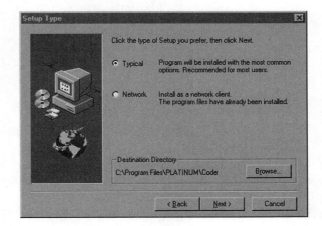

17. The next dialog box asks you to select a program group for the Coder. (See Figure 38.10.) Click Next to accept the default location.

FIGURE 38.10.
The Select Program Folder dialog.

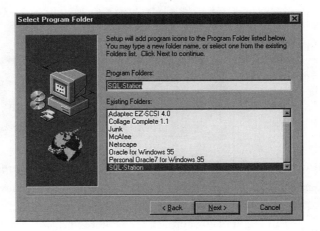

18. For each database (referred to a server) that Coder will access, you must perform a server-side installation. (See Figure 38.11.) You can do this now or later. If this is the first install, choose Yes.

FIGURE **38.11.**

The Coder Server Side
Install dialog.

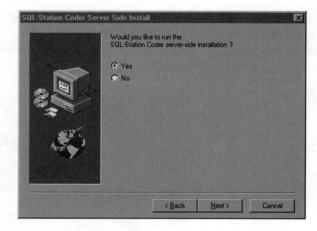

19. You now need to choose which database server to install. (See Figure 38.12.) If you use Personal Oracle, click the Oracle checkbox. Click all others that apply.

FIGURE **38.12.**

The Coder Server
Installation(s) dialog.

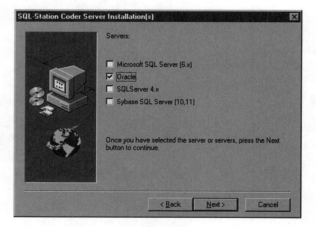

20. A dialog summarizes everything to be installed. (See Figure 38.13.)

21. Scroll down the summary to see the components on the lower end of the list. (See Figure 38.14.)

22. An Install Login dialog appears. (See Figure 38.15.) Complete the sys password.

23. You are asked whether the install should go into an existing schema or into a new one. (See Figure 38.16.) The Coder tables should be in their own schema; therefore, New Schema is the right choice. If this is a reinstall, however, use that schema name.

FIGURE 38.13.
Install summary part 1.

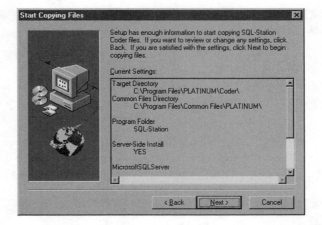

FIGURE 38.14.
Install summary part 2.

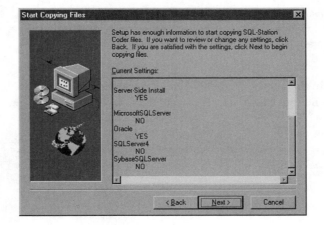

FIGURE 38.15.
Install Login dialog.

FIGURE 38.16.
The Schema dialog.

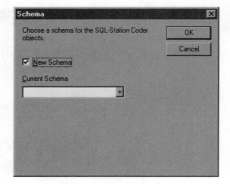

> **NOTE**
>
> Schema, user, and owner are the same here. The name inserted for schema is used to create a user in whose schema the necessary objects—tables, views, and so on—are created. The user is also the owner of these objects.

24. In the next box, you need to set the characteristics of that user—a name, a password, and the default and temporary tablespaces. (See Figure 38.17.)

FIGURE 38.17.
The Specify Objects Owner dialog.

25. If you want to use Debugger, you see another set of dialogs. Using Debugger is beyond the scope of the book, so I do not describe it further. However, if you plan to do PL/SQL programming, you probably want to install that portion as well.

26. If you want to customize your Start Menu, you can right-click the taskbar, select Properties | Advanced, and move shortcuts within that directory structure.

TIP

I moved the few programs that I use all the time into the top level of the Start Menu and keep a few vendor-specific submenus there as well. That way I can avoid submenus that take up several columns.

Everything should be working properly, but you still need to install the Plan Analyzer server objects. You do this with a separate executable, DBInstall, which appears in the SQL Station program group.

1. Start DBInstall. Click Start.

2. An empty window with a menu on the top appears. (See Figure 38.18.) Select Install | SYS Views & Repository.

FIGURE 38.18.

Starting the install.

3. Fill in the sys password and the name of the connect string. (See Figure 38.19.) On a local database, you either leave this empty or use the string 2:. Some programs, including the Reports option of Plan Analyzer, need the 2:.

4. Enter a new user account for the plan tables or enter an existing account. (See Figure 38.20.) Click Continue.

5. Set default and temporary tablespace for these accounts. (See Figure 38.21.) Click Continue.

FIGURE 38.19.
The sys user connect dialog.

FIGURE 38.20.
The Plan Analyzer owner connect dialog.

FIGURE 38.21.
The user characteristics dialog.

6. The objects are now installed under this user. Depending on how your initialization parameters are set, the warning shown in Figure 38.22 might appear.

FIGURE 38.22.
The TIMED_STATISTICS warning dialog.

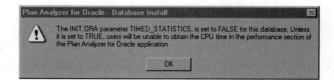

7. To fix the problem, open your `initsid.ora` file that sets the parameters for your installation. Using Personal Oracle in Windows 95 with everything installed on C:, start Notepad and open the file `c:\orawin95\Database\initorcl.ora`. In Windows NT, replace `orawin95` with `orant`. In this file, find the line that starts with `# timed_statistics = true`. Delete the `#` and the space. Click OK. Don't shut down and restart the database right now.

8. The next dialog asks you how much space to set aside for the Plan Analyzer tables. (See Figure 38.23.) At this point, a setting of 1MB should be sufficient. Click Continue.

FIGURE 38.23.
The initial storage allocation dialog.

9. If you want all users to be able to capture and store SQL statements, click Yes on the next dialog. (See Figure 38.24.) In Personal Oracle, this is something you probably want.

FIGURE 38.24.
The permission to all users dialog.

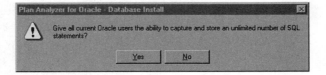

10. Now you see a spread table where you can set individual users' limits. Click Yes.

11. The installation is now complete. Click Exit on the last dialog box. Exit the program.

12. Shut down and restart the database to activate the time statistics setting.

Using Plan Analyzer

To start Plan Analyzer, open the Start Menu and select Programs | SQL Station | SQL Station Plan Analyzer. In the customized Start Menu, shown in Figure 38.25, a Plan Analyzer icon is also directly included in the top level of the Start Menu, so you can start it there. The Start Menu shown was adapted as explained in step 26 of "Installing SQL Station," earlier in this chapter.

When the program starts, a Connect dialog box appears. Enter the user and password. The Database Connect String is the SQL*Net identifier for your database. If you use Personal Oracle or any version of Oracle on the local machine and this connect string is not defined, either leave it empty or enter `2:`, as shown in Figure 38.26.

FIGURE 38.25.
The Start Menu for Plan Analyzer.

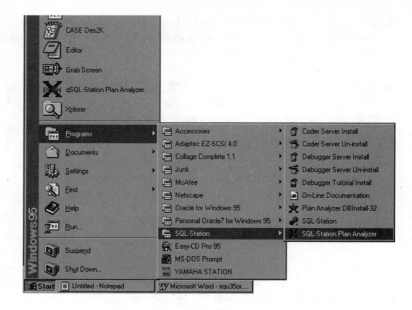

FIGURE 38.26.
The Plan Analyzer Connect dialog.

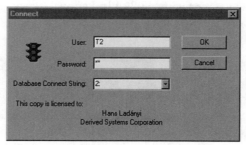

If the database on a local machine is not already started, it is automatically started now.

Analyzing a Simple Query

When the Plan Analyzer was installed, it created a user PAFU in whose schema several tables and queries were loaded. These tables and queries can be used as samples when learning to use the tool. We, however, will use tables that we got to know in the course of this book. To help you understand Plan Analyzer, this section starts with some simple queries against the lawyer2 table.

When Plan Analyzer has loaded, you will see a menu bar, a button bar, a pane labeled with SQL, and a pane labeled with Retrieve data. Click the Edit SQL tab in the SQL pane and type select * from lawyer2. Do not include comments, and do not end with a ;. You do not need to worry about formatting; instead, select SQL | Format, and the statement is formatted by Plan Analyzer. It looks slightly different from the standards used in this book, but it is consistent.

After you apply the formatting, the statement looks as follows

```
SELECT *
FROM lawyer2
```

Now click the Rule tab. The SQL statement is changed slightly:

```
SELECT /*+ RULE */  *
FROM lawyer2
```

The `/*+ RULE */` is a hint for the optimizer to use a rule-based optimization scheme when creating the execution plan. The bottom window says Rule Plan. If you click the left button, which shows the tip "Rule Plan" when you move the cursor over it, the execution plan is displayed. Just one step is performed, a full table scan in which all the rows of the table are read and displayed. Click the Visualize button with the film strip icon to display a Visualize dialog. Click Next Step, and you see a plain English explanation of the step. (See Figure 38.27.)

FIGURE 38.27.

The Visualize dialog.

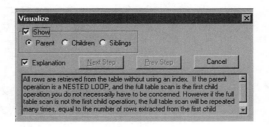

The visualization hint explains that a full table scan might be okay if this is the first step performed. If this step is a child operation, however, which is performed for each row of a parent process, then many lengthy table scans affect performance badly.

Close the Visualize dialog box and click First Row. The bottom window is titled First Row Plan. If you click the left button, now associated with the tip text "First Row Plan," the same plan is revealed. The execution plan is optimized using a cost-based approach based on table statistics that minimize the cost of retrieving the first row.

Click the All Rows button and click the left button in the bottom pane. You see the same approach. The visualize explanation in all cases is the same because the plan is the same as well.

Creating Object Statistics

For the cost-based optimizer to work, you must generate statistics on the affected table's columns and indexes. Depending on the size of a table and the distribution of key and index values, the cost-based optimizer can then choose better execution plans.

With SQL, you analyze an object using the `analyze table` command. In Plan Analyzer, you can do this interactively. Click the SQL tab and select DB Objects Analysis, and an analysis screen appears. Its left window has an object hierarchy structure that contains the objects referenced in the SQL statement. If you click the table you want to analyze—in this case, `lawyer2`—

some of the buttons on the bottom that were grayed out become active. Click Analyze, and a warning dialog appears. (See Figure 38.28.)

FIGURE 38.28.

A Plan Analyzer warning dialog.

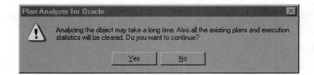

Because this is a tiny table, click Full analysis and click Analyze. The full table statistics are available in the upper-right window. (See Figure 38.29.)

FIGURE 38.29.

Analysis screen with Compute Statistics dialog.

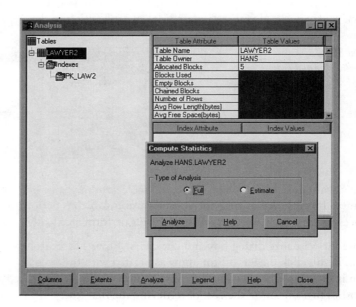

Now the table is analyzed. The area in the statistics window that had been black—indicating that no statistics were available—now contains numbers. If you click the Columns button, another table called Column Analysis appears. No column statistics are available at this point.

Gathering Table Statistics in SQL

You can run the analyze table command within SQL as well:

```
analyze table lawyer2 compute statistics;
```

The preceding command returns

```
Table analyzed.
```

If the table is large, it is preferable to estimate statistics instead. This option is much faster yet yields almost the same information. The sample can be stated as a number of rows or as a percentage:

```
analyze table lawyer2 estimate statistics sample 100 rows;
```

The preceding command samples 100 rows of the table, whereas the following statement samples 15% of the table's rows:

```
analyze table lawyer2 estimate statistics sample 15 percent;
```

Analyzing Indexes

The table `lawyer2` has one index, its primary key `pk_law2`. You need to analyze this index as well. Highlight the index in the object hierarchy, click the Analyze button, click the Yes button in the warning dialog, and click Full analysis and the Analyze button. (See Figure 38.30.)

FIGURE 38.30.

Analysis screen set for index analysis.

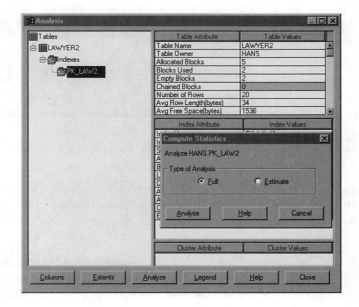

The second window on the right side contains the index statistics.

Analyzing a Sorted Query

The same query is sorted by the indexed column in descending order. To that end, close the Analysis screen and click the Edit SQL tab. Add `order by id` to the statement and select SQL | Format. The statement now appears as follows:

```
SELECT *
FROM lawyer2
ORDER by id desc
```

Click the Rule tab and then the Rule button. Then repeat the same steps for the First Row and All Rows tabs. The execution plans are the same in all three cases. (See Figure 38.31.)

FIGURE 38.31.

The Execution Plan and Visualize dialog.

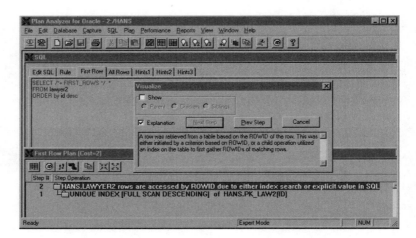

The execution now starts with a full scan on the index `pk_law2`. Then, in the second step, the rows are retrieved in order by row ID.

Considering the small size of the table, it might be preferable to perform a full table scan and a sort. In the SQL version as in Plan Analyzer, you accomplish this with hints that are included in the SQL statement. To create a hint in Plan Analyzer, select Plan | Hints | Specify Hints. (See Figure 38.32.)

A Hints dialog appears. Click the Add Hint Button. An Add Hint dialog appears, containing a scroll list with possible hints. Select Full. Click the Specify button. A Full Hint dialog appears. Highlight the table and click the OK button. (See Figure 38.33.)

In the Hints dialog, click the Apply Changes button and click OK. Look at how the hint is incorporated in the SQL window. You can issue the same statement in SQL and it executes the same way. You can now display the rule plan and the hint plan side by side. This is shown in Figure 38.34.

FIGURE 38.32.
The Specify Hints menu tree.

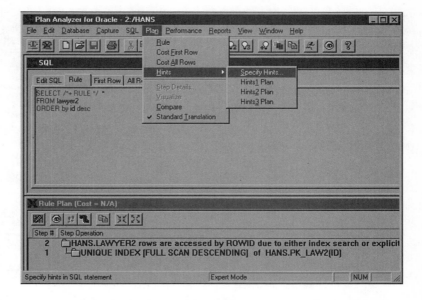

FIGURE 38.33.
Specify a hint.

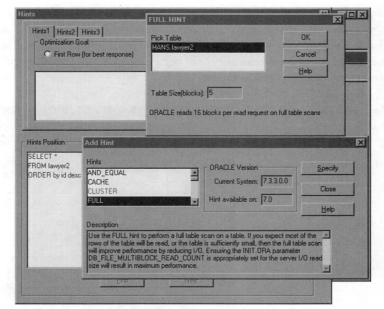

FIGURE 38.34.

*Rule versus full table
scan and sort execution
plan.*

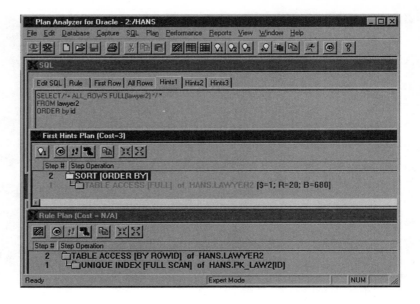

If you click the Performance menu and select Execution Statistics, you can benchmark the two
approaches side by side. Up pops a Server Statistics dialog. Click the Rule tab. The Server Statistics dialog now shows a summary of performance information in table format. Most values
are zero because the statement has not been timed yet. Click the Test button. You see statistics
similar to what is shown in Figure 38.35.

FIGURE 38.35.

*Rule-based execution
statistics.*

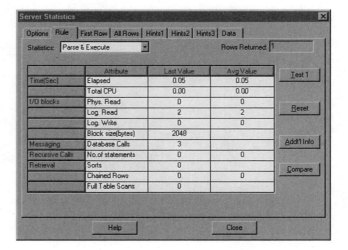

This execution took 5/100 of a second to execute two logical reads and three database calls, which requires network packet round trips if this happens in a networked environment. Click the Hints 1 button and the Test button to repeat the same testing procedure for the Hints 1 execution plan.

Now click the Compare button and Text Summary, and you can see the performance statistics side by side, as shown in Figure 38.36.

FIGURE 38.36.

Comparison of rule-based and full table scan execution statistics.

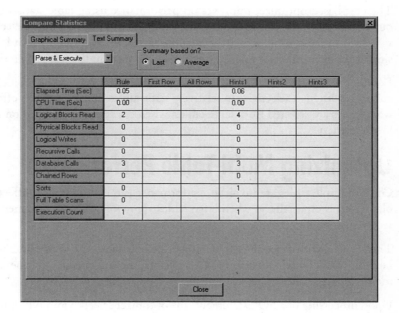

The second approach took more time to execute. It performed four logical reads instead of two in the rule-based approach and one full table scan and one sort, which were not used in the index scan.

Criteria for Using Index Versus Full Table Scans

The examples in the preceding section used the most frequently used method to retrieve rows—the full table scan and the index lookup. When deciding which approach you should use, consider a few trade-offs:

■ If you need to retrieve only one row or a few rows and you can identify them through an index, an index lookup is probably the most efficient approach.

■ If you need to retrieve a considerable portion of a table's rows, a full table scan is more efficient.

According to Harrison, the gray zone is between 5% and 20% of a table's rows to be retrieved. Below that, the index lookup will probably perform better, and above that, the full table scan will perform better. You should test the queries in the gray zone.

The rule-based optimizer almost always uses available indexes. This might result in somewhat slower performance but avoids the possibility of dramatically reduced performance due to an inappropriate full table scan.

The cost-based optimizer improves on performance using table statistics. If the statistics are out of date or, in the case of index histograms, are not used because the corresponding value is in a bind variable, a full table scan might be used where an index scan is the better choice. A similar problem results if the optimizer goal is not set to first row when that is what's needed.

Besides the B-tree index, Oracle offers two other index types. The hash cluster works well for columns with high selectivity in relatively static tables. Bitmap indexes offer good performance where rows are selected from large tables, when the selection is based on multiple columns of low selectivity.

Optimizing Multi-Table Performance

Once multiple tables are involved, performance can be much more affected by the execution plan. This is especially so when large tables are involved. Such statements should, therefore, receive heightened attention.

This uses a series of examples to demonstrate how tables are joined and how performance can be optimized. Three join options are available: the sort merge join, the nested loop join, and the hash join.

Upon processing of a SQL statement, the optimizer selects a join type based either on rules or existing statistics. Through hints, the optimizer can be directed to choose a different execution plan. The way to specify hints in Plan Analyzer was shown in Chapter 35, "Providing and Controlling Access to Database Objects Through Views," in Figure 35.27.

The Sort Merge Join

A sort merge join of two tables sorts both tables by the values of the join column(s) as the sorting criteria, then merges the rows to a joined logical table. Starting with a query adapted from examples in Chapter 17, which can be found on the CD-ROM, a query with an outer join of `inc2` and `inclu2` is copied into the SQL pane of Plan Analyzer. The original query was as follows:

```
select
   name inc_type,
decode (sum(amount),NULL,'ZILCH',to_char(sum(amount))) total
from
   inc2   i,
   inclu2 l
where i.type (+) = l.type
```

```
group by
    sortorder,
    name
order by sortorder
;
```

The query is then reformatted via the SQL | Format Menu option. To get a rule-based execution plan, click the Rule tab and then click the Rule Plan button. A plan is now displayed (see Figure 38.37).

FIGURE 38.37.

A sort merge join of two tables.

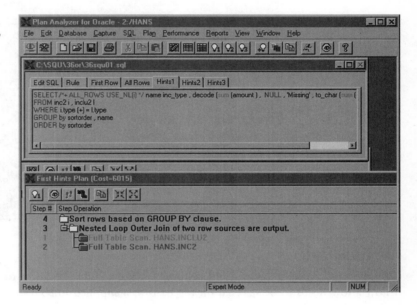

The execution plan in Figure 38.37 indicates that the `inclu2` table is read and sorted according to the join criterion. The same happens with the `inc2` table. Then the two sorted sets are merged. Finally, the output of this operation is sorted according to the `group by` clause. Because this is a rule-based approach, no analysis of the objects is necessary.

The Nested Loops Join

In a nested loops join, a full-table scan is performed on one table. For each row returned, the matching row(s) of the other table is retrieved. This second table should have an index or be very small; otherwise, the repeated full-table scans will likely have dramatic performance implications. If the table is small enough to fit in memory, its blocks will likely remain cached there, and the join operation will not cause a lot of disk accesses. If an index is available, each row of the table can be retrieved with just a few accesses. If, however, the table is larger than what can stay in memory, many datablocks will have to be read from disk, which could become a massive job. Figure 38.38 shows an execution plan based on a nested loops join.

First, a full-table scan of `inclu2` is performed for each row of the matching row of `inc2` is found, again through a full-table scan, because there is no index to go by. The rows are then joined and sorted.

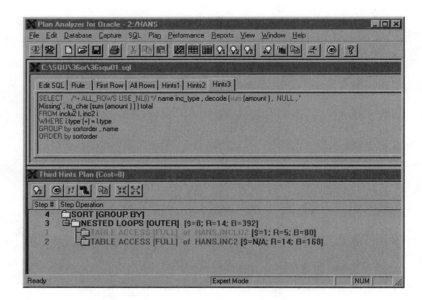

The Hash Join

Hashing translates an index or a join-column value to an offset and then to a database address. If now a row needs to be selected on the basis of a supplied index value, it can be done by converting the index value through the hash algorithm, to an offset which can then be added to the `rowid` of the first row to provide the address of the block where the information is stored. Thus a row can be identified through the key value without applying an index and without having to do a full table span. This mechanism can be used in a hash cluster, which keeps rows with the same hash value together. In certain circumstances, hash clusters can provide considerable performance advantages over indexing.

A hash join uses a similar mechanism. The process starts to create a hash table for the smaller of the tables to be joined. The other table is read in a full-table scan and, through the use of the hash table, the matching row(s) of the first table is retrieved. Hash joins can be very fast, especially if the hash table can be kept in memory but the smaller table would be too large to fit. Figure 38.39 shows an execution plan based on a hash join.

Again, `inclu2` is read one time in a full-table scan. Then `inc2` is read, also in a full-table scan, and the hash join performed. In the last step, the output is sorted.

FIGURE 38.39.

A hash join of two tables.

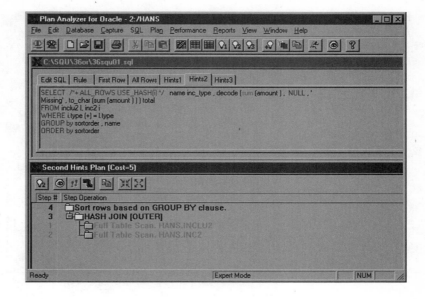

Performance Criteria

Guy Harrison in *Oracle SQL High Performance Tuning* provides a few pages of criteria as to which type of join is most efficient given a certain situation. Provided that an index can support a nested loops join, this type should be considered if only a subset of rows is processed, if quick response time rather than throughput is required (meaning that the user wants to see the first row quickly), and if only limited memory and CPU resources are available for sorting.

When a nested loops join is not advisable, a hash join should perform as well as or better than the sort merge join. It should perform better in cases when one table is much larger than the other. The biggest gain would occur if, due to limited memory, the smaller of the original tables could not fit in memory, but the hash table could.

As was shown in Chapter 35, SQL Station allows you to test all approaches and then display the performance statistics side by side. Figure 38.40 presents performance data graphically.

The left-most bars in each graph represent a merge sort join, the right-most bars represent a nested loops join, and the four bars in between represent a hash join. For this query, the hash join is most efficient, the sort merge join has the most sorts, and the nested loops join has the most logical reads. In the graph shown here, all blocks are already in memory, so no physical reads are reported. Obviously, in such a small table, the difference does not matter. In a production system, however, especially where large tables are involved, such statistics should be run periodically in order to proactively eliminate bottlenecks.

FIGURE 38.40.

Joins—a performance comparison.

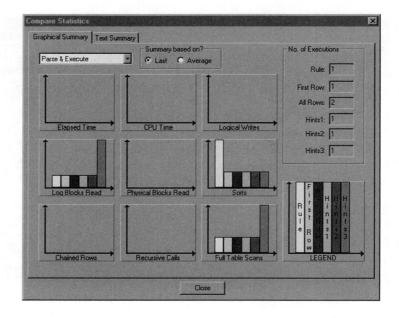

In his article "Managing Multitable Joins" (*Oracle Magazine*, November/December 1996), Eyal Aronoff points out that merge joins are usually not appropriate in multi-user systems because all the processing must be completed before the first row can be displayed to the user. Often, only the first or first few rows are wanted, and waiting until everything is processed is not desirable. Furthermore, the results are the least likely to stay in memory, and contention for temporary tablespace might occur. For batch jobs or large reports and in cases where full-table scans are preferable, the merge sort join may provide the best performance.

Summary

This chapter focuses on execution plans for SQL statements and the way the optimizer workings can be affected. This is done through an interactive process between analyzing performance and affecting the execution plan through hints.

While Oracle provides a few basic utilities for performance analysis, this chapter uses the much more convenient Plan Analyzer from Platinum for this purpose. After the install of the tool, it is used to display the execution plan, assign hints to SQL statements in a convenient menu and dialog-driven way, test different execution plans, and show statistics side by side.

In select statements against multiple tables, performance can be affected much more by the execution plan, especially when tables involved are large. When processing a SQL statement, the optimizer selects a join type based on rules, on existing statistics, or as specified through hints. Three kinds of joins are available:

- A sort merge join sorts both tables by the values of the join column(s) and merges the rows to a joined logical table.

- A nested loops join first performs a full-table scan on one table. For each row returned, the matching row(s) of the other table is retrieved.

- A hash join first creates a hash table for the smaller of the tables to be joined. The other table is read in a full-table scan and, through the use of the hash table, the matching row(s) of the first table is retrieved.

CHAPTER 39

Testing and Scrubbing Loaded Data

Most people who have ever done analysis on real data have become painfully aware of one of its most cumbersome issues—what to do if your data is not pure, error free, and complete. Generally, if the data is garbage, the results will likely be garbage, too. If the former is not known, the latter will be plainly dangerous.

This chapter first briefly discusses data quality issues and then presents a series of steps that can be used to test, improve, and sometimes assure data quality.

Data Quality Issues

The issue of data quality is not very well covered by the basic statistical-analysis books and software manuals that most students are exposed to in college. The typical examples there calculate measures such as mean, mode, and variance of the height of a sampling of people. But they assume that the base data is clean and do not, therefore, cover the case in which a value might be something like 720 inches.

Data quality issues and concerns, however, are addressed in depth in research design and methodology texts and training programs, and have been so since long before the advent of computers. Research-method handbooks contain sections on how to detect and deal with problems such as unreliable data collectors, as data-collection procedures are an extremely important part of designing experiments. In the game of scientific research, competitors of a researcher will frequently latch onto data-collection and data-handling procedures that they consider improper and cite them as the reason why the findings of a study should be rejected, especially if they contradict a study of their own. Thus, much so-called objective research and analysis ultimately depends on interpretation and judgment calls. A careful, skilled, and ethical researcher will do all he or she can to eliminate undue influence on data, interpretations, and, ultimately, findings.

Some standard methods exist to cope with data that has problems—simply eliminating a case from the sample is usually the preferred choice. Many statistical methods also assume that there are errors in the observations, but that these errors balance each other. This is one of the reasons why random sampling is so important. While some statistical procedures such as those that calculate correlation matrices assume that each record has valid values in all variables under analysis, some statistical software packages provide the option of eliminating the record only in those calculations where that variable is affected.

In real life as a data analyst, you will see values that are obviously wrong, and you will encounter values that are equally wrong but not obviously so. Where a value is obviously wrong, and where it is important, it is possible to follow the data trail back and have the value corrected. This has the added advantage that the originating source gets feedback and improvement too. Where following up is not possible, the only option remaining is to test the data for values that are implausible, impossible in the context of other variables, out of range, or missing and deal with them in some rule-based or more intuitive fashion. Just as a compiler can check only for the syntax of code and not for its logic, these procedures cannot detect errors that are plausible or complete, or for items that fall within check ranges yet are still plain wrong. Such errors can be the result of purposeful action, human error, or bad procedures.

REAL-WORLD EXPERIENCES

The state of California has a fairly comprehensive reporting system for higher-education data. Under this system, each public university has to report teaching certificates that have been granted through recommendation, and therefore supposedly coursework, of that university. Therefore, every year, a credential file is created from records in the respective credentialing offices and sent on to the central statewide administration.

One day, as result of a legislative inquiry, the credential reports of a university system were compared with those of the statewide credentialing agency and found to understate the state's numbers by about a third.

After much puzzlement and embarrassment, it turned out that the definition of which students a university should consider for reporting was not clear. Furthermore, some students applied to the credentialing agency directly for a certificate, which was never even known to the universities.

All care for the data could not compensate for a systemic error resulting from inappropriate reporting points and procedures. Ultimately, the problem was fixed as it should have been, by treating the state agency data as the source and feeding it back to the universities for reporting.

Ultimately, you will find that much of this work involves judgment calls that require the same care, ethics, and reasoning that a good researcher would use. Some data can be fixed. Some data cannot be fixed, but it doesn't matter. Sometimes data can be fixed within the data set, but has been collected in such a way that many cases did not get recorded. Sometimes, data can be fixed but it is preferable to take care of the originating system. Sometimes, nothing helps.

It is your professional responsibility to decide which case you are dealing with, and then take the necessary steps. If you don't, at best you expend a lot of effort and money but end up with nothing to show for it. In the worst case, you end up with wrong reports that put your employer or customer out of business—or even worse, create a huge liability. The impact of such a case on you, and on your career, should be obvious.

Dealing with Data Derived from Other Systems

Ideally, a system should have checks and procedures in place to ensure that the data it contains is reasonably accurate. Just as is the case with original data, however, there are many reasons why that might not be the case. Some are listed here; for more, pick up any book on data warehousing:

- The original system is poorly designed.
- The original system does not enforce any integrity standards.

- If there are integrity standards, they are temporarily disabled.
- The original system is not used correctly.
- The downloads from the system might have been done at the wrong time or in the wrong state, thus leading to conflicting data. Dealing with this issue is probably the most important contribution of data warehousing.
- The downloads from different systems that should have matching data don't.

REAL-WORLD EXPERIENCES

I used to work for a university where the administrative computing system ran off a central mainframe some 150 miles away that was shared by several other colleges as well. During the registration period, which was the same for all the universities, the system was hopelessly overloaded. So, as a quick fix, the data center simply switched off all the error checking and constraint enforcing. Thus, while error checks were supposedly in place, they were not for the periods when they would have mattered most.

What it boils down to is that you must never completely trust the quality of data that you get from somewhere else.

Hard Facts of Life for Data Analysts; or, Bad Data Can Put You Out of Business

If you perform or support data analysis and, therefore, data control, you should consider a few basic, hard facts of life for data analysis. They all support the theory that, in the role of developer, bad data will put you out of business. Whereas fancy analysis and reporting are usually the fun part of a project, data scrubbing can be rather tedious. The latter, however, will determine whether your fancy analyses and reports will have any value. This is one of the points where the term *data warehouse* is totally misleading. To have all the data in the world sitting in storage is useless until someone comes to organize, clean up, and integrate it.

TIP

Count on the fact that in a typical project you will spend 80% of your time on data issues, 5% on analysis, and the rest on cleaning up the reports.

You can never know for sure whether your data is clean. You can, however, test whether certain problems are present and fix those problems. In other words, you can certify the absence of certain problems but not the total correctness of your data. In the language of statistical inference testing, a significance level of 0.01 means that there is a 1 in 100 probability that your findings are the result of random effects, such as the random impact of variables not included in the model, measuring errors, and the like. Therefore, you keep eliminating these other effects to the extent you can.

Contrary to popular myth, denormalization is of very little help for SQL-based reporting, and usually gets in the way. Report writers that extract data from relational databases assume a normalized structure and build standard reports with those in mind. If you have array structures in your tables, you are asking for trouble. Keeping redundant values, however, is okay.

CAUTION

One of the adages of data warehousing is to replace non-intuitive codes such as 0, 1, and 2 with longer codes that are immediately meaningful to a user of data. If the warehouse is based on an RDBMS, there is really no reason for doing this, and there are quite a few against it:

- A longer code might be desirable in one context but not so in a different one. If there is little space left on a page, abbreviated values are preferable. As a result, each value will likely need an abbreviated label, a less-abbreviated label, and a full-length label. This is very easy to do with a code table.

- Some codes are nested. For example, many years ago, the federal government made up a rough set of ethnic codes. In some places, these are broken out to subcodes, referring to subgroups such as Korean or Chinese rather than just Asian. Some reports are needed by detail, others by the original codes. Following the data-warehousing conventions, when working with such codes you would need to maintain an additional column because you would need one for original codes and one for detailed codes. With one code table that joins on detailed codes, you can break out on either one.

- Space is cheap, but it is still not worthwhile to blow it on bad design.

Referential integrity ensures the integrity of analyses that depend on table joins, which are most of the analyses you'll perform. The indexing that most integrity constraints require can speed up retrieval considerably. Therefore, although reporting on tables without referential constraints enforced is possible, it should be avoided. If you maintain historical data on an ongoing basis, and if you don't have all your constraints enforced (because of loading, performance issues, and so on), you need to retest your data once in a while. Write a batch job and run it during off hours.

If you have to choose between efficiency and reliability, choose the latter. Most of the stages here are performed once in a while, and it does not matter if they take a little bit longer. Unreliable programs and routines that take extra human intervention will ultimately cost you much more time.

Use a modular approach such as the one shown here. Beware of the biggest trap for those with a procedural programming background, where everything tends to be done in one large and complicated program. You cannot maintain such a program efficiently in a once-in-a-blue-moon situation. Small modules of just a few lines are easy to understand, and you can batch them in a script.

If you have not used batch scripts, now is the time to get used to them. (Refer to Chapter 23, "Generating SQL Statements Through SQL.") Many scrubbing processes have to be repeated every time data is loaded. With a batch script, most of the process can be done unsupervised.

Last but not least, clean up data before you move it to its final destination. Otherwise, you risk that an analyst who writes a report against this table will use it when he or she should not. Also, ensure the quality of data positively; don't wait until an integrity constraint rejects a row. At that point, you will have to go and figure out why. If you take care of data quality in the early stages, you know what you are after from the outset, which will help you to find problems right away.

The Stages of Data Scrubbing

After data from from external sources is imported or loaded into database tables, Figure 39.1 shows how to take it from there. If the data is clean, the pieces can be loaded directly into their respective tables. It is usually preferable, though, to load the data into a staging table, where it can be tested and cleaned up. From there the data can be inserted into its final destination(s).

As shown in the figure, the typical scrubbing process starts with the original data file, which can be converted and sorted through utilities such as UNIX shell scripts. The data is then loaded to a staging table, where a number of steps are performed:

- Checking of codes for allowable values
- Checking of codes for allowable ranges
- Checking of codes for plausible values, based on other combinations of values in the table
- Code conversions
- Checking for uniqueness of codes that should be unique
- Deleting extraneous records

TIP

If you work from data files, you will have to make a judgment call on whether to clean up data in the file before loading or to clean it in the staging table.

Generally, if the data file can be printed on one or two sheets of paper, you would want to clean it up there. Usually, data sets that fit such short files will be used for code tables and the like, for which the sources should be maintained accurately anyway.

If you deal with a massive data file, it might be useful to do a few global replacements through batch processes, such as the elimination of extra spaces at the ends of lines, the global conversion of special characters, and the global elimination of extraneous lines or rows. You might want to do a sort on the file, because this is one of the few opportunities you get for guaranteeing that records will be stored in sorted order. Remember, the database does not guarantee the order of records.

Conversions and checks beyond that, however, especially those on individual data fields, are usually much better performed in the database.

FIGURE 39.1.

Stages of data scrubbing.

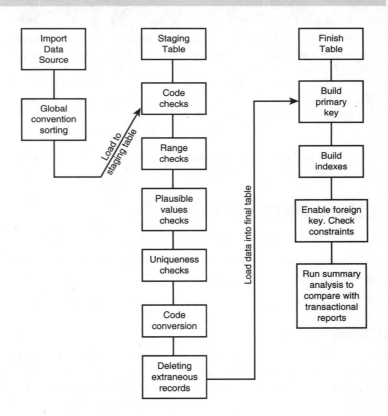

Now the cleaned data can be moved to the final table. At this point, the data should not violate the constraints on the final table, so it should be possible to load it with all the constraints of the table enabled. For performance reasons, you might want to load the data first, without constraints enforced. After the load, you would enable the constraints in the following order:

- ■ Check constraints
- ■ Foreign-key constraints

- Primary-key constraints
- Unique-key constraints
- Non-unique indexes

The final stage is to run a few summary reports on the cleaned data and to compare them with reports on the same data from the originating system. If there are no discrepancies, you can be reasonably (but not completely) sure that your table is fine. Otherwise, you should at least be able to determine the reason for the discrepancies. If you can't do that, it's debugging time.

> **CAUTION**
>
> Never, ever report on data that you have not tested this way to an acceptable level of accuracy. You might be a hero because you whipped out a report in a frenzy, but if that report has glaring errors, it can cost you your reputation, your job, and perhaps even your career. As far as your boss is concerned, if data is not tested, it is not yet available. If you are asked to report on untested data, *state on every page of the report that this is a draft report using unverified data.*

All data scrubbing should be performed through scripts that can be reused and improved over time, and that can be run periodically to check the quality of the data in the database.

Testing Data for Integrity

The purpose of integrity testing is threefold:

- To ensure that the essential codes of a table are valid and plausible
- To ensure the completeness of the data
- To ensure the uniqueness of the columns that will serve as primary or unique keys

Distinct Codes

Most variables and table columns have a rather limited range of defined codes that should be documented in code tables for the originating data system. If you have lookup tables for these codes, this task is half done. All it takes is to retrieve the rows whose values in this column do no appear in the results of a subquery from the lookup table.

Listing 39.1 demonstrates this approach: It runs against the `lawyer3` table, which contains the data about lawyers who work for a firm that just joined forces with yours. The lookup table against which you will work is `office2`.

 If you have not run the following scripts, you need to do so now: `crlaw3.sql` creates and loads `lawyer3`, and `croff2` creates and loads `office2`.

Listing 39.1. Testing for validity of codes.

```
--        Filename: 39squ01.sql
--           Purpose: tests for validity of office codes
--
select
    *
from   lawyer3
where  office not in
       (select office
        from office2)
;
```

This script returns four rows:

ID	BOSS	NAME	OFFICE	BHRS	BGROSS	VI
8	9	Stearns	Neu York	1984	298733	
15	10	Ewald	Bostox	2984	471938	
16	14	Daneshgar	Seattle	1120	118973	
17	7	Bielski	Seattle	3311	559399	

The first two are examples of wrong codes—in this case misspelled—that are easy to fix. The Seattle office is not yet in the code table. In this case, you would have to know whether Seattle is a valid code. Listing 39.2 assumes that Seattle is valid and adds a row to office2 to that effect.

Listing 39.2. Correcting invalid entries in a table.

```
--        Filename: 39squ02.sql
--           Purpose: fix invalid office entries in lawyer3
--                    add 'Seattle' as valid office code into office2.
--
update lawyer3
set office = 'Boston'
where office = 'Bostox';

update lawyer3
set office = 'New York'
where office = 'Neu York';

insert into office2 values (5, 'Seattle',    5);

commit;
```

39

TESTING AND
SCRUBBING
LOADED DATA

The changed script returns

```
1 row updated.

1 row updated.

1 row created.

Commit complete.
```

Next, you look at the contents of the `office2` table to make sure that every row is as desired:

```
select * from office2;
```

It turns out that they are

```
        ID OFFICE            BOSSID
---------- --------------- ---------
         1 Boston                  1
         2 Los Angeles             7
         3 New York                9
         4 Houston                 5
         5 Seattle                 5
```

Finally, you rerun the original query, which confirms that all office codes can be found in `office2`:

```
SQL> @43squ01

no rows selected
```

If you do not have a code table, this would be a good time to create one. If this is contrary to your *Weltanschauung* or if the database administrator has yanked your `create table` privilege, you could test the codes through a straight `in` query, as shown in Listing 39.3.

Listing 39.3. Testing code using an `in` query.

```
--        Filename: 39squ03.sql
--         Purpose: tests for validity of office codes
--
select
    *
from   lawyer3
where  office not in
       ('Boston',
        'Los Angeles',
        'New York',
        'Houston',
        'Seattle')
;
```

This returns the same result:

```
no rows selected
```

Finally, you could run a `select distinct` on the code

```
select distinct office from lawyer3;
```

and eyeball the results,

```
OFFICE
--------------
Boston
Houston
Los Angeles
New York
Seattle
```

which appear to be correct. This latter method is okay if you know your codes well, and if there are only a handful of codes. Otherwise, overlooking problems is quite easy.

Ranges of Codes and Plausichecks

Allowable ranges of codes can be defined in code tables as well. Such a definition would have to have a *low value* and a *high value* column as is implemented in Designer/2000 domains. Often, however, allowable ranges are only represented in the check constraints in the Data Dictionary.

 You can use the `tcons.sql` utility, which is described in Chapter 29, "Keys, Indexes, Constraints, and Table/Column Comments," to display check constraint names and to display the nature of this constraint. The script will also retrieve check constraints with lists of values, such as the constraints used in the previous section.

ORACLE vs SQL

Regardless of whether they are defined as a check constraint, all allowable ranges can be tested through just one statement. Listing 39.4 assumes that there was a policy at the joining firm that no lawyer could have more than 2,500 billable hours a year, and that the maximum amount per hour charged was $200.

Listing 39.4. Testing for allowable ranges.

```
--        Filename: 39squ04.sql
--          Purpose: tests for ranges of office codes
--
col rate format 999

select
  id,
  name,
  office,
  bhrs,
  bgross,
  bgross/bhrs rate
from  lawyer3
where
  bhrs > 2500  or
  bhrs/bgross > 200
;
```

The output should raise a red flag:

ID	NAME	OFFICE	BHRS	BGROSS	RATE
3	Hayward	Los Angeles	3003	683392	228
6	Vanatta	Los Angeles	3401	649022	191
7	Carlson	Los Angeles	3219	873922	271
9	Shubeck	New York	2583	487399	189
11	Bishop	Boston	2939	308299	105
15	Ewald	Boston	2984	471938	158
17	Bielski	Seattle	3311	559399	169
18	Young	Los Angeles	2783	419833	151
20	Kinney	Boston	2672	288739	108

9 rows selected.

39

TESTING AND SCRUBBING LOADED DATA

Because so many of the rows (45%) were returned, it begs the question whether the policy was not enforced or was off the books altogether, or whether the data is simply wrong. In this situation, it is again in order to check with the original data source, and then either change the criteria or fix the data.

Plausichecks—checks for plausibility of data—are usually range checks as well, and can be performed similarly. The example of the person who is 720 inches tall would fall under this category. In all likelihood, such a value reflects a decimal error.

REAL-WORLD EXPERIENCES

Addresses always pose a problem because misspellings of street names or other slight inaccuracies can lead to a totally wrong destination, which is one of the reasons the postal service pushes the ZIP + 4 system. In a previous life, I was responsible for a project in which we created a map that showed the spread of employee residences around the work site. I had a really talented geographer on the project. He used a GIS (geographic information system) address-matching process to obtain the latitude and longitude of each address. About 15% of the addresses, however, could not be matched. The personnel office was really pleased to get a list of these employees, because it allowed them to verify the addresses before the W2 forms were mailed out.

Testing for Null Values

Unexpected null values can indicate missing values, which will result in errors for check and foreign-key constraints. Therefore, codes should be checked for null values and be corrected as applicable. Obviously, where columns are defined as allowing nulls, this is not an issue. Listing 39.5 checks the data for null values.

Listing 39.5. Testing for null values.

```
--       Filename: 39squ05.sql
--        Purpose: tests for null values
--
col rate format 999

select * from lawyer3 where id is null;

select * from lawyer3 where boss is null;

select * from lawyer3 where name is null;

select * from lawyer3 where office is null;

select * from lawyer3 where bhrs is null;

select * from lawyer3 where bgross is null;
```

This script returns

```
no rows selected
         ID      BOSS NAME              OFFICE              BHRS     BGROSS VI
  --------- --------- --------------- --------------- --------- --------- --
         7               Carlson        Los Angeles         3219     873922

no rows selected

no rows selected

no rows selected

no rows selected
```

If this were a large table, it would be advisable to start with a single run:

```
select
    *
from lawyer3
where
    id     is null or
    boss   is null or
    name   is null or
    office is null or
    bhrs   is null or
    bgross is null
;
```

This returns the following:

```
ID        BOSS NAME              OFFICE              BHRS     BGROSS VI
--------- --------- --------------- --------------- --------- --------- --
        7               Carlson        Los Angeles         3219     873922
```

After some inquiry, it appears that Carlson was the boss of the acquiring firm, and will now report to Easton. The following script

```
update lawyer3
set boss = 7
where boss is null;

commit;
```

will update Carlson's record and return this:

```
1 row updated.
```

```
Commit complete.
```

If the single-run statement is issued again, it will indicate that no null values are left:

```
no rows selected
```

Testing for Uniqueness

The very definition of a unique or primary key is that a value may occur only once per column. When adding data to a new table, this is a two-step process:

1. Check the uniqueness of values within the staging table. Basically, the new data should at least be unique in its own right.

2. Check the uniqueness of values between the staging table and the final table.

If only a few values are added, or if the final table has no data, the first step will be omitted.

Testing for Unique Values Within the Staging Table

Listing 39.6 tests for the uniqueness of the ID column values in lawyer3. First it counts all rows in the table, and then it counts the distinct values.

Listing 39.6. Testing for unique columns in a staging table.

```
--          Filename: 39squ06.sql
--            Purpose: tests for uniquness of columns in the staging table
--
select
   count(1)
from lawyer3
;

select
   count(distinct id)
from lawyer3
;
```

Because the value returned by the first query is 20, and that returned by the second one is 19, one value must be represented twice:

```
COUNT(1)
--------
      20

COUNT(DISTINCTID)
----------------
              19
```

The second option is even better:

```
select
   id,
   count(1)
from lawyer3
having count(1) > 1
group by id;
```

because it identifies the culprit—ID 19 is represented twice:

```
      ID  COUNT(1)
--------  --------
      19         2
```

A further improvement is to display all information in duplicate ID rows—the previous query is simply inserted as a subquery into a select *:

```
select
    *
from lawyer3
where id =
     (select
          id
      from lawyer3
      having count(1) > 1
      group by id)
     ;
```

This query returns

ID	BOSS	NAME	OFFICE	BHRS	BGROSS	VI
19	14	Gerardi	New York	1093	189733	
19	7	Kinney	Boston	2672	288739	

Kinney is assigned ID number 20,

```
update lawyer3
set id = 20
where id = 19 and
      name = 'Kinney'
;

commit;
```

which returns

```
1 row updated.
```

```
Commit complete.
```

and fixes the problem. The first two queries return the same value, and the third one returns 0 rows:

```
COUNT(1)
--------
      20
```

```
COUNT(DISTINCTID)
-----------------
               20
```

```
no rows selected
```

The last two sections of this chapter return to this example and demonstrate updating by rowid and rownum.

Testing for Unique Values Between the Staging Table and the Final Table

The battle is half won—the staging table ID values are unique. Because these values will share a column with the ID values in the final table, however, uniqueness across both tables has to be tested for. This is done by enhancing the queries in 39squ06.sql with set operators (for a review of these, please see Chapter 18, "Combining Output from Similar Tables Through Set and Pseudoset Operators"), as shown in Listing 39.7.

Listing 39.7. Testing for unique columns across a staging table and a final table.

```
--        Filename: 39squ07.sql
--        Purpose: tests for uniquness of columns across staging table
--                 and final table
--
select
   count(1)
from lawyer2
union all
select
   count(1)
from lawyer3
;
```

The script returns the following:

```
COUNT(1)
---------
      20
      20
```

A view could be defined on the basis of the previous statement. A `select` from this view would yield the same result, already added up:

```
create or replace view lawtot as
select
   id
from lawyer2
union all
select
   id
from lawyer3
;

select count(*) from lawtot;

drop view lawtot;
```

It returns a total of 40 rows:

```
View created.

  COUNT(1)
---------
        40
```

Instead of the `having count(1) > 1` construct, it is only necessary to replace the `union all` of this query with `union`, which will return a count of duplicate rows:

```
create or replace view lawdis as
select
   id
```

```
from lawyer2
union
select
    id
from lawyer3
;
```

```
select count(1) from lawdis;
```

This returns a count of 20 common rows:

```
 COUNT(1)
---------
       20
```

Using intersect to query ID values of lawyer2 and lawyer3, like this,

```
select
    id
from lawyer2
intersect
select
    id
from lawyer3
;
```

identifies the duplicated ID values:

```
        ID
---------
         1
         2
         3
         4
         5
         6
         7
         8
         9
        10
        11
        12
        13
        14
        15
        16
        17
        18
        19
        20
```

```
20 rows selected.
```

Finally, the full information on duplicate rows is displayed:

```
select
    *
from lawyer2
```

```
where id in
    (select
         id
    from lawyer2
    intersect
    select
         id
    from lawyer3)
union all
select
    id,
    boss,
    name,
    office,
    bhrs,
    bgross
from lawyer3
where id in
    (select
         id
    from lawyer2
    intersect
    select
         id
    from lawyer3)
order by 1
;
```

This statement combines a `union all` select of `lawyer2` and `lawyer3` with the same `intersect` subquery on these tables used twice to identify culprit ID values. The output is as follows:

ID	BOSS	NAME	OFFICE	BHRS	BGROSS
1	20	Dewey	Boston	2856	426800
1	20	Ronstadt	Boston	2444	410210
2	8	Cheetham	New York	1398	280435
2	8	Beene	New York	1678	242100
3	7	Howe	Los Angeles	3480	569338
3	7	Hayward	Los Angeles	3003	683392
4	5	Clayton	Houston	1789	190045
4	5	Nazar	Houston	1979	192828
5	7	Roach	Houston	2349	269844
5	7	Straus	Houston	2132	344909
6	3	Roll	Los Angeles	3203	498084
6	3	Vanatta	Los Angeles	3401	649022
7		Easton	Los Angeles	3800	654832
7	7	Carlson	Los Angeles	3219	873922
8	9	Bonin	New York	1678	346892
8	9	Stearns	New York	1984	298733
9	7	Frankie	New York	2134	469843
9	7	Shubeck	New York	2583	487399
10	1	Greene	Boston	2854	289435
10	1	Rhodes	Boston	2123	297382
11	1	Cardinal	Boston	2694	277952

```
       ID    BOSS NAME              OFFICE              BHRS      BGROSS
---------- --------- --------------- --------------- ---------- ---------
       11       1 Bishop            Boston              2939      308299
       12       6 Chandler          Los Angeles         2987      423878
       12       6 Pesacov           Los Angeles         2131      379254
       13      18 Martinez          Los Angeles         2659      403488
       13      18 Leyva             Los Angeles         2425      468920
       14       9 Earl              New York            2320      434801
       14       9 Herrera           New York            2098      389279
       15      10 Wright            Boston              2789      204133
       15      10 Ewald             Boston              2984      471938
       16      14 Chabot            New York            1680      310897
       16      14 Daneshgar         Seattle             1120      118973
       17       7 Miller            Los Angeles         3153      503582
       17       7 Bielski           Seattle             3311      559399
       18      17 Ming              Los Angeles         2492      359021
       18      17 Young             Los Angeles         2783      419833
       19      14 Chatham           New York            1759      367944
       19      24 Gerardi           New York            1093      189733
       20       7 Paul              Boston              2198      239855
       20       7 Kinney            Boston              2672      288739
```

40 rows selected.

> **TIP**
>
> If the tables `lawyer2` and `lawyer3` had been really big, it would have been preferable to store the results of the `union` operation in an intermediate table.

The results show what should have been obvious a few queries earlier—that both tables use the values 1 through 20 as key values. However, if there had been only a few duplicate values, going through all these steps would have been very helpful.

> **TIP**
>
> When duplicate values result from less-than-perfect source data, the information returned through the previous query is truly helpful for those in charge of the source data systems. Just don't rub it in. Ask gently whether they could help you clarify a few codes.

In this case it is easy to fix the ID column by adding 20 to each ID value in the `lawyer3` table:

```
update lawyer3
set id = id + 20
;

commit;
```

This returns the following:

```
20 rows updated.

Commit complete.
```

Rerunning the first few queries shows that the problem no longer exists:

```
SQL> @43squ07

  COUNT(1)
  --------
        20
        20

View created.

  COUNT(1)
  --------
        40

View dropped.

View created.

  COUNT(1)
  --------
        40

View dropped.

no rows selected
```

The remaining problem is that the values in the boss column have to be updated in order to reflect the change in ID values. After checking with personnel, it turns out that the 7 in Carlson's boss column means she reports to Easton, but all other "new" lawyers will maintain their reporting lines, at least for the time being. The necessary updates are shown in Listing 39.8. The boss column in everyone's but Carlson's record (ID value of 2) is augmented by 20. Carlson's boss value remains the same.

Listing 39.8. Correcting data in a table.

```
--        Filename: 39squ08.sql
--         Purpose: fix reporting lines in lawyer3 table
--
update lawyer3
set boss = boss + 20
where id <> 27
;

commit;
```

This script returns

```
19 rows updated.

Commit complete.
```

Checking Foreign-Key Values

For any column that references a foreign-key column in another table and will ultimately be a key, two conditions must be met:

- All entries must have a matching entry in the referenced column or be null (such as is the case with Easton, who reports to no one).
- The referenced values must be unique.

In our ongoing example, the second condition is already met because the uniqueness of the ID codes, the referenced values, was established in the previous section. The first condition can be easily tested through a subquery. (See Listing 39.9.)

Listing 39.9. Verifying matching entries in referenced columns.

```
--      Filename: 39squ09.sql
--      Purpose: verify existence of boss IDs in ID fields
--
select * from lawyer3 where boss not in
    (select id from lawyer3
         union
      select id from lawyer2)
;
```

This script returns

```
    ID      BOSS NAME          OFFICE            BHRS     BGROSS VI
--------  -------- ---------------  ---------------  --------  --------- --
    39       44 Gerardi          New York           1093     189733
```

If the column queried in the inner query contains a null value, however, this statement will return an erroneous

```
no rows selected
```

just as the following statements would produce:

```
update lawyer3
set violation = id - 10
where id > 23
;

commit;

select * from lawyer3 where boss not in
    (select to_number(violation) from lawyer3
         union
      select id from lawyer2
         union
      select id from lawyer3)
;
```

Note that `violation` is an unused character column; therefore, the `to_number` is necessary to make the `union` operation work.

These statements return the following:

```
17 rows updated.

Commit complete.

no rows selected
```

Use the nvl function if you cannot exclude the possibility of null values on the key field with certainty,

```
select * from lawyer3 where boss not in
    (select nvl(to_number(violation),-9) from lawyer3
        union
    select nvl(id,-9) from lawyer2
        union
    select nvl(id,-9) from lawyer3)
;
```

and it will return the familiar row:

```
       ID     BOSS NAME            OFFICE           BHRS   BGROSS VI
--------- --------- --------------- --------------- --------- --------- --
       39       44 Gerardi         New York          1093   189733 29
```

A further consultation with personnel yields that Gerardi reports to Chatham, ID 34, which is easily fixed. This script

```
update lawyer3
set boss = 34
where id <> 39
;

commit;

select * from lawyer3 where boss not in
    (select id from lawyer3
        union
    select id from lawyer2)
;
```

returns this:

```
1 row updated.

Commit complete.

no rows selected
```

Copying Records and Enabling Constraints

Because all the problems were eliminated in the previous steps, this section is short, as it should be (refer back to the section titled "Hard Facts of Life for Data Analysts; or, Bad Data Can Put You Out of Business"). The lawyer3 data can be copied to the lawyer2 table with a simple insert statement, as shown in Listing 39.10.

Listing 39.10. Copying records using `insert`.

```
--          Filename: 39squ10.sql
--          Purpose: copy lawyer3 values to lawyer2
--                   create/enable primary and
--                   recursive key constraints
--
insert into lawyer2
    (id,
     boss,
     name,
     office,
     bhrs,
     bgross)
select
    id,
    boss,
    name,
    office,
    bhrs,
    bgross
from lawyer3
;

commit;
```

It returns the following:

```
20 rows created.
```

```
Commit complete.
```

The integrity constraints are defined and enabled through two `alter table` statements:

```
alter table lawyer2
    add constraint pk_law2
        primary key (id)
;

alter table lawyer2 add (
    constraint fk_law2_law2 foreign key (boss)
        references lawyer2 (id))
;
```

They return

```
Table altered.
```

```
Table altered.
```

Finally, the job is complete. Although not all data-scrubbing jobs are as bad as this example, the creation of large code tables can easily take as much effort.

Inconsistent Coding Schemes

The most frequent reasons why coding schemes might be inconsistent are

- Data originates from different systems with conflicting schemes. One might use m and f for sex codes, the next might use M and F, and yet another might use 1 and 0.

- The objects that are described by the codes have changed over time, and a new code has been assigned.

The first case is easy: A decision must be made as to which scheme should be used. An update script will then do the job.

Updating with decode

If one short coding scheme is to be replaced with a long one, a straight update combined with a decode expression works well. Listing 39.11 does that: It changes the full office names to two-letter abbreviations, then shows the content of the table, and then rolls back because you really do not want to maintain the new scheme.

Listing 39.11. Updating data using decode.

```
--        Filename: 39squ11.sql
--         Purpose: updating lawyer3 values to 2 byte office codes
--
update lawyer3
set office = decode(office, 'Boston',      'BX',
                            'New York',    'NY',
                            'Los Angeles','LA',
                            'Seattle',     'SE',
                            'Houston',     'HO','XX')
;

select
    *
from lawyer3
where rownum < 8
;

rollback;
```

This script returns

```
20 rows updated.
```

ID	BOSS	NAME	OFFICE	BHRS	BGROSS	VI
21	40	Ronstadt	BX	2444	410210	
22	28	Beene	NY	1678	242100	
23	27	Hayward	LA	3003	683392	
24	25	Nazar	HO	1979	192828	14
25	27	Straus	HO	2132	344909	15
26	23	Vanatta	LA	3401	649022	16
27	7	Carlson	LA	3219	873922	17

```
7 rows selected.

Rollback complete.
```

The second situation arises when only some codes have to be changed. The `decode` operator does provide a throughput option by repeating the column name as the default expression. In Listing 39.12, Boston and New York are converted to two-digit codes, but the other codes remain unchanged.

Listing 39.12. Updating selective data using decode.

```
--         Filename: 39squ12.sql
--          Purpose: selective updating of
--                   lawyer3 values to 2 byte office codes
--
update lawyer3
set office = decode(office, 'Boston',    'BX',
                            'New York',  'NY',
                            office)
;

select
     *
from lawyer3
where rownum < 8
;

rollback;
```

This is a terrific option if just a few codes have to be updated—the statement can be quickly written, and the whole update performs in one run.

It returns the following:

```
20 rows updated.

    ID    BOSS NAME            OFFICE            BHRS   BGROSS VI
--------- ---- --------------- ----------------- ------ ------- --
    21      40 Ronstadt        BX                2444   410210
    22      28 Beene           NY                1678   242100
    23      27 Hayward         Los Angeles       3003   683392
    24      25 Nazar           Houston           1979   192828 14
    25      27 Straus          Houston           2132   344909 15
    26      23 Vanatta         Los Angeles       3401   649022 16
    27       7 Carlson         Los Angeles       3219   873922 17

7 rows selected.

Rollback complete.
```

This option is a good one if only a handful of a large number of codes have to be changed. You could add a `where in` clause and list all values that are explicitly listed in decode. In this case, fewer rows, and likely database blocks would be updated, which would reduce writes and related rollback segment activity. In this case, the default option can be omitted. Such a selective update is demonstrated in Listing 39.13.

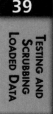

39

TESTING AND
SCRUBBING
LOADED DATA

Listing 39.13. Updating selective data using decode and where in.

```
--         Filename: 39squ13.sql
--          Purpose: selective updating of
--                   lawyer3 values to 2 byte office codes
--                   limit rows updated
--
update lawyer3
set office = decode(office, 'Boston',     'BX',
                            'New York',    'NY')
where office in ('Boston','New York')
;

rollback;
```

This script returns

```
10 rows updated.
```

```
Rollback complete.
```

You can fix all your code schemes with one run, because there is no practical limit to the number of columns you can update, and the database work overhead results mostly from reads and writes that are not affected by the number of columns decoded.

Recall from Chapter 4, "Operator Conversions and Value Decoding," that decode is limited to a total of 255 arguments. Therefore, if a column contains more than 126 codes to be converted, it would be necessary to perform one update cycle per 126 values in a single column. This is no problem on a small table, but is hardly the thing to do on a large one. Lookup and code-conversion tables offer a solution in that situation.

Using Lookup Tables

Lookup tables offer three major advantages:

- They can handle an almost unlimited number of codes
- They can be maintained independently of conversion scripts
- They are useful in subsequent reporting steps where base tables and code tables can be conveniently joined

Their major disadvantage is that to date, there is no fast or direct way to update a table with values from a lookup table other than using subqueries, although the indirect ways described here should not be that terribly inefficient either.

NOTE

This issue will disappear when updateable multi-table views are available.

Even with these drawbacks, in a production situation, lookup tables are likely the best way to go. The code tables have to be maintained anyway, and the data-conversion scripts can be written so that they depend solely on database values. Therefore, there will be no unpleasant surprises if a few codes change and the data control technician (who might be you) forgets to update the script. Working with lookup tables allows you to keep data and code completely separate, which is usually preferable. In most cases, you will probably lose some efficiency but gain a lot in terms of reliability.

 Run the script `croff3.sql` to create the lookup table `office3`. This table has the following layout and content:

```
    ID OFFICE            NEWOFFICE         SH ST    BOSSID
---------- ---------------- ---------------- -- -- ----------
     1 Boston           Cambridge         CB MA         1
     2 Los Angeles      Los Angeles       LA CA         7
     3 New York         New York          NY NY         9
     4 Houston          Houston           HO TX        17
     5 Seattle          Bellevue          BV WA         5
```

> **TIP**
>
> If it is available to you, use the cache option for lookup and code-conversion tables. That way the entire table will likely remain in memory, which provides a major performance gain.
>
> If you do not have a cache option available but you have several disk drives, put the lookup table on a disk other than the one where the tables are located. That way, at least you can avoid the disk contention.
>
> If you have to update more than one column, do them all at the same time. That way, you have the writing overhead only once.

Updating with Subqueries

A subquery update from a code table uses a regular update with a subquery on the lookup table for each value replaced. The following example assumes that due to the merger, a few offices had to be moved to larger premises, which resulted in new office names as well. The Boston office was moved to Cambridge, and the Seattle office to Bellevue. You now need to use a code table to update the `lawyer3` table to reflect that change. As has been and will be done in this section, the changes are shown, and the data is rolled back to re-create the official state. (See Listing 39.14.)

Listing 39.14. Updating data using subqueries.

```
--          Filename: 39squ14.sql
--          Purpose: updating of lawyer3 using office codes
--                   to new office codes using office3 table
--                   and update subquery
--
update lawyer3 l
set office =
       (select newoffice
        from office3 o
        where o.office = l.office)
;

select
      *
from lawyer3
where id < 24 or
      id > 35
;

rollback;
```

This script returns the following:

```
20 rows updated.

      ID     BOSS NAME             OFFICE               BHRS    BGROSS VI
--------- -------- --------------- ---------------- --------- --------- --
      21       40 Ronstadt         Cambridge             2444    410210
      22       28 Beene            New York              1678    242100
      23       27 Hayward          Los Angeles           3003    683392
      36       34 Daneshgar        Bellevue              1120    118973 26
      37       27 Bielski          Bellevue              3311    559399 27
      38       37 Young            Los Angeles           2783    419833 28
      39       34 Gerardi          New York              1093    189733 29
      40       27 Kinney           Cambridge             2672    288739 30

8 rows selected.

Rollback complete.
```

Considering that those conversions are likely to happen infrequently, this method should be sufficiently efficient, especially with the cache option. If you do not have the cache option, try to place the lookup tables on a disk drive different from the table disk drive (see the preceding tip and the discussion in Chapter 28, "Creating Tables").

Try the subquery update first. If it is unacceptable, in terms of performance, use one of the other three options described in the following sections.

Updating into an Intermediate Table

The strategy of updating data into an intermediate table involves the creation of another (temporary) table by selecting from a join of the original table and the lookup table. In terms of code, this is a very straightforward case, but without the cache option, the lookup table will likely be read over and over because the written data blocks in the new table will have priority over the preexisting code table's data blocks. Therefore, the written data blocks in the new table will force the preexisting data blocks out of memory. Listing 39.15 creates the `lawyer4` table from `lawyer3` and `office3`. After the script displays some of the table's data, the table will be dropped.

Listing 39.15. Updating data into an intermediate table.

```
--      Filename: 39squ15.sql
--      Purpose: creating lawyer4 table from
--               join of lawyer3 and office3 table
--
create table lawyer4 as
select
   l.id,
   l.boss,
   l.name,
   o.newoffice office,
   bhrs,
   bgross
from lawyer3 l,
     office3 o
where o.office = l.office
;

select
    *
from lawyer4
where id < 24 or
      id > 35
;

drop table lawyer4;
```

This script returns

```
Table created.

     ID    BOSS NAME            OFFICE            BHRS     BGROSS
--------- ------- -------------- ---------------- -------- ---------
     21      40 Ronstadt        Cambridge         2444     410210
     40      27 Kinney          Cambridge         2672     288739
     23      27 Hayward         Los Angeles       3003     683392
     38      37 Young           Los Angeles       2783     419833
     22      28 Beene           New York          1678     242100
     39      34 Gerardi         New York          1093     189733
     36      34 Daneshgar       Bellevue          1120     118973
     37      27 Bielski         Bellevue          3311     559399

8 rows selected.

Table dropped.
```

39

TESTING AND SCRUBBING LOADED DATA

Working with Translation Views

If you do not have the space for an intermediate table, you can create the same logic through a view. This might actually be more efficient, because in an intermediate table you have two write operations, one when you create it and one when you write to the final table. Because a view is a virtual table, the first write never happens. Because you need to do the second one anyway, a translation view may be your most efficient option, especially when combined with the cache option. Listing 39.16 creates a translation view, shows its content, and then drops the view.

> **NOTE**
>
> Note that the example is identical to the previous one, except that the keyword `table` is replaced with the keyword `view`. Except for the same substitutions, the output is identical, too, and is therefore not shown.

Listing 39.16. Updating data into an intermediate table.

```
--        Filename: 39squ16.sql
--        Purpose: creating lawyer4 view from
--                 join of lawyer3 and office3 table
--
create or replace view lawyer4 as
select
   l.id,
   l.boss,
   l.name,
   o.newoffice office,
   bhrs,
   bgross
from lawyer3 l,
     office3 o
where o.office = l.office
;

select
    *
from lawyer4
where id < 24 or
      id > 35
;

drop view lawyer4;
```

Updating from a Join Directly into the Final Table

Updating from a join directly into your final table is the most dangerous option, and you should use it only if you are sure about what you are doing. It combines the insert script, such as `39squ10.sql`, with the view-creation script. In essence, it creates the information on-the-fly from two tables and loads them directly into the final table. You have no way to check the intermediate output, as you could from a table or view, except that you can check your final table and roll back the transaction if you need to.

Listing 39.17 loads into the `lawyer2` table from the `lawyer3` and `office3` tables. To avoid a primary-key violation, the ID values are augmented by 20. After showing the results, the transaction will be rolled back.

Listing 39.17. Updating data into a final table from a join of two tables.

```
--        Filename: 39squ17.sql
--         Purpose: loading directly into the lawyer2 table from a
--                  join of lawyer3 and office3 table
--
insert into lawyer2
    (id,
     boss,
     name,
     office,
     bhrs,
     bgross)
select
   l.id + 20,
   l.boss,
   l.name,
   o.newoffice office,
   bhrs,
   bgross
from lawyer3 l,
     office3 o
where o.office = l.office
;

select
    *
from lawyer2
where id > 40 and
     (id < 44 or
     id > 55)
;

rollback;
```

This script returns

```
20 rows created.
```

ID	BOSS	NAME	OFFICE	BHRS	BGROSS
41	40	Ronstadt	Cambridge	2444	410210
42	28	Beene	New York	1678	242100
43	27	Hayward	Los Angeles	3003	683392
56	34	Daneshgar	Bellevue	1120	118973
57	27	Bielski	Bellevue	3311	559399

39

TESTING AND
SCRUBBING
LOADED DATA

```
58          37 Young         Los Angeles        2783    419833
59          34 Gerardi       New York           1093    189733
60          27 Kinney        Cambridge          2672    288739
```

8 rows selected.

Rollback complete.

Creating a SQL Generating SQL Script

The final approach is to use SQL to generate a statement similar to `39squ11.sql` from the code table. It combines the performance of the direct, single-table update approach with the flexibility of lookup and code-conversion tables. This option is definitely one to consider and is demonstrated in Listing 39.18.

Listing 39.18. Creating a SQL generating SQL script.

```
--          Filename: 39squ18.sql
--          Purpose: Create a SQL statement that will
--                   update lawyer3 office values to new office values
--                   using code table information
--
set termout off
set feedback off
set trimspool on
ttitle ''
set pagesize 0
--set the following to the directory of your choice
spool c:\squ\39or\39squ19a.sql

select
    'update lawyer3' || chr(10) ||
    'set office = decode(office, '
from dual
union all
select
    '''' || office || ''', ''' || newoffice || ''','
from office3
union all
select
    '''wrong'');'
from dual
;

spool off
set linesize 80
set termout on
set feedback on
set pagesize 25
```

This creates the following code in the file `39squ19a.sql`:

```
update lawyer3
set office = decode(office,
'Boston', 'Cambridge',
'Los Angeles', 'Los Angeles',
```

```
'New York', 'New York',
'Houston', 'Houston',
'Seattle', 'Bellevue',
'wrong');
```

If you strip out the line after `office`, the code will do the conversion.

Dealing with Duplicate Rows in Historical Data

In an earlier section of this chapter you learned how occasional or erroneous duplicate values can be identified and corrected. This section deals with the situation in which the feeder system creates duplicate rows by default, and some decision has to be made about which rows to maintain and which to delete.

A typical example is a series of snapshots of data that remains essentially the same but has portions that change. In any case, the changing portion would likely be kept as new, time-based records. There is little use in maintaining several copies of the stable portion, though, which creates the need and the opportunity to select the copy that is most accurate. But there is no way of telling which copy that is.

For example, consider the stable portion of personnel data. The date of birth remains the same, as do the sex, the parents' names, and the Social Security number. If there are several snapshots of this information available, you probably want to keep the later ones. In this case, maintaining the latest snapshot is usually preferable because initially wrong data could have been corrected over time. In other cases, you might be primarily interested in the initial stages of data, as might be the case with parents' names if you are interested with birth parents only. Whichever the case may be, the duplicate values must be dealt with.

Overwriting Data

Overwriting data is the easiest way of dealing with duplicate data. As new data comes in, each row in the old data set gets overwritten with data from the new one.

 `lawyer5`, a duplicate (but corrected) version of the table `lawyer3`, is created through the script `crlaw5.sql`.

Listing 39.19 overwrites the values of `lawyer3` with those of `lawyer5`. It is similar to `39squ15.sql`, where the `office` column was updated with the new values from the lookup table.

Listing 39.19. Overwriting data.

```
--       Filename: 39squ19.sql
--       Purpose: updating of lawyer3 using values from the
--                new lawyer5 table
--
update lawyer3 l3
set (id,
     boss,
```

continues

Listing 39.19. continued

```
       name,
       office,
       bhrs,
       bgross,
       violation) =
         (select
             id + 20,
             boss + 20,
             name,
             office,
             bhrs,
             bgross,
             duplicate
          from lawyer4 l5
         where l3.id = l5.id + 20)
;

select
     *
from lawyer3
where id < 24 or
      id > 35
;

rollback;
```

It returns the following:

```
20 rows updated.

        ID     BOSS NAME            OFFICE                 BHRS    BGROSS VI
--------- -------- --------------- ---------------- ---------- --------- --
       21       40 Ronstadt        Boston                 2444    410210  2
       22       28 Beene           New York               1678    242100  2
       23       27 Hayward         Los Angeles            3003    683392  2
       36       34 Daneshgar       Seattle                1120    118973  2
       37       27 Bielski         Seattle                3311    559399  2
       38       37 Young           Los Angeles            2783    419833  2
       39       34 Gerardi         New York               1093    189733  2
       40       27 Kinney          Boston                 2672    288739  2

8 rows selected.

Rollback complete.
```

Eliminating Redundant Rows

The situation in which you need to eliminate redundant rows arises when a historical database is to be created from periodic snapshots such as could be recovered from backup tapes. The information from a series of tapes is loaded into a table and broken into subtables, some of which will have redundant rows.

 lawyer6 is a duplicate version of the lawyer5 table. Eighty redundant rows have been added, distinguished from their look-alikes through an enumeration in the duplicate column. `lawyer6` is created through the `crlaw6.sql` script. Note that this script will return an error the first time you run it, which can be disregarded:

```
ERROR at line 1:
ORA-00942: table or view does not exist
```

In this example, the duplicate column can be used to order each occurrence of an otherwise identical row. A date of creation or some other indication could serve the same purpose. The task is now to delete all duplicates but the last one.

The best way to do that is to identify the rows to be retained through a subquery, view, or table, and then delete all the others. Listing 39.20 is a simple query that selects the ID and the maximum duplicate value.

Listing 39.20. Identifying rows with highest duplicate values.

```
--        Filename: 39squ20.sql
--         Purpose: identifying the rows of lawyer6
--                  with the highest duplicate value.
--
select
   id,
   max(duplicate) dupmax
from lawyer6
group by
   id
;
```

It returns this:

```
     ID    DUPMAX
--------- ---------
        1        93
        2        65
        3        72
        4        82
        5        92
        6        74
        7        84
        8        94
        9        95
       10        85
       11        93
       12        65
       13        72
       14        82
       15        92
       16        74
       17        84
       18        94
       19        95
       20        91

20 rows selected.
```

Listing 39.21 inserts this query as a subquery into a `delete` statement.

Listing 39.21. Eliminating redundant rows.

```
--         Filename: 39squ21.sql
--         Purpose: eliminating redundant rows of lawyer6, keeping only
--                  the ones with the highest duplicate value.
--
delete from lawyer6
where (id, duplicate) not in
    (select
        id,
        max(duplicate) dupmax
    from lawyer6
    group by
        id)
;
```

It returns this:

```
80 rows deleted.
```

Now, selecting from `lawyer6`

```
select
    *
from lawyer6
;

rollback;
```

returns the same 20 rows identified by `39squ21.sql`:

ID	BOSS	NAME	OFFICE	BHRS	BGROSS	DUPLICATE
20	7	Kinney	Boston	2672	288739	91
3	7	Hayward	Los Angeles	3003	683392	72
4	5	Nazar	Houston	1979	192828	82
5	7	Straus	Houston	2132	344909	92
13	18	Leyva	Los Angeles	2425	468920	72
14	9	Herrera	New York	2098	389279	82
15	10	Ewald	Boston	2984	471938	92
1	20	Ronstadt	Boston	2444	410210	93
11	1	Bishop	Boston	2939	308299	93
6	3	Vanatta	Los Angeles	3401	649022	74
7		Carlson	Los Angeles	3219	873922	84
8	9	Stearns	New York	1984	298733	94
16	14	Daneshgar	Seattle	1120	118973	74
17	7	Bielski	Seattle	3311	559399	84
18	17	Young	Los Angeles	2783	419833	94
2	8	Beene	New York	1678	242100	65
9	7	Shubeck	New York	2583	487399	95
10	1	Rhodes	Boston	2123	297382	85
12	6	Pesacov	Los Angeles	2131	379254	65
19	14	Gerardi	New York	1093	189733	95

```
Rollback complete.
```

The task can also be accomplished with the methods used earlier in the section of this chapter titled "Inconsistent Coding Schemes," when codes had to be updated.

Dealing with Changed Organizational Structures

Changed organizational structures are a fact of life in a time when mergers and acquisitions are a way of business life, and incompetent CEOs can stir up a lot of dust to camouflage their shortcomings through an incessant stream of consultants, retreats, and the reorganizations that invariably follow, whether they make sense or not. These changes pose a challenge to the interpretation of aggregate time-based comparisons.

For the initiated who deal well with numbers and charts, a footnote that explains and reports the size of the change's impact is usually sufficient. Because few of the decision makers, on the other hand, have time to read anything in detail, such reports, although correct, are misleading. In most cases, if a reader cannot make sense of a report instantly, the report is useless. There are sometimes cases when are report must be complex anyway, but that should be the exception.

An example can illuminate the issue: Let's assume that Kinney in Boston decides that she never liked lawyering too much and that, perhaps, life as a small-scale executive might be more fun. Indeed, she is successful in convincing management that the original part of the firm should be organized into an Eastern division, consisting of New York, Boston, and Houston, and a Western division based in Los Angeles and Seattle.

Within a reasonably short time it turns out that she is not that adept at managing at a distance, especially when she is annoyed by many delays due to fog when she flies out of Boston International. It is therefore decided that at the end of the fiscal year, the Houston office will become part of the Western division. A year later, Carlson wants to compare how the divisions are doing in terms of billable hours and revenues for the year before and after the change.

The problem the change poses is that neither division before the change is the same as after. A solution to this problem is to provide three reports:

- A comparison of the totals as they are, including the effect of the change
- A comparison of the totals as they would have been if the organizational change had never happened
- A comparison of the totals as they would have been if the organizational change had happened a year earlier

This report can be easily done through a lookup table that reports both old and new organizational structures.

lawyer7 is a duplicate version of the table lawyer2 that is augmented by a Year column coded as 1 for the first year and 2 for the second. This code has been added, as well as 20 rows of data for the second year. lawyer6 is created through the script crlaw7.sql.

office4 now contains two records per office, one for year 1 and the other for year 2. It also has two new columns, one for the year and one for the division:

```
    ID   YEAR OFFICE          DIVI SH ST   BOSSID
--------- ----- --------------- ---- -- -- ---------
     1      1 Boston          East BO MA       1
     1      2 Boston          East BO MA       1
     2      1 Los Angeles     West LA CA       7
     2      2 Los Angeles     West LA CA       7
     3      1 New York        East NY NY       9
     3      2 New York        East NY NY       9
     4      1 Houston         East HO TX      17
     4      2 Houston         West HO TX      17
     5      1 Seattle         West SE WA       5
     5      2 Seattle         West SE WA       5
```

 office4 is created through the croff4.sql script, which you can find on the CD-ROM that accompanies this book.

The first example shows a matrix of how the offices are assigned to their current divisions, the old scheme, the new scheme, and the gross receipts of the offices in each year. Listing 39.22 joins the lawyer7 table to the office4 table three times.

Listing 39.22. Eliminating redundant rows and keeping rows with the highest duplicate value.

```
--       Filename: 39squ22.sql
--        Purpose: eliminating redundant rows of lawyer6, keeping only
--                 the ones with the highest duplicate value.
--
select
    l.office,
    o1.division curr,
    o2.division old,
    o3.division new,
    sum(decode(l.year,1,bgross,0)) gross1,
    sum(decode(l.year,2,bgross,0)) gross2
from lawyer7 l,
    office4 o1,
    office4 o2,
    office4 o3
where l.office = o1.office and l.year    = o1.year and
      l.office = o2.office and o2.year    = 1         and
      l.office = o3.office and o3.year    = 2
group by
    l.office,
    o1.division,
    o2.division,
    o3.division
order by office
;
```

It returns

```
OFFICE          CURR OLD  NEW     GROSS1     GROSS2
--------------- ---- ---- ---- ---------- ----------
Boston          East East East    1776568    1794333
Houston         East East West     537737          0
Houston         West East West          0     689216
Los Angeles     West West West    3474343    2753357
New York        East East East    1607244    1836299
Seattle         West West West     678372     779409
```

6 rows selected.

The next three examples summarize this information. The first reports by current division:

```
select
    o1.division curr,
    sum(decode(l.year,1,bgross,0)) gross1,
    sum(decode(l.year,2,bgross,0)) gross2
from lawyer7 l,
    office4 o1
where l.office = o1.office and l.year   = o1.year
group by
    o1.division
;
```

It returns this:

```
CURR     GROSS1     GROSS2
-----  --------- ---------
East    3921549    3630632
West    4152715    4221982
```

The next example reports the totals as they would have been if the change had not occurred:

```
select
    o2.division old,
    sum(decode(l.year,1,bgross,0)) gross1,
    sum(decode(l.year,2,bgross,0)) gross2
from lawyer7 l,
    office4 o2
where l.office = o2.office and o2.year    = 1
group by
    o2.division
;
```

It returns

```
OLD     GROSS1     GROSS2
----  --------- ---------
East    3921549    4319848
West    4152715    3532766
```

39

TESTING AND
SCRUBBING
LOADED DATA

The final part shows the totals as they would have been if the structure had always been as it was in year 2:

```
select
    o3.division new,
    sum(decode(l.year,1,bgross,0)) gross1,
    sum(decode(l.year,2,bgross,0)) gross2
from lawyer7 l,
    office4 o3
where l.office = o3.office and o3.year   = 2
group by
    o3.division
;
```

It returns the following:

```
NEW     GROSS1     GROSS2
----    ---------- ----------
East    3383812    3630632
West    4690452    4221982
```

Summary

There are a myriad of reasons why data received from another source could be in less-than-desirable shape. Data analysis follows the garbage in, garbage out principle. Bad data will therefore likely put you out of business. This chapter covers the steps necessary to test and clean up a data set before doing further processing. These steps need to be performed, even if they are tedious at times.

In the second half of this chapter, you examined rule-based data conversions performed within the database, such as code conversions, updates of records from redundant sources, and deletion of duplicate rows. Finally, you were presented with a methodology for dealing with changing organizational structures in your reports.

I

INDEX

Symbols

Sams Teach Yourself SQL in 21 Days,
Second Edition

—*Bryan Morgan & Jeff Perkins*

Fully updated and revised to include coverage of PL/SQL and Transact-SQL, this easy-to-understand guide teaches users everything they need to know—from database concepts and processes to implementing security and constructing and optimizing queries. Q&A sections, step-by-step instructions, and review sections make learning easy and fun. Shows how to create tables, modify data, incorporate security features, and tune the database for optimum performance. Emphasizes common database concepts, including SQL functions and queries.

$39.99 USA/$56.95 CDN   *User Level: New–Casual*
ISBN: 0-672-31110-0   *624 pages*

Microsoft SQL Server 6.5 Unleashed,
Second Edition

—*David Solomon, Ray Rankins, et al.*

This comprehensive reference details the steps needed to plan, design, install, administer, and tune large and small databases. Covers programming topics, including data structures, stored procedures, referential integrity, large table strategies, and more. Includes updates to cover all new features of SQL Server 6.5 including the new transaction processing monitor and Internet/database connectivity through SQL Server's new Web Wizard.

CD-ROM includes source code, libraries, and administration tools.

$59.99 USA/$84.95 CDN   *User Level: Accomplished–Expert*
ISBN: 0-672-30956-4   *1,272 pages*

Sams Teach Yourself Transact-SQL in 21 Days

—Bennett Wm. McEwan & David Solomon

Based on the best-selling *Sams Teach Yourself* series, this comprehensive book provides readers with the techniques they need to not only write flexible and effective applications that produce efficient results but also decrease the performance demands on the server. In no time, users will master methods that will improve productivity and maximize performance. Explores topics such as coding standards, the CASE function, bitmaps, and more. Covers Transact-SQL for Microsoft SQL Server and Sybase SQL Server.

$35.00 USA/$49.95 CAN   *User Level: New–Casual*
ISBN: 0-672-31045-7   *592 pages*

Microsoft BackOffice Unleashed, Second Edition

—Joe Greene, et al.

As an update to the highly successful first edition, this all-in-one, how-to guide helps users master the individual products within the BackOffice family and shows how to successfully integrate those pieces to build a robust, information resource for corporations. Highlights the significant improvements in Exchange Server, including ActiveX programming support. Covers the phases instrumental in the development, integration, and administration of the BackOffice environment. Explores new commercial Internet servers, such as Proxy Server, Index Server, Merchant Server, and Conference Server.

CD-ROM includes source code, third-party products, and utilities to help readers take full advantage of Microsoft BackOffice.

$89.99 USA/$126.95 CAN   *User Level: Accomplished–Expert*
ISBN: 0-672-31085-6   *1,500 pages*

Add to Your Sams Library Today with the Best Books for Programming, Operating Systems, and New Technologies

ISBN	Quantity	Description of Item	Unit Cost	Total Cost
0-672-31110-X		Sams Teach Yourself SQL in 21 Days, 2E	$39.99	
0-672-30956-4		Microsoft SQL Server 6.5 Unleashed, 2E	$59.99	
0-672-31045-7		Sams Teach Yourself Transact-SQL in 21 Days	$35.00	
0-672-31085-6		Microsoft BackOffice Unleashed, 2E	$89.99	
		Shipping and Handling: See information below.		
		TOTAL		

Shipping and Handling: $5.00 for Standard shipping or $10.00 for Second Day shipping. If you need to have it NOW, we can ship product to you in 24 hours for $17.50. International shipments are $40.00. Prices subject to change.

201 W. 103rd Street, Indianapolis, Indiana 46290
1-800-882-8583 — Fax

Book ISBN 0-672-31133-X

What's on the CD-ROM

What's on the Disc

The companion CD-ROM contains all of the authors' source code and samples from the book and many third-party software products.

Windows 3.1 and Windows NT 3.5.1 Installation Instructions

1. Insert the CD-ROM disc into your CD-ROM drive.

2. From File Manager or Program Manager, choose Run from the File menu.

3. Type `<drive>\SETUP.EXE` and press Enter, where `<drive>` corresponds to the drive letter of your CD-ROM. For example, if your CD-ROM is drive D:, type `D:\SETUP.EXE` and press Enter.

4. Installation creates a program named "SQL Unleashed." This group will contain icons to browse the CD-ROM.

Windows 95 and Windows NT 4.0 Installation Instructions

1. Insert the CD-ROM disc into your CD-ROM drive.

2. From the Windows 95 desktop, double-click on the My Computer icon.

3. Double-click on the icon representing your CD-ROM drive.

4. Double-click on the icon titled `SETUP.EXE` to run the installation program.

5. Installation creates a program group named "SQL Unleashed." This group will contain icons to browse the CD-ROM.

> **NOTE**
>
> If Windows 95 is installed on your computer, and you have the AutoPlay feature enabled, the `SETUP.EXE` program starts automatically whenever you insert the disc into your CD-ROM drive.